THE ANNUAL DIRECTORY OF AMERICAN
AND CANADIAN BED & BREAKFASTS

The West

Includes
WESTERN CANADA

2000 EDITION • VOLUME V

THE ANNUAL DIRECTORY OF AMERICAN AND CANADIAN BED & BREAKFASTS

The West

Includes
WESTERN CANADA

2000 EDITION • VOLUME V

Tracey Menges, *Compiler*

PUBLISHING, INC.
Uhrichsville, Ohio

Copyright © 1989, 1990, 1991, 1992, 1993, 1994, 1995, 1996, 1997, 1998, 1999 by Barbour Publishing, Inc.

ISBN 1-57748-775-3

All rights reserved. Written permission must be secured from the publisher to use or reproduce any part of this book, except for brief quotations in critical reviews or articles.

Published by Barbour Publishing, Inc., P.O. Box 719, Uhrichsville, Ohio 44683
http://www.barbourbooks.com

Cover design and book design by Harriette Bateman
Page composition by Roger A. DeLiso, Rutledge Hill Press®

Printed in the United States of America.

1 2 3 4 5 6—02 01 00 99

Contents

Introduction	*vii*		New Mexico	261
Alaska	2		Oregon	279
Arizona	18		Texas	303
California	78		Utah	334
Colorado	184		Washington	347
Hawaii	215		Wyoming	387
Idaho	239		Alberta	395
Montana	246		British Columbia	401
Nevada	257		Saskatchewan	430

Introduction

The 2000 edition of *The Annual Directory of Western Bed & Breakfasts* is one of the most comprehensive directories available today. Whether planning your honeymoon, a family vacation or reunion, or a business trip (many bed and breakfasts provide conference facilities), you will find what you are looking for at a bed and breakfast. They are all here just waiting to be discovered.

Once you know your destination, look for it, or one close by, to see what accommodations are available. Each state has a general map with city locations to help you plan your trip efficiently. There are listings for all 50 states, Canada, Puerto Rico, and the Virgin Islands. Don't be surprised to find a listing in the remote spot you thought only you knew about. Even if your favorite hideaway isn't listed, you're sure to discover a new one.

How to Use This Guide

The sample listing below is typical of the entries in this directory. Each bed and breakfast is listed alphabetically by city and establishment name. The description provides an overview of the bed and breakfast and may include nearby activities and attractions. *Please note that the descriptions have been provided by the hosts. The publisher has not visited these bed and breakfasts and is not responsible for inaccuracies.*

Following the description are notes that have been designed for easy reference. Looking at the sample, a quick glance tells you that this bed and breakfast has four guest rooms, two with private baths (PB) and two that share a bath (SB). The rates are for two people sharing one room. Tax may or may not be included. The specifics of "Credit Cards" and "Notes" are listed at the bottom of each page.

GREAT TOWN

Favorite Bed and Breakfast
123 Main Street, 12345
(800) 555-1234

This quaint bed and breakfast is surrounded by five acres of award-winning landscaping and gardens. There are four guest rooms, each individually decorated with antiques. It is close to antique shops, restaurants, and outdoor activities. Breakfast includes homemade specialties and is served in the formal dining room at guests' leisure. Minimum stay of two nights.

Hosts: Sue and Jim Smith
Rooms: 4 (2 PB; 2 SB) $65-80
Full Breakfast
Credit Cards: A, B
Notes: 2, 5, 8, 10, 11, 12, 13

For example, the letter A means that MasterCard is accepted. The number 10 means that tennis is available on the premises or within 10 to 15 miles.

In many cases, a bed and breakfast is listed with a reservation service that represents several houses in one area. This service is responsible for bookings and can answer other questions you may have. They also inspect each listing and can help you choose the best place for your needs.

Before You Arrive

Now that you have chosen the bed and breakfast that interests you, there are some things you need to find out. You should always make reservations in advance, and while you are doing so you should ask about the local taxes. City taxes can be an unwelcome surprise. Make sure there are accommodations for your children. If you have dietary needs or prefer nonsmoking rooms, find out if these requirements can be met. Ask about check-in times and cancellation policies. Get specific directions. Most bed and breakfasts are readily accessible, but many are a little out of the way.

When You Arrive

In many instances you are visiting someone's home. Be respectful of their property, their schedules, and their requests. Don't smoke if they ask you not to, and don't show up with pets without prior arrangement. Be tidy in shared bathrooms, and be prompt. Most places have small staffs or may be run single-handedly and cannot easily adjust to surprises.

With a little effort and a sense of adventure you will learn firsthand the advantages of bed and breakfast travel. You will rediscover hospitality in a time when kindness seems to have been pushed aside. With the help of this directory, you will find accommodations that are just as exciting as your traveling plans.

We would like to hear from you about any experiences you have had or any inns you wish to recommend. Please write us at the following address:

> Barbour Publishing, Inc.
> P.O. Box 719
> Uhrichsville, Ohio 44683

THE ANNUAL DIRECTORY OF AMERICAN
AND CANADIAN BED & BREAKFASTS

The West

Includes
WESTERN CANADA

2000 EDITION • VOLUME V

Alaska

Alaska

ANCHORAGE

Alaskan Frontier Gardens Bed & Breakfast

P.O. Box 241881, 99503
(907) 345-6556; FAX (907) 562-2923
e-mail: afg@alaska.net
www.alaskaone.com/akfrontier

The ultimate location for a getaway, honeymoon, or wedding, this elegant Alaska hillside estate on peaceful scenic three acres by Chugach State Park meets every expectation. A museum-like environment with a warm and relaxing atmosphere, exceptional comfort, and gourmet breakfast, Ivory suite is particularly exquisite with its inviting amenities: king-size bed, a fireplace, multi-person Jacuzzi, sauna, double shower, cable TV, and view. A unique Alaskan adventure awaits guests.

Host: Rita Gitlins
Rooms: 3 (2 PB; 1 SB) $75-195
Full Breakfast
Credit Cards: A, B, C, D, E, F
Notes: 2, 5, 6, 7, 8, 9, 10, 11, 12, 13, 14, 15

Coastal Trail Bed & Breakfast

3100 Iliamna Drive, 99517
(907) 243-5809; FAX (907) 243-5514
e-mail: info@coastaltrail.com

Coastal Trail Bed and Breakfast invites guests to a comfortable Alaskan homestay with gardens, featherbeds, and full breakfast. Centrally positioned between airport and downtown. Hunting and fishing trips are provided by traditional Alaskan hosts. Coastal Trail adjoins an urban walking trail where guests may enjoy wildflowers, migratory birds, whales, and views of Denali.

Hosts: Sherry and Derek Tomlinson
Suite: 2 (PB) $90
Full Breakfast
Cards: A, B, C, D
Notes: 2, 5, 7, 8, 9, 10, 13, 14

Elderberry Bed & Breakfast

8340 Elderberry, 99502
(907) 243-6968 (phone/FAX)
e-mail: 103260.3221@compuserve.com

Close to airport, bike and walking trails, bus route, and local restaurants. Beautiful summer flowers. Moose frequently seen. Breakfast prepared to guests' taste—homemade. Special diets accommodated. Big-screen TV. Alaska videos. Rooms tastefully decorated in matching decor. Hosts, Norm and Linda, love to talk to guests about their 20 years of Alaskan experiences.

Hosts: Norm and Linda Seitz
Rooms: 3 (PB) $70-90
Full and Continental Breakfasts
Credit Cards: A, B
Notes: 2, 5, 7, 8, 9, 11, 12, 13, 14

NOTES: Credit cards accepted: A MasterCard; B Visa; C American Express; D Discover; E Diner's Club; F Other; 2 Personal checks accepted; 3 Lunch available; 4 Dinner available; 5 Open all year; 6 Pets welcome; 7 No smoking; 8 Children welcome; 9 Social drinking allowed; 10 Tennis nearby; 11 Swimming nearby; 12 Golf nearby; 13 Skiing nearby; 14 May be booked through a travel agent; Handicapped accessible.

A Homestay at Homesteads

341 West Tudor, Suite 250, 99503
(907) 272-8644; FAX (907) 274-8644

A1. A premier country inn in the heart of downtown Anchorage. Overlooking Bootleggers Cove, the inn offers spectacular views of Cook Inlet, the Alaska Range, and Redoubt volcano. This newly restored historic building is within walking distance to the museum, shops, restaurants, courthouse, business district, and train station. A Continental plus breakfast is included. Sightseeing tours and in-house mountain bike rentals available. Open year-round. Seasonal rates. $55-100.

A2. Just at the tree line with a great trail across the creek lies this delightful home. In the winter ski, from the porch. In the summer, climb the mountains surrounding this unique getaway. A wood stove provides the warmth. Homemade quilts. No smoking. Full breakfast. $65-95.

The Lilac House

950 P Street, 99501
(907) 278-2939; FAX (907) 278-4939
e-mail: lilac@pobox.alaska.net

An exceptional bed and breakfast, the Lilac House was designed for the convenience and comfort of all guests and is perfect for both the business and pleasure traveler. In a quiet, prestigious residential neighborhood across the street from Delaney Park and a short walk to downtown Anchorage restaurants, shops, and the beautiful coastal trail. Spacious rooms offer views of Cook Inlet and the Chugach Mountains. A separate entrance assures guests' privacy.

Host: Debi Shinn
Rooms: 3 (1 PB; 2 SB) $75-120
Continental Breakfast
Credit Cards: A, B, C
Notes: 2, 5, 7, 8, 9, 10, 12, 13, 14

ANCHORAGE—(EAGLE RIVER)

A Homestay at Homesteads

341 West Tudor, Suite 250, 99503
(907) 272-8644; FAX (907) 274-8644

ER1. Wonderful wood stove and fireplace await travelers after the drive up the seven and one-half tree-lined miles from the main highway. Close to Anchorage, yet surrounded by wilderness, guests can ski from the house or hike across the creek to the Chugach Wilderness trail head. Shared or private half-bath. Full breakfast by the back valley window with a view of two glaciers. Nonsmoking. $65-90.

ER2. One of the most spectacular views in all of Alaska will welcome guests to this log home inside Chugach State Park. The home, in the wilderness, offers a cozy suite, solitude with the friendliness of a bed and breakfast. Hike or ski from the door in a glaciated valley with a rushing river where salmon spawn and the moose, bear, and sheep call home. A suburb of Anchorage, Eagle River is a short commute. Families welcomed. Nonsmoking. $95-115.

ER3. On a clear day guests can see the Alaska Range and Sleeping Lady as they sit by the fire or enjoy the spacious yard at this split-level home. Stay a few days for great hiking, berry picking, fishing, rafting, and cross-country skiing. Two bedrooms, shared or private bath. Continental breakfast. Nonsmoking. $65-85.

NOTES: Credit cards accepted: A MasterCard; B Visa; C American Express; D Discover; E Diner's Club; F Other; 2 Personal checks accepted; 3 Lunch available; 4 Dinner available; 5 Open all year; 6 Pets welcome;

ER4. On the north shore of Peters Creek, this newly built bed and breakfast sits in the middle of two and one-half acres of parklike terrain where king salmon spawn in the creek. Designed with the physically challenged in mind, this spacious home is furnished with Victorian antiques and Alaskan memories. Enjoy a full Alaskan breakfast, then hike or ski on the nearby trails. Family-friendly. Non-smoking. Secluded area set aside for the business traveler. E-mail access and conference room available. $75-85.

BETHEL

Bentley's Bed & Breakfast Inn

624 First Avenue, Box 529, 99559
(907) 543-3552; (907) 543-5923; (907) 543-2257
FAX (907) 543-3561

Experience the warmth of Alaskan hospitality during a stay in southwest Alaska. Bentley's is on the beautiful Kuskokwim River in Bethel. Comfortable rooms, homelike atmosphere, full breakfasts, smoke-free and alcohol-free environment, and reasonable rates are what guests may expect at this home away from home. Connection with kayak and rafting tours June through September. Advance reservations are advisable.

Host: Millie D. Bentley
Rooms: 24 (SB) $95-128
Full Breakfast
Credit Cards: A, B, C, D, E
Notes: 2, 5, 7, 14

CHUGIAK

Peters Creek Bed & Breakfast

22626 Chambers Land, 99567
(888) 688-3465; FAX (907) 688-3466
e-mail: pcbnb@alaska.net
www.alaska.net/~pcbnb

Stay with long-time Alaskans in their large, spacious, newly built home on the north shore of Peters Creek on two and one-half wooded acres. Smoke-free environment, designed with physically challenged in mind. Furnished with Victorian antiques, 1800s square grand piano, and fireplace in living room. Large home theater in family room for guests' use. Guest rooms have cable TV, VCR, refrigerator, private bath, robes and slippers, iron and board, and are theme decorated.

Hosts: Bob and Lucy Moody
Rooms: 4 (PB) $85-100
Full Breakfast
Credit Cards: A, B, C, D
Notes: 2, 5, 7, 8, 10, 11, 13, 14, 15

Peters Creek Inn

Peters Creek Inn

22635 Davidson Road, P.O. Box 671487, 99567
(907) 688-2776; (800) 680-2776
FAX (907) 688-5031
www.alaska.net/~pcibnb

A rural, wooded setting that suggests remoteness, yet possesses metropolitan convenience. Only 20 minutes from Anchorage from the bed and breakfast's private entrance. Choose from the five Alaskan themed rooms, each with a private bath. Beverage service available 24 hours. A barbecue is available for the one that didn't get away. Walk along the creek's edge or through the woods to see picturesque mountains and Cook Inlet. Nordic ski trails abound in the winter.

Hosts: Martha and Burl Rogers
Rooms: 5 (PB) $75-90
Full Breakfast
Credit Cards: A, B
Notes: 2, 3, 4, 5, 6, 7, 8, 9, 10, 11, 12, 13, 14

---

7 No smoking; 8 Children welcome; 9 Social drinking allowed; 10 Tennis nearby; 11 Swimming nearby; 12 Golf nearby; 13 Skiing nearby; 14 May be booked through a travel agent; 15 Handicapped accessible.

COOPER LANDING

Gwin's Lodge

14865 (Milepost 52) Sterling Highway, 99572
(907) 595-1266; FAX (907) 595-1681

Built more than 50 years ago, historic Gwin's Lodge is beautifully preserved as one of Alaska's few remaining traditionally built log roadhouses. Centralized location on Kenai Peninsula. Closest lodge to Kenai and Russian Rivers confluence, the world's most prolific sockeye salmon sportfishery. Comfortable, modern log cabins feature two double beds, bath/shower. Full RV hookups. World renowned restaurant and bar, package store, fishing tackle/licenses, gifts, ice, fish freezing/smoking services, fishing and scenic rafting charters booked.

Hosts: The Siter Family
Rooms: 9 (7 PB) $119
Full Breakfast
Credit Cards: A, B, D
Notes: 2, 3, 4, 8, 9, 12, 14, 15

Gwin's Lodge

DENALI NATIONAL PARK

Earth Song Lodge

P.O. Box 89, Healy, 99743
(907) 683-2863; FAX (907) 683-2868
www.earthsonglodge.com

North of Denali National Park, close enough for convenience, far enough for peace and quiet. Spectacular views. Ten charming cabins with handcrafted furniture and private baths. Lodge made with honey-colored Alaskan logs

Earth Song Lodge

features a library, TV/VCR for viewing Alaskan videos, spacious living room. There's lots to do: walk, hike, view wildlife, photography, pick berries, visit a working sled dog kennel, dog mushing adventures, and watch evening naturalist slide shows. Gift shop. Prepackaged lunch may be purchased. Come and share the dream. Continental breakfast served.

Hosts: Karin and Jon Nierenberg
Rooms: 10 (PB) $105-125
Continental Breakfast
Credit Cards: A, B
Notes: 2, 5, 6, 7, 8, 9, 13, 14

DENALI NATIONAL PARK AREA

A Homestay at Homesteads

341 West Tudor, Suite 250, Anchorage, 99503
(907) 272-8644; FAX (907) 274-8644

1. Guests' very own Alaska log cabin overlooking the Nenana River, wildlife, and glaciated mountains. Get away from the usual crowds. Relax on one of the three riverside sun decks, the hot tub, or sauna. The cozy western cedar cabins have private baths, double beds, or one double plus futon sofa. Continental breakfast by the fireplace in the new River Lodge. Cappuccino bar, periodic night programs, exclusive Alaskan art, restaurant next door, outdoor grills on premises. Arriving by

---

NOTES: Credit cards accepted: A MasterCard; B Visa; C American Express; D Discover; E Diner's Club; F Other; 2 Personal checks accepted; 3 Lunch available; 4 Dinner available; 5 Open all year; 6 Pets welcome;

train or bus? Shuttle service included, of course. $149-159.

2. Choose the old hotel inside the park. Many hikers and the locals, so dress informally. Most rooms have two double beds and private baths. Walk to park headquarters. Meals available, but not included. Short walk up from the train station. Complimentary shuttles to other hotels. Shoulder season rates available. Call for quotes.

FAIRBANKS

A Homestay at Homesteads

341 West Tudor, Suite 250, Anchorage, 99503
(907) 272-8644; FAX (907) 274-8644

F1. This spacious comfortable apartment with a spectacular panoramic view awaits travelers looking for a unique bed and breakfast. This well-known Fairbanks home is nestled on a cliff directly above the beautiful Tanana River where the riverboat *Discovery* cruises. Guests can enjoy breakfast and relax on a large private cliffside deck. Two bedrooms with full bath, kitchen, living room, nature trails, and large yard. Nonsmoking. Children over seven welcome. $105-160.

F2. Elegant home in a surprisingly refreshing riverside niche. Gracious, long-time Alaskan hosts pride themselves on friendly accommodations with breakfast, of course. Private entrance, private or shared baths, guest kitchenette. Children welcome. Smoking permitted on outside deck and in the yard. Weekly and monthly rates available. $65-90.

F3. Bordering on a small pond, the house with large deck enables guests to enjoy the many hours of summer sun in this lovely residential section of town. On the city bus line and convenient to Alaskaland, University of Alaska, riverboat *Discovery,* airport, and train depot. Four spacious and impeccably clean rooms, shared or private bath, plus an apartment.

Enjoy breakfast with this fifth generation Alaskan family. $65-100.

Lennies Lair Bed & Breakfast

2034 Eagan Avenue, 99701
(907) 456-5931

Guests will find this bed and breakfast in the heart of the city with a partial forest setting. Close to Alaskaland, public bus routes, and restaurants.

Host: Lennie Johnson
Rooms: 2 (PB) $40-75
Continental Breakfast
Credit Cards: A, B
Notes: 2, 5, 7, 8, 10, 11

7 Gables

7 Gables Inn

P.O. Box 80488, 99708
(907) 479-0751

Historically, Alaska's 7 Gables Inn was a fraternity house within walking distance to the UAF campus, yet is near the river and airport. This spacious 10,000-square-foot Tudor-style home features a floral solarium, antique stained glass in the foyer with an indoor waterfall, cathedral ceilings, a meeting room, and rooms and suites. A gourmet breakfast is served daily. Other amenities include cable TV/VCR and telephone in each room, laundry facilities, Jacuzzis, bikes, and canoes.

Hosts: Paul and Leicha Welton
Rooms: 12 (PB) $50-120
Full Breakfast
Credit Cards: A, B, C, D, E, F
Notes: 2, 5, 7, 8, 9, 14

---

7 No smoking; 8 Children welcome; 9 Social drinking allowed; 10 Tennis nearby; 11 Swimming nearby; 12 Golf nearby; 13 Skiing nearby; 14 May be booked through a travel agent; 15 Handicapped accessible.

GIRDWOOD

Cross Country Meadows Bed & Breakfast

Timberline and Alta Drive, P.O. Box 123, 99587-0123
(907) 783-3333; FAX (907) 783-3335
e-mail: XCountryBB@aol.com
www.XCountryBB.com

Cross Country Meadows Bed and Breakfast is nestled in the heart of Alaska's prime skiing community of Girdwood. The home was designed and built specifically as a bed and breakfast and furnished for the convenience of all the guests. The hosts cater to those who seek quiet, peaceful accommodations with a luxurious and private atmosphere. The bed and breakfast is a great place for staging day trips to Prince William Sound or the Kenai Peninsula, enjoying a romantic retreat, or just mixing business with pleasure.

Hosts: Brent and Sylvia Stonebraker
Rooms: 2 (PB) $85-125
Continental Breakfast
Credit Cards: A, B, C, D
Notes: 2, 5, 7, 9, 10, 11, 13, 14

GUSTAVUS (GLACIER BAY)

Good River Bed & Breakfast

Box 37, 99826
(907) 697-2241 (phone/FAX)
e-mail: acbb@goodriver.com; www.goodriver.com

Elegant log home on Gustavus' Good River. Adjacent to the Sandhill Crane Refuge, Glacier Bay National Park, Southeast Alaska's Tongass Rainforest and wildlife viewing. Comfortable country accommodations. Hearty breakfast with homemade breads and jams—ask about their nagoonberry jelly. Activities? What's your pleasure? Hosts will arrange Glacier Bay Tours, whale watching, kayaking, charter fishing, and more—no charge for the service. In business since 1986. One of the first and finest bed and breakfasts near Glacier Bay.

Good River

Rooms: 5 (1 PB; 4 SB) $60-80
Continental Breakfast
Credit Cards: None
Notes: 2, 8, 12, 14

Gustavus Inn

Box 60, 99826
(800) 649-5220; FAX (907) 697-2255

Glacier Bay's historic homestead, newly renovated, full-service inn accommodates 26. Family-style meals, seafood, garden produce, wild edibles. Boat tours of Gla-cier Bay, charter fishing, and air transportation from Juneau arranged. Kayaking and hiking nearby. Bikes and airport transfers included in the daily rates. Lunch and dinner included. American plan only. Closed September 15 through May 1.

Hosts: David and Jo Ann Lesh
Rooms: 13 (11 PB; 2 SB) $135
Full Breakfast
Credit Cards: A, B, C
Notes: 2, 3, 4, 7, 8, 9, 14, 15

Gustavus Inn

NOTES: Credit cards accepted: A MasterCard; B Visa; C American Express; D Discover; E Diner's Club; F Other; 2 Personal checks accepted; 3 Lunch available; 4 Dinner available; 5 Open all year; 6 Pets welcome;

Meadow's Glacier Bay Guest House

P.O. Box 93, 99826
(907) 697-2348; FAX (907) 697-2454
e-mail: meadowguest@iname.com
www.glacier-bay-alaska.com

A stunning setting and warm welcome await guests at Meadow's Glacier Bay Guest House. Every window of this architect-designed home is filled with views of Alaska's Inside Passage or snow-capped mountains in Glacier Bay. Step outside the front door and fish in a river, ride a bike, or beachcomb. Trophy salmon and halibut fishing, Glacier Bay excursions, kayaking, golf, and restaurants are nearby. Gourmet breakfasts and concierge services are the specialty.

Hosts: Meadow Brook and Chris Smith
Rooms: 5 (4 PB; 1 SB) $99-179
Full Breakfast
Credit Cards: A, B
Notes: 2, 3, 4, 5, 7, 8, 9, 12, 13, 14, 15

A Puffin's Bed & Breakfast Lodge

P.O. Box 3, 99826
(907) 697-2260; FAX (907) 697-2258
e-mail: ad@puffintravel.com

Guests stay in their own modern cottage on a seven-acre, partially wooded homestead adorned with wild flowers and berries. Full country breakfast served in central lodge. Covered picnic area with barbecue. Coin-operated laundry available. Special diets accommodated. Hike beaches or bicycle miles of country roads. See marine life from a charter cruiser or kayak. Glacier Bay tours, complete packages with air or ferry, lodging and activities. Special rates for seniors and children. Travel service year-round. Social drinking permitted in cabins only.

Hosts: Chuck and Sandy Schroth
Cottages: 6 (PB) $85-125
Full Breakfast
Credit Cards: None
Notes: 2, 3, 4, 6, 7, 8, 9, 14

HAINES

The Summer Inn Bed & Breakfast

117 Second Avenue, P.O. Box 1198, 99827
(907) 766-2970 (phone/FAX)
www.summerinn@wytbear.com

This charming, historic farmhouse has an infamous beginning, it was built by a member of a gang of claimjumpers who operated during the Gold Rush. The home affords stunning mountain and water views. The home is comfortably furnished, and one guest bathroom includes a claw-foot tub original to the home. A full homemade breakfast is served daily. Be a guest at the Summer Inn, big enough for privacy—small enough for conversation.

Hosts: Bob and Mary Ellen Summer
Rooms: 5 (SB) $70-80
Full Breakfast
Credit Cards: A, B
Notes: 2, 5, 7, 8, 10, 11, 12, 13, 14

HOMER

A Homestay at Homesteads

341 West Tudor, Suite 250, Anchorage, 99503
(907) 272-8644; FAX (907) 274-8644

H1. Come to this spacious log house and a bit of Alaskan nostalgia in this exceptionally beautiful part of Alaska. Nestled under the tall spruce trees in a quiet neighborhood, walking distance from downtown. Just the perfect place to enjoy another Alaskan day fishing or hiking in inviting Kachemak Bay. The hosts will make arrangements for ferry, fishing, dog sledding, and other activities. The Home Stage will pick-up and drop off at the door. Nonsmoking. Private and shared baths. Full Alaskan breakfast. Open May 1 through September 30.

H3. Just spin on in to this delightful home. It has facilities to fit guests' every taste. Choose between cozy private rooms with a full breakfast

---

7 No smoking; 8 Children welcome; 9 Social drinking allowed; 10 Tennis nearby; 11 Swimming nearby; 12 Golf nearby; 13 Skiing nearby; 14 May be booked through a travel agent; 15 Handicapped accessible.

or the dormitory-type room with a Continental breakfast. For the folks that like seclusion, the two-bedroom Chalet is a few miles from Homer up the Sterling highway and will sleep up to eight. The Chalet has a two-night minimum. Open year-round. A short walk to to the museum and town. $28-135.

H4. What a view! This three-bedroom private cottage overlooks the Kenai Mountains, glaciers, and beautiful Kachemak Bay. A kitchen, full bath, and living room make this the perfect "home away from home." What a honeymoon spot. Open all year.

HOPE

Hope GoldRush Bed & Breakfast

P.O. Box 36, 99605
(907) 782-3436 (Hope)
(907) 248-4563 (Anchorage)
e-mail: fayrene@alaska.net
www.advenalaska.com/hope/

Hope GoldRush Bed and Breakfast provides a quiet, restful sleep with a delicious home-style breakfast. Enjoy the historic pioneer ambiance of the Hirshey Barn (built 1916) while the charming guest cabin provides a living room, full bath with sleeping accommodations for up to five persons. Historic Hope, started by gold miners in 1896, is 88 scenic miles from Anchorage, and is close to fishing, sightseeing, hiking/biking, gold panning, kayaking/boating, and camping on the Kenai Peninsula.

Hosts: Fayrene and Scott Sherritt
Rooms: 1 (PB) $85
Full Breakfast
Credit Cards: A, B
Notes: 2, 7, 8, 14

JUNEAU

Alaska Wolf House

P.O. Box 21321, 99802
(907) 586-2422

Enjoy gourmet breakfasts in the Glass Room and Great Room while eyelevel with Alaskan aircraft and eagle. Each room or suite in the AAA-rated cedar log home has a distinct Alaskan theme, pillow mattresses, and feather pillows. Old-fashioned hospitality with all modern amenities: romantic spa, hot tub in the Sitka forest. Just one and one-half miles from downtown Juneau, yet quietly secluded on Mount Juneau with beautiful views of Gastineau Channel and mountains on Douglas Island.

Hosts: Philip and Clovis Dennis
Rooms: 6 (4 PB; 2 SB) $85-145
Full Breakfast
Credit Cards: A, B, C, D
Notes: 2, 5, 7, 8, 9, 10, 11, 12, 13, 14

A Homestay at Homesteads

341 West Tudor, Suite 250, Anchorage, 99503
(907) 272-8644; FAX (907) 274-8644

J1. This home away from home nestles up to Mount Juneau overlooking the Gastineau Channel and, of course, there are stairs up to the house. The ferry is a long way out of town, so ask the hosts about arranging transportation or a rental car. Breakfast is included (most of the time). Open year-round, yet booked to assist the legislature when in session. Laundry, cooking, sauna, and picnic area. Nonsmoking. $70-95.

Pearson's Pond Luxury Inn & Garden Spa

4541 Sawa Circle, 99801-8723
(907) 789-3772; (888) 6 JUNEAU (658-6328)
FAX (907) 789-6722
e-mail: pearsons.pond@juneau.com
www.juneau.com/pearsons.pond

NOTES: Credit cards accepted: A MasterCard; B Visa; C American Express; D Discover; E Diner's Club; F Other; 2 Personal checks accepted; 3 Lunch available; 4 Dinner available; 5 Open all year; 6 Pets welcome;

Pearson's Pond

Award-winning bed and breakfast resort is perfect getaway for nature and privacy lovers. Enjoy a hot tub overlooking Mendenhall Glacier and a massage at this breathtaking waterfront retreat. Photograph wildlife between naps on the dock, or row on the peaceful pond surrounded by gardens and sparkling fountains. Bike or walk the adjacent river trail. Garden or water view mini-suites have private entry, kitchens, and every imaginable amenity. Health club access. Frommer's Best B&B of Alaska. Fodor's Best of America. AAA/ABBA Excellence.

Hosts: Steve and Diane Pearson
Rooms: 1 (PB) $89-189
Suite: 2 (PB) $99-429
Continental Breakfast
Credit Cards: A, B, C, D, E, F
Notes: 2, 5, 7, 9, 10, 11, 12, 13, 14

Silverbow Inn

120 Second Street, 99801
(907) 586-4146; (800) 586-4146
FAX (907) 586-4242

In the heart of historic downtown, this unique 1914 building was converted to an inn in 1984. Enjoy modern amenities while being surrounded by beautiful antique furniture. Each room has private bath, telephone, and cable TV. Fresh bagels and bread are served hot for breakfast from the bakery next door. Museums, waterfront, shopping, and hiking are all within walking distance. Continental plus breakfast served.

Hosts: Jill Ramiel and Ken Alper
Rooms: 6 (PB) $75-125
Continental Breakfast
Credit Cards: A, B, C
Notes: 2, 3, 4, 5, 7, 8, 9, 13, 14

KENNICOTT

A Homestay at Homesteads

341 West Tudor, Suite 250, Anchorage, 99503
(907) 272-8644; FAX (907) 274-8644

In the heart of the St. Elias Wilderness lies this "old" newly made antique inn just waiting for adventurous souls to enjoy the gourmet dining and tales of the mining days. Share baths as in the olden times. Plan to spend at least two nights; the hosts and the area are worth it. Most people drive in, but guests may fly in (weather permitting). Public transportation available from Glennallen, Valdez, and Anchorage. Overnight with or without meals available. Day rates vary with the size of the traveling group, but calculate per person with meals at $125.

KETCHIKAN

A Homestay at Homesteads

341 West Tudor, Suite 250, Anchorage, 99503
(907) 272-8644; FAX (907) 274-8644

K1. In the quiet woods overlooking Knudson Cove marina, guests will feel "almost home" in the privacy and comfort in own apartment. The apartment has a kitchen, linens, washer/dryer, telephone, cable TV, gas barbecue, and deck. Downstairs has three bedrooms and two baths. Upstairs has a bedroom with private bath. Breakfast foods provided for a self-cook breakfast. Nonsmoking. No pets. Rates begin at $85.

---

7 No smoking; 8 Children welcome; 9 Social drinking allowed; 10 Tennis nearby; 11 Swimming nearby; 12 Golf nearby; 13 Skiing nearby; 14 May be booked through a travel agent; 15 Handicapped accessible.

K2. In town in the midst of all the action. Cruise ships, float planes, fishing boats, eagles and whales—on one of Ketchikan's unique stairway streets (not handicapped accessible). Choice of two beautiful rooms with exotic Jacuzzi bathroom; guest bathrobes provided. Also available is a fully outfitted apartment with separate entrance, double bed, futon for two, cot, barbecue, TV, telephone, washer/dryer. Choose Continental or breakfast with hosts. Nonsmoking. Late arrivals OK by arrangement. Open year-round. $50-90.

K3. View Tongass Narrows in the privacy and comfort of own apartment. Kitchen, cable TV, telephone, private baths, gas barbecue. Upstairs apartment has a cathedral ceiling, two double beds, one twin bed and a queen-size sofa bed. Downstairs apartment has three twin and a double bed, a queen-size sofa bed. Knudson Cove marina and Clover Pass resort are just a few minutes north for charters and fine dining. Generous Continental breakfast on arrival. Rates begin at $85.

KODIAK

A Homestay at Homesteads

341 West Tudor, Suite 250, Anchorage, 99503
(907) 272-8644; FAX (907) 274-8644

KA2. Enjoy the country flavor of this bed and breakfast right in the middle of a wonderful coastal town. Hosts love to cook and plan great breakfasts for all the guests. These long-time Kodiak folks know where to hike, fish, and sightsee. They also know the best pilots in the air and skippers on the sea. Open year-round. Nonsmoking. $65-95.

Kodiak Bed & Breakfast

308 Cope Street, 99616
(907) 486-5367; FAX (907) 486-6557
e-mail: monroe@ptialaska.net
www.ptialaska.net/~monroe

Visitors enjoy a spectacular view of Kodiak's busy fishing fleet in a location just above the boat harbor. Mary's home is easy walking distance from a historic Russian church, art galleries, Baronov Museum, air charters, and Kittiwake Rookery. Enjoy this fishing city with its Russian heritage, stunning beaches, cliffs, and abundant fish and bird life. Fresh local fish is often a breakfast option.

Host: Mary A. Monroe
Rooms: 2 (PB) $70-82
Full Breakfast
Credit Cards: A, B
Notes: 2, 5, 6, 7, 8, 9, 14

KOTZEBUE

A Homestay at Homesteads

341 West Tudor, Suite 250, Anchorage, 99503
(907) 272-8644; FAX (907) 274-8644

Come, enjoy this town right on the ocean so the walk on the street is always refreshing. Tours of one day or overnight stays from Anchorage. There are no roads across Alaska, so a flight is necessary. Private baths, two beds to a room. Restaurant in the two-story hotel. Breakfast is available, but not included. Call for quotes.

PALMER

Timberlings Bed & Breakfast

P.O. Box 732, 99645
(907) 745-4445

A treasure among bed and breakfasts. Log house on 150 acres of wooded hills with panoramic mountain views, exotic birds and plants, alpacas, and a friendly dog. Artists/hosts serve a full gourmet breakfast. Timberlings is the perfect place to return to after a day of hiking, wandering around old gold mines, flying over Mount McKinley, exploring glaciers, river rafting, or shopping and sightseeing in Anchorage.

NOTES: Credit cards accepted: A MasterCard; B Visa; C American Express; D Discover; E Diner's Club; F Other; 2 Personal checks accepted; 3 Lunch available; 4 Dinner available; 5 Open all year; 6 Pets welcome;

Hosts: Buz and Alma Blum
Rooms: 1 (SB) $75
Full Breakfast
Credit Cards: D
Notes: 2, 5, 7, 9, 12, 13, 14

PAXSON (DENALI HIGHWAY)

A Homestay at Homesteads

341 West Tudor, Suite 250, Anchorage, 99503
(907) 272-8644; FAX (907) 274-8644

Old-time Alaskan hospitality awaits guests here. A favorite stage stop in the early 1900s now offers the same warm place to sleep at night plus the restaurant with the best pie around. Stopping for the night before traveling on the most scenic route to Denali National Park? Why not stay a few days to fish, ski, and enjoy peace and quiet. Open year-round. Gas, towing, cocktails, gifts, and rooms with a bath. $80-95.

PETERSBURG

A Homestay at Homesteads

341 West Tudor, Suite 250, Anchorage, 99503
(907) 272-8644; FAX (907) 274-8644

"We know the Alaska Ferry schedule!" So in the middle of the night, the beds are warm and coffee pots are always on. If guests are traveling light, just walk on over to this lovely home or take a very short taxi ride. Breakfast with the family. Stay a few days on this island and enjoy the change of pace here. $55-90.

SEWARD

A Homestay at Homesteads

341 West Tudor, Suite 250, Anchorage, 99503
(907) 272-8644; FAX (907) 274-8644

S1. Guests' very own log cabin is nestled in the trees next to a rushing salmon spawning stream. Fresh pastries, fruit, and juice are delivered to the door. Lounge in bed and watch the wilderness from the picture windows. So the pipes do not freeze in the winter, there is a year-round heated central bath and shower. There are camping spots available, too. Creekside is a treat worth waiting for. Families are welcome. Just off the highway on the road to Exit Glacier. $65-130.

S2. Surrounded by a panoramic mountain view. This wonderful two-story inn is a bed and breakfast not to be missed. Each room has its own atmosphere sharing a fully equipped kitchen and TV common areas. Private and shared baths. Breakfast is an ample self-serve buffet. In the center for Exit Glacier hiking, fishing, and the Kenai Fjords National Park excursions. Seasonal rates. $60-100.

S3. An eagle's nest is in the tree just outside the upstairs living room wall of windows. This new home is in a rural area but close to town. The hosts love to cook and visit, so plan to join them in the glassed-in formal dining area or out on the upstairs porch. Twin-size beds with shared bath. Nonsmoking. $65-85.

S4. Guests have their own six-room log house with spacious bedrooms, private bath, two double beds covered with handmade quilts. Hiking and exploring on dirt roads and streams. Close to Seward and the Kenai Fjords National Park but still in the wilds. Rushing stream on both sides of the property hum in the night. Continental breakfast. Nonsmoking. $75-95.

SHEEP MOUNTAIN

A Homestay at Homesteads

341 West Tudor, Suite 250, Anchorage, 99503
(907) 272-8644; FAX (907) 274-8644

SM. Half-way between Anchorage and Glennallen in the mountains, take a few days away from the crowds to explore, hike, and enjoy a typical Alaskan experience. Make these individual

---

7 No smoking; 8 Children welcome; 9 Social drinking allowed; 10 Tennis nearby; 11 Swimming nearby; 12 Golf nearby; 13 Skiing nearby; 14 May be booked through a travel agent; 15 Handicapped accessible.

log cabins home. All have private baths. Dorm rooms are available with shared bath (call for quotes). Finest meals around with homemade pastries and pies available, but not included. $95 plus 4.75 tax.

SITKA

Alaska Ocean View Bed & Breakfast

1101 Edgecumbe Drive, 99835
(907) 747-8310; FAX (907) 747-3440
e-mail: aovbb@hotmail.com
www.wetpage.com/oceanview

Enjoy casual elegance and affordable rates at this superior quality bed and breakfast where guests experience a high degree of personal comfort, privacy, and friendly helpful hosts. Very comfortable king- and queen-size beds. Open the day with the tantalizing aroma of freshly baked breads, freshly ground coffee, and a delicious complimentary buffet-style breakfast. Close the day with a relaxing soak under the stars in the bubbling patio hot tub/spa. Recipient of Alaska's Best award.

Hosts: Carole and Bill Denkinger
Rooms: 3 (PB) $69-139
Full and Continental Breakfast
Credit Cards: A, B, C
Notes: 2, 5, 7, 8, 9, 10, 11, 14

A Homestay at Homesteads

341 West Tudor, Suite 250, Anchorage, 99503
(907) 272-8644; FAX (907) 274-8644

ST1. This home is downtown and up the hill so that the rooms have some of the finest views around. The hosts have been here for years and love to talk about their adventures. Breakfast is included. Shared bath. $55-90.

SKAGWAY

A Homestay at Homesteads

341 West Tudor, Suite 250, Anchorage, 99503
(907) 272-8644; FAX (907) 274-8644

How nice to come home to quiet rooms, fresh sheets, and in the morning to restart the day with a delicious Continental breakfast. Hosts have integrated the old with the new and it's all right downtown. Shared bath. Open year-round. $75-95.

SOLDOTNA

Denise Lake Lodge Bed & Breakfast

41680 Denise Lake Road, P.O. Box 1050, 99669
(907) 262-1789; (800) 478-1789
FAX (907) 262-7184
www.bbonline.com/ak/deniselake

On Denise Lake three miles from Soldotna and the Kenai River. The hosts offer package deals on lodging with fishing or hunting. Fly-out trips are available. The immaculate rooms have private baths, and a full breakfast is included. There is a fish-cleaning area and freezer space for fish and an exercise room and coin-operated laundry. Bring warm clothing and rain gear.

Hosts: Elaine and Jim
Rooms: 10 (PB) $89-149
Full Breakfast
Credit Cards: A, B, C, D
Notes: 2, 7, 8, 9, 11, 12, 13, 14, 15

SOLDOTNA (KENAI AREA)

A Homestay at Homesteads

341 West Tudor, Suite 250, Anchorage, 99503
(907) 272-8644; FAX (907) 274-8644

KS2. Enjoy the view from the home which is right on the bank of the Kenai River. The captain and host provide early, early breakfast for the fishing and Bidding aficionados. Charters

---

NOTES: Credit cards accepted: A MasterCard; B Visa; C American Express; D Discover; E Diner's Club; F Other; 2 Personal checks accepted; 3 Lunch available; 4 Dinner available; 5 Open all year; 6 Pets welcome;

for bird watching and/or fishing available (not included). Bring oneself, binoculars, and poles for a truly Alaskan experience. $85-95.

Posey's Kenai River Hideaway

Posey's Kenai River Hideaway Bed & Breakfast Lodge

P.O. Box 4094-ABB, 99669
(907) 262-7430; FAX (907) 262-7430
e-mail: hideaway@alaska.net
www.alaska.net/~hideaway/

On the bank of the Kenai River with its world-record king salmon, guests enjoy good, wholesome breakfast served before fishing. Hosts will arrange guided salmon or halibut charter, also fly-out fishing or sightseeing trips. After catching fish, relax on the sun deck built out over the river and swap fish stories. Hosts will freeze and pack fish for the return trip home. Seasonal rates available.

Hosts: Ray and June Posey
Rooms: 10 (3 PB; 7 SB) $110-130
Full Breakfast
Credit Cards: A, B
Notes: 2, 5, 9, 12, 13, 14

STEPHEN LAKE

A Homestay at Homesteads

341 West Tudor, Suite 250, Anchorage, 99503
(907) 272-8644; FAX (907) 274-8644

SL. The hosts will pick up guests in their plane and fly them to the dock in front of the main house. Great fishing in the stream nearby. The hosts love to cook gourmet meals; all meals are included. Because of the flight time, guests stay for an unforgettable experience for two or more nights (three or more days). Nonhunting or nonfishing guests may receive reduced rates. Fly-out cabins available; hosts will bring meals out to guests. Call for rates.

TOK

A Homestay at Homesteads

341 West Tudor, Suite 250, Anchorage, 99503
(907) 272-8644; FAX (907) 274-8644

Guest rooms are tiny but the host has a big heart in this log home on the highway. Open year-round and has camping places for RVs and tents. One-half mile from the Y in the highway, this hostel offers private baths with double beds or shared baths in the rooms with bunk beds. Warm hospitality is here in the middle of nowhere. Stay awhile and hike, fish, hunt, or enjoy all the winter sports. RV and tent camping $15. Bunk rooms $25. Bed and breakfast $50-75.

VALDEZ

A Homestay at Homesteads

341 West Tudor, Suite 250, Anchorage, 99503
(907) 272-8644; FAX (907) 274-8644

V1. The hosts love to travel too! They know what it is like to come home at night and be welcomed into the best of all bed and breakfasts. Come stay for a few days in the lovely fjord town to explore the waterways, glaciers, wilderness mountains, white-water rivers. Taking the ferry? The hosts are used to guests leaving at the crack of dawn and/or arriving late. The hospitality door is always open. $75-95.

---

7 No smoking; 8 Children welcome; 9 Social drinking allowed; 10 Tennis nearby; 11 Swimming nearby; 12 Golf nearby; 13 Skiing nearby; 14 May be booked through a travel agent; 15 Handicapped accessible.

V4. If guests have a family looking for the perfect stop, the hosts have the right rooms with double and bunk beds. What a joy to find a fun family stop that loves and welcomes well-behaved kids as well as their parents. Families and large groups are welcomed. From $85.

WASILLA

Yukon Don's Bed & Breakfast Inn

1830 East Parks Highway, Suite 386, 99654 (mail)
2221 Yukon Circle
(907) 376-7472; (800) 478-7472
e-mail: yukondon@alaska.net

All rooms are decorated with authentic Alaskana. Stay in the Iditarod, Fishing, Denali, and Southeast Rooms, or in the Matanuska or Klondike Suites. Or enjoy the cozy cabin. Alaska Room offers Alaskan historic library, video library, pool table, cable TV, and gift bar. The all-glass View Room on the second floor offers the grandest view in the Matanuska Valley. Telephones in each room. Continental plus breakfast bar. Sauna and exercise room. Alaska's award-winning bed and breakfast inn: Alaska's Family Business of the Year, 1994; Top 50 Inns in America, 1991; ABBA Award of Excellence; Wasilla's Official Bed and Breakfast Accommodation. AAA-approved 1996, three diamonds. Ask about our oyster farm.

Hosts: Yukon Don and Beverly Tanner
Rooms: 8 (3 PB; 5 SB) $85-135
Continental Breakfast
Credit Cards: A, B
Notes: 2, 5, 7, 9, 12, 14

WHITTIER

A Homestay at Homesteads

341 West Tudor, Suite 250, Anchorage, 99503
(907) 272-8644; FAX (907) 274-8644

1. Guests have a world-class view of the spectacular fjord at this warm-water port where two-thirds of the population live in the high rise built for troops during World War II. The ferry and train both leave from the docks below. Enjoy plenty of winter skiing, summer hiking, kayaking, and fishing. Come for overnight or stay a few days. Kitchen, living room in each suite. Continental breakfast and/or early hot meal delivered to the condo suite.

2. See Prince William Sound with a retired commercial fisherman and his wife. Enjoy this very stable boat on Prince William Sound, around the islands for wilderness hiking, glacier viewing, and shrimping or fish without new electric reels. Meals and accommodations for up to six lucky folks. They have two boats so could accommodate more. Call early to get your pick of days.

3. Why not try this bed and breakfast on a boat while touring the beautiful Prince William Sound. Captain is the foremost authority on bird habitats in Prince William Sound and is an expert on where to camp as well as the area's forest service cabins and kayaking. The boat is wheelchair and kayak accessible. Come spend a few days on the water exploring remote islands in Alaska. Open year-round. Call for quote.

WILLOW

Willow Winter Park Bed & Breakfast

P.O. Box 251, 99688
(907) 495-7547; FAX (907) 495-7638
e-mail: winterpark@matnet.com

An hour and a half north of Anchorage on the Parks Highway. Overlooking Winter Park Lake, this beautiful bed and breakfast is the perfect home base for the Alaskan adventure. Three hours south of Mount McKinley Park, four hours north of Seward. Rooms are furnished with antiques, and flannel sheets. Hot tub on outdoor deck. Great salmon and trout fishing, mountain biking, hiking, canoeing in

---

NOTES: Credit cards accepted: A MasterCard; B Visa; C American Express; D Discover; E Diner's Club; F Other; 2 Personal checks accepted; 3 Lunch available; 4 Dinner available; 5 Open all year; 6 Pets welcome;

the summer; skiing, dog-sled rides, and snowmobiling in the winter.

Host: Kurt Stenehjem
Rooms: 5 (PB) $75
Full Breakfast
Credit Cards: A, B, C, D, E
Notes: 2, 5, 7, 8, 9, 11, 13, 14

WRANGELL

Grand View Bed & Breakfast

P.O. Box 927, 99929
(907) 874-3225 (phone/FAX)
e-mail: Judy@GrandViewBnB.com
e-mail: bakerj@seapac.net
www.GrandViewBnB.com

Nestled in the woods, quiet, secluded, courtesy transportation. Four guest rooms with private baths and entrances, common dining, living, kitchen area with kitchen privileges. Rooms include cable TV, VCR, touch-tone telephone, extra-long twin or queen-size beds, spa, bicy-

Grand View

cles. Activity planning—i.e., charter fishing, kayaking, jet boat tours, guided walking tours, or car rental. Sack lunches provided on request for an additional fee.

Hosts: Judy and John Baker
Rooms: 4 (PB) $75-105
Full and Continental Breakfast
Credit Cards: None
Notes: 2, 3, 5, 7, 8, 9, 10, 11, 12, 14

---

7 No smoking; 8 Children welcome; 9 Social drinking allowed; 10 Tennis nearby; 11 **Swimming nearby**; 12 Golf nearby; 13 Skiing nearby; 14 May be booked through a travel agent; 15 Handic**apped accessible**.

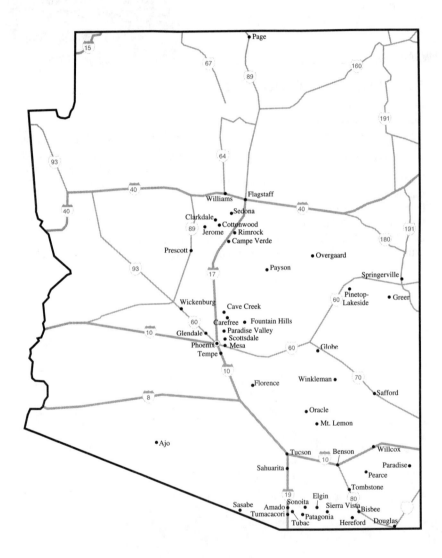

Arizona

Arizona

AJO

Mi Casa Su Casa/Old Pueblo Homestays Bed & Breakfast Reservation Service

P.O. Box 950, Tempe, AZ 85280-0950
(602) 990-0682; (800) 456-0682
FAX (602) 990-3390
e-mail: micasa@primenet.com
www.azres.com

4011. Near Organ Pipe Cactus National Monument and 50 minutes from Mexico. Originally built in 1925 to accommodate visiting company officials for Phelps Dodge, this inn has four guest rooms, private baths, a reputation for warm hospitality, and excellent breakfasts. The furnishings reflect the rich traditions of Arizona. There is a guest cottage with living room, kitchen, full hall bath, and three bedrooms. Rollaway beds available. Children welcome. No smoking. No pets. Ten dollars for third person in room. $69-79.

AMADO

Amado Territory Ranch Inn

3001 East Frontage Road, P.O. Box 81, 85645
(800) 398-8684
e-mail: info@amado-territory-inn.com
www.amado-territory-inn.com

The Amado Territory Inn bed and breakfast has nine gorgeous rooms with private baths and one private suite. This bed and breakfast is only one-year-old, nestled on 17 acres of lush landscaping, with more than 53 varieties of birds, pond, waterfalls, antique shop, meeting rooms, wedding locations, chip and putt area. Cafe, nursery. Excellent locations for bird watching. AAA-rated. Lunch and dinner available next door.

Rooms: 10 (PB) $105-135
Full Breakfast
Credit Cards: A, B, C, D
Notes: 2, 5, 7, 9, 10, 11, 12, 14, 15

Arizona Trails Bed & Breakfast Reservation Service

P.O. Box 18998, Fountain Hills, 85269-8998
(480) 837-4284; (888) 799-4284
FAX (480) 816-4224
e-mail: aztrails@arizonatrails.com
www.arizonatrails.com

AZ 024. Relax in this cozy nine-room western inn south of Tucson. Five acres of riparian habitat with award-winning landscaping, walking trails and adjacent artists studios. Just five miles of Tubac and great for hikers and bird watchers. Decorated in a simple but warm mission style. All rooms have private baths and hand-carved furnishings. Guests may also enjoy on-site chip and putt, spa facilities, library, and restaurant. Handicapped accessible. $105-135.

NOTES: Credit cards accepted: A MasterCard; B Visa; C American Express; D Discover; E Diner's Club; F Other; 2 Personal checks accepted; 3 Lunch available; 4 Dinner available; 5 Open all year; 6 Pets welcome; 7 No smoking; 8 Children welcome; 9 Social drinking allowed; 10 Tennis nearby; 11 Swimming nearby; 12 Golf nearby; 13 Skiing nearby; 14 May be booked through a travel agent; 15 Handicapped accessible.

BENSON

Mi Casa Su Casa/Old Pueblo Homestays Bed & Breakfast Reservation Service

P.O. Box 950, Tempe, AZ 85280-0950
(602) 990-0682; (800) 456-0682
FAX (602) 990-3390
e-mail: micasa@primenet.com
www.azres.com

4031. This bed and breakfast, built in 1995, is adjacent to a privately owned amateur astronomical observatory housing six modern telescopes from six to twenty inches in diameter and a two mile nature trail that includes the San Pedro River and ponds that attract many species of waterfowl. Three guest bedrooms each have a bed, sofa bed, and bathroom. Smaller studio with kitchenette also available. Forty-seven miles east of the Tucson International Airport. Full breakfast. Smoking permitted outside only. No pets. Children welcome with close adult supervision. Ten dollars for each additional person. $65-99.

4032. Comfortable and welcoming, this southwestern-themed bed and breakfast ranch-style house is located on one acre where guests might see javelina, jack rabbits, or deer. Forty-seven miles from Tucson, it is near Kartchner Caverns, the world's largest Caverns. An old steam train departs from Benson for the San Pedro River Valley excursion. Three guest rooms with private or shared full baths. Accredited massage therapist available by appointment. Full breakfast. Children welcome. Smoking permitted outside only. No pets. $65-85.

BISBEE

Arizona Trails Bed & Breakfast Reservation Service

P.O. Box 18998, Fountain Hills, 85269-8998
(480) 837-4284; (888) 799-4284
FAX (480) 816-4224
e-mail: aztrails@arizonatrails.com
www.arizonatrails.com

AZ 118. This Mediterranean-style bed and breakfast is just minutes from Old Town Bisbee. Choose from one of four guest rooms. Two rooms have a private bath and two share the full hall bath. One has a balcony. The common area features a fireplace with TV. Enjoy the local mine tour or visit the quaint antique shops and boutiques in downtown Bisbee. Full breakfast. $50-70.

Bisbee Grand Hotel

P.O. Box 825, 85603
(602) 452-5900

Capture the ambiance of downtown historic Bisbee by staying at Bisbee's most elegant turn-of-the-century hotel. Each room is individually appointed with antiques featuring Victorian, oriental, garden, and captain's suites. Old West bar. Within walking distance to all fine restaurants, shopping, and the famous copper mine tour.

Host: Bill W. Thomas
Rooms: 11 (PB) $55-150
Full Breakfast
Credit Cards: A, B, C, D, E, F
Notes: 2, 5, 7, 8, 9, 10, 11, 12, 14

Hotel La More/The Bisbee Inn

45 OK Street, P.O. Box 1855, 85603
(888) 432-5131; FAX (520) 432-5343
e-mail: bisbeeinn@aol.com

Designated by *Tucson Lifestyle* magazine as "one of the most romantic getaways in Arizona," Hotel La More/*The* Bisbee Inn has reno-

---

NOTES: Credit cards accepted: A MasterCard; B Visa; C American Express; D Discover; E Diner's Club; F Other; 2 Personal checks accepted; 3 Lunch available; 4 Dinner available; 5 Open all year; 6 Pets welcome;

vated 16 rooms to include private baths. The "best breakfast in Bisbee" is included in the price of the room. For the business guests as well as families and friends who enjoy traveling together there are now fully furnished suites/apartments available. Above a tree-lined walkway, nestles the newest historic addition, the Hotel La More Annex, a 1905 brick building which survived the Chihuahua Hill fire of 1908. Antiques furnishings and hand-sewn quilts combine with modern TV/VCR and private telephone with fax/modem hookups to provide style, charm, comfort, and convenience. The one- or two-bedroom suites include fully equipped kitchens.

Hosts: Al and Elissa Strati
Rooms: 25 (21 PB; 4 SB) $50-165
Full Breakfast
Credit Cards: A, B, C, D, E, F
Notes: 5, 6, 7, 9, 11, 12, 14

The Inn at Castle Rock

The Inn at Castle Rock

112 Tombstone Canyon Road, P.O. Box 1161, 85603
(520) 432-4449; (800) 566-4449
FAX (520) 432-7868
e-mail: castlerock@theriver.com

A romantic return to Bisbee's past, with an acre of hillside gardens, fish ponds, a silver mine shaft complete with water and fish, eclectic decor, and original art. This one of a kind 1890 restored miner's boarding house is a must see. "We're not normal."

Rooms: 14 (PB) $59-87
Full Breakfast
Credit Cards: A, B, C, D, E
Notes: 2, 5, 6, 7, 8, 9, 12

Mi Casa Su Casa/Old Pueblo Homestays Bed & Breakfast Reservation Service

P.O. Box 950, Tempe, AZ 85280-0950
(602) 990-0682; (800) 456-0682
FAX (602) 990-3703
e-mail: micasa@primenet.com
www.azres.com

4042. Spanish Mission-style two story home designed by famous architect was built in 1906. Spacious rooms with lofty crowned ceilings, oak and maple flooring, fireplaces, and Victorian decor. Six bedrooms with private or shared baths. Kitchenette for guests on the second floor. A generous breakfast offering many homemade items is included. Afternoon refreshments are served. First floor rooms may be partially handicapped accessible. Smoking permitted outside. Children welcome. No pets. Fifteen dollars per extra guest. $60-70.

4043. This 1910 two-story Mediterranean-style home, 10 minutes from the quaint shopping district, is in a quiet residential area across from a park. Four spacious bedrooms, two with balconies. Roses and fruit trees grace the front and back lawns. Two guest rooms have private baths. The host couple serves a four-course gourmet breakfast. Smoking permitted outside. Inquire about accommodations for children and pets. Ten dollars per each additional guest. $50-70.

School House Inn

818 Tombstone Canyon, P.O. Box 32, 85603
(520) 432-2996; (800) 537-4333

Historic schoolhouse built in 1918 and converted into lovely large rooms and suites with 12-foot ceilings and private baths. High up Tombstone Canyon, the 5,600-foot elevation provides spectacular scenery, clean air, and a relaxing retreat. A full breakfast is served on the shaded patio or in the spacious family room. The inn is close to mine tours, art galleries, antique shops, hiking, bird watching,

---

7 No smoking; 8 Children welcome; 9 Social drinking allowed; 10 Tennis nearby; 11 Swimming nearby; 12 Golf nearby; 13 Skiing nearby; 14 May be booked through a travel agent; 15 Handicapped accessible.

and much more. Recommended by *Arizona Republic* as "Best Place to Stay in Southern Arizona." In-state personal checks accepted.

Hosts: Jeff and Bobby Blankenbeckler
Rooms: 9 (PB) $55-80
Full Breakfast
Credit Cards: A, B, C, D, E
Notes: 5, 7, 9, 11, 12, 15

CAMP VERDE

Arizona Trails Bed & Breakfast Reservation Service

P.O. Box 18998, Fountain Hills, 85269-8998
(480) 837-4284; (888) 799-4284
FAX (480) 816-4224
e-mail: aztrails@arizonatrails.com
www.arizonatrails.com

AZ 113. Privacy plus at this bed and breakfast guest house on the site of an award-winning winery adjacent to Prescott National Forest. Room features sitting area, wood-burning stove, CD player, two-person whirlpool tub with shower and all European fixtures, and a breakfast nook for in-room breakfast. Relax on the deck or enjoy a meal at the on-site restaurant for lunch or dinner. Close to area attractions. Guests receive a complimentary bottle of wine. $125-150.

Mi Casa Su Casa/Old Pueblo Homestays Bed & Breakfast Reservation Service

P.O. Box 950, Tempe, AZ 85280-0950
(602) 990-0682; (800) 456-0682
FAX (602) 990-3390
e-mail: micasa@primenet.com
www.azres.com

4071. This bed and breakfast was built in 1996 on 20 acres in high chaparral surrounded by forest service land. On the property is an award-winning boutique winery dedicated to the production of fine varietal wines. It is an easy drive to historic Fort Verde, Prescott, Jerome, and Sedona. The large open guest room has a private entrance and is separate from the main house. It has a double whirlpool tub with shower, and a wood burning stove. No smoking. No pets. No children. $150.

CAREFREE

Mi Casa Su Casa/Old Pueblo Homestays Bed & Breakfast Reservation Service

P.O. Box 950, Tempe, AZ 85280-0950
(602) 990-0682; (800) 456-0682
FAX (602) 990-3390
e-mail: micasa@primenet.com
www.azres.com

4081. In a secluded valley, this bed and breakfast is near scenic Cave Creek and Carefree. Spectacular views of the mountains and great hiking and bird watching along the creek. Stable nearby where guests can rent horses and ride some of the most beautiful trails in Arizona. The carriage house has a private entrance, living room with large TV, bedroom, and bath with tub/shower. The full kitchen is stocked with Continental plus breakfast fixings. No smoking. No pets. Children 10 and older welcome. Ten dollars for each additional person. $85-100.

4082. This deluxe executive retreat is on 20 acres surrounded by the scenic Tonto National Forest. Convenient to golf, horseback riding, hiking, biking, jeep tours, and fine dining. Four extra-large guest rooms include private entrance and private bath, stereo with CD, cassette, and radio, TV/VCR, full concierge services, and afternoon snacks. Large fireplace in common room; heated outside spa; pool for seasonal swimming. Heart-healthy breakfast served by chef. Smoking is permitted outside. No children. No pets. Twelve dollars for each additional guest. $270.

NOTES: Credit cards accepted: A MasterCard; B Visa; C American Express; D Discover; E Diner's Club; F Other; 2 Personal checks accepted; 3 Lunch available; 4 Dinner available; 5 Open all year; 6 Pets welcome;

CAVE CREEK

Arizona Trails Bed & Breakfast Reservation Service

P.O. Box 18998, Fountain Hills, 85269-8998
(480) 837-4284; (888) 799-4284
FAX (480) 816-4224
e-mail: aztrails@arizonatrails.com
www.arizonatrails.com

AZ 019. Comfort and charm abound at this three-guest room bed and breakfast close to the Phoenix border and only 10 minutes to the freeway, yet nestled in a lush desert landscape that is quiet and relaxing. Two guest rooms have TVs and private baths with stand up showers. The Dream Catcher suite has sliding glass doors leading to a private patio, private hall bath and private living room with TV, fireplaces, and guest refrigerator stocked with cold drinks. An indoor hot tub adjoins the large outside deck. Continental breakfast is served Monday through Friday, with a full breakfast served on the weekends. $85-95.

AZ 075. Experience the Old West at this guest house adjacent to Tonto National Forest. The main room features a sitting area with TV/VCR. Full kitchen is stocked daily for a self-serve breakfast and the private bath has both tub and shower. Private entrance, great views. Stables and trail rides across the street. Site was once an old gold mine. The main house is Victorian and has been featured in a Disney/Mirimax film. $100.

AZ 098. For a true taste of the Southwest, stay at this lovely, new two-guest-room bed and breakfast in the Spur Cross area of Cave Creek. One room offers a private bath. The upstairs suite has a bed, sleeper sofa, full bath with whirlpool tub, kitchenette, and balcony. The grounds are spacious, the views panoramic. Close to town with shops and restaurants. Horse boarding also available. A buffet Continental plus breakfast is served. $95-125.

Mi Casa Su Casa/Old Pueblo Homestays Bed & Breakfast Reservation Service

P.O. Box 950, Tempe, AZ 85280-0950
(602) 990-0682; (800) 456-0682
FAX (602) 990-3390
e-mail: micasa@primenet.com
www.azres.com

4101. Casual, friendly host couple welcomes guests to a large rambling house on a five-acre horse ranch. Their large suite has a living room, TV, large bedroom, full bath en suite. The second bedroom is small and has a hall bath. The compact apartment has a private entrance, bath, kitchenette, and two bedrooms. Pool available for in-season swimming. Spa. Cookouts, barbecues, and hay rides available by appointment. Continental breakfast weekdays; full breakfast on weekends. Resident dog. Smoking permitted outside. No pets. Children 10 and older welcome. $65-85.

4102. This two-story pueblo-style house constructed in 1997 is on two acres surrounded by state land and the Tonto National Forest. The second-floor El Grande Suite has a bedroom, TV, a bathroom with jetted tub and shower, a separate sitting room, small microwave, and refrigerator. The suite has a private deck to view the pristine desert and mountains. The Cowboy Room on the first floor has a queen-size bed, bath with tub/shower, and a small refrigerator. Smoking permitted outside. No pets. Children welcome. Ten dollars for each additional guest. $95-125.

4103. This seven-acre private horse ranch offers a high desert retreat minutes from Cave Creek's historic Old West center. Each of the three rooms has a separate entrance and patio, kitchenette, TV, VCR, personal telephone line, and private bathroom. A private outdoor spa is accessible to guests in the Pinto Suite. Horse boarding available. Delectable buffet breakfast. No smoking. Small children and pets are considered on an individual basis. $99-130.

---

7 No smoking; 8 Children welcome; 9 Social drinking allowed; 10 Tennis nearby; 11 Swimming nearby; 12 Golf nearby; 13 Skiing nearby; 14 May be booked through a travel agent; 15 Handicapped accessible.

4105. The large Southwestern homes in this area are surrounded by pristine desert with a variety of desert trees, cacti, and bushes. Luxurious, spacious two-bedroom, two-bath guest house set in scenic mountain area has a private entrance, living and dining room, full kitchen, laundry. Room one has a full bath. Room two has a full hall bath. The pool and lounge area is surrounded by majestic palm trees. The Continental plus breakfast is "creatively delectable." Non-smoking. No pets. No children. Weekly and monthly rates available. Add $10 for one night stay. $100-120.

FAX (602) 990-3390
e-mail: micasa@primenet.com
www.azres.com

4125. At 4,200 feet, this five-acre ranchette is built of unique energy-efficient "strawbale" construction, and has a front porch view of the Cochise Stronghold in the Dragoon Mountains. Area attractions include the immense Kartchner Caverns, golf, shopping, hiking, a museum, and an art gallery. Two guest rooms share a bath. Hot tub. Full home-style breakfast. No alcohol. No pets. Smoking permitted outside. Children 12 and older welcome. $65.

CLARKDALE

Arizona Trails Bed & Breakfast Reservation Service

P.O. Box 18998, Fountain Hills, 85269-8998
(480) 837-4284; (888) 799-4284
FAX (480) 816-4224
e-mail: aztrails@arizonatrails.com
www.arizonatrails.com

AZ 053. Relax in this charming three guest room bed and breakfast on a hillside in Clarkdale, just 12 minutes to Jerome and 20 minutes from Sedona. Spectacular panoramic views include the red rocks of Sedona. Close to a golf course and shopping, great for hiking. Two rooms feature sitting area, TV, and private bath with tub and shower. The guest house has a private bath with shower only, full kitchen, TV, wood-burning stove, and great views. An outdoor hot tub is great for viewing the stars at night. Cooking class weekends also available. Full gourmet breakfast. $79-89.

COCHISE

Mi Casa Su Casa/Old Pueblo Homestays Bed & Breakfast Reservation Service

P.O. Box 950, Tempe, AZ 85280-0950
(602) 990-0682; (800) 456-0682

COTTONWOOD

Arizona Trails Bed & Breakfast Reservation Service

P.O. Box 18998, Fountain Hills, 85269-8998
(480) 837-4284; (888) 799-4284
FAX (480) 816-4224
e-mail: aztrails@arizonatrails.com
www.arizonatrails.com

AZ 073. Relax at this two room bed and breakfast in a farm setting, close to the Verde River in Cottonwood. One room in the main house has a dressing room, private bath with tub and shower, and private balcony overlooking the pasture. The guest house has a sitting area, TV, private bath with tub and shower, and is decorated with antiques. Only 20-25 minutes from Sedona and close to the Verde Canyon scenic trail ride. Full breakfast. $85.

Mi Casa Su Casa/Old Pueblo Homestays Bed & Breakfast Reservation Service

P.O. Box 950, Tempe, AZ 85280-0950
(602) 990-0682; (800) 456-0682
FAX (602) 990-3390
e-mail: micasa@primenet.com
www.azres.com

4131. Delightful hostess has pleasant three-bedroom, two-bath stucco house built in 1981

NOTES: Credit cards accepted: A MasterCard; B Visa; C American Express; D Discover; E Diner's Club; F Other; 2 Personal checks accepted; 3 Lunch available; 4 Dinner available; 5 Open all year; 6 Pets welcome;

in quiet residential neighborhood. Landscaped with rock, trees, shrubs, and rose bushes. Large guest room with full bath en suite, TV, radio, coffee maker. Continental plus or full breakfast. Resident parakeet. Two nights preferred. No smoking. No pets. Children six and older welcome. Fifteen dollars for additional person on rollaway. $65.

4132. Large, elegant country home in a serene setting surrounded by mountain views and acres of manicured green pastures. Fourteen miles from Sedona, 15 minutes from Jerome. Spacious 600-square-foot guest cottage with exterior stairs to private entrance on the second floor of a building separate from the main house. Private bath, ample sitting and dining areas, balcony, refrigerator, and small microwave for warming snacks. In the main house is a spacious master bedroom with cable TV, dressing room, tub/shower, balcony deck. Refreshments. Sumptuous breakfasts. Twenty-five dollars for third person in cottage. Ten dollars for children under two years. $85.

DOUGLAS

Mi Casa Su Casa/Old Pueblo Homestays Bed & Breakfast Reservation Service

P.O. Box 950, Tempe, AZ 85280-0950
(602) 990-0682; (800) 456-0682
FAX (602) 990-3390
e-mail: micasa@primenet.com
www.azres.com

4142. This working ranch is on the northeastern slope of the Chiricahua Mountains near many historic sites, museums, and Old Mexico. Forty two miles from Douglas, 150 miles from Tucson. Guests can choose to relax, trail ride, fish in the three-acre catfish pond or take part in the general ranch life including working with cattle. Home-cooked country style meals served family style. Bunk houses have one or two rooms and baths. Seasonal swimming pool. No pets. Children 12 and older welcome. Rates include room, three daily meals and horseback riding. Inquire about rates for breakfast only. $125.

FLAGSTAFF

Arizona Trails Bed & Breakfast Reservation Service

P.O. Box 18998, Fountain Hills, 85269-8998
(480) 837-4284; (888) 799-4284
FAX (480) 816-4224
e-mail: aztrails@arizonatrails.com
www.arizonatrails.com

AZ 010. Enjoy the quiet atmosphere of northern pines at this lovely ranch-style bed and breakfast. This ranch house was originally moved from Texas with its large stone fireplace and high ceilings. Close to historic downtown Flagstaff but far enough away to enjoy the peace and relaxation of the pines. Four rooms all with private baths and antiques. The upstairs suite will accommodate up to four. Downstairs suite has a private entrance, sitting room, and kitchenette. Close to parks, a lake, stables, and skiing. Breakfast and afternoon snacks served in the dining area. Children welcome. $80-120.

AZ 018. Experience this authentic Victorian style bed and breakfast in Flagstaff. Four rooms with antiques and private baths with claw-foot tubs will take guests back to a time of grace and charm. In a quiet residential area, only minutes to parks, downtown shops and restaurants, or skiing. Three guest rooms available, one with fireplace and two with porch access. The parlor houses an old book library. Handmade glycerin soaps in all rooms. Gourmet breakfast served each morning. $95-125.

AZ 025. Luxury abounds in this uniquely historic nine-room inn near downtown. Elegantly appointed with antiques mixed with a touch of southwest. All rooms have a different theme

---

7 No smoking; 8 Children welcome; 9 Social drinking allowed; 10 Tennis nearby; 11 Swimming nearby; 12 Golf nearby; 13 Skiing nearby; 14 May be booked through a travel agent; 15 Handicapped accessible.

with private baths—some with whirlpool tubs and some with gas fireplaces. All rooms have coffee makers and refrigerators. Walk to shops and restaurants in historic downtown Flagstaff. A full breakfast is served each morning. Handicapped accessible. $125-175.

AZ 097. Stay at this 10-room lodge-style inn adjacent to national forest land. There are two sitting areas, one with a fireplace, board games, and library. Relax in the sauna or the outdoor hot tub. Two suites can sleep up to six. A hearty full breakfast is served each morning with all-day coffee service and afternoon cappuccino. Ask about adventure packages including hiking, rock climbing, mountain biking, dog sledding, and cross-country skiing (in season). Handicapped accessible. $99-169.

Birch Tree Inn

824 West Birch Avenue, 86001-2240
(520) 774-1042; (888) 774-1042
e-mail: birch@flagstaff.az.us

The Birch Tree Inn, circa 1917, offers guests comfortable surroundings in one of the city's finest historic homes. The inviting parlor offers a retreat to read, converse, or relax in front of a warm fire. Each bedroom features its own atmosphere blending antiques and heirloom furnishings or southwestern decor. An outdoor whirlpool tub is great for relaxing the weary hiker or skier. A hearty full breakfast is served in the dining room; in early morning coffee/tea is served upstairs. Afternoon refreshments offer guests a time to acquaint themselves with each other and the hosts. Children over 10 are welcome.

Hosts: Sandy and Ed Znetko; Donna and Rodger Pettinger
Rooms: 5 (3 PB; 2 SB) $69-129
Full Breakfast
Credit Cards: A, B, C, D
Notes: 2, 5, 7, 9, 10, 12, 13, 14

Comfi Cottages of Flagstaff

1612 North Aztec Street, 86001
(520) 774-0731; (888) 774-0731
e-mail: pat@comficottages
www.comficottages.com

In historic downtown Flagstaff, cottages are beautifully decorated and furnished with antique pieces having a touch of the Southwest. These one-, two-, and three-bedroom cottages are equipped with everything guests need for comfortable daily living. Breakfast foods are placed in the refrigerator to be prepared at their leisure. All cottages have picnic tables, lawn chairs, and barbecue grills; some have fireplaces. Bicycles are available. Chosen by the *Arizona Republic* as the Best Week-End Getaway. Special recommendation Fodor's 1998 and 1999. Inquire about accommodations for pets. Smoking permitted outside only. Limited accessibility for handicapped.

Hosts: Pat and Ed Wiebe
Cottages: 6 (PB and SB) $105-210
Full Breakfast
Credit Cards: A, B, C, D
Notes: 2, 5, 7, 8, 9, 10, 11, 12, 13, 14, 15

The Inn at 410

410 North Leroux Street, 86001
(800) 774-2008

Explore the Grand Canyon, Indian ruins, and Sedona, then relax at "the Place with the Personal Touch." The Inn at 410 offers award-winning hospitality in a charming 1907 Craftsman home. Scrumptious gourmet breakfasts and freshly baked cookies featured on PBS. Nine distinctive guest rooms with private bath; some

The Inn at 410

NOTES: Credit cards accepted: A MasterCard; B Visa; C American Express; D Discover; E Diner's Club; F Other; 2 Personal checks accepted; 3 Lunch available; 4 Dinner available; 5 Open all year; 6 Pets welcome;

with fireplace or oversized Jacuzzi. Walk two blocks to restaurants and shops in historic downtown Flagstaff. Hike, bike, or ski in the San Francisco Peaks.

Hosts: Howard and Sally Krueger
Rooms: 9 (PB) $125-175
Full Breakfast
Credit Cards: A, B
Notes: 2, 5, 7, 8, 9, 10, 11, 12, 13, 14

Jeanette's

Jeanette's Bed & Breakfast

3380 East Lockett Road, 86004
(520) 527-1912; (800) 752-1912

Imagine stepping back in time to a place where crackling fires welcome guests, fresh flowers adorn guest rooms, and large luxurious clawfoot tubs await guests' travel-weary body. Imagine staying at Jeanette's Bed and Breakfast, a Victorian-style house nestled among the pines at the foot of Mount Elden. Guests will love the old-fashioned romance of the antique-filled rooms, the delicious complimentary fresh-squeezed lemonade and homemade sugar cookies, and the friendliness of the hosts, Ray and Jeanette West. This charming inn is acclaimed as Flagstaff's most romantic inn. Rediscover romance—discover Jeanette's Bed and Breakfast.

Hosts: Jeanette and Ray West
Rooms: 4 (PB) $95-125
Full Breakfast
Credit Cards: A, B, C, D
Notes: 2, 5, 7, 8, 9, 12, 13, 14

Lake Mary Bed & Breakfast

5470 South "J" Diamond Road, 86001
(520) 779-7054; (888) 241-9550
FAX (520) 779-7054

Two and one-half miles outside Flagstaff, this country ranch-type house hosts a large wrap-around front/side porch. Guest facilities include four large guest rooms with private baths. Start the day with one of the hosts' full home-cooked gourmet breakfasts. Need to unwind before dinner? Relax in one of two common rooms with a good book or by the fireplace with a cup of coffee and a slice of homemade bread or a handful of cookies. Smoking is permitted outside only.

Hosts: Frank and Christine McCollum
Rooms: 4 (PB) $80-100 plus tax
Full Breakfast
Credit Cards: A, B
Notes: 2, 5, 7, 8, 9, 12, 13, 14

Mi Casa Su Casa/Old Pueblo Homestays Bed & Breakfast Reservation Service

P.O. Box 950, Tempe, AZ 85280-0950
(602) 990-0682; (800) 456-0682
FAX (602) 990-3390
e-mail: micasa@primenet.com
www.azres.com

4181. This award-winning historic two-story house built in 1917 offers guests comfortable surroundings. There are five guest rooms on the second floor, each with its own atmosphere blending antiques and heirloom furnishings or southwestern decor. Three guest rooms have a private bath; two share a bath. Outside heated spa. Full breakfast is served in the dining room. Afternoon refreshments. Inviting parlor offers a retreat to read or relax in front of the fireplace. Game room with pool table. Children 10 and older are welcome. Smoking permitted outside only. No pets. $79-129.

4182. Rambling five-level home built on a hillside with views of historic downtown, the San

Francisco Peaks, and Mars Hill. Within walking distance of shops, restaurants, and train and bus stations. The suite includes a private entrance, deck, living room with sofa bed and cable TV, bedroom with king bed, bath, and fully equipped kitchen stocked for a self-serve Continental plus breakfast. The other guest room has a shared hall bath and is served a Continental plus breakfast. This inn caters to the chemically and environmentally sensitive. Children over eight are welcome. No pets. Smoking is not permitted on premises. Suite has two-night minimum, with $15 for each person over two persons. $65-95.

4183. This three-story house was built in 1915 in the original town of Flagstaff. Many large trees shade the yard. Five blocks from downtown Flagstaff in quiet residential neighborhood near Thorpe Park. Two suites on the second floor are reached by exterior stairs and have a private entrance. Each has a bedroom with queen bed, a sitting room with sofa bed, private bath with shower, cable TV, telephone, small refrigerator, and wet bar. Bicycles and tennis racquets available. Full breakfast is served. No smoking. No pets. Children 14 and older welcome. $95.

4185. This inn offers well-planned comfortable surroundings in one of the city's finest historic homes built in 1907. There are four suites and five guest rooms, all with private bath, refrigerator, and coffee maker. Several have a fireplace and double whirlpool tub. Some can accommodate three or four people. One is handicapped accessible. Guests are pampered with afternoon snacks with oven-fresh cookies and gourmet breakfasts. Children are welcome. No smoking. No pets. Ten dollars for each additional guest. $125-175.

4186. This recently built bed and breakfast in a scenic, quiet area was designed in a 1912-style post-Victorian-era recalling Arizona's first statehood days. Four bedrooms each with its own delightful atmosphere blends antiques, heirlooms with contemporary for a comfortable stay. Three bedrooms are on the second floor; one is on the first floor. Private baths reflect the style of the era. The breakfast is served with the flair and detail of a fine Sunday dinner. Smoking outside. No pets. Children welcome with prior approval. $95-125.

4187. As guests step onto this vine covered porch they see the lovely old door of the historic England house (ca. 1905), which has welcomed travelers for nearly a century. Two blocks from downtown and six blocks from N.A.U. Accommodating hosts are always ready to assist guests with whatever adventure brings them to town. Three guest accommodations have private baths, original pressed tin ceilings, antiques, and comfortable turn-of-the-century decor. King, queen, twin beds. One room has whirlpool tub and another a wood stove. Full home-cooked breakfast. No smoking. No pets. Children welcome. $95-105.

4188. This bed and breakfast is on five acres in a peaceful, wooded area on Mars Hill, five minutes from downtown. The host couple lives in the main house and have turned a second building which was originally used as an observatory into a guest house. Bedroom with bath with shower, and living room with "flip" couch. Futon available for child. Kitchenette has small refrigerator, microwave, coffee maker, and seating. Full breakfast brought to guest house. Smoking permitted outside. Well behaved pets possible. Ten dollars for each additional person. $125.

FLORENCE

Arizona Trails Bed & Breakfast Reservation Service

P.O. Box 18998, Fountain Hills, 85269-8998
(480) 837-4284; (888) 799-4284
FAX (480) 816-4224
e-mail: aztrails@arizonatrails.com
www.arizonatrails.com

NOTES: Credit cards accepted: A MasterCard; B Visa; C American Express; D Discover; E Diner's Club; F Other; 2 Personal checks accepted; 3 Lunch available; 4 Dinner available; 5 Open all year; 6 Pets welcome;

AZ 065. This six-room historic inn was originally built in the 1930s and is a great midway stopping point between Phoenix and Tucson in the beauty of the Sonoran Desert. The adobe-style inn is centered on a main courtyard with gardens and fountain. Each room has a private bath, private entrance, and individual themes. There are also three guest cottages, furnished with one or two bedrooms, living room, kitchen, and bathroom. Outside swimming pool. Continental breakfast. $69-125.

Mi Casa Su Casa/Old Pueblo Homestays Bed & Breakfast Reservation Service

P.O. Box 950, Tempe, AZ 85280-0950
(602) 990-0682; (800) 456-0682
FAX (602) 990-3390
e-mail: micasa@primenet.com
www.azres.com

4201. This 1930s adobe guest ranch was recently renovated to its original charm. Four miles south of Florence, 60 miles from Phoenix or Tucson. Ten golf courses and horseback riding within 30 minutes. Three cottages with kitchens, a pool to use in season, and seven guest rooms. All have individual heating and air conditioning, private baths, and TVs. New RV park has full hook-ups and laundry facilities. Barbecue area. Continental breakfast buffet. Smoking is permitted in designated areas only. Children are welcome. Inquire about accommodations for pets. Weekly and monthly rates are available. $69-95.

FOUNTAIN HILLS

Arizona Trails Bed & Breakfast Reservation Service

P.O. Box 18998, Fountain Hills, 85269-8998
(480) 837-4284; (888) 799-4284
FAX (480) 816-4224
e-mail: aztrails@arizonatrails.com
www.arizonatrails.com

AZ 037. This charming two-guest room bed and breakfast sits high on a hill with great mountain views. Both rooms have private entrances, full private baths, TVs, and in-room coffee makers. The downstairs suite is decorated in an antique theme with four-poster bed. The upstairs suite is done in southwestern theme and outside balcony with swing. Relax on the patio and enjoy the pool. Full breakfast. $95-105.

AZ 049. This 42-room inn offers golf course views and all the amenities one can imagine. A variety of rooms offer guests the choice of bed size, one- and two-room suites, fireplaces, whirlpool jetted tubs in full private baths, data port telephones, TV/VCRs, in-room coffee makers, and private patios or decks with up to 50-mile views. Golf and spa packages available. Continental plus breakfast buffet. Pool and spa overlook the golf course. Handicapped accessible. $149-345.

AZ 145. Cozy and private guest suite offers guests great views of the yard and surrounding mountains. The room features a sitting area with library, TV/VCR, and private bath. There is a small desk with private telephone. Yard offers lush landscaping with a pool and koi pond. Close to bird watching, hiking, the Verde River, and a variety of shops and restaurants. Pet friendly. Full breakfast. $95.

Mi Casa Su Casa/Old Pueblo Homestays Bed & Breakfast Reservation Service

P.O. Box 950, Tempe, AZ 85280-0950
(602) 990-0682; (800) 456-0682
FAX (602) 990-3390
e-mail: micasa@primenet.com
www.azres.com

4222. As elegant and beautiful as a swan is this large home built on a hill in a scenic area with 50- to 80-mile panoramic mountain views. Luxurious, simple decor. Ten minutes to Mayo Clinic and Taliesen West, 25 minutes to central

---

7 No smoking; 8 Children welcome; 9 Social drinking allowed; 10 Tennis nearby; 11 Swimming nearby; 12 Golf nearby; 13 Skiing nearby; 14 May be booked through a travel agent; 15 Handicapped accessible.

Scottsdale, 45 minutes to Phoenix Sky Harbor Airport. Master suite has cable TV, bath with large shower, whirlpool tub for two, fireplace. Apartment has private entrance, bedroom, full bath and fully furnished kitchen. Continental plus breakfast. No smoking. No pets. No children. Weekly and monthly rates available. $75-175.

4223. This luxurious hillside bed and breakfast sits on two and one-half acres with magnificent mountain views. The number of guests has been limited to four. Only two of the four guest rooms rented at any one time. The largest suite has a large sitting area, large bath with a sunken tub and separate shower. The Merry Lane room has a private bath and shower, and a separate entrance. Two smaller rooms share a hall bath. Private outside spa, putting green, barbecue grill, cabana with fireplace and kitchenette, bicycles, and a lighted tennis court available. Inside is a brick fireplace, a TV connected to a satellite dish, VCR, and pool table. Guests have kitchen privileges. Continental breakfast. Nearby are three golf courses, horseback riding, jeep tours, a wildlife park, casino gambling. No smoking. No pets. Children are welcome. $75-165.

GLOBE

Mi Casa Su Casa/Old Pueblo Homestays Bed & Breakfast Reservation Service

P.O. Box 950, Tempe, AZ 85280-0950
(602) 990-0682; (800) 456-0682
FAX (602) 990-3390
e-mail: micasa@primenet.com
www.azres.com

4252. This bed and breakfast was formerly a schoolhouse, started in 1907 and completed in 1917. The two guest rooms are nicely arranged and very large as they are former classrooms. There are 12-foot windows with views, comfortable furniture, and private baths. Hearty southwestern or Sonoran-style breakfast. The host couple are knowledgeable about mining and historic Arizona. Smoking permitted outside. Possible handicapped accessibility. Ten dollars for each additional person. $75.

GOODYEAR

Mi Casa Su Casa/Old Pueblo Homestays Bed & Breakfast Reservation Service

P.O. Box 950, Tempe, AZ 85280-0950
(602) 990-0682; (800) 456-0682
FAX (602) 990-3390
e-mail: micasa@primenet.com
www.azres.com

4255. This bed and breakfast is southwest of Phoenix, a short driving distance from the Phoenix International Raceway and 35 minutes from the Phoenix Sky Harbor Airport. Built in 1974, the two-story Spanish Hacienda and guest house is on a large property with some fruit trees as well as natural desert. It is adjacent to a golf course and the 18,000 acre Estrella Park with horse back riding, hiking, bird watching, and climbing. Decorated with Spanish/Mexican furnishings, four rooms each have a private bath. Pool for seasonal swimming. Continental plus breakfast. Smoking permitted outside only. No pets. $75-85.

GREER

Arizona Trails Bed & Breakfast Reservation Service

P.O. Box 18998, Fountain Hills, 85269-8998
(480) 837-4284; (888) 799-4284
FAX (480) 816-4224
e-mail: aztrails@arizonatrails.com
www.arizonatrails.com

AZ 103. This lodge in the White Mountains is the oldest building in Greer. The main lodge features seven rooms all with private baths. Four housekeeping cabins surround the property, some with fireplaces, one with two bed-

---

NOTES: Credit cards accepted: A MasterCard; B Visa; C American Express; D Discover; E Diner's Club; F Other; 2 Personal checks accepted; 3 Lunch available; 4 Dinner available; 5 Open all year; 6 Pets welcome;

rooms and jetted tubs, and all with full kitchens. Enjoy warm hospitality, soak in the therapeutic hot tub, wander down to the beaver pond and just relax. Great for fishing, bird watching, and hiking. Full breakfast for those staying in the lodge. $79-145.

Red Setter Inn

8 Main Street, P.O. Box 133, 85927
(520) 735-7441; (888) 994-7337
FAX (520) 735-7425; www.redsetterinn.com

This 7,000-square-foot log bed and breakfast inn is close to skiing, fishing, bird watching, and hiking. Some guest rooms have private fireplaces and jetted tubs. The lodge was built in 1995 on the Little Colorado River in a beautiful pine forest and is filled with antiques and an extensive toy collection. The lodge is on the boundary of one million acres of national forest. Picnic lunch included with all guest stays of two nights or longer. Voted Arizona's Best Bed and Breakfast by the *Arizona Republic*. A 3,000-square-foot four-bedroom, three-bath cabin is available on the river.

Hosts: Jim Sankey and Ken Conant
Rooms: 12 (PB) $130-195
Full Breakfast
Credit Cards: A, B, C
Notes: 2, 5, 7, 9, 13, 15

White Mountain Lodge

140 Main Street, P.O. Box 143, 85927
(520) 735-7568; FAX (520) 735-7498

The 1892 farmhouse was residence to the Lund family until 1940. The Basts purchased the farmhouse in 1993 and remodeled during 1994-95. Each bedroom is individually decorated and the common rooms reflect their southwestern country heritage. Overlooking the Greer meadow and Little Colorado River, the Lodge affords guests spectacular scenery and country hospitality. All breakfasts are made from scratch and include homemade

White Mountain Lodge

baked goods. In the afternoon, homemade sweets are provided and hot drinks are always available. Sack lunch is available.

Hosts: Charles and Mary Bast
Rooms: 7 (PB) $69-119
Full Breakfast
Credit Cards: A, B, C, D, E
Notes: 2, 3, 5, 6, 7, 8, 9, 13, 14

HEREFORD

Arizona Trails Bed & Breakfast Reservation Service

P.O. Box 18998, Fountain Hills, 85269-8998
(480) 837-4284; (888) 799-4284
FAX (480) 816-4224
e-mail: aztrails@arizonatrails.com
www.arizonatrails.com

AZ 016. Along the San Pedro River on five acres of riparian habitat, this 10-room inn is a bird-watcher's paradise with more than 100 species of resident birds and 300 species of migrating birds. All rooms are centered on the courtyard. Each has a private bath and hand-carved Mexican furnishings. Great for group meetings, with a meeting room and A/V screen. The common areas feature a fireplace, library, telescope, and a computer with birder software. Full breakfast with regional dishes served. Handicapped accessible. $119.

---

7 No smoking; 8 Children welcome; 9 Social drinking allowed; 10 Tennis nearby; 11 Swimming nearby; 12 Golf nearby; 13 Skiing nearby; 14 May be booked through a travel agent; 15 Handicapped accessible.

JEROME

The Ghost City Inn

541 North Main Street, 86331
(520) 63 GHOST (phone/FAX); (888) 63 GHOST
e-mail: ghostcityinn@yahoo.com
www.ghostcityinn.com

Experience the elegance of days gone by in this unique "living ghost town." The home was originally built in 1898 and has been lovingly restored to include five antique-filled rooms, complete with two common guest areas. Gourmet breakfast and afternoon tea and cookies are served in the dining room or on the spacious veranda with "take-your-breath-away" views.

Host: Joy Beard
Rooms: 5 (1 PB; 4 SB) $75-95
Full Breakfast
Credit Cards: A, B, C, D
Notes: 2, 5, 7, 8, 10, 11, 12, 13, 14

Mi Casa Su Casa/Old Pueblo Homestays Bed & Breakfast Reservation Service

P.O. Box 950, Tempe, AZ 85280-0950
(602) 990-0682; (800) 456-0682
FAX (602) 990-3390
e-mail: micasa@primenet.com
www.azres.com

4281. This historic two-story white stucco inn with red tile roof and arched windows was constructed in 1917 for the chief surgeon of a very large mining company. The three guest rooms are on the second floor; all have double beds and private baths. The master suite has a sitting room with oversized day bed, dressing room, and full bath. There is a guest cottage with a full bath, kitchenette, and secluded patio. Complimentary snacks. Smoking outside. Crib and rollaway bed available. Well-behaved children welcome. Spectacular full breakfast. Thirty-five dollars for each additional person. Dog possible in guest cottage with additional charge. $95-125.

4282. This inn, built in 1898, continues to offer the legendary hospitality of Arizona's most famous ghost town. Just a few steps away are art galleries and clothing and jewelry boutiques. There are five guest rooms, each with a delightful decor. There are two shared hall baths and one room has a private bath. All rooms have TVs, ceiling fans, outside verandas. Guests are welcome to use two common areas with telephones and fax, courtyard, and outside spa. Children 10 and older welcome. Smoking permitted outside. Fifteen dollars for each additional person. Refreshments. Full breakfast. $75-95.

4283. This house was built in 1925 of hand-poured concrete, a popular style in 1920s boomtown Jerome. Panoramic views. The delightful hostess with an Irish background welcomes guests to a bed and breakfast which has fine built-in cabinetry of the Arts and Crafts fashion of the era. The Copper Suite has two bedrooms, private bath and large sitting room. The Jerome View Suite has a large bedroom with private bath, deck and views. The cottage is separate, with private bath and kitchenette. Full breakfast. No smoking. Fifteen dollars for each additional persons. Children and pets by prior arrangement. $85-100.

LAKE MONTEQUMA

Arizona Trails Bed & Breakfast Reservation Service

P.O. Box 18998, Fountain Hills, 85269-8998
(480) 837-4284; (888) 799-4284
FAX (480) 816-4224
e-mail: aztrails@arizonatrails.com
www.arizonatrails.com

AZ 125. This quaint Victorian-style homestay offers guests serene, natural surroundings with warm hospitality. The upstairs suite features an authentic antique bed, adjacent full bath, and in-room TV. The Strawberry kitchen will bring back delightful childhood memories. Sit on the

---

NOTES: Credit cards accepted: A MasterCard; B Visa; C American Express; D Discover; E Diner's Club; F Other; 2 Personal checks accepted; 3 Lunch available; 4 Dinner available; 5 Open all year; 6 Pets welcome;

deck overlooking Beaver Creek, play a round on the local golf course, or go for a hike and you may run in to the resident elk. Just 20 minutes to Sedona and close to Montezuma's well. Full breakfast. $95.

LAVEEN

Mi Casa Su Casa/Old Pueblo Homestays Bed & Breakfast Reservation Service

P.O. Box 950, Tempe, AZ 85280-0950
(602) 990-0682; (800) 456-0682
FAX (602) 990-3390
e-mail: micasa@primenet.com
www.azres.com

4298. Delightfully quiet two-bedroom guest house on a two-acre mini-ranch is perfect for business travelers and families. Twenty minutes from downtown Phoenix, Tempe, and Phoenix Sky Harbor Airport. Completely remodeled in 1999, guests will enjoy the privacy. Full hall bath, living room with TV/VCR, fully equipped kitchen, telephone with answering machine, private entrance and patio, laundry facilities. Small pets are possible. Smoking permitted outside. Continental breakfast. $65.

MESA

Mi Casa Su Casa/Old Pueblo Homestays Bed & Breakfast Reservation Service

P.O. Box 950, Tempe, AZ 85280-0950
(602) 990-0682; (800) 456-0682
FAX (602) 990-3390
e-mail: micasa@primenet.com
www.azres.com

4301. Friendly host couple welcomes guests to their very large, contemporary Spanish home on one acre. The compact guest suite has a private entrance, living room, private bath, TV, dining area, sink, and refrigerator. Unheated swimming pool available. Resident dog. Handicapped facilities possible. Inquire about accommodations for children. Smoking permitted outside. Full breakfast. $60.

4302. Friendly, caring Scandinavian host couple from Minnesota welcomes guests to a spacious Spanish-style home. In a quiet, handsome neighborhood, one mile to the golf course, three miles to baseball spring training, and an easy drive to the Superstition Mountains and Apache Trail. Decor is traditional with some Scandinavian accents. The two guest rooms share a hall bath. Only one party accepted at a time. Full breakfast. Children 12 and older are welcome. No smoking. $60.

4303. Spacious stucco Mediterranean home is in well-kept neighborhood within walking distance to a small park. Two guest rooms are available in a private guest wing that has one bath. Only one party at a time. Guests are welcome to use the family room with stereo and fireplace or living room that has cable TV and VCR. Pool for seasonal swimming. Small resident dog and parrot. Smoking permitted outside. Fifteen dollars extra for children over 10. Possible handicapped accessibility. $65-84.

4304. In East Mesa, near Apache Junction, the Superstition Mountains, a large chain of lakes, golf, and the Apache Trail, is this contemporary home on an acre of land. Two guest rooms share a hall bath. Swim in the solar-heated swimming pool or relax by the living room fireplace. Full breakfast. Children two and older are welcome. Pre-arranged baby-sitting available. Resident cat. Smoking permitted outside. Special rates are available for longer stays. $40-60.

4305. This ranch-style house was built in the late 1970s with an attached suite. In a residential neighborhood within walking distance of the Mormon Temple or the Genealogy Library. Two guest rooms in the main house have private baths. The suite has a living room with a

---

7 No smoking; 8 Children welcome; 9 Social drinking allowed; 10 Tennis nearby; 11 Swimming nearby;
12 Golf nearby; 13 Skiing nearby; 14 May be booked through a travel agent; 15 Handicapped accessible.

sofa bed, bedroom, bath, and fully equipped kitchen. Full southwestern breakfast is served. Weekly rates available. No smoking. Pets possible with prior arrangement. $75-125.

ORACLE

Arizona Trails Bed & Breakfast Reservation Service

P.O. Box 18998, Fountain Hills, 85269-8998
(480) 837-4284; (888) 799-4284
FAX (480) 816-4224
e-mail: aztrails@arizonatrails.com
www.arizonatrails.com

AZ 064. Just 30 minutes from Tucson in the midst of Coronado National Forest, this historic ranch offers six adobe casitas. Units have one or two bedrooms, full kitchens, and a bathroom. Meeting room available for groups with kitchen. The outdoor ramada features an original, brick barbecue area great for cowboy cookouts. Hike the trails, then cool off in the swimming pool or ease into one of the relaxing hammocks around the property. Inquire about group rates. Meal plan available. $95-175.

OVERGAARD (HEBER)

Arizona Trails Bed & Breakfast Reservation Service

P.O. Box 18998, Fountain Hills, 85269-8998
(480) 837-4284; (888) 799-4284
FAX (480) 816-4224
e-mail: aztrails@arizonatrails.com
www.arizonatrails.com

AZ 095. Nestled in the Pines of the White Mountains this country inn provides gracious charm to the wilderness area. Three elegantly appointed guest rooms all upstairs from the restaurant and sitting area which occupy the main level of the inn. All rooms have full baths with garden tubs, TV/VCR with video libraries, mini-refrigerators, coffee makers, and balconies. A full breakfast is included each morning. Golf at the nearby golf course or relax on the patio café with outdoor fireplace. $125-150.

PAGE

Arizona Trails Bed & Breakfast Reservation Service

P.O. Box 18998, Fountain Hills, 85269-8998
(480) 837-4284; (888) 799-4284
FAX (480) 816-4224
e-mail: aztrails@arizonatrails.com
www.arizonatrails.com

AZ 108. This charming bed and breakfast is the closest bed and breakfast to Lake Powell. Three large, lovely rooms all have private baths. One room has a jetted tub. Another also sleeps up to four with an in-room bath and the third room has a private hall bath. All rooms have TV/VCR with an extensive video library. and refrigerators. Full breakfast. $65-85.

Mi Casa Su Casa/Old Pueblo Homestays Bed & Breakfast Reservation Service

P.O. Box 950, Tempe, AZ 85280-0950
(602) 990-0682; (800) 456-0682
FAX (602) 990-3390
e-mail: micasa@primenet.com
www.azres.com

4341. Friendly, hospitable couple have a bed and breakfast within walking distance of downtown Page. Three guest rooms each have cable TV, VCR, and private bath. An extensive video library plus commercial videos of Lake Powell and the southwest canyon areas are available. Guests are welcome to use the patio, barbecue grill, or pool for seasonal swimming. Refreshments might include salsa and chips or homemade cookies and iced tea. A dog and cat are inside only in the winter time, but not allowed in the guest rooms. Full breakfast served. Smoking permitted in designated areas only. Partially handicapped access possible. Seasonal rates are available. $50-85.

NOTES: Credit cards accepted: A MasterCard; B Visa; C American Express; D Discover; E Diner's Club; F Other; 2 Personal checks accepted; 3 Lunch available; 4 Dinner available; 5 Open all year; 6 Pets welcome;

4342. From the area where this handsome two-story home was built, guests can see the sheer sandstone of the Vermillion Cliffs beyond a wide expanse of open desert, the blue waters of Lake Powell, and the impressive face of Glen Canyon Dam. The extra large guest room on the second floor has a sitting area, private bath, and private balcony. Roll-away bed available. Continental plus breakfast is served. No smoking, no pets. Ten dollars for each additional person. $75.

4343. This hospitable host couple enjoys helping guests discover and enjoy the wonder and beauty of this area. Each guest room is luxurious and spacious with vaulted ceilings and sitting areas. The Southwest Room is extra large, has a full bath en suite. The Rose Room has a shower and large tub en suite, private deck and sitting area with a 180 degree view of Lake Powell, surrounding buttes and mesas. Full breakfast. Children welcome. No pets. Smoking permitted outside. Five dollars for each child under six. Ten dollars for each additional person over 16. $95-105.

4344. Hostess welcomes guests to a two-story Victorian-style house with arched fretwork, wraparound porch with rocking chairs and views of Lake Powell and the Vermillion cliffs. The yard has been featured in the Flower Gardens of Page tour. The three rooms each have a private bath, writing desk, cable TV, VCR, and small refrigerator. On the second floor is the large Lake View Room which has a private balcony with a view of the lake and cliffs, and a full bath en suite. The second floor Garden Room has a full bath en suite. Very private outside hot tub. Full breakfast and afternoon refreshments. No smoking. No pets. Children 12 and older welcome. Ten dollars for each additional person. $95-125.

4345. This handsome two-story home is decorated with early American antiques, some going back to the 1850s. The host couple are very knowledgeable about the Glen Canyon Recreation Area. The first floor suite has two bedrooms, one bath, and cable TV/VCR. It can be reserved as a two bedroom suite or as 2 individual bedrooms. On the second floor is an extra large room with a full bath en suite and a deck with a view of the cliffs. Continental plus breakfast. Smoking outside. No pets. Children welcome. $75-125.

PARADISE VALLEY

Arizona Trails Bed & Breakfast Reservation Service

P.O. Box 18998, Fountain Hills, 85269-8998
(480) 837-4284; (888) 799-4284
FAX (480) 816-4224
e-mail: aztrails@arizonatrails.com
www.arizonatrails.com

AZ 099. This exclusive inn was originally built by one of the famous "cowboy artists." The luxurious grounds include 35 rooms, casitas and villas, a swimming pool, tennis courts, two in-ground spas, gardens, and a southwestern cuisine restaurant. Choose from a basic room with private bath, private patio, fireplace, and TV/VCR, or go to the top of the line with a villa that equals a home away from home with living room, kitchen, two bedrooms, two baths, fireplaces, kitchenettes, and private patios. Close to Phoenix and Scottsdale, area golf courses, shops, and restaurants. Continental breakfast is served. Small meeting room available. Handicapped accessible. Children welcome. $160-595.

PATAGONIA

Mi Casa Su Casa/Old Pueblo Homestays Bed & Breakfast Reservation Service

P.O. Box 950, Tempe, AZ 85280-0950
(602) 990-0682; (800) 456-0682
FAX (602) 990-3390
e-mail: micasa@primenet.com
www.azres.com

---

7 No smoking; 8 Children welcome; 9 Social drinking allowed; 10 Tennis nearby; 11 Swimming nearby; 12 Golf nearby; 13 Skiing nearby; 14 May be booked through a travel agent; 15 Handicapped accessible.

4351. This turn-of-the-century two-story adobe house, built as miners' apartments when Patagonia was a thriving mining town, has been restored into comfortable, charming accommodations. It is within walking distance of the famous Nature Conservancy bird sanctuary and one block from the town square. It is a 20-minute drive to Nogales. On the first floor there are two suites. Each has a private entrance, living room, a bedroom, and a bath with shower. A third suite is on the second floor has two bedrooms with a bath in between. Guests have access to the living room with cable TV. Full breakfast. Smoking permitted outside. Children are welcome. Twenty dollars for each additional person. No pets. $75.

PAYSON

Arizona Trails Bed & Breakfast Reservation Service

P.O. Box 18998, Fountain Hills, 85269-8998
(480) 837-4284; (888) 799-4284
FAX (480) 816-4224
e-mail: aztrails@arizonatrails.com
www.arizonatrails.com

AZ 043. Elegance and relaxation are the specialty of this five-room inn. All rooms have private baths. Three suites all have private patios or deck, full private bath, gas fireplaces, and sitting areas. There is an outdoor hot tub with the gazebo. Gourmet breakfast including latté or cappuccino is served each morning. Handicapped accessible. $85-155.

AZ 066. This rustic lodge style bed and breakfast is the oldest bed and breakfast in Payson. Wraparound porch with gardens and a pond create a relaxed atmosphere. Five rooms all have private baths with original fixtures, some with TVs and antiques. one suite offers a larger room with sitting area. Breakfast is served in the main part of the lodge. Close to town. $70-85.

Mi Casa Su Casa/Old Pueblo Homestays Bed & Breakfast Reservation Service

P.O. Box 950, Tempe, AZ 85280-0950
(602) 990-0682; (800) 456-0682
FAX (602) 990-3390
e-mail: micasa@primenet.com
www.azres.com

4361. On two wooded acres, perfect for a romantic getaway. Many excursions, natural wonders and a casino nearby. Five unique rooms with private entrances and baths. Three rooms have a fireplace and private patio. Secluded hot tub. Gourmet breakfast on weekend; weekdays are Continental. Two-night minimum on weekends. No smoking. No children. No pets. $85-155.

4362. Set in the pines just below the Mogollon Rim at an elevation of 5,000 feet. Guests at this family-friendly inn have full use of the main lodge and its two-acre grounds. Choose from four theme-oriented bedrooms, each with a private bath and cable TV. Three of the rooms each have space for two guests; the fourth is a suite for four guests. Full breakfast. Smoking permitted outside. Handicapped possible. Horses and medium-size dogs welcome with prior arrangement. $69-89.

4363. In Star Valley, four miles north of Payson, this ranch style house with wraparound porch is surrounded by pines and mountains. Guests can hike along the creek in the adjacent forest or bring their own horses to ride the many area trails. Completely private, extra large, guest room on the first level has a private entrance, private bath, cable TV/VCR, refrigerator. Children over 10 are welcome. Pets including horses welcome with prior arrangements. Continental breakfast. Fifteen dollars for each additional guest. $85.

NOTES: Credit cards accepted: A MasterCard; B Visa; C American Express; D Discover; E Diner's Club; F Other; 2 Personal checks accepted; 3 Lunch available; 4 Dinner available; 5 Open all year; 6 Pets welcome;

PEARCE

Mi Casa Su Casa/Old Pueblo Homestays Bed & Breakfast Reservation Service

P.O. Box 950, Tempe, AZ 85280-0950
(602) 990-0682; (800) 456-0682
FAX (602) 990-3390
e-mail: micasa@primenet.com
www.azres.com

4370. Guest ranch offering the comforts of today and the ranch traditions of yesterday. Amenities included in the cost are horseback riding, sightseeing, swimming pool, pool table, TV/VCR, guest laundry, hiking, bird watching, rock hounding, and three meals a day. Casitas consist of a bedroom, sitting area, full bathroom, refrigerator, coffee pot, private porch, and sun deck. Cabins offer a spacious single room with queen bed and sofa bed, bath, coffee pot, private porch, and sun deck. Conference rooms available. Smoking permited outside. No pets. Children 12 and older welcome. Inquire about rates for additional persons. $130-170.

PEORIA

Arizona Trails Bed & Breakfast Reservation Service

P.O. Box 18998, Fountain Hills, 85269-8998
(480) 837-4284; (888) 799-4284
FAX (480) 816-4224
e-mail: aztrails@arizonatrails.com
www.arizonatrails.com

AZ 108. This charming two-room historic red brick Colonial style homestay with white picket fence will provide guests with a great experience when visiting the Phoenix area. Close to the Glendale antique district, restaurants, and the Peoria Sports Complex. Two rooms both share the hall bath. Spacious patios and gardens surround the bed and breakfast—great for weddings and group gatherings. The guest parlor is decorated with Victorian antiques and features a TV/VCR and stereo. Continental breakfast served weekdays; full breakfast served weekends. $75.

Mi Casa Su Casa/Old Pueblo Homestays Bed & Breakfast Reservation Service

P.O. Box 950, Tempe, AZ 85280-0950
(602) 990-0682; (800) 456-0682
FAX (602) 990-3390
e-mail: micasa@primenet.com
www.azres.com

4375. This 1940s red brick home is set in the middle of historic downtown on a one-half-acre orchard park with two patios, barbecue grills, a basketball court, and a porch swing. Nearby to golf, Glendale's renowned antique mecca, Peoria Sports Complex, Arrowhead Towne Center, White Tank Mountain, and Lake Pleasant. The two guest rooms feature antique four-poster beds and share a bath. Full breakfast on weekends; Continental plus on weekdays. Smoking permitted outside only. No pets. $75.

PHOENIX

Arizona Trails Bed & Breakfast Reservation Service

P.O. Box 18998, Fountain Hills, 85269-8998
(480) 837-4284; (888) 799-4284
FAX (480) 816-4224
e-mail: aztrails@arizonatrails.com
www.arizonatrails.com

AZ 042. Enjoy the feel of an English country home in the city at this English Tudor-style bed and breakfast. Lush landscaping and rose gardens surround the inn. Close to public transportation, shops, restaurants, and just minutes to downtown. Five rooms all with private baths. Antiques throughout. Full breakfast. $85-115.

---

7 No smoking; 8 Children welcome; 9 Social drinking allowed; 10 Tennis nearby; 11 Swimming nearby; 12 Golf nearby; 13 Skiing nearby; 14 May be booked through a travel agent; 15 Handicapped accessible.

AZ 057. Relax with the "at home" feeling of this charming homestay. A private suite of rooms awaits guests in this home owned by a retired actress from England. The bedroom features a private bath with tub and shower; sliding glass door leads to a private roof-top patio. The sitting room features cable TV and the ability to sleep a third guest. Full breakfast. High tea available on request for a small charge. $85.

AZ 059. Convenience and privacy are featured at this charming guest cottage on the Phoenix/Paradise Valley border. Decorated in a Ralph Lauren floral pattern, guests have a queen-size bed, sitting area with sleeper-sofa, cable TV, telephone, a minikitchen with refrigerator, cook top, microwave, sink, coffee maker, and cooking utensils. Private bath features a tub and shower. A Continental plus breakfast is delivered to guests' room each morning. Relax by the pool or travel just minutes to area golf courses, restaurants, shops, and museums. $135.

AZ 061. Nothing equals the views from this private bed and breakfast guest house designed by a student of Frank Lloyd Wright on Camelback Mountain. The private suite features a private bath with tub and shower, TV/VCR, stereo system, kitchenette, and fireplace. Unequaled views from the patio, the pool, or spa. Also available is a sports/game room with large screen TV, pool table, and more. Close to shops and restaurants. Continental breakfast. $175.

AZ 062. This guest house offers quiet, private accommodations close to the Phoenix/Scottsdale border. Close to the Phoenix Mountain Preserve, it's also great for hikers. Decorated in a southwestern decor, guests will enjoy a bedroom with queen-size bed, living room/kitchenette area with TV, telephone, sleeper-sofa, refrigerator, microwave, and sink, and private bath with tub and shower. The grounds are surrounded with mature landscaping, a swimming pool, in-ground spa, and badminton/volleyball court. Continental plus breakfast. $95.

AZ 155. This bed and breakfast is a work in progress with the restoration of an old farmhouse in the agricultural area of Phoenix. The guest suites have private entrances with queen-size beds, kitchenettes, cable TV, and private baths. The downstairs suite also features a whirlpool tub and fireplace. The upstairs suite has an additional sitting room with day bed to sleep additional guests. Close to South Mountain recreational area and Tempe. In-room Continental breakfast. $94-125.

AZ 179. In the historic Roosevelt district, this private guest studio is close to all activities of downtown Phoenix including Civic Plaza, the Arizona Center, sports arenas, theaters, and the airport. The studio features a queen-size bed, full kitchen, private bath with original tile and fixtures, cable TV, and telephone. Decorated in a mix of country and 1950s period decor. Relax in the yard with lush landscape. Continental self-serve breakfast. $95-125.

Ashton House

85028
(602) 996-4147

A townhome in private community on the border of Paradise Valley and four minutes from Route 51, Squaw Peak Parkway and Shea Boulevard. The beautifully appointed suite of rooms on the second floor has two twin-size or a king-size bed in large bedroom with TV and sun deck. The sitting room has a day bed for extra guest and contains cable TV, small refrigerator, coffee and tea supplies. Private bathroom, walk-in closets. Private and quiet. Full English breakfast, choice of items served by the Scottish hostess—sorry, no haggis! Afternoon tea for minimum of four persons by arrangements. Garage parking. Call for brochure. Rates $85 May–Dec; $95 Jan–Apr. Prefer traveler's checks or currency.

NOTES: Credit cards accepted: A MasterCard; B Visa; C American Express; D Discover; E Diner's Club; F Other; 2 Personal checks accepted; 3 Lunch available; 4 Dinner available; 5 Open all year; 6 Pets welcome;

Host: Avis Ashton Baransky
Full Breakfast
Credit Cards: None
Notes: 5, 7, 9, 10, 11, 12, 14

The Harmony House Bed & Breakfast Inn

7202 North 7th Avenue, 85021
(602) 331-9554; FAX (602) 395-8528
e-mail: jfontaine@sprintmail.com

The Harmony House was built in 1934 as a doctor's residence among acres of citrus trees on the outskirts of bustling downtown Phoenix. Today, the Harmony House is in the very heart of the Valley of the Sun. Buses offer easy access to downtown, the convention center, and the capitol complex. Theaters, museums, and churches are all close by and the internationally renowned shopping centers and golf courses of the region are all just minutes away.

Hosts: Mike and Jennifer Fontaine
Rooms: 5 (PB) $65-115
Full Breakfast
Credit Cards: A, B
Notes: 2, 5, 7, 8, 9, 12, 13, 14

Maricopa Manor

15 West Pasadena Avenue, 85013
(602) 274-6302; (800) 292-6403

Six luxury suites, spacious public rooms, patios, decks, and the gazebo spa and pool offer an intimate Old World atmosphere in an elegant urban setting. Maricopa Manor is in the heart of the Valley of the Sun, convenient to shops, restaurants, museums, churches, and civic and government centers. The Spanish-style manor house, built in 1928, houses beautiful art, antiques, and a warm southwestern hospitality. Advance reservations required.

Hosts: Mary Ellen and Paul Kelley
Suites: 6 (PB) $89-229
Continental Breakfast
Credit Cards: A, B, C, D
Notes: 2, 5, 7, 8, 9, 10, 12

Mi Casa Su Casa/Old Pueblo Homestays Bed & Breakfast Reservation Service

P.O. Box 950, Tempe, AZ 85280-0950
(602) 990-0682; (800) 456-0682
FAX (602) 990-3390
e-mail: micasa@primenet.com
www.azres.com

4401. Separate guest cottage with its own heat and air conditioning. Bath with shower, sofa bed, small refrigerator, and microwave. The business guest will find a desk, fax, and private telephone. Near museums, downtown business and government centers, and Encanto Park with its golf courses, tennis courts, and bike paths. One bicycle to loan. Shopping and restaurants are easily accessible. Continental plus breakfast, self-catering. Two-night minimum. No smoking. No children. No pets. Possible handicapped accessibility. Fifteen dollars for third person. $85.

4402. In a handsome historic central Phoenix neighborhood within walking distance of the Heard Museum. Unique, romantic English Tower has a private entrance, formal living room with high ceilings, mahogany walls adorned with fine tapestry, TV, small refrigerator, microwave and coffee maker, and curved open staircase to second floor bedroom with bath. The two-bedroom, two-bath, two-level guest house is in a lush garden setting with tall palms. There is an enclosed sun room. Full kitchen. Living room has a TV. No smoking. No pets. Continental plus breakfast. Twenty-five dollars for extra person. $125.

4404. Near Central and Camelback. Beautifully landscaped Spanish-style manor house offers six luxury two-room suites and "breakfast in a basket" delivered to guests' door. Enjoy the spacious gathering room with outside deck, formal living, dining and music rooms, patio, gazebo spa, and heated pool. All suites have a private entrance, TV and telephone. Some have double-jetted tubs and fireplaces. Ten minutes

---

7 No smoking; 8 Children welcome; 9 Social drinking allowed; 10 Tennis nearby; 11 Swimming nearby; 12 Golf nearby; 13 Skiing nearby; 14 May be booked through a travel agent; 15 Handicapped accessible.

Mi Casa Su Casa/Old Pueblo Homestays Bed & Breakfast Reservation Service (continued)

to downtown Phoenix, 15 minutes from the airport. Smoking outside. No pets. Roll-away available. Children over seven welcome. Seasonal rates. Twenty-five dollars for each additional person. $129-229.

4405. The extra large guest suite with a private entrance is romantic and private. This rambling 1950s ranch style home has a sitting area, fireplace, a table and chairs, cable TV, bath with shower, kitchenette. Ten minutes from airport, near the Heard and Phoenix Art Museums and Phoenix College. Walk to bike paths, tennis, park, golf, shopping, and churches or temple. Continental plus breakfast. A computer/modem and fax are available. No smoking. No children. Inquire about accommodations for pets. Two-night minimum stay. $85.

4453. Gracious hostess welcomes guests to a very large southwestern ranch-style home. This house was built beside a golf course in a handsome neighborhood near many activities. One guest room has a TV and a full hall bath; another has a TV and shares the full hall bath. Only one party is accepted at a time. Guests are welcome to use the large living room with fireplace, cable TV, VCR, or pool. Full breakfast. No pets. Smoking is permitted outside only. Inquire about accommodations for children. $70-75.

4454. The main house was built in 1924 on a very large property. The second-story cottage offers a living room with TV, a kitchen, an extra large bedroom, a private bath with claw-foot tub, and a porch with a view of the pool for seasonal swimming. Ten minutes from the Heard Museum, 20 minutes from the airport. Continental plus breakfast is self-catered. Smoking is permitted outside only. Children over five who can swim are welcome. Special rates for longer stays. $75.

4455. Handsome two-story home near the Hilton Pointe Tapatio. Two guest rooms, each have a private hall bath. Sofa bed is also available on the second floor on the balcony. Heated pool, tennis, golf course, and stables are nearby. Spanish spoken. Continental plus breakfast. Children are welcome. Smoking allowed outside. No pets. Five dollars for one-night stays. Ten-dollar charge per child. $70.

4456. On a mountainside overlooking Phoenix, this stunning home was built to take advantage of the beautiful views. Switchback flagstone stairs take guests up to the spacious house perched on the mountainside. Private, luxurious suite has fireplace, TV, large bath with double whirlpool tub, and separate shower. Full breakfast. No smoking. No children. No pets. $150.

4457. Gracious hostess has attractive town home in a very nice private community. Heated swimming pool and spa, tennis courts on grounds. Easy access to downtown Phoenix, Scottsdale and Phoenix Sky Harbor Airport. The beautifully appointed suite of rooms on the second floor has a large, tranquil bedroom that has sun deck with views. The sitting room has a day bed for an extra guest and contains cable TV, small refrigerator, coffee, and tea supplies. Private full bath, walk-in closets. Full breakfast. Kitchen privileges. Garage parking. Smoking permitted outside only. No pets. Children 12 and older welcome. Twenty dollars for additional person. Weekly Rates. $85.

4458. The Spanish-style adobe house has an inviting courtyard with a Mediterranean air. Easy access to downtown Phoenix, Scottsdale, and the airport. The romantic guest cottage is in the courtyard and has beautifully appointed decor, a TV, and private bath with shower. The pool and spa are available for seasonal swimming. Smoking outside. No pets. No children.

NOTES: Credit cards accepted: A MasterCard; B Visa; C American Express; D Discover; E Diner's Club; F Other; 2 Personal checks accepted; 3 Lunch available; 4 Dinner available; 5 Open all year; 6 Pets welcome;

Public transportation one block. Continental plus breakfast. $85-115.

4459. Built in 1934 as an impressive country residence in a citrus area, this English Tudor-style house surrounded by large trees, lawns, and rose gardens is now in the heart of the Phoenix metro area. Near public transportation. It offers easy access to downtown, the convention center, theaters, museums, fine shopping and dining. Golf courses and hiking are minutes away. Beautiful Victorian antiques fill five elegantly furnished bedrooms each has a private bath. Cable TV. Full breakfast served family style. One outside dog. Smoking outside. No pets. Children 12 and older welcome. $85-115.

4501. An exceptional value, this friendly, helpful host couple has a contemporary two-story townhouse in a small complex near Camelback Mountain, 20 minutes from downtown Phoenix, Scottsdale, or airport. Near public transportation. The large guest room is up a spiral staircase on the second floor and has a pleasant southwestern decor, private bath, telephone, and TV. Computer, fax, and internet available. The community pool for seasonal swimming is next door. Full breakfast. Smoking permitted outside only. No pets. Airport pick up. Children 10 and older (swimmers) welcome. Two nights preferred. $70.

4502. Gracious, helpful hostess has a spacious and comfortable ranch-style house built in 1959 in a very quiet, up-scale neighborhood "near everything." Twenty minutes from downtown Phoenix and Sky Harbor Airport. Five minutes from Scottsdale. Room one is large and shares full hall bath with room two. Only one party accepted at a time. Guests are welcome to use the pool table in the family room, the TV in the den with fireplace, or the large covered patio. Fenced, unheated diving pool. Full breakfast. Smoking permitted outside only. No pets. Two-night minimum stay. Special rates for children. $85.

4503. This handsome, historic adobe house, built in 1916, is on the south side of Camelback Mountain. Twenty minutes to downtown Phoenix or Sky Harbor Airport and five minutes to Scottsdale. The separate guest house has contemporary southwest art and decor. There are two accommodations, both with private entrance and bath. The Camelback Suite has a living room with sofa bed, fireplace, full kitchen and bedroom. The Papago Suite has an extra large room with a sitting area. Full breakfast served in main house. Smoking outside. Children 12 and older welcome. Partially handicapped possible in Papago Suite. Two-night minimum stay. $115-150.

4504. Gracious hosts welcome guests to luxurious accommodations in a country club area. Handsome two-story main house has large lawns with palm and citrus trees, flowering shrubs. Near fine dining and shopping. The two-story guest house has a private entrance, large living room with TV/VCR, full kitchen, dining area, two baths. One bedroom also has a balcony. The 1,500 square foot Library Suite in the main house has a private entrance, a bedroom, bath, and a library/living room with TV, VCR, small refrigerator, and coffee bar. Gourmet Continental plus buffet breakfast. Heated swimming pool, attractive lawn furniture, barbecue. No smoking. No pets. No children. Twenty-five dollars for each additional person. $150-250.

4505. This very nice home with a view of Camelback Mountain is in a quiet, beautiful neighborhood near everything. Downtown Phoenix 15 minutes, central Scottsdale 10 minutes, Sky Harbor Airport 15 minutes. The sitting room/bedroom has a private entrance, cable TV, private bath and telephone, small refrigerator, and microwave. Unfenced pool for seasonal swimming. Two blocks to public transportation. Smoking outside. Inquire about accommodations for pets. Inquire about accommodations for children. Partially handicapped possible. Stocked Continental plus

---

7 No smoking; 8 Children welcome; 9 Social drinking allowed; 10 Tennis nearby; 11 Swimming nearby; 12 Golf nearby; 13 Skiing nearby; 14 May be booked through a travel agent; 15 Handicapped accessible.

breakfast. Three night minimum preferred. Nightly, weekly, and monthly rates available. $65-70.

4551. A real "find" for the traveler. Friendly and helpful host couple welcomes guests to a bed and breakfast host home with a large patio where one can observe hummingbirds, an unheated swimming pool, and a view of Camelback Mountain. Near downtown Phoenix, Scottsdale, and airport. Award-winning southwestern-design guest room with a TV, telephone, and bath en suite with shower. Full breakfast. Smoking permitted outside only. No pets. Children eight and older welcome. Two-night minimum stay preferred. Five dollars extra for one-night stay. $60.

4552. This is an excellent value. The host couple welcomes guests to a one- or two-bedroom suite in a quite neighborhood a few minutes from downtown Phoenix, Scottsdale, Camelback Mountain, and Sky Harbor Airport. There is a private patio and entrance, full kitchen, and private baths. Bountiful breakfast stocked in kitchen. Guests welcome to pick all the citrus they can eat from the orange, grapefruit, lemon, and tangelo trees! Pool for seasonal swimming. Near public transportation. Smoking permitted outside. No pets. Children eight and older (swimmers only) welcome. Three nights preferred. $75-95.

4601. Built in 1987, this large Spanish-style house is near South Mountain Park, hiking, biking, tennis, and golf. The very private large guest room is separate from the main house. It has a private hall bath with shower, private entrance, cable TV, telephone, small refrigerator, and microwave. Continental breakfast. Two-night minimum. Infants only, no extra charge. Crib, Port-a-crib, and high chair available. Easy drive to Tempe, Gilbert, Chandler, and 15 to 25 minutes from Sky Harbor Airport. Fenced pool. No smoking. Weekly and no-breakfast rates available. $65.

4602. Retired host enjoys his theater organ and musical instrument collecting. This extra-large home with an overview of Phoenix is in a quiet rural setting with natural desert landscaping adjacent to the South Mountain Preserve. Bird watching is excellent. Ten minutes to Sky Harbor Airport. Within 15 to 30 minutes of downtown Phoenix, Tempe, and Mesa. Room one has a TV, ceiling fan, and a private hall full bath. Room two has a TV, ceiling fan, and shares the hall bath with room one. Only one party accepted at a time. Bicycles to loan. Full breakfast. No smoking. No pets. No children. Two-night minimum. $65-70.

4802. Ranch-style home in quiet cul-de-sac near biking, hiking, downtown, and airport. The guest apartment is attached to but separate from the main house. Private entrance, living room with cable TV, bathroom with roll-in shower, and well-equipped kitchenette. Continental plus breakfast. Handicapped welcome. Smoking permitted outside only. No pets. Children over eight are welcome. $75.

4803. An excellent value. Friendly host couple welcomes guests to their modest neighborhood. They have a one-story home with three guest rooms. One room has a private bath and the other two rooms share a bath. Private guest telephone. Continental plus breakfast. No smoking. No pets. Public transportation one block away. $50-65.

PINETOP (LAKESIDE)

Arizona Trails Bed & Breakfast Reservation Service

P.O. Box 18998, Fountain Hills, 85269-8998
(480) 837-4284; (888) 799-4284
FAX (480) 816-4224
e-mail: aztrails@arizonatrails.com
www.arizonatrails.com

AZ 063. Charming two-room bed and breakfast close to town yet nestled in the tall pines.

NOTES: Credit cards accepted: A MasterCard; B Visa; C American Express; D Discover; E Diner's Club; F Other; 2 Personal checks accepted; 3 Lunch available; 4 Dinner available; 5 Open all year; 6 Pets welcome;

One room sleeps up to four with a queen-size bed and sleeper-sofa, private bath, TV, refrigerator, and adjacent game room in the loft. The other has a queen-size bed and private bath, also with refrigerator and TV. Relax in the main room with lofted beam ceiling or among the gardens, pond, or in the hot tub. Full breakfast and picnic lunches. $95-105.

AZ 120. On Rainbow Lake this three-room bed and breakfast offers a private and relaxing getaway. All feature private baths with in-room TVs. One suite features a Jacuzzi tub with lake view; the other suite has an adjacent sitting room that will sleep two additional people. Outdoor hot tub on the deck overlooks the lake. Great for bird watching, fishing, and canoeing. Full breakfast. $100-150.

Mi Casa Su Casa/Old Pueblo Homestays Bed & Breakfast Reservation Service

P.O. Box 950, Tempe, AZ 85280-0950
(602) 990-0682; (800) 456-0682
FAX (602) 990-3390
e-mail: micasa@primenet.com
www.azres.com

4854. Nestled in the ponderosa pines of Pinetop with breathtaking scenery, and offers a full-service dining room featuring gourmet foods prepared by an award-winning chef and staff. The inn has seven luxurious rooms with private baths. Several rooms have access to an outside deck. Also one room offers a separate living room with fireplace and TV, and a kitchenette with dining area, microwave, refrigerator, and coffee pot. The downstairs sitting room features a fireplace, antique Victrola, and organ. The upstairs library has more than 300 books, a TV with small video library, games, and puzzles. Minimum stay of two nights; three-night minimum during holidays. Smoking permitted outside in designated areas only. Pets are not permitted. Inquire about accommodations for children. $85-120.

PRESCOTT

Arizona Trails Bed & Breakfast Reservation Service

P.O. Box 18998, Fountain Hills, 85269-8998
(480) 837-4284; (888) 799-4284
FAX (480) 816-4224
e-mail: aztrails@arizonatrails.com
www.arizonatrails.com

AZ 021. Enjoy a peaceful retreat in the Granite Dells of Prescott. This four-room rustic log cabin will take guests back to a time in Western history, where old wagon trains used to run. At night contemplate the stars from the outdoor hot tub. Two suites can sleep up to four with queen-size beds, private baths, and fireplaces. Two other rooms feature queen-size beds, sitting areas, and private baths. Less than five miles from downtown Prescott. Full country breakfast. $85-125.

AZ 050. Relax in this international country decor three-guest room bed and breakfast near downtown Prescott. One room is done in Italian countryside, one in French countryside, and one in English countryside decor. A private massage therapist is on call 24 hours for guest convenience at an extra charge. Professional chefs prepare a wonderful full breakfast and an afternoon social hour. One room is a two-room suite that will accommodate up to four. All rooms have private baths with tubs and shower. $90-100.

AZ 116. This historic inn is walking distance to Whiskey Row, the courthouse, and downtown Prescott. Twenty rooms on two floors offer guests a variety of room types with queen-, king-, or twin-size beds. All have private baths, TVs, ceiling fans, and telephones, water purifiers, and air filters. The lobby features a wine bar and sitting area. Two verandas off the front of the building offer a relaxed setting. Smoking and nonsmoking rooms. Children welcome. Continental breakfast. $99-179.

---

7 No smoking; 8 Children welcome; 9 Social drinking allowed; 10 Tennis nearby; 11 Swimming nearby; 12 Golf nearby; 13 Skiing nearby; 14 May be booked through a travel agent; 15 Handicapped accessible.

Hassayampa Inn

Hassayampa Inn

122 East Gurley Street, 86301
(520) 778-9434; (800) 322-1927

Locally known as "Prescott's Grand Hotel," the inn offers a full-service restaurant and lounge. Built in 1927 and completely renovated in 1985, its lobby is acknowledged as one of the most beautiful in Arizona. Features tile floors, oriental rugs, oversize easy chairs, and potted palms; the focal point, however, is the beamed ceiling decorated with Spanish and Indian motifs. The renowned Peacock Room serves breakfast, lunch, and dinner. Overnight rooms include daily breakfast and an evening cocktail.

Hosts: Bill and Georgia Teich
Rooms: 68 (PB) $99-175
Full Breakfast
Credit Cards: A, B, C, D, E
Notes: 2, 3, 4, 5, 8, 9, 10, 11, 12, 13, 14, 15

Hotel Vendome

230 South Cortez Street, 86303
(520) 776-0900; (888) 468-3583
FAX (520) 771-0395

Hotel Vendome is a historic landmark in the heart of Prescott. Built in 1917, the inn is fully refurbished to an immaculate condition. It is very distinctive with an aura of history and tradition. A cozy, intimate bar, warm, comfortable lobby, and inviting guest rooms all create unique ambiance. Perfect for leisure or corporate travel. Within walking distance to restaurants, antique shops, western shopping, entertainment, museums, etc. Special occasion romance packages available on request. Hiking and picnic packages also available. European-style breakfast. Smoking and nonsmoking rooms available. AAA-listed.

Host: Rama Patel
Rooms: 16 (PB) $69-149
Suites: 4
Continental Breakfast
Credit Cards: A, B, C, D, E
Notes: 2, 3, 4, 5, 7, 8, 9, 10, 11, 12, 14

Lynx Creek Farm Bed & Breakfast

P.O. Box 4301, 86302
(520) 778-9573; (888) 778-9573

Secluded country hilltop setting with great views overlooking Lynx Creek, it has spacious suites in separate guest house. Organic garden and orchard supply fresh fruit and produce for full gourmet breakfasts. Hot tub, cold pool, croquet, volleyball, horseshoes, gold-panning, big swing, animals, and exotic birds. Light cocktails and hors d'oeuvres each evening. Also available for weddings and cooking classes. Voted Best Bed and Breakfast in Arizona by the *Arizona Republic* newspaper in November 1994. Smoking is permitted in designated areas only.

Hosts: Greg and Wendy Temple
Rooms: 6 (PB) $75-140
Full Breakfast
Credit Cards: A, B, C, D
Notes: 2, 5, 6, 8, 9, 10, 11, 12, 14

Mi Casa Su Casa/Old Pueblo Homestays Bed & Breakfast Reservation Service

P.O. Box 950, Tempe, AZ 85280-0950
(602) 990-0682; (800) 456-0682
FAX (602) 990-3390
e-mail: micasa@primenet.com
www.azres.com

NOTES: Credit cards accepted: A MasterCard; B Visa; C American Express; D Discover; E Diner's Club; F Other; 2 Personal checks accepted; 3 Lunch available; 4 Dinner available; 5 Open all year; 6 Pets welcome;

4871. Join the hosts on the veranda of a magnificently restored turreted Queen Anne Victorian in Arizona's first capital. A short walk to the courthouse, museums, galleries, restaurants, and antiquing. The two-bedroom Ivy Suite on the first floor has a private bath. Three guest rooms are on the second floor. The Tea Rose has a private bath in the hall. The Princess Victoria has a private bath with an 1800s bathhouse-style copper tub. The Queen Anne Suite has a private bath. Rates include afternoon refreshments and a full breakfast. Smoking outside. No children. No pets. $75-120.

4872. A wonderfully romantic bed and breakfast has rural luxury and scenic views on a 25-acre, wooded, hilly property. The two guest cottages have six suites. The cottages can accommodate up to 18 guests. Amenities include decks, spas, hiking, and volleyball. Families welcome. Children enjoy seeing the farm animals. Full country breakfast served in the main house. Smoking outside. Twenty dollars for additional adult. Fifteen dollars for children. $85-130.

4873. This two-story bed and breakfast inn, an easy walk from historic downtown, was built in 1906. Gracious hostess welcomes guests to tranquil, well-appointed setting. On the first floor, the two-room Terrace Suite has a bedroom with private deck. Upstairs, there are three guest rooms. The two-room Pine View Suite has a sitting room with a sofa bed and fireplace. The Garden Room has a private bath en suite. The Coventry Room has a private bath in the hall. Full breakfast and afternoon refreshments are served. Available for seminars, meetings, and weddings. Smoking permitted outside only. No pets. Inquire about accommodations for children. $85-135.

4875. People stop to take photographs of this restored 1883 two-story Victorian bed and breakfast with white picket fence and rose garden in Arizona's largest Victorian neighborhood. A lovely curving staircase takes guests to the four nicely decorated guest rooms on the second floor, each with a private bath. Also available is the Carriage House apartment with private entrance and bath, living room and fully furnished kitchen. Guests are welcome to use the cable TV in the parlor, or to enjoy games, movies, books, and puzzles. Refreshments. Full breakfast. Smoking permitted in designated areas only. Children 12 and over welcome. No pets. Twenty dollars for each additional person. Rates higher during special events. $89-129.

Prescott Pines Inn

Prescott Pines Inn

901 White Spar Road, 86303
(520) 445-7270; (800) 541-5374 (reservations)
FAX (520) 778-3665
www.prescottpinesinn.com

Formerly the Haymore Dairy in the 1930s, the inn continues the tradition as a gathering place for family and friends. Eleven guest rooms, each with private bath and entry, are in one of three guest houses around the main house. The 1300-square-foot chalet has three bedrooms, two baths, full kitchen, dining and living room with wood-burning stove, and can sleep up to four couples. Whether for a

---

7 No smoking; 8 Children welcome; 9 Social drinking allowed; 10 Tennis nearby; 11 Swimming nearby; 12 Golf nearby; 13 Skiing nearby; 14 May be booked through a travel agent; 15 Handicapped accessible.

romantic getaway, a comfortable business stay, or just an escape to rejuvenate, the inn's acre of pines, cedars, roses, and wildflowers will "welcome you home." Fresh coffee, teas, seasonal beverages, and homemade cookies are always available. A full breakfast, optional, is served by reservation, at 8:00 or 10:00 A.M. Only a mile and a third south of the courthouse square and excellent restaurants and shops.

Hosts: Jean Wu and Michael Acton
Rooms: 11 (PB) $75-119
Chalet: 1; $249
Full Breakfast
Credit Cards: A, B
Notes: 5, 7, 12

SAFFORD

Mi Casa Su Casa/Old Pueblo Homestays Bed & Breakfast Reservation Service

P.O. Box 950, Tempe, AZ 85280-0950
(602) 990-0682; (800) 456-0682
FAX (602) 990-3390
e-mail: micasa@primenet.com
www.azres.com

4901. Western Colonial-type brick house built in 1890 has wide verandas that run across the front of the house. Three guest rooms on the second floor share a large hall bath with shower. Guests are welcome to enjoy the sitting room and veranda on the second floor. Two guest cottages are also available, each with a bath with shower. Both cottages have a refrigerator, microwave, cable TV, and telephone. Heated spa. Full breakfast. Smoking is not permitted on premises. Ten-dollar charge for each additional person over two people. Children over toddler age and under 12 in guest cottage only. Children 12 and older welcome in main house. Credit cards accepted. $80.

SAHUARITA

Mi Casa Su Casa/Old Pueblo Homestays Bed & Breakfast Reservation Service

P.O. Box 950, Tempe, AZ 85280-0950
(602) 990-0682; (800) 456-0682
FAX (602) 990-3390
e-mail: micasa@primenet.com
www.azres.com

4913. This inn is surrounded by the National Forest and is at an elevation of 5,200 feet in the heart of Madera Canyon in the Santa Rita Mountains 40 miles southeast of Tucson. Renowned for its scenic beauty, more than 200 species of birds have been sighted in Madera Canyon. The bed and breakfast is a retreat for romantic couples, nature lovers, and hiking and biking enthusiasts. Area attractions include Nogales, historic Tombstone and Bisbee, and the artist community at Tubac. Three guest rooms, each with a private entrance, private bath, and kitchenette. Full gourmet breakfast in the privacy of guests' room. Smoking permitted outside only. No pets. Children over 12 welcome. $80-90.

Mi Gatita Bed & Breakfast

HCR 70, Box 3401, 85629
(520) 648-6129; e-mail: jpace71896@aol.com

Enjoy a pampered respite, sumptuous breakfasts, easy comfort, and abundant wildlife. This adobe-hued, Mexican-style hacienda rests on five acres carved from the historic Navarro Ranch which still runs cattle nearby. Overlooking Tucson, convenient to the city, the high desert setting is wonderful for bird watching, hiking, and stargazing. Spacious rooms and suites, fireplaces, gardens, southwestern arts and antiques, Tarahumara carvings. Pool.

Hosts: Jean and Bentley Pace
Rooms: 3 (PB) $85-125
Full Breakfast
Credit Cards: None
Notes: 2, 3, 4, 5, 7, 9, 11, 12

NOTES: Credit cards accepted: A MasterCard; B Visa; C American Express; D Discover; E Diner's Club; F Other; 2 Personal checks accepted; 3 Lunch available; 4 Dinner available; 5 Open all year; 6 Pets welcome;

SASABEE

Mi Casa Su Casa/Old Pueblo Homestays Bed & Breakfast Reservation Service

P.O. Box 950, Tempe, AZ 85280-0950
(602) 990-0682; (800) 456-0682
FAX (602) 990-3390
e-mail: micasa@primenet.com
www.azres.com

4921. Reaching 3,800 feet high in the Sonoran Desert, this fascinating 250 year old ranch is one of the last great Spanish haciendas still standing in the United States. There are 16 fully modernized guest rooms, each with its own private bath and fireplace. Heated pool, spa, hot tub, variety of recreational activities on site, including horseback riding. Three meals are served a day. Horseback riding package available at additional charge. $60.

SCOTTSDALE

Arizona Trails Bed & Breakfast Reservation Service

P.O. Box 18998, Fountain Hills, 85269-8998
(480) 837-4284; (888) 799-4284
FAX (480) 816-4224
e-mail: aztrails@arizonatrails.com
www.arizonatrails.com

AZ 060. Nestled in the lush desert between Scottsdale and Carefree, this hideout has combined the best of a luxury resort with the atmosphere and activities of the finest guest ranches in one spectacular setting. Sit under a rock waterfall in the pool/spa, enjoy a campfire, or play one of the many championship golf courses nearby. The guest house has a private bath with claw-foot tub and rock-walled shower, full kitchen including washer and dryer, and a living room with gas fireplace, TV, and stereo. A second unit with Jacuzzi tub, in-room refrigerator, TV, and balcony is available for parties of four. Panoramic views. Full breakfast. $250.

AZ 067. This charming guest house is close to shops, restaurants, golf, and only minutes to Phoenix or Paradise Valley. Enjoy the views from the sparkling pool. The guest house has full kitchen that is stocked daily for a self-serve full breakfast. The private bath has a stand-up shower. No daily maid service is provided unless otherwise requested. $95.

AZ 077. Convenience and comfort are the key in this convenient bed and breakfast guest house, close to Scottsdale Fashion Square and the Camelback corridor. Private entrance, covered parking, queen-size bed, sitting area with TV/VCR and stereo system, large work area with desk and telephone line for business travelers, kitchen, private patio with outdoor fireplace, and swimming pool. Breakfast is stocked in the private kitchen so guests can help themselves according to their schedule. $135.

AZ 110. This charming homestay is conveniently located in central Scottsdale close to a city park and golf courses. Enjoy own private suite of rooms within the main house. The suite offers a bedroom with queen-size bed, private bath, and sitting room with a TV/VCR, library, games, and a dining area for in-room breakfast if desired. Close by make use of the heated pool/spa, fitness center, and sauna. Full breakfast. $100.

AZ 123. Luxury abounds in north Scottsdale at this exclusive 11-room inn close to the Pinnacle Peak area. All rooms have private entrances, queen- or king-size beds, TV/VCR, telephone, robes, mini-bars, private marble baths, many with fireplaces, sitting rooms, balconies, and one with a Jacuzzi tub. The inner courtyard features lovely gardens with a pond and footbridge. A day spa, art gallery, and restaurant share the property. Continental breakfast. Pet friendly. $109-335.

AZ 135. Enjoy the finest accommodations and hospitality at this bed and breakfast in central Scottsdale with two guest rooms. Each suite

---

7 No smoking; 8 Children welcome; 9 Social drinking allowed; 10 Tennis nearby; 11 Swimming nearby; 12 Golf nearby; 13 Skiing nearby; 14 May be booked through a travel agent; 15 Handicapped accessible.

has a private entrance, king- or queen-size bed, private bath, TV, telephone, wet bar, iron and ironing board. On arrival guests are greeted with a bowl of fruit, bottle of wine, and fresh flowers. The yard features lush rose gardens, a pool, hot tub, firepit, and patio area. Continental breakfast. $135-155.

Inn at the Citadel

8700 East Pinnacle Peak Road, 85255
(800) 927-8367; FAX (602) 585-3436
www.arizonaguide.com/citadelinn

A combination of pleasures of distinctive boutiques, galleries, and restaurants surrounding the elegant inn. The inn offers 11 luxuriously appointed suites. Enjoy a suite with a private Jacuzzi on the terrace overlooking the foothills of the McDowell Mountain Range. Fireplaces, balconies, and terraces combine to form a tapestry of unequaled ambiance.

Hosts: Lorraine Irving and staff
Rooms: 11 (PB) $109-295
Continental Breakfast
Credit Cards: A, B, C, D, E
Notes: 5, 6, 7, 8, 9, 10, 11, 12, 14, 15

La Paz in Desert Springs

6309 East Ludlow Drive, 85254
(602) 922-0963; (888) 922-0963
e-mail: lapaz-desertsprings@juno.com
www.bbonline.com/az/desertsprings

Enjoy peace, comfort, and warm hospitality in this home bed and breakfast. Three guest accommodations are offered. The Arizona Suite has a private entrance, a large master king-size bedroom, and private bath. The living room has a sleeper sofa and cable TV/VCR. The Desert Spring Room is queen-size bed, and the Old West Room accommodates two on twin beds. These two rooms are in the main part of the home and share a common bath. La Paz is in north Scottsdale close to Old Scottsdale, Westworld, Rawhide, restaurants, golf, and shopping malls. Close to the desert, hiking, rafting, and horseback riding. Within one day's travel to Sedona, the Petrified Forest, Painted Desert and Sunset Craters, and the Grand Canyon. Continental plus breakfast. Complimentary snacks and hot tea and coffee. Reservations required. Seasonal rates.

Hosts: Luis and Susan Cuevas
Rooms: 3 (1 PB; 2 SB) $55-165
Continental Breakfast
Credit Cards: A, B, C
Notes: 2, 5, 7, 8, 9, 10, 11, 12, 14

Mi Casa Su Casa/Old Pueblo Homestays Bed & Breakfast Reservation Service

P.O. Box 950, Tempe, AZ 85280-0950
(602) 990-0682; (800) 456-0682
FAX (602) 990-3390
e-mail: micasa@primenet.com
www.azres.com

5011. A hostess from New Zealand welcomes guests to this home in a quiet neighborhood, convenient to downtown Scottsdale, near art galleries, theaters, restaurants, and shopping. There is one guest room with a private bath en suite. Please reserve outdoor hot tub in advance for heating. Full breakfast. Resident cat and dog. No smoking. No pets. No children. $85.

5012. Three-level condominium in a very nice complex one mile from Scottsdale Fashion Square. Extra large room on the first level has sitting area and private bath up a few steps. On the third level is a guest bedroom with a shared hall full bath. Community pool is heated except December through February. Continental breakfast. Two-night stay preferred. No children. No pets. Smoking permitted outside. $65-75.

5013. In a nice neighborhood, guests have enjoyed this attractive, light-filled suite which is attached but separate from the main house. A short distance to the canal path in a park for walking or jogging, the Desert Botanical Gardens, downtown Scottsdale, Tempe, Sky Harbor Airport. The suite has a private entrance,

---

NOTES: Credit cards accepted: A MasterCard; B Visa; C American Express; D Discover; E Diner's Club; F Other; 2 Personal checks accepted; 3 Lunch available; 4 Dinner available; 5 Open all year; 6 Pets welcome;

bay window, large sitting area, TV, bath with shower, and kitchenette. There is a private telephone, separate climate controls, and cabinet for hanging clothes. Guests welcome to use patio. Resident AKC Maltese dogs. Continental breakfast stocked in kitchen. Smoking outside. No pets. No children. Three-night minimum. Weekly and monthly rates available. Seasonal rates $67.50-75.

5014. This u-shaped handsome house is in a very nice neighborhood within easy driving distance of downtown Phoenix, Scottsdale, or Sky Harbor Airport. There is a landscaped desert front yard, and a lush back yard with a scenic buttes view and a pool for seasonal swimming. The two-bedroom guest suite has a private entrance, living room with cable TV, private telephone, complete kitchen, and private patio. Room one has a private bath en suite. Room two has a hall bathroom with shower. A starter Continental breakfast is provided for self-serve breakfast for two mornings. Near public transportation. Weekly and seasonal rates. Three night minimum. No smoking. No pets. Children 10 and over (swimmers) welcome. Possible handicapped accessibility. German spoken. $95-125.

5016. This beautifully landscaped, light and airy guest house is attached to but separate from the main house in a very nice neighborhood close to Fashion Square and Old Town Scottsdale. There is a private entrance, sitting area with cable TV/VCR and stereo, pull-down bed, large work area with desk and private telephone for business travelers, full kitchen, private patio with outdoor fireplace, and pool for seasonal swimming. Self-serve Continental plus breakfast. No smoking. No pets. No children. Two-night minimum, add $10 for one-night stay. Weekly rates available. Seasonal rates. $100-125.

5051. Hafod-y-Gwynt means "shelter from the wind" in Welsh. On 10 acres with mountains in every direction, the guest apartment with private entrance is connected to the main house in a remote, scenic area. Air conditioned. Comfortable combined living room and bedroom with TV, and traditional decor. Bathroom has shower. Fully equipped kitchen stocked for first few days' breakfasts. Resident pets include horses, dogs, and one cat. Closed May 15 through October 15. No smoking. No pets. No children. Two night minimum stay. $65.

5052. In a handsome neighborhood on an acre in north central Scottsdale is a charming guest house with a bedroom/living room, fully equipped kitchen, full bath, and contemporary furnishings. French doors lead to pool. Guests enjoy jogging or hiking along the nearby scenic canal. Walk to Hilton Village, public transportation. For short stays, breakfast items are stocked in the kitchen. For longer stays, self-catering. Smoking outside. No children. No pets. Three-night minimum stay preferred. $85.

5053. This charming stone-front guest house was built in 1985 and is opposite the main house with the pool in between. Well maintained yard with flowering bushes. Cottage has own climate controls, compact living room-bedroom, TV, full kitchen with all appliances, bath with shower, contemporary furniture. Kitchen stocked with selfcatering Continental plus breakfast items. Telephone, water purifier, and air purifier. Near shopping centers and aquatic center. No smoking. No pets. Adults only. Weekly, monthly rates are available. $85.

5055. Handsome home in the very nice residential area of McCormick Ranch. Heated pool overlooks a beautiful man-made lake. The private three-room suite has a bedroom, bath, and separate sitting room has a TV. Guests welcome in large living room. Restaurants, shopping, and golf courses nearby. Gentle, elderly dog in residence. Full breakfast. No smoking. No pets. No children. Two-night stay preferred. $110.

---

7 No smoking; 8 Children welcome; 9 Social drinking allowed; 10 Tennis nearby; 11 Swimming nearby; 12 Golf nearby; 13 Skiing nearby; 14 May be booked through a travel agent; 15 Handicapped accessible.

5057. Unobstructed views of the McDowell Mountains from this comfortable patio home with contemporary decor is what gave it the name "Ancala" meaning "haven in the distance." Twenty-five minutes from Sky Harbor Airport, 20 minutes from downtown Scottsdale, three miles from the Tournament Players Club. Six blocks from Frank Lloyd Wright's Taliesen West, and a short distance from the Mayo Clinic. Shopping and restaurants nearby. The mini-suite has a bedroom, private bath, and a sofa-bed in den. Full breakfast. No smoking. No pets. Children 10 and older welcome. Twenty-five dollars for extra person in den or a child $10. Seasonal rates. $65-80.

5058. In a prestigious residential area, guests return to this very private, luxury guest house with a private entrance, living room with sofa bed, cable TV, bedroom, bathroom with oversized tub and shower, custom kitchen, private telephone, washer and dryer. There is a delightful patio with views, pool for seasonal swimming, outside grill, sports court. Near fine shopping and restaurants, as well as McDonald Park and jogging track. Continental plus breakfast placed in kitchen. Minimum two nights. No children. No smoking. No pets. Possible handicapped accessibility. $100-150.

5060. Two private custom suites each with private entrance in this one story house in a nice residential area. The secluded yard and garden are made for relaxation with outdoor adobe fireplace, heated whirlpool spa, swimming pool for seasonal swimming, barbecue, and Mexican fire pits. Each suite has a sitting and dining area, walk-in closet, bath with shower, wet bar, refrigerator, microwave, cable TV, VCR, and telephone. Continental plus breakfast. Smoking outside. No pets. No children. Closed May 16-October 1. $129-149.

5061. A gracious host couple welcomes guests to a tranquil stay at this southwestern home in an upscale residential neighborhood. There is one guest room with a Scandinavian motif, TV, and private hall bath with tub and shower. The hostess is knowledgeable about flora of the Southwest, and has created a beautiful outside garden. Refreshments include kringlas, a delectable Norwegian treat. Special gourmet breakfasts. No smoking. No pets. No children. Two-night minimum stay. $85.

5063. In a scenic area, hospitable couple welcomes guests to a large, new home with attractive contemporary furniture. There are 10 golf courses in the vicinity. Thirty minutes to Phoenix Sky Harbor Airport. All guest rooms have cable TV and large closets. The master suite has a luxurious bath, and sliding glass doors to the patio. In another wing, there are three guest rooms. Two-night minimum. Full breakfast. Smoking permitted outside only. No pets. Children six and older welcome. $60-150.

Southwest Inn at Eagle Mountain

Southwest Inn at Eagle Mountain

9800 North Summer Hill Boulevard, Fountain Hills, 85268
(480) 816-3000; (800) 992-8083
FAX (480) 816-3090
e-mail: info@southwestinn.com
www.southwestinn.com

Experience the southwest in this beautiful new luxury bed and breakfast resort on the 18th fairway of the Golf Club at Eagle Mountain. All rooms have two-person whirlpool tubs, gas fireplaces, 25-inch TVs with 60-plus channels and VCRs; rooms have digital modem lines, computer desks, and private decks with 50-

---

NOTES: Credit cards accepted: A MasterCard; B Visa; C American Express; D Discover; E Diner's Club; F Other; 2 Personal checks accepted; 3 Lunch available; 4 Dinner available; 5 Open all year; 6 Pets welcome;

mile views. A Continental plus breakfast is served daily. Relax in total privacy while enjoying total luxury. "See our web-site for special internet rates."

Hosts: Sheila and Joel Gilgoff
Rooms: 42 (PB) $99-345
Continental Breakfast
Credit Cards: A, B, C, D, E
Notes: 5, 7, 8, 9, 10, 11, 12, 14, 15

The Temporary Teepee

Scottsdale, AZ (location)
P.O. Box 24132, Tempe, AZ 85285 (mailing)
(602) 991-6630; FAX (602) 991-9757

Large beautifully decorated suites with private facilities and entrances. Very quiet. Close-in location with magnificent garden area. Pool and spa on grounds. Every conceivable amenity including TV, wet bar, telephone, coffee maker, microwave, and stocked no-charge refrigerator in each suite. Specializing in making the guest feel at home and in providing the highest degree of personalized service, while allowing complete privacy. Smoking permitted in garden area only. Resident cat is not permitted in guest suites. Continental plus breakfast served. Cash, traveler's checks, and personal checks accepted. No children. No pets.

Host: Robert S. Mayer
Rooms: 2 (PB) $149-169
Continental Breakfast
Credit Cards: none
Notes: 2, 7, 9, 10, 11, 12, 14

SEDONA

Apple Orchard Inn

656 Jordan Road, 86336
(800) 663-6968; FAX (520) 204-0044
e-mail: appleorc@sedona.net
www.appleorchardbb.com

AAA's newest four-diamond inn, nestled in the heart of Sedona, sits on the site of the historic Jordan apple orchard. The new waterfall "cooling" pool and outdoor spa sit under the pine

Apple Orchard Inn

trees, secluded on nearly two acres of wooded, red-rock view property. The unparalleled location allows easy access to uptown galleries, shops, restaurants, and direct hiking trails off the property. The inn features king-sized beds, whirlpool tubs, TV/VCRs, complimentary videos, bathrobes, mini-refrigerators, private patios, fireplaces, massage room, full gourmet breakfast, and more. Walk to shops and Sedona Heritage Museum.

Hosts: Bob and Paula Glass
Rooms: 7 (PB) $135-230
Full Breakfast
Credit Cards: A, B, C
Notes: 2, 5, 7, 9, 10, 11, 12, 13,1 4, 15

Arizona Trails Bed & Breakfast Reservation Service

P.O. Box 18998, Fountain Hills, 85269-8998
(480) 837-4284; (888) 799-4284
FAX (480) 816-4224
e-mail: aztrails@arizonatrails.com
www.arizonatrails.com

AZ 003. Enjoy the friendly atmosphere of this five-room ranch-style bed and breakfast with spectacular red rock views in Sedona. Property backs up to national forest land for hiking and bird watching. All rooms have private baths and queen-size beds. One has two twin beds, and each has a different theme. Two rooms share a common kitchen and living room area with fireplace. Close to shops, galleries, and restaurants in the Village of Oak Creek and only minutes to uptown Sedona. Full breakfast. Children welcome. $95-115.

AZ 044. Relax in this elegant and special seven-room inn near uptown Sedona. Walking distance to shops and restaurants, but in a quiet

---

7 No smoking; 8 Children welcome; 9 Social drinking allowed; 10 Tennis nearby; 11 Swimming nearby; 12 Golf nearby; 13 Skiing nearby; 14 May be booked through a travel agent; 15 Handicapped accessible.

area with red rock views and hiking nearby. Each room features a king-size bed, private bath, in-room refrigerator, and TV/VCR with video library. Six of the rooms have whirlpool tubs. Five rooms offer private patios and two have gas fireplaces. Massage therapist on call. Outdoor patio for dining and separate pool/spa patio area. Full breakfast. Handicapped accessible. $135-220.

AZ 048. Combine bed and breakfast hospitality with hotel-style accommodations and guests have this wonderful 28-room inn in West Sedona. The property features rooms with queen-size beds, dual queen-, king-size beds and king-size suites. There are a pool and outdoor hot tub for relaxation. Great red rock views and all rooms are equipped with mini-refrigerators, TV/VCRs, telephones, robes, and fireplaces. Handicapped accessible. Children welcome. Continental breakfast. $115-195.

AZ 052. This elegant Victorian five-room inn sits on Oak Creek. Wander the grounds down to the creek for a relaxing afternoon. A gourmet breakfast is served on the expansive deck overlooking the creek or in the dining room. All rooms have queen-size beds, private baths with Jacuzzi tubs, private entrances, and some have fireplaces. Authentic 19th century antiques can be found throughout the inn. Dinner can be arranged on weekends with advance notice. Handicapped accessible. $175-275.

AZ 111. This charming four-room bed and breakfast offers great hospitality not far from downtown Sedona. Decorated in a country French decor, choose from king- or queen-size beds, standard rooms or suites all with private baths and TV. One suite offers a cozy fireplace sitting area and kitchenette; the other is a two-bedroom suite, with a full kitchen, living room, and bath. Outdoors enjoy the courtyard with gardens, fountain, and red rock views. Full breakfast. $105-195.

Boots & Saddles Bed & Breakfast

2900 Hopi Drive, 86336
(520) 282-1944; (800) 201-1944
FAX (520) 204-2230

Boots and Saddles Bed and Breakfast, completely remodeled, offers the charm of the Old West in a magnificent setting among Sedona's spectacular red rock country. Each room is distinctly furnished with cowboy decor to take guests back to those thrilling days of yesteryear. Rooms with fireplaces and jetted tubs. Full breakfast is served in the dining room with beautiful red rock views. All private baths. Rooms with deck or balcony access. Area orientation provided.

Hosts: John and Linda Steele
Rooms: 4 (PB) $135-205
Full Breakfast
Credit Cards: A, B, C, D
Notes: 2, 5, 7, 8, 9, 10, 11, 12, 13, 14

The Canyon Wren— Cabins for Two

6425 North HIGHWAY 89A, 86336
(520) 282-6900; (800) 437-WREN (9736)
e-mail: cnynwren@sedona.net
www.canyonwrencabins.com

Six miles north of Sedona, four cabins are set against the parklike frame of red rock cliffs and green canyon landscape. Specializing in one to two adults only for private retreats or romantic getaways. The cabins offer kitchens, fireplaces, whirlpool bathtubs, decks, and patios. Gas grills. No TVs or telephones. Continental plus breakfast. Away from bustle of Sedona, yet close enough to enjoy town benefits. Personal, friendly service. Nonsmoking property inside and outside. Creek swimming, hiking, and fishing are a stone's throw away.

Hosts: Milena Pfeifer and Mike Smith
Cabins: 4 (PB) $125-140
Continental Breakfast
Credit Cards: A, B, C, D
Notes: 2, 5, 7, 9, 10, 11, 12, 13, 14

NOTES: Credit cards accepted: A MasterCard; B Visa; C American Express; D Discover; E Diner's Club; F Other; 2 Personal checks accepted; 3 Lunch available; 4 Dinner available; 5 Open all year; 6 Pets welcome;

Casa Sedona

55 Hozoni Drive, 86336
(520) 282-2938; (800) 525-3756

Casa Sedona offers fabulous red rock views from an acre of wooded property. The rooms are spacious, luxurious, and include private baths, spa tubs, and a delightful fireplace. Guests are served a hearty southwestern breakfast and afternoon appetizers in a smoke-free environment (inside and out). Casa Sedona offers a tranquil, serene experience. Enjoy a soak in the outdoor hot tub. Children over 10 are welcome.

Hosts: John and Nancy True
Rooms: 16 (PB) $130-210
Full Breakfast
Credit Cards: A, B, C
Notes: 2, 5, 7, 9, 10, 11, 12, 14, 15

Cathedral Rock Lodge Bed & Breakfast

61 Los Amigos Lane, 86336
(520) 282-7608; (800) 352-9149
FAX (520) 282-4505; www.cathrockbnb.com

Welcome to our world of awesome red rock canyons with spectacular views of mountains and western skies. This rambling country home is a shady oasis nestled at the base of a crimson cliff. A classic bed and breakfast home with classic rates, the hosts serve scrumptious breakfasts—hot breads and homemade jams are their speciality. All guest rooms have private baths and queen-size beds which feature family quilts. The Southwestern Amigos Suite with kitchen and private deck is great for families. Ask about the getaway cottage.

Hosts: Samyo Shannon and Carol Shannon
Rooms: 4 (PB) $80-150
Full Breakfast
Credit Cards: A, B, C, D
Notes: 2, 5, 7, 8, 9, 10, 11, 12, 14

The Graham Bed & Breakfast Inn

150 Canyon Circle Drive, 86351
(520) 284-1425; (800) 228-1425
FAX (520) 284-0767; e-mail: graham@sedona.net

The Graham Inn is an impressive, award-winning southwestern inn with huge windows providing views of Sedona's famous red rock formations. Six guest rooms with private baths, CD players, TV/VCRs, balconies with red rock views, fireplaces, and whirlpool tubs. Four new luxury casitas with waterfall showers and bath fireplaces. Enjoy wonderful breakfasts, afternoon refreshments, and videos. Pool, Jacuzzi, and bicycles are available for guests' use.

Hosts: Roger and Carol Redenbaugh
Rooms: 6 (PB) $169-369
Casitas: 4
Full Breakfast
Cards: A, B, C, D
Notes: 2, 5, 7, 9, 10, 11, 12, 14

The Graham

---

7 No smoking; 8 Children welcome; 9 Social drinking allowed; 10 Tennis nearby; 11 Swimming nearby; 12 Golf nearby; 13 Skiing nearby; 14 May be booked through a travel agent; 15 Handicapped accessible.

The Inn on Oak Creek

556 Highway 179, 86336
(520) 282-7896; (800) 499-7896
FAX (520) 282-0696

The Inn on Oak Creek is a luxurious 11-room bed and breakfast overlooking beautiful Oak Creek. All 11 rooms have private baths, gas fireplaces, whirlpool tubs, TVs, and VCRs. Most rooms have private decks overlooking the water and scenic red rocks. Within walking distance of Tlaquepaque shopping village, art galleries, and fine restaurants. A creekside park, full gourmet breakfast, and afternoon refreshments all serve to pamper the guests. Smoking is not permitted.

Hosts: Pam Harrison and Rick Morris
Rooms: 11 (PB) $155-245
Full Breakfast
Credit Cards: A, B, C, D
Notes: 2, 5, 7, 9, 10, 11, 12, 13, 14, 15

The Lodge at Sedona

125 Kallof Place, 86336
(800) 619-4467; FAX (520) 204-2128
e-mail: lodge@sedona.net
www.lodgeatsedona.com

"It's the nearest to heaven you'll come at 4,500 feet," wrote the *Arizona Republic* when naming the Lodge "Arizona's Best Bed and Breakfast Inn." Elegantly rustic, it offers secluded privacy on three wooded acres of gardens, lawns, and labyrinth. Fourteen guest rooms and large, elegant common rooms with country pine antiques provide a comfortable and nurturing experience. Some rooms have private decks, fireplaces, and Jacuzzi tubs. A full gourmet breakfast is served on the morning porch. Refreshments, appetizers, and dessert are served every afternoon and evening. Romantic dinners are available. Twenty percent discount available to Canadian guests.

Hosts: Barb and Mark Dinunzio
Rooms: 14 (PB) $125-245
Full Breakfast
Credit Cards: C
Notes: 5, 7, 8, 9, 11, 12, 14, 15

Mi Casa Su Casa/Old Pueblo Homestays Bed & Breakfast Reservation Service

P.O. Box 950, Tempe, AZ 85280-0950
(602) 990-0682; (800) 456-0682
FAX (602) 990-3390
e-mail: micasa@primenet.com
www.azres.com

5151. From this five-bedroom inn, guests have marvelous views of the red rock formations. All bedrooms have private baths. Each pair of bedrooms has a private entrance, shares a sitting room with a fireplace and small kitchen. The fifth bedroom is in the main part of the building. Full breakfasts served. Children welcome. Smoking permitted outside only. No pets. Handicapped accessible. $95-115.

5152. Ten miles from I-17, six miles south of center of Sedona. Large contemporary home built in 1993 on quiet cul-de-sac has breathtaking views of the red rock formations. Talented artist-hostess who knows the vicinity hiking trails offers one guest bedroom which has a bath and cable TV. Self-serve Continental plus breakfast. Resident cat. No children. No pets. No smoking. Two-night minimum stay preferred. Additional $10 charge for one-night stay. Weekly and monthly rates available. $85.

5153. Under tall trees along the spring fed waters of Oak Creek in scenic Oak Creek Canyon is this delightful inn with 18 separate and private cottages. Winding paths lead guests to these handcrafted, delightful cabins with southwestern decor. Private baths. Many of the cabins have sitting areas, fireplaces, and kitchens. Full breakfast. Smoking restricted. No pets. Children possible. Partially handicapped accessible. Twenty-five dollars for each additional person. $149-295.

5154. Chosen as "Arizona's Best Bed and Breakfast Inn" by the *Arizona Republic* readers in 1993 and 1994, this inn is known for its "wealth of creature comforts, beautiful sur-

---

NOTES: Credit cards accepted: A MasterCard; B Visa; C American Express; D Discover; E Diner's Club; F Other; 2 Personal checks accepted; 3 Lunch available; 4 Dinner available; 5 Open all year; 6 Pets welcome;

roundings, and gracious reception and attention from the innkeepers." Enjoy 14 beautifully appointed guest accommodations, of which three are luxury suites. Several have private outdoor decks, brick fireplaces, mountain or wooded views, Jacuzzi tubs. Smoking outside only. No pets. Afternoon appetizers. Sumptuous breakfasts. $125-245.

5155. This adobe hacienda was built in 1996 with a courtyard and fountain, verandas, red rock and golf course views. Each of the five spacious rooms has a private entrance. All rooms have private baths and phones; some with whirlpool tubs and double sinks and fireplaces. Southwestern-style breakfasts. No smoking. No pets. One room is handicapped accessible. The host couple will arrange for a balloon ride, or *Verde Valley* steam train trip, or offer guests swimming and tennis privileges at the neighboring Sedona Golf Resort for an additional fee. $129-159.

5156. This bed and breakfast offers fabulous red rock views from each of its 15 terrace guest rooms. Each luxurious room is individually appointed to please and pamper with a private bath, refrigerator, and telephone, some with a whirlpool tub and fireplace. A hearty Southwestern breakfast is served outside most of the year. Children 10 and older are welcome. Twenty-five dollars for each additional guest. No smoking. No pets. $125-190.

5157. This bed and breakfast is convenient to hiking, shops, art galleries, and restaurants. Guests enjoy private tennis club privileges and by special arrangement may use the facilities. All accommodations feature ground-level rooms, private bath, secured entry, and TV. Two rooms share a private deck with a view. Five minutes away is a one-bedroom apartment. Full breakfast. Italian and English spoken. Children welcome. Fifteen dollars for each additional guest. No smoking. No pets. $105-135.

5158. This host home bed and breakfast has remarkable views. The accommodations include the elegant Sedona Suite with a large whirlpool tub, marble shower, and TV. The suite was designed with a deck so that guests could enjoy the incredibly beautiful red rock formations. Another room has a private bath, TV, and can be used in combination with a third room. Two-night minimum on weekends. Smoking outside. No pets. Inquire about accommodations for children. Full breakfast served. $85-135.

5159. In beautiful Oak Creek Valley, this host home "castle" is surrounded by rock gardens and flagstone pathways; the interior has slate floors, rock fireplaces, and much woodwork. Two suites are available, each with private bath, fireplace and balcony overlooking Oak Creek. TV in main living area and hot tub in private courtyard. Full breakfast including many specialties. No smoking. No pets. Children welcome when both rooms are rented. $129-200.

Rose Tree Inn

376 Cedar Street, 86336
(888) 282-2065

"The best kept secret in Sedona..." is the Rose Tree Inn, conveniently in uptown Sedona, steps away from shops and dining. Five comfortable rooms; kitchens, fireplaces available. TV/VCR, telephone, and bath with shower in each room. Quiet, cozy, and friendly. Attractive gardens and patios, outdoor hot tub, barbecue area. The knowledgeable hosts can help guests plan their activities.

Host: Gary Dawson
Rooms: 5 (PB) $65-135
Continental Breakfast
Credit Cards: A, B, C
Notes: 5, 7, 9, 10, 11, 12, 14

---

7 No smoking; 8 Children welcome; 9 Social drinking allowed; 10 Tennis nearby; 11 Swimming nearby; 12 Golf nearby; 13 Skiing nearby; 14 May be booked through a travel agent; 15 Handicapped accessible.

Saddle Rock Ranch

255 Rock Ridge Drive, 86336
(520) 282-7640; FAX (520) 282-6829
e-mail: saddlerock@sedona.net

History. Romance. Antiques. Views. Sedona's only historic landmark bed and breakfast. Enjoy fabulous views from this centrally located secluded hillside estate. The perfect adult retreat features quiet, romantic rooms with wood-burning fireplaces, canopied beds. All private baths have terry-cloth robes; luxurious amenities. Savor scrumptious breakfasts, fabled cookies, and afternoon snacks. Bubble in the whirlpool spa; lounge by the sparkling pool cantilevered over the hillside. Gardens, birds, and hiking. Warm service; individualized itineraries. A true gem.

Host: Fran (Bruno) Jackson
Rooms: 3 (PB) $130-175
Full Breakfast
Credit Cards: None
Notes: 2, 5, 7, 9, 10, 11, 12, 13

Saddle Rock Ranch

Southwest Inn at Sedona

3250 West Highway 89A, 86336
(520) 282-3344; (800) 483-7422
FAX (520) 282-0267; e-mail: info@swinn.com
www.swinn.com

The Southwest Inn is a wonderful combination of a small luxury hotel and a bed and breakfast.

Southwest Inn at Sedona

The inn has large, beautifully decorated rooms with king- or queen-size beds, fireplaces, and decks or patios facing dramatic red rock views. The inn has a swimming pool and spa and is close to all the varied activities Sedona has to offer, including hiking, horseback riding, jeep tours, hot-air balloon rides, and helicopter rides. Several restaurants, galleries, and theaters are within walking distance. AAA four-diamond rating.

Hosts: Joel and Sheila Gilguff
Rooms: 28 (PB) $99-195
Continental Breakfast
Credit Cards: A, B, C, D
Notes: 5, 7, 8, 9, 10, 11, 12, 13, 14. 15

Territorial House: An Old West Bed & Breakfast

65 Piki Drive, 86336
(520) 204-2737; (800) 801-2737
FAX (520) 204-2230

The Territorial House is built of native stone and cedar. Each unique room is comfortably decorated with a theme depicting Sedona's territorial history. Guests enjoy western hospitality as they relax around the large native-stone fireplace, watch numerous birds from the veranda, soak in the hot tub, or just rest in the peaceful, serene setting. Rooms available with fireplace, balcony, deck, whirlpool tub, and

---

NOTES: Credit cards accepted: A MasterCard; B Visa; C American Express; D Discover; E Diner's Club; F Other; 2 Personal checks accepted; 3 Lunch available; 4 Dinner available; 5 Open all year; 6 Pets welcome;

Sonoita, AZ   57

Territorial House

TV. Full gourmet breakfasts are served in the Saltillo-tiled dining room. Late afternoon snacks are available after a full day of exploring Sedona's red rock country.

Hosts: John and Linda Steele
Rooms: 4 (PB) $115-165
Full Breakfast
Credit Cards: A, B, C, D
Notes: 2, 5, 7, 8, 9, 10, 11, 12, 13, 14

SHOW LOW

Arizona Trails Bed & Breakfast Reservation Service

P.O. Box 18998, Fountain Hills, 85269-8998
(480) 837-4284; (888) 799-4284
FAX (480) 816-4224
e-mail: aztrails@arizonatrails.com
www.arizonatrails.com

AZ 186. This bed and breakfast sits on a hill overlooking Fool Hollow Lake. Choose from two suites or a standard guest room, all with lake views. Relax on the deck, in the garden, or on the courtyard patio. One suite features a king-size bed, sitting area with TV, large bath with jetted tub, and a romantic decor. Another has a private entrance, queen-size bed, TV, and kitchenette. The standard room is done in a patriotic country decor with a queen-size bed, TV, and private bath. Full breakfast. $85-125.

SIERRA VISTA

Mi Casa Su Casa/Old Pueblo Homestays Bed & Breakfast Reservation Service

P.O. Box 950, Tempe, AZ 85280-0950
(602) 990-0682; (800) 456-0682
FAX (602) 990-3390
e-mail: micasa@primenet.com
www.azres.com

5181. Guests will enjoy this secluded two-story ranch house and separate guest casita in a peaceful river valley amid the San Pedro Riparian National Conservation Area. Both guest rooms have private baths, microwaves, and refrigerators. The casita has a private entrance, sitting area, and gas fireplace. It is quiet, cozy, and romantic. The common room provides a TV, pool table, and small library. Enjoy the shaded courtyard and walled patio area with swimming pool (in season) and hot tub. Outside dog in residence. Two-night minimum stay. Smoking restricted. No pets. Children over 12 welcome. Full breakfast. Ten dollars extra for a one-night stay. $85.

SONOITA

Mi Casa Su Casa/Old Pueblo Homestays Bed & Breakfast Reservation Service

P.O. Box 950, Tempe, AZ 85280-0950
(602) 990-0682; (800) 456-0682
FAX (602) 990-3390
e-mail: micasa@primenet.com
www.azres.com

5192. Built in 1916 on a hilltop surrounded by acres of producing vineyards, the handsome main house has been updated but maintains the ambiance of the original hacienda. There are three attractive bedrooms with private baths. The attached guest house has a sitting room, bedroom with bath and private entrance. Full breakfast. Smoking permitted outside only. No pets. Children 12 and older welcome. $85-95.

---

7 No smoking; 8 Children welcome; 9 Social drinking allowed; 10 Tennis nearby; 11 Swimming nearby; 12 Golf nearby; 13 Skiing nearby; 14 May be booked through a travel agent; 15 Handicapped accessible.

5194. In the gorgeous high desert grasslands, this unique western country lodge is rich in local history. All furniture was custom made in Mexico; each room is decorated differently. Close to cultural and historic communities, the inn is near wineries, lakes, bird watching, hiking, horseback riding, golf, excellent dining, and Kartchner caverns, the largest caverns known in the world. Mexico is just 30 miles away. Eighteen spacious rooms named in honor of area ranches. Each has a private bath, TV/VCR, in-house movie ordering service, air conditioning, telephone, and spectacular views of surrounding meadows and mountains. Continental breakfast. No smoking. No pets. Handicapped possible in one room. Fifteen dollars for additional guests. $99-145.

SPRINGERVILLE/EAGER

Arizona Trails Bed & Breakfast Reservation Service

P.O. Box 18998, Fountain Hills, 85269-8998
(480) 837-4284; (888) 799-4284
FAX (480) 816-4224
e-mail: aztrails@arizonatrails.com
www.arizonatrails.com

AZ 104. This charming red brick Colonial home is listed in the historic register. It features four guest rooms all in a Victorian decor. Choose from double, queen-, or king-size beds, all with private baths and robes in each room. Relax in the parlor with TV/VCR, or enjoy a fun visit in the soda shop with an authentic working soda fountain and antique jukebox. Relax outdoors in the hot tub under the gazebo or browse in the plant nursery. Full breakfast. $65-95.

AZ 107. Elegance is classic at this three-room bed and breakfast on five secluded acres. Relax in any of the common rooms from the atrium with indoor fountain to the formal living room, dining room, casual breakfast room, or great room with a large fireplace and TV. Each room has a private bath with an in-room refrigerator. Choose from two queen-size beds or a king-size bed. Weekend dinner packages available along with on-site massage treatments. Wander down to the canal or sit on the roof top patio. Full breakfast. $100-130.

Mi Casa Su Casa/Old Pueblo Homestays Bed & Breakfast Reservation Service

P.O. Box 950, Tempe, AZ 85280-0950
(602) 990-0682; (800) 456-0682
FAX (602) 990-3390
e-mail: micasa@primenet.com
www.azres.com

4161. Carefully restored Colonial Revival home, circa 1910, allows a visitor to step back in time to the Victorian era. Four bedrooms on the second floor have private baths furnished with antiques, handmade quilts, and goose-down pillows. King, queen, double beds. Full breakfast is served. Seventeen miles from Sunrise, Arizona's largest ski resort, and 13 miles from Lyman Lake. Two miles from Casa Malpais Pueblo, prehistoric Indian structures. Children welcome at an additional charge. Smoking outside. No pets. $65-85.

SURPRISE

Mi Casa Su Casa/Old Pueblo Homestays Bed & Breakfast Reservation Service

P.O. Box 950, Tempe, AZ 85280-0950
(602) 990-0682; (800) 456-0682
FAX (602) 990-3390
e-mail: micasa@primenet.com
www.azres.com

5197. In a quiet, new golf community near Sun City. Spacious bedroom has sliding glass doors to the patio overlooking the 17th tee and offers view of spectacular sunsets. TV/VCR, writing desk and recliner, large full bath. Full break-

---

NOTES: Credit cards accepted: A MasterCard; B Visa; C American Express; D Discover; E Diner's Club; F Other; 2 Personal checks accepted; 3 Lunch available; 4 Dinner available; 5 Open all year; 6 Pets welcome;

fast. Smoking outside, no children, pets possible. Seasonal $65-75.

TEMPE

Arizona Trails Bed & Breakfast Reservation Service

P.O. Box 18998, Fountain Hills, 85269-8998
(480) 837-4284; (888) 799-4284
FAX (480) 816-4224
e-mail: aztrails@arizonatrails.com
www.arizonatrails.com

AZ 151. This charming homestay is conveniently located close to ASU, Scottsdale, and Phoenix Sky Harbor Airport in a quiet residential area. Enjoy a private southwestern suite complete with a private entrance, two bedrooms, bath, and living room. One bedroom features a queen-size bed, the other two bedrooms have twin-size beds. The cowboy living room has a TV/VCR, refrigerator, microwave, and coffee maker. Outside, enjoy the pool and patio area. Full breakfast. Children welcome. $80-100.

Mi Casa Su Casa/Old Pueblo Homestays Bed & Breakfast Reservation Service

P.O. Box 950, 85280-0950
(602) 990-0682; (800) 456-0682
FAX (602) 990-3390
e-mail: micasa@primenet.com
www.azres.com

5201. This bed and breakfast is in an older, quiet, well-kept neighborhood two blocks from ASU and downtown Tempe. The main house was built in 1939. A new addition with a private entrance onto the patio blends well with the old house. This area consists of large open space with sitting room/bedroom with TV, VCR, microwave, and small refrigerator. The private bath has a whirlpool tub. Full breakfast served in the main house. Smoking outside. Children and infants are welcome; Port-a-crib available. Minimum stay is two nights. Ten dollars each additional person. $75.

5202. This homey one story bed and breakfast is in a nicely maintained, quiet neighborhood which is near "everything." One of the two guest rooms has a TV. Guests have private full hall bath. There is also a private half bath available. Guests are welcome to watch TV in the living room or the family room. Refreshments. Full country style breakfast. Smoking outside. No pets. Infants only. Minimum stay two nights. $55-$70.

5203. A spacious home in an area of mini-ranches complete with Arabian horses and chickens. The private guest suite has two bedrooms, private full bath, and a living room with a TV and a sofa bed to accommodate children. Full breakfast. Resident cat. Minimum two nights stay. Only one party at a time. Three blocks from public transportation, airport pickup available. Smoking outside. Children six and older welcome. Ten dollars for each additional person. $90-110.

5204. Large ranch-style home in a quiet, pretty neighborhood. Two guest rooms on the second floor share a bath. Small guest room on first floor has crib and private hall bath. Pool for seasonal swimming. Prize winning breakfasts. No smoking. No pets. Infants and children 12 and older (swimmers only) are welcome. Infants stay free. Twenty dollars each additional guest. Weekly rates. $50-80.

5205. This extra large ranch-style home is in a nice, quiet neighborhood five minutes from Arizona State University and downtown Tempe and 20 minutes from Sky Harbor Airport. The private two-bedroom guest suite has a sitting room, private entrance and bath, TV/VCR, mid-size refrigerator, microwave, and coffee maker. Full breakfast. Port-a-crib available. Inquire about accommodations for pets. Smoking outside. $80-100.

---

7 No smoking; 8 Children welcome; 9 Social drinking allowed; 10 Tennis nearby; 11 Swimming nearby; 12 Golf nearby; 13 Skiing nearby; 14 May be booked through a travel agent; 15 Handicapped accessible.

Valley O' the Sun Bed & Breakfast

P.O. Box 2214, Scottsdale, 85252
(602) 941-1281; (800) 689-1281 (phone/FAX)

This bed and breakfast is in the college district of Tempe but still close enough to Scottsdale for guests to enjoy the glamour of its shops, restaurants, and theaters. Valley O' the Sun Bed and Breakfast offers clean, comfortable rooms at reasonable and affordable rates. Continental plus breakfast is served. Personal checks accepted on second visit. Discount for seniors.

Host: Kathleen Curtis
Rooms: 3 (1 PB; 2 SB) $45
Continental Breakfast
Credit Cards: None
Notes: 5, 9, 10, 11, 12, 13, 14

TOMBSTONE

Mi Casa Su Casa/Old Pueblo Homestays Bed & Breakfast Reservation Service

P.O. Box 950, Tempe, AZ 85280-0950
(602) 990-0682; (800) 456-0682
FAX (602) 990-3390
e-mail: micasa@primenet.com
www.azres.com

5241. Originally Emily Morton's Boarding House, this house was totally renovated in 1994-95 to become a charming bed and breakfast. It is next door to the famous 1880 County Courthouse, now a museum. Three guest rooms with private baths and cable TV. Outside cat and dog. Arrangements can be made for a small wedding at the bed and breakfast, stage coach rides, desert trail horseback rides, mine tours, train trips to the San Pedro River, and Kartchner Caverns tours. Full breakfast. Smoking permitted outside. No children. No pets. $65-75.

5242. This accommodation consists of two 1880s adobe houses surrounded by a picket fence. An artist's studio is also available. A hearty breakfast is served. Each of the six rooms, plus a small miners' cabin, have private entrances and most have private baths. Smoking permitted outside. Children welcome. Inquire about accommodations for pets. Ten dollars for each additional guest. $55-80.

5243. This 1904 home was restored and retains all the original wood, some of the gas lighting fixtures, and a large oak staircase. It is the only remaining two-story clapboard Victorian house in the county. The three rooms upstairs share the shower bath on the same floor. A guest room downstairs has a private bath and TV. Smoking permitted outside. Children welcome. No pets. $40-100.

5244. This 1880 adobe home, listed in the National Register of Historic Places, was originally built as a boarding house. The common room is filled with antiques, memorabilia, puzzles, games, and books. A barbecue area is available. Each of the four guest rooms is filled with antiques or various themes and provides a private or shared bath. Full breakfast. Smoking permitted outside. Children negotiable. No pets. $65-85.

5246. This is a newly remodeled 1927 homestead and working cattle ranch that has retained its Old West atmosphere in the San Pedro Riparian National Conservation Area. Its newly constructed western town consists of 14 buildings, each filled with antiques and memorabilia. Horseback tours, wagon rides, and chuck wagon suppers with musical western stage shows entertain guests. The "hotel" offers six large rooms, private shower baths, and sleeping porch. There are also four themed cottages. Prices include three meals per day and 15% gratuity will be added. Smoking permitted in designated areas. Children and trained pets welcome. $280.

NOTES: Credit cards accepted: A MasterCard; B Visa; C American Express; D Discover; E Diner's Club; F Other; 2 Personal checks accepted; 3 Lunch available; 4 Dinner available; 5 Open all year; 6 Pets welcome;

TUBAC

Mi Casa Su Casa/Old Pueblo Homestays Bed & Breakfast Reservation Service

P.O. Box 950, Tempe, AZ 85280-0950
(602) 990-0682; (800) 456-0682
FAX (602) 990-3390
e-mail: micasa@primenet.com
www.azres.com

5262. On three acres of gardens with two fish ponds, this inn is a 1978/1992 Spanish Colonial located in the Historic District of Tubac within easy walking distance of 75 art galleries, boutiques, and restaurants. There are two units, each with refrigerator, wet bar and coffee maker. The Queen's Wreath suite has a private bath, patio, a fireplace, TV/VCR, microwave oven, electric range. The Jasmine Suite has a private bath, TV/VCR, a refrigerator, wet bar, and coffee maker. Continental breakfast. No smoking. No pets. Children welcome. Ten dollars per additional guest. Seasonal rates. $89-99.

Tubac Country Inn

Corner Plaza and Burruel, P.O. Box 1540, 85646
(520) 398-3178

Visit the 75 art galleries, boutiques, and restaurants all within walking distance of the inn. Or drive a few minutes to shop in Mexico, or visit missions, museums, national parks, or play golf at one of seven courses within easy access. Or if quiet relaxation is what is desired, then sit on the patio and enjoy the sounds of the birds singing while the sun sets in the west. "Since we do not sell drinks you are encouraged to bring your own favorites."

Hosts: Jim and Ruth Goebel
Rooms: 4 (PB) $75-95
Continental Breakfast
Credit Cards: None
Notes: 2, 7, 8, 9, 10, 11, 12

TUCSON

Adobe Rose Inn

940 North Olsen Avenue, 85719
(520) 318-4644; (800) 328-4122
FAX (520) 325-0055

Causal comfort best describes the atmosphere of this beautifully restored 1933 adobe home in a prestigious older neighborhood just two blocks from the University of Arizona. There are three charming, lodge-pole-furnished rooms in the main house, two which have cozy beehive fireplaces and stained-glass windows. There are also two private cottages that are ideally suited for the longer stay. All the rooms have cable TV and access to the very private bougainvillaea-draped swimming pool and hot tub.

Host: Diana Graham
Rooms: 5 (PB) $55-125
Full Breakfast
Credit Cards: A, B, C, D, F
Notes: 2, 5, 7, 9, 10, 11, 12, 13, 14

Arizona Trails Bed & Breakfast Reservation Service

P.O. Box 18998, Fountain Hills, 85269-8998
(480) 837-4284; (888) 799-4284
FAX (480) 816-4224
e-mail: aztrails@arizonatrails.com
www.arizonatrails.com

AZ 005. Enjoy this Spanish hacienda on 16 acres in the beautiful Tucson desert with spectacular views. Hiking trails and bird watching are favorites. Two suites and one private two-bedroom casita all with private baths, antique stoves/fireplaces and kitchenettes. Decorated with Mexican influence and southwest decor. Private courtyard with fountain and flowers. Two therapeutic outdoor hot tubs. Close to attractions, restaurants, and shopping. Full breakfast. Children welcome. Outdoor cats wander the property along with other desert wildlife. $95-145.

---

7 No smoking; 8 Children welcome; 9 Social drinking allowed; 10 Tennis nearby; 11 Swimming nearby; 12 Golf nearby; 13 Skiing nearby; 14 May be booked through a travel agent; 15 Handicapped accessible.

AZ 006. Southwestern home in a quiet desert neighborhood nestled on the threshold of the Catalina Mountains. Four rooms all with private baths and contemporary southwestern decor. All the rooms can sleep up to four comfortably with queen-size beds and queen-size pullouts, TVs, and private baths. Enjoy the pool or spa and keep favorite snacks in the separate guest refrigerator that is available. Minutes to Tucson shops, restaurants, and other area attractions. Full breakfast. Children welcome. $95-110.

AZ 007. On six acres of desert with mountain views, this southwestern bed and breakfast has been called the Ritz Carlton of bed and breakfasts. Three guest rooms in the main house and one separate casita. All have private baths and TVs. The casita features a full kitchen, fireplace, and sleeper-sofa for parties of four. Panoramic views of the Catalina Mountains offset the pool and patio area. Full breakfast. $95-150.

AZ 008. Enjoy the convenience of this downtown Tucson location in a nice neighborhood close to the bus line. One room with queen-size bed and a private bath, and one suite which sleeps up to four with a private bath; washer/dryer privileges for extended stays. An eclectic collection of art and artifacts from South America and Africa adds to the southwestern decor. Minutes to the university, shopping, and restaurants. Continental breakfast served each morning. $65-85.

AZ 020. This 1940s ranch-style home in central Tucson hosts four lovely guest rooms and is only minutes to shopping, restaurants, and a small city park. Two rooms share a full hall bath, one with queen-size bed and one with a king-size or two twin beds. Two separate guest cottages have private entrances and baths. One features a queen-size bed with Hollywood couch and small library, the other has king-size bed with a trundle, Jacuzzi tub, and is handicapped accessible. Common areas feature large, inviting, sitting rooms, TV/VCR, and library. Full breakfast. $80-125.

AZ 033. Two-room bed and breakfast ideal for those who appreciate the outdoors and are train enthusiasts. Nestled in the desert of Northwest Tucson, this bed and breakfast sits on a beautiful site with hiking trails and Indian ruins. Pool and patio area features a delightful model train that chugs around the patio. Inside room offers twin beds with a private hall bath. The guest cottage has its own model train display and features a queen-size bed, private bath, private patio, and Ben Franklin stove. Sleeps up to four. Full breakfast. $65-85.

AZ 054. Relax in northwest Tucson at this outstanding four-room bed and breakfast nestled in the glorious Tucson desert. All rooms have private entrances, king-size beds, in-room refrigerators, cable TV, telephone, and private baths. The master suite also has a large sitting area and two-person jetted tub. Cool off with a dip in the pool, soak in the therapeutic hot tub, and start the day with a healthy Continental plus breakfast buffet. $80-100.

AZ 078. On three acres this immaculate four-room bed and breakfast is convenient and comfortable. The main house features two rooms that combine for a family unit with hall bath featuring a sunken tub and shower. Three other rooms all with private entrances are adjacent. One features a queen-size bed, private bath, and color cable TV. The Sonoran suite (handicapped accessible) has a king-size bed, king-size sleeper-sofa, sitting area, microwave, and mini-refrigerator, cable TV, and large bath. The Eastlake suite has a queen-size bed, sitting area, two-person jetted tub, and stand-up shower, microwave, refrigerator, and cable TV. Relax by the pool, take a dip in the spa, or try your luck on the putting green. Full breakfast. $95-165.

AZ 081. Relax in quiet and solitude at this four-room bed and breakfast close to Old Tuc-

NOTES: Credit cards accepted: A MasterCard; B Visa; C American Express; D Discover; E Diner's Club; F Other; 2 Personal checks accepted; 3 Lunch available; 4 Dinner available; 5 Open all year; 6 Pets welcome;

son Studios. Great views of the Tucson Mountains provide a perfect backdrop to the pool and spa area. Two rooms have queen-size beds, fireplaces, private baths, and sitting areas with TV/VCR. Two rooms share a bath, one with a queen-size bed, and one with a double bed. All rooms are decorated in rustic southwest style. Full breakfast. $65-125.

AZ 088. In central Tucson, this bed and breakfast is close to shops, restaurants, and the historic district. Each room has a private bath. Two rooms share a common sitting room with TV/VCR and guest refrigerator. Two suites both have queen-size beds, double sleeper-sofas, TV/VCRs, and sitting areas. Two common rooms give guests plenty of space to spread out. Outside relax by the pool or use the exercise room. A guest kitchen is also available for longer stays. Full breakfast. Children welcome. $85-105.

AZ 096. Escape the world and retreat to this two-room bed and breakfast overlooking Saguaro National Park Annex in the far southeast corner of Tucson. Owned by an artist and photographer, original works of art decorate the rooms. One room is done in a Victorian theme; the other replicates a southwest garden with private patio area. Both have full private baths. Relax in the common area with TV/VCR, library, wet bar, and great views. Full healthy breakfast. $85-95.

AZ 140. In downtown Tucson, this restored adobe six-room inn exudes all the charm and grace of the Victorian era. Each room has a private bath, sitting area, TV, mini-refrigerator, and exquisite, pristine antiques. The suite features a spa room with jetted tub and wet bar. Most rooms have private entrances. The back courtyard features lush landscaping with a heated pool and spa. Walking distance to downtown and visitors center. Gourmet breakfast. $120-180.

AZ 142. Rest in the far north area of Oro Valley close to Catalina State Park. This warm and friendly two-room bed and breakfast is steeped in colorful southwestern decor with murals on the guest room walls. Both suites have private baths with king-size beds, TV, mini-refrigerators, and coffee makers. One is a two-bedroom suite that sleeps up to four. The back yard is adjacent to Catalina State Park and offers great bird watching and hiking. Continental breakfast. $139.

AZ 172. This quaint, natural sun-baked adobe home bed and breakfast provides a delightful stay. Located on the southwest side of Tucson with great views and close to area attractions. Two guest rooms; each room has a queen-size bed, private bath, private entrance, sitting area, and antiques. The location is great for bird watching and hiking. Enjoy an outdoor therapeutic hot tub and large patios. Full breakfast. $85.

Casa Alegre

Casa Alegre
Bed & Breakfast Inn

316 East Speedway, 85705
(520) 628-1800

This charming 1915 Craftsman-style home is between the University of Arizona and downtown Tucson. A scrumptious full breakfast is served in the formal dining room or poolside on the serene patio. Casa Alegre allows easy access to Tucson's many historical, cultural, and recreational attractions, state and national parks, as well as great shopping and fantastic eateries.

---

7 No smoking; 8 Children welcome; 9 Social drinking allowed; 10 Tennis nearby; 11 Swimming nearby; 12 Golf nearby; 13 Skiing nearby; 14 May be booked through a travel agent; 15 Handicapped accessible.

Host: Phyllis Florek
Rooms: 5 (PB) $80-125
Full Breakfast
Credit Cards: A, B, D
Notes: 2, 5, 7, 9, 10, 11, 12, 14

Car-Mar's Southwest Bed & Breakfast

6766 West Oklahoma, 85735
(520) 578-1730; (888) 578-1730
e-mail: CarMarBB@aol.com
www.members.aol.com/carmarbb

Southwestern by design, close to popular attractions, such as Arizona-Sonora Desert Museum and Old Tucson Movie Studios. Each room is uniquely decorated with lodgepole and saguaro rib furniture. Hot tub under the stars, poolside refreshments, and luxurious robes may be relished during guests' stay. Freshly baked treats at turndown. Full, scrumptious breakfast served in dining room or garden by request. Super Summer special in effect May 15 through August 31. (Buy two nights and get the third consecutive night free.)

Host: Carole Martinez
Rooms: 4 (2 PB; 2 SB) $65-125
Full Breakfast
Credit Cards: A, B
Notes: 2, 5, 7, 8, 9, 10, 11, 12, 14

Casa Tierra Adobe Bed & Breakfast Inn

11155 West Calle Pima, 85743
(520) 578-3058; FAX (520) 578-8445
e-mail: casatier@azstarnet.com

On five acres of beautiful Sonoran Desert, Casa Tierra is 30 minutes west of Tucson. This secluded area has hundreds of Saguaro cacti, spectacular mountain views, and fiery sunsets. The rustic and elegant Spanish adobe hacienda features entryways with vaulted brick ceilings, an interior arched courtyard with fountain, Mexican furnishings, hot tub overlooking the dessert, telescope, fully equipped gym. Great hiking and bird watching. Near Arizona-Sonora Desert Museum, Saguaro National Park. Gourmet vegetarian breakfast. AAA three-diamond rating.

Hosts: Barb and Dave Malmquist
Rooms: 5 (PB) $95-150
Full Breakfast
Credit Cards: A, B
Notes: 2, 5, 7, 8, 9, 12, 14

Catalina Park Inn

309 East First Street, 85705
(520) 792-4541; (800) 792-4885
e-mail: cpinn@flash.net
www.catalinaparkinn.com

Exceptional architectural details abound in this elegant 1927 historic district jewel. Six guest rooms are smartly appointed sanctuaries of privacy that combine time-tested comforts and modern conveniences. Savor the day while relaxing on own private porch or in the fragrant lush gardens. Each morning enjoy a glorious breakfast prepared and garnished with herbs and flowers from the garden. The superb central location is handy to many of Tucson's attractions. Recommended by Fodor's and Frommer's guidebook.

Hosts: Mark Hall and Paul Richard
Rooms: 6 (PB) $95-115
Full Breakfast
Credit Cards: A, B, D
Notes: 2, 5, 7, 9, 10, 11, 12, 14

Catalina Park Inn

NOTES: Credit cards accepted: A MasterCard; B Visa; C American Express; D Discover; E Diner's Club; F Other; 2 Personal checks accepted; 3 Lunch available; 4 Dinner available; 5 Open all year; 6 Pets welcome;

Copper-Bell Bed & Breakfast

25 North Westmoreland Avenue, 85745
(520) 629-9229 (phone/FAX)

Copper Bell is a unique turn-of-the-century lava stone home which was built from 1907 to 1920 providing a unique blend of architectural styles. The owner, relocated here from Germany, has created the inn by combining the Old World with the New. Four of the six guest rooms have a private ground-level entry and are in separate guest houses. Each has a private bath and climate control. A private honeymoon suite is also available. Guests will enjoy the homemade German breakfast in the large and sunny dining room with beautiful stained-glass windows.

Host: Gertrude M. Eich
Rooms: 6 (4 PB; 2 SB) $79-95
Full Breakfast
Credit Cards: None
Notes: 2, 5, 7, 10, 11, 12, 14

El Presidio Bed & Breakfast

297 North Main Street, 85701
(520) 623-6151; (800) 349-6151

A Victorian adobe, this inn is a splendid example of American-Territorial style and is listed in the National Register of Historic Places. In El Presidio historic district. Walk to the best restaurants, museums, and shops. Guests enjoy true southwestern charm in spacious suites, two with kitchens that open onto large courtyards and gardens, fountains, and lush floral displays. A tranquil oasis with the ambiance of Old Mexico. Three-star rating from Mobil and AAA. Awarded "Best Bed and Breakfast in Southern Arizona," 1998.

Host: Patti Toci
Rooms: 3 (PB) $95-115
Full Breakfast
Credit Cards: None
Notes: 2, 5, 7, 9, 10, 11, 12, 14

Hacienda Bed & Breakfast

5704 East Grant Road, 85712-2235
(520) 290-2224; (888) 236-4421 (outside Tucson)
FAX (520) 721-9066; e-mail: Hacienda97@aol.com
www.members.aol.com/hacienda97/index.html

Four quiet, air-conditioned rooms with private baths. Two rooms have TV/VCR, refrigerator, full-size Hide-a-Bed, and outside entrance. One is handicapped accessible with coffee maker and microwave. Two bedrooms share a sitting room with TV/VCR, private courtyard, barbecue, solar pool, spa, exercise room. Computer, fax, copier, fireproof file for valuables. No smoking. Supervised children are welcome. AAA-rated. Member of the Tucson Convention Bureau, the Chamber of Commerce, and AABBI and PAII.

Hosts: Barbara and Fred Shamseldin
Rooms: 4 (PB) $85-105
Full Breakfast
Credit Cards: A, B, C, D
Notes: 2, 5, 7, 9, 10, 11, 12, 14, 15

Karrels Double K Ranch

3930 North Smokey Topaz Lane, 85749
(520) 749-5345; www.doublekranch.com

Bird watchers paradise. People who enjoy this bed and breakfast most are hikers, nature lovers, rail fans, and star gazers. Friendly host couple welcomes guests to relax among stately saguaros in this territorial-style home on four acres. Splendid bird watching from guest room and adjacent desert oasis. Explore the Sonoran Desert and ancient Hohokam sites on private trail or venture off to nearby national forest

El Presidio

trails. Railroading theme. Enjoy full breakfast on patio with garden railway.

Hosts: Ken and Mary Karrels
Rooms: 2 (PB) $69-95
Full Breakfast
Credit Cards: None
Notes: 2, 7, 8, 9, 10, 11, 12, 13, 14

La Posada Del Valle

1640 North Campbell Avenue, 85719
(520) 795-3840 (phone/FAX); (888) 404-7113
e-mail: laposadabandbinn@hotmail.com
www.bbhost.com/laposadadelvalle

An elegant 1920s inn nestled in the heart of the city has five guest rooms with private baths and private entrances. Mature orange trees perfume the air as guests enjoy a gourmet breakfast and sip tea each afternoon on the patio overlooking the Santa Catalina Mountains. Children over eight are welcome. *Wir sprechen Deutsch.* Private off-street parking is available.

Hosts: Tom and Karin Dennen
Rooms: 5 (PB) $90-135
Full Breakfast
Credit Cards: A, B
Notes: 2, 5, 7, 8, 9, 10, 11, 12, 13, 14

Mi Casa Su Casa/Old Pueblo Homestays Bed & Breakfast Reservation Service

P.O. Box 950, Tempe, AZ 85280-0950
(602) 990-0682; (800) 456-0682
FAX (602) 990-3390
e-mail: micasa@primenet.com
www.azres.com

5351. Guests enjoy experiencing the beautiful grounds of this historic downtown mansion built in 1886. Convenient to shops, theaters, museums, and restaurants. Gracious hostess serves gourmet breakfasts. The Carriage House has a living room/kitchen, bedroom, and private bath. In the main house, the Gate House suite has a living room/bedroom, Pullman kitchen, private bath, and private entrance. The Victorian Suite has a sitting room and bedroom and private bath. The Quilt Room has a private bath. Smoking outside. No pets. Children age 15 and older welcome. Two-night minimum stay. Weekly and monthly rates. $85-120.

5352. Guests enjoy the private guest area in this Santa Fe-style patio home, built in 1993, in a quiet north central area with unobstructed views of the Catalina Mountains. Landscaped back yard with desert plantings and access to community pool. The guest room has a private hall bath. Guests are welcome in the living room with fireplace. Laundry privileges. Enclosed garage parking. Full breakfast. Smoking outside. Children over three welcome. $65.

5353. Warm, outgoing hostess welcomes guests to a delightfully restored Spanish Colonial two-story home built around 1900 in a quiet, well-kept neighborhood near the University of Arizona. On the first floor, room one has a private entrance, sitting area, and a private bath. Room two on the second floor shares the hall bath. Light kitchen privileges available. Near public transportation. Continental plus breakfast. Smoking outside. Weekly rates. Children welcome. $65-75.

5354. The friendly, helpful hostess has a large 1915 Craftsman-style bungalow near the University of Arizona. She offers three bedrooms with private baths. The Arizona room offers a TV/VCR and opens onto the patio, swimming pool, and spa. The Buchanan House, next door, has two guest rooms with private baths, which can be individually occupied or rented as a suite, and an upstairs guest room with bath. For the guests occupying the suite there is a kitchen, dining room, and living room. Full breakfasts. Inquire about accommodations for children. Smoking outside. $80-125.

5355. Knowledgeable about local artists, the friendly hostess lives in a pre-Santa Fe home built in 1928 and has a charming, updated guest cottage in an older quiet neighborhood

---

NOTES: Credit cards accepted: A MasterCard; B Visa; C American Express; D Discover; E Diner's Club; F Other; 2 Personal checks accepted; 3 Lunch available; 4 Dinner available; 5 Open all year; 6 Pets welcome;

with a view of the Catalina Mountains. Three blocks north of the University of Arizona Medical Center and near shopping and theaters. The cottage has a private entrance, southwestern decor, living room/kitchen, bedroom with bath with shower, TV, private telephone, and small patio. Off street parking. Continental plus breakfast. No smoking. No pets. Children 14 and older welcome. Weekly and monthly rates. $85.

5356. This is a 1933 adobe southwestern-style home with antiques, stained glass, tile, attractive gardens, patios, and pool surrounded by a six-foot wall in a quiet neighborhood east of the University of Arizona. Three guest rooms, a studio, an upstairs apartment, and a separate cottage, each with private bath and cable TV. The hostess takes pride in her gourmet breakfast. Smoking outside. No pets, no children. Seasonal rates. $45-125.

5357. Built in the 1920s as a corner market, the adobe structure, in one of Tucson's historic barrios, is furnished with antiques and folk art. The great room has a fireplace, books, and music. Guests are invited to relax outside in an enclosed garden with well-established desert plants. The downtown arts district, Tucson Museum of Art, shops, restaurants, and the convention center are just blocks away. Two suites each have two bedrooms and each suite has a shared bath. The larger suite has a kitchen. Continental breakfast. Smoking permitted outside. Children welcome. No pets. Rates quoted are per bedroom occupancy. $65-75.

5359. This gracious English hostess has a Southwestern inn in the early Santa Fe-style built in 1929. It is within walking distance of the University of Arizona and its medical center. A cottage with kitchenette and four large rooms, each offering private outside entrance and private bath. A gourmet breakfast and afternoon tea are served. Children welcome. No smoking. No pets. $90-125.

5360. Minutes from downtown, the University of Arizona, and the medical center is this restored Victorian home built in 1905. Three rooms (one in the main house, and two in a 1917 bungalow adjacent to it which includes a living room) have private baths. Each of two two-bedroom guest houses has a living room, dining area, full kitchen, laundry, private patio, telephone, and TV. A one-bedroom apartment for monthly rental does not include breakfast. Gourmet breakfast served, special dietary needs provided for with advance notice. Smoking permitted outside. Children welcome. No pets. $85-175.

5361. A warm welcome is provided at this quiet home filled with period antiques. The guest room has an antique vanity, TV, radio, telephone, air conditioning, rocking chair, and private hall bath with whirlpool tub. Delight in a tastefully prepared breakfast in a charming dining area or on the front patio with mountain view. High tea can be served in the late afternoon, if desired. No smoking. No children. No pets. $70.

5362. This 1940s family ranch, with Saltillo tile throughout, is convenient to sightseeing, restaurants, shopping, and recreation. A spacious living room with fireplace offers relaxing diversions. Two guest rooms share a Mexican tiled bath. A guest house offers a yard, patio, and Mexican tiled private shower bath. Full gourmet breakfast served. Picnics can be arranged on request. Cat in residence. Open September through May and by special arrangement in the summer. Discount stays of three or more nights. No smoking. No pets. Inquire about accommodations for children. Ten dollars for extra guests. $65-100.

5365. This meticulously renovated 1878 historic Victorian mansion is in the heart of downtown. All spacious guest rooms feature period antiques, Victorian decor, private baths, air conditioning, telephones and TV. Four of the six rooms are two room suites and most can be made into adjoining suites. Pool and hot tub

---

7 No smoking; 8 Children welcome; 9 Social drinking allowed; 10 Tennis nearby; 11 Swimming nearby; 12 Golf nearby; 13 Skiing nearby; 14 May be booked through a travel agent; 15 Handicapped accessible.

Mi Casa Su Casa/Old Pueblo Homestays Bed & Breakfast Reservation Service *(continued)*

heated by request. Continental breakfast in addition to main entrée. Evening wine and cheese. Smoking permitted outside. Inquire about accommodations for pets. Well-behaved children welcome. Discounted rates based on length of stay. Seasonal rates $85-170.

5401. Stunningly beautiful home with 360 degree views. Guests are welcome to use common room with cable TV, VCR, and fireplace. The Quail's Nest Honeymoon Suite has views, private patio, TV, fireplace, and private bath with double tub. The Cactus Wren has views, private hall bath with whirlpool tub, and TV. Rollaway and cot available for small additional fee. Continental plus breakfasts. Smoking outside. Resident pets. Handicapped accessible. No children. No pets. Two-night minimum. $75-95.

5402. Delightful, gracious hostess welcomes guests to this beautiful, spacious adobe-style home in fashionable north Tucson. Very private extra large room has semi-private entrance, sofa, TV and small refrigerator. Bath with shower. Sliding glass doors lead to private patio and unheated pool. Continental plus breakfast. Two-night stay preferred. A child 10 and older welcome. Maximum two guests. No pets. Smoking permitted outside. $80.

5403. This handsome two-level home in the Catalina Foothills is in a quiet neighborhood with mountain and city views. Guests have a private entrance from the large pool/patio area into a large guest living room, dining, and kitchen area. In the living room are a private telephone, TV/VCR, and small library with books and brochures. There are four guest rooms with private baths. For guests' use, there is a large refrigerator, sink, microwave, toaster, coffee maker, and dishes. Smoking permitted in designated areas only. No pets. Children over eight who can swim welcome. Full breakfast. $70-75.

5404. A getaway in a quiet northwest neighborhood below the Catalina Mountain cliffs. Nearby are golf, a state park, restaurants, and a health club. Guests can relax on the patio, in the spa, or in the solar heated pool. This Territorial home provides a large entryway living room with fireplace. Five guest rooms, each with cable TV. Private and shared baths. Full breakfast served. Smoking permitted outside. Inquire about accommodations for children. No pets. $65-80.

5405. A spectacular view of the mountains and the city can be enjoyed from a quiet patio at this accommodation. Four rooms, all light and cheerful, are tastefully furnished with cherry and walnut antiques, oriental rugs, telephones, a TV on request, and private baths. Two bedrooms have a private entrance and Jacuzzi. A full breakfast served. Smoking outside. Children 12 and older welcome. Pets welcome. $65-95.

5406. Five miles north of Tucson, this ranch house has breathtaking views, as it is in the shadow of the Santa Catalina Mountains at the edge of thousands of acres of state and national forest land. The bunkhouse room has a loft that can sleep four and has a private hall bath with tub, shower, and double sinks. Two other rooms share a bath with a whirlpool tub. All rooms feature luxury linens, ceiling fans, and cable TV/VCR. Full breakfast. Host couple speaks Spanish and will pick guests up at the airport. Smoking permitted outside. Inquire about accommodations for children. No pets. $95-110.

5409. At the base of the Catalina Mountains, this cozy suite has easy access to shops, restaurants, and the University of Arizona. The suite consists of TV, private bath and entrance, and kitchenette including microwave, toaster oven,

---

NOTES: Credit cards accepted: A MasterCard; B Visa; C American Express; D Discover; E Diner's Club; F Other; 2 Personal checks accepted; 3 Lunch available; 4 Dinner available; 5 Open all year; 6 Pets welcome;

and mini-refrigerator. Enjoy the views of the mountains from the front patio or the city lights at night while relaxing in the pool or spa. The refrigerator is stocked with ingredients for a Continental plus breakfast. Resident dog. No smoking. Inquire about accommodations for pets and children. $80.

5451. Sixteen miles north of Tucson, four miles from Biosphere 2. Hostess welcomes guests to a very large stucco home built in 1990 in a resort community in a scenic area. Available are a club house with a restaurant, tennis courts, 9- and 18-hole golf course, two heated swimming pools, driving range, and health club with spa. Guests have private use of the living room with fireplace, dining room, and den. Room one has private full hall bath. Room two has a sofa bed for additional guests and shares the hall bath. Full breakfast. Children welcome with children's rates. Guest pets welcome by arrangement. Smoking permitted. Weekly rates are available. $85.

5452. Host couple lives in scenic areas and welcome guests to their guest house which has mountain and city views. On the porch of the guest house, guests overlook a beautifully landscaped tropical yard with a pool with waterfall for seasonal swimming and heated spa. One hour to skiing on Mt. Lemmon. The guest house has climate controls, a living room with cable TV, a bedroom, bath with shower, telephone, and large kitchenette. Outside gas grill. A mountain bike and a 10-speed bike available. Continental plus breakfast. Smoking permitted in designated areas only. No pets. Infants welcome and children who are swimmers. Three-night minimum. Weekly rates. $115.

5454. Casual southwestern Territorial-style home in a desert setting on four acres. The main house and guest cottage are separated by a patio. The guest cottage has a private entrance, private bath, refrigerator, TV, telephone, library of bird and western lore, and private patio. There is a smaller room in the main house with private full bath in the hall. Full breakfast. Pool for seasonal swimming. Heated spa. Children two and under free. Smoking permitted outside. Ten dollars for additional guests. Horses boarded. $69-95.

5455. Friendly, helpful host couple has a spacious Territorial adobe home on three acres in the northeast quadrant of Tucson with beautiful mountain views. Two guest rooms are in a private wing of the house. Each has a private hall bath, a sitting room with TV and writing desk. Reading material is shared by both. Pool for seasonal swimming. Washer/dryer. The breakfast menu caters to low-cholesterol, low-fat, gluten-free diets, but not exclusively. Infants and supervised children six and older (swimmers only) welcome. Smoking permitted outside. Inquire about pets. $75.

5456. Awaken to spectacular views of the Catalina and Rincon Mountains from the private and secluded foothills suites. Three guest suites each have private entrance, bath with shower, and kitchenette. Pool, barbecue, heated spa, and acres of adjacent trails. Continental breakfast plus complimentary fresh fruit, coffee, and tea are available 24 hours a day. Children 13 and older welcome. Smoking permitted outside. Pets negotiable. $70-90.

5458. A warm welcome awaits guests at this non-smoking home in a quiet neighborhood with a bird's-eye view of the mountains from guests' private patio. The accommodations consist of a private entrance, small sitting room with TV, refrigerator and microwave, private bath, and two bedrooms. Continental plus breakfast. Only one party accepted at a time. No pets. Children nine and older welcome. Near public transportation. $60.

5460. This brick home with Mexican and oriental influence is in a quiet neighborhood. Enjoy the mountain and desert views, private walled gardens, hammock, pool and spa. The oversized recreational room has a Ping-Pong

---

7 No smoking; 8 Children welcome; 9 Social drinking allowed; 10 Tennis nearby; 11 Swimming nearby; 12 Golf nearby; 13 Skiing nearby; 14 May be booked through a travel agent; 15 Handicapped accessible.

Mi Casa Su Casa/Old Pueblo Homestays Bed & Breakfast Reservation Service *(continued)*

table, mini-trampoline, and TV/VCR. Two bedrooms share a hall bath with double sink, tub, and shower. Terry-cloth robes for adult guests. Telephone in each room and TV/VCR available on request. No smoking. Full breakfast. Inquire about accommodations for children. $70-80.

5461. This newly constructed elegant inn is on 3.3 acres nestled on the threshold of the Catalina Mountains. It offers five rooms, each with TV, radio, telephone, and private bath en suite with shower. Each of the four largest rooms has a sitting area. Shared hall refrigerator, pool (add $10/day to heat the pool), and heated spa are available. Full breakfast. No smoking. No pets. Children welcome. Seasonal rates. $65-110.

5462. This spacious new southwestern contemporary home sits on six acres of beautiful Sonoran Desert. The guest suite has a private bath, a sitting room with TV/VCR, stereo, telephone, and opens onto a private adjoining patio. The Sabino Canyon recreation area is minutes away, as are hiking and riding trails, golf courses, and many exceptional restaurants. A full or Continental breakfast catering to guests' special dietary needs is served. No children. No pets. No smoking. $55-75.

5463. This handsome Southwestern-style home with beautiful landscaping is located on four acres in east Tucson. The attached but separate apartment has private entrance, living room with TV, sofa bed, bedroom, bath, kitchen, fireplace. The second accommodation has antiques, TV, and bath. Solar heated pool, barbecue. Laundry facilities available. No smoking. No pets. Children 16 and older welcome. Continental plus breakfast. $85-125.

5465. In a scenic, quiet residential area, this secluded nicely decorated two-bedroom guest cottage has mountain views. Country quiet, but near city amenities. Great area for walking and wildlife. Near Sabino Canyon. Living room has fireplace, CD player, TV/VCR. Private telephone. The large bath has a shower. Full kitchen. Private laundry facilities, barbecue, seasonal pool, and spa. Self-catered Continental plus breakfast. No smoking. No pets. Children 12 and older welcome. Monthly rates. $95.

5466. This guest studio apartment is attached to the main house in a scenic residential area 25 minutes from the airport. Great views of the city, desert, and mountains from the patio area. Private entrance, sofa-bed, extra large walk-in closet, cable TV, VCR, CD/cassette stereo, private full bath and full kitchen. Unheated pool, spa. Full breakfast. No smoking. No pets. Children welcome. Five dollars for one-night stay. Fifteen dollars for each additional persons. Long term and senior rates. Seasonal $85-110.

5467. This two-bedroom townhouse is in the Catalina Foothills, one of Tucson's nicest areas. The guest room has firm waterbed and full bath en suite. Guest privileges in the complex include use of two pools, an extra large jetted hot tub, and tennis courts. Full breakfast on weekends; Continental weekdays. No smoking. No children. Guest pet negotiable. Seasonal $55-70.

5468. This converted, somewhat historic ranch in Sabino Canyon offers peaceful, scenic, rustic Southwestern atmosphere and simply furnished, comfortable rooms. The large banquet center often hosts weddings in the beautiful courtyard lawn and fountain patio area. Nearby are riding stables and restaurant row. The 1920s six-unit bed and breakfast building is a completely remodeled, plastered adobe hacienda. A two-bedroom guest cottage with living room, kitchen, bath is also available. All rooms have private baths, heating and cooling

NOTES: Credit cards accepted: A MasterCard; B Visa; C American Express; D Discover; E Diner's Club; F Other; 2 Personal checks accepted; 3 Lunch available; 4 Dinner available; 5 Open all year; 6 Pets welcome;

units, and covered porches with beautiful mountain views. Cable TV arranged at no charge. Continental breakfast. Smoking permitted outside only. No pets. $105-170.

5469. Hospitable artist couple welcomes guests to this exceptionally beautiful home and guest house on 20 acres. It was built on a hilltop with panoramic views and designed in hacienda style around a courtyard with a fountain and many flowers. The main house has two guest rooms, each with TV and private bath. Guests welcome in the living room with fireplace. The guest house has a living room with TV and sofa bed, fireplace, bedroom, complete kitchen, and private walled patio. Heated pool. Full breakfast. No pets. Non-smoking guests only. Children 16 and older with prior permission. Three-night minimum in cottage. $120-175.

5502. This bed and breakfast is in a quiet east-side location minutes from the university, walking distance to shopping, restaurants and near the bus stop. An outstanding collection of art and crafts from Central and South America and Africa adds to the southwestern decor. The air-conditioned mini-suite has a private entrance, private bath, microwave, refrigerator, washer and dryer, and sitting room. Another room in the main residence has a private bath. Continental plus breakfast. No smoking. Well-behaved children and small pets welcome. Rates are slightly higher during the Tucson International Gem and Mineral show. $65-85.

5503. Two-story inn has many extras which include a heated pool, spa, patio, exercise room, covered parking, fax, copier, computer and telephones. On the first floor are two rooms, one of which is handicapped accessible. They have private baths and entrances. Four guest rooms are on the second floor, and each pair of rooms has its own living room, one pair shares a bath. In the first great room there are a fireplace and areas for visiting, reading, or TV/VCR. A second great room, a patio and kitchen are available for small weddings and conferences. Full breakfasts included in the rates for short stays. No smoking. No pets. Infants and well-behaved children (swimmers) welcome. Seasonal, weekly and monthly rates available. $85-105.

5551. This tri-level French chateau-style home is a mile from Saguaro National Park East on three acres. It offers unobstructed views of the beautiful Sonoran Desert, private courtyard, and convenience to shopping, restaurants, and local points of interest. A separate apartment offers living room with sofa bed, TV/VCR, radio, telephone, private dining area, full kitchen stocked for Continental plus breakfast, and full bath. A room in the main house offers TV/VCR, radio, and private full bath in hall. English, French, German, and Spanish spoken. Smoking permitted on the patio only. Children over six welcome. No pets. Ten dollars for each additional guest. $70-90.

5553. This lovely hacienda is on six acres of Sonoran Desert near Saguaro National Park East. air conditioning, telephones, robes and hair dryers in rooms. One suite has a sitting room, cable TV, full bath, mountain views. The Rincon Room has a large private bath. The casita has a living room with cable TV, fireplace, a bedroom, full bath, and fully furnished kitchen. Heated spa and solar heated lap-pool. Full breakfast. Available for special occasions, business meetings, and retreats. Children 10 and older (swimmers) welcome. No smoking. No pets. Complimentary horse facilities available. $90-150.

5554. This two-bedroom guest house on four acres has views of the Rincon Mountains from each window. Relax on the covered porch or explore the desert on trails just outside the door. There is a great room, fully furnished kitchen, washer and dryer, two private baths, a two-car garage, heated spa, and pool (small extra charge for heating). Self-serve Continental plus breakfast. No smoking. No pets.

---

7 No smoking; 8 Children welcome; 9 Social drinking allowed; 10 Tennis nearby; 11 Swimming nearby; 12 Golf nearby; 13 Skiing nearby; 14 May be booked through a travel agent; 15 Handicapped accessible.

Mi Casa Su Casa/Old Pueblo Homestays Bed & Breakfast Reservation Service (continued)

Closed July 15-August 15. Seasonal, weekly, and monthly rates. $125.

5701. Two hostesses welcome guests to a guest house built among many saguaro cacti and desert trees. The adobe main house and guest house were built recently on 6.3 acres with mountain views. The guest house is a two room suite with private entrances and patio, sitting room, bedroom, private bath, air conditioning, telephone, and two TVs. Relax and enjoy the mountains or the stars in the hot tub. Two-day minimum. Continental plus breakfast. No pets. Smoking permitted on patio only. $75.

5702. This working ranch was originally built in the early 1900s. Marvelous place for families as well as singles or couples. Many extra amenities and activities. Heated pool and indoor redwood hot tub. Rates include three meals, hayrides, and all ranch activities per person. There are 29 units, all with private baths and air conditioning. Some deluxe suites have fireplaces and whirlpool tubs. Rollaway beds available. Laundry facilities. No smoking in dining room. Free airport transportation. Closed May 1 through October 1. Four-night minimum. Weekly rates. Families and children welcome. Seventy-nine dollars for third person in room. $97-159.

5704. This comfortable home is on a cul-de-sac in a quiet neighborhood three miles from the University of Arizona and close to a bus stop, a beautiful park, golf, and driving range. The attractive guest room has a TV, radio, telephone, and private hall bath. There are limited kitchen and laundry privileges. Continental breakfast served, although a full breakfast can be requested for an additional $5 per person. Smoking permitted outside. No pets. No children. $55.

5705. This southwestern-style home is on 10 acres in the heart of the Tucson Mountains and on the edge of Saguaro National Park West, 30 minutes from downtown Tucson. The home has high ceilings, tile floors, a large Arizona room, satellite TV, and several fireplaces to create an inviting environment. Both guest rooms have private entrances, share a large shower bath, and have coffee makers. Continental plus breakfast served. Smoking permitted outside. No pets. Inquire about accommodations for children. $75-80.

5751. Attached but separate, very large, charming guest cottage with private patio is in the Catalina Mountain Foothills. Living room/bedroom has fireplace, and large private bath. Private telephone. Full kitchen. For short stays, the kitchen is stocked, and guests serve themselves during the week. Full breakfasts are served on the weekends. Two-night minimum. Resident dog in main house. Smoking outside. Ten dollars for well-behaved children 12 and older (swimmers only). Weekly rates available. Possible handicapped accessibility. Swedish spoken. $95.

5753. This extra large Spanish hacienda is a desert paradise nestled on six acres close to Saguaro National Park West, hiking and walking trails. The main house has a luxury suite with a large sitting area, fireplace, whirlpool tub for two, cable TV, and a wet bar with microwave and refrigerator. Two guest rooms have a private bath. A large separate two bedroom, two bath apartment is also available. Continental plus breakfast served. Pool, spa, and very large great room with fireplace and a baby grand piano. Near stables for horseback riding. Smoking permitted outside. Inquire about accommodations for pets. Children welcome. $85-195.

5754. An original property in the Orange Grove homes built in the 1930's, the guest cottage was refurbished by the architect-owner and his wife. It has saltillo tile floors with inset

NOTES: Credit cards accepted: A MasterCard; B Visa; C American Express; D Discover; E Diner's Club; F Other; 2 Personal checks accepted; 3 Lunch available; 4 Dinner available; 5 Open all year; 6 Pets welcome;

carpet in the living room and bedroom. The roomy living room has fireplace, cable TV, and private telephone. Private bath with tub and shower, air conditioning. A roll away bed and crib available. The Pullman-style kitchenette is completely equipped. Kitchen stocked with Continental plus breakfast. Guests are welcome to swim in the fenced pool in season. Ten dollars additional for one-night stay or third person. No smoking. No pets. Children welcome. Special summer rates. $95.

5755. Friendly host couple welcomes guests to this spacious, southwestern-style home a short drive from El Conquistador Resort. The guest wing has a large bedroom, separate den, and private hall bath with tub and shower. The den has cable TV, VCR, telephone, and writing desk. Near restaurants, two shopping malls, golf, tennis, hiking trails, horseback riding, and bird watching trails. Gourmet breakfast served in dining area with mountain views. No smoking. No pets. No children. $85.

5757. This scenic 30-acre family-owned guest ranch resort is in the Tucson Mountains under Sombrero Peak. The ranch is adjacent to the acre Saguaro National Park. Perfect place for weddings, family reunions, retreats. The two-story adobe and rock main house, built in 1931, contains a library, baby grand piano, fireplace, TV, telephone, dining room, and two guest rooms. Separate from the main house is a large house containing seven rooms all with private baths and entrances. There are also back-to-back casitas containing seven suites; all have private baths and entrances. Other amenities include a heated swimming pool and spa, large patio, shaded hammocks, hiking and walking trails, and horseback riding. Full breakfast. Lunch and dinner also available at an additional cost. Smoking permitted outside. Children welcome. No pets. $100-335.

5758. This ranch-style home is 10 miles from downtown Tucson. The spacious home has a patio, spa, pool, and Arizona room with guest kitchen facilities. The living room has a fireplace and cable TV. The suite has a private entrance with outside sitting area, cable TV, and a large two-person sunken tub with shower. One guest room boasts a private entrance, tile floor, cable TV, and full bath. Three other rooms share two full hall baths. A self-served Continental breakfast is provided. Dog on premises. Open October through June. Smoking outside. Inquire about accommodations for children. No pets. Add $10 per day to heat spa. $55-80.

5759. This bed and breakfast is within walking distance of Saguaro National Park West, 20 minutes from downtown Tucson, and 18 miles from the airport. Outdoors is a pavilion and barbecue area (which can accommodate reunions or gatherings), hiking and walking trails, and horse facilities. Five private luxurious adobe casitas each offer covered parking, complete kitchens, fireplaces, air conditioning, TV/VCR, stereo, and a refrigerator stocked with ingredients for a Continental breakfast. Hosts speak English and Greek. Smoking outside. Children welcome. Inquire about pets. $175.

5760. This ranch home on a secluded acre surrounded by citrus, pine, and desert trees is in what used to be an orange grove estate and is convenient to the University of Arizona, downtown, shops, and restaurants. Amenities include a pool, spa, barbecue, cable TV, newspaper, and piano. The guest room has a private bath, radio, and refrigerator and opens onto a patio/pool area. Continental plus breakfast. A dachshund and a cat are owned by the host. Smoking permitted outside. No children. No pets. $85.

5761. A large adobe ranch-style home at the foothills on five desert landscaped acres in the Tucson Mountains, yet just minutes from shopping, dining, and sights rich in history and culture. Four rooms with private entrances, private bath, cable TV, small refrigerator, and coffee

---

7 No smoking; 8 Children welcome; 9 Social drinking allowed; 10 Tennis nearby; 11 Swimming nearby; 12 Golf nearby; 13 Skiing nearby; 14 May be booked through a travel agent; 15 Handicapped accessible.

maker. The master room can be combined with a twin-size room to make a suite. Relax in the spacious Grand Room, on the patio, or by the seasonal pool. A high-energy Continental breakfast served. Smoking permitted outside. Inquire about accommodations for children. No pets. Seasonal rates. $75-105.

5762. Friendly hostess and excellent cook has a bed and breakfast in Tucson's northwestern area which is convenient to restaurants, shops, and excellent golf courses. A guest house with two guest rooms and private baths share a sitting room and kitchenette. A large room offers a private shower bath, TV, telephone, radio alarm clock, and dresser. One other room shares a bath. Guests welcome in living room with fireplace and TV/VCR. A refrigerator, coffee pot, and exercise bicycle are available in the Arizona rooms. Full breakfast. Smoking is permitted outside. Children 10 and older welcome. No pets. $60-85.

5763. This 1996 southwestern, hacienda-style home with central courtyard brings back the flavor of Old Mexico. Each of the spacious rooms has a private outside entrance, covered patio, TV, telephone, and full bath. Guests have access to a library, games, and laundry facilities. A full or Continental breakfast at guests' request, plus a snack bar with drinks, fruits, and goodies are available. Will cater to vegetarian diets. Smoking is permitted outside only. Sorry, pets and children cannot be accommodated. $75-85.

5764. This working miniature horse operation is only minutes away from the Arizona-Sonora Desert Museum, Avra Valley Airport and Skydiving Center, and Saguaro National Park West. Fabulous for walkers. Relax in a luxury mobile home with a private bath, a kitchen/dining/living room with air conditioning, cable TV, and sofa bed. Continental breakfast provided. English and Spanish spoken. No smoking. No pets. Children over 10 welcome. $75.

5765. An intimate ranch nestled in the mountains offers 23 rooms, all with individual air conditioning and private full bath. Rates include three meals, horseback riding daily, airport transfers and use of ranch facilities, such as the swimming pool and spa, lighted tennis courts, shuffleboard, horseshoe courts, Ping-Pong, billiards, library, bar, piano, and TV/VCR. Activities include cookouts, hayrides, picnic rides, western dancing, and sightseeing. Golf courses are nearby. Fifteen percent gratuity will be added. Three-night minimum stay required. Smoking permitted. Children are welcome. Extra guest are an additional $25-85. No pets. Seasonal rates. $185-300.

5769. This romantic inn captures the serenity and magic of the desert with casual elegance. Amenities include family heirlooms and antiques, shaded patios for outdoor relaxation and dining, seasonal pool and heated spa, and a putting green. All accommodations have private entrance and bath. There are two suites, each with refrigerator and microwave, one with two-person whirlpool tub. There are also three rooms, two of which can be combined into a suite. Full hearty breakfast. Smoking permitted outside only. No pets. Limited accommodations for children. Seasonal rates. $80-165.

Natural Bed & Breakfast

3150 East Presidio Road, 85716
(520) 881-4582

At Natural Bed and Breakfast, the word "natural" is true in all senses of the word. Attention is paid to a natural, non-toxic, and non-allergenic environment. For example, this home is water cooled rather than air conditioned, and only natural foods are served. Shoes are not worn inside. The natural home environment is very nurturing. Professional massages are available. Guests are invited to share the large, homey living room with fireplace. "You'll feel at home."

NOTES: Credit cards accepted: A MasterCard; B Visa; C American Express; D Discover; E Diner's Club; F Other; 2 Personal checks accepted; 3 Lunch available; 4 Dinner available; 5 Open all year; 6 Pets welcome;

Host: Marc Haberman
Rooms: 3 (2 PB; 1 SB) $65-75
Full Breakfast
Credit Cards: A, B
Notes: 2, 3, 4, 5, 7, 8, 10, 11, 12, 13, 14

TUCSON/MOUNT LEMMON

Mi Casa Su Casa/Old Pueblo Homestays Bed & Breakfast Reservation Service

P.O. Box 950, Tempe, AZ 85280-0950
(602) 990-0682; (800) 456-0682
FAX (602) 990-3390
e-mail: micasa@primenet.com
www.azres.com

5301. High in the Catalina Mountains this attractive mountain lodge is at 8100 feet on Mt. Lemmon, only one hour but a world away from Tucson. The three rooms in the main house each has a two-person spa, fireplace and private bath. The Family Cabin has two bedrooms, two baths, living room with additional sleeping space and fireplace, and fully equipped kitchen. The romantic Casita Linda has a two-person spa and fireplace in the spacious bedroom, and fully equipped kitchen. Full breakfast and dinner included for main house guests only. Meeting facilities available. No smoking. No pets. Two-night minimum. $155-360.

TUMACACORI

Mi Casa Su Casa/Old Pueblo Homestays Bed & Breakfast Reservation Service

P.O. Box 950, Tempe, AZ 85280-0950
(602) 990-0682; (800) 456-0682
FAX (602) 990-3390
e-mail: micasa@primenet.com
www.azres.com

5261. This charming bed and breakfast was constructed in the 1920s and served as a grocery store, post office, and gathering place until the 1960s. It is adjacent to a design studio featuring work by regional artists and is near Tumacacori National Historic Park and the ruins of an old Spanish Colonial Mission. The south wing consists of a breakfast/sitting room with small refrigerator, bedroom, TV, private bath, private entrance, and patio. A full breakfast is served. Host owns a cat. Children are welcome. Twenty dollars for each additional guest. No smoking. No guest pets. $65.

WICKENBURG

Mi Casa Su Casa/Old Pueblo Homestays Bed & Breakfast Reservation Service

P.O. Box 950, Tempe, AZ 85280-0950
(602) 990-0682; (800) 456-0682
FAX (602) 990-3390
e-mail: micasa@primenet.com
www.azres.com

5802. This historic 1937 ranch house on forty-nine acres has breathtaking 360-degree views of this unique western town. In the area are horseback riding, golf and tennis, hiking, excursions, shopping, and restaurants. Near Lake Pleasant, Prescott, and Sedona. Transportation available for travel and entertainment needs. Four guest rooms with private baths and entrances. Pool for seasonal swimming. Continental plus breakfast. Smoking permitted outside only. No pets. Ten dollars each for extra guests. $75-85.

WILLCOX

Mi Casa Su Casa/Old Pueblo Homestays Bed & Breakfast Reservation Service

P.O. Box 950, Tempe, AZ 85280-0950
(602) 990-0682; (800) 456-0682
FAX (602) 990-3390
e-mail: micasa@primenet.com
www.azres.com

---

7 No smoking; 8 Children welcome; 9 Social drinking allowed; 10 Tennis nearby; 11 Swimming nearby; 12 Golf nearby; 13 Skiing nearby; 14 May be booked through a travel agent; 15 Handicapped accessible.

5811. This bed and breakfast is a large eastern Colonial-style home near Willcox on 70 acres. The guest suite offers a private bath, private entrance, air conditioning, TV, and kitchenette with a refrigerator, hot plate, and coffee maker. Two rooms each have a bed and sofa bed in bedroom and share a bathroom and sitting room with TV/VCR, books and magazines. Continental plus breakfast. No smoking, no alcohol, no pets. Children over two welcome. Ten dollars per each additional guest. $65-80.

WILLIAMS

Arizona Trails Bed & Breakfast Reservation Service

P.O. Box 18998, Fountain Hills, 85269-8998
(480) 837-4284; (888) 799-4284
FAX (480) 816-4224
e-mail: aztrails@arizonatrails.com
www.arizonatrails.com

AZ 055. Treat yourself to a grand experience at this eight-room inn. Luxury and outstanding hospitality abound at this great hillside retreat. Work out in the exercise room, and then take a dip in the outdoor patio spa. Relax in the game room each evening during happy hour with an open bar, hot and cold hors d'oeuvres and billiard table. All rooms feature cable TV/VCR, CD players, and private marble baths. Some with views stretching to the Grand Canyon. Full breakfast. Children welcome. $110-225.

AZ 082. Visit this log cabin-style bed and breakfast with four guest rooms and a wraparound porch. Just minutes to the Grand Canyon Railroad. Two rooms have a fireplace, one has a whirlpool-jetted tub and all four have king-size beds and private baths. Socialize in the parlor area by the fireplace, sit on the front porch and watch the stars from one of the rockers or relax out back in the barbecue gazebo. Full breakfast. $100-130.

Mi Casa Su Casa/Old Pueblo Homestays Bed & Breakfast Reservation Service

P.O. Box 950, Tempe, AZ 85280-0950
(602) 990-0682; (800) 456-0682
FAX (602) 990-3690
e-mail: micasa@primenet.com
www.azres.com

5821. The breakfasts prepared by the host, a retired chef, are "to write home about" at this three-story house in the pines within walking distance of downtown. The luxurious accommodations have private baths, cable TV with HBO, VCR, and CD equipped stereo systems. In the main house are three guest rooms, one with private entrance. In the two story guest house there is one suite and three rooms, two of which can be combined as a suite. Fitness room, pool table, piano and hot tub available to guests. Smoking outside. Well behaved children welcome, guest dog negotiable. Extra person $15. $95-225.

5822. This spacious, two-story log inn has a delightful decor. Endless activities nearby include the old steam train ride to the Grand Canyon, golf, hiking and rafting, fishing, and the historic downtown with shops and restaurants. There are four sizeable guest rooms, each with comfortable country-Victorian decor and private baths. The host couple is knowledgeable about Northern Arizona, Indian lore, jewelry, rugs and pottery, as her father worked on the Hopi and Navajo reservations. Full ranch-style breakfast. Children welcome. No smoking, alcohol, or pets. Possible handicapped accessibility. Seasonal rates. $90-130.

NOTES: Credit cards accepted: A MasterCard; B Visa; C American Express; D Discover; E Diner's Club; F Other; 2 Personal checks accepted; 3 Lunch available; 4 Dinner available; 5 Open all year; 6 Pets welcome;

WINKLEMAN

Arizona Trails Bed & Breakfast Reservation Service

P.O. Box 18998, Fountain Hills, 85269-8998
(480) 837-4284; (888) 799-4284
FAX (480) 816-4224
e-mail: aztrails@arizonatrails.com
www.arizonatrails.com

AZ 090. Escape to the solitude and beauty of this natural setting just outside Aravaipa Canyon Wilderness area. Two rooms with private entrances, kitchenettes, fireplaces, queen-size beds with room for an additional twin. Primitive decor, outdoor patios, and barbecue areas grace the charm of these comfortable and colorful rooms. This bed and breakfast sits on acres of orchards across from a year-round running creek. The packages includes all three meals with breakfast served in the room, a picnic lunch and dinner in the main house. Great for bird watching, hiking, or just relaxing. $200.

Mi Casa Su Casa/Old Pueblo Homestays Bed & Breakfast Reservation Service

P.O. Box 950, Tempe, AZ 85280-0950
(602) 990-0682; (800) 456-0682
FAX (602) 990-3390
e-mail: micasa@primenet.com
www.azres.com

5831. Perfect for the traveler seeking the excellent hiking and bird watching in the Aravaipa Canyon Wilderness. Guests enjoy fording a creek and seeing the orchards surrounding this oasis. Each of the two guest houses has queen beds, a fireplace, bath, and delightful country furnishings. Outdoor barbecue and sitting area. The hostess is an excellent cook and the rates include three delicious meals with local organically grown produce. A dog and flock of sheep share the farm. Smoking outside. Inquire about children. No pets. $200.

---

7 No smoking; 8 Children welcome; 9 Social drinking allowed; 10 Tennis nearby; 11 Swimming nearby; 12 Golf nearby; 13 Skiing nearby; 14 May be booked through a travel agent; 15 Handicapped accessible.

California

California

AHWAHNEE

Silver Spur Bed & Breakfast

44625 Silver Spur Trail, 93601
(559) 683-2896; (888) 359-9178

The Silver Spur Bed and Breakfast is nestled in the Sierra Nevadas of California, just off historic Highway 49. Key to the California gold country and the south and west gates of famed Yosemite National Park, it is only minutes from many outdoor sports. It features beautiful, clean rooms with private baths and entrances and comfortable beds and is tastefully decorated in American Southwest. Outdoor rest and dining areas boast outstanding Sierra views. Come enjoy Yosemite, and be treated to old-fashioned hospitality and great value.

Hosts: Patty and Bryan Hays
Rooms: 2 (PB) $60
Continental Breakfast
Credit Cards: A, B, D
Notes: 2, 5, 7, 8, 9, 11, 12, 13

ALBION

Albion River Inn

P.O. Box 100, 95410
(707) 937-1919; (800) 479-7944
e-mail: ari@mcn.org; www.albionriverinn.com

On the ocean, six miles south of the historic town of Mendocino, this romantic clifftop inn, on 10 acres of coastal bluffs, offers beauty, serenity, and luxury in New England-style cottages with stunning ocean views, garden entrances, fireplaces, decks, and hot tubs. Complimentary wine, morning newspaper, fresh coffee, and full breakfast are included in the rates. The restaurant is open nightly serving the celebrated coastal cuisine of Chef Stephen Smith and an award-winning wine list. Weddings welcome!

Hosts: Flurry Healy and Peter Wells
Rooms: 20 (PB) $180-260
Full Breakfast
Credit Cards: A, B, C, D, E
Notes: 2, 4, 5, 7, 8, 9, 10, 11, 12, 15

The Wool Loft

32751 Navarro Ridge Road, 95410
(707) 937-0377; e-mail: woolloft@mcn.org
www.designjk.com/woolloft

The Wool Loft is a "casual, comfortable, contemporary" bed and breakfast. Located high on Navarro Ridge, cooled by ocean mists, the views of the river and the ocean are ever changing. The sunroom features large windows for unobstructed views of the green forested hills, ocean, river, the resident sheep, various birds, and possibly sea lions as they rest on the beach below. Located seven miles south of the town of Mendocino off Highway One. All rooms have queen-size beds, down comforters, bed warmers, and private baths, plus there is an outdoor spa to refresh guests.

Hosts: Richard and Roberta Ollenberger
Rooms: 4 (PB) $85-150
Full Breakfast
Credit Cards: A, B, C
Notes: 2, 5, 7, 9, 10, 11, 12

NOTES: Credit cards accepted: A MasterCard; B Visa; C American Express; D Discover; E Diner's Club; F Other; 2 Personal checks accepted; 3 Lunch available; 4 Dinner available; 5 Open all year; 6 Pets welcome; 7 No smoking; 8 Children welcome; 9 Social drinking allowed; 10 Tennis nearby; 11 Swimming nearby; 12 Golf nearby; 13 Skiing nearby; 14 May be booked through a travel agent; 15 Handicapped accessible.

AMADOR CITY

Imperial Hotel

Box 195, 95601
(209) 267-9172

"There is a rich, almost seductive opulence to this brick 1879 hostelry that comes at you in whispers and peeks"—*Sunset* magazine, April 1997. The restored Imperial Hotel offers six handsome guest rooms with full breakfast, air conditioning, and modern private baths. The original bar has a large selection of spirits and California wines. The elegant, nationally acclaimed dining room is open for dinner nightly from 5:00 to 9:00 P.M. Skiing is one hour away.

Hosts: Bruce Sherrill and Dale Martin
Rooms: 6 (PB) $75-105
Full Breakfast
Credit Cards: A, B, C, D
Notes: 2, 4, 5, 7, 9, 10, 11, 12, 14, 15

APTOS

Apple Lane Inn

6265 Soquel Drive, 95003-3117
(831) 475-6868; (800) 649-8988
www.applelaneinn.com

Apple Lane Inn is a historic Victorian farmhouse restored to the charm and tranquility of an earlier age. It is just south of Santa Cruz on two and one-half acres of grounds, with gardens, a romantic gazebo, and fields. Explore the many miles of beaches within walking distance. Golf, hiking, fishing, shopping, and dining are all nearby.

Hosts: Doug and Diana Groom
Rooms: 5 (PB) $70-175
Full Breakfast
Credit Cards: A, B, C, D
Notes: 2, 5, 6, 7, 8, 9, 10, 11, 12, 14

Bayview Hotel

8041 Soquel Drive, 95003
(800) 422-9843; FAX (831) 688-5128
e-mail: lodging@bayviewhotel.com
www.bayviewhotel.com

An 1878 beautiful Victorian hotel. Each room was renovated and refurbished during 1992-1995, in keeping with its historic grandeur. The tastefully appointed rooms provide charming antiques, cozy beds with feather mattresses, comfortable sitting areas, and fireplaces as well as private baths (some with two-person soaking tubs), telephones with modem capacity, some built-in TVs (other TVs and business conveniences are available upon request). Complimentary Continental plus breakfast served in the Vintage Room or brought to guests' room. Restaurant on-site. Adjacent to the Forest of Nisene Marks State Park.

Host: Gwen Burkard
Rooms: 11 (PB) $90-160
Continental Breakfast
Credit Cards: A, B, C
Notes: 5, 7, 10, 11, 12, 14

Mangels House

Mangels House

570 Aptos Creek Road, Box 302, 95001
(831) 688-7982

A large Southern Colonial, on four acres of lawn and orchard and bounded by a 10,000-acre redwood forest, is less than a mile from the

---

NOTES: Credit cards accepted: A MasterCard; B Visa; C American Express; D Discover; E Diner's Club; F Other; 2 Personal checks accepted; 3 Lunch available; 4 Dinner available; 5 Open all year; 6 Pets welcome;

beach. The five large, airy rooms are eclectic in decor and European in feel, reflecting the owners' background. Closed December 24 through 26. Inquire about accommodations for pets. Limited smoking allowed on outside porch. Inquire about accommodations for children.

Hosts: Jacqueline and Ronald Fisher
Rooms: 6 (PB) $125-165
Full Breakfast
Credit Cards: A, B, C
Notes: 2, 7, 9, 10, 11, 12, 14

Power's Mansion Inn

ARROYO GRANDE

House of Another Tyme Bed & Breakfast

227 Le Point Street, 93420
(805) 489-6313

On a quarter-acre of hillside with gardens to allow sunlight in and create a tranquil area containing natural rock wall, exotic finches, and 100-year-old palms, the House of Another Tyme reflects its name. Circa 1916, the single-walled-construction home was renovated by upgrading bathrooms and kitchen. All bedrooms have queen-size beds and private baths and are furnished in antiques. A full country breakfast is served. One block from historic village with antique shops and fine restaurants.

Hosts: Jack and Judy
Rooms: 3 (PB) $95
Full Breakfast
Credit Cards: A, B, D
Notes: 5, 7, 11, 12

AUBURN

Power's Mansion Inn

164 Cleveland Avenue, 95603
(916) 885-1166; FAX (916) 885-1386

This magnificent mansion was built from a gold fortune in the late 1800s. It has easy access to I-80 and off-street parking. Close to gold country, antiquing, water sports, hiking, horseback riding, skiing, and restaurants. Smoking permitted outside only.

Owners: Arno and Jean Lejnieks
Rooms: 13 (PB) $79-149
Full Breakfast
Credit Cards: A, B, C
Notes: 2, 5, 7, 8, 9, 10, 11, 12, 13, 14

BALLARD

The Ballard Inn

2436 Baseline Avenue, 93463
(805) 688-7770; (800) 638-2466
FAX (805) 688-9560
e-mail: innkeeper@ballardinn.com
www.ballardinn.com

Comfortably elegant accommodations in the heart of the Santa Barbara wine country. Just 40 minutes from Santa Barbara, yet nestled in country orchards and vineyards, the Ballard Inn offers an intimate retreat. Each of the 15 guest rooms possesses its own special charm and character reflecting local history. Cafe Chardonnay serving creative wine-country cuisine, located on the property. Rates include a full breakfast and hors d'oeuvres.

Host: Kelly Robinson
Rooms: 15 (PB) $170-250
Full Breakfast
Credit Cards: A, B, C
Notes: 2, 4, 5, 7, 10, 11, 12, 14, 15

---

7 No smoking; 8 Children welcome; 9 Social drinking allowed; 10 Tennis nearby; 11 Swimming nearby; 12 Golf nearby; 13 Skiing nearby; 14 May be booked through a travel agent; 15 Handicapped accessible.

BASS LAKE

Jonnie's Inn at Bass Lake

P.O. BOX 717, 93604
(559) 642-4966; FAX (559) 641-6043
e-mail: jonnie@sierratel.com

A beautiful setting at pristine Bass Lake at the Pines Village makes Jonnie's Inn an exceptional bed and breakfast on the way to Yosemite National Park just 14 miles from the park entrance. Enjoy a gourmet breakfast on the large front porch overlooking the lake. The guest rooms are uniquely designed and have a large deck nestled in the mountain rocks and trees. Exceptional hosts are just waiting to greet guests.

Hosts: Gene and Jonnie Baker
Rooms: 2 (PB) $95-135
Full Breakfast
Credit Cards: None
Notes: 2, 5, 9, 11, 12, 13

BENICIA

Bed & Breakfast California

P.O. Box 2247, Saratoga, 95070
(408) 867-9662; (800) 872-4500
FAX (408) 867-0907; e-mail: info@bbintl.com
www.bbintl.com

Charming Victorian in Benicia's historic district filled with antiques. Amenities include quilts and comforters, a lovely garden available for dining in good weather, port and sherry in rooms in the evenings. Peace and serenity are the key factors at work at this inn. Just a short drive to Napa. $75-90.

BERKELEY

Bed & Breakfast California

P.O. Box 2247, Saratoga, 95070
(408) 867-9662; (800) 872-4500
FAX (408) 867-0907; e-mail: info@bbintl.com
www.bbintl.com

A. Ideal for the single woman traveler! Completed in 1936, this home is a well-architected ranch-style house with spacious rooms in a well defined setting which separate bedrooms from living and dining areas. It is in a quiet neighborhood of well-kept homes. $75.

B. A spacious Mediterranean-style home, with a pool and a hot tub in a landscaped setting, which has been featured in *Los Angeles Times Home* magazine. The home is beautifully furnished and has floor-to-ceiling bookcases and views of the bay. The Casablanca Suite on the first floor is adjacent to the front door and includes a sitting room plus an en suite bath. The Spinnaker Room on the second floor has a view of the bay and twin beds. $75-85.

C. This inn is like an elegant home filled with warmth and charm. The two front buildings are gorgeous Victorians which have been wonderfully restored. It has 40 beautifully decorated guest rooms between five separate buildings which surround a beautiful central garden filled with roses. It is only seven blocks from UC-Berkeley. $99-195.

D. This spacious four-bedroom home was built in 1911 and is located in the Claremont area of Berkeley, close to public transportation and within walking distance of shops and restaurants. All guest rooms have private baths, and there is also a charming dormer-style sitting room on the same floor available for guests. $85-95.

E. This 1904 Craftsman-style inn is close to the University campus, restaurants, hiking and public transportation. The light-filled house is furnished with antiques in the bedrooms and in an eclectic style in common rooms. All rooms have a private bath and telephones with voice mail. Relax in the parlor or patio with deck overlooking the lovely gardens. $95-110.

NOTES: Credit cards accepted: A MasterCard; B Visa; C American Express; D Discover; E Diner's Club; F Other; 2 Personal checks accepted; 3 Lunch available; 4 Dinner available; 5 Open all year; 6 Pets welcome;

F. This 1904 Craftsman-style inn is close to the university campus, restaurants, hiking, and public transportation. Relax in the parlors or patio areas on the lovely grounds. Five guest rooms with private baths and king- or queen-size or twin beds. No smoking. Continental plus breakfast. $80-110.

BIG BEAR LAKE

Apples Bed & Breakfast Inn

42430 Moonridge Road, P.O. Box 7172, 92315-7172
(909) 866-0903; www.bigbear.com/apples

A slice of hospitality awaits guests at this 9,000-square-foot country Victorian inn, specifically designed and built for the discriminating bed and breakfast traveler. This 12-room inn, nestled on one acre of pine trees and flowers, boasts king-size beds, private baths (four with Jacuzzi tubs for two), TVs, VCRs, and comfy chairs. Relax in the garden complete with outdoor hot tub, game court, and hammocks in the trees. Delight in their sumptuous breakfasts, all day snack and beverage bar, afternoon cider and cheese, and evening desserts. Guests are not allowed to go away hungry from this bed and breakfast.

Hosts: Jim and Barbara McLean
Rooms: 12 (PB) $125 and up
Full Breakfast
Credit Cards: A, B, C, D
Notes: 5, 7, 9, 10, 11, 12, 13, 14, 15

Apples

Gold Mountain Manor

Gold Mountain Manor Historic Bed & Breakfast

117 Anita, P.O. Box 2027, 92314
(800) 509-2604

Gold Mountain Manor is Big Bear's only historic 1928 log mansion bed and breakfast. At the end of the 1920s on Northshore, Alexander Buchanan Barret, a wealthy Los Angeles movie investor, built Gold Mountain Manor. Set in a forest of pine trees, the house is three stories high with birds-eye maple floors and beamed ceilings. Eight fireplaces, antiques, and romantic ambiance. Mentioned in *The Best Places to Kiss* and *Fifty Most Romantic Places* books. Hiking nearby.

Rooms: 6 (PB) $120-190
Full Breakfast
Credit Cards: A, B, C, D
Notes: 5, 7, 11, 13

The Inn at Fawnskin Bed & Breakfast

880 Canyon Road, P.O. Box 378, Fawnskin, 92333
(909) 866-3200; (888) 329-6754
e-mail: tmurphy@bigbear.net
www.bajalife.com/fawnskin/index.htm

The Inn at Fawnskin, on the quiet north shore of Big Bear Lake, is a beautiful custom-built

---

7 No smoking; 8 Children welcome; 9 Social drinking allowed; 10 Tennis nearby; 11 Swimming nearby; 12 Golf nearby; 13 Skiing nearby; 14 May be booked through a travel agent; 15 Handicapped accessible.

log home nestled in its own pine forest only steps from the lake and forest trails. Living room has big stone fireplace, decks with lake and forest views. Enjoy a gourmet breakfast next to fireplace in dining room. Game room has wide-screen TV, video library, pool and game table. Breathtaking master suite with fireplace and balcony. Handmade quilts and terry-cloth robes.

Hosts: Kathy and Todd Murphy
Rooms: 4 (2 PB: 2 SB) $85-175
Full Breakfast
Credit Cards: A, B, C
Notes: 2, 5, 7, 9, 10, 11, 12, 13, 14

Knickerbocker Mansion Country Inn

869 Knickerbocker Road, P.O. Box 1907, 92315
(909) 878-9190; (877) 423-1180
FAX (909) 878-4248; e-mail: knickmail@aol.com
www.knickerbockermansion.com/

The historic Knickerbocker Mansion Country Inn was originally built by the first damkeeper of the Big Bear Lake Dam in 1920. This magnificently restored unique log private home and carriage house is now a well-known bed and breakfast with rustic elegance, a quiet atmosphere and personal attention from the innkeepers. Two historic buildings sitting on 2.5 private heavily treed acres backing to the national forest, yet walking distance to the village. The moment you arrive you will realize the Knickerbocker is a very special place.

Knickerbocker Mansion

Hosts: Stanley R. Miller & Thomas F. Bicanic
Rooms: 11 (PB) $110-280
Credit Cards: A, B, C, D
Notes: 2, 5, 7, 9, 10, 11, 12, 13, 14, 15

BODEGA

Bed & Breakfast California

P.O. Box 2247, Saratoga, 95070
(408) 867-9662; (800) 872-4500
FAX (408) 867-0907; e-mail: info@bbintl.com
www.bbintl.com

The Villa. Guests eager to experience the simple elegance of country living will enjoy the quiet peacefulness of the Villa. Terraced grounds, terra-cotta stucco, red-tiled roofs, and an expansive veranda give the inn a distinct Mediterranean atmosphere. Twelve beautifully appointed guest rooms offer beamed ceilings and wood-burning fireplaces. A landscaped courtyard with a swimming pool and a large indoor Jacuzzi are just steps from guests' room. $185-295.

BOONVILLE

Anderson Creek Inn

12050 Anderson Valley Way, P.O. Box 217, 95415
(707) 895-3091; (800) LLAMA-02
www.andersoncreekinn.com

Elegant and secluded, this spacious inn is on 16 lovely acres with views from every room. Guests are treated to wine and appetizers in the evenings, and a memorable breakfast is served in the dining room, the patio, or in a basket brought to the room. Lazy days can be spent walking the grounds, visiting the animals, or lounging around the Olympic-size pool. Wine tasting, shopping, restaurants, hiking, and the Mendocino Coast are just minutes away.

Hosts: Rod and Nancy Graham
Rooms: 5 (PB) $110-170
Full Breakfast
Credit Cards: A, B
Notes: 2, 5, 7, 9, 10, 11, 12

NOTES: Credit cards accepted: A MasterCard; B Visa; C American Express; D Discover; E Diner's Club; F Other; 2 Personal checks accepted; 3 Lunch available; 4 Dinner available; 5 Open all year; 6 Pets welcome;

BURLINGAME

Burlingame Bed & Breakfast

1021 Balboa Avenue, 94010
(650) 344-5815

Burlingame Bed and Breakfast is in a pleasantly quiet neighborhood. Three miles south of the San Francisco Airport and 12 miles of San Francisco. Bus and train service are one to six blocks away, freeway one block further. Ten dollars for each additional person.

Hosts: Joe and Elnora Fernandez
Room: 1 (PB) $60
Continental Breakfast
Credit Cards: None
Notes: 2, 5, 7, 8, 10, 11, 12

CALISTOGA

Bear Flag Inn

2653 Foothill Boulevard, 94515
(707) 942-5534; FAX (707) 942-8761
www.bearflaginn.com

This historical turn-of-the-century farmhouse has fabulous views. Luxuriate in period furnishings, queen-size beds, and private baths. Enjoy a gourmet breakfast served in the marvelous dining room. Complimentary wine and hors d'oeuvres served poolside or fireside. Experience local wine tasting, hiking, or biking, and top off the day with one of the award-winning local restaurants close by. Enjoy outdoor hot tub.

Rooms: 5 (PB) $150-200
Full Breakfast
Credit Cards: A, B, C, D
Notes: 2, 5, 7, 8, 9, 10, 11, 12, 14

Bed & Breakfast California

P.O. Box 2247, Saratoga, 95070
(408) 867-9662; (800) 872-4500
FAX (408) 867-0907; e-mail: info@bbintl.com
www.bbintl.com

A. Very close to Napa Valley wineries, 1900 country farmhouse on several acres offers quiet and comfort. Each of the guest accommodations has a private entrance. Full breakfast and afternoon refreshments are served in guests' room, suite, or on the tree-shaded pool deck. One guest room and two suites have private baths and queen-size beds. No smoking. $125-185.

B. Uniquely decorated rooms, some with fireplaces and whirlpool tubs, and a pool fed by the inn's own hot springs are some of the special offerings at this wine country estate. A Continental plus breakfast and afternoon refreshments are provided. Nine guest rooms with private baths and king- or queen-size beds. No smoking. $185-270.

C. Bungalow offers six suites all with private bath. Walk to restaurants and shops in this charming small town at the northern end of Napa Valley. Inn is convenient to wineries, tennis, golf, spas, hiking, and biking areas. $125-150.

"Culvers," A Country Inn

1805 Foothill Boulevard, 94515
(707) 942-4535

A lovely Victorian residence built in 1875, filled with antiques and offering a full country breakfast. Jacuzzi and seasonal pool available for guests' enjoyment. Within minutes of wineries, mud baths, and downtown Calistoga. Lovely view of St. Helena mountain range from the veranda. Sherry and hors d'oeuvres are offered in the afternoon, with an afternoon beverage and baked treats offered upon arrival. Closed December through January, and Thanksgiving and New Year's. Reservations are held for seven days on a credit card, with payment by personal or traveler's check. Children 16 and older are welcome.

Hosts: Meg and Tony Wheatley
Rooms: 6 (PB) $156.80-179.20
Full Breakfast
Credit Cards: None
Notes: 2, 7, 9, 10, 11, 14, 15

---

7 No smoking; 8 Children welcome; 9 Social drinking allowed; 10 Tennis nearby; 11 Swimming nearby; 12 Golf nearby; 13 Skiing nearby; 14 May be booked through a travel agent; 15 Handicapped accessible.

The Elms Bed & Breakfast Inn

1300 Cedar Street, 94515
(707) 942-9476; (800) 235-4316

This 1871 French three-story Victorian is one-half block from town next to a park on the Napa River. It is very quiet and peaceful, yet within walking distance of restaurants, spas, gliders, bike rentals, golf, and tennis. The rooms are very romantic—decorated with antiques. All have coffee makers, bathrobes, chocolates, and port for after dinner. The feather beds are piled high with pillows and down comforters. Most rooms have fireplaces, TV, and some have whirlpool tubs. A huge gourmet breakfast is served, and wine and cheese are served in the afternoon. Limited handicapped accessibility.

Hosts: Stephen and Karla Wyle
Rooms: 7 (PB) $115-210
Full Breakfast
Credit Cards: A, B
Notes: 2, 7, 9, 10, 11, 12, 14

The Elms

Foothill House

3037 Foothill Boulevard, 94515
(707) 942-6933; (800) 942-6933

"The most romantic inn of the Napa Valley," according to the *Chicago Tribune* travel editor. In a country setting, Foothill House offers spacious suites individually decorated with

Foothill House

antiques, each with private bath and entrance, fireplace, and small refrigerator. Three suites offer whirlpool tubs. Complimentary wine and hors d'oeuvres each evening. Elegant private cottage is also available.

Hosts: Doris and Gus Beckert
Rooms: 3 (PB) $150-300
Full Breakfast
Credit Cards: A, B, C, D
Notes: 2, 5, 7, 9, 10, 11, 12, 14

Hillcrest

3225 Lake County Highway, 94515
(707) 942-6334

Breathtaking view of Napa Valley countryside. Hiking, swimming, and fishing on 40 acres. Family-owned property since 1860. Hilltop modern country home decorated with heirlooms from family mansion. Rooms have balconies. Fireplace and grand piano, rare artwork, silver, crystal, china, and oriental rugs. Family photo albums date back to 1870s. Breakfast is served weekends on a 12-foot

Hillcrest

NOTES: Credit cards accepted: A MasterCard; B Visa; C American Express; D Discover; E Diner's Club; F Other; 2 Personal checks accepted; 3 Lunch available; 4 Dinner available; 5 Open all year; 6 Pets welcome;

antique table fit for a king. Enjoy the outdoor spa and large pool. Water skiing is a 45-minute drive away. Some fireplaces. Smoking permitted outside on balcony. Inquire about accommodations for children.

Host: Debbie O'Gorman
Rooms: 4 (1 PB; 3 SB) $60-165
Continental Breakfast
Credit Cards: None
Notes: 2, 5, 6, 9, 10, 11, 12, 13, 14

Quail Mountain

Quail Mountain Bed & Breakfast Inn

4455 North St. Helena Highway, 94558
(707) 942-0316

A secluded luxury bed and breakfast on 26 heavily wooded idyllic acres on a mountain top between St. Helena and Calistoga. Three guest rooms, each with king-size bed, private bath, and private deck. Cabernet vineyard and fruit orchard on property. Full breakfast and complimentary wine with gracious, personalized hospitality. Close to world-class restaurants, wineries, and golf. A two-night minimum stay on weekends and holidays. Advance reservations recommended. Under new ownership.

Hosts: Eric and Kathy Amadei
Rooms: 3 (PB) $130-150
Full Breakfast
Credit Cards: A, B, C
Notes: 2, 5, 7, 9, 10, 11, 12, 14

Scarlett's Country Inn

Scarlett's Country Inn

3918 Silverado Trail, 94515
(707) 942-6669 (phone/FAX)
e-mail: scarletts@aol.com

Three exquisitely appointed suites set in the quiet mood of green lawn and tall pines overlooking the famed Napa Valley Vineyards. Seclusion, romance, queen-size beds, private baths, antiques, fireplace, air conditioning, secluded woodland swimming pool. Telephone and TV available in rooms on request. Home-baked breakfast and afternoon refreshments served in rooms or under the apple trees by the pool. Close to wineries and spas. Children welcome at no charge.

Host: Scarlett Dwyer
Rooms: 3 (PB) $115-175
Full Breakfast
Credit Cards: None
Notes: 2, 5, 8, 9, 10, 11, 12, 14

Trailside Inn

4201 Silverado Trail, 94515
(707) 942-4106; FAX (707) 942-4702
www.trailsideinn.com

A charming 1930s farmhouse in the country with three very private suites. Each suite has its own entrance, porch with vineyard view, bedroom, bath, fireplace, and air conditioning. Fresh home-baked breads provided in guests' fully equipped kitchen. Complimentary wine, lovely pool and spa, soft terry-cloth robes. Close to all major wineries and restaurants. Smoking permitted outside only. Children over 12 welcome.

Hosts: Randy and Lani Gray
Suites: 3 (PB) $165-185
Continental Breakfast
Credit Cards: A, B, C, D
Notes: 2, 5, 7, 9, 10, 11, 12, 14

Zinfandel House

Zinfandel House

1253 Summit Drive, 94515
(707) 942-0733

Zinfandel House is in a wooded setting on a western hillside with a spectacular view of the famous Napa Valley vineyards. Halfway between St. Helena and Calistoga. Choose from three tastefully decorated rooms with a private or shared bath. Breakfast is served on the deck or in the solarium.

Hosts: Bette and George Starke
Rooms: 3 (PB or SB) $95-125
Full Breakfast
Credit Cards: A, B, D
Notes: 2, 5, 7, 9, 10, 11, 12

CAMARILLO

Bed & Breakfast California

P.O. Box 2247, Saratoga, 95070
(408) 867-9662; (800) 872-4500
FAX (408) 867-0907; e-mail: info@bbintl.com
www.bbintl.com

Pick oranges and avocados at this three-acre ranch just 15 minutes south of Ventura or 30 minutes to Santa Barbara. There are two guest wings surrounded by orchards. From rooms with balconies, guests can see the ocean on a clear day. A huge deck offers a hot tub for relaxing. $65.

CAMBRIA

Bed & Breakfast California

P.O. Box 2247, Saratoga, 95070
(408) 867-9662; (800) 872-4500
FAX (408) 867-0907; e-mail: info@bbintl.com
www.bbintl.com

A. Watch the ocean from the hot tub. The entire lower level of this luxury home in Cambria is designed for bed and breakfast pampering. There is a bedroom with queen-size bed, living room with fireplace, stereo and TV systems, dining area, fully equipped kitchen (including goodies), and two decks—both with ocean view and one with guests' own hot tub. British hostess bakes fresh scones as part of every gourmet breakfast. Walking distance to town. There is even a secret, private entrance. $110.

B. This brand new home was built in 1998. Stunning white-water ocean views greet guests upon arrival. The guest studio has a full ocean view, a private entrance, a private stone patio, and direct access to paths through the English garden. Furnished in antiques in country French style, the studio offers a king-size bed, sitting/dining area, a coffee bar with small refrigerator, and a private bath. Within walking distance of the ocean, and also only seven miles from Hearst Castle. $125.

C. In the scenic town of Cambria and only minutes from Hearst Castle, this picturesque inn is perfect for a romantic getaway. Some rooms feature Jacuzzi baths, fireplaces, private patios, and/or ocean views. There is a common area for gathering and a Jacuzzi

---

NOTES: Credit cards accepted: A MasterCard; B Visa; C American Express; D Discover; E Diner's Club; F Other; 2 Personal checks accepted; 3 Lunch available; 4 Dinner available; 5 Open all year; 6 Pets welcome;

room open to the sky for all guests to use. A delightful light country breakfast is brought to guests' door for an intimate breakfast in bed. $95-210.

D. Romantic room in a contemporary hillside home, surrounded by the forest and located one mile from the ocean and six miles from Hearst Castle. The room has a separate entrance, a fireplace, and is attractively furnished in country style. Breakfast and afternoon refreshments are served either on the deck or in the sun room with views of the lovely garden and the many birds in the forest. If guests are lucky, the deer will stop for a visit. $125-135.

J. Patrick House

2990 Burton Drive, 93428
(800) 341-5258; FAX (805) 927-6759
e-mail: jph@jpatrickhouse.com
www.jpatrickhouse.com

Discover the charming and romantic hidden secret of the central coast. The J. Patrick House is a beautiful log home that blends with its wooded setting above the old village of Cambria. The inn overlooks a forest of tall Monterey pines and yet the ocean is only minutes away. All rooms have wood-burning fireplaces and private baths. Homemade hors d'oeuvres are served and complemented by fine wines. A lovely breakfast is served in the garden room. Inquire about accommodations for children.

Hosts: Barbara and Mel Schwimmer
Rooms: 8 (PB) $115-180
Full Breakfast
Credit Cards: A, B, C, D
Notes: 2, 5, 7, 10, 12, 14

The Pickford House Bed & Breakfast

2555 Macleod Way, 93428
(805) 927-8619

Only eight miles from Hearst Castle, Pickford House is decorated with antiques reminiscent of the golden age of film. Eight rooms have king- or queen-size beds, private baths, fireplaces, and views of the mountains. Parlor with an 1860 bar is used for wine and tea bread at 5:00 p.m. TV in rooms. All baths have clawfoot tubs and showers. Enjoy wine tasting nearby or rock collecting on the beach. Twenty dollars for each additional person any age. Plenty of off-street parking.

Host: Anna Larsen
Rooms: 8 (PB) $99-145
Full Breakfast
Credit Cards: A, B
Notes: 2, 5, 7, 8, 9, 10, 11, 12

CAPITOLA BY THE SEA

Inn at Depot Hill

250 Monterey Avenue, 95010
(831) 462-3376; (800) 572-2632
FAX (831) 462-3697
e-mail: lodging@innatdepothill.com
www.innatdepothill.com

Near a sandy beach in a quaint Mediterranean-style resort, this award-winning inn was named one of the top 10 inns in the country. A decorator's delight, upscale rooms resemble different parts of the world: Côte d'Azur, a chic auberge in St. Tropez; Paris, a romantic French hideaway; Portofino, an Italian coastal villa; and a traditional English garden room named Sissinghurst. All rooms have fireplaces, TV/VCR, stereo systems, telephones, modems, robes, featherbeds, and flowers. Most have private hot tubs in garden patios.

Hosts: Suzie Lankes and Dan Floyd
Rooms: 12 (PB) $190-275
Full Breakfast
Credit Cards: A, B, C, D
Notes: 2, 5, 7, 9, 10, 11, 12, 14, 15

---

7 No smoking; 8 Children welcome; 9 Social drinking allowed; 10 Tennis nearby; 11 Swimming nearby; 12 Golf nearby; 13 Skiing nearby; 14 May be booked through a travel agent; 15 Handicapped accessible.

CARDIFF BY THE SEA

Bed & Breakfast California

P.O. Box 2247, Saratoga, 95070
(408) 867-9662; (800) 872-4500
FAX (408) 867-0907; e-mail: info@bbintl.com
www.bbintl.com

A. Charming couple host an elegant bed and breakfast with a relaxed atmosphere near Hearst Castle and midcoast beaches. First floor is guests' domain with large bedroom/sitting room in English country decor. A gourmet breakfast and afternoon refreshments are provided. Private bath and twin or king-size bed. No smoking. $125.

B. Contemporary oceanfront bed and breakfast inn on the beach has antique furnishings, ocean views, and outdoor decks. Afternoon refreshments and a full breakfast are served. No smoking. Seven guest rooms. Private bath. $125-175.

C. Just south of Hearst Castle at the ocean, this bed and breakfast features rooms with fireplaces, private patios, and baths en suite. A full breakfast is served with an ocean view. No smoking. Three guest rooms. Private bath. $75.

D. Set on three wooded acres five minutes from the ocean, this bed and breakfast has one quiet suite and another guest room, each with a private deck. Host is docent at the Hearst Castle. A Continental breakfast is served. $105.

E. Private entrance and fireplace in individually decorated room can be found at Cape Cod-style bed and breakfast in quiet seaside village 100 yards from the beach. Full breakfast served. $90-180.

F. Individually decorated guest rooms at family-run inn, one block from the beach in a serene seaside village. An easy commute to San Diego and most tourist attractions in San Diego and Orange Counties. Continental plus breakfast served. $126-350.

CARLSBAD

Pelican Cove Bed & Breakfast

320 Walnut Avenue, 92008
(760) 434-5995; (888) PEL COVE

Sun, blue skies, endless beaches, glorious sunsets, and the wide Pacific welcome guests to Pelican Cove Bed and Breakfast Inn at the Village of Carlsbad By-the-Sea. Only 200 yards from the ocean, the inn is strolling distance from the fine restaurants and pleasant shops of this intimate Village. Carlsbad is a vacation delight, with quiet streets and uncrowded beaches. Rooms at this small and romantic inn feature individual baths and fireplaces, optional Scandia feather beds and down comforters, TVs, some whirlpool tubs, and a pleasing blend of antique and contemporary furnishings. The inn is surrounded by gardens of flowers and trees. Guests will enjoy a complete breakfast, with fresh fruit, juices, excellent coffee and tea, and cereals in the inside nook, or take a tray to their room, the garden patio, or sun porch. Individual room entrances and the Sunset Deck are added features. Beach chairs, towels, and picnic baskets are available for the use of guests.

Rooms: 8 (PB) $90-180
Full Breakfast
Credit Cards: A, B, C
Notes: 2, 5, 7, 8, 9, 11, 12, 15

CARMEL

Absolutely Accommodations

P.O. Box 641471, San Francisco, 94164-1471
(415) 677-9789; (888) 982-2632
e-mail: travelinfo@iname.com
www.citysearch.com/sfo/accommodations

This is a free reservation service committed to assisting travelers in finding the best possible accommodations in California. It offers access to private homestay bed and breakfasts and inns. It can help guests find the proper accommodations that meet their individual needs. The service's goal is to provide both

---

NOTES: Credit cards accepted: A MasterCard; B Visa; C American Express; D Discover; E Diner's Club; F Other; 2 Personal checks accepted; 3 Lunch available; 4 Dinner available; 5 Open all year; 6 Pets welcome;

its clients and hosts with the best possible customer service.

Carmel 101. This inn is convenient in the heart of Carmel-by-the-Sea. Within walking distance to shops, restaurants, and art galleries. Each one of the 24 rooms features a fireplace, refrigerator, and TV. All private baths. $95-180.

Carmel 102. This inn features a collection of cottages among lush gardens. Eighteen rooms with each room appointed in a unique country style with a private bath and private entrance. Some rooms feature fireplaces. Four blocks away from the beach and a few blocks from downtown Carmel. $105-225.

Bed & Breakfast California

P.O. Box 2247, Saratoga, 95070
(408) 867-9662; (800) 872-4500
FAX (408) 867-0907; e-mail: info@bbintl.com
www.bbintl.com

A. Snug within the heart of Carmel, this family of inns gives guests Old World service and a charming setting. Spacious rooms and suites are designed to accommodate the whole family, and one inn even takes pets! Many rooms have full kitchens and wood-burning fireplaces, and some have Jacuzzis. A short stroll to the shops, restaurants, and galleries of downtown Carmel. A Continental breakfast and complimentary newspaper are delivered to the door each morning. With rates ranging from affordable to luxurious, these inns have something to offer everyone. $109-249.

B. Guests will feel like visiting royalty while staying at this lovely four-diamond property. Perfect for that romantic getaway, guest rooms are spacious and beautiful with king-size beds and wood-burning fireplaces. Fresh flowers welcome guests. Some rooms also have Jacuzzi tubs. Complimentary wine and hors d'oeuvres are offered each evening. A Continental breakfast and complimentary newspaper are delivered to guests' door each morning. $229-299.

C. Built in 1900 in the heart of Carmel, just three blocks from the beach, the Spanish Mission-style inn is within walking distance of the shops and restaurants in Carmel, and includes small garden areas for guests to enjoy. Ten rooms, cozy and comfortable, all have private baths, and are decorated in bright colors. $99-155.

D. Tucked away in a quiet corner of town, the 24 romantic guest rooms wraparound a slate courtyard and English gardens. French doors welcome guests to the lobby complete with a huge stone fireplace and overstuffed furniture. Hot and cold beverages and a cookie jar are always available to guests. All rooms have a stone fireplace, sitting chair, telephone, TV, refrigerator stocked with beverages. $105-180.

E. Fireplace and mini-refrigerator are available in all rooms of this lovely English Tudor-style inn built around a courtyard. Within walking distance to beaches, shops, and restaurants. Several suites have a kitchenette. Continental breakfast is served. $95-165.

Carriage House Inn

Junipero between 7th and 8th, 93921
(800) 433-4732

Fresh flowers and country inn flavor. Continental plus breakfast and newspaper delivered to the room each morning. Wood-burning fireplaces, down comforters. Spacious rooms, many with open-beam ceilings and whirlpools or soaking tubs. Wine and hors d'oeuvres each evening in the library. Carmel's AAA four-diamond inn. A romantic getaway! Two-night minimum stay required for weekends and holidays.

Host: Cathy Lewis
Rooms: 13 (PB) $189-315
Continental Breakfast
Credit Cards: A, B, C, D
Notes: 2, 5, 7, 9, 12, 14

---

7 No smoking; 8 Children welcome; 9 Social drinking allowed; 10 Tennis nearby; 11 Swimming nearby; 12 Golf nearby; 13 Skiing nearby; 14 May be booked through a travel agent; 15 Handicapped accessible.

Cypress Inn

Cypress Inn

Lincoln and 7th Streets, P.O. Box Y, 93921
(831) 624-3871

Built in 1929, this classic Spanish-Mediterranean-style inn in the heart of Carmel by the Sea, within walking distance to all shops, restaurants, galleries, and the beautiful Carmel beach. The spacious living room lobby with fireplace and the garden courtyard are ideal for enjoying a complimentary Continental breakfast or a cocktail from the full-service Library Lounge. A variety of rooms are available, all with private baths, TVs, and telephones, and some with gas-burning fireplaces, sitting areas, wet bars, verandas, and ocean views. Smoking permitted in designated areas only. Limited handicapped accessibility.

Innkeeper: Hollace Thompson
Owners: Doris Day, Terry Melcher, and Dennis Levett
Rooms: 33 (PB) $115-295
Continental Breakfast
Credit Cards: A, B, C, D
Notes: 2, 5, 6, 8, 9, 10, 11, 12, 14

Green Lantern Inn

Cassanova and Seventh, (P.O. Box 1114), 93921
(831) 624-4392; FAX (831) 624-9591
e-mail: info@greenlanterninn.com

Eighteen charming rooms all with private baths nestled among beautiful terraced and landscaped gardens. Buffet breakfast and afternoon refreshments. Four short blocks to sandy beach, shops, and restaurants. All rooms have refrigerator and hair dryer. Some fireplaced units. Children welcome. No pets. No smoking

Host: Cathy Matthews
Rooms: 18 (PB) $85-195
Continental Breakfast
Credit Cards: A, B, C, D
Notes: 5, 7, 8, 11, 12, 14

Happy Landing Inn

Monte Verde between 5th & 6th Avenues (location)
P.O. Box 2619, 93921 (mailing)
(831) 624-7917

Built as a family retreat in 1926, this early-Comstock-design inn has evolved into one of Carmel's most romantic places to stay. The Hansel and Gretel look is accentuated by a central garden and gazebo, pond, and flagstone paths. There are cathedral ceilings and the rooms are filled with antiques. Breakfast is taken to guests' rooms.

Hosts: Robert Ballard and Dick Stewart
Rooms: 7 (PB) $90-170
Continental Breakfast
Credit Cards: A, B
Notes: 2, 5, 7, 9, 10, 11, 12, 15

The Sandpiper Inn-at-the-Beach

2408 Bay View Avenue, 93923
(831) 624-6433; (800) 633-6433
FAX (831) 624-5964; www.sandpiper-inn.com

The inn closest to Carmel beach with views across the bay to Pebble Beach. Rooms and cottage rooms are filled with country antiques and fresh flowers. Some have glorious ocean views, others have gas fireplaces. Beautiful Continental plus buffet breakfast and afternoon tea and sherry served in the parlor area. No pets. No smoking. Award-winning gardens, patios. Like being a houseguest in someone's exclusive seaside home. A special place for special occasions. Children over 12 welcome.

Host: Audie Haousman
Rooms: 16 (PB) $105-285
Continental Breakfast
Credit Cards: A, B, C, D
Notes: 2, 5, 7, 9, 10, 11, 12, 14

NOTES: Credit cards accepted: A MasterCard; B Visa; C American Express; D Discover; E Diner's Club; F Other; 2 Personal checks accepted; 3 Lunch available; 4 Dinner available; 5 Open all year; 6 Pets welcome;

Sea View Inn

P.O. Box 4138, 93921
(831) 624-8778

The Sea View Inn, a simple country Victorian, has been welcoming guests for more than 70 years. A quiet, cozy bed and breakfast, the Sea View has eight individually decorated rooms, six with private baths. Near the village and the beach, the Sea View provides a welcoming retreat. A generous Continental breakfast and afternoon tea are complimentary. Children over 12 welcome.

Hosts: Diane and Marshall Hydorn
Rooms: 8 (6 PB; 2 SB) $90-155
Continental Breakfast
Credit Cards: A, B, C
Notes: 2, 5, 7, 9, 10, 11, 12, 14

The Stonehouse Inn

8th below Monte Verde, P.O. Box 2517, 93921
(831) 624-4569; (800) 748-6618

Experience this luxurious country house in a quiet neighborhood setting. All one hears at night is the ocean! The Stonehouse Inn offers a tastefully restored turn-of-the-century vacation retreat. Superior accommodations and attention await guests' pleasure on the Monterey Peninsula by beautiful Carmel Bay. A generous home-cooked breakfast is served each morning in the sunny dining room. Carmel's world-famous shops and restaurants are only two blocks away.

Hosts: Kevin and Terri Navaille
Rooms: 6 (PB) $110-199
Full Breakfast
Credit Cards: A, B, C
Notes: 5, 7, 9, 10, 11, 12, 14

Vagabond's House Inn

4th and Dolores, P.O. Box 2747, 93923
(831) 624-7738; (800) 262-1262
FAX (831) 626-1243

The stone courtyard here is almost a magical experience, with the great oak and cascading waterfalls surrounded by award-winning flower gardens. Around the courtyard are unique rooms with fireplaces, antiques, designer fabrics, and fresh flowers. All the natural beauty and fascinating shops of Carmel are just around the corner. Inquire about accommodations for pets.

Hosts: Dennis Levett (owner) Dawn Dull (innkeeper)
Rooms: 11 (PB) $125-185
Continental Breakfast
Credit Cards: A, B, C
Notes: 2, 7, 12

CARMEL BY THE SEA

Briarwood Inn

5th Street at San Carlos Street, Box 5245, 93921
(831) 626-9056; (800) 999-8788
FAX (831) 626-8900

Be spoiled! At an upscale delightful bed and breakfast set amid flowers and shrubs. With fireplaces, 27-inch TVs, VCRs, free movies, irons, and much much more. Recently refurbished and with a sumptuous breakfast. Sherry and port wine too. In the heart of the village. A minute's walk to charming shops, galleries, and numerous restaurants. Continental plus breakfast.

Host: George Costa, Innkeeper
Rooms: 12 (PB) $115-295
Continental Breakfast
Credit Cards: A, B, C
Notes: 2, 5, 7, 8, 9, 10, 12

CARMEL VALLEY

Carmel Valley Lodge

Carmel Valley Road and Ford Road, 93924
(831) 659-2261; (800) 641-4646

A warm, sunny Carmel Valley welcome awaits guests. Relax in a garden patio room or cozy one- or two-bedroom cottage with fireplace/kitchen. Enjoy a sumptuous Continental breakfast, heated swimming pool, sauna, hot tub, and free S'mores every night.

---

7 No smoking; 8 Children welcome; 9 Social drinking allowed; 10 Tennis nearby; 11 Swimming nearby; 12 Golf nearby; 13 Skiing nearby; 14 May be booked through a travel agent; 15 Handicapped accessible.

Walk to fine restaurants and quaint shops, or visit wine-tasting rooms or local wineries on a self-guided walking tour. Tennis and golf are nearby. Dog-friendly. Smoking and nonsmoking rooms available.

Host: Michael Cawdrey
Rooms: 31 (PB) $109-299
Continental Breakfast
Credit Cards: A, B, C
Notes: 2, 5, 6, 8, 9, 10, 11, 12, 14, 15

COLOMA

The Coloma Country Inn

345 High Street, P.O. Box 502, 95613
(530) 622-6919; www.colomacountryinn.com

Charming 1852 farmhouse inside 300-acre historic gold rush park and one block from American River. Includes five guest rooms in main inn and two deluxe suites in carriage house. Decorated throughout with American antiques and treasures. Recreational packages include hot-air ballooning and white-water rafting. Grounds include five acres of gardens and a pond. Featured in *Country Living* and *Country Inns* magazines. Walk to Sutter's Mill, museums, and visitor center. Families welcome.

Hosts: Alan and Cindi Ehrgott
Rooms: 7 (5 PB; 2 SB) $90-130
Continental Breakfast
Credit Cards: None
Notes: 2, 5, 7, 8, 9, 11, 12, 13, 14

COLUMBIA

Columbia City Hotel

Box 1870, 95310
(209) 532-1479; e-mail: info@cityhotel.com
www.cityhotel.com

In the heart of a historic gold rush town that is preserved and protected by the state of California, this impeccable inn is surrounded by relics of the past. All rooms have been restored to reflect the 1850s. Downstairs, the highly acclaimed restaurant and always inviting What

Columbia City Hotel

Cheer Saloon provide a haven for travelers seeking comfort and gracious hospitality. All rooms have half-baths; hall showers. Buffet-style breakfast served. Closed Christmas Eve and Christmas Day.

Host: Tom Bender
Rooms: 10 (PB) $95-115
Continental Breakfast
Credit Cards: A, B, C, D
Notes: 2, 4, 7, 8, 9, 10, 11, 12, 13, 14

Fallon Hotel

Washington Street, 95310
(209) 532-1470; e-mail: info@cityhotel.com
www.cityhotel.com

Since 1857, the historic Fallon Hotel has provided a home away from home to countless visitors. Authentically restored to its Victorian grandeur, most of the furnishings are original to the inn. Several rooms have private balconies, and all rooms have half-baths. Baskets of toiletries, robes, and slippers are provided for the showers off the hallway. One room available for handicapped guests. In the heart of a state-restored gold rush town. Adjacent to the Fallon Theatre, which provides year-round productions. Call or write for price information.

NOTES: Credit cards accepted: A MasterCard; B Visa; C American Express; D Discover; E Diner's Club; F Other; 2 Personal checks accepted; 3 Lunch available; 4 Dinner available; 5 Open all year; 6 Pets welcome;

Host: Tom Bender
Rooms: 14 (SB) $50-115
Continental Breakfast
Credit Cards: A, B, C, D
Notes: 2, 4, 5, 7, 8, 9, 10, 11, 12, 13, 14, 15

CROWLEY LAKE

Rainbow Tarns Bed & Breakfast at Crowley Lake

HC 79, Box 1053, 93546
(760) 935-4556; (888) 588-6269
www.rainbowtarns.com

Near Mammoth Lakes, at an altitude of 7,000 feet, Rainbow Tarns is a secluded retreat amid three acres of ponds, open meadows, and the

Rainbow Tarns

Sierra Nevada mountains. Country-style lodge includes luxury touches, such as double Jacuzzi, queen-size beds, down pillows and comforters, and a skylight for star-gazing. Afternoon hors d'oeuvres and wine. Gourmet restaurants nearby. The area provides excellent fishing, hiking, horseback riding, and winter skiing. Rainbow Tarns Road, off Crowley Lake Drive near Tom's Place. Closed March. Children 12 and older welcome.

Hosts: Brock and Diane Thoman
Rooms: 3 (PB) $90-140
Full Breakfast
Credit Cards: None
Notes: 2, 3, 7, 9, 11, 12, 13, 15

DAVENPORT

Davenport Bed & Breakfast Inn

31 Davenport Avenue, 95017
(831) 425-1818; (800) 870-1817
FAX (831) 423-1160; e-mail: inn@swanton.com
www.swanton.com/BnB

Halfway between Carmel-Monterey and San Francisco, on Coast Highway 1. Small rural coastal town noted for whale watching, windsurfing, Ano Nuevo State Elephant Seal Reserve, hiking, bicycling, and beach access. Wonderful restaurant and gift store with unusual treasures and jewelry. Personal checks accepted two weeks prior to stay.

Hosts: Bruce and Marcia McDougal
Rooms: 12 (PB) $85-130
Full Breakfast
Credit Cards: A, B, C
Notes: 3, 4, 5, 7, 8, 9, 11, 12, 14

DAVIS

University Inn Bed & Breakfast

340 "A" Street, 95616-4103
(530) 756-8648; (800) 756-8648
FAX (530) 753-6920; e-mail: yancher@aol.com

Adjacent to the University of California at Davis, this country inn offers a charming

---

7 No smoking; 8 Children welcome; 9 Social drinking allowed; 10 Tennis nearby; 11 Swimming nearby; 12 Golf nearby; 13 Skiing nearby; 14 May be booked through a travel agent; 15 Handicapped accessible.

escape from a busy college town in a homelike setting. Each room has a private bath, telephone, refrigerator, cable TV; off-street parking; a microwave oven is available. A generous Continental plus breakfast is served. Complimentary chocolates, beverages, and flowers. Inquire to see what type of pets accepted. Smoking permitted outside only. Special university events rates.

Hosts: Lynda and Ross Yancher
Rooms: 4 (PB) $55-135
Continental Breakfast
Credit Cards: A, B, C, D, E
Notes: 2, 5, 6, 7, 8, 9, 10, 11, 12, 14, 15

DEL MAR

The Blue Door

13707 Durango Drive, 92014
(858) 755-3819

Enjoy New England charm in a quiet southern California setting. Lower-level two-room suite with king-size bed, private bath, and cozy sitting room opening onto bougainvillaea-splashed patio with open vista of Torrey Pines Reserve Canyon. Only 20 miles north of San Diego. Creative full breakfast. Children over 16 welcome.

Hosts: Bob and Anna Belle Schock
Suite: 1 (PB) $70-80
Full Breakfast
Credit Cards: None
Notes: 2, 5, 7, 9, 11, 12

DESERT HOT SPRINGS

Travellers Repose

66920 First Street, P.O. Box 655, 92240
(760) 329-9584

Bay windows, gingerbread trim, and stained glass decorate this two-story Victorian home. The interior is color coordinated throughout, blending natural woods and wallpapers. The three individually decorated bedrooms are spacious and all have queen-size beds. Guests enjoy the view of desert floor and mountains rising to 11,000 feet. Amenities include a patio, gardens, and spa. Desert Hot Springs is famous for its natural hot mineral waters. Palm Springs is only minutes away, with its museums, shopping, famous restaurants, celebrities, golf tournaments, tennis tournaments, theaters, and stage shows. Closed July and August.

Host: Marian Relkoff
Rooms: 3 (PB) $65-85
Continental Breakfast
Credit Cards: None
Notes: 2, 7, 9, 10, 11, 12, 14

DULZURA

Brookside Farm Bed & Breakfast Inn

1373 Marron Valley Road, 91917
(619) 468-3043; FAX (619) 468-9145

A country farmhouse furnished with collectibles, handmade quilts, and stained glass. Tree-shaded terraces by a stream, farm animals, gardens, hot tub in the grape arbor. Perfect for country walks. Close to Tecate, Mexico, and 35 minutes from San Diego. Two-night minimum stay required for holidays and some rooms. Many guests come for the gourmet country weekend.

Rooms: 10 (PB) $85-120
Full Breakfast
Credit Cards: A, B, C, D, E
Notes: 2, 4, 5, 7, 9, 12, 14, 15

Brookside Farm

NOTES: Credit cards accepted: A MasterCard; B Visa; C American Express; D Discover; E Diner's Club; F Other; 2 Personal checks accepted; 3 Lunch available; 4 Dinner available; 5 Open all year; 6 Pets welcome;

ELK

Elk Cove Inn

6300 South Highway 1, P.O. Box 367, 95432
(707) 877-3321; (800) 275-2967
FAX (707) 877-1808; www.elkcoveinn.com

The Elk Cove Inn is an 1883 lumber baron's oceanfront estate on the Mendocino Coast, with gardens, gazebo, roof deck, and private steps down to the beach. Antique-filled rooms, cottages and suites all offer private baths, fireplaces, bathrobes, coffee makers. All have either dramatic ocean views or lovely garden views. House has common room with TV/VCR, refrigerator, microwave, books, and games. A cocktail bar is also in the house. A huge, multi-course gourmet breakfast is served in the oceanfront dining room. Wineries, redwoods, whale watching, unique shops, and gourmet restaurants are just minutes away. Dinner is available Tuesdays and Wednesdays during the winter.

Hosts: Elaine Bryant and Jim Carr
Rooms: 15 (PB) $108-278
Full Breakfast
Credit Cards: A, B, C
Notes: 2, 5, 7, 9, 10, 12, 14, 15

ENCINITAS

Bed & Breakfast California

P.O. Box 2247, Saratoga, 95070
(408) 867-9662; (800) 872-4500
FAX (408) 867-0907; e-mail: info@bbintl.com
www.bbintl.com

In a renowned flower-growing area in southern California, this bed and breakfast has ocean views, a southwestern decor, and a relaxed atmosphere with large rooms, an apartment, and penthouse with Jacuzzi. All baths are private and rooms have a queen- or king-size bed. A Continental plus breakfast and afternoon refreshments are served. Walking distance to the ocean. $75-150.

Sea Breeze Bed & Breakfast

121 North Vulcan Avenue, 92024
(760) 944-0318
www.compuvar.com/internet/seabreeze

Encinitas's first bed and breakfast. "An absolute treasure," said KABC talk radio. Features in this contemporary two-story ocean-view home are three bedrooms, a common sitting room with a fireplace, and kitchenette. A new addition to the inn is the penthouse, a true "boudoir," with cable TV, VCR, whirlpool tub and shower, plus an eight-foot spa on an ocean-view balcony. Also, an upstairs one-bedroom apartment with fireplace, kitchen, and double soaking tub. Sun deck in the front yard with a waterfall and fish pond. Intimate wedding grotto available. Make reservations early.

Host: Kirsten Richter
Rooms: 5 (PB) $75-150
Continental Breakfast
Credit Cards: A, B, D
Notes: 2, 5, 8, 9, 10, 11, 12, 14

EUREKA

Abigail's Elegant Victorian Mansion

1406 C Street, 95501
(707) 444-3144; FAX (707) 442-5594
www.eureka-california.com

An award-winning 1888 national historic landmark featuring spectacular gingerbread exteriors, opulent Victorian interiors, antique furnishings, and an acclaimed French-gourmet breakfast. Breathtakingly authentic, with all the nostalgic trimmings of a century ago, this meticulously restored Victorian masterpiece offers both history and hospitality, combined with romance and pampering. With "the most stunningly spectacular interiors in the state," *World Traveler* magazine calls it "the best lodging value in California." Ocean views, beaches, Redwood National Park nearby.

---

7 No smoking; 8 Children welcome; 9 Social drinking allowed; 10 Tennis nearby; 11 Swimming nearby; 12 Golf nearby; 13 Skiing nearby; 14 May be booked through a travel agent; 15 Handicapped accessible.

Abigail's Elegant Victorian Mansion

Hosts: Doug and Lily Vieyra
Rooms: 4 (2 PB; 2 SB) $75-185
Full Breakfast
Credit Cards: A, B
Notes: 5, 7, 9, 10, 11, 12, 14

Bed & Breakfast California

P.O. Box 2247, Saratoga, 95070
(408) 867-9662; (800) 872-4500
FAX (408) 867-0907; e-mail: info@bbintl.com
www.bbintl.com

A. This 1883 Victorian offers old-fashioned hospitality, wonderful gardens, and features a studio of a fiber artist. Full breakfast is served. Four guest rooms have king- or queen-size, or twin beds. Private and shared baths. No smoking. $75-125.

B. These charming 1981 and 1986 re-creations of 1880 Victorian mansions offer superb hospitality and excellent full breakfasts. This seaport town offers many recreational activities, including fishing, hiking, golf, biking, and museums. One site has seven guest rooms and the other has 23 guest rooms with private and shared baths. King- or queen-size or double beds available. No smoking. $154-497.

The Carter House Victorians

301 L Street, 95501
(707) 444-8062; FAX (707) 444-8067
e-mail: carter52@carterhouse.com

On the northern border of Eureka, California's historic Old Town, the Carter House Victorians and Restaurant 301 have been welcoming travelers to the Redwood Empire with world-class accommodations and cuisine since 1981. An enclave of four unique, magnificent Victorian homes perched alongside Humboldt Bay, guests are greeted with a special brand of hospitality imbued with the friendly, easy-going spirit of the North Coast. The accommodations and service are unparalleled; the cuisine and wine list award winning.

Rooms: 30 (PB) $120-495
Full Breakfast
Credit Cards: A, B, C, D, E
Notes: 2, 4, 5, 7, 8, 9, 10, 11, 12, 13, 14, 15

Old Town Bed & Breakfast Inn

1521 Third Street, 95501
(707) 445-3951; (800) 331-5098
FAX (707) 268-0231
www.oldtownbnb.com

The uniquely Victorian seaport of Eureka is the setting for this 1871 Greek Revival Italianate two-story Victorian. A short stroll to Humboldt Bay brings nostalgic memories of the great fleets of sailing ships that once carried loads of redwood lumber to San Francisco and the world and brought the bounty of the fishing fleets home. Only two blocks from lumber baron William Carson's famous mansion. Teak hot tub, evening tea, and award-winning breakfast treats. Bring cameras and appetites. Single and corporate rates available. Children under 10, please pre-arrange.

Hosts: Leigh and Diane Benson
Rooms: 6 (4 PB; 2 SB) $95-185
Full Breakfast
Credit Cards: A, B, C, D, E, F
Notes: 2, 5, 7, 9, 10, 11, 12, 14

A Weaver's Inn

1440 B Street, 95501
(707) 443-8119; (800) 992-8119
FAX (707) 443-7923
e-mail: weavrinn@humboldt1.com
www.humboldt1.com/~weavrinn

NOTES: Credit cards accepted: A MasterCard; B Visa; C American Express; D Discover; E Diner's Club; F Other; 2 Personal checks accepted; 3 Lunch available; 4 Dinner available; 5 Open all year; 6 Pets welcome;

A Weaver's Inn

Circa 1883. A stately Queen Anne with beautiful gardens and spacious lawn. Four lovely guest rooms furnished in antiques, with down comforters and fresh flowers from the garden. The charm of the Victorian parlor and elegant dining room, fireplaces, and delicious full breakfasts reflect the genteel elegance of a bygone era. The Eureka area offers many fine restaurants, antique and speciality import stores, and the special treat of the Victorian era ambiance in Old Town—fish from a boat, enjoy a tour of the harbor, or comb a beach. Inquire about accommodations for pets and children. Smoking is permitted outside only.

Hosts: Lea L. Montgomery, Shoshana McAvoy, and Lee Montgomery
Rooms: 4 (2 PB; 2 SB) $75-125
Full Breakfast
Credit Cards: A, B, C, D, E
Notes: 2, 5, 7, 9, 12, 14

FERNDALE

The Gingerbread Mansion

400 Berding Street, P.O. Box 40, 95536
(707) 786-4000; (800) 952-4136

The Gingerbread Mansion inn is well known as one of America's most photographed homes. Its striking Victorian architecture trimmed with gingerbread, its colorful peach and yellow paint, and its surrounding English gardens all make the Gingerbread Mansion a photographer's delight. It is an understatement to say that the interiors are also spectacular. AAA-rated four diamonds. Rates are subject to change.

Host: Ken Torbert
Rooms: 5 (PB) $140-180
Suites: 5 (PB) $150-350
Full Breakfast
Credit Cards: A, B, C
Notes: 2, 5, 7, 8, 9, 14

The Gingerbread Mansion

FISH CAMP

Karen's Yosemite Bed & Breakfast

1144 Railroad Avenue, P.O. Box 8, 93623
(800) 346-1443

Two miles south of Yosemite on Highway 41, Karen's is nestled in the towering pines and whispering cedars at 5,000 feet. Each room has private bath and individual heat control. A bountiful country breakfast is served family-style each morning. Refreshments, in harmony with the season, are available throughout the evening. Karen's offers a unique blend of contemporary-country hospitality.

Host: Karen Bergh
Rooms: 3 (PB) $90
Full Breakfast
Credit Cards: None
Notes: 2, 5, 7, 8, 9, 10, 11, 12, 13, 14

---

7 No smoking; 8 Children welcome; 9 Social drinking allowed; 10 Tennis nearby; 11 Swimming nearby; 12 Golf nearby; 13 Skiing nearby; 14 May be booked through a travel agent; 15 Handicapped accessible.

FORT BRAGG

Bed & Breakfast California

P.O. Box 2247, Saratoga, 95070
(408) 867-9662; (800) 872-4500
FAX (408) 867-0907; e-mail: info@bbintl.com
www.bbintl.com

Landmark redwood building has 14 guest rooms, all with private baths. King, queen, double, and twin beds are available. Near scenic railway, state parks, beaches, fishing, and hiking, and within walking distance to shops and galleries. Full breakfast. No smoking. $88-165.

Grey Whale Inn

615 North Main Street, 95437
(707) 964-0640; (800) 382-7244 (reservations)
e-mail: stay@greywhaleinn.com
www.greywhaleinn.com

Handsome Mendocino Coast landmark since 1915. Cozy rooms to expansive suites, all private baths, telephones, TVs, and coffee makers. Ocean, garden, or hill and city views. Some have fireplaces; one has whirlpool tub. Recreation area: pool table, fireside lounge, TV/VCR room. Conference room seats 16 people. Friendly, helpful staff. Full buffet breakfast. Walk to beach, Skunk train, restaurants, shops, microbrewery. Three-star rating from Mobil. ABBA-rated three crowns. AAA three-diamond-rated. Inquire about accommodations for children.

Grey Whale Inn

Host: Colette Bailey
Rooms: 14 (PB) $100-180
Full Breakfast
Credit Cards: A, B, C, D, F
Notes: 2, 5, 7, 9, 10, 11, 12, 14, 15

The Historic Old Coast Hotel, Bar & Grill

101 North Franklin Street, 95437
(707) 961-4488; (888) 468-3550
FAX (707) 961-4480

Sixteen romantic Victorian suites. Fireplaces, complimentary Continental breakfast. The Historic Old Coast Hotel has been newly restored. Close to downtown Fort Bragg, shopping, beaches, antique shops, museums, and the Skunk Trail. AAA-rated three diamonds. Steaks, seafood, Italian specialties, pizza are available at the 49er's theme Sports Bar.

Rooms: 16 (PB) $95-175
Continental Breakfast
Credit Cards: None
Notes: 4, 5, 7, 8, 15

FREMONT

Lord Bradley's Inn

43344 Mission Boulevard, 94539
(510) 490-0520; (877) 567-3272
www.lordbradleysinn.com

This Victorian is nestled below Mission Peak, adjacent to the Mission San Jose. Numerous olive trees on the property were planted by the Ohlone Indians. Common room, garden, patio. Parking in rear. Take the bus or Bay Area Rapid Transit to San Francisco for a day. Close to San Jose airport.

Hosts: Susie and Steve Wilson
Rooms: 8 (PB) $85-135
Continental Breakfast
Credit Cards: A, B, C, D
Notes: 2, 5, 7, 9, 10, 12, 14

NOTES: Credit cards accepted: A MasterCard; B Visa; C American Express; D Discover; E Diner's Club; F Other; 2 Personal checks accepted; 3 Lunch available; 4 Dinner available; 5 Open all year; 6 Pets welcome;

GEORGETOWN

American River Inn

Main at Orleans Streets, P.O. Box 43, 95634
(800) 245-6566; FAX (916) 333-9253
e-mail: ari@pcweb.net; www.pcweb.net/ari

In the heart of gold country nine miles off Highway 49 between I-80 and I-50, this "Jewel of the Mother Lode" is a totally restored 1853 miners' boarding house. Each room is individually decorated with Victorian and turn-of-the-century antiques, and feather beds. Gorgeous natural gardens, a refreshing mountain stream pool and Jacuzzi, a dove aviary, and mountain bikes. Enjoy a full breakfast in the morning, local wines and treats in the evening. Antique shop on the premises. Other amenities include a croquet field, putting green, and mini-driving range. Georgetown is a Sierra foothills village with real flavor and only six miles from Gold Discovery Park in Coloma. Retreat and conference facility.

Hosts: Will and Maria
Rooms: 17 (6 PB; 11 SB) $85-115
Suites: 8 (PB)
Full Breakfast
Credit Cards: A, B, C, D, E
Notes: 2, 5, 8, 9, 10, 11, 12, 13, 14, 15

GILROY

Country Rose Inn Bed & Breakfast

P.O. Box 2500, 95021
(408) 842-0441; FAX (408) 842-6646
www.bbonline.com/ca/countryrose

Country Rose Inn Bed and Breakfast is nestled in San Martin between Morgan Hill and Gilroy in the original California wine region in south Santa Clara Valley. Is is just minutes from historic San Juan Baulita boasting the only California mission with its original plaza. The heart of Silicon Valley, San Jose, is just 25 miles north. Its rural setting and gracious hostess create a warm hospitable feeling to be remembered. "Every window is a living postcard. It is beautifully simple."

Host: Rose Hernandez
Rooms: 5 (PB) $129-189
Full Breakfast
Credit Cards: A, B, D, E
Notes: 2, 5, 7, 12, 14

GRASS VALLEY

Murphy's Inn

318 Neal Street, 95945
(530) 273-6873; (800) 895-2488
FAX (530) 273-5157

Manicured ivy trims the 1866 Colonial Revival classic built by one of the gold barons as a wedding present for his wife. Eight rooms, four with fireplaces and four with dual shower heads, are decorated in Victorian elegance. Large outside deck and wraparound porch. Inquire about accommodations for children.

Hosts: Ted and Nancy Daus
Rooms: 8 (PB) $105-155
Full Breakfast
Credit Cards: A, B, C
Notes: 2, 5, 7, 9, 10, 11, 12, 13, 14

Murphy's Inn

GUALALA

North Coast Country Inn

34591 South Highway One, 95445
(707) 884-4537; (800) 959-4537

A cluster of rustic redwood buildings with ocean views. Rooms feature king- and queen-size

---

7 No smoking; 8 Children welcome; 9 Social drinking allowed; 10 Tennis nearby; 11 Swimming nearby; 12 Golf nearby; 13 Skiing nearby; 14 May be booked through a travel agent; 15 Handicapped accessible.

North Coast Country

beds, fireplaces, private baths, decks, and private entries. The inn has a hot tub and gazebo. Full breakfast is served in common room. Golf, hiking, horseback riding, fishing, and beaches are nearby. Minimum stay requirements for weekends and holidays.

Hosts: Loren and Nancy Flanagan
Rooms: 6 (PB) $150-175
Full Breakfast
Credit Cards: A, B, C
Notes: 2, 5, 7, 9, 10, 12, 14

The Old Milano Hotel & Restaurant

38300 South Highway One, 95445
(707) 884-3256; FAX (707) 884-4249
e-mail: lll@mcn.org
www.cristalen.com/oldmilano

One hundred miles north of San Francisco, the inn is on a three-acre oceanfront estate with incredible white-water views. Built in 1905, it has been beautifully refurbished in Victorian elegance. Accommodations include lovely ocean view rooms, a master suite, and private cottages appointed with canopied beds, fireplaces, and whirlpool tubs. There is also a caboose tucked in the cypress trees for privacy. Features include English gardens, cliff side hot tub by reservation, and intimate candlelight dining at its finest.

Host: Leslie Linscheid
Room: 13 (7 PB; 6 SB) $115-210
Full Breakfast
Credit Cards: A, B
Notes: 2, 4, 5, 7, 9, 10, 12, 14, 15

GUERNEVILLE

Bed & Breakfast California

P.O. Box 2247, Saratoga, 95070
(408) 867-9662; (800) 872-4500
FAX (408) 867-0907; e-mail: info@bbintl.com
www.bbintl.com

A. Warm and welcoming accommodation nestled in the redwoods along the Russian River in the heart of Sonoma County's great northwest. Guests may enjoy the use of the bright, cheerfully furnished living room and lounge, both of which have fireplaces and feature original works of art. The more formal living room boasts Art Deco furniture and a lovely bay window which fills the room with light. The lounge and its adjacent poolside patio are more casual and relaxed. $75-149.

B. Amidst the beauty of the redwoods, apple tree, and vineyards, this is a great place to unwind and relax. The estate is a short distance to the wine country or the coast, and opportunities for hiking, horseback riding, canoeing,

NOTES: Credit cards accepted: A MasterCard; B Visa; C American Express; D Discover; E Diner's Club; F Other; 2 Personal checks accepted; 3 Lunch available; 4 Dinner available; 5 Open all year; 6 Pets welcome;

fishing, and swimming are nearby. All rooms have private baths, and some have views, fireplaces, and/or Jacuzzis. An excellent full breakfast is served, and there is also a restaurant on the property. $135-275.

Fern Grove Cottages

Fern Grove Cottages

16650 Highway 116, 95446
(707) 869-8105; FAX (707) 869-1615
e-mail: ferngrov@tomatoweb.com
www.tomatoweb.com/ferngrov

Spend the night in an authentic 1920s cottage under towering redwood trees. Most cottages have fireplaces and original knotty pine paneling, some have double-size whirlpool tubs in the bedroom. Studios, one- and two-bedroom units suitable for families are available. All the cottages have their own deck and an all-you-can-eat buffet Continental breakfast is served. Guests can walk to the river and town and wineries are nearby.

Hosts: Simon and Anne Lowings
Rooms: 20 (PB) $69-159
Continental Breakfast
Credit Cards: A, B, C, D
Notes: 2, 5, 6, 8, 9, 11, 12, 14

Ridenhour Ranch House Inn

12850 River Road, 95446
(707) 887-1033

A 1906 inn on more than two acres of trees, gardens, and meadow in the Russian River area of northern California. More than 50 wineries and the dramatic Sonoma Coast are a short, scenic drive away. The inn and guest rooms are decorated with an eclectic assortment of antiques, folk art, and collectibles.

Hosts: Chris Bell and Meilani Naranjo
Rooms: 8 (PB) $95-145
Full Breakfast
Credit Cards: A, B, C
Notes: 2, 5, 7, 8, 9, 11, 12, 14

Rio Inn

444 Wood Road, 95446
(707) 869-4444; (800) 344-7018
FAX (707) 869-4443
e-mail: reservations@rioinn.com

Epitomizing the grace, history, and charm of the Russian River Wine Road, the 1890s vintage Rio Inn is nestled in the redwoods just one hour's drive north of San Francisco. More than 100 wineries and the superb Sonoma coast are within half an hour's drive from this landmark Tudor building. Each unique room is furnished with antiques and original artwork, and has a private bath. The Rio Inn also has substantial indoor and outdoor facilities for banquets, weddings, and company retreats for between 15 and 400 people.

Host: Dawson Church
Rooms: 10 (PB) $89-149
Continental Breakfast
Credit Cards: A, B, C, D
Notes: 2, 5, 6, 7, 8, 9, 10, 11, 12, 14, 15

HALF MOON BAY

Bed & Breakfast California

P.O. Box 2247, Saratoga, 95070
(408) 867-9662; (800) 872-4500
FAX (408) 867-0907; e-mail: info@bbintl.com
www.bbintl.com

A. Revel in the ultimate in beach-side living. Every room has a seaside view. Guests just step outside the door and sink their toes into a five-mile stretch of sandy beach. Run or walk it.

---

7 No smoking; 8 Children welcome; 9 Social drinking allowed; 10 Tennis nearby; 11 Swimming nearby; 12 Golf nearby; 13 Skiing nearby; 14 May be booked through a travel agent; 15 Handicapped accessible.

Amidst the colorful collection of native folk art, each of the 12 rooms captures the essence of California beach-side living. Listen to the sound of waves. Warm yourself by the fire. Or unwind with a massage by the in-house massage therapist. Explore the coast's myriad activities. Picnicking on the beach. Sailing, sport fishing, whale watching, etc. All of these activities are within 5-10 minutes away. $170-275.

B. Beach house offers 54 beautifully appointed ocean lofts with patio or balconies, 30 minutes south of San Francisco overlooking seven miles of sandy beach. Each loft includes a king-size bed and queen-size sleeper-sofa and a wood-burning fireplace. Wet bar with granite counters, stereo system with CD changer. Separate shower and ultra-deep tub. Double sinks with granite counters. Two line telephone with voice mail, modem, and fax capabilities. Swimming pool and spa overlooking the Pacific Ocean. $175-350.

C. The oldest building still standing in Half Moon Bay, built circa 1859. It is conveniently located in a garden-like setting in the heart of downtown Half Moon Bay. On the same block are two of the finest restaurants on the coast and the shopping and browsing district is just steps from the door. A variety of guest rooms including three beautifully appointed and spacious suites are available. $90-250.

Cypress Inn on Miramar Beach

407 Mirada Road, 94019
(650) 726-6002; (800) 83-BEACH
FAX (650) 712-0380
e-mail: lodging@cypressinn.com
www.cypressinn.com

Ten steps to the sand. The Bay area's only oceanfront bed and breakfast on five miles of sandy beach 30 minutes south of San Francisco. Private decks, most with unobstructed, breathtaking views of the ocean; all with fireplaces, private baths, telephones. Natural pine and wicker furniture and sky lights. A palette of nature's colors from the sea, sky, and earth, and colorful folk art capture the essence of California contemporary beachside living. Complimentary wine and hors d'oeuvres, and evening dessert. In-house massage therapist. Conference room.

Hosts: Suzie Lankes and Dan Floyd
Rooms: 12 (PB) $165-275
Full Breakfast
Credit Cards: A, B, C, D
Notes: 5, 7, 10, 11, 12, 14, 15

The Goose and Turrets

The Goose and Turrets

835 George Street, Box 937, Montara, 94037-0937
(650) 728-5451; e-mail: rhmgt@montara.com
www.montara.com/goose.html

A quiet, historic bed and breakfast catering to readers, nature lovers, pilots—and enthusiastic eaters who appreciate afternoon tea and four-course breakfasts. On an acre of gardens, this traditional bed and breakfast offers comfortable rooms, conversation, and pampering. Only 30 minutes from San Francisco airport and 5 minutes from the beach, it is convenient to San Francisco and the Bay Area. Special attractions include tide pools, bird watching, elephant seals, and whales. French spoken.

Hosts: Raymond and Emily Hoche-Mong
Rooms: 5 (PB) $100-150
Full Breakfast
Credit Cards: A, B, C, D, E
Notes: 2, 5, 7, 8, 9, 10, 11, 12, 14

NOTES: Credit cards accepted: A MasterCard; B Visa; C American Express; D Discover; E Diner's Club; F Other; 2 Personal checks accepted; 3 Lunch available; 4 Dinner available; 5 Open all year; 6 Pets welcome;

Old Thyme Inn

779 Main Street, 94019
(650) 726-1616; (800) 720-4277
FAX (650) 726-6394
e-mail: innkeeper@oldthymeinn.com

Your coastal garden of herbal delight: the fully restored Old Thyme Inn is a beautiful 1899 Queen Anne Victorian Bed and breakfast. Its aromatic English garden, with more than 50 varieties of herbs and colorful flowers, was designed to help guests slip effortlessly into the easy pace of the coastside. The inn, with its seven distinctively decorated rooms, is furnished with antiques and the innkeepers's collection of fine art. Available amenities include Jacuzzis-for-two, fireplaces, feather beds with down duvets, and TV/VCRs. Full gourmet breakfast served every morning; white wine and sherry in the afternoon. "We're looking forward to the pleasure of your company!"

Hosts: Rick and Kathy Ellis
Rooms: 7 (PB) $100-255
Full Breakfast
Credit Cards: A, B, C, D, F
Notes: 2, 5, 7, 9, 11, 12, 14

HEALDSBURG

Bed & Breakfast California

P.O. Box 2247, Saratoga, 95070
(408) 867-9662; (800) 872-4500
FAX (408) 867-0907; e-mail: info@bbintl.com
www.bbintl.com

A. This contemporary architect-designed home has a lovely guest suite with a private entrance. It is on the site of an old winery and boasts a 1908 wine cellar in the garden. The suite is attractively furnished in a mix of modern and antique styles and the walls are covered with handmade wallpaper. The home is surrounded by beautiful hills and vineyards with private deck and Jacuzzi for guests. $135.

B. Distinguished by a sense of homey elegance, combining the graciousness one might feel at a friend's home and the luxurious amenities of thick terry-cloth robes, an expansive breakfast buffet, stately antique furniture, elegant decor found in European lodgings. Full breakfast. All nine rooms have fireplaces. Five have antique furniture of the first owner. $155-220.

C. An 1869 Italianate Victorian townhouse on one-half acre has landscaped grounds with pool and large antique-filled guest rooms. Breakfast with freshly baked breads and afternoon refreshments are served. Nine guest rooms. Shared and private baths. $80-165.

D. This 1902 Queen Anne Victorian offers an elegant return to a bygone era. Upstairs rooms have roof windows and view of the lovely grounds. Full country breakfast. Seven guest rooms. Private bath. No smoking. $150-185.

Bed & Breakfast San Francisco

P.O. Box 420009, San Francisco, 94142
(415) 931-3083; FAX (415) 921-BBSF (2273)
e-mail: bbsf@linex.com; www.bbsf.com

24. A wonderful bed and breakfast hideaway near the center of town. The owners grow their own grapes and bottle their own wines. The beautiful accommodation has a private entrance and a private bath. Full breakfast. Enjoy the deck and hot tub. $100-135.

Sonoma County Wine and River Country. Jane's place is in rustic Healdsburg in the heart of the wine country, just minutes from some of

---

7 No smoking; 8 Children welcome; 9 Social drinking allowed; 10 Tennis nearby; 11 Swimming nearby; 12 Golf nearby; 13 Skiing nearby; 14 May be booked through a travel agent; 15 Handicapped accessible.

California's finest wineries, close to the Russian River beaches and resorts, and only one-half hour from the Pacific Coast. There are three quaintly furnished rooms on an estate overlooking vineyards. All the bedrooms have private baths. If guests are lucky, they will be entertained by the wild turkeys while enjoying a home-cooked full breakfast in the morning. $85.

Belle de Jour Inn

16276 Healdsburg Avenue, 95448
(707) 431-9777; FAX (707) 431-7412
www.belledejourinn.com

Sonoma County wine country hospitality at its finest. This six-acre hilltop location is home to four cottage accommodations and a deluxe carriage house suite. Bountiful breakfast is served each day in the Italianate farmhouse. Whirlpool tubs for two, gas fireplaces, privacy, privacy, privacy! Wineries and great restaurants nearby.

Hosts: Tom and Brenda Hearn
Rooms: 5 (PB) $165-275
Full Breakfast
Credit Cards: A, B, C
Notes: 2, 5, 7, 9, 10, 11, 12, 14

Calderwood Inn

25 West Grant Street, 95448
(707) 431-1110; (800) 600-5444
www.calderwoodinn.com

A romantic 1902 Victorian Inn, just blocks from the plaza and renowned wineries. Grand porches, fountains, koi ponds, and gardens in a lush forested estate. Full breakfast with gourmet coffees and teas is served at 9:00 a.m. Appetizers and port are served in the evenings. Beautiful yet comfortable antiques throughout. Hand-stenciled Victorian wall and ceiling papers. Private baths in each room with either whirlpool, claw-foot tub/showers, or tiled showers. Fireplaces available. Air conditioned. Walk to plaza and wine tastings.

Hosts: Jennifer and Paul Zawodny
Rooms: 6 (PB) $135-185
Full Breakfast

Credit Cards: None
Notes: 2, 5, 7, 8, 9, 10, 11, 12, 13, 14

Camellia Inn

211 North Street, 95448
(707) 433-8182; (800) 727-8182
FAX (707) 433-8130
e-mail: info@camelliainn.com
www.camelliainn.com

Italianate Victorian townhouse, built in 1869, elegantly decorated with antiques. Nine rooms with private baths, several with double whirlpools and gas fireplaces. Full buffet breakfast is served in the dining room beneath massive mahogany mantel. Fifty camellia varieties plus roses on half-acre. Afternoon refreshments in double parlors or by swimming pool. Forty-five-minute drive to coast through redwoods. Walking distance to town square for shopping, restaurants, wineries.

Hosts: Ray, Del, and Lucy Lewand
Rooms: 9 (PB) $80-165
Full Breakfast
Credit Cards: A, B, C
Notes: 2, 5, 7, 8, 9, 10, 11, 12, 14

The Grape Leaf Inn

539 Johnson Street, 95448
(707) 433-8140; FAX (707) 433-3140
e-mail: grapeleaf.pacbell.net

A beautifully restored warm and cozy 1900 Queen Anne Victorian home. Seven elegant, antique furnished guest rooms, five of which

The Grape Leaf Inn

NOTES: Credit cards accepted: A MasterCard; B Visa; C American Express; D Discover; E Diner's Club; F Other; 2 Personal checks accepted; 3 Lunch available; 4 Dinner available; 5 Open all year; 6 Pets welcome;

have whirlpool tubs/shower for two. All private. King- or queen-size beds, air conditioned, fireplace. Wine tasting nightly. Sumptuous country breakfasts. Four blocks to restaurants, antique shops, and winery tasting rooms.

Hosts: Richard and Kae Rosenberg
Rooms: 7 (PB) $105-185
Full Breakfast
Credit Cards: A, B
Notes: 2, 5, 7, 9, 10, 11, 12, 14

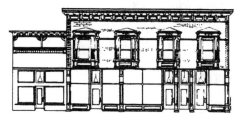

Healdsburg Inn on the Plaza

Haydon Street Inn

Haydon Street Inn

321 Haydon Street, 95448
(707) 433-5228; FAX (707) 433-6637

Turn-of-the-century Queen Anne home in old, quiet neighborhood within walking distance of downtown historic plaza and a short drive to many fine wineries. The main house has six comfortable and tastefully decorated guest rooms, all with private baths. A Victorian Gothic-style two-story cottage with two luxurious rooms with private baths and double whirlpool tubs. Abundant, delicious, home-cooked breakfasts served in the sunlit dining room. Air conditioned. Special midweek rates. Canine greeter.

Rooms: 8 (PB) $95-175
Full Breakfast
Credit Cards: A, B
Notes: 2, 5, 7, 9, 10, 11, 12, 14

Healdsburg Inn on the Plaza

110 Matheson Street, P.O. Box 1196, 95448
(707) 433-6991; (800) 431-8663
www.healdsburginn.com

This 1900 brick Victorian, formerly a Wells Fargo stagecoach express station, has been restored and is now elegantly furnished as a bed and breakfast. Features include bay windows with a view of the plaza or open balconies, fireplaces, and central heat/air. Solarium for snacks, popcorn, wine, music. Coffee and cookies available all day. Champagne breakfasts on weekends. TV, VCR, telephone, and gift certificates. Family owned and operated; close to everything. Midweek and winter rates are discounted 20 to 30 percent.

Hosts: Genny Jenkins and LeRoy Steck
Rooms: 10 (PB) $185-265
Full Breakfast
Credit Cards: A, B
Notes: 2, 5, 7, 10, 11, 12, 14

The Raford House

10630 Wohler Road, 95448
(707) 887-9573; (800) 887-9503
FAX (707) 887-9597
www.rafordhouse.com

This charming landmark Victorian summer house overlooks award-winning vineyards and is surrounded by towering palm trees and old-fashioned flower gardens. Guest rooms are furnished with turn-of-the-century antiques. A full breakfast is served in the dining room. The sunroom and front porch entice guests to enjoy the splendid view and complimentary evening wine and hors d'oeuvres. Near many fine wineries, restaurants, the Russian River, and the rugged northern California coast.

Hosts: Carole and Jack Vore
Rooms: 5 (PB) $110-175

---

7 No smoking; 8 Children welcome; 9 Social drinking allowed; 10 Tennis nearby; 11 Swimming nearby; 12 Golf nearby; 13 Skiing nearby; 14 May be booked through a travel agent; 15 Handicapped accessible.

Suite: 1 (PB) $200-250
Full Breakfast
Credit Cards: A, B, C, D
Notes: 2, 7, 9, 10, 11, 12, 14

HOLLYWOOD

Bed & Breakfast California

P.O. Box 2247, Saratoga, 95070
(408) 867-9662; (800) 872-4500
FAX (408) 867-0907; e-mail: info@bbintl.com
www.bbintl.com

A. Historic West Hollywood neighborhood is the setting for very private self-hosted one-bedroom guest house with kitchen, living room, private bath, double bed, and pool. Central to most tourist attractions, and good public transportation is available. No smoking. $120.

B. A 1910 California bungalow on a quiet palm-tree-lined street close to Hollywood's well-known attractions. There are two second-floor guest rooms, both with private bath and one with a sun deck. Well-traveled hosts speak several languages. Good public transportation. Resident dog. Continental breakfast. $70-75.

HOPLAND

Fetzer Bed & Breakfast Inn at Valley Oaks Ranch

13601 East Side Road, 95449
(707) 744-1250; FAX (707) 744-7488

Nestled in the vineyards of historic Valley Oaks Ranch is the charming bed and breakfast at Fetzer Visitor Center. The inn has four standard deluxe rooms and six suites. Spacious, beautifully furnished, the rooms feature stunning views of the surrounding vineyards. Several rooms feature separate bedrooms, private patio, kitchenette, whirlpool tub, CD player, TV, and fireplace. Rooms include Continental breakfast, telephones, and seasonal access to the pool. The Hopland location makes it ideal for day trips throughout the Redwood Empire.

Hosts: Jo Gennaso, Ines Guevara, and Jacqueline Guevara
Rooms: 10 (PB) $120-200
Continental Breakfast
Credit Cards: A, B, C, D
Notes: 3, 5, 7, 8, 9, 11, 12, 14, 15

IDYLLWILD

Strawberry Creek Inn

26370 Highway 243, P.O. Box 1818, 92549
(909) 659-3202; (800) 262-8969

The Strawberry Creek Inn is a mile high in the peaceful San Jacinto Mountains of southern California. All rooms have queen-size beds and private baths; most have fireplaces. The honeymoon cottage by the creek has an in-room spa, fireplace, living room, and full kitchen. Full breakfasts await guests each morning—such specialties as Jim's baked German French toast with smoked bratwurst or Diana's tasty herb baked eggs. There are 100 miles of hiking trails nearby.

Hosts: Diana Dugan and Jim Goff
Rooms: 10 (PB) $75-150
Full Breakfast
Credit Cards: A, B, D
Notes: 2, 5, 7, 15

Strawberry Creek Inn

NOTES: Credit cards accepted: A MasterCard; B Visa; C American Express; D Discover; E Diner's Club; F Other; 2 Personal checks accepted; 3 Lunch available; 4 Dinner available; 5 Open all year; 6 Pets welcome;

INVERNESS

Bed & Breakfast California

P.O. Box 2247, Saratoga, 95070
(408) 867-9662; (800) 872-4500
FAX (408) 867-0907; e-mail: info@bbintl.com
www.bbintl.com

A long driveway takes guests to one of the most beautiful and romantic original Inverness homes. Perched on a hill just beyond the village of Inverness, this inn is a Craftsman-style home built in 1916 offering decks with sweeping views overlooking Tomales Bay and the Marin Hills beyond. The guest rooms feature clawfoot tubs, pedestal sinks, and French showers. Guests are invited to plunk on the upright piano or relax in front of the massive river rock fireplace or in the hot tub. Weekends a delicious and hearty breakfast awaits, and on weekdays a Continental breakfast served. $98-167.

Fairwinds Farm Bed & Breakfast Cottage & Dan's En Suite Room

82 Drake's Summit, P.O. Box 581, 94937
(415) 663-9454; FAX (415) 663-1787
e-mail: fairwind@svh.net

Overlooking 75,000 acres of national seashore with direct access. Only visible light is the lighthouse on Farallon Islands. Private cottage, more than 100 square feet, fully equipped kitchen, full bath, fireplace, TV/stereo/VCR (500-plus movies), library, beach umbrella, toys, playhouse, barnyard animals, garden with ponds, waterfalls, giant swing. Hot tub on private deck. Queen-size bed, two doubles, crib, and two futons. Dan's En Suite Room has a private entrance, wraparound decks, fireplace, TV/VCR, movies, microwave, refrigerator, deck-top hot tub with ocean view. Continental breakfast and evening treats.

Cottage: 1 (PB) $148.50
En Suite Room: 1 (PB) $100
Full Breakfast/Continental Breakfast
Credit Cards: None
Notes: 2, 5, 7, 8, 9, 10, 11, 12

Rosemary Cottage

75 Balboa Avenue, P.O. Box 273, 94937
(415) 663-9338; (800) 808-9338
e-mail: rosemarybb@aol.com
www.nbn.com/people/rosemary

Romantic French country pied-à-terre. Two-room private cottage in a sunny secluded spot adjacent to Point Reyes National Seashore Park. Hauntingly beautiful forest canyon view. Large deck, herb garden. Main living space features cathedral ceiling, many windows, skylight. Antiques, oriental rugs, artwork, French fabrics, handmade cabinets, and tiles create inviting ambiance. Kitchen well equipped. Woodstove functions as open fireplace and main source of heat. Private bath. Queen-size and two twin beds. Hot tub.

Rooms: 3 (PB)
Full Breakfast
Credit Cards: None
Notes: 2, 5, 6, 8, 10, 11, 12

Ten Inverness Way

10 Inverness Way, P.O. Box 63, 94937-0063
(415) 669-1648; FAX (415) 669-7403
e-mail: inn@teninvernessway.com
www.teninvernessway.com

Built in 1904, this handsome redwood-shingled bed and breakfast features a stone fireplace, sunny library with many good books, gourmet breakfasts, picnic lunches, and access to a diverse recreational area. Enjoy a relaxing soak in the garden hot tub after an afternoon hike. Just 45 minutes from San Francisco's Golden Gate Bridge, the inn is nestled in a nostalgic waterfront village abutting the Point Reyes National Seashore.

Hosts: Teri Moweny
Rooms: 5 (PB) $145-180
Full Breakfast
Credit Cards: A, B
Notes: 3, 5, 7, 11, 12

---

7 No smoking; 8 Children welcome; 9 Social drinking allowed; 10 Tennis nearby; 11 Swimming nearby; 12 Golf nearby; 13 Skiing nearby; 14 May be booked through a travel agent; 15 Handicapped accessible.

IONE

The Heirloom
214 Shakeley Lane, 95640
(209) 274-4468

Travel down a country lane into a romantic English garden where a petite Colonial mansion (circa 1863) is shaded by century-old trees and scented by magnolias and gardenias. Fireplaces and balconies. Breakfast has a French flair. Enjoy gracious hospitality. Closed Thanksgiving, Christmas Eve, and Christmas Day. Children over 10 welcome.

Hosts: Patricia Cross and Melisande Hubbs
Rooms: 6 (4 PB; 2 SB) $65-98
Full Breakfast
Credit Cards: A, B, C
Notes: 2, 7, 9, 11, 12, 14

The Heirloom

JACKSON

Bed & Breakfast California
P.O. Box 2247, Saratoga, 95070
(408) 867-9662; (800) 872-4500
FAX (408) 867-0907; e-mail: info@bbintl.com
www.bbintl.com

Within walking distance to gold rush town's historic area and near wineries, this 1872 Victorian inn has a lovely rose garden and spa and serves a full breakfast. Private or shared baths. $95-190.

JAMESTOWN

Jamestown Hotel
18153 Main Street, P.O. Box 539, 95327
(209) 984-3902; (800) 205-4901
FAX (209) 984-4149
e-mail: info@jamestownhotel.com

The Jamestown Hotel lets guests sample the flavor of life in the gold rush days. From the old brick exterior and wooden veranda-style balcony, to the exquisitely furnished suites, the hotel has been carefully restored to the elegance of the mid-1800s. Here is the perfect place for city-weary people seeking a country retreat. Eight of the guest rooms feature furnishings indicative of the gold rush era, with antiques and private Victorian bath with brass shower. The other three guest rooms have whirlpool tubs, TVs, and VCRs. The hosts offer the charm of a small country inn, friendly staff, and full-service lounge and bar. Continental plus breakfast is served. Skiing is one hour away.

Hosts: Jerry and Lucille Weisbrot
Rooms: 11 (PB) $70-135
Continental Breakfast
Credit Cards: A, B, C, D, E
Notes: 2, 5, 7, 8, 9, 10, 11, 12, 14, 15

The Palm Hotel Bed & Breakfast
10382 Willow Street, 95327
(209) 984-3429; FAX (209) 984-4929
e-mail: innkeeper@palmhotel.com
www.palmhotel.com

This 100-year-old Victorian, off Main Street, graces Jamestown with its rare arched windows and five-story tower. Eight unique rooms have private baths. Relax in a bubble bath in a claw-foot tub or enjoy double-headed marble showers. High vaulted ceilings and sunny sitting areas recall days past. Walk to antique shops, gourmet restaurants, and Railtown 1897 State Historic Park.

Hosts: Rick and Sandy Allen
Rooms: 8 (PB) $85-145
Full Breakfast
Credit Cards: A, B, C
Notes: 5, 7, 8, 9, 11, 12, 13, 14, 15

NOTES: Credit cards accepted: A MasterCard; B Visa; C American Express; D Discover; E Diner's Club; F Other; 2 Personal checks accepted; 3 Lunch available; 4 Dinner available; 5 Open all year; 6 Pets welcome;

Royal Hotel

18239 Main Street, 95327
(209) 984-5271; FAX (209) 984-1675

Best value in the second oldest mining town in the west. Victorian-style rooms, nicely appointed, larger, secluded cottages. Close to golf, fishing, white-water rafting, steam trains, and Yosemite. Visit the many fine antique stores, restaurants, and pan gold right on Main Street. Specializing in golf play and stay packages.

Hosts: Richard and Cora Riddell
Rooms: 20 (17 PB; 3 SB) $55-100
Continental Breakfast
Credit Cards: A, B
Notes: 2, 5, 7, 11, 12, 13

JENNER

Bed & Breakfast California

P.O. Box 2247, Saratoga, 95070
(408) 867-9662; (800) 872-4500
FAX (408) 867-0907; e-mail: info@bbintl.com
www.bbintl.com

A. Enjoy the adventure and romance of Jenner, a quiet, protected village blessed with the warmest weather on the North Coast. Enjoy the warm hospitality and cozy bed and breakfast accommodations in a collection of California- and New England-style cottages throughout the village. The heart of the inn is its lodge parlor where guests gather for breakfast and drop in to enjoy teas and apéritifs by the fire in the afternoons and evenings. $135-185.

JULIAN

Bed & Breakfast California

P.O. Box 2247, Saratoga, 95070
(408) 867-9662; (800) 872-4500
FAX (408) 867-0907; e-mail: info@bbintl.com
www.bbintl.com

This intimate, petite Colonial mansion sits among tree-lined country roads just a few miles from town. Four guest rooms are appointed with antiques, each with private bath. The honeymoon suite is spacious with mountain views, a claw-foot slipper tub, and white canopied bed. Full breakfast served in the dining room or in room upon request. Freshly baked cookies are a terrific tuck-in treat. $105-165.

Julian Gold Rush Hotel

2032 Main Street, P.O. Box 1856, 92036
(760) 765-0201; (800) 734-5854
FAX (760) 765-0327; e-mail: b&b@julianhotel.com

Selected one of *Sunset* magazine's "Best of the West Bed and Breakfast." This historically designated 100-year-old Victorian hotel offers hosted afternoon tea and breakfast served in the original dining room. The patio cottage, located in the garden area and the exclusive honeymoon house both have fireplaces.

Hosts: Steve and Gig Ballinger
Rooms: 15 (PB) $72-175
Full Breakfast
Credit Cards: A, B, C
Notes: 2, 5, 7, 8, 9, 14

Orchard Hill Country Inn

2502 Washington Street, P.O. Box 425, 92036
(760) 765-1700; FAX (760) 765-0290
e-mail: information@orchardhill.com

Award-winning, premiere inn in heart of Julian historic district. Magnificent hilltop vistas, colorful gardens, meadows, lush grounds with hiking trails leading to abandoned gold mines. Oversized deluxe rooms with private porches, patios. Some with dual-sided fireplaces serving both bed and bath. view rooms in lodge with common room reminiscent of America's great national park lodges. Dining room features gourmet menu and impeccable service. The ultimate romantic getaway. AAA four-diamond rated. Dinner available on select nights.

Hosts: Pat and Darrell Struabe
Rooms: 22 (PB) $160-265
Full Breakfast
Credit Cards: A, B, C
Notes: 2, 5, 7, 12, 14, 15

---

7 No smoking; 8 Children welcome; 9 Social drinking allowed; 10 Tennis nearby; 11 Swimming nearby; 12 Golf nearby; 13 Skiing nearby; 14 May be booked through a travel agent; 15 Handicapped accessible.

Kern River Inn

KERNVILLE

Kern River Inn Bed & Breakfast

119 Kern River Drive, P.O. Box 1725, 93238
(760) 376-6750; (800) 986-4382

Charming, classic country riverfront bed and breakfast on the Wild and Scenic Kern River in the southern Sierra Nevada three hours north of Los Angeles. All bedrooms have private baths and feature river views; most have whirlpool tubs or fireplaces. Full breakfast. Walk to shops, restaurants, parks, museum. Short drive to giant sequoias. An all-year vacation area with white-water rafting, fishing, and kayaking; golf, skiing, hiking, and biking; water skiing, boating, wind surfing, and fishing. Senior and business discounts.

Hosts: Jack and Carita
Rooms: 6 (PB) $89-109
Full Breakfast
Credit Cards: A, B, C
Notes: 2, 5, 7, 8, 9, 11, 12, 13, 14, 15

LAGUNA BEACH

Bed & Breakfast California

P.O. Box 2247, Saratoga, 95070
(408) 867-9662; (800) 872-4500
FAX (408) 867-0907; e-mail: info@bbintl.com
www.bbintl.com

A. Romantic Cape Cod-style inn at water's edge is renowned for its hospitality and gourmet breakfasts. A fireplace and Jacuzzi tub and robes are featured in each room as is a view of the ocean, harbor, or hills. Excellent restaurants and shops nearby. $135-350.

B. This New Orleans-style Colonial inn with central courtyard and subtropical plants is two blocks from the beach. It is in the heart of the village and within walking distance to shops and galleries. The six guest rooms have private baths and queen-size beds. Continental plus breakfast. $95-150.

C. Imaginatively decorated rooms with Paradise Island themes are featured in unique bed and breakfast at the ocean. Several rooms have Jacuzzis, fireplaces, and ocean views. Honeymoon suites available. Midweek rates available. Full breakfast. $120-350.

D. Terraced on a hillside amid tropical gardens and flower splashed patios, this inn exudes an ambiance of bygone days when Laguna Beach was developing its reputation as an artists' colony and hideaway for Hollywood film stars. The romantic mission-style architecture set below towering palms framing views of the blue Pacific invites guests to linger, to slow their pace to that of another less hurried era. Decorated in a mixture of early 20th-century and contemporary furnishings. The many beautiful garden areas include the aviary patio beneath a family of magnificent queen palms, the bougainvillaea-splashed courtyard, and the ocean view pool deck with its banana and avocado trees. $105-225.

The Carriage House of Laguna Beach

1322 Catalina Street, 92651
(949) 494-8945

The Carriage House features all private suites with living room, bedroom, bath, and some kitchen facilities. Two-bedroom suites available. All surround a courtyard of plants and flowers, two blocks from the ocean. Close to

---

NOTES: Credit cards accepted: A MasterCard; B Visa; C American Express; D Discover; E Diner's Club; F Other; 2 Personal checks accepted; 3 Lunch available; 4 Dinner available; 5 Open all year; 6 Pets welcome;

The Carriage House

art galleries, restaurants, and shops. Minimum-stay requirements for weekends and holidays. Inquire about accommodations for pets.

Hosts: Lesley and Andy Kettley
Suites: 6 (PB) $95-150
Continental Breakfast
Credit Cards: A, B, C
Notes: 2, 5, 7, 8, 9, 10, 11, 12, 14

LA JOLLA

Bed & Breakfast California

P.O. Box 2247, Saratoga, 95070
(408) 867-9662; (800) 872-4500
FAX (408) 867-0907; e-mail: info@bbintl.com
www.bbintl.com

A. Tastefully decorated contemporary bed and breakfast designed by the architect/host in La Jolla features views of San Diego and beaches from the pool and Jacuzzi. Two guest rooms with private baths and private entrances. No smoking. Full breakfast served. $125.

B. Beautifully decorated bed and breakfast inn with ocean views and attractive gardens offers an elegant, comfortable way to enjoy this seaside paradise. Private bathrooms have queen-size or twin beds and some rooms have a fireplace. Continental plus breakfast and afternoon refreshments served. $85-200.

C. This Mediterranean-style home is set in an exclusive area with a stunning view of the Pacific. Hosts have two rooms with private baths. Hosts are an architect and a retired teacher who also collect modern art. Full breakfast on the terrace by the pool. $125.

The Bed & Breakfast Inn at La Jolla

7753 Draper Avenue, 92037
(858) 456-2066; (800) 582-2466 (reservations only)
www.innlajolla.com

Offering deluxe accommodations in 15 charmingly decorated rooms, one block from the beach in the heart of La Jolla by the Sea, the Bed and Breakfast Inn at La Jolla is listed as Historical Site 179 on the San Diego registry. Fireplaces and ocean views are featured in many rooms. Fresh fruit, sherry, fresh flowers, and terry-cloth robes await in each guest room. Savor a large breakfast in the dining room, on the patio, or in the bedroom. A picnic basket to add the finishing touch to the day is also available. Children 12 and older welcome. Limited handicapped accessibility.

Rooms: 15 (PB) $109-329
Full Breakfast
Credit Cards: A, B, C
Notes: 2, 5, 7, 9, 10, 11, 12, 14

Inn at La Jolla

---

7 No smoking; 8 Children welcome; 9 Social drinking allowed; 10 Tennis nearby; 11 Swimming nearby; 12 Golf nearby; 13 Skiing nearby; 14 May be booked through a travel agent; 15 Handicapped accessible.

Prospect Park Inn

1110 Prospect Street, 92037
(619) 454-0133; (800) 433-1609
FAX (619) 454-2056
www.tales.com/ca/prospectparkinn

Twenty-two-room inn in the heart of La Jolla, one block from the beach. Most rooms offer ocean views. Decor is contemporary with queen-size bed, cable TV, air conditioning, and private bath. Room rates include Continental breakfast and parking. Two beautiful penthouse suites available. Nonsmoking property.

Rooms: 22 (PB) $110-400
Continental Breakfast
Credit Cards: A, B, C, D, E, F
Notes: 5, 7, 8, 9, 10, 11, 12, 14

LAKE ARROWHEAD

Bracken Fern Manor

815 Arrowhead Villas Road, 92352
(909) 337-8557; FAX (909) 337-3323

Relax and enjoy the historic ambiance at this unique bed and breakfast. Restored to its 1929 grandeur with amenities that include art gallery/library, game parlor, wine tasting cellar, garden spa, sauna, patios, and sun decks. Ten guest rooms with private baths include attic suites and a bridal suite with whirlpool tub for two. Healthy and delicious full breakfast. Enjoy an Afternoon Hospitality Social. Perfect setting for intimate weddings/receptions. Angelic children considered. No smoking or pets. Official appointment property three-diamond rated. Member Lake Arrowhead Wedding Association. Certified historic landmark.

Host: Cheryl Weaver
Rooms: 10 (10 PB; 1 SB) $85-222
Full Breakfast
Credit Cards: A, B
Notes: 5, 7, 13

LAKEPORT

Forbestown Inn

825 Forbes Street, 95453
(707) 263-7858; FAX (707) 263-7878
e-mail: forbestowninn@zapcom.net
www.innaccess.com/fti

A charming Civil War-era Victorian farmhouse with four bedrooms and a separate carriage house all furnished with oak antiques. Lovely, secluded garden with pool. Afternoon treats as well as wine and cheese are served daily. Enjoy beautiful Clear Lake for water sports and fishing, and downtown Lakeport for shopping and dining, both within easy walking distance. Many fun local events throughout the year, as well as big name entertainers in concert at nearby Konocti Harbor Resort. Listed in many publications including "North California Best Places." Boating nearby. Children welcome with prior arrangement.

Hosts: Wally and Pat Kelley
Rooms: 5 (3 PB; 2 SB) $85-150
Full Breakfast
Credit Cards: A, B, C, D, E
Notes: 2, 5, 7, 9, 11, 12, 14

LAKE TAHOE

Bed & Breakfast California

P.O. Box 2247, Saratoga, 95070
(408) 867-9662; (800) 872-4500
FAX (408) 867-0907; e-mail: info@bbintl.com
www.bbintl.com

A. Very large sunny charming up-to-date rooms. All rooms are on the second floor. Very private and quiet. One mile from the beach, heavenly ski area, and the Casinos. Also nearby are hiking trails, golf, tennis, bicycling trails, and horseback riding. $125.

B. Built in 1932 by Norman Mayfield, Lake Tahoe's pioneer builder. Newly refinished hardwood floors, wood walls and beams, and a rustic mountain decor throughout. The large living room has an original stone fireplace, baskets hanging from wood beams, comfortable chairs and sofas, and plenty of reading materials. $95-225.

C. This 1934 Old Tahoe-style house with French country decor has private beach privileges, terry-cloth robes, guest refrigerator, dining area, and Continental plus breakfast. Choice of queen- or king-size bed and private or shared baths. Additional accommodations nearby include a guest cottage with a lake view. $95-180.

LA SELVA BEACH

Inn at Manresa Beach

1258 San Andreas Road, 95076
(831) 728-1000; (888) 523-2244

The Inn at Manresa Beach is an 1867 restored replica of Abraham Lincoln's Springfield home, located between Santa Cruz and Carmel on Monterey Bay. Eight elegant rooms and suites include fireplaces, TV, VCR, stereo, two-line telephone, two-person whirlpool tubs, and king- or queen-size adjustable massage beds. The inn has two clay tennis courts, grass volleyball, and croquet. A quarter mile from Manresa Beach, swimming, walking, fishing, surfing, and biking are just outside the door. Wheelchair accessible.

Hosts: Susan Van Horn and Brian Denny
Rooms: 8 (PB) $150-215
Full Breakfast
Credit Cards: A, B, C, D
Notes: 2, 3, 5, 7, 8, 9, 10, 11, 12, 14, 15

LONG BEACH

Bed & Breakfast California

P.O. Box 2247, Saratoga, 95070
(408) 867-9662; (800) 872-4500
FAX (408) 867-0907; e-mail: info@bbintl.com
www.bbintl.com

A. This perfectly restored 1912 Craftsman home has two big guest rooms and one smaller one: perfect for a family. On a quiet residential street, just two blocks from the beach. Antique furnishings are simple and serene. Breakfast is sumptuous on weekends, self-serve during the week. $80.

B. Private retreat in a 1920s California Craftsman home. Enjoy the entire second floor in guests' own private suite. The bedroom adjoins the sitting room and includes the most comfortable king-size bed guests will ever sleep on. The bath is equipped with a glass-enclosed shower as well as a double-size bathtub sunken in marble. If guests must work, there is an office area off the sitting room which features a magnificent wood-burning fireplace. Guests may use an outdoor spa at any time. $95-140.

C. This 1920s California Craftsman, in historic Bluff Park features a very private guest suite that is the entire second story. Amenities include a fireplace, sitting room, balcony, king-size bed, large bath/dressing room, and full breakfast on weekends. A patio and hot tub are available. Hosts can assist with arrangements for a unique gondola cruise through the canals of nearby Naples, tickets to Civic Light Opera, and other events. Convenient for business people weekdays, as suite offers a small office with fax and telephone. $95-140.

Lord Mayor's Inn Bed & Breakfast

435 Cedar Avenue, 90802
(562) 436-0324 (phone/FAX)
e-mail: innkeepers@lordmayors.com
www.lordmayors.com

This elegantly restored 1904 home of the first mayor of Long Beach invites guests to enjoy the ambiance of years gone by. Recipient of awards in 1991 for restoration and beautification. The inn's rooms have ten-foot ceilings and are all tastefully decorated with period antiques. Each unique bedroom has a private

---

7 No smoking; 8 Children welcome; 9 Social drinking allowed; 10 Tennis nearby; 11 Swimming nearby; 12 Golf nearby; 13 Skiing nearby; 14 May be booked through a travel agent; 15 Handicapped accessible.

bath and access to a large sun deck. A full breakfast is prepared by the hosts and served in the dining room or on the deck overlooking the garden area. Convenient to beaches, the convention center, civic center, and theaters.

Rooms: 11 (PB) $85-125
Full Breakfast
Credit Cards: A, B, C, E
Notes: 2, 5, 7, 8, 9, 10, 11, 12, 14

LOS ANGELES

Bed & Breakfast California

P.O. Box 2247, Saratoga, 95070
(408) 867-9662; (800) 872-4500
FAX (408) 867-0907; e-mail: info@bbintl.com
www.bbintl.com

1. This 1930s custom home is on manicured grounds in prestigious Hancock Park. Elegant guest suite has sitting area, king-size bed, and huge original tile bath. Full breakfast in the formal dining room on weekends; Continental on weekdays. Very, very beautiful architecture. $85.

2. This stunning California Spanish mansion is on a residential street one block from Sunset Boulevard and has four guest rooms, two with private bath and two sharing a bath. Telephones and TVs available. Amenities include terraced garden, gazebo, hot tub, and gated parking. The host is a gourmet chef and can provide meals in addition to the full breakfast upon arrangement. $75-85.

3. Just a few minutes from the airport, this condo is shared with the interior decorator hostess. The bedroom has a private bath and is appointed with bent-willow furniture and country charm. The hostess can pick up guests at the airport and help with other arrangements. Full breakfast. $65.

4. This elegant mansion was built when Los Angeles still had rolling hills and UCLA was a budding university. Just a block from Wilshire Boulevard and a mile from the campus, two bedrooms are impeccably decorated, including the original hand-painted bathroom tile. Full breakfast in the dining room or in the country garden. $95.

5. A 1927 completely restored Spanish-style building with European interior. This 3,000-square-foot home is on the second floor. The dining room opens onto a small patio on one side and a large gourmet kitchen on the other side. Guest room has a king-size bed which converts to twins and a private bath; second room with king-size bed sometimes available as well. Very high quality. Close to Century City, downtown, Beverly Hills. Fifteen minutes to the ocean. $85.

6. Close to the USC campus, this 1910 Craftsman historic registry home has two upstairs guest rooms, with a bath between them. There's a shaded porch in front, a sunny deck in the rear, and a small sun porch off one guest room. Close to the freeways and Music Center, and very close to the convention center. $50-60.

7. Enjoy 360-degree views from the multilevel deck/patio of this spacious hillside house. The Western Room can accommodate a family of four; the other comes with sunken double tub. Start the day with a full gourmet breakfast and then enjoy the attractions of Los Angeles, Pasadena, and the San Gabriel Mountains. $75-95.

8. Third-floor penthouse with high ceilings and spacious rooms in a secure building in a safe area. Ideally located on a quiet tree-lined street within walking distance of UCLA and Westwood Village, and close to the freeways, Beverly Hills, and beaches. Tastefully furnished in high quality pieces, a grand piano, and decorator touches. The guest rooms all have private baths. Breakfast is served in the main dining area. $100.

NOTES: Credit cards accepted: A MasterCard; B Visa; C American Express; D Discover; E Diner's Club; F Other; 2 Personal checks accepted; 3 Lunch available; 4 Dinner available; 5 Open all year; 6 Pets welcome;

9. At the foot of the Hollywood Hills near West Hollywood restaurants and attractions, this Mediterranean-style house with a music room, interesting artifacts, and antiques offers four guest rooms with queen-size, double, or twin beds and private or shared baths. Amenities include a full breakfast, patio areas, hot tub, and off-street parking. Good public transportation is available. No smoking. $75-85.

10. Beautifully restored Craftsman-style house in the National Register of Historic Places is close to USC and civic and convention centers. Two comfortable guest rooms, lovely gardens, and patio are available for guests to enjoy. Shared and private baths. No smoking. $65.

11. Spacious apartment, on the border of Westwood and Century City, offers convenience and homey comfort. Just minutes from the Getty Museum, Santa Monica, and Beverly Hills. Well-traveled host makes a wonderful concierge. Continental breakfast. $70-80.

California Home Hospitality

P.O. Box 661804, 90066
(310) 390-1526 (phone/FAX)
e-mail: htop2@aol.com

This hilltop home enjoys a spectacular view of the Santa Monica Mountains and the entire northern portion of the city, including Beverly Hills, Westwood, and Century City. The city lights in the evening are lovely. Guests are just 15 minutes from the beach at Santa Monica and adjacent to Marina del Rey Yacht Harbor and Santa Monica Municipal Airport. Hostess stresses comfort, cleanliness, secure surroundings, and lots of TLC! For enthusiastic sightseers, a rental car is suggested, although public transportation is within easy walking distance.

Room: 1 (PB) $60
Full Breakfast
Credit Cards: None
Notes: 5, 7, 9, 10, 11, 12, 14

Inn at Playa del Rey

435 Culver Boulevard, Playa del Rey, 90293
(310) 574-1920; FAX (310) 574-9920
e-mail: playainn@aol.com

The Inn at Playa del Rey is close to the beach and overlooks both the main channel of Marina del Rey and a 200-acre bird sanctuary. The inn was the only California bed and breakfast inn featured on America Online's "Inn of the Week." All 21 rooms are just as refreshing as the views, with distinctive decor. Rooms facing the wetlands have fireplaces, decks, marina sailboat views, and whirlpool tubs. Two "romance suites" feature a fireplace in the bathroom next to a bubbling oversized whirlpool tub for two. Recently pictured in *Country Inns* as an "Urban Oasis." The village of Playa del Rey offers a variety of restaurants and shops and is just five minutes from Los Angeles International Airport.

Hosts: Lauren Cresto and Donna Donnelly
Rooms: 21 (PB) $130-285
Full Breakfast
Credit Cards: A, B, C, F
Notes: 2, 3, 5, 8, 9, 10, 11, 12, 13, 14, 15

The Woodbine

11471 Woodbine Street, 90066
(310) 398-9695 (phone/FAX)

Three large rooms—one with private bath, two with shared baths. Fireplaces in dining and sitting rooms. Beautifully landscaped gardens with stream, waterfall, and fish ponds; sunning, barbecue facilities. Adjacent to park with tennis, soccer, and softball fields, and seasonal pool. Continental breakfast, afternoon wine and cheese. Near Century City, Beverly Hills, Santa Monica, and Marina del Rey with shopping, movies, theaters, and beaches. Walk to public transportation. Car desirable.

Host: Carole Gentile
Rooms: 3 (1 PB; 2 SB) $65-80
Continental Breakfast
Credit Cards: None
Notes: 5, 7, 10, 11, 12

---

7 No smoking; 8 Children welcome; 9 Social drinking allowed; 10 Tennis nearby; 11 Swimming nearby; 12 Golf nearby; 13 Skiing nearby; 14 May be booked through a travel agent; 15 Handicapped accessible.

Kristalberg

LUCERNE

Kristalberg Bed & Breakfast

P.O. Box 1629, 95458
(707) 274-8009

Tranquil country inn, incredible view of clear lake; deluxe room, in Early American decor, has Jacuzzi tub, Victorian dining room, elegant Italian parlor. Full breakfast, congenial host speaks German, French, and Spanish. Discount on extended stays.

Hosts: Merv Myers (since 1988)
Rooms: 3 (2 PB) $60-150
Full Breakfast
Credit Cards: A, B, C, D
Notes: 2, 5, 7, 11, 12, 14

MALIBU

Bed & Breakfast California

P.O. Box 2247, Saratoga, 95070
(408) 867-9662; (800) 872-4500
FAX (408) 867-0907; e-mail: info@bbintl.com
www.bbintl.com

A. Nestled in the Santa Monica Mountains with a beautiful view of Malibu Canyon, this spacious ranch-style home is just five miles from Malibu Beach. With access to local hiking trails as well, this is a perfect location for guests who love the out-of-doors. The guest room is furnished in antiques and offers a king-size bed and a large wood-burning fireplace. $85.

B. This spectacular home sits at the top of a bluff overlooking the Malibu coastline. Built in 1995 by renowned architects Charles and Steve Kanner, the home is artfully furnished in contemporary style and offers a 180-degree view of the ocean. Guests are welcome to enjoy the quiet and beautiful garden, pool, and deck areas. One guest room offers a spacious sitting area and private bath with Jacuzzi tub, and the other has a private bath. Both rooms offer wonderful ocean and mountain views and have private entrances. For fitness buffs, there is also a treadmill and stationary bicycle available. $95-150.

Casa Larronde

Box 86, 90265
(213) 456-9333

This is the area of the "famous," so the locals call this beach "Millionaires Row." The Ocean Suite has 40 feet of windows adjoining its deck. Features include TV, telephone, fireplace, kitchenette, ceiling fan over a king-size bed, floor-to-ceiling three-way mirrors in the dressing room, and a large bathroom with twin basins. Cocktails are offered in the evening, and a full American breakfast is served leisurely in the morning. Closed July through mid-October. Inquire about arrangements for children.

Host: Charlou Larronde
Rooms: 2 (PB) $115-150
Full Breakfast
Credit Cards: None
Notes: 2, 7, 9, 10, 11, 12, 15

MAMMOTH LAKES

Absolutely Accommodations

P.O. Box 641471, San Francisco, 94164-1471
(415) 677-9789; (888) 982-2632
e-mail: travelinfo@iname.com
www.citysearch.com/sfo/accommodations

This is a free reservation service committed to assisting travelers in finding the best possible

---

NOTES: Credit cards accepted: A MasterCard; B Visa; C American Express; D Discover; E Diner's Club; F Other; 2 Personal checks accepted; 3 Lunch available; 4 Dinner available; 5 Open all year; 6 Pets welcome;

accommodations in California. It offers access to private homestay bed and breakfasts and inns. It can help guests find the proper accommodations that meet their individual needs. The service's goal is to provide both its clients and hosts with the best possible customer service.

Mammoth 101. A perfect location for visiting Mammoth Lakes. Walk to shops and restaurants. All individually decorated rooms with antiques, quilts, and private baths. Some have fireplaces and kitchens. $63-98.

Snow Goose Inn Bed & Breakfast

57 Forest Trail, P.O. Box 387, 93546
(760) 934-2660; (800) 874-7368
e-mail: snowgoose@9net.com
www.snowgoose-inn.com

This traditional-style bed and breakfast inn has been in business since 1980. The inn has 15 guest rooms, some with kitchenettes, and four townhouse suites. There is an outdoor Jacuzzi and some guest rooms have whirlpool bathtubs. The full breakfast includes cold cereal, hot cereal, fruit tray, toast and jam, fresh-baked banana breads or cinnamon rolls or coffee cakes, and main dishes that include quiche, banana pecan pancakes, stuffed French toast, Snowgoose eggs Benedict, etc. "At the Snow Goose you are once a guest always a friend."

Rooms: 19 (PB) $68-168
Full Breakfast
Credit Cards: A, B, C, D
Notes: 2, 3, 5, 7, 8, 9, 10, 11, 12, 13, 14

MANHATTAN BEACH

Bed & Breakfast California

P.O. Box 2247, Saratoga, 95070
(408) 867-9662; (800) 872-4500
FAX (408) 867-0907; e-mail: info@bbintl.com
www.bbintl.com

On a hilly, tree-lined street only one mile from the beach, this bright and airy southwestern-style home was built in 1989 and is decorated in a mix of antique and contemporary motifs. The guest room is on the second floor and is furnished with antiques. Guest has entire second floor. There is a private deck directly off of the guest room as well as a common courtyard with a fountain and outdoor fireplace for relaxing. A rustic walking/jogging trail is within walking distance, and also nearby is the quaint downtown area with many shops and restaurants. The local beach is one of the prettiest in California. $95.

MARINA DEL REY (VENICE BEACH)

Bed & Breakfast California

P.O. Box 2247, Saratoga, 95070
(408) 867-9662; (800) 872-4500
FAX (408) 867-0907; e-mail: info@bbintl.com
www.bbintl.com

A. Ocean and mountain views are spectacular from contemporary Malibu bed and breakfast with interesting art work. Very large guest suite has private entrance and Jacuzzi tub. Continental plus breakfast. $95-150.

B. All 43 rooms feature a lovely French-country decor, stocked refreshment centers, TV with AM/FM clock radio, luxury amenities, and hair dryers in vanity area. Also, the inn is just a few blocks to the Venice beach strand, Muscle Beach, and the marina, and a 10-minute drive to LAX. Only a 50-minute drive to Disneyland and Knott's Berry Farm. Unique shops and eclectic restaurants are within easy walking distance. $99-120.

C. One block from the Marina del Rey Harbor, this two-story home was designed and built in 1989 by the host. The spacious and sunny suite has a queen-size bed, sitting area, kitchenette, dining area, and private bath. There is a rooftop deck for enjoying the sun, as well as a private entrance. Walk to Fisherman's Village or Restaurant Row, or explore the area on skates or bicycles...the 40-mile bike path between

---

7 No smoking; 8 Children welcome; 9 Social drinking allowed; 10 Tennis nearby; 11 Swimming nearby;
12 Golf nearby; 13 Skiing nearby; 14 May be booked through a travel agent; 15 Handicapped accessible.

Santa Monica and Long Beach passes by right across the street. Motorcoach tours to points of interest in the greater LA area are available from hotels within walking distance. $80-90.

Inn at Venice Beach

327 Washington Boulevard, 90291
(310) 821-2557; (800) 828-0688 (reservations)
FAX (310) 827-0289; www.innatvenicebeach.com

A charming European-style hotel just two blocks from Venice Beach. The hotel has queen-size and twin-bed standard rooms and five bi-level loft suites. All rooms have air conditioning, refrigerators, irons and ironing boards, hair dryers in the vanity areas, full baths and showers, telephones, TVs, and in-room movies each night. All rooms have been completely renovated and are decorated in an upbeat, cheerful, fun beach decor. A very generous Continental plus breakfast is included each morning in the café in the cobblestone courtyard. Nonsmoking rooms available. Four rooms handicapped accessible.

Rooms: 43 (PB) $69-139
Continental Breakfast
Credit Cards: A, B, C, D, E
Notes: 5, 8, 11, 14

MARIPOSA

Bed & Breakfast California

P.O. Box 2247, Saratoga, 95070
(408) 867-9662; (800) 872-4500
FAX (408) 867-0907; e-mail: info@bbintl.com
www.bbintl.com

A. Contemporary bed and breakfast on an old stagecoach route, hosted by long-time residents, is on four acres and offers gold panning and hiking on the inn's property. Three guest rooms have private baths. Mini-refrigerator, TV, VCR, and many other amenities are available. The inn is near museums, wineries, and Yosemite National Park. Handicapped accessible. Continental breakfast is served. $90-115.

B. European chalet-style home with floor to ceiling windows in living and dining areas looking out towards the scenic splendor of the Sierra foothills, gateway to Yosemite National Park. Three guest rooms are comfortable and cozy, tastefully decorated and have quality beds, private baths, and lovely views. Guests can also enjoy the relaxing hot tub under a romantic gazebo. $85.

MENDOCINO

Bed & Breakfast California

P.O. Box 2247, Saratoga, 95070
(408) 867-9662; (800) 872-4500
FAX (408) 867-0907; e-mail: info@bbintl.com
www.bbintl.com

A. These 1882 Victorian inn and garden cottages are furnished with Persian rugs and Tiffany lamps and offer a true bed and breakfast experience. Adjacent barn has contemporary accommodations. Several rooms have a fireplace, others a wood-burning stove. $100-190.

B. Offering views of the ocean and the country, this classic little bed and breakfast inn is run by devoted owner-occupants who take satisfaction in making a stay memorable. There are four bedrooms, all with private baths, two with ocean views. In the little town of Fort Bragg, near Mendocino. Try whale watching from December through March, or charter a boat at Noyo Harbor. Hiking, beachcombing, riding, canoeing, cycling, or just relaxing to the sound of the ocean. Full breakfast. $99-169.

c.o. Packard House Bed & Breakfast

45170 Little Lake Street, P.O. Box 1065, 95460
(707) 937-2677; (888) 453-2677
FAX (707) 937-1323

One of four landmark homes on "Executive Row" in the historic town of Mendocino. This Carpenter Gothic was built in 1878 for the

---

NOTES: Credit cards accepted: A MasterCard; B Visa; C American Express; D Discover; E Diner's Club; F Other; 2 Personal checks accepted; 3 Lunch available; 4 Dinner available; 5 Open all year; 6 Pets welcome;

town's chemist. It has undergone a complete renovation and reopened in October 1998. All of the rooms, elegantly and professionally decorated, either have king- or queen-size beds, fireplaces, luxurious baths with jet tubs and separate showers, some ocean views, telephones, TV/VCR, and full gourmet breakfasts, wine and hors d'oeuvres in the afternoon. "Come and be pampered!"

Hosts: Maria and Dan Levin
Rooms: 5 (PB) $105-210
Full Breakfast
Credit Cards: A, B, D
Notes: 2, 7, 9, 10, 11, 12, 14

Joshua Grindle Inn

44800 Little Lake Road, P.O. Box 647, 95460
(707) 937-4143; (800) GRINDLE
e-mail: stay@joshgrin.com
www.joshgrin.com

On two acres in a historic village overlooking the ocean, the Joshua Grindle Inn is a short walk to the beach, art center, shops, and fine restaurants. Stay in the lovely two-story Victorian farmhouse, a New England-style cottage, or a three-story water tower. Six rooms have fireplaces; all have private baths, antiques, and comfortable reading areas. Enjoy a full breakfast served around a 10-foot 1830s harvest table. Off-street parking.

Hosts: Jim and Arlene Moorehead
Rooms: 10 (PB) $100-205
Full Breakfast
Credit Cards: A, B
Notes: 2, 5, 7, 9, 10, 12, 14

John Dougherty House

571 Ukiah Street, P.O. Box 817, 95460
(707) 937-5266

Historic John Dougherty House was built in 1867 and is one of the oldest houses in Mendocino. On land bordered by Ukiah and Albion Streets, the inn has some of the best ocean and bay views in the historic village; steps away from great restaurants and shopping, but years removed from 20th-century reality. The main house is furnished with period country antiques taking guests back to 1867. Enjoy quiet, peaceful nights seldom experienced in today's urban living.

Hosts: David and Marion Wells
Rooms: 8 (PB) $95-205
Full Breakfast
Credit Cards: A, B, D
Notes: 2, 5, 7, 9, 10, 11, 12, 14

John Dougherty House

---

7 No smoking; 8 Children welcome; 9 Social drinking allowed; 10 Tennis nearby; 11 Swimming nearby; 12 Golf nearby; 13 Skiing nearby; 14 May be booked through a travel agent; 15 Handicapped accessible.

MacCallum House Inn

MacCallum House Inn

P.O. Box 206, 95460
(800) 609-0492; www.maccallumhouse.com

In 1882 William Kelley built the MacCallum House in the heart of historic Mendocino Village as a wedding present for daughter Daisy, the town belle. Guests enjoy delightful rooms, richly appointed with sleigh beds, cherry wardrobes and claw-foot tubs for two in the main house, as well as unique accommodations in the Carriage House, Water Tower, Greenhouse, or Barn, offering amenities including fireplaces and ocean and garden view balconies. Superb fine dining on premises.

Rooms: 19 (PB) $100-190
Continental Breakfast
Credit Cards: A, B, D
Notes: 2, 4, 5, 7, 8, 9, 10, 11, 12, 14, 15

McElroy's Inn

P.O. Box 1881, 95460
(707) 937-1734; (888) 262-3576
www.mcn.org/r/mcelroy

McElroy's Inn is in the beautiful and historic village of Mendocino and faces the spectacular Mendocino coastline. There are trails to the cliffs overlooking the ocean and paths leading to the beach. Within easy walking distance to restaurants, bakeries, historical museums, and galleries. This intimate inn offers pleasant rooms and suites; all with private baths, at affordable prices.

Hosts: Bonnie Novakov Lawlor and Larry Lawlor
Rooms: 4 (PB) $70-110
Credit Cards: A, B
Notes: 2, 5, 7, 8, 9, 10, 11, 12, 14

Mendocino Village Inn

44860 Main Street, P.O. Box 626, 95460
(707) 937-0246; (800) 882-7029

The inn was built for the first physician and his family in 1882. In the heart of the historic district, the building was lovingly restored in the early 1980s and is filled with antiques and some contemporary pieces. The three-story watertower was built in 1992. The house is surrounded by lush gardens. There is a frog pond with waterfall in the southeast portion of the garden. The town is within an easy walk. A full two-course breakfast is served 8:30-10:30 A.M. (9:00-10:00 A.M. winter hours). Guests may help themselves to afternoon tea in the parlor from 4:00 P.M. Evening refreshments in the common room are served 5:00-7:00 P.M. (5:00-6:00 P.M. winter hours).

Rooms: 10 (8 PB; 2 SB) $75-175
Full Breakfast
Credit Cards: None
Notes: 2, 5, 7, 9, 15

Mendocino Village Inn

NOTES: Credit cards accepted: A MasterCard; B Visa; C American Express; D Discover; E Diner's Club; F Other; 2 Personal checks accepted; 3 Lunch available; 4 Dinner available; 5 Open all year; 6 Pets welcome;

Sea Rock Bed & Breakfast Inn

11101 Lansing Street, P.O. Box 906, 95460
(707) 937-0926; (800) 906-0926 (reservations)

Country cottages on a hillside overlooking the ocean—spectacular white-water ocean views. All units have fireplaces, cable TV, and VCRs. Feather beds in many rooms and all rooms furnished with fine linens, down comforters, and pillows. The cozy cottages are surrounded by cypress trees, beautifully landscaped gardens, and spacious lawns. Continental plus breakfast.

Hosts: Susie and Andy Plocher
Rooms: 14 (PB) $89-259
Continental Breakfast
Credit Cards: A, B, C, D, E
Notes: 2, 5, 7, 8, 10, 12, 15

MILL VALLEY

Bed & Breakfast Exchange of Marin County—Referral Service

45 Entrata, San Anselmo, 94960
(415) 485-1971; FAX (415) 454-7179

Cottage Bed and Breakfast. Private cottage in the redwoods. Full kitchen and fireplace. Garden view. Walk to town. Great value. Suitable for short or longer stays. No smoking. $110 per night.

Mill Valley Village Studio. Private guest suite with king- or twin-size beds. Extra bed for families traveling with children. Private entrance. Walk to lovely old-fashioned village of Mill Valley. Refrigerator and small kitchen. $95.

Mountain Home Inn

810 Panoramic Highway, 94941
(415) 381-9000

A romantic country inn high atop Mount Tamalpais, offering spectacular views of the Marin Hills and San Francisco Bay. Ten guest rooms, some offering Jacuzzi baths, private decks, and fireplaces. Just outside the front door is Mount Tamalpais State Park, offering miles of hiking trails. Muir Woods National Monument, Muir Beach, and Stinson Beach are a short drive away, with downtown San Francisco only 45 minutes away. Restaurant on premises. Smoking permitted in designated areas only.

Rooms: 10 (PB) $139-249
Full Breakfast
Credit Cards: A, B, C
Notes: 2, 3, 4, 5, 8, 9, 10, 11, 12, 14, 15

MILL VALLEY (MARIN COUNTY)

Bed & Breakfast San Francisco

P.O. Box 420009, San Francisco, 94142
(415) 931-3083; FAX (415) 921-BBSF (2273)
e-mail: bbsf@linex.com; www.bbsf.com

Tree Top Bed and Breakfast. The charming town of Mill Valley, nestled beneath Mount Tamalpais in Marin County, is the location of this bed and breakfast. The three guest rooms designed by the hostess, an interior designer, offer all the amenities such as private baths, private decks, TVs, a large living room with fireplace, and a full breakfast. $125-250.

MODESTO

Vineyard View

2837 Michigan Avenue, 95358
(209) 523-9009

Rambling split-level home in the country a few miles from downtown overlooking vineyard and almond orchards. Three guest rooms with private or shared baths. Swimming pool. Quiet location away from traffic, subject only to bird songs and, in season, crickets, frogs, etc. Within commute distance of Sacramento, San Francisco, and Yosemite. Full breakfast, when guests want it served, by friendly elderly hosts.

Hosts: Bob and Martha Garvin
Rooms: 3 (PB) $70-85
Full Breakfast
Credit Cards: A, B, D
Notes: 2, 5, 6, 7, 8, 9, 11, 12, 15

---

7 No smoking; 8 Children welcome; 9 Social drinking allowed; 10 Tennis nearby; 11 Swimming nearby; 12 Golf nearby; 13 Skiing nearby; 14 May be booked through a travel agent; 15 Handicapped accessible.

MONTEREY (CARMEL)

Bed & Breakfast San Francisco

P.O. Box 420009, San Francisco, 94142
(415) 931-3083; FAX (415) 921-BBSF (2273)
e-mail: bbsf@linex.com; www.bbsf.com

Barlockers Rustling Oaks Ranch. Stay on a beautiful horse ranch in the picturesque Salinas Valley, a 25-minute ride east of Monterey. The hostess offers her three guest rooms, each with private bath, and a big country breakfast each morning. The views and surrounding area are beautiful. The ranch has chickens, dogs, cats, pigs, goats, and lots of horses. Horseback riding is available. This is a wonderful place for a family. There is even a pool for summertime use. $90-150.

The Jabberwock

598 Laine Street, 93940
(831) 372-4777; (888) 428-7253
FAX (831) 655-2946

Alice's Wonderland just four blocks above Cannery Row and Monterey Bay Aquarium. The Jabberwock has one-half acre of lush gardens, a waterfall, and overlooks the bay. Each room has down pillows and comforters. Hors d'oeuvres at 5:00 P.M. and cookies and milk at bedtime.

Hosts: Joan and John Kiliany
Rooms: 7 (5 PB; 2 SB)
Full Breakfast
Credit Cards: A, B
Notes: 2, 5, 7, 9, 10, 11, 12

MORAGA

Hallman Bed & Breakfast

309 Constance Place, 94556
(925) 376-4318

Bed and breakfast on a quiet cul-de-sac in the beautiful Moraga Valley. Bed down in one of the tastefully appointed rooms. Awake refreshed with breakfast in the comfortable dining room. Take off and "do" San Francisco or any other Bay Area attractions. There are two guest rooms with queen-size beds and shared bath available. Both rooms are used only when guests are in the same party.

Host: Virginia Hallman
Rooms: 2 (SB) $60
Full Breakfast
Credit Cards: None
Notes: 2, 5, 7, 9, 11

MORRO BAY

Bed & Breakfast California

P.O. Box 2247, Saratoga, 95070
(408) 867-9662; (800) 872-4500
FAX (408) 867-0907; e-mail: info@bbintl.com
www.bbintl.com

On Morro Bay on the scenic California coastline just 10 miles northwest of San Luis Obispo, close to Hearst Castle, Montana de Oro State Park, Morro Bay Bird Sanctuary, and the great wineries of Templeton and Paso Robles. The inn is nestled in a tranquil neighborhood overlooking the beautiful Morro "back" Bay. $80-160.

MOSS BEACH

Seal Cove Inn

221 Cypress Avenue, 94038
(415) 728-4114; FAX (415) 728-4116
e-mail: sealcove@coastside.net

Set among wildflowers, Seal Cove Inn looks out to the ocean over acres of parkland. Paths lead to secluded beaches, tidal pools, and windswept ocean bluffs. The inn is decorated with antiques and each guest room has private bath, wood-burning fireplace, and views of park and ocean. This four-star and four-diamond inn is set in the quiet coastal town of Moss Beach, just 30 minutes south of San Francisco.

NOTES: Credit cards accepted: A MasterCard; B Visa; C American Express; D Discover; E Diner's Club; F Other; 2 Personal checks accepted; 3 Lunch available; 4 Dinner available; 5 Open all year; 6 Pets welcome;

Seal Cove Inn

Hosts: Karen Brown and Rick Herbert
Rooms: 10 (PB) $190-270
Full Breakfast
Credit Cards: A, B, C, D
Notes: 2, 5, 7, 8, 12, 14, 15

MOUNT SHASTA

Bed & Breakfast California

P.O. Box 2247, Saratoga, 95070
(408) 867-9662; (800) 872-4500
FAX (408) 867-0907; e-mail: info@bbintl.com
www.bbintl.com

This 1923 two-story ranch house is near fishing, hiking, boating, and skiing areas. Full breakfast and afternoon refreshments served. Hot tub. Nine guest rooms with queen-size and twin beds and private and shared baths. No smoking. $60-95.

Mount Shasta Ranch

1008 W. A. Barr Road, 96067
(530) 926-3870; e-mail: alpinere@snowcrest.net

This northern California historic two-story ranch house offers affordable elegance. There are four spacious guest rooms in the main house, each with private bath. Carriage house accommodations include five rooms. Two-bedroom vacation cottage available year-round. Guests are invited to enjoy the rec room with Ping-Pong, pool table, and piano. Relax in the hot-spring spa. Close to lake, town, and ski slopes. Full country-style breakfasts each morning.

Hosts: Bill and Mary Larsen
Rooms: 9 (4 PB; 5 SB) $55-95
Cottage: 1
Full Breakfast
Credit Cards: A, B, C, D
Notes: 2, 5, 6, 7, 8, 9, 10, 11, 12, 13, 14

MUIR BEACH

Bed & Breakfast California

P.O. Box 2247, Saratoga, 95070
(408) 867-9662; (800) 872-4500
FAX (408) 867-0907; e-mail: info@bbintl.com
www.bbintl.com

Architecturally interesting contemporary home with panoramic views of the Pacific Ocean. On Muir Overlook, a bluff overlooking Muir Beach and near Muir Woods. Just over the hill from charming Sausalito and the Golden Gate Bridge. Stinson Beach is nearby in the other direction. The guest unit is on the second floor and has a private entrance. The guest suite is a spacious, light room with a fireplace and a spectacular view of the ocean. $125.

Bed & Breakfast Exchange of Marin County—Referral Service

45 Entrata, San Anselmo, 94960
(415) 485-1971; FAX (415) 454-7179

See the ocean from the bedroom. This carefully crafted cottage is totally surrounded by the Golden Gate National Recreation Area. Private entrance. Includes separate Japanese tatami meditation room. Loll in front of the fire in the large hammock and see the rolling hills across the valley and the whitecaps of the surf. Walk to dinner at an English inn. Twenty minutes from the Golden Gate Bridge. $165.

The Butterfly Tree

P.O. Box 790, Sausalito, 94966
(415) 383-8447

Guests are staying at the home of Karla Andersdatter, local poet, novelist, author, and

---

7 No smoking; 8 Children welcome; 9 Social drinking allowed; 10 Tennis nearby; 11 Swimming nearby; 12 Golf nearby; 13 Skiing nearby; 14 May be booked through a travel agent; 15 Handicapped accessible.

artist. Walking distance to the beach, ocean views, surrounded by the Golden Gate National Recreation Area, and Muir Woods. The monarch butterflies return here each year. This is a secluded, fragile environment, a perfect hideaway for lovers, friends, and "time out!" Only 30 minutes from San Francisco, 15 minutes to Sausalito shopping, an hour to Sonoma wineries. Enjoy a coastal paradise.

Host: Karla Andersdatter
Rooms: 1 (PB) $150
Full Breakfast
Credit Cards: None
Notes: 2, 5, 7, 11, 14

NAPA

Absolutely Accommodations

P.O. Box 641471, San Francisco, 94164-1471
(415) 677-9789; (888) 982-2632
e-mail: travelinfo@iname.com
www.citysearch.com/sfo/accommodations

This is a free reservation service committed to assisting travelers in finding the best possible accommodations in California. It offers access to private homestay bed and breakfasts and inns. It can help guests find the proper accommodations that meet their individual needs. The service's goal is to provide both its clients and hosts with the best possible customer service.

Napa 111. This 1889 three-story grand mansion stands on an acre of well-cared-for lawns and rose gardens. Each of the 11 rooms feature luxurious private baths. Full breakfast. $115-189.

Napa 112. This elegant 1886 Queen Anne mansion is in walking distance to the historic district of Napa. It has been lovingly restored and offers guests a blend of romance and Victorian elegance. Relax in one of the parlors or by the pool and outdoor spa. Fourteen rooms. $159-289.

Napa 113. This luxury inn is just north of Napa where the vineyards begin. Twenty rooms are individually decorated with quality antiques, fine designer linens, some with working fireplaces, patios, or verandas. Relax by the pool and spa. Charming and convenient to all the splendors of the valley, this inn is the best choice for the discriminating traveler. Full breakfast. $165-235.

Napa 114. Start the day with a gourmet breakfast served in an elegant candlelit dining room. This landmark Queen Anne-style inn is one of the finest examples of Victorian architecture in Napa. Elegantly appointed accommodations, including a magnificent collection of fine period antiques, oriental carpets, and beautiful stained-glass windows. Within walking distance of Old Town Napa and a variety of restaurants and shops. Excellent location to explore the wine country.

Beazley House

1910 First Street, 94559
(800) 559-1649; FAX (707) 257-1518
e-mail: innkeeper@beazleyhouse.com

Guests sense the hospitality as they stroll the walk past verdant lawns and bright flowers. The landmark 1902 mansion is a chocolate brown masterpiece. Visitors feel instantly wel-

Beazley House

NOTES: Credit cards accepted: A MasterCard; B Visa; C American Express; D Discover; E Diner's Club; F Other; 2 Personal checks accepted; 3 Lunch available; 4 Dinner available; 5 Open all year; 6 Pets welcome;

come as they are greeted by a smiling innkeeper. The view from each room reveals beautiful gardens. All rooms have a private bath; some have a private spa and a fireplace. Napa's first bed and breakfast and still its best!

Hosts: Carol and Jim Beazley
Rooms: 11 (PB) $115-225
Full Breakfast
Credit Cards: A, B, C
Notes: 2, 5, 7, 8, 9, 10, 11, 12, 14, 15

Bed & Breakfast California

P.O. Box 2247, Saratoga, 95070
(408) 867-9662; (800) 872-4500
FAX (408) 867-0907; e-mail: info@bbintl.com
www.bbintl.com

A. Experience the stately elegance of this historic landmark taking guests back to 1879. Four large elegantly decorated bedroom suites with private baths offer guests comfort in a classic ambiance. Fine European antiques and authentic chandeliers. This is wine country at its finest. A full breakfast is served in the formal dining room with handcrafted ornate ceilings. Complimentary wine and hors d'oeuvres in the early evening. Call for rates.

B. The inn sits in half an acre of lawns and gardens. Guests will see why it has been a Napa landmark sine 1902 as they walk past verdant lawns and bright flowers. Guests will feel at once welcome as the huge stained-glass door opens and a smiling innkeeper greets them. The guest rooms are large and individually decorated with beautiful antiques. $115-250.

C. One hour drive from both San Francisco and Sacramento, an ideal base from which to explore both Napa and Sonoma Valleys. Hiking, horseback riding, gliding, and mud baths are all available in addition to the local wineries. This eight-room inn welcomes guests with a carafe of local wine and features tea time delights and early evening appetizers. Enjoy the outdoor Jacuzzi at day's end. $160-275.

D. Built in 1929, the inn is a lovely English Tudor on a serene one-acre, park-like setting. The elegant living room features high contoured ceilings and a fireplace for guests' evening relaxation. A delicious full breakfast served in the dining area at individual tables by canlelight, and there is a friendly social hour in the late afternoon. Enjoy the view of the garden through French doors or watch TV by the soapstone woodstove. $125-260.

E. Bed and breakfast in the heart of wine country is offered in the 1889 mansion that has been designated a national historic landmark. The nine guest rooms are individually decorated and have private baths. Enjoy a Continental plus breakfast, and relax on the veranda with evening refreshments. No smoking. $125-195.

Blue Violet Mansion

443 Brown Street, 94559-3348
(800) 959-2583; FAX (707) 257-8205

This 1886 Victorian mansion, in the National Register of Historic Places, was awarded the 1996 gold award for Best Bed and Breakfast in North America. Rooms with spas. Balconies, fireplaces, antique furnishings, and oriental carpets. Deluxe Camelot-theme floor; faux- and mural-painted stained glass. Hot beverages bar, ice, wine, and snacks available. Fountains. Enjoy the heated swimming pool and spa. Picnic baskets available. In-room candlelight dinner and massage services. Complimentary afternoon teas, cookies, and hot beverage service. Evening enjoy mulit-course fine dining in Violette's. In historic Old Town near shops, the Napa Valley Wine Train, hot-air balloons, and wine tastings.

Hosts: Bob and Kathy Morris
Rooms: 17 (PB) $169-339
Suites: 3
Full Breakfast
Credit Cards: A, B, C, D, E
Notes: 2, 3, 4, 5, 7, 8, 9, 10, 11, 12, 14, 15

---

7 No smoking; 8 Children welcome; 9 Social drinking allowed; 10 Tennis nearby; 11 Swimming nearby; 12 Golf nearby; 13 Skiing nearby; 14 May be booked through a travel agent; 15 Handicapped accessible.

Cedar Gables Inn

486 Coombs Street, 94559
(707) 224-7939; (800) 309-7969
www.cedargablesinn.com

In Old Town Napa, this 106-year-old home is styled after English country manors of the 16th century. Antique furnishings are throughout the house. Some rooms have fireplaces and whirlpool tubs. Huge family room with large fireplace and big-screen TV are also available for guests. Minutes from wineries, restaurants, and the Napa Valley Wine Train.

Hosts: Margaret and Craig Snasdell
Rooms: 6 (PB) $139-199
Full Breakfast
Credit Cards: A, B, C, D
Notes: 2, 7, 12, 14

Cedar Gables Inn

Churchill Manor Bed & Breakfast Inn

485 Brown Street, 94559
(707) 253-7733

Churchill Manor, an 1889 mansion, is listed in the National Register of Historic Places. Elegant parlors boast carved-wood ceilings and columns, leaded-glass windows, oriental rugs, brass and crystal chandeliers, four fireplaces, and a grand piano. Guest rooms are individually decorated with gorgeous antiques; five of the guest rooms have fireplaces. Enjoy freshly baked cookies and refreshments in the after-

Churchill Manor

noon, complimentary wines and cheeses in the evening, and a delicious gourmet breakfast. Complimentary tandem bicycles and croquet.

Hosts: Joanna Guidotti and Brian Jensen
Rooms: 10 (PB) $95-205
Full Breakfast
Credit Cards: A, B, D
Notes: 2, 5, 7, 9, 10, 11, 12, 14, 15

La Belle Epoque Bed & Breakfast

1386 Calistoga Avenue, 94559
(707) 257-2161; FAX (707) 226-6314

This 1893 Queen Anne features an extensive display of vintage and contemporary stained glass. Fine Victorian antiques grace each of the six guest rooms and extend into the common areas. A full gourmet breakfast is served in the elegant formal dining room or on the plant-filled sun porch. Complimentary wine and

La Belle Epoque

NOTES: Credit cards accepted: A MasterCard; B Visa; C American Express; D Discover; E Diner's Club; F Other; 2 Personal checks accepted; 3 Lunch available; 4 Dinner available; 5 Open all year; 6 Pets welcome;

appetizers are served nightly in the on-premises wine-tasting parlor. The inn is within an easy walk of Old Town Napa and the Napa Valley Wine Train.

Host: Georgia Jump
Rooms: 6 (PB) $159-229
Full Breakfast
Credit Cards: A, B, C, D
Notes: 2, 5, 7, 9, 10, 11, 12, 14

The Laurel Street Inn

The Laurel Street Inn

1737 Laurel Street, 94559
(707) 251-0617; FAX (707) 259-5463
e-mail: laurelstin@aol.com

On historic Fuller Park, this lovely old Colonial Revival Victorian with Tuscan columns was built in 1906. The inn has two guest rooms, each with a private bath. Antiques throughout. Early morning risers can relax on the porch and watch the hot-air balloons glide over the tree tops above the park. Enjoy a stroll to historic downtown Napa. A gourmet breakfast is served by candlelight in the formal dining room. Complimentary wine and cheese are served each evening.

Hosts: Lynnette and Steve Sands
Rooms: 2 (PB) $139-159
Full Breakfast
Credit Cards: A, B
Notes: 5, 7, 12, 14

Napa Inn

1137 Warren Street, 94559
(707) 257-1444; (800) 435-1144
FAX (707) 257-0251; e-mail: info@napainn.com
www.napainn.com

Napa Inn

This beautiful Queen Anne Victorian is in the historic section of Napa. Furnished with turn-of-the-century antiques, the inn features a large parlor and a formal dining room. Each bedroom has its own private bath, and three suites feature fireplaces. Convenient to the Napa, Sonoma, and Carneros wine regions, hot-air ballooning, gliding, biking, hiking, many fine restaurants, and the Napa Valley Wine Train.

Hosts: Brooke and Jim Boyer
Rooms: 6 (PB) $140-185
Full Breakfast
Credit Cards: A, B, C, D, E
Notes: 2, 5, 7, 9, 10, 11, 12, 14

Oak Knoll Inn

2200 East Oak Knoll Avenue, Napa Valley, 94558
(707) 255-2200

Tall French windows, rustic stone walls, and vaulted ceilings distinguish the four spacious guest rooms at this luxurious inn, set well off the bustle of the main roads and surrounded by

Oak Knoll Inn

---

7 No smoking; 8 Children welcome; 9 Social drinking allowed; 10 Tennis nearby; 11 Swimming nearby; 12 Golf nearby; 13 Skiing nearby; 14 May be booked through a travel agent; 15 Handicapped accessible.

600 acres of Chardonnay vineyards. The rooms have king-size beds, marble fireplaces, private baths, and sitting areas with overstuffed chairs and sofas. A full breakfast is served at guests' leisure in the room, dining room, or on the veranda surrounding the heated pool, spa, and magnificent views. In-state personal checks accepted.

Hosts: Barbara Passino and John Kuhlmann
Rooms: 4 (PB) $250-395
Full Breakfast
Credit Cards: A, B
Notes: 5, 7, 9, 10, 11, 12

The Old World Inn

1301 Jefferson Street, 94559
(707) 257-0112

For a holiday of romance and plentiful gourmet delights, plan a stay at this charming Victorian inn. Relax in the outdoor spa or choose a room with a sunken spa tub. Guests are pampered with home-baked treats throughout their stay: savor afternoon tea and cookies when one arrives, unwind during the wine and cheese social, treat oneself to a chocolate lover's dessert buffet before retiring, and awaken to a gourmet breakfast.

Host: Sam VanHoeve
Rooms: 8 (PB) $115-150
Cottage: 1-$205
Full Breakfast
Credit Cards: A, B, C, D
Notes: 2, 5, 7, 9, 10, 11, 12, 14

NAPA VALLEY

Bartels Ranch and Bed & Breakfast Country Inn

1200 Conn Valley Road, St. Helena, 94574
(707) 963-4001; FAX (707) 963-5100
e-mail: Bartelsranch@WEBTV.net
www.bartelsranch.com

In the heart of Napa Valley, a peaceful 60-acre estate overlooks oak hillsides and vineyards. Six minutes east of St. Helena's finest wineries, restaurants, and shopping. In *Best Places to Stay in California* and *Frommers*. Three uniquely decorated rooms and honeymoon suite. Amenities: fireplaces, movies, coffee, robes, bicycles, library, living room with piano, entertainment room. Breakfast served in formal dining room terraces. Telephone, fax, and refrigerator. ABBA Award of Excellence. Dinner catered. Designated smoking areas.

Host: Jami Bartels
Rooms: 4 (PB) $185-425
Full Breakfast
Credit Cards: A, B, C, D, E, F
Notes: 2, 3, 5, 8, 9, 10, 11, 12, 14

La Residence Country Inn

4066 St. Helena Highway, Napa, 94558
(707) 253-0337

Accommodations, most with fireplaces, are in two structures: a Gothic Revival home, decorated in traditional American antiques, and the "French barn," decorated with European pine antiques. Two acres of grounds with large spa and a heated swimming pool include a gazebo and trellis. Complimentary wine is served each evening.

Hosts: David Jackson and Craig Claussen
Rooms: 20 (PB) $175-295
Full Breakfast
Credit Cards: A, B, C, E
Notes: 5, 7, 8, 12, 14, 15

NEVADA CITY

Deer Creek Inn

116 Nevada Street, 95959
(530) 265-0363; (800) 655-0363
FAX (530) 265-0980; e-mail: deercreek@gv.net

At the edge of downtown Nevada City guests will find Deer Creek Inn. A spectacular Queen Anne Victorian, it sits majestically high above historic Deer Creek. As guests wander among the romantic rose gardens and creekside setting, one's mind will release itself of present day concerns. A kiss on the hand, a glance of

---

NOTES: Credit cards accepted: A MasterCard; B Visa; C American Express; D Discover; E Diner's Club; F Other; 2 Personal checks accepted; 3 Lunch available; 4 Dinner available; 5 Open all year; 6 Pets welcome;

Deer Creek Inn

the eye, can say it all...Romance and elegance...Deer Creek Inn. The gourmet breakfasts and evening hors d'oeuvres that await guests are only a sampling of the treats in store. Smoking is permitted on balcony only. Inquire about accommodations for children.

Hosts: Elaine and Chuck Matroni
Rooms: 5 (PB) $95-150
Full Breakfast
Credit Cards: A, B, C
Notes: 2, 5, 9, 10, 11, 12, 13, 14

The Parsonage Bed & Breakfast

427 Broad Street, 95959
(530) 265-9478; FAX (530) 265-8147

This home, dating back to 1865, offers six guest rooms with private baths. Each guest room honors a California pioneer ancestor of the owner. The entire home is furnished with family antiques that date back to the 1850s. A Continental breakfast, including freshly baked muffins and croissants, homemade jam, yogurt, fresh fruit, juice, and coffee, is served at a table with line-dried and hand-pressed linens. In every way, the hosts like to transport their guests back 100 years to a gentler era where people cared about each other. A full breakfast served on weekends and holidays. Lunch and dinner are available nearby. Inquire about accommodations for children.

Rooms: 6 (PB) $80-135
Full Breakfast
Credit Cards: A, B
Notes: 2, 5, 7, 9, 10, 11, 12, 13, 14

NEWPORT BEACH

Bed & Breakfast California

P.O. Box 2247, Saratoga, 95070
(408) 867-9662; (800) 872-4500
FAX (408) 867-0907; e-mail: info@bbintl.com
www.bbintl.com

A. Crow's nest with 360-degree view tops this trilevel beach home. Two guest rooms. Private baths. The third level is a large guest deck with barbecue and refrigerator. Stained glass is featured throughout the house. Perfect for beach and bay activities; bicycle and beach chairs available. Full or Continental breakfast and afternoon refreshments. $65-85.

B. This charming home in a quiet neighborhood on the Balboa Peninsula of Newport Beach features stained glass, used bricks, and natural wood surroundings. Upstairs loft room has a private bath and access to a large sun deck with ocean and beach views. Downstairs brass bedroom offers a large private bath. Just steps from the beach and bay. Bicycles and beach chairs are available. Full breakfast. $65-85.

Island Cottage

1305 Park Avenue, P.O. Box 5853, 92662
(949) 723-0266 (phone/FAX); (714) 658-2663 (cell)
e-mail: islandetg@aol.com

On historic Balboa Island, Island Cottage with romantic Cape Cod ambiance in the heart of Newport Beach. One block from bay for harbor cruise, sailing, electric boats, and jet skis. A short walk to ferry boat that takes you across the bay for a two-block walk to the Pacific Ocean. The town of Balboa Island features more than 70 gift shops, galleries, and restaurants. Includes fresh flowers, a fruit bowl, and Balboa Island breakfast for two. Skiing is one

---

7 No smoking; 8 Children welcome; 9 Social drinking allowed; 10 Tennis nearby; 11 Swimming nearby; 12 Golf nearby; 13 Skiing nearby; 14 May be booked through a travel agent; 15 Handicapped accessible.

hour away. Downstairs unit is handicapped accessible.

Host: Anne Lemen
Rooms: 2 (1 PB; 1 SB) $175
Continental Breakfast
Credit Cards: None
Notes: 5, 8, 9, 10, 11, 12, 13, 14, 15

NICE

Featherbed Railroad Company

2870 Lakeshore Boulevard, P.O. Box 4016, 95464
(707) 274-4434; (800) 966-6322

Nine lovingly refurbished theme cabooses reflect the Casablanca Orient Express. Most have Jacuzzi tubs for two. All have small refrigerators, cable TV (all with VCRs). Small sitting areas, coffee pot, assorted complimentary beverages, private pool, and spa are available. Full breakfast. Year-round fishing. Enjoy serene country setting.

Hosts: Len and Lorraine Bassignani
Rooms: 9 (PB) $90-140
Full Breakfast
Credit Cards: A, B, C, D
Notes: 2, 5, 7, 9, 10, 11, 12, 14

NIPOMO

Kaleidoscope Inn

130 East Dana Street, P.O. Box 1297, 93444-1297
(805) 929-5444; FAX (805) 929-5440
e-mail: kaleidoscope@pronet.org

Circa 1887. The sunlight that streams through the stained-glass windows of this charming Victorian creates a kaleidoscope effect and thus the name. The inn is surrounded by an acre of gardens. Each romantic guest room is decorated with antiques; the library offers a fireplace, and the parlor has an 1866 Steinway upright piano. Fresh flowers add a special touch. A full breakfast is served on porcelain and crystal in the dining room or gardens. *Los*

Kaleidoscope Inn

Angeles Times readers voted the inn as one of the best lodging spots for under $100 per night.

Hosts: Edward and Carol DeLeon
Rooms: 3 (PB) $95
Full Breakfast
Credit Cards: A, B, C, D
Notes: 2, 5, 8, 10, 11, 12

NIPTON

Hotel Nipton

107355 Nipton Road, 92364
(760) 856-2335; e-mail: hotel@nipton.com
www.nipton.com

Hotel Nipton, originally built in 1904, was restored in 1986. In the Mojave National Preserve, 1.4 million acres of California desert,

NOTES: Credit cards accepted: A MasterCard; B Visa; C American Express; D Discover; E Diner's Club; F Other; 2 Personal checks accepted; 3 Lunch available; 4 Dinner available; 5 Open all year; 6 Pets welcome;

65 miles southwest of Las Vegas between the Grand Canyon and Death Valley. Enjoy the beautiful panoramic views of Ivanpah Valley and New York Mountains. Outside Jacuzzi for star gazing. Only bed and breakfast in the preserve. Historic mining town has a population of 60.

Hosts: Jerry and Roxanne Freeman
Rooms: 4 (SB) $59.95
Continental Breakfast
Credit Cards: A, B, D
Notes: 5, 7, 8, 9, 11, 12, 14

OAKLAND

Washington Inn

495-10th Street, 94607
(510) 452-1776

The Washington Inn is a charming turn-of-the-century historic landmark located in the heart of Old Oakland. The inn features 47 traditionally furnished guest rooms all with private baths, a full-service bar and restaurant, and meeting facilities, all in a warm and friendly atmosphere. Conveniently across from the Oakland Convention Center. Full breakfast served weekdays; Continental breakfast served weekends.

Notes: 47 (PB) $80-140
Full or Continental Breakfast
Credit Cards: A, B, C
Notes: 3, 4, 5, 8, 9, 14, 15

OCCIDENTAL

The Inn at Occidental

3657 Church Street, 95465
(707) 874-1047; (800) 522-6343
FAX (707) 874-1078
e-mail: innkeeper@innatoccidental.com
www.innatoccidental.com

In a charming village near the spectacular Sonoma coast and wine country, the Inn at Occidental is a completely renovated 1877 Victorian with European ambiance and antique furnishings and goose-down comforters. Each room features original art, antiques, and fresh flowers. Amenities include a courtyard garden, fireplaces, in-room Jacuzzis and a hot tub, afternoon refreshments, and sumptuous breakfast. Two-night minimum stay required for weekends and holidays. Dinner is available with prior arrangements. Children over 10 are welcome. One room is handicapped accessible.

Hosts: Jack, Bill, and Jean Bullard
Rooms: 16 (PB) $175-270
Full Breakfast
Credit Cards: A, B, C, D
Notes: 2, 5, 7, 9, 10, 12, 14, 15

OJAI

Bed & Breakfast California

P.O. Box 2247, Saratoga, 95070
(408) 867-9662; (800) 872-4500
FAX (408) 867-0907; e-mail: info@bbintl.com
www.bbintl.com

A. This 1887 New England-style farmhouse on seven acres is close to town center. Enjoy the buffet breakfast and afternoon refreshments. Rooms have private or shared bath. Relax on the screened patio or at the swimming pool or Jacuzzi. Good hiking and biking areas and restaurants and art galleries are nearby and it is a short commute to Santa Ynez wineries and local lakes for boating and fishing. $85-120.

B. A beautiful large 6,300-square-foot custom-built home in the canyon. Windows (no drapes) look out onto gorgeous intimate and serene five-acre estate with spa, swimming pool, and glorious gardens nestled next to a running creek in the foothills of the Los Padres National Forest. An ideal spiritual retreat only half-hour from beautiful Santa Barbara. Ojai features golf courses, shops, and award-winning restaurants only seven minutes away. Hiking and biking trails galore right outside the door. $130.

---

7 No smoking; 8 Children welcome; 9 Social drinking allowed; 10 Tennis nearby; 11 Swimming nearby; 12 Golf nearby; 13 Skiing nearby; 14 May be booked through a travel agent; 15 Handicapped accessible.

PACIFIC GROVE

Absolutely Accommodations

P.O. Box 641471, San Francisco, 94164-1471
(415) 677-9789; (888) 982-2632
e-mail: travelinfo@iname.com
www.citysearch.com/sfo/accommodations

This is a free reservation service committed to assisting travelers in finding the best possible accommodations in California. It offers access to private homestay bed and breakfasts and inns. It can help guests find the proper accommodations that meet their individual needs. The service's goal is to provide both its clients and hosts with the best possible customer service.

Pacific Grove 101. A charming Victorian designated as a historical landmark is within walking distance from Lover's Point in Pacific Grove. All of the 20 rooms are tastefully decorated and have private baths.

Bed & Breakfast California

P.O. Box 2247, Saratoga, 95070
(408) 867-9662; (800) 872-4500
FAX (408) 867-0907; e-mail: info@bbintl.com
www.bbintl.com

A. Cozy, private cottages with fireplaces, claw-foot tubs, and wet bars...airy attic suites...elegant rooms...intimate hideaways with Jacuzzi tubs...for more than 100 years, this award-winning inn has been the destination of choice for charm and romance. Stroll down to Lover's Point or over to Cannery Row, or visit the historic town of Pacific Grove, famous for its annual migration of monarch butterflies. $89-229.

B. The suites offer comfort and luxury at its finest. This boutique Cape Cod-style village is the Monterey Peninsula's best kept secret. Each suite offers a king- or queen-size bed with down pillows, fireplace, Jacuzzi tub, and plush robes. Awaken each morning to a chef-prepared breakfast, cooked to order and served in the elegant dining room. Complimentary wine and hors d'oeuvres are offered in the afternoon. $169-575.

C. Century-old Victorian boarding house is now a refurbished award-winning bed and breakfast inn. Beautifully decorated rooms, private baths, delicious breakfast, and afternoon refreshments. $89-229.

D. This 1884 Victorian with ocean view was renovated and opened its doors in 1990 to become a Pacific Grove bed and breakfast inn close to the beach. Each room is uniquely decorated and features views or sun decks and private baths. Delicious full breakfast and afternoon refreshments are provided. No smoking. $110-225.

E. This 1888 Queen Anne-style mansion-by-the-sea has a panoramic view of Monterey Bay. Delicious breakfast and afternoon refreshments. Shared and private baths. $110-165.

F. Beautifully preserved 1887 Victorian in the National Register of Historic Places can now be enjoyed as a bed and breakfast inn. Wonderful breakfast, afternoon hors d'oeuvres, and wine or tea served. $100-160.

G. Four rooms in this 1910 Cape Cod-style inn have ocean views. Convenient to the aquarium, beaches, and most local attractions. Full breakfast served. $110-195.

Gatehouse Inn

225 Central Avenue, 93950
(831) 649-8436; (800) 753-1881
FAX (831) 648-8044

This historic home, built in 1884, was the summer residence of Senator Langford. Each of the nine guest rooms is individually decorated in grand Victorian style. Many of the rooms have ocean views, fireplaces, and claw-foot tubs. Enjoy the gourmet full breakfast or relax on the garden patio at teatime while soaking in the view of Monterey. Near excellent restaurants,

---

NOTES: Credit cards accepted: A MasterCard; B Visa; C American Express; D Discover; E Diner's Club; F Other; 2 Personal checks accepted; 3 Lunch available; 4 Dinner available; 5 Open all year; 6 Pets welcome;

Pacific Grove, CA

Gatehouse Inn

shopping, and activities. Just 100 yards away from the ocean.

Hosts: Lois DeFord, Lewis Shaefer, and Susan Kuslis
Rooms: 9 (PB) $110-165
Full Breakfast
Credit Cards: A, B, C, D
Notes: 2, 5, 7, 9, 10, 11, 12, 14

Grand View Inn

557 Ocean View Boulevard, 93950
(831) 372-4341

Built in 1910, the Grand View Inn is at the edge of Monterey Bay. The inn was completely restored in 1994 by the Flatley family, owners of the Seven Gables Inn is next door. Guests enjoy a tradition of warm personal service, spectacular natural surroundings, comfortably appointed accommodations, irresistible breakfasts, and sociable gatherings at afternoon tea. A feeling of quiet elegance encompasses the inn. Along with unsurpassed views of Monterey Bay from each room, guests enjoy the comfort of marble tiled private baths, patterned hardwood floors, beautiful antique furnishings, and lovely grounds.

Hosts: Susan Flatley and Ed Flatley
Rooms: 10 (PB) $155-285
Full Breakfast
Credit Cards: A, B
Notes: 2, 5, 7, 9, 10, 11, 12, 15

The Martine Inn

255 Ocean View Boulevard, 93950
(831) 373-3388; (800) 852-5588
FAX (831) 373-3896
www.martineinn.com

The Martine Inn is a grand 1890s home overlooking the rocky coastline of Pacific Grove on Monterey Bay. All 23 rooms have private bathroom, authentic museum-quality antiques, a fresh rose, a silver Victorian bridal basket with fresh fruit, and a telephone. Some rooms overlook the waves crashing against the rocks and/or have a wood-burning fireplace. Breakfast is served on Old Sheffield silver, Victorian-style china, crystal, and lace. Play pool in the game room, lounge in the spa, or view vintage cars from the Martine's collection.

Host: Don Martine
Rooms: 23 (PB) $150-295
Full Breakfast
Credit Cards: A, B, C, D
Notes: 2, 5, 9, 10, 11, 12, 14, 15

The Old St. Angela Inn

321 Central Avenue, 93950
(831) 372-3246; (800) 748-6306

The Old St. Angela's Inn, built as a country home in 1910, was converted to a rectory and convent in 1920. Within this Cape Cod home, overlooking Monterey Bay, are rooms of distinctive individuality and warmth to provide guests with comfort and serenity. Enjoy afternoon wine and teatime by the fireplace. Relax on the garden patio amidst flowers, butterflies, and sunshine. Just 100 yards from the ocean and only minutes from excellent restaurants, shopping areas, and the Monterey Bay Aquarium.

Hosts: Lewis Shaefer and Susan Kuslis
Rooms: 8 (PB) $110-225
Full Breakfast
Credit Cards: A, B, D
Notes: 2, 5, 7, 8, 9, 10, 11, 12, 14

---

7 No smoking; 8 Children welcome; 9 Social drinking allowed; 10 Tennis nearby; 11 Swimming nearby; 12 Golf nearby; 13 Skiing nearby; 14 May be booked through a travel agent; 15 Handicapped accessible.

Seven Gables Inn

555 Ocean View Boulevard, 93950
(831) 372-4341

It's hard to imagine a more picturesque and romantic location than that of Seven Gables. The waves crashing along the rocky shoreline, the sea otters frolicking just offshore, the whales spouting, the surrounding mountains lit up by the sunset...these are the images seen from each guest room of this century-old Victorian inn. Such natural beauty is complemented on the inside by an unmatched array of museum-quality European, Asian, and American antiques. A bountiful breakfast, enjoyable afternoon tea, outstanding guest service, and the comfort of all private baths combine to make Seven Gables, truly, one of the most outstanding inns in California.

Hosts: Susan Flatley and Ed Flatley
Rooms: 14 (PB) $155-350
Full Breakfast
Credit Cards: A, B
Notes: 2, 5, 7, 9, 10, 11, 12

PALM DESERT

Tres Palmas Bed & Breakfast

73135 Tumbleweed Lane, 92260
(760) 773-9858; (800) 770-9858
www.innformation.com/ca/trespalmas

Tres Palmas is one block south of El Paseo, the "Rodeo Drive of the Desert," where guests will find boutiques, art galleries, and restaurants. Or stay "home" to enjoy the desert sun in and around the pool and spa. Guest rooms, featuring queen- or king-size beds, color cable TVs, are decorated in southwestern style. Lemonade and iced tea are always available. Snacks are provided in the late afternoons. Rated A-plus by ABBA and three diamonds by AAA.

Hosts: Terry and Karen Bennett
Rooms: 4 (PB) $120-185
Continental Breakfast
Credit Cards: A, B, C
Notes: 2, 5, 7, 9, 10, 11, 12, 14

PALM SPRINGS

Bed & Breakfast California

P.O. Box 2247, Saratoga, 95070
(408) 967-9662; (800) 872-4500
FAX (408) 867-0907; e-mail: info@bbintl.com
www.bbintl.com

A. Nestled peacefully in the sheltered area between South Palm Canyon Drive, the hub of Palm Springs shopping and dining activity, and the picturesque San Jacinto Mountains to the west, the beautiful Orchid Tree evokes the charm, tranquility and comfort of Old Palm Springs. Two swimming pools are ready for guests to take a cooling dip after a hot shopping spree. $95-290.

B. A romantic, historic hideaway nestled against the spectacular San Jacinto Mountains in the heart of Palm Springs Village. Completely redecorated in Santa Fe decor. Twenty-three ground level units consisting of hotel rooms, studio suites, one- and two-bedroom suites with private patios; fireplaces, fully equipped tiled kitchens, cable TV, and telephones, two pools and whirlpool spa. $89-209.

C. Nestled against the magnificent San Jacinto Mountains, this romantic villa provides charming accommodations in comfortable suites with lots of relaxing and secluded privacy. These suite villas are lovely and spacious. The villas specialize in family and small group reunions. Two swimming pools and fireplaces

Tres Palmas

NOTES: Credit cards accepted: A MasterCard; B Visa; C American Express; D Discover; E Diner's Club; F Other; 2 Personal checks accepted; 3 Lunch available; 4 Dinner available; 5 Open all year; 6 Pets welcome;

in many units; air conditioning, cable TV, and Continental breakfast. Units with kitchen will have microwave. Continental is only on Saturday and Sunday. Guests love the cozy interior charm and the flowers, gardens, and privacy. $99-300.

D. Japanese-style inn and decor create a relaxed bed and breakfast stay. Shoji windows open to the pool. Three guest rooms have private baths. Shiatsu massage, kimonos, and additional amenities available. Choice of American or Japanese breakfast. No smoking. $65-75.

Casa Cody Bed & Breakfast Country Inn

175 South Cahuilla, 92262
(760) 320-9346

This romantic and historic hideaway is in the heart of the village of Palm Springs. Beautifully redecorated in Santa Fe style, with kitchens, wood-burning fireplaces, patios, two pools, and a spa. Close to the Desert Museum, Heritage Center, and Moorten Botanical Garden. Nearby hiking in Indian canyons, horseback riding, tennis, golf, polo, ballooning, helicopter and desert Jeep tours. Near celebrity homes, date gardens, and Joshua Tree National Monument.

Hosts: Therese Hayes and Frank Tysen
Rooms: 23 (PB) $79-299
Continental Breakfast
Credit Cards: A, B, C, D, E
Notes: 2, 5, 6, 8, 9, 10, 11, 12, 13, 14, 15

L'Horizon Garden Hotel

1050 East Palm Canyon, 92264
(760) 323-1858; (800) 377-7855
FAX (760) 327-2933

The serenity of gentler times lives on at L'Horizon Garden Hotel, a secluded resort at the foot of the spectacular Mount San Jacinto. Twenty-two luxurious rooms and suites decorated to reflect the pastel beauty of the desert surround the refreshing pool and Jacuzzi. Amenities include complimentary Continental breakfast, an extensive library, table games, afternoon refreshments by the pool, and a hotel staff dedicated to guests' comfort. Experience a true oasis in the desert at L'Horizon Garden Hotel.

Host: Sandi Howell
Rooms: 22 (PB) $95-140
Continental Breakfast
Credit Cards: A, B, C, D, E
Notes: 7, 9, 10, 12, 14

Villa Royale Inn

1620 Indian Trail, 92264
(760) 327-2314; (800) 245-2314
FAX (760) 322-3794; e-mail: info@villaroyale.com
www.villaroyale.com

This romantic European-style country inn is an oasis in the desert, with a series of interior courtyards framed with pillars, cascading bougainvillaea, and hovering shade trees. Many rooms have wood-burning fireplaces and private spas. Each accommodation represents a different European country. There are two pools and a spa. The main courtyard has a terrace for the complimentary Continental breakfast served daily, and in the evening, dinner is served outside or in the romantic, internationally renowned Europa Restaurant. Brunch is available.

Villa Royale Inn

---

7 No smoking; 8 Children welcome; 9 Social drinking allowed; 10 Tennis nearby; 11 Swimming nearby; 12 Golf nearby; 13 Skiing nearby; 14 May be booked through a travel agent; 15 Handicapped accessible.

Rooms: 31 (PB) $105-325
Continental Breakfast
Credit Cards: A, B, C, D, E
Notes: 4, 5, 7, 9, 10, 11, 12, 14

The Willows Historic Palm Springs Inn

412 West Tahquitz Canyon Way, 92262
(760) 320-0771; FAX (760) 320-0780
e-mail: innkeeper@thewillowspalmsprings.com

AAA four-diamond, Mobil four-star small luxury hotel, the Willows recreates the ambiance and elegance of Palm Springs in the 1930s. Albert Einstein, Marion Davies, Clark Gable, and Carole Lombard slept here. Accommodations feature luxurious linens, fine antique furnishings, sumptuous bathrooms with handmade tiles and claw-foot tubs, hardwood floors, fireplaces, private patios, pool, and spa. Lush gardens with spectacular views and fine cuisine complete the magic.

Rooms: 8 (PB) $250-500
Full Breakfast
Credit Cards: A, B, C, D, E
Notes: 2, 3, 4, 5, 7, 9, 10, 11, 12, 14

PALO ALTO

The Victorian on Lytton

555 Lytton Avenue, 94301
(650) 322-8555

Special amenities include down comforters, Battenberg lace canopies, botanical prints, Blue Willow china, and claw-foot tubs. Wander through the English country garden with over 900 perennial plants. Five king-size and five queen-size beds are available. Relax in the parlor with a picture book or a novel and a cup of tea while listening to classical music. One room is handicapped accessible.

Hosts: Maxwell and Susan Hall
Rooms: 10 (PB) $148-225
Continental Breakfast
Credit Cards: A, B, C
Notes: 5, 7, 10, 11, 12, 14, 15

PASADENA

Bed & Breakfast California

P.O. Box 2247, Saratoga, 95070
(408) 867-9662; (800) 872-4500
FAX (408) 867-0907; e-mail: info@bbintl.com
www.bbintl.com

A. This very private guest house is set in a nicely landscaped yard of quiet, lovely neighborhood near the Huntington Library and has a small kitchen with self-hosted Continental breakfast. The trundle bed provides two twin beds and there is a private bath. Quick commute time to Los Angeles Civic Center, Pasadena, and many tourist attractions. Weekly rates are available. $65.

B. Georgian Colonial style estate built in 1925 is on an acre of garden in a beautiful quiet residential area. There are two guest rooms with private baths (baths are in hall right outside room), handsomely decorated with antiques. A Continental breakfast is served in sunny breakfast nook or on terrace overlooking the gardens. Nearby hiking and nature tours. Convenient locations to the Rose Bowl, Old Town Pasadena, and Huntington Library. Twenty minutes from downtown Los Angeles. $75.

C. Large contemporary home with Old World wine cellar has Angeles National Forest as its back yard. Two guest rooms with private baths. Host teaches wine classes and is a gourmet cook. Wine dinners and wine tastings available upon request. Continental or full breakfast served. No smoking. $85.

D. Dramatic contemporary bed and breakfast within walking distance of the Rose Bowl offers a quiet setting near most tourist attractions. The guest room has queen-size bed and a private bath. Continental breakfast is served. Smoking is not permitted. $85-95.

E. This Craftsman-style house near Orange Grove's historic Millionaire's row offers gracious surroundings and friendly well-traveled

---

NOTES: Credit cards accepted: A MasterCard; B Visa; C American Express; D Discover; E Diner's Club; F Other; 2 Personal checks accepted; 3 Lunch available; 4 Dinner available; 5 Open all year; 6 Pets welcome;

hosts. Guest room has king-size beds, private bath. Walk to Old Town, restaurants, and museums. Continental breakfast is served. Smoking is not permitted. $70-100.

F. Only a short walk to Pasadena Civic and Convention Center, this bed and breakfast is an older, well-kept California bungalow with first-floor guest accommodations, as well as a separate, private apartment. Private and shared baths. Hosts who enjoy travel have lived abroad and speak Swedish. Continental or full breakfast served. Smoking is not permitted. $60-85.

G. Half-timbered Tudor-style home was designed and built by the host, who is a magician, yoga enthusiast, and vegetarian gourmet cook. One guest room with private bath. Lovely community with good hiking is close to museums and tourist attractions. Smoking is not permitted. $75.

H. This 1895 Victorian farmhouse has been refurbished and decorated to recall the heritage of the home and city. Four guest rooms with double, queen- or king-size beds and private baths. Full breakfast is served and afternoon refreshments are available. Smoking is not permitted. $110-165.

I. Restored elegant Victorian in the National Register of Historic Places close to Old Town, museums, and restaurants offers gracious hospitality, lovely grounds, and a full or Continental breakfast served in the dining room or patio areas. The three guest rooms on the top floor each have a queen-size bed, sitting area, and private bath en suite. Two additional guest rooms have twin beds and shared bath. A short commute to Los Angeles Civic Center, Hollywood, beaches, and most tourist destinations. $115-160.

J. A 400-square-foot redwood guest house shares patio and Jacuzzi with host's home, which faces Arroyo Seco natural recreation area. Horse stable, par three golf course, racquetball, and tennis courts are within walking distance. Cottage has cooking facilities and TV. Private bath. Twelve-minute drive to Los Angeles. Smoking is not permitted. $85.

PESCADERO

Bed & Breakfast California

P.O. Box 2247, Saratoga, 95070
(408) 867-9662; (800) 872-4500
FAX (408) 867-0907; e-mail: info@bbintl.com
www.bbintl.com

Halfway between Half Moon Bay and Santa Cruz, this romantic retreat provides an atmosphere of rustic elegance and historic interest. It is on one of many old saw mill sites dating back to the late 1800s and early 1900s. A full gourmet buffet breakfast and afternoon wine and hors d'oeuvres are included in the room rate. $105-175.

PETALUMA

Bed & Breakfast California

P.O. Box 2247, Saratoga, 95070
(408) 867-9662; (800) 872-4500
FAX (408) 867-0907; e-mail: info@bbintl.com
www.bbintl.com

Step back in time in this charming riverfront Victorian town. Weary travelers can unwind and forget about their cares at this inn, which is in walking distance from historic downtown Petaluma. The elegant main home, built in 1902, is paneled with rare heart redwood. Climb the beautiful staircase to a stunning octagonal landing which opens into four lovely guest rooms. The three-room cottage next door has a more casual garden cottage theme, complete with a lush garden mural. A luscious gourmet breakfast is served. Afternoon wine and sweets at bedtime provide the finishing touches. $85-130.

---

7 No smoking; 8 Children welcome; 9 Social drinking allowed; 10 Tennis nearby; 11 Swimming nearby; 12 Golf nearby; 13 Skiing nearby; 14 May be booked through a travel agent; 15 Handicapped accessible.

Cavanagh Inn

Cavanagh Inn

10 Keller Street, 94952
(707) 765-4657; (888) 765-4658
FAX (707) 769-0466
e-mail: info@cavanaghinn.com
www.cavanaghinn.com

Step back into the romantic past and enjoy the warmth and charm of Petaluma's first bed and breakfast. Appreciate the rare redwood-heart paneling in both the 1902 Georgian Revival home and the 1912 California Craftsman cottage. Award-winning chef Jeanne Farris prepares a gourmet breakfast guests will long remember. Local wines are served in the evening. Cavanagh Inn is in the historic downtown area and within walking distance of restaurants, shops, and the riverfront. AAA three-diamond-rated property. San Francisco is 42 miles south across the Golden Gate Bridge. *Se habla español.*

Hosts: Ray and Jeanne Farris
Rooms: 7 (5 PB; 2 SB) $85-130
Full Breakfast
Credit Cards: A, B, C
Notes: 2, 5, 7, 12, 14

PISMO BEACH

Bed & Breakfast California

P.O. Box 2247, Saratoga, 95070
(408) 867-9662; (800) 872-4500
FAX (408) 867-0907; e-mail: info@bbintl.com
www.bbintl.com

White-washed exteriors tastefully complemented inside by sea foam blues and taupes ever in harmony with the sand and shore provide an understated elegance reminiscent in mood and style of a romantic Mediterranean villa. Sweeping ocean views from generous windows and attached outdoor patios are available from almost every room. Relax and enjoy the view from the glass enclosed outdoor spa or third floor sun deck. Each room has refrigerator, coffee maker, video cassette player. Complimentary Continental breakfast of fruit and fresh-baked pastries. In the evening, relax and reflect in the atrium. Just steps away from the water's edge. $80-250.

PLACERVILLE

The Chichester-McKee House

800 Spring Street, 95667
(530) 626-1882; (800) 831-4008
www.innacess.com/cmh/

This elegant home was built in 1892 by the lumber baron D. W. Chichester. Enjoy the fireplaces, fretwork, stained glass, antiques, and relaxing hospitality. A "special" full breakfast is served in the dining room. Four air-conditioned guest rooms, two with private baths and two

The Chichester-McKee House

NOTES: Credit cards accepted: A MasterCard; B Visa; C American Express; D Discover; E Diner's Club; F Other; 2 Personal checks accepted; 3 Lunch available; 4 Dinner available; 5 Open all year; 6 Pets welcome;

with private half-baths. Robes are available. Downtown near Apple Hill, Gold Discovery Site, and white-water rafting. Subject of artist Thomas Kinkade's *Victorian Christmas III.*

Hosts: Doreen and Bill Thornhill
Rooms: 4 (PB) $90-125
Full Breakfast
Credit Cards: A, B, C, D
Notes: 2, 5, 7, 8, 9, 10, 11, 12, 13, 14

Combellack Blair House

3059 Cedar Ravine Road, 95667
(530) 622-3764; FAX (530) 621-4165
e-mail: comblair@c-zone.net
www.c-zone.net/comblair

This gracious Queen Anne Victorian, featured in Thomas Kinkade's painting *Victorian Christmas III*, sits atop a hill in historic Placerville. The house, built in 1895, is in the national register and features a magnificent spiral staircase and original stained glass, woodwork, and fixtures. The home is surrounded by beautiful gardens. Rooms feature zoned heating and air conditioning, queen-size beds, private baths, and period decor. A full breakfast is served in the dining room. Walk to town to visit unique shops, galleries, and restaurants. Visit wineries, the Gold Discovery site, and Apple Hill.

Hosts: Loren and Marlene De Laurenti
Rooms: 3 (PB) $110
Full Breakfast
Credit Cards: A, B
Notes: 2, 5, 7, 9, 12, 13

River Rock Inn

1756 Georgetown Road, 95667
(530) 622-7640

A comfortable country inn on the banks of the American River. Rooms open on to the deck over the river. Gold County activities near—gold panning, antique shops, museums, and good restaurants to enjoy. White-water rafting and hot-air ballooning available. Two half baths.

Hosts: Dorothy Irvin
Rooms: 4 (2 PB; 2 SB) $80-110
Full Breakfast
Credit Cards: None
Notes: 2, 5, 7, 8, 12, 13, 14

PLAYA DEL REY

Bed & Breakfast California

P.O. Box 2247, Saratoga, 95070
(408) 867-9662; (800) 872-4500
FAX (408) 867-0907; e-mail: info@bbintl.com
www.bbintl.com

Old World-style home with an Elizabethan Tudor appearance. Completed in 1987, the four-level home is intricately decorated and offers many hand-painted and hand-carved touches to delight the eye. Antiques from England, Mexico, and elsewhere create a fairy tale ambiance. The family room features a high ceiling and a river rock fireplace, and the parlor has an old piano and Victrola. Two guest rooms on the first floor share a lovely sitting room, and each room has a private bath. Through French doors guests will find a charming courtyard leading to a lovely garden with a cascading waterfall. $75-115.

---

7 No smoking; 8 Children welcome; 9 Social drinking allowed; 10 Tennis nearby; 11 Swimming nearby; 12 Golf nearby; 13 Skiing nearby; 14 May be booked through a travel agent; 15 Handicapped accessible.

POINT REYES STATION

Bed & Breakfast California

P.O. Box 2247, Saratoga, 95070
(408) 867-9662; (800) 872-4500
FAX (408) 867-0907; e-mail: info@bbintl.com
www.bbintl.com

The Country House. This three-bedroom, two-bath inn, in the picturesque Point Reyes Station, features a huge country kitchen fireplace. All linens, dishes, cooking utensils, and firewood are provided. An acre of orchards and gardens overlooks Inverness Ridge. Full breakfast. $125-250.

Bed & Breakfast Exchange of Marin County—Referral Service

45 Entrata, San Anselmo, 94960
(415) 485-1971; FAX (415) 454-7179

Gallery Cottage. Charming self-contained cottage within walking distance to town. It backs up to open space and sits in a pretty garden. This bed and breakfast has its own kitchen and includes coffee/tea only. Fireplace, queen-size bed, quiet. $125.

Cricket Cottage

Box 627, 94956
(415) 663-9139; FAX (415) 663-9090
e-mail: pinc@nbn.com; www.nbn.com/people/pinc

A cozy, romantic country cottage set in an intimate garden overlooking a meadow, surrounded by elegant cypress and eucalyptus trees. The cottage is furnished with antique furniture, original art, library, Franklin fireplace, and just outside the front door, a private redwood hot tub under the stars. A stay at the cottage also provides an opportunity to explore the permaculture garden including an earthen bread oven, orchard, pond, ducks, and beds of herbs, vegetables, and berries.

Hosts: James Stark and Penny Livingston
Cottage: 1 (PB) $115-145
Full Breakfast
Credit Cards: None
Notes: 2, 5, 7, 8, 9, 10, 11, 12

Gray's Retreat

P.O. Box 56, 94956
(415) 663-1166

Private cottage quarters on the ground floor of a classic barn converted to elegant living—floor to ceiling windows for a view of the Inverness Ridge and sunset, two garden patios, Franklin fireplace, full tile kitchen with gas stove, dishwasher, microwave, and service for eight. Four-poster queen-size bed in bedroom, double and trundle in living room sleep six. High chair, crib, and stroller available. Tub and shower in bath. Secluded garden spa. Cable TV with VCR available. Private telephone. Walk to town. Large nature library; laundry. Stocked kitchen. Pets welcome by prior arrangements. Partially handicapped accessible.

Host: Karen Gray
Cottage: $185
Credit Cards: A, B, C
Notes: 2, 3, 4, 5, 6, 8, 12, 14

Holly Tree Inn & Cottages

3 Silverhills Road, P.O. Box 642, 94956
(415) 663 1554; FAX (415) 663-8566
www.hollytreeinn.com

This inn's setting is a 19-acre valley of lawns, herbs, and wooded hillsides with a gazebo and

Holly Tree Inn

NOTES: Credit cards accepted: A MasterCard; B Visa; C American Express; D Discover; E Diner's Club; F Other; 2 Personal checks accepted; 3 Lunch available; 4 Dinner available; 5 Open all year; 6 Pets welcome;

garden hot tub. Spacious living and dining rooms decorated in flowery prints and antiques have vast couches, French doors, and fireplaces. Two cottages, the Sea Star Cottage on Tomales Bay and Vision Cottage in the Bishop pine forest, each have queen-size beds, hot tub, and fireplace. The Cottage-in-the-Woods is a magical two-room getaway, with fireplace and claw-foot soaking tub. Outstanding breakfasts, afternoon tea.

Hosts: Diane and Tom Balogh
Rooms: 4 (PB) $120-250
Cottages: 3 (PB)
Full Breakfast
Credit Cards: A, B, C
Notes: 2, 5, 7, 8, 9, 11, 12, 14

JASMINE COTTAGE
Bed & Breakfast

Jasmine Cottage

P.O. Box 56, 94956
(415) 663-1166

A complete garden cottage all for guests: full kitchen, fireplace, secluded flower gardens with barbecue, large nature library, garden spa under the stars, and lots of sunshine. Full breakfast is provided as well as a stocked kitchen with coffees, teas, herbs, spices, and lots of cooking gear. An equipped picnic basket, beach chairs, and beach barbecue included. TV with cable and VCR by request. A Jasmine Cottage stay always includes bouquets of fresh flowers. High chair, crib, and stroller available. Walk to town. Dogs welcome with prior arrangements. Partially handicapped accessible.

Host: Karen Gray
Cottage: $185
Full Breakfast
Credit Cards: A, B, C
Notes: 2, 5, 7, 8, 9, 14

QUINCY

The Feather Bed

542 Jackson Street, P.O. Box 3200, 95971
(530) 283-0102; (800) 696-8624
e-mail: feathrbd@pslan.com

Relax, refresh, revitalize. Choose a romantic cottage or a comfy upstairs room in the Queen Anne-styled inn. Relax on the porch with homemade cookies and fudge. Tour Quincy on complimentary bicycles. Hike and fish uncrowded Feather River and Plumas Forest. Walk to restaurants, museum, and theater. Savor the homegrown berry smoothies and gourmet breakfasts. All rooms have private baths and telephones, must have a fireplace and air conditioning. Gansner Airfield pick-up.

Hosts: Bob and Jan Janowski
Rooms: 7 (PB) $80-130
Full Breakfast
Credit Cards: A, B, C, D, E
Notes: 2, 5, 7, 8, 9, 10, 11, 12, 14,1 5

The Feather Bed

7 No smoking; 8 Children welcome; 9 Social drinking allowed; 10 Tennis nearby; 11 Swimming nearby; 12 Golf nearby; 13 Skiing nearby; 14 May be booked through a travel agent; 15 Handicapped accessible.

REDDING

Palisades Paradise Bed & Breakfast

1200 Palisades Avenue, 96003
(530) 223-5305

Guests will love the breathtaking view of the Sacramento River, the city, and surrounding mountains from this beautiful contemporary home with its spa, fireplace, in-room TV, and homelike atmosphere. Palisades Paradise is a serene setting for a quiet hideaway, yet one mile from shopping and I-5, with water skiing and river rafting nearby. Inspected and approved by the CABBI. Inquire about accommodations for pets. Smoking permitted outside only. Children welcome when booking both rooms. Small dog in residence.

Host: Gail Goetz
Rooms: 2 (SB) $65-100
Continental and Full Breakfasts
Credit Cards: A, B, C
Notes: 2, 5, 7, 9, 10, 11, 12, 13, 14

Palisades Paradise

REDONDO BEACH

Bed & Breakfast California

P.O. Box 2247, Saratoga, 95070
(408) 867-9662; (800) 872-4500
FAX (408) 867-0907; e-mail: info@bbintl.com
www.bbintl.com

A. Walk to Redondo Beach from this cozy, comfortable bed and breakfast in quiet, residential neighborhood. Sunny guest room has private entrance, private bath, deck, and hot tub. Continental plus breakfast. $75-85.

B. Hosts have remodeled their home to include a guest suite with private bath. Quiet, residential neighborhood, close to LA International Airport and not far from the beach or tourist attractions. Hosts are both teachers and, in the summer, guests may have breakfast served at the Jacuzzi on their deck. $75-85.

Breezy Inn

122 South Juanita Avenue, 90277-3435
(310) 316-5123

In a quiet upscale neighborhood. Large suite with private entrance, private bath with spa, oriental carpet, California king-size bed. Breakfast area with microwave, toaster oven, and stocked refrigerator. Good ventilation with skylight and ceiling fan. Also other guest room with twin beds, private bath, TV, and refrigerator.

Host: Betty Binding
Rooms: 2 (PB)
Continental Breakfast
Credit Cards: None
Notes: 2, 5, 7, 8, 9, 10, 11, 12

RUNNING SPRINGS

Bed & Breakfast California

P.O. Box 2247, Saratoga, 95070
(408) 867-9662; (800) 872-4500
FAX (408) 867-0907; e-mail: info@bbintl.com
www.bbintl.com

In the San Bernardino Mountains, this quaint bed and breakfast is just 10 minutes from Lake Arrowhead and 30 minutes from Big Bear. The house was originally built as part of a sawmill and is open for winter skiing and summer sunning and hiking. The three guest rooms offer antique furnishings and comfortable quilts, as well as a full breakfast served by the fireplace or on the deck. Wine and cheese are available in the afternoon and brandy is served in the evening. $95-130.

NOTES: Credit cards accepted: A MasterCard; B Visa; C American Express; D Discover; E Diner's Club; F Other; 2 Personal checks accepted; 3 Lunch available; 4 Dinner available; 5 Open all year; 6 Pets welcome;

SACRAMENTO

Amber House Bed & Breakfast Inn

1315 22nd Street, 95816
(916) 444-8085; (800) 755-6526
e-mail: innkeeper@amberhouse.com

Sacramento's only AAA four-diamond inn, just eight blocks from the capitol and convention center in a quiet neighborhood of historic homes. Three turn-of-the-century homes have been beautifully restored and decorated all with marble tiled private baths, 11 with two person Jacuzzi, TVs, telephones, bathrobes. A full gourmet breakfast is served at the time and place of guests' choice: in the guest room, the dining room, or the garden.

Hosts: Michael and Jane Richardson
Rooms: 14 (PB) $139-259
Full Breakfast
Credit Cards: A, B, C, D, E
Notes: 5, 7, 9, 10, 11, 12, 14

Amber House

Bed & Breakfast California

P.O. Box 2247, Saratoga, 95070
(408) 867-9662; (800) 872-4500
FAX (408) 867-0907; e-mail: info@bbintl.com
www.bbintl.com

A. In the historic district, this 1912 Colonial Revival offers spacious, airy rooms with antiques. Walk to the capitol or restaurants; relax in the hot tub; enjoy gourmet full breakfasts and afternoon refreshments. Five guest rooms have private baths and king- or queen-size beds. No smoking. $105-175.

B. Just eight blocks from the capitol, this inn is on a quiet tree-lined street of historic homes. Cozy rooms or elegant suites have private baths, double, king- or queen-size beds. Full breakfast; afternoon refreshments help guests relax after a day of business or sightseeing. No smoking allowed. $139-259.

C. Spacious two-story traditional home in Sacramento's finest neighborhood, convenient to the capitol, Sacramento State University, and other places of interest. It has a swimming pool and lovely garden which includes a bonsai collection. Two guest rooms share one bath. $75-85.

Hartley House Bed & Breakfast Inn

700 22nd Street, 95816
(916) 447-7829; (800) 831-5806
FAX (916) 447-1820

A stunning turn-of-the-century mansion with the sophisticated elegance of a small European hotel in historic Boulevard Park in midtown. Offering exquisitely appointed rooms, the inn is near the capitol, Old Town, the convention center, the city's finest restaurants, and coffee and dessert cafés. Step back in time and ride a horse and carriage to a restaurant and back to

Hartley House

the inn. The host also has a cookie jar filled with freshly baked cookies!

Host: Randy Hartley
Rooms: 5 (PB) $120-175
Full Breakfast
Credit Cards: A, B, C, D, E, F
Notes: 5, 7, 9, 10, 11, 12, 13, 14

ST. HELENA

Bartels Ranch and Bed & Breakfast Country Inn

1200 Conn Valley Road, St. Helena, 94574
(707) 963-4001; FAX (707) 963-5100
e-mail: Bartelsranch@WEBTV.net
www.bartelsranch.com

In the heart of Napa Valley, a peaceful 60-acre estate overlooks oak hillsides and vineyards. Six minutes east of St. Helena's finest wineries, restaurants, and shopping. In *Best Places to Stay in California* and *Frommers*. Three uniquely decorated rooms and honeymoon suite. Amenities: fireplaces, movies, coffee, robes, bicycles, library, living room with piano, entertainment room. Breakfast served in formal dining room terraces. Telephone, fax, and refrigerator. ABBA Award of Excellence. Dinner catered. Designated smoking areas.

Host: Jami Bartels
Rooms: 4 (PB) $185-425
Full Breakfast
Credit Cards: A, B, C, D, E, F
Notes: 2, 3, 5, 8, 9, 10, 11, 12, 14, 15

Bartels Ranch

Bed & Breakfast California

P.O. Box 2247, Saratoga, 95070
(408) 867-9662; (800) 872-4500
FAX (408) 867-0907; e-mail: info@bbintl.com
www.bbintl.com

A. A 1950s home surrounded by vineyards and fruit trees. Enclosed pool and spa. Extensive rose, vegetable, and herb gardens for use by guests. Fireplace, ceiling fans, barbecue, stunning views. Two comfortable bedrooms with designer touches make guests' stay in the wine country more enjoyable. The whole house is for guests to enjoy! $200-250.

B. This inn is ideally positioned in the Napa Valley, furnished with antiques and fine linens to make an elegant country atmosphere. The details at this inn make lasting memories, whether its the 100-year-old wisteria vine that covers the column-enclosed patio, or the sumptuous champagne breakfast offered daily. Fine wines and cheese in the evening, fresh cut flowers, croquet in the garden are all part of the experience. $175-215.

C. Fashioned after the inns of New England, was designed and is operated as an integral part of one of the truly great wine producing areas of the world. Most of the 25 rooms are oriented to rural views, many overlooking nearby vineyards. Some rooms have patios, gracefully surrounded by lawns and privacy landscaping; others have intimate balconies; most are provided with fireplaces. Combining the old and the new, all rooms are individually decorated with country antique furnishings and lovely, fresh colors. $146-268.

D. Visitors to California's Napa Valley will find a charming, comfortable, and delightfully individual retreat in historic St. Helena. Thickets of oak, pine, magnolia, and madrone on the resort's 265-acre grounds provide a serene backdrop for the Cape Cod-style Croquet Lodge, which houses 13 guest rooms, and the

---

NOTES: Credit cards accepted: A MasterCard; B Visa; C American Express; D Discover; E Diner's Club; F Other; 2 Personal checks accepted; 3 Lunch available; 4 Dinner available; 5 Open all year; 6 Pets welcome;

17 gabled guest cottages, each containing four suites clustered around the studio. Accommodations feature private porches, vaulted ceilings, and skylights. Most also have fireplaces. $490-650.

E. Secluded in a forest above vineyards, yet near town, this small bed and breakfast offers a peaceful, rustic retreat. Guest room has private entrance and fireplace. Carriage Room, studio, and two-room cottage are decorated with antiques and are very private. Private baths. Full breakfast is served. Sorry, smoking is not permitted. $130-175.

F. This New England-style inn offers large, comfortable rooms and elegant hospitality. There are 20 guest rooms and suites, many with a fireplace, whirlpool, patio, balcony, and beautiful view. Private baths. Continental plus buffet breakfast is served. No smoking. $140-210.

Cinnamon Bear Bed & Breakfast

1407 Kearney Street, 94574
(707) 963-4653; (888) 963-4600
FAX (707) 963-0251

Historic Craftsman bungalow, circa 1904, the Metzner Estate is now a cozy, inviting bed and breakfast. Two blocks from Main Street, discover the best wineries, shopping, and restaurants in Napa Valley. The guest rooms are filled with antiques, king- or queen-size beds,

Cinnamon Bear

all with private baths. Relax after a day of tasting and touring on the spacious front porch or by the fireplace in the sitting room. Great hospitality. A wonderful breakfast awaits guests in the morning.

Host: Cathye Ranieri
Rooms: 3 (PB) $115-190
Full Breakfast
Credit Cards: A, B, C, E
Notes: 2, 5, 7, 9, 10, 11, 12, 14

Deer Run Inn

P.O. Box 311, 94574
(707) 963-3794; (800) 843-3408
FAX (707) 963-9026

Old World hospitality awaits guests at Deer Run Inn tucked away in the forest on Spring Mountain Road in the wine country of Napa Valley. A cedar-shingled bungalow on four lush acres, lovingly restored, offers comfort, friendly ambiance, and gracious personal service. Rooms are fully carpeted, decorated with family antiques and heirlooms. Feather beds, fine linens, decks, fireplaces, private baths, down quilts, evening brandy, mints, coffee and tea service, air conditioning, refrigerators, robes, and hair dryers. Lunch and dinner available by local delivery service. Heated swimming pool on grounds.

Hosts: Tom and Carol Wilson
Rooms: 4 (PB) $140-195
Full Breakfast
Credit Cards: A, B, C
Notes: 2, 5, 7, 9, 10, 11, 12, 14

Hilltop House Bed & Breakfast

9550 St. Helena Road, P.O. Box 726, 94574
(707) 944-0880; FAX (707) 571-0263

Poised at the very top of a ridge that separates the famous wine regions of Napa and Sonoma, Hilltop House is a country retreat with all the comforts of home, with a view that must be seen to be believed. The host built this contemporary home with this mountain panorama in mind, and the vast deck allows guests to enjoy

---

7 No smoking; 8 Children welcome; 9 Social drinking allowed; 10 Tennis nearby; 11 Swimming nearby; 12 Golf nearby; 13 Skiing nearby; 14 May be booked through a travel agent; 15 Handicapped accessible.

it at leisure with a glass of wine in the afternoon, with breakfast in the morning, or with a long soak in the hot tub. From this vantage point sunrises and sunsets are simply amazing. Guests will cherish the natural setting, caring hospitality, and prize location.

Host: Annette Gevarter
Rooms: 4 (PB) $135-195
Full Breakfast
Credit Cards: A, B, C
Notes: 2, 5, 7, 8, 9, 10, 11, 12, 14

Meadowood

Meadowood Napa Valley

900 Meadowood Lane, 94574
(800) 458-8080; FAX (707) 963-3532

To find a place which reflects the peaceful nature and innate beauty of the wine country, look to Meadowood Napa Valley, an exquisite property reminiscent of a grand country estate. Meadowood offers 85 cottages, suites and lodges, all nestled among the oaks and pines of the estate's 250 acre setting, and all the amenities consistent with its standing as a Relais et Chateaux property, including croquet, tennis, golf, a complete health spa, and fine dining in the Restaurant at Meadowood. Either full or Continental breakfast option at additional cost via room service or in the Grill.

Host: Seamu McManus (Managing Director)
Rooms: 85 (PB) $345-670
Full or Continental Breakfast
Credit Cards: A, B, C, D, E
Notes: 2, 3, 4, 5, 8, 9, 10, 11, 12, 14, 15

The Wine Country Inn

1152 Lodi Lane, 94574
(707) 963-7077; FAX (707) 963-9018
e-mail: romance@winecountryinn.com
www.winecountryinn.com

Perched on a knoll overlooking manicured vineyards and the nearby hills, this country inn offers 24 individually decorated guest rooms. The host used family-made quilts, local antiques, fireplaces, and balconies to create an atmosphere of unparalled comfort. Closed Christmas.

Host: Jim Smith
Rooms: 24 (PB) $145-275
Full Breakfast
Credit Cards: A, B
Notes: 2, 7, 9, 10, 11, 12, 14

SAN ANDREAS

The Robin's Nest

247 West St. Charles Street, P.O. Box 1408, 95249
(209) 754-1076; (888) 214-9202
FAX (209) 754-3975
www.robinest.com

A homey 1895 Queen Anne Victorian mansion. Traditional yet informal. Gourmet five-course breakfast. Hot tub. Central to seven wineries, three caverns, four golf courses, eight public lakes, historic gold-mining towns, giant redwoods, and more.

The Robin's Nest

NOTES: Credit cards accepted: A MasterCard; B Visa; C American Express; D Discover; E Diner's Club; F Other; 2 Personal checks accepted; 3 Lunch available; 4 Dinner available; 5 Open all year; 6 Pets welcome;

Hosts: Karen and William Konietzny
Rooms: 9 (7 PB; 2 SB) $65-115
Full Breakfast
Credit Cards: A, B, C, D
Notes: 2, 4, 5, 7, 8, 9, 10, 11, 12, 13, 14, 15

SAN ANSELMO

Bed & Breakfast Exchange of Marin County—Referral Service

45 Entrata, 94960
(415) 485-1971; FAX (415) 454-7179

The Lamortes San Anselmo Bed and Breakfast. Be the exclusive guests at this charming bed and breakfast apartment. Within walking distance to town, shops, fine restaurants, and even a lake. This is a great spot for visiting anywhere in Marin County—it is only 15 miles north of San Francisco and one hour to the wine country. Sleeps up to four people. Full kitchen. Discount for longer stays. Full breakfast. No smoking. Children welcome. $85.

San Anselmo Village Cottage. Private cottage on a tree-lined street close to town. Completely self-contained. Off-street parking. Full kitchen, including dishwasher and bath. Queen-size bed. Walk to restaurants and parks. $110.

SAN DIEGO

Bed & Breakfast California

P.O. Box 2247, Saratoga, 95070
(408) 867-9662; (800) 872-4500
FAX (408) 867-0907; e-mail: info@bbintl.com
www.bbintl.com

A. This charming house and cottage in a quiet residential neighborhood is on a bluff less than 10 minutes from downtown, the beach, and all local tourist attractions. The 65-foot deck features a spa and a superb view of Hotel Circle below. All accommodations have 14-foot ceilings, antique furnishings, color TV/VCR, telephones, refrigerators, and bathrobes. $115-130.

B. Designated a historical site in 1984, this charming inn has eight bedrooms and five baths. There is a pool and Jacuzzi for guests' use; some of the rooms are at poolside. The home is furnished in antiques and with oriental rugs. A Continental breakfast is served in the morning. There are also two studios and a two-bedroom apartment across the street. The inn is less than one mile from the zoo and also within walking distance of Balboa Park. $69-150.

C. Ten minutes from downtown, beaches, and local tourist attractions. Relax and enjoy views from the 75-foot deck with spa. Four guest rooms with private baths. Robes, mini-refrigerator, TV, and VCR are provided. Gourmet breakfast and afternoon refreshments. Smoking is not permitted. $115-130.

D. Separate guest house with turn-of-the-century furnishings assures privacy in central San Diego and offers a bedroom, sitting room with wood-burning stove, and dining area where a delicious Continental breakfast is served. Additional guest room with private entrance is available. Private bath. $65-89.

E. Enchanted cottage nestled away on quiet cul-de-sac is just minutes away from zoo, Balboa Park, and golf course. Bed and breakfast is also convenient to downtown and many tourist attractions. Suites have a private entrance and patios overlooking a wooded canyon and a fragrant herb garden. Full breakfast is served. $75-95.

F. Just a five-minute drive from Harbor Island Convention Center and 10 minutes from the Downtown Convention Center, beaches, and other attractions, this beautiful Mediterranean-style bed and breakfast is in the Point Loma neighborhood. Two suites have private baths. Full breakfast is served. Pool, Jacuzzi, and kitchen for guests. $95.

---

7 No smoking; 8 Children welcome; 9 Social drinking allowed; 10 Tennis nearby; 11 Swimming nearby; 12 Golf nearby; 13 Skiing nearby; 14 May be booked through a travel agent; 15 Handicapped accessible.

Carole's

Carole's Bed & Breakfast Inn

3227 Grim Avenue, 92104
(619) 280-5258; (800) 975-5521

Historic 1904 two-story Craftsman home built by the city's mayor is furnished with antiques and a piano; a rose garden is on the grounds. Swimming pool, hot tub, and gas barbecue. Less than one mile to zoo. Close to all major attractions. Continental plus breakfast is served in guest room or dining area. Refreshments served in the evening. A garden studio apartment and a two-bedroom apartment are available across the street. Dinner is available but not included in the rate. Smoking on designated patio only. Senior rates are available. Reservation deposit is required. Traveler's checks are accepted.

Hosts: Carole Dugdale and Michael O'Brien
Rooms: 6 (2 PB; 4 SB) $69-89
Apartments: 2 (PB) $99-159
Continental Breakfast
Credit Cards: A, B, C, D
Notes: 5, 8, 9, 10, 11, 12, 14

Harbor Hill Guest House

2330 Albatross Street, 92101
(619) 233-0638

Overlooking the San Diego Harbor is the ideal location for business, weekend getaways, honeymoons, and family reunions. Accommodates 16 adults. The Carriage House is a separate hideaway for two. Private baths. Continental breakfast. Each level has a semiprivate entry. A kitchen is on each level.

Rooms: 6 (PB) $65-90
Continental Breakfast
Credit Cards: A, B
Notes: 2, 5, 8, 9, 14

Mi Casa Su Casa/Old Pueblo Homestays Bed & Breakfast Reservation Service

P.O. Box 950, Tempe, AZ 85280-0950
(602) 990-0682; (800) 456-0682
FAX (602) 990-3390
e-mail: micasa@primenet.com
www.azres.com

7551. Don't go boatless in San Diego! The boat and breakfast at Cabrillo Isle Marina offers boat and breakfast accommodations as well as harbor tours, custom charter, sunset cruises all under the supervision of licensed captains. The 42-foot Carver motor yacht and the 33-foot Sea Ray are attractively furnished including kitchenette, lounge, and sleeping areas. Off-season. November 1 to May 1. Can rent boats by the hour, with a two-hour minimum. Rates for boat and breakfast are $150-200.

SAN FRANCISCO

Absolutely Accommodations

P.O. Box 641471, San Francisco, 94164-1471
(415) 677-9789; (888) 982-2632
e-mail: travelinfo@iname.com
www.citysearch.com/sfo/accommodations

This is a free reservation service committed to assisting travelers in finding the best possible accommodations in California. It offers access to private homestay bed and breakfasts and inns. It can help guests find the proper accommodations that meet their individual needs. The service's goal is to provide both its clients and hosts with the best possible customer service.

NOTES: Credit cards accepted: A MasterCard; B Visa; C American Express; D Discover; E Diner's Club; F Other; 2 Personal checks accepted; 3 Lunch available; 4 Dinner available; 5 Open all year; 6 Pets welcome;

San Francisco 101. Experience one of San Francisco's finest painted ladies in North Beach. This beautiful home is furnished throughout with fine antiques and designer linens. Walk four blocks to Fisherman's Wharf, Pier 39, and a block and a half from the cable cars. Guests are also within a 10-minute walk to Coit Tower and Chinatown. Don't miss out on all of the wonderful restaurants in the heart of North Beach. $105-275.

San Francisco 102. Built in 1907 as a private home, this inn has been lovingly restored and is furnished with hand-picked antiques. Convenient to Union Square, cable cars, and Chinatown. Twenty-one rooms with private baths. $99-249.

San Francisco 103. Restored to its true Victorian elegance, this home was built in the late 1800s and is furnished with heirloom antiques. Convenient to all tourist attractions. Walk to the cable cars or dine at fine restaurants within a short walk from this bed and breakfast. Two shared baths and two private baths. $88-125.

San Francisco 104. Stay in own private suite in downtown San Francisco. Walk to Union Square and the cable cars. Easily accessible to all tourist attractions. Fully furnished in a true San Francisco style. Three rooms with private baths. $150-175.

San Francisco 105. This 1908 Edwardian in the Corona Heights/Castro has been restored and decorated with an eclectic mix of contemporary and antique furniture of the Mission Revival and Arts and Crafts movement. Most rooms have hardwood floors and oriental rugs. Many ceilings boast Bradbury and Bradbury hand silk-screened papers coordinated with Ralph Lauren paints. Each apartment provides a queen-size bed, full kitchen, private bathroom, living room with a fold-out sofa and fireplace. Sleeps two to four. $150-200.

The Andrews Hotel

624 Post Street, 94109
(415) 563-6877; (800) 926-3739
FAX (415) 928-6919; www.andrewshotel.com

Two blocks west of Union Square, the Andrews Hotel is at the heart of the shopping and theater districts. Built as the Sultan Turkish Baths in 1905 and converted into a hotel in the 1920s, this Queen Anne structure features bay windows in 10 of the 48 guest rooms. Continental breakfast is served buffet style in the hallways. complimentary wine is included with rate and served in the acclaimed Italian restaurant, Fino. Twenty-four hour coffee and tea service are also available. Additional charge for parking. Nonsmoking hotel.

Hosts: Barbara, Yvonne, Jessica, and Susan
Rooms: 48 (PB) $89-129
Continental Breakfast
Credit Cards: A, B, C, E, F
Notes: 4, 5, 7, 8, 9, 11, 14

Bed & Breakfast California

P.O. Box 2247, Saratoga, 95070
(408) 867-9662; (800) 872-4500
FAX (408) 867-0907; e-mail: info@bbintl.com
www.bbintl.com

A. Three-story turn-of-the-century home that has been pictured in *Sunset* magazine. Favorite spot for many returning guests. Only 15 minutes from Union Square and an equal distance to an ocean beach. Within walking distance to Golden Gate Park, the Presidio, and the many shops and restaurants on Clement Street. One room with sitting area and private bath. Two rooms with shared bath. $80-90.

B. This 1876 Victorian is "eccentrically, eclectically, and very tastefully decorated." This home is truly San Francisco and is close to shops and restaurants in popular Pacific Heights. There is a guest room with private bath, minikitchen, and sitting room. In the back garden, a guest cottage affords privacy and opens onto the patio. $105.

---

7 No smoking; 8 Children welcome; 9 Social drinking allowed; 10 Tennis nearby; 11 Swimming nearby; 12 Golf nearby; 13 Skiing nearby; 14 May be booked through a travel agent; 15 Handicapped accessible.

Bed & Breakfast California (continued)

C. This quintessential 1896 Victorian in Pacific Heights has been lovingly restored and is close to downtown and within walking distance to shops and restaurants on popular Fillmore Street. High quality antiques and linens are used in four guest rooms. One guest room has a private bath and two guest rooms share a bath. A suite with a private entrance and private bath was added last year. $90-120.

D. Built in 1910, this home was built in the Craftsman style and has been remodeled to give it a very spacious and open feeling. The apartments are individually decorated and are open and sunny, with a parlor, vanity area, and separate entrances. The host prepares luscious gourmet breakfasts served in his dining room, which has a panoramic view of the city including the Bay Bridge. $110.

E. Recently renovated large Queen Anne Victorian within walking distance of Golden Gate Park, close to good public transportation and restaurants in the "Greenwich Village" of San Francisco. Its six guest rooms are spacious, sunny, and include kitchenettes; two also have fireplaces. Guests are pampered with robes and slippers provided for their use. $115.

F. In a quiet residential neighborhood, this pleasant home was built in 1923 and is just three blocks from Golden Gate Park and six blocks from Ocean Beach with its famous Cliff House restaurant. The home has a fireplace, ocean view, and a deck, and there are always homemade cookies in the cookie jar. The guest rooms are inviting and cozy, with antique beds, down comforters, and plush robes. $95-115.

G. This elegant, contemporary, two-bedroom flat is part of a Mediterranean-style building built in the mid-1900s. It includes a kitchen, a front room with fireplace, cable TV, VCR, a cozy deck with a garden, and a wonderful bay view. The flat is decorated with original and unusual artwork. The building is in a quiet residential neighborhood, ideally within walking distance of the crooked part of Lombard Street, Fisherman's Wharf, the Marina, Chinatown, and downtown. $150.

H. Lovely studio apartment on the ground floor of an attractive 1879 Victorian built by Charles Eastridge. Looks out onto a private patio and garden. The charming, contemporary suite has a private entrance, is furnished with a sleigh bed, and has a full kitchen and dining area. In the sunny heart of San Francisco, guests are minutes from many restaurants and shops. $130.

I. This spectacular home is the anchor of the famous "Postcard Row" in San Francisco's historic Alamo Square district. Built in 1892 by carpenter-builder Matthew Kavanaugh for his family, it has been meticulously restored and has appeared in numerous films and TV shows. The guest apartment is large and beautifully decorated in contemporary style, with a sunken living room that looks out over the garden, a large kitchenette, and a large bedroom with a canopied bed. A wonderful two-bedroom house with garden next door is also available. $175-300.

J. Unique small cottage to the rear of the host home atop one of San Francisco's highest points near Golden Gate Park. Fireplace and kitchen. Private bath. Car essential. Three-night minimum stay. Continental breakfast is self-catered. $100.

K. This 1913 turn-of-the-century Edwardian family-run bed and breakfast with antique furnishings is two blocks from Union Square and the cable cars. Twenty-three guest rooms with private and shared baths offered. Continental breakfast is served. $75-110.

L. This four-story Victorian hotel, now a Marina District bed and breakfast inn, features

NOTES: Credit cards accepted: A MasterCard; B Visa; C American Express; D Discover; E Diner's Club; F Other; 2 Personal checks accepted; 3 Lunch available; 4 Dinner available; 5 Open all year; 6 Pets welcome;

four-poster beds and modern amenities. Thirty guest rooms with private baths. Continental breakfast is served. $65-125.

M. Two unique bed and breakfast inns, one country French and the other formal English, are two blocks from Union Square and offer beautifully appointed rooms, hospitality, afternoon refreshments, and wonderful breakfasts. Twenty-six guest rooms with private baths. $110-250.

N. Hilltop home in Diamond Heights area has glorious view of the bay and city from the two-story living room. Enjoy a full breakfast in the Scandinavian dining area. Each of three guest rooms has a balcony. Two baths. $65-70.

O. This restored Edwardian home was built in 1900. It has lovely hardwood floors in the living room, as well as a covered ceiling. The bedroom has a queen-size canopied bed and there is a full kitchen. There is a garden in back, perfect for enjoying the San Francisco sunshine (liquid or otherwise!). The neighborhood has many shops and restaurants, and is easily accessible to transportation downtown. $110.

P. The 21 individually decorated guest rooms can only be described as 20ish, vaudeville, unique, some oppulent, not for all. This is a fun, different Victorian frequented by movie stars, the Hollywood set, and eccentrics. Museum quality art and antique furnishings and fixtures surround guests with nostalgia and house ghost. $227-368.

Q. A delightful three-story European-style inn, only blocks from San Francisco's yacht harbor. Unpretentious and small, the hotel was originally built to house guests who attended the 1915 Panama-Pacific International Exposition. A Continental breakfast is served in the main floor's old-world bakery, and guests can enjoy complimentary sherry in the small pub in the evening. Guest rooms range from pension-style rooms with shared bath to opulent suites with Jacuzzi tubs. $75-99.

R. Light and airy, this hotel offers European style comfort in the heart of the city, just minutes from Union Square, the theater district, and the cable cars. The hotel has 65 rooms, as well as an indoor heated lap swimming pool and fitness room for guests to enjoy. $89-159.

S. This inn is an 1890 landmark which has been beautifully restored with 49 individually designed, luxuriously appointed rooms and suites. The inn also features a large parlor, a grand staircase, and meeting rooms. Amenities include a Continental breakfast, nightly tea and sherry, morning newspaper, and exercise facilities. $120-275.

T. Beautiful house built in 1876 remodeled in a Beaux Arts style in 1918. Interior is a magazine quality with 12-14 foot ceilings, stained glass, and leaded glass doors and windows. Furnishings are an eclectic mixture of old, new, and whimsical with an antebellum southern flair. Neighborhood is one of San Francisco's finest with trendy shops and restaurants as well as parks just blocks away. The quiet and spacious guest room is charming with a queen-size metal poster bed and antiques with private bath just outside the door. $105.

U. Constructed in 1908, this 153-room hotel has been newly renovated in theater-deco style combined with Victoriana. The interiors feature velvets and brocades in rich jewel tones with savvy stripes and precocious plaids as accents. Hotel amenities include reception, concierge services, and a full-service restaurant and bar. Located in the heart of Union Square, the hotel is steps away from theater row, the cable car line, the Financial District, and some of the world's finest shopping. $129-675.

V. This bed and breakfast is a home away from home for the discerning hotel-weary traveler. Six beautifully decorated rooms welcome

---

7 No smoking; 8 Children welcome; 9 Social drinking allowed; 10 Tennis nearby; 11 Swimming nearby; 12 Golf nearby; 13 Skiing nearby; 14 May be booked through a travel agent; 15 Handicapped accessible.

business travelers and families alike. A landscaped deck in the front of the house invites breakfast al fresco, and a hot tub in the back garden provides relaxation after a hard day's work or shopping. $99-169.

W. This contemporary multi-level home has three rooms. The upper level large open room with private bath has gorgeous wall-to-wall full window view of the Pacific Ocean. The lowest level room has a queen-size sofa bed, private bath, and small personal kitchen. Furnishings are Scandinavian. $85-150.

X. This beautiful 1869 Victorian survived the 1906 earthquake and was completely renovated in 1998, at which time the guest apartment was added. A private entrance leads guests to a spacious one-bedroom apartment with a full kitchen, living room, and private deck. The apartment is bright and sunny, furnished in modern European-style and decorated with original artwork. Just across the street is one of the lovely city parks providing tennis courts, walking trails through its 36 acres and stunning views of downtown San Francisco and the Pacific Ocean. $150.

Y. Small boutique hotel located in the heart of downtown San Francisco. Walk to cable cars, Chinatown, Union Square. There are 48 rooms in this traditional Victorian building that offer a floral motif in the rooms and a comfortable lobby with concierge. There is an Italian restaurant on premises that guests won't want to miss. $90-142.

Z. Built in 1904, the spirit of this inn is delightfully romantic and relaxing. It is centrally positioned on a beautiful park and surrounded by lovely Victorian homes. Most rooms have fireplaces, and the delicious Continental breakfast is delivered to guests' room. Afternoons offer complimentary wine service in the parlor, accompanied by piano music. $139-249.

AA. Classic 1908 Edwardian that has been featured in several "Painted Ladies" revisited guidebooks and is on one of the city's motorized cable car tours. The recently renovated Junior Suite is furnished in fine antiques and beautifully decorated, and guests will enjoy sleeping on designer linens. The location is one of the best in San Francisco, putting guests within walking distance to Coit Tower, Pier 39, Fisherman's Wharf, cable cars, and all the wonderful Italian restaurants and coffee houses in North Beach. $135.

BB. This 100-year-old Edwardian was formerly the neighborhood candy store. This home has been wonderfully restored in the past few years. The guest unit is very spacious offering a large bedroom, kitchen, sitting room, French doors, and two decks with views. The furnishings are a mix of high quality furniture and heirloom antiques. $135.

CC. Guests will find plenty of peace and quiet at this lovely 1910 Edwardian home only two blocks from Golden Gate Park. Walk to the DeYoung Museum, the Steinhart Aquarium, and the Strybing Arboretum. The home is tastefully furnished with antiques and chandeliers, and guests will be delighted by their host's collection of fine silver and stemware. Two roomy guest rooms with private baths have brass beds, and bathrobes are provided for their comfort. $95.

Bed & Breakfast San Francisco

P.O. Box 420009, 94142
(415) 931-3083; FAX (415) 921-BBSF (2273)
e-mail: bbsf@linex.com; www.bbsf.com

3. A cozy country-style bed and breakfast in the heart of San Francisco has four guest rooms that are comfortably furnished with country antiques and brass beds. The house is at the end of a quiet street, away from the city noise. There is a small patio with trees and birds for the guests to enjoy. A full breakfast is served in the sunny kitchen each morning, and complimentary wine is always available. Four guest rooms share two full baths. $69-79.

NOTES: Credit cards accepted: A MasterCard; B Visa; C American Express; D Discover; E Diner's Club; F Other; 2 Personal checks accepted; 3 Lunch available; 4 Dinner available; 5 Open all year; 6 Pets welcome;

4. In one of the most photographed areas of San Francisco, the historic district of Alamo Square, the bed and breakfast is close to the Civic Center, Opera House, Davies Symphony Hall, Union Square, and all of the sights that make the city famous. Guest rooms feature fireplaces, and private baths have been tastefully decorated to show the charm of old San Francisco. One room features an antique Chinese wedding bed. In the evening guests can help themselves to wine, relax in the hot tub, and perhaps enjoy a surprise visit from Nosey, the neighborhood resident raccoon. Two-bedroom family apartment with fireplace and kitchen is also available. Full breakfast. $69-125.

5. In one of San Francisco's most beautiful neighborhoods, Jay's place is atop the Broadway tunnel. Walk down the steps to North Beach Italian restaurants, Fisherman's Wharf, and Chinatown. Cable cars are only one block away. This exclusive, quiet location offers San Francisco sights just minutes away. Jay's one bed-and-breakfast guest room is traditionally furnished and has a private bath. Full breakfast. $100.

10. A million-dollar panoramic view of San Francisco Bay and the Golden Gate Bridge plays host to this upscale Presidio Heights bed and breakfast. This prestigious area offers a wealth of wonderful restaurants, interesting walks, and the historic Presidio. Two rooms with private baths are available. Full breakfast. $85-125.

11. A scenic location in San Francisco with a panoramic view. Two bathrooms are available. Each room is equipped with a TV. The spacious family room also has a sitting area and a piano. Guests have ample on-street parking in a quiet neighborhood. Public transportation is nearby. Crib available. Full breakfast. $70-95.

12. High atop charming Russian Hill, a two-bedroom Victorian apartment has a spectacular view of the bay. A great place for two couples or a family includes a living room, sunny solarium, a full kitchen, and bath. A futon is also available. The living room has TV, fireplace, and telephone. The area is great for walking. Cable cars are on the corner, and the wharf is just a short distance away. Special rates for stays over seven days. Full breakfast. $150-200.

14. One of San Francisco's most enjoyable neighborhoods, Noe Valley is a local treasure of restaurants and shops. This beautifully renovated, charming San Francisco home offers a bed and breakfast suite. Private entrance, king-size bed, and full kitchen. Transportation to the center of downtown (15 minutes away) is excellent. Full breakfast. $95.

15. A wonderful bed and breakfast penthouse with a panoramic view of the city, the bay, and Alcatraz in San Francisco's nicest neighborhood. It's a full flat with kitchen, full bath, balcony, and private entrance. There is a queen-size bed in one room and a set of twin beds in a separate room. The hosts offer TV, VCR, and stereo. All of this within walking distance of the famous sites of San Francisco. Full breakfast. $150-200.

Cole Valley/Golden Gate Park Bed and Breakfast. This is a 1922 Edwardian home, with original fixtures and an Italianate garden atrium. It is style that Robert offers, mostly, as well as wall-to-wall books, art work, charm, and warmth. There are four guest rooms; one room boasts a panoramic view of Golden Gate Park, the Golden Gate Bridge, and the bay. Cole Valley is adjacent to the Haight Ashbury district and close to the Castro and to the UCSF Med Center. It takes only about 10 to 15 minutes to get to the center of downtown. Full breakfast. $75-85.

Luxurious Pacific Heights Victorian. In one of San Francisco's most upscale neighborhoods, this Victorian offers three fabulously furnished guest rooms. Room one is a master suite with a queen-size poster bed, private

---

7 No smoking; 8 Children welcome; 9 Social drinking allowed; 10 Tennis nearby; 11 Swimming nearby; 12 Golf nearby; 13 Skiing nearby; 14 May be booked through a travel agent; 15 Handicapped accessible.

bath with claw-foot tub, a sitting area with fireplace, and a private deck. There are also two additional guest rooms, each with fireplace, TV, and VCR. One room has a deck overlooking the back garden. Cable cars are only four blocks away and the center of downtown is just 10 minutes away. Full breakfast. $150-180.

Noe Valley Garden Studio. The hostess offers a beautiful and peaceful garden studio with a private entrance and private bath. Guests sleep in a cozy queen-size bed, and prepare breakfast at their own leisure. French doors lead to quiet garden. One block from the streetcar in the quaint Noe Valley area where there are restaurants and shops within walking distance. Only a 15-minute ride to Moscone Center and downtown sights. Full breakfast provided. $95-115.

Richmond District. Still in the heart of San Francisco, the Richmond District offers a wealth of wonderful things to do from bike riding and walking trails to excellent restaurants. Two guest rooms with TVs, VCRs, and private baths. One room offers an ocean view and accommodates a third person. The living room has a fireplace and ocean view. The world-famous Cliff House restaurant, Seal Rocks, and Ocean Beach are just a few blocks away. Transportation to downtown is excellent. Express bus to Union Square in 15 minutes. Full breakfast. $95-115.

Romantic Garden Cottage. A beautifully decorated, romantic cottage with a private entrance and patio. It's furnished with queen-size bed, stereo, TV, and small kitchen. The location near Golden Gate Park offers many wonderful shops and restaurants. Full breakfast. $95.

Russian Hill Victorian Cottage. Enjoy the privacy of a large cottage suite with private bath and queen-size bed. The living room has a fireplace, skylight, TV, and stereo. French doors lead out to a deck and garden. Cable cars are only one-half block away. The Wharf, North Beach, and Chinatown are within walking distance. Full breakfast. $125.

Brady Acres

649 Jones Street, 94102
(415) 929-8033; (800) 6 BRADY 6 (627-2396)
FAX (415) 441-8033; e-mail: staff@bradyacres

Small hotel in theater district three blocks northwest of Union Square. Close to shopping and cable car. Fully accessorized with kitchenware, all rooms have wet bar with microwave, refrigerator, coffee maker, and toaster. Six very sunny rooms with bay windows are decorated with antiques. All rooms are fully furnished with kitchenettes and have private baths with tub and shower. All have private-line telephone with answering machine, color TV, and cassette player. Laundry facilities available. Weekly rates are also available.

Host: Joey Wolosz
Rooms: 25 (PB) $75-95
Credit Cards: A, B
Notes: 2, 5, 8, 14

The Chateau Tivoli

1057 Steiner Street, 94115
(415) 776-5462; (800) 228-1647
FAX (415) 776-0505
e-mail: mail@chateautivoli.com
www.chateautivoli.com

This prize-winning restored Victorian townhouse is in the Alamo Square historic district near the center of San Francisco. The ornate gold-leaf trim and 22 colors of the exterior are prelude to the splendor inside. Elaborate woodwork, a grand oak staircase, and period antique furnishings return guests to the opulence and comfort of San Francisco's golden age. Continental plus breakfast weekdays; champagne brunches on weekends. Dinners available by request.

Hosts: Victoria, Soraya, Erica
Rooms: 9 (5 PB; 4 SB) $109-250

NOTES: Credit cards accepted: A MasterCard; B Visa; C American Express; D Discover; E Diner's Club; F Other; 2 Personal checks accepted; 3 Lunch available; 4 Dinner available; 5 Open all year; 6 Pets welcome;

The Chateau Tivoli

Continental Breakfast
Credit Cards: A, B, C
Notes: 2, 4, 5, 7, 8, 9, 14

Country Cottage Bed & Breakfast

5 Dolores Terrace, 94110
(415) 479-1913; (800) 452-8249
FAX (415) 921-2273

A cozy country-style bed and breakfast in the heart of San Francisco. The four guest rooms are comfortably furnished with antiques and brass beds. The house is at the end of a quiet street, away from the city noise. There is a small patio with trees and birds. A full breakfast is served in the sunny kitchen.

Hosts: Susan and Richard Kreibich
Rooms: 4 (S2B) $69
Full Breakfast
Credit Cards: A, B, C
Notes: 2, 5, 7, 8, 9, 10, 14

The Golden Gate Hotel

775 Bush Street, 94108
(415) 392-3702; (800) 835-1118
FAX (415) 392-6202

The ambiance, location, and price make the Golden Gate Hotel an extraordinary find in the heart of San Francisco. Dedicated to a high standard of quality and personal attention, the hosts keep fresh flowers in all the rooms. Rates include a Continental breakfast of fresh croissants and the city's strongest coffee and afternoon tea.

Hosts: John and Renate Kenaston
Rooms: 23 (14 PB; 9 SB) $65-115
Continental Breakfast
Credit Cards: A, B, C, E
Notes: 5, 7, 8, 9, 11, 14

The Grove Inn

890 Grove Street, 94117
(415) 929-0780; (800) 829-0780
www.jps.net/grovinn/

The Grove Inn is a charming, intimate, and affordable Victorian bed and breakfast. Close to public transportation. The owners and managers are always available for information, help in renting cars, booking shuttles to the airport, and city tours. Parking is available at $5 additional charge. A two-room suit, with private bath sleeps four to five persons. Closed December. No smoking.

Hosts: Klaus and Rosetta Zimmermann
Rooms: 18 (14 PB; 4 SB) $80-135
Continental Breakfast
Credit Cards: A, B, C
Notes: 2, 7, 8, 9, 10, 12, 14

The Inn at Union Square

440 Post Street, 94102
(415) 397-3510; (800) 288-4346
www.unionsquare.com

An elegant, small European-style hotel in the heart of San Francisco's financial, theater, and shopping districts. Each floor has an intimate lobby and fireplace where guests enjoy complimentary afternoon tea and wine and hors d'oeuvres in the evening. Rooms are individually decorated with beautiful fabrics and comfortable contemporary furniture, and soft terry-cloth robes are provided. All bathrooms have just been remodeled. Penthouse accommodations include a cozy sauna, whirlpool bath, fireplace,

---

7 No smoking; 8 Children welcome; 9 Social drinking allowed; 10 Tennis nearby; 11 Swimming nearby; 12 Golf nearby; 13 Skiing nearby; 14 May be booked through a travel agent; 15 Handicapped accessible.

and wet bar. Personalized service and attention to detail. "We are a nonsmoking and a nontipping hotel." Open year-round.

Host: Brooks Bayly
Rooms: 30 (PB) $175-350
Penthouse: 1 (PB) $350
Credit Cards: A, B, C, D, E
Notes: 2, 5, 7, 9, 11, 14, 15

The Inn San Francisco

943 South Van Ness Avenue, 94110
(415) 641-0188; (800) 359-0913
FAX (415) 641-1701; e-mail: innkeeper@innsf.com
www.innsf.com

Authentic historic Italianate Victorian mansion, circa 1872. Ornate woodwork, oriental carpets, marble fireplaces, and lovely antiques. Charming buffet breakfast served 7:00-11:00 A.M. Enjoy redwood hot tub in the peaceful English garden or reserve a room with a private whirlpool tub—the perfect romantic escape! Two-night minimum stay may be required for weekends and holidays. Limited smoking permitted.

Hosts: Marty Neely and Connie Wu
Rooms: 21 (19 PB; 2 SB) $85-235
Full Breakfast
Credit Cards: A, B, C, D, E, F
Notes: 2, 5, 8, 14

The Monte Cristo

600 Presidio Avenue, 94115
(415) 931-1875; fax (415) 931-6005

The elegantly restored Monte Cristo was originally built in 1875 as a saloon and hotel. It has served as a bordello, a refuge after the 1906 earthquake, and a speakeasy. Only two blocks from Victorian shops, restaurants, and antique stores on Sacramento Street; 10 minutes to any other point in the city. Buffet breakfast served. Two-night minimum stay required for weekends and holidays. Smoking in designated areas only.

Host: George
Rooms: 14 (11 PB; 3 SB) $73-118
Continental Breakfast
Credit Cards: A, B, C, D, E
Notes: 5, 8, 14

No Name Victorian

847 Fillmore Street, 94117
(415) 479-1913; FAX (415) 921-2273
e-mail: bbsf@linex.com
www.bbsf.com

In one of the most photographed areas of San Francisco, the historic district of Alamo Square, the bed and breakfast sits close to all the sights that make this city famous. Most of the guest rooms feature fireplaces and private baths. All the rooms have been tastefully decorated to show the charm of old San Francisco homes. One room features an antique Chinese wedding bed. In the evening, guests are encouraged to help themselves to wine and relax in the hot tub where many a guest has had a surprise visit from Nosey, the neighborhood resident raccoon. Open year-round. Also, a two-room family apartment with kitchen is available. Children are welcome. This is a nonsmoking establishment.

Hosts: Susan and Richard Kreibich
Rooms: 6 (4 PB; 2 SB) $79-125
Full Breakfast
Credit Cards: A, B, C
Notes: 2, 5, 7, 8, 9, 14

Red Victorian Bed, Breakfast & Art

1665 Haight Street, 94117
(415) 864-1978; FAX (415) 863-3293
e-mail: redvic@linex.com

The Red Victorian is in the geographic heart of San Francisco on famous Haight Street. Near Golden Gate Park, it welcomes creative people from everywhere. Breakfast is served family style around a big table. Beloved for its 18 lighthearted and fanciful guest rooms, some meditative, like the Japanese Tea Garden Room and the Redwood Forest Room, some funny, like the Playground or Friends, some

---

NOTES: Credit cards accepted: A MasterCard; B Visa; C American Express; D Discover; E Diner's Club; F Other; 2 Personal checks accepted; 3 Lunch available; 4 Dinner available; 5 Open all year; 6 Pets welcome;

romantic, some historic. All celebrate the Summer of Love (1967 peace and ecology movement) and Golden Gate Park. The most friendly small hotel in San Francisco. Plan to stay awhile. Open year-round. No smoking. Children are welcome.

Host: Sami Sunchild
Rooms: 18 (6 PB; 12 SB) $86-200
Continental Breakfast
Credit Cards: A, B, C
Notes: 2, 5, 7, 8, 10, 11, 12, 14

Stanyan Park Hotel

750 Stanyan Street, 94117
(415) 751-1000; FAX (415) 668-5454
e-mail: info@stanyanpark.com
www.stanyanpark.com

The Stanyan Park Hotel, listed in the National Register of Historic Places, is an elegant, thoroughly restored Victorian Hotel, that will take guests back to a bygone era of style, grace, and comfort. The 36 romantic rooms and suites come in a lovely variety of period decor and are equipped with a color cable TV, direct-dial telephone with a data port, and a full, modern bath. Their suites all have a full kitchen, dining room, and living room. Enjoy their complimentary Continental plus breakfast and evening tea service.

Rooms: 36 (PB) $110-300
Continental Breakfast
Credit Cards: A, B, C, D, E
Notes: 5, 7, 8, 10, 11, 12, 14, 15

Stanyan Park Hotel

Victorian Inn on the Park

Victorian Inn on the Park

301 Lyon Street, 94117
(415) 931-1830; (800) 435-1967
e-mail: vicinn@aol.com
www.citysearch.com/ffol/victorianinn

Queen Anne Victorian near Golden Gate Park, decorated with Victorian antiques. Many rooms have fireplaces, and the Belvedere Room features a private balcony overlooking the park. The inn features fireplaces, dining room with oak paneling, and a parlor with fireplace. Complimentary wine served nightly. Parking is available. Continental plus breakfast including fresh breads served daily. No smoking. Children are welcome.

Hosts: Lisa and William Benau
Rooms: 12 (PB) $124-174
Continental Breakfast
Credit Cards: A, B, C, D, E
Notes: 2, 5, 7, 8, 9, 10, 11, 12, 14

SAN GREGORIO

Rancho San Gregorio

Route 1, Box 54 (Highway 84), 94074
(650) 747-0810; FAX (650) 747-0184
e-mail: rsgleebud@aol.com

Five miles inland from the Pacific off SR 1 in a rural valley, Rancho San Gregorio welcomes

---

7 No smoking; 8 Children welcome; 9 Social drinking allowed; 10 Tennis nearby; 11 Swimming nearby; 12 Golf nearby; 13 Skiing nearby; 14 May be booked through a travel agent; 15 Handicapped accessible.

Rancho San Gregorio

travelers to share relaxed hospitality. This country getaway has 15 acres, an old barn, creek, gardens, decks, and gazebo. Full country breakfast features home-grown specialties. Only 45 minutes from San Francisco, Santa Cruz, and the Bay Area. Smoking is permitted outside only. Children are welcome.

Hosts: Bud and Lee Raynor
Rooms: 4 (PB) $90-120
Suite: $150
Full Breakfast
Credit Cards: A, B, C, D
Notes: 2, 5, 7, 8, 9, 11, 12, 14

SAN JOSE

The Hensley House

456 North Third Street, 95112
(408) 298-3537; (800) 498-3537
FAX (408) 298-4676
e-mail: henhouse@ix.netcom.com
www.hensleyhouse.com

Three-story Queen Anne Victorian and a two-story Craftsman-style home with a 40-foot living room with hand-painted beam ceilings and walls, 10-foot fireplace, antique crystal and brass chandeliers, and hand-painted and gilded walls and ceilings. Queen-size beds, TV, VCR, telephones, voice mail, separate modem hookups, speaker telephones, outdoor hot tub Jacuzzi, air conditioning, whirlpools, fireplace, and gourmet breakfasts. In downtown historical district, with restaurants, museums, and theaters also close.

Innkeepers: Ron Evans and Tony Contreras
Rooms: 9 (PB) $135-265
Full Breakfast
Credit Cards: A, B, C, D, E
Notes: 2, 3, 4, 5, 7, 9, 10, 11, 12, 14

The Hensley House

SAN LUIS OBISPO

Arroyo Village Inn

407 El Camino Real, Arroyo Grande, 93420
(805) 489-5926; (800) 563-7762
www.centralcoast.com/ArroyoVillageInn

Elegant and romantic, award-winning English country-style inn offering a delightful blend of yesterday's charm and hospitality with today's comforts and conveniences. Spacious suites are decorated with Laura Ashley prints and antiques with private baths, spas, fireplaces, window seats, and skylights. In the heart of California's central coast, halfway between Los Angeles and San Francisco. Near beaches, wineries, San Luis Obispo; less than one hour to Hearst Castle. "The greatest little secret on the Central Coast," says the *Los Angeles Times*.

Host: Gina Glass
Rooms: 7 (PB) $135-375
Full Breakfast
Credit Cards: A, B, C, D, E
Notes: 2, 5, 7, 9, 10, 11, 12, 14

NOTES: Credit cards accepted: A MasterCard; B Visa; C American Express; D Discover; E Diner's Club; F Other; 2 Personal checks accepted; 3 Lunch available; 4 Dinner available; 5 Open all year; 6 Pets welcome;

Baywood Bed & Breakfast Inn

1370 2nd Street, Baywood Park, 93402
(805) 528-8888; FAX (805) 528-8887
e-mail: innkeeper@baywoodinn.com
www.baywoodinn.com

This inn is on Morro Bay, 12 miles west of San Luis Obispo in a small neighborhood on a tiny peninsula. The inn is close to kayaking, golfing, hiking, bicycling, and picnicking. Beautiful Montana de Oro State Park and Hearst Castle are minutes away. The inn features 15 suites which have lovely bay views, cozy seating areas, fireplaces, and private baths. Guests are treated to afternoon wine and cheese, room tours, and breakfast in bed.

Hosts: Suzanne McCollom; Pat and Alex Benson
Rooms: 15 (PB) $90-160
Full Breakfast
Credit Cards: A, B
Notes: 2, 4, 5, 7, 9, 12, 14, 15

SAN LUIS OBISPO (ARROYO GRANDE)

Bed & Breakfast California

P.O. Box 2247, Saratoga, 95070
(408) 867-9662; (800) 872-4500
FAX (408) 867-0907; e-mail: info@bbintl.com
www.bbintl.com

A. One block from the 1772 San Luis Mission, this restored 1887 Italianate Queen Anne home is near shops and restaurants. Spacious rooms, some with gas fireplace and whirlpool tub, individually decorated. Eleven guest rooms and four suites. Private baths. A full breakfast and afternoon refreshments are served in the dining room or patio areas. No smoking. $90-160.

B. Experience the romance of a turn-of-the-century inn while being pampered with home-style hospitality. Nine guest rooms; each room has its own special touch. All rooms are decorated cheerfully with interesting antiques. Three rooms have private baths, and six rooms have sinks in the room and offer three spacious baths "down the hall" with luxurious claw-foot tubs. Enjoy an intimate breakfast for two or chat with fellow guests in the fireside dining room each morning. The parlor with its large bay window and fireplace is always available for guests relaxation and socializing. $85-110.

C. Built in 1984 and styled after an old English country Victorian, this inn offers a delightful blend of yesterday's charm and hospitality with today's comforts and conveniences. Each of the seven unique garden-themed suites has its own private bath, queen-size bed, and an abundance of candles for that romantic ambiance. A full gourmet breakfast is served each morning, and hors d'oeuvres and beverages are provided in the parlor each afternoon. Only two miles from Pismo Beach and 15 minutes from San Luis Obispo. $125-375.

D. Just north of San Luis Obispo on Highway 101, the quaint little town of Templeton takes guests back 100 years. The country inn is a perfectly restored two-story Victorian house built in 1886. There are five guest rooms, two in the main house with shared baths and three in the carriage house with private baths. The house is on an acre of land surrounded by green lawns and shaded by old oak trees. A full breakfast is served. $85-95.

E. Experience this hospitality through the unique blend of a charming country Victorian inn with the luxury of a AAA four-diamond hotel. Or take advantage of the Victorian charm and convenience of our three-diamond Trellis Court motel. All rooms in both facilities have a fireplace and cozy traditional decor. At the inn arrive to welcome baskets, robes, and hot beverages with wake-up call. Breakfast in bed is available. At the Trellis Court receive a complimentary Continental breakfast. Watch the 14-foot waterwheel harness water power to grind the wheat and coffee and make old-fashioned ice cream. $79-199.

---

7 No smoking; 8 Children welcome; 9 Social drinking allowed; 10 Tennis nearby; 11 Swimming nearby; 12 Golf nearby; 13 Skiing nearby; 14 May be booked through a travel agent; 15 Handicapped accessible.

SAN MATEO

Bed & Breakfast California

P.O. Box 2247, Saratoga, 95070
(408) 867-9662; (800) 872-4500
FAX (408) 867-0907; e-mail: info@bbintl.com
www.bbintl.com

Hidden quietly in the San Francisco peninsula's reflective past, guests will find this Tudor Revival bed and breakfast that offers rustic pleasures of days gone by. Built in 1891 by noted English architect Ernest Coxhead, it brings to life a bit of England in a leisurely atmosphere with gardens to enjoy and comfortably elegant accommodations. The beautifully furnished guest rooms offer antiques, period furnishings, and hand-painted murals. Full breakfast. Every evening refreshments are served in the great room, inviting guests to relax after a long day of work or play. $129-169.

SAN RAFAEL

Bed & Breakfast Exchange of Marin County—Referral Service

45 Entrata, San Anselmo, 94960
(415) 485-1971; FAX (415) 454-7179

Barr Mansion Bed and Breakfast. Be the exclusive guests in this historic Victorian in a lovely leafy area of San Rafael. Guest will have a private hot tub in the private bath. Full breakfast is served. Swimming pool is available. Lovely garden setting. $125.

464 Mission Bed and Breakfast. This Victorian bed and breakfast has four guest rooms and a hot tub. Gourmet full breakfasts are served. Kitchen is available. Great location near Dominican College. $110.

SANTA ANA

Bed & Breakfast California

P.O. Box 2247, Saratoga, 95070
(408) 867-9662; (800) 872-4500
FAX (408) 867-0907; e-mail: info@bbintl.com
www.bbintl.com

Built in the early 1920s, this registered historic home has been decorated for beauty and romance. One private guest suite features private bath, French doors to the deck, garden, and koi pond. A wonderful full gourmet breakfast is served in the guests' room or on the deck. Host is an artist with an eye for sunshine and perfection. $85.

SANTA BARBARA

Bed & Breakfast California

P.O. Box 2247, Saratoga, 95070
(408) 867-9662; (800) 872-4500
FAX (408) 867-0907; e-mail: info@bbintl.com
www.bbintl.com

A. Antiques and period furnishings highlight each of the 50 guest rooms and suites. All accommodations have private baths, color cable TV, and radios and are individually decorated with rich colors, soft lines, and cozy comforters. Guest rooms and suites are located in the main building, the five Garden Cottages and the Carriage House. Garden cottage units feature porches or secluded patios and several have gas fireplaces. $130-375.

B. Enjoy the elegance of the Victorian era at this historic 1874 bed and breakfast set on an acre of English gardens, only a five-minute walk to restaurants, theaters, museums, and shops. Rooms in the house, cottages and barn suites each offer quiet and privacy. Enjoy a leisurely, full breakfast and afternoon hors d'oeuvres on the veranda or in the dining room. $120-325.

NOTES: Credit cards accepted: A MasterCard; B Visa; C American Express; D Discover; E Diner's Club; F Other; 2 Personal checks accepted; 3 Lunch available; 4 Dinner available; 5 Open all year; 6 Pets welcome;

C. Relaxation begins the moment guests arrive. Leave the car and stroll to exclusive downtown shops, restaurants, galleries, clubs, and museums. Classic antiques and period furnishings welcome guests throughout this lovingly restored 1898 Victorian home. All seven guest rooms are individually decorated and feature queen-size beds with a choice of fireplaces, whirlpool spas, and garden or mountain views. $125-225.

D. Ten-acre coastal ranch is surrounded by three and one-half acres of flowers planted by commercial flower-growers, avocado, lemon, and Fuyu persimmon trees. There is a downstairs two-room suite for guests with an ocean view, private deck, and spa. A full ranch breakfast is served upstairs. $105.

E. Beautifully restored Spanish-Colonial inn provides a quiet retreat only a few steps from the heart of town. The bridal suite offers a fireplace and private veranda, while family and executive rooms are tailored for guests' comfort. All rooms include cable TV with free movie channel, refrigerator, coffee maker, and microwave oven, and some come complete with fully equipped kitchens. The inn is within an easy walk to fine dining and just one block from the beach between Stearns Wharf and the yacht harbor. $80-169.

F. Secluded quarters behind high hedges, hidden pathways and romantic gardens. Originally built for a large family in 1905, then renovated and opened in 1980. Each guest room and cottage is lovingly furnished with Early American antiques and wicker appointments, chintz quilts, and cushions. Claw-foot antique baths enhance all the bathrooms which have modern shower attachments. Indulge in a leisurely breakfast either in bed, on the privacy of own garden patio, or beneath the lacey intertwined branches of the persimmon and avocado trees. $110-145.

Casa Del Mar Inn

18 Bath Street, 93101
(805) 963-4418; (800) 433-3097
FAX (805) 966-4240
www.casadelmar.com

Walk to all beach activities, sailing, shopping, and fine restaurants from this beautiful Mediterranean-style inn. Lush gardens year-round. Twenty-one rooms offer a variety of accommodation options. One room is newly remodeled for full wheelchair access. All rooms feature private baths, telephones, and color remote-control TV. Amenities include a garden courtyard spa and sun deck, buffet-style breakfast, evening wine and cheese social hour. Golf and day spa packages available. Newly decorated in 1997. All rooms are nonsmoking.

Hosts: Yun and Yessy Kim
Rooms: 21 (PB) $69-239
Continental Breakfast
Credit Cards: A, B, C, D, E
Notes: 5, 6, 7, 8, 9, 10, 11, 12, 14, 15

Cheshire Cat Inn & Cottages

36 West Valerio Street, 93101
(805) 569-1610; FAX (805) 682-1876
e-mail: cheshire@cheshirecat.com
www.cheshirecat.com

Two elegant Victorian Queen Anne houses and a coach house surrounded by flower-filled gardens, brick patios, decks, and fountains comprise the Cheshire Cat. Wedgewood china, English antiques, Chinese rugs, and Laura Ashley furnishings add to the sophisticated ambiance. Enjoy a delicious gourmet breakfast which includes coddled eggs, seasonal fruits, yogurt, freshly baked breads and pastries, cereal, and fresh fruit juices. Afternoon

---

7 No smoking; 8 Children welcome; 9 Social drinking allowed; 10 Tennis nearby; 11 Swimming nearby; 12 Golf nearby; 13 Skiing nearby; 14 May be booked through a travel agent; 15 Handicapped accessible.

Cheshire Cat

wine hour with brie, hors d'oeuvres, and crudités. Seventeen guest rooms, cottages, and suites, some with Jacuzzi, fireplaces, TV/VCRs, and private balconies. Only four blocks from shops, restaurants, and theaters. No smoking.

Hosts: Christine Dunstan (owner); Amy Taylor (manager)
Rooms: 17 (PB) $140-300
Full Breakfast
Credit Cards: A, B, C, D
Notes: 2, 5, 7, 8, 9, 10, 11, 12, 14, 15

Glenborough Inn

1327 Bath Street, 93101
(805) 966-0589; (800) 962-0589

Experience the ultimate in romance. Three Victorian/California Craftsman-era homes, each featuring gardens and sitting areas for guests' enjoyment. Full hot breakfast served in guest rooms. Secluded spa for private use. All rooms with private baths, coffee makers, robes, and telephones; many with private entrances and mini-refrigerators; some with fireplaces, Jacuzzi, and hot tubs. Daily evening cookies and beverages; weekend evening social hour including hors d'oeuvres. Walk three blocks to fine shops, restaurants, and theaters. In-state personal checks accepted. No smoking. Children are welcome.

Hosts: Michael and Steve
Rooms: 13 (PB) $110-300
Vacation Cottage: 1-$300-360

Full Breakfast
Credit Cards: A, B, C, D, E
Notes: 5, 7, 8, 9, 10, 11, 12, 14

Long's Sea View Bed & Breakfast

317 Piedmont Road, 93105
(805) 687-2947

Overlooking Santa Barbara's prestigious north side, this ranch-style home is in a quiet, residential neighborhood. Breakfast is usually served on the patio, where guests can see the ocean, Channel Islands, and the small family citrus orchard and garden. Convenient to the beach, Solvang, and Santa Ynez Valley, the large, airy bedroom is cheerfully furnished with antiques and king-size bed. The breakfast menu varies from Southern dishes to Mexican specialties. Continental breakfast served after 9:30 A.M.

Host: LaVerne Long
Rooms: 1 (PB) $80
Full Breakfast
Credit Cards: None
Notes: 2, 7, 9, 11, 12

The Old Yacht Club Inn

431 Corona Del Mar Drive, 93103
(805) 962-1277; (800) 549-1676 (CA)
(800) 676-1676 (US)

The Old Yacht Club Inn has 12 guest rooms in two houses: a 1912 California Craftsman and a 1920s Early California-style building. The inn opened as Santa Barbara's first bed and breakfast in 1980 and is now world renowned for its hospitality and warmth in comfortable surroundings and for its fine food. Within a block of the beach, the inn is close to tennis, swimming, boating, fishing, and golf. Evening wine, bikes, and beach chairs. Dinner available Saturdays.

Hosts: Nancy Donaldson and Sandy Hunt
Rooms: 12 (PB) $110-190
Full Breakfast
Credit Cards: A, B, C, D
Notes: 2, 5, 7, 8, 9, 10, 11, 12

NOTES: Credit cards accepted: A MasterCard; B Visa; C American Express; D Discover; E Diner's Club; F Other; 2 Personal checks accepted; 3 Lunch available; 4 Dinner available; 5 Open all year; 6 Pets welcome;

Olive House Inn

1604 Olive Street, 93101
(805) 962-4902; (800)786-6422
FAX (805) 962-9983; e-mail: olivehse@aol.com

Enjoy the quiet comfort and gracious hospitality at this restored 1904 Craftsman-style house in a quiet residential neighborhood near the mission and downtown. Ocean and mountain views, terraced garden, large sun deck, off-street parking. Gracious living room replete with bay windows, redwood paneling, fireplace. Private decks, hot tubs. Afternoon wine, evening tea, sherry, and treats. Credit card is required for reservations.

Host: Ellen Schaub
Rooms: 6 (PB) $110-180
Full Breakfast
Credit Card: A, B, C, D
Notes: 5, 7, 9, 10, 11, 12

The Parsonage

1600 Olive Street, 93101
(805) 962-9336; (800) 775-0352
FAX (805) 962-2285; www.parsonage.com

The Parsonage Bed and Breakfast, built in 1892, is a romantic getaway, quiet and secluded, with all the beauty and splendor of the Queen Anne Victorian period. Each room is elegantly decorated and distinctive to the period with some of the finest antique furnishings in the area. Located just minutes from the scenic Pacific Ocean and historic Santa Barbara Mission, the Parsonage is within walking distance of theaters, dining, and shopping in beautiful Santa Barbara.

Rooms: 6 (PB) $130-305
Full Breakfast
Credit Cards: A, B, C, D, E
Notes: 5, 10, 11, 12, 14

Simpson House Inn

121 East Arrellaga, 93101
(805) 963-7067; (800) 676-1280
www.simpsonhouseinn

Beautifully restored 1874 Victorian estate secluded on an acre of English gardens. Only a five-minute walk to historic downtown, restaurants, and shopping. Cottages, suites, and rooms elegantly furnished with antiques and oriental rugs feature private patios with fountains, fireplaces, and Jacuzzis. Full spa service and health club with pool available. Rates include concierge services, afternoon beverages, lavish Mediterranean hors d'oeuvres buffet, evening wine, bicycles, and croquet. Minimum-stay requirements for weekends and holidays. North America's only five-diamond AAA bed and breakfast. No smoking.

Hosts: Glyn and Linda Davies; Dixie Budke
Rooms: 14 (PB) $160-375
Full Breakfast
Credit Cards: A, B, C, D
Notes: 2, 5, 7, 9, 10, 11, 12, 14, 15

Tiffany Inn

1323 De La Vina Street, 93101
(805) 963-2283; (800) 999-5672
FAX (805) 963-0994; e-mail: tiffanyinn@aol.com
www.sbinns.com/tiffany

A charming 1898 Victorian home filled with classic antiques and period furnishings. All seven guest rooms are individually decorated and feature queen-size beds, private bathrooms, choice of fireplaces, whirlpool spas, and garden or mountain views. A short walk to downtown shops and restaurants. Full breakfast served on veranda overlooking garden. No smoking.

Hosts: Carol and Larry MacDonald (owners)
    Janice Hawkins (manager)
Rooms: 7 (PB) $125-250
Full Breakfast
Credit Cards: A, B, C, D
Notes: 5, 7, 9, 11, 12, 14

The Upham Hotel and Garden Cottages

1404 de la Vina Street, 93101
(800) 727-0876

Established 1871, this beautifully restored Victorian hotel is on an acre of gardens. Guest

---

7 No smoking; 8 Children welcome; 9 Social drinking allowed; 10 Tennis nearby; 11 Swimming nearby; 12 Golf nearby; 13 Skiing nearby; 14 May be booked through a travel agent; 15 Handicapped accessible.

Santa Barbara, CA

The Upham Hotel

rooms and suites feature period furnishings and antiques. Continental breakfast and afternoon wine and cheese. Walk to museums, galleries, historic attractions, shops, and restaurants downtown. Some rooms are nonsmoking.

Host: Jan Martin Winn
Rooms: 50 (PB) $130-375
Continental Breakfast
Credit Cards: A, B, C, D, E
Notes: 3, 4, 5, 8, 9, 11, 12, 14

SANTA BARBARA AREA

Carpinteria Beach Condo

1825 Cravens Lane, Carpinteria, 93013
(805) 684-1579

In a lush flower-growing valley and across the street from "the world's safest beach." Unit has mountain view. Tropical island decor has a sunset wall mural. Fully furnished kitchen, queen-size bed, and color cable TV. Pool, spa, and gas barbecue on complex. Self-catering with beverage provided and fruit from host's ranch. Sleeps four. Eleven miles south of Santa Barbara. Hosts available for tennis, bridge, or tour of their semitropical fruit ranch.

Hosts: Bev and Don Schroeder
Suite: 1 (PB) $80-90
Continental Breakfast
Credit Cards: None
Notes: 2, 5, 7, 8, 9, 10, 11, 12

D&B Schroeder Ranch Bed & Breakfast

1825 Cravens Lane, Carpinteria, 93013
(805) 684-1579

Nestled in the foothills of Carpinteria one mile from Highway 101 with an ocean view, the Schroeder ranch produces avocados and semitropical fruit. The guest accommodation has a separate entrance, color TV, small refrigerator, and private bath. There are decks for viewing the Pacific Ocean, Channel Islands, and gorgeous sunsets. Guests may enjoy strolling around the 10 acres, discovering fruit trees and a year-round creek. There is a spa in a lush tropical setting to soothe weary travelers. The world's safest beach is 2 miles away. Santa Barbara is 12 miles away. Inquire about accommodations for children. No smoking.

Hosts: Bev and Don Schroeder
Room: 1 (PB) $85-95
Full Breakfast
Credit Cards: None
Notes: 2, 5, 7, 9, 10, 11, 12

SANTA BARBARA (CARPINTERIA)

Prufrocks Garden Inn By the Sea

600 Linden Avenue, 93013
(805) 566-9696

Historic Santa Barbara area award-winning inn (1904). "Most Romantic Getaway" *Santa Barbara Independent*. Voted "Reader's Favorite," *Los Angeles Times*. Photographed for *Land's End®* Catalog. Jacuzzis, fireplaces, in-room fresh flowers, sunset hor d'oeuvres, chocolates on pillows. Best bed and breakfast location, one block to state beach park. Restaurants, boutiques, antique stores. Santa Barbara area festival packages. Historic Theme Romance packages including coastal train rides, beach picnics, wharf lunches, and classic dinners. Amtrak, bicycles, beach amenities.

Hosts: Judy and Jim Haluorsen
Rooms: 7 (5 PB; 2 SB) $69-229
Full Breakfast

NOTES: Credit cards accepted: A MasterCard; B Visa; C American Express; D Discover; E Diner's Club; F Other; 2 Personal checks accepted; 3 Lunch available; 4 Dinner available; 5 Open all year; 6 Pets welcome;

SANTA CRUZ

Bed & Breakfast California

P.O. Box 2247, Saratoga, 95070
(408) 867-9662; (800) 872-4500
FAX (408) 867-0907; e-mail: info@bbintl.com
www.bbintl.com

A. Most rooms at this charming, unique inn with French country decor have a fireplace and private entrance. Several rooms also have a whirlpool tub. All have a private bath and a king- or queen-size bed. A great breakfast and afternoon refreshments are served. The inn is close to the beach and boardwalk. A garden stream and gazebo serve as a picturesque place for a wedding. $145-195.

B. Vacation home in the redwoods. This 1,600-square-foot home in a breathtaking natural environment is just 10 minutes from the Santa Cruz beaches. Two bedrooms, both with private bath and spa robes, a fully equipped kitchen, cable TV, VCR, stone fireplace, and redwood deck with hot tub—even a piano. The hosts stock the refrigerator with breakfast supplies and a welcoming bottle of wine for guests. $195.

C. This inn lies nestled between spectacular beaches and lush green strawberry fields just 10 minutes from the Santa Cruz Beach Boardwalk. The beautifully furnished guest rooms all offer fireplaces, private baths, and two-line telephones, and some have double Jacuzzi tubs. Resort activities include two clay tennis courts, volleyball, croquet, and badminton; a driving net awaits the golfer prepping for a round at one of the local championship golf courses. $150-195.

D. Sanctuary created to provide guests the serene environment they deserve. This spectacular retreat with sweeping views of Monterey Bay and redwood forests is the perfect gateway to the Monterey Peninsula. Hike through redwood forests or enjoy a peaceful time on the deck with a favorite book. Art work and antiques from around the world create a warm and inviting atmosphere. $150-250.

Credit Cards: A, B, D
Notes: 5, 7, 8, 9, 10, 11, 12, 15

Chateau Victorian, A Bed & Breakfast Inn

118 First Street, 95060
(831) 458-9458

Chateau Victorian was built in the 1880s as a family home. Only one block from the beach and Monterey Bay. The house was opened in June 1983 as an elegant bed and breakfast inn. Each room has a private bath, fireplace, queen-size bed, carpeting, and individual heating system. A Continental plus breakfast is served each morning. Each room is furnished in Victorian style. Within walking distance of downtown, the municipal wharf, the Boardwalk amusement park, and fine dining. Cash or checks preferred. No smoking.

Hostess: Alice June
Rooms: 7 (PB) $115-145
Continental Breakfast
Credit Cards: A, B, C, F
Notes: 2, 5, 7, 9, 10, 11, 12

Chateau Victorian

---

7 No smoking; 8 Children welcome; 9 Social drinking allowed; 10 Tennis nearby; 11 Swimming nearby; 12 Golf nearby; 13 Skiing nearby; 14 May be booked through a travel agent; 15 Handicapped accessible.

Pleasure Point Inn
Bed & Breakfast

2-3665 East Cliff Drive, 95062
(408) 475-4657

This beachfront home overlooks the beautiful Monterey Bay. Guest rooms have ocean views, private baths, whirlpool tubs, and fireplaces. Forty-foot motor yacht for fishing or cruising daily. Within walking distance of Capitola Beach and three miles to the Santa Cruz Beach boardwalk. Innkeepers love to share their inn with guests.

Hosts: Margaret and Sal Margo
Rooms: 4 (PB) $125-155
Continental Breakfast
Credit Cards: A, B
Notes: 5, 7, 10, 11, 12, 15

Valley View

P.O. Box 67438, 95067
(650) 321-5195; FAX (650) 325-5121
www.valleyviewinn.com

Romantic, secluded, fabulous view overlooking 20,000 acres of redwoods. Ten minutes to Santa Cruz and beaches. This unhosted bed and breakfast can make a guest's fantasy a reality. Walls of glass reflect the gorgeous view. Large viewing deck features hot tub. Interior features luxury furnishings, white carpet, fully equipped kitchen, and stone fireplace for elegant evenings. Continental breakfast and wine are left in the refrigerator. Read, hike, or head for the beach. No smoking indoors. Rate includes entire house.

Host: Tricia Young
Rooms: 2 (PB) $225
Continental Breakfast
Credit Cards: A, B, C, E
Notes: 2, 5, 7, 9, 10, 11, 12, 14

SANTA MARIA

Historic Santa Maria Inn

801 South Broadway, 93454
(805) 928-7777; (800) 462-2276
FAX (805) 928-0418

The Historic Santa Maria Inn is a registered landmark with 166 beautiful guest rooms. Built in 1917, and meticulously maintained, the inn offers a combination of enchanting nostalgia and modern comfort. Relax in the heated pool and spa, surrounded by award-winning gardens, shaded cobblestone courtyards, and cascading fountains. Other amenities include a restaurant, Old English Tap Room, wine cellar, fitness center, masseuse, laundry service, and champagne Sunday brunch. Smoking and non-smoking rooms available.

Rooms: 166 (PB) $69-139
Full Breakfast
Credit Cards: A, B, C, D, E, F
Notes: 3, 4, 5, 6, 8, 9, 10, 11, 12, 14, 15

SANTA MONICA

Bed & Breakfast California

P.O. Box 2247, Saratoga, 95070
(408) 867-9662; (800) 872-4500
FAX (408) 867-0907; e-mail: info@bbintl.com
www.bbintl.com

A. Near Santa Monica Canyon and the beach, this 1910 shingle-clad Colonial Revival inn offers gracious hospitality and an excellent location. Fourteen guest rooms with private baths. Some of the amenities provided are a spa, bicycles, and a full breakfast. No smoking. $125-245.

B. This turn-of-the-century beach estate is now a lovely bed and breakfast inn. Guest rooms and suites are individually decorated with antiques and hand-detailed furnishings. Ten guest rooms have shared and private baths. Large Continental breakfast and evening refreshments are served. No smoking. $95-160.

C. This is a designer-built addition to the second floor of a renovated 1920 California bungalow. There is a nice deck and the apartment has contemporary furnishings with natural wood, as well as a kitchenette. It is close to the Venice Boardwalk and one mile from Santa

---

NOTES: Credit cards accepted: A MasterCard; B Visa; C American Express; D Discover; E Diner's Club; F Other; 2 Personal checks accepted; 3 Lunch available; 4 Dinner available; 5 Open all year; 6 Pets welcome;

Monica Pier. It is within two blocks of the beach. $85.

Channel Road Inn

219 West Channel Road, 90402
(310) 459-1920; FAX (310) 454-9920
e-mail: channellinn@aol.com
www.channelroadinn.com

Named by the readers of *Sunset* magazine as one of the best bed and breakfast inns in the West and recently featured in *Country Inns*, the Channel Road Inn is just one block from the beach. All 14 rooms are richly decorated and all have private baths. Some rooms have blue ocean views and fireplaces; some have sun-warmed decks; all offer telephones, TV, fine linens, and a respite from the outside world. A flowering garden Jacuzzi and bicycles for exploring the 30-mile oceanside bike path are available. Several of the city's well-known restaurants are within walking distance; fashionable shops along Montana Avenue, and the new Getty Center are both close by.

Host: Heather Suskin
Rooms: 14 (PB) $145-275
Full Breakfast
Credit Cards: A, B
Notes: 2, 3, 5, 8, 9, 10, 11, 12, 14, 15

SANTA ROSA

The Gables Inn

4257 Petaluma Hill Inn, 95404
(707) 585-7777

A beautifully restored Victorian mansion sits grandly on three and one-half acres in the center of Sonoma wine country. Elegant guest rooms feature fluffy goose-down comforters, antiques, and private bathrooms. A separate cozy creekside cottage features a whirlpool tub for two. Sumptuous four-course gourmet breakfast is included. Easy access to 140 premium wineries, the giant redwoods, the Russian River Resort, the craggy north coastline, and just one hour north of San Francisco.

The Gables

Hosts: Mike and Judy Ogne
Rooms: 8 (PB) $135-225
Full Breakfast
Credit Cards: A, B, C, D, E
Notes: 2, 5, 7, 9, 10, 11, 12, 14, 15

Melitta Station Inn

5850 Melita Road, 95409
(707) 538-7712; (800) 504-3099

Late 1800s restored railroad station, this American country bed and breakfast is on a country road in the Valley of the Moon and the center

Melitta Station Inn

---

7 No smoking; 8 Children welcome; 9 Social drinking allowed; 10 Tennis nearby; 11 Swimming nearby; 12 Golf nearby; 13 Skiing nearby; 14 May be booked through a travel agent; 15 Handicapped accessible.

of wine country. Decorated with antiques and country collectibles. Within minutes of many fine restaurants and wineries. Next to two major parks offering hiking, biking, and jogging. Center of Sonoma County and only 12 miles from Calistoga.

Hosts: Diane Crandon and Vic Amstadter
Rooms: 5 (PB) $95-160
Full Breakfast
Credit Cards: A, B, C
Notes: 2, 5, 7, 9, 10, 11, 12, 14

Vintners Inn

4350 Barnes Road, 95403
(707) 575-7350; (800) 421-2584
www.vintnersinn.com

Amid a 45-acre vineyard in the Sonoma wine country, this four-diamond, 44-room, European-style inn features antique furnishings, modern private baths, fireplaces if desired, balconies or patios, vineyard and plaza views, along with a complimentary breakfast. Beautiful sun deck and Jacuzzi. Also the home of the nationally acclaimed John Ash & Co. restaurant.

Hosts: John and Cindy Duffy
Rooms: 44 (PB) $172.22-270.32
Continental Breakfast
Credit Cards: A, B, C, E
Notes: 3, 4, 5, 7, 8, 9, 10, 11, 12, 14, 15

SAUSALITO

Bed & Breakfast California

P.O. Box 2247, Saratoga, 95070
(408) 867-9662; (800) 872-4500
FAX (408) 867-0907; e-mail: info@bbintl.com
www.bbintl.com

A. Charming separate guest unit adjacent to host's home up on a hill above the town of Sausalito. The unit consists of a bedroom/living room with an alcove, free-standing fireplace, and queen-size bed. There is also a fully equipped kitchen and lovely deck filled with flowers and views of Richardson's Bay. It is light, sunny, and offers complete privacy. $145.

B. A 1907 houseboat in Sausalito's famous floating homes community. Charming bed and breakfast has a full kitchenette, queen-size and single beds, and a private entrance, catwalks/decks. For those with eclectic tastes. Excellent location near all amenities. Breakfast included. $150.

C. An evolving part of Sausalito history since 1915 features rooms in the French Riviera style. Sixteen stylish rooms and suites with park and/or harbor views. Furnishings are custom-designed and handcrafted by local artisans. $135-270.

D. Enjoy the quiet pace and romantic charm of this historic little hamlet...a world apart from the pleasures of city life, yet only a brief drive across the Golden Gate Bridge or lovely ferry ride from San Francisco. Elegant and secluded, it is designed for the most discriminating traveler. $195-485.

E. Originally built in 1869, it has recently been completely renovated into a cozy bed and breakfast offering nine distinctive suites artfully decorated in a timeless elegance. In the heart of Sausalito, guests will be within strolling distance of more than 200 quaint shops, art galleries, and world-class restaurants. $155-250.

F. This 1885 Victorian-style inn with restaurant can be found in the hills. There are 35 guest rooms with private baths, some with fireplaces. Continental breakfast served. No smoking permitted. $138-260.

Bed & Breakfast Exchange of Marin County—Referral Service

45 Entrata, San Anselmo, 94960
(415) 485-1971; FAX (415) 454-7179

Bed and Breakfast Houseboat—White Elephant. Come aboard this two-bedroom hosted houseboat on the loveliest dock on Sausalito waterfront. Private bath, deck with

---

NOTES: Credit cards accepted: A MasterCard; B Visa; C American Express; D Discover; E Diner's Club; F Other; 2 Personal checks accepted; 3 Lunch available; 4 Dinner available; 5 Open all year; 6 Pets welcome;

view of the water. Flower-filled walkways. No smoking. $95.

Cottage by the Bay. Stay in a private cottage built on a pier with a peaceful water view. Separate entrance, private bath, and deck. Guests may feel as if they are far away from the hustle and bustle of town but they are actually within walking distance to all the sights and the ferry boat to San Francisco. $150.

Bed & Breakfast San Francisco

P.O. Box 420009, San Francisco, 94142
(415) 931-3083; FAX (415) 921-BBSF (2273)
e-mail: bbsf@linex.com; www.bbsf.com

17. The Marin County picturesque village of Sausalito offers wonderful restaurants, quaint shops, and a romantic view of San Francisco. Stay aboard a houseboat, a permanently moored home on the bay. There are decks on three sides, living room with fireplace, full kitchen, and a full bath. The home is unhosted but all items for a full breakfast are supplied. Enjoy the view as the city lights come on and the sun slips behind Mount Tamalpais. $150.

The Honor Mansion

14891 Grove Street, 95448
(707) 433-4277; (800) 554-4667
www.honormansion.com

The Honor Mansion is a historic Italianate Victorian mansion in the heart of the Sonoma County wine country. The architecture and decor blend to create a sense of turn-of-the-century grace and elegance. Bask in the solitude of the gardens, decks, and koi pond. A stay is not complete without a tour of the wine country or a canoe trip down the nearby Russian River. "From mints on your pillow, to a full gourmet breakfast...Come let us pamper you."

Host: Cathi Fowler
Rooms: 6 (PB) $150-300
Full Breakfast
Credit Cards: A, B, D
Notes: 5, 7, 9, 10, 11, 12, 14, 15

SEAL BEACH

Bed & Breakfast California

P.O. Box 2247, Saratoga, 95070
(408) 867-9662; (800) 872-4500
FAX (408) 867-0907; e-mail: info@bbintl.com
www.bbintl.com

A bed and breakfast inn with the look and ambiance of an elegant European inn is surrounded by lovely gardens. Inn has a brick courtyard, pool, library, and a gracious dining room for large Continental breakfasts and evening refreshments. Twenty-four guest rooms all have individual decor and private baths. This lovely, quiet beach community is a well-kept secret. $155-325.

The Seal Beach Inn

The Seal Beach Inn and Gardens

212 5th Street, 90740-6115
(562) 493-2416; (800) HIDEAWAY (reservations)
FAX (562) 799-0483
e-mail: hideaway@sealbeachinn.com
www.sealbeachinn.com

Elegant historic southern California inn, one block from ocean beach in charming prestigious seaside town next to Long Beach. Lush gardens, lovely estate appearance. Exquisite rooms and suites. Pool, library, kitchens available. Free full breakfast/social hour. Modern amenities. Short walk to restaurants, shops, beach pier. Three freeways close by. Easy drive to Disneyland and major L.A. attractions and business center. Meeting rooms (24 max.).

---

7 No smoking; 8 Children welcome; 9 Social drinking allowed; 10 Tennis nearby; 11 Swimming nearby;
12 Golf nearby; 13 Skiing nearby; 14 May be booked through a travel agent; 15 Handicapped accessible.

Convenient to LAX, Long Beach, and Orange County airports.

Host:s Marjorie and Harty Schmaehl
Rooms: 23 (PB) $155-325
Full Breakfast
Credit Cards: A, B, C, D, E
Notes: 5, 7, 10, 11, 12, 14

SEQUOIA NATIONAL PARK

Bed & Breakfast California

P.O. Box 2247, Saratoga, 95070
(408) 867-9662; (800) 872-4500
FAX (408) 867-0907; e-mail: info@bbintl.com
www.bbintl.com

A. Sequoia National Park is very near this lovely, quiet, rural community. Self-contained cottage adjacent to hosts' home offers fireplace and private bath. Continental breakfast served. No smoking. $75.

B. Built in 1876, this Victorian inn is constructed of redwood from the Sequoias. Guests enjoy the ambiance of the Victorian era along with the comforts of in-room cable TV, private telephones with computer connections, refrigerators, and other amenities. Swimming pool/spa. Full breakfast. Sequoia National Park is only 40 minutes away. $85-95.

Mesa Verde Plantation Bed & Breakfast

33038 Sierra Highway 198, Lemoncove, 93244
(800) 240-1466; www.plantationbnb.com

Only 16 miles from Sequoia National Park. Nestled in the foothills of the Sierra Nevada among acres of orange groves. Heated swimming pool, hot tub, fireplaces, gazebos, and verandas. Rooms are named after characters from *Gone With the Wind* and decorated accordingly. Full gourmet breakfast served in the formal dining room or outside on the 5,000-square-foot brick courtyard. Freshly squeezed orange juice served every morning, picked from bed and breakfast's own orchard.

Hosts: Scott and Marie Munger
Rooms: 8 (6 PB; 2 SB) $69-159
Full Breakfast
Credit Cards: A, B, C, D, E
Notes: 2, 5, 9, 11, 12, 13, 14

SOLVANG

The Alisal Guest Ranch and Resort

1054 Alisal Road, 93463
(805) 688-6411; (800) 425-4725
FAX (805) 688-2510

The Alisal combines first-class accommodations with the rustic charm of a working cattle ranch and is California's only full-service guest ranch. Tucked away among 10,000 acres of picturesque countryside the Alisal offers two championship golf courses, seven tennis courts, boating and fishing on a private lake, horseback riding, 6,000-square-feet of conference/meeting facilities, swimming pool, Western barbecues, theme parties, group rodeos, and supervised activities for children. Breakfast and dinner are always included and children are most welcome.

Host: David S. Lautensack, general manager
Rooms: 73 (PB) $355-435 MAP
Full Breakfast
Credit Cards: A, B, C, E
Notes: 2, 3, 4, 5, 7, 8, 9, 10, 11, 12, 14, 15

Bed & Breakfast California

P.O. Box 2247, Saratoga, 95070
(408) 867-9662; (800) 872-4500
FAX (408) 867-0907; e-mail: info@bbintl.com
www.bbintl.com

A. In the rolling hills above Solvang, this spacious home is on one acre. A lovely guest room with large bath en suite is available. Relax in the living room or on the screened patio surrounded by 100-year-old oak trees. Walk a mile into town or bicycle or drive to nearby Lake Cachuma and Santa Ynez wineries. Horseback riding, golf, and boating are all nearby. $85-95.

NOTES: Credit cards accepted: A MasterCard; B Visa; C American Express; D Discover; E Diner's Club; F Other; 2 Personal checks accepted; 3 Lunch available; 4 Dinner available; 5 Open all year; 6 Pets welcome;

B. This English Tudor is decorated with Hans Christian Andersen story themes and antique furnishings. Many rooms have fireplaces, and several have whirlpool tubs. Nine guest rooms are available. Each of the guest rooms has a private bath. Full breakfast is served. Smoking is not permitted. $90-180.

C. This lovely nonsmoking home has a guest room with a view of the mountains. Full breakfast served. Guests may sit and relax on the screened porch in good weather. Just a short walk to the little Danish town of Solvang. $85.

SONOMA

Bed & Breakfast California

P.O. Box 2247, Saratoga, 95070
(408) 867-9662; (800) 872-4500
FAX (408) 867-0907; e-mail: info@bbintl.com
www.bbintl.com

A. An old stonecutter's cottage in a garden setting that has been renovated for guests. An ideal location for walking to the Sonoma Plaza and gourmet restaurants. There are wineries within walking distance and hot springs nearby. The cottage is spacious and has a Franklin stove and large deck for guests to enjoy. $150.

B. This inn is a turn-of-the-century bed and breakfast in the heart of California's renowned wine country. The old estate was originally the home of one of Sonoma's pioneer families. The inn is furnished with antique pieces and each room has its own special charm. The landscaped grounds feature gardens of colorful flowers and enormous trees. A full breakfast is served each morning and complimentary wine and hors d'oeuvres in the afternoon. Bicycles are available for guests' use, as is an outdoor Jacuzzi. $135-150.

C. Nestled in the Valley of the Moon, one of the first bed and breakfast inns established in Sonoma. This quaint Swiss-style farmhouse and country cottage are surrounded by three acres of 100-year-old eucalyptus trees, lawns and flower gardens, and overlook a 200-acre ranch. The town square of Sonoma is only three-quarters-of-a-mile away. Built in the 1940s, this inn is colorfully decorated with hand-painted murals throughout the main house and cottages. $95-170.

D. These 1900 Victorian vintage houses furnished with antiques circa 1910 and Arts and Crafts furniture are very close to the plaza. Some rooms have a fireplace and Jacuzzi tub. A full breakfast, afternoon refreshments, garden hot tub, and complimentary bicycles are available. Wineries are nearby. $115-210.

Sparrow's Nest Inn

424 Denmark Street, 95476
FAX (707) 938-5023; e-mail: sprwwsnest@aol.com

Sparrow's Nest Inn0 is a pretty country cottage, one mile from Sonoma's historic plaza. A respite from a busy world. Privacy, flowers, chocolates, cozy bed, scrumptious Continental plus breakfast, an English garden wraps around the cottage. Equipped kitchenette and air conditioning. Close to wineries, historic sites, wonderful restaurants, and little shops. Pets are welcome with prior arrangements. Smoking permitted outside only.

Hosts: Thomas and Kathleen Anderson
Cottage: 1 (PB) $100-150
Continental Breakfast
Credit Cards: A, B, C, D
Notes: 2, 5, 7, 8, 10, 12

Trojan Horse Inn

19455 Sonoma Highway, 95476
(707) 996-2430; FAX (707) 996-9185
e-mail: trojaninn@aol.com

Enjoy a wine country getaway at the Trojan Horse Inn, an 1887 Victorian home that sits on the banks of Sonoma Creek. The inn is furnished with antiques and its six rooms, all with private baths, offer queen-size beds, plush linens, ceiling fans, and air conditioners. A

---

7 No smoking; 8 Children welcome; 9 Social drinking allowed; 10 Tennis nearby; 11 Swimming nearby; 12 Golf nearby; 13 Skiing nearby; 14 May be booked through a travel agent; 15 Handicapped accessible.

delicious full breakfast is prepared each day; beverages and hors d'oeuvres are offered each evening. The lower patio offers a spa for guest use and bicycles are available. No smoking. Open year-round

Hosts: Joe and Sandy Miccio
Rooms: 6 (PB) $135-165
Full Breakfast
Credit Cards: A, B, C, D
Notes: 2, 5, 7, 12, 14, 15

Victorian Garden Inn

316 East Napa Street, 95476
(707) 996-5339; (800) 543-5339
FAX (707) 996-1689
www.victoriangardeninn.com

Nestled beside Nathanson Creek on an acre of beautiful gardens with private patios and winding paths, this lovely and historic (1870) farmhouse is just one and one-half blocks from Sonoma's historic plaza and the Sebastiani Winery. The comfortable and artfully decorated rooms are designed for comfort. A gourmet California breakfast is served in garden, guests' room, or dining room. A therapeutic spa and full-size swimming pool in the gardens are available for guests' enjoyment. Concierge services are provided. Inquire about accommodations for children.

Host: Donna Lewis
Rooms: 4 (3 PB; 1 SB) $99-185
Full Breakfast
Credit Cards: A, B, C, E
Notes: 2, 5, 7, 9, 10, 11, 12, 14

SONORA

Hammons House Inn Bed & Breakfast

22963 Robertson Ranch Road, 95370
(209) 532-7921; (888) 666-5329
e-mail: hammons@hammonshouseinn

Enjoy panoramic views from the decks of this secluded hilltop setting overlooking the lower Sierra foothills. Guest rooms include the Platinum suite with fireplace, two-person Jacuzzi tub, Casa Blanca fans, and color TV; the Oak room with large two-person Jacuzzi tub, separate shower area, and color TV; and the two-story Bungalow with oaken spiral staircase, fireplace, private bath and deck, color TV, full kitchen facilities, Casa Blanca fans, and much more. All rooms have private entrances, decks, and parking. The Hammons House is extremely popular for weddings/receptions, private dinner events, business retreat. Groups up to 100 are easily accommodated. Coffee/tea service to all guest rooms prior to breakfast and refreshments during stay.

Owner/innkeeper: Linda Cahill-Hammons
Rooms: 3 (PB) $130-165
Full Breakfast
Credit Cards: A, B, C, D
Notes: 2, 5, 6, 7, 8, 9, 11, 12, 13

Lavender Hill

683 South Barretta, 95370
(209) 532-9024; (800) 446-1333 ext. 290
e-mail: lavender@sonnet.com
www.lavenderhill.com

Delightfully restored 1900 Victorian with four lovely guest rooms, all with private baths. Full hearty breakfast served in antique dining room. Formal parlor with baby grand piano, sitting room with TV, wraparound porch with swing, beautiful gardens. Walking distance of shops, restaurants, live repertory theater, and historical Highway 49. Close to golf, gold panning, white-water rafting, and steam train rides. Dinner/theater packages available.

Hosts: Charlie and Jean Marinelli
Rooms: 4 (PB) $75-95
Full Breakfast
Credit Cards: A, B, C
Notes: 2, 5, 7, 8, 9, 11, 12, 13, 14

SOQUEL

Blue Spruce Inn

2815 Main Street, 95073
(831) 464-1137; (800) 559-1137

NOTES: Credit cards accepted: A MasterCard; B Visa; C American Express; D Discover; E Diner's Club; F Other; 2 Personal checks accepted; 3 Lunch available; 4 Dinner available; 5 Open all year; 6 Pets welcome;

Blue Spruce Inn

FAX (831) 475-0608
e-mail: innkeeper@bluespruce.com

Spa tubs, fireplaces, and quiet gardens foster relaxation for guests. The Blue Spruce is four miles south of Santa Cruz, one mile inland from Capitola Beach—an ideal location for a romantic getaway, special celebration, business travel, or an important business meeting. Hike in the redwoods. Bike through country fields. Walk to fine dining. Relax in the outdoor hot tub. Professional, personal attention is the hallmark of this inn. Visit soon!

Hosts: Pat and Tom O'Brien
Rooms: 6 (PB) $85-150
Full Breakfast
Credit Cards: A, B, C, D
Notes: 2, 5, 7, 9, 10, 11, 12, 14

SOUTH LAKE TAHOE

Inn at Heavenly

1261 Ski Run Boulevard, 96150
(530) 544-4244; (800) 692-2246
FAX (530) 544-5213; e-mail: mycabin@siera.net

"Come join us at our unique mountain getaway in beautiful South Lake Tahoe." The pleasant accommodations offered consist of 14 individual rooms, which for 27 years have been hiding away some very satisfied guests. Each room has a private bath, fireplace, kitchenette, TV, and VCR. All rooms are decorated in country mountain-style with log furniture and patchwork quilts. Rates vary upon season and length of stay.

Hosts: Paul Gardner and Sue Ogden
Rooms: 14 (PB) $125-165
Continental Breakfast
Credit Cards: A, B, C, D
Notes: 5, 6, 7, 9, 11, 12, 13, 14

SUMMERLAND

Inn on Summer Hill

2520 Lillie Avenue, 93067
(805) 969-9998; (800) 845-5566
FAX (805) 565-9946
e-mail: denisel@innonsummerhill.com

Nestled in the rolling foothills of Santa Barbara, in the charming sea-side village of

Inn on Summer Hill

7 No smoking; 8 Children welcome; 9 Social drinking allowed; 10 Tennis nearby; 11 Swimming nearby; 12 Golf nearby; 13 Skiing nearby; 14 May be booked through a travel agent; 15 Handicapped accessible.

Summerland, lies a quiet retreat; a reminder of yesteryears when the world moved a bit slower and the people were more friendly. The rooms all offer commanding ocean and island views, fireplaces, romantic canopied beds with lavish custom fabrics, imported furniture, sitting areas, TV/VCRs, stereo cassette players and other world class amenities. Each has a private bath with whirlpool tub.

Hosts: Denise LeBlanc (general manager) and Angie Sumpter (assistant manager)
Rooms: 16 (PB) $215-325
Full Breakfast
Credit Cards: A, B, C, D
Notes: 5, 7, 10, 11, 12, 14

SUSANVILLE

The Roseberry House Bed & Breakfast

609 North Street, 96130
(530) 257-5675

Everything is coming up roses at the Roseberry House. Delicate rose patterns cover the walls and floors and accent the Victorian furnishings. The four upstairs bedrooms are spacious and comfortable, with queen-size beds and choice antiques. Early morning coffee is available in the upstairs hall, with a full breakfast served in the formal dining room. Susanville is on the eastern slopes of the Sierra Nevadas, with warm summer days, spectacular autumn colors, and often a white Christmas.

Hosts: Bill and Maxine Ashmore
Rooms: 4 (PB) $60-85
Full Breakfast
Credit Cards: A, B
Notes: 2, 5, 7, 10, 12, 13

SUTTER CREEK

The Foxes in Sutter Creek

77 Main Street, P.O. Box 159, 95685
(209) 267-5882; (800) 987-3344
FAX (209) 267-0712; e-mail: foxes@cdepot.net
www.foxesinn.com

Foxes Bed and Breakfast Inn is in the gold rush town of Sutter Creek, known as "the nicest town in Mother Lode." There are seven spacious guest rooms, all with private baths. Some with private entrances, wood-burning fireplaces and all with air conditioning. A full breakfast is cooked to order and served on silver service to each guest room or in the garden at the time guest chooses. Covered parking is available. "The Gold Country's most elegant inn"—*Motorland* magazine/CSAA-AAA. Skiing is an hour and fifteen minutes away. Closed Christmas Eve and Christmas day.

Hosts: Pete and Min Fox
Rooms: 7 (PB) $125-185
Full Breakfast
Credit Cards: A, B, D
Notes: 2, 7, 9, 10, 11, 12, 14

Sutter Creek Inn

75 Main Street, P.O. Box 385, 95685
(209) 267-5606; FAX (209) 267-9287
e-mail: info@suttercreekinn.com
www.suttercreekinn.com

The Sutter Creek Inn is full of surprises. Eighteen rooms with baths, 10 with fireplaces, some with hot tubs and TV. Some rooms have swinging beds that can be stabilized. A full hot breakfast is served each morning. Tree-shaded lawns with hammocks. Living room with library, piano, and game tables. Handwriting

Sutter Creek Inn

NOTES: Credit cards accepted: A MasterCard; B Visa; C American Express; D Discover; E Diner's Club; F Other; 2 Personal checks accepted; 3 Lunch available; 4 Dinner available; 5 Open all year; 6 Pets welcome;

Chaney House

analysis and massages available. An hour's drive east of Sacramento on Highway 49.

Rooms: 18 (PB) $65-175
Full Breakfast
Credit Cards: A, B
Notes: 2, 5, 7, 9, 12, 13, 14

TAHOE CITY

Chaney House

4725 West Lake Boulevard, P.O. Box 7852, 96145
(530) 525-7333; FAX (530) 525-4413
e-mail: gary@chaneyhouse.com
www.chaneyhouse.com

Built on the Lake Tahoe shore by Italian stonemasons, Chaney House has an almost medieval quality with its dramatic arched windows, 18-inch-thick stone walls, and enormous fireplace. The private beach and pier beckon guests. Bicycling, hiking, boating, fishing, and 19 ski areas are close at hand. Scrumptious breakfasts are served on the patio overlooking the lake on mild days. Children over 12 welcome.

Hosts: Gary and Lori Chaney
Rooms: 4 (PB) $110-195
Full Breakfast
Credit Cards: A, B
Notes: 2, 5, 7, 9, 10, 11, 12, 13, 14

The Cottage Inn

1690 West Lake Boulevard, Box 66, 96145
(530) 581-4073; (800) 581-4073
FAX (530) 581-0226; e-mail: cottage@sierra.net
www.thecottageinn.com

Nestled among towering pines, the Cottage Inn is just a stone's throw from the lake and private beach. Its cozy cottages offer rooms and suites with knotty pine paneling throughout. All rooms have private entrances, private bathrooms, gas fireplaces, TV/VCR. Sauna on the

The Cottage Inn

---

7 No smoking; 8 Children welcome; 9 Social drinking allowed; 10 Tennis nearby; 11 Swimming nearby; 12 Golf nearby; 13 Skiing nearby; 14 May be booked through a travel agent; 15 Handicapped accessible.

property. The Cottage Inn is close to all summer and winter activities, such as boating, swimming, hiking, skiing, and nearby is a bountiful array of restaurants.

Host: Susanne Muhr
Rooms: 15 (PB) $145-225
Full Breakfast
Credit Cards: A, B
Notes: 2, 5, 7, 11, 12, 13, 14

TAHOE VISTA

The Shore House at Lake Tahoe

7170 North Lake Boulevard, P.O. Box 343, 96148
(530) 546-7270; (800) 207-5160
FAX (530) 546-7130
e-mail: shorhse@inntahoe.com
www.inntahoe.com

On the north shore of Lake Tahoe, the Shore House is the ultimate romantic getaway, with a lakefront hot tub, private gardens and lawns, pier, and adjoining beach. Each floor is surrounded by balconies and decks offering views of the lake and snow-capped mountains. Each guest room has a private outdoor entrance, private bath, and mini-refrigerator. Decorated with gas log fireplaces, knotty pine walls and custom-built log beds, Scandia down comforters, and feather beds. There are 10 ski areas within 20 miles. Water sports, hiking, and biking are all within a few miles.

Hosts: Marty and Barb Cohen
Rooms: 9 (PB) $160-255
Full Breakfast
Credit Cards: A, B, D
Notes: 2, 5, 7, 8, 9, 10, 11, 12, 13

The Shore House

TEMECULA

Loma Vista Bed & Breakfast

33350 La Serena Way, 92591
(909) 676-7047

Loma Vista, in the heart of Temecula's wine country, is convenient to any spot in southern California. This beautiful new Mission-style home is surrounded by citrus groves and premium vineyards. All six rooms have private baths; most have balconies. A full champagne breakfast is served. Closed Christmas day.

Hosts: Walt and Sheila Kurczynski
Rooms: 6 (PB) $100-150
Full Breakfast
Credit Cards: A, B
Notes: 2, 7, 9, 10, 11, 12, 14

TIBURON

Bed & Breakfast Exchange of Marin County—Referral Service

45 Entrata, San Anselmo, 94960
(415) 485-1971; FAX (415) 454-7179

Max's Place. Be the exclusive guests at this convenient Tiburon location. The private bedroom has water view and private bath. Walk to town and take the ferry boat to San Francisco and many fine restaurants. Off-street parking and breakfast included. No smoking. $125.

NOTES: Credit cards accepted: A MasterCard; B Visa; C American Express; D Discover; E Diner's Club; F Other; 2 Personal checks accepted; 3 Lunch available; 4 Dinner available; 5 Open all year; 6 Pets welcome;

TRINIDAD

The Lost Whale Bed & Breakfast

3452 Patrick's Point Drive, 95570
(800) 677-7859; www.lostwhaleinn.com

Gorgeous oceanfront bed and breakfast on four wooded acres with a private beach and trail. Wake to barking sea lions and a spectacular ocean view. Chosen by *San Francisco Chronicle* as "one of the top ten dream vacation spots in California." Amenities include outdoor hot tub, afternoon tea, private baths, and queen-size beds. Fifteen minutes from the largest redwood forests in the world. Enjoy the gardens, decks, and gourmet breakfast. Families welcome.

Hosts: Lee Miller and Susanne Lakin
Rooms: 8 (PB) $100-180
Full Breakfast
Credit Cards: A, B, C, D
Notes: 2, 5, 7, 8, 10, 11, 12, 14

TRUCKEE

Richardson House Bed & Breakfast Inn

10154 High Street, P.O. Box 2011, 96160
(916) 587-5388; (888) 229-0365
FAX (916) 587-0927

Fully restored Victorian, built by Warren Richardson, lumber baron, in the 1880s. Furnished with treasured antiques and fine linens. Victorian strolling garden, complete with gingerbread-adorned gazebo for weddings. On a hill overlooking the Sierras and Old Town Truckee. Train whistles and fresh mountain air to lull guests to sleep each night. Steeped in history and romance. Close to Lake Tahoe, Donner Lake, skiing, hiking, fishing, river rafting, and Amtrak. Twenty-four-hour snack bar, player piano. Children over 10 welcome.

Host: Jeannine Karnofsky
Rooms: 8 (6 PB; 2 SB) $100-150
Full Breakfast
Credit Cards: A, B, C, D
Notes: 2, 5, 7, 13, 14, 15

UKIAH

Bed & Breakfast California

P.O. Box 2247, Saratoga, 95070
(408) 867-9662; (800) 872-4500
FAX (408) 867-0907; e-mail: info@bbintl.com
www.bbintl.com

This 1854 California historic landmark, once a favorite retreat of writers and U.S. presidents, still features warm, naturally carbonated mineral baths. The bed and breakfast is on 700 acres and features an Olympic-size pool, large Jacuzzi, indoor and outdoor mineral tubs, and massages. There are 12 guest rooms and two cottages with private baths and queen-size or twin beds. Hike or bike on the property. Many recreational opportunities are at nearby coast. Continental plus breakfast. No smoking. $139-179.

Vichy Hot Springs Resort & Inn

2605 Vichy Springs Road, 95482-3507
(707) 462-9515; FAX (707) 462-9516
e-mail: vichy@pacific.net
www.vichysprings.com

Vichy Hot Springs Resort, a delightful two-hour drive north of San Francisco, has 17 rooms and three self-contained cottages that have been renovated and individually decorated. All accommodations have their own heating and air-conditioning and either queen- or twin-size beds. Nearby are 10 mineral baths built in 1860. Vichy features naturally sparkling mineral baths, a communal hot pool, Olympic-size pool, 700 private acres with a waterfall, trails, and roads for hiking, jogging, picnicking, and mountain bicycling. Swedish massage, reflexology, and herbal facials. Lunch and dinner available nearby. Smoking permitted outside only.

Hosts: Gilbert and Marjorie Ashoff
Rooms: 22 (PB) $99-225
Full Breakfast
Credit Cards: A, B, C, D, E, F
Notes: 2, 5, 7, 8, 9, 10, 11, 12, 14, 15

---

7 No smoking; 8 Children welcome; 9 Social drinking allowed; 10 Tennis nearby; 11 Swimming nearby; 12 Golf nearby; 13 Skiing nearby; 14 May be booked through a travel agent; 15 Handicapped accessible.

VENICE BEACH

Bed & Breakfast California

P.O. Box 2247, Saratoga, 95070
(408) 867-9662; (800) 872-4500
FAX (408) 867-0907; e-mail: info@bbintl.com
www.bbintl.com

A world of warmth and hospitality awaits guests at this turn-of-the-century lodge with nine elegant guest rooms and suites. Modern comfort and convenience blend with the beauty of antiques and hand-detailed furnishings. Perhaps nowhere in the world can visitors find a communtiy as interesting as Venice Beach. Venice offers a unique and unforgettable travel experience. $95-160.

VENTURA

Bed & Breakfast California

P.O. Box 2247, Saratoga, 95070
(408) 867-9662; (800) 872-4500
FAX (408) 867-0907; e-mail: info@bbintl.com
www.bbintl.com

A. Three blocks from the beach, this inn with Mediterranean decor offers comfort and convenience. Seventeen rooms with private baths. Full breakfast and afternoon refreshments. $75-150.

B. Bavarian-style hospitality is featured at this lovely bed and breakfast near the beach. Five guest rooms have queen- or king-size beds and private baths. Walking or biking distance from shops, restaurants, and attractions. Short commute to Santa Barbara, Ojai, and Santa Ynez Valley. Full breakfast. No smoking. $110-160.

Bella Maggiore Inn

67 South California Street, 93001
(805) 652-0277

This 1920s northern Italian-style inn was designed by A. C. Martin, architect of the Los Angeles City Hall. The inn is in the old business district near Mission San Buenaventura. Full breakfast served in the dining room or courtyard. Appetizers with beverages served in the afternoon. Telephone, TV in all rooms. Whirlpool, fireplace, and air conditioning in some rooms.

Host: Thomas Wood
Rooms: 24 (PB) $75-150
Full Breakfast
Cards: A, B, C, D, E
Notes: 3, 4, 5, 8, 9, 11, 14, 15

La Mer Bed & Breakfast

411 Poli Street, 93001
(805) 643-3600; FAX (805) 653-7329

Nestled on a green hillside, this Cape Cod-style Victorian house overlooks the heart of historic Ventura and the spectacular California coastline. Originally built in 1890, La Mer has been faithfully decorated by host Gisela Baida to create an Old World atmosphere. Each guest room has been furnished to capture the feeling of a specific European country: France, Germany, Austria, Norway, and England. Wine or champagne and a Bavarian-buffet breakfast are included.

Hosts: Gisela and Mike Baida
Rooms: 5 (PB) $90-185
Full Breakfast
Credit Cards: A, B, C
Notes: 2, 5, 7, 9, 10, 11, 12, 14

WESTPORT

The Blue Victorian Inn and Antique Shop

38911 Main Street, Hwy. 1 North, 95488
(707) 964-6310 (phone/FAX); (800) 400-6310

The Blue Victorian Inn and Antique Shop was built from California redwood in the 1880s. The building carries a wonderful history. At the turn of the century, Westport was the largest seaport between San Francisco and Eureka. Now the inn is one of only two hotels that remain from the town's heyday. This is the

---

NOTES: Credit cards accepted: A MasterCard; B Visa; C American Express; D Discover; E Diner's Club; F Other; 2 Personal checks accepted; 3 Lunch available; 4 Dinner available; 5 Open all year; 6 Pets welcome;

best-kept secret on the Mendocino's Northern Coast. Our awesome panoramic view of the Pacific Ocean and period-furnished rooms will provide a wonderful escape from the modern world. Come to California and "...unwind on Pacific Coast time." Inquire about accommodations for pets.

Hosts: Bill R. Sullivan and Terry M. Anderson
Rooms: 5 (3 PB; 2 SB) $65-150
Full Breakfast
Credit Cards: None
Notes: 2, 5, 7, 15

Howard Creek Ranch

DeHaven Valley Farm

39247 North Highway One, 95488
(707) 961-1660; FAX (707) 961-1677
e-mail: dehavenval@ad.com
www.dehaven-valley-farm.com

Eight comfortable rooms and cottages, private baths, hot tub, fireplaces. Twenty acres of hills, meadows, streams, and woods nestled next to the Pacific Ocean. Restaurants serving fresh, fabulous four-course dinners. Convenient to Mendocino, the Lost Coast, and the giant redwoods. A menagerie of animals provides endless entertainment. Full country-style breakfast included with fresh fruit, specialties like apple pancakes and kaiserschmaren. Mild climate (no snow!).

Host: Christa Stapp
Rooms: 8 (6 PB; 2 SB) $85-140
Full Breakfast
Credit Cards: A, B
Notes: 2, 4, 5, 7, 8, 9, 11, 12, 14

Howard Creek Ranch

Box 121, 95488
(707) 964-6725; FAX (707) 964-1603
www.howardcreekranch.com

A historic 1867 farm on 40 acres, only 100 yards from the beach. A rural retreat adjoining wilderness. Suite and cabins; views of ocean, mountains, creek, or gardens; fireplace/wood stoves; period furnishings; hot tub, sauna, heated swimming pool, and horseback riding nearby. Gift certificates available. Pets welcome with prior arrangements. Inquire about accommodations for children. Limited smoking permitted.

Hosts: Charles (Sunny) and Sally Grigg
Rooms: 11 (9 PB; 2 SB) $75-160
Full Breakfast
Credit Cards: A, B
Notes: 2, 5, 6, 7

WOODACRE

Bed & Breakfast Exchange of Marin County—Referral Service

45 Entrata, San Anselmo, 94960
(415) 485-1971; FAX (415) 454-7179

Country Retreat. This lovely private accommodation has a separate entrance, queen-size bed, breakfast in a lovely garden, and a private hot tub. Woodacre is a semi-rural location yet still close to all of Marin County, San Francisco, and the wine country. $85.

YOSEMITE

Bed & Breakfast California

P.O. Box 2247, Saratoga, 95070
(408) 867-9662; (800) 872-4500
FAX (408) 867-0907; e-mail: info@bbintl.com
www.bbintl.com

A. A little corner of paradise on 11 acres of land has stunning surroundings. Three large

7 No smoking; 8 Children welcome; 9 Social drinking allowed; 10 Tennis nearby; 11 Swimming nearby; 12 Golf nearby; 13 Skiing nearby; 14 May be booked through a travel agent; 15 Handicapped accessible.

suites and a guest house for four, all with private baths, private entrances, TV/VCR, refrigerator, and microwave. Full breakfast. Enjoy fishing in the pond or swimming in the pool. Barbecue area can accommodate 10 people at a time. Great for a family reunion. Forty-five minutes from Yosemite, 10 minutes from beautiful Mariposa. $85-105.

B. Halfway between Yosemite Valley and Wawona is this beautiful new bed and breakfast with uniquely decorated rooms, each with fireplace and one with Jacuzzi for two. The three guest rooms have double, queen-, and king-size beds and private baths. Outdoor decks offer serenity, views, and a hot tub. Full breakfast. No smoking. $95-160.

C. Two miles from park entrance, this inn is five minutes from Mariposa Grove of giant sequoias and the narrow gauge railroad excursion. Full country breakfast. $90.

D. A new vacation home. Hidden in the trees with magnificent sunset views, the home provides everything for a perfect vacation in Yosemite. The mural of Yosemite Valley that adorns the carport wall, the art gallery in the entry area, and, best of all, the breathtaking views all tell guests that this 1700-square-foot home was designed by an artist. Indeed, the clerestory windows, colorful walls and original art and furnishings are unique for a vacation rental. Prepare a full gourmet meal in the fully equipped kitchen and enjoy it on the deck under the stars with no lights or noise to disturb guests. $75-300.

Château du Sureau

48688 Victoria Lane, P.O. Box 577, Oakhurst, 93644
(209) 683-6860; FAX (209) 683-0800

On the rim of Yosemite National Park commanding extraordinary views of the Sierra Nevada sits this seven-and-one-half-acre French country estate. An enchanting, authentic European castle, the hotel offers exquisite guest rooms, all lovingly decorated with period antiques, canopied beds, wood-burning fireplaces, CD and stereo systems, and gorgeous baths with deep Roman tubs. On the grounds, pathways meander through wildflower gardens, a European pool, and an outdoor chess and checkers court. Open year-round, except for three weeks in January. Now available is the two-bedroom-two-bath exclusive Villa Sureau.

Host: Mrs. Erna Kubin-Clanin
Rooms: 10 (PB) $315-515
Full Breakfast
Credit Cards: A, B, C
Notes: 3, 4, 7, 9, 11, 12, 13, 14, 15

Château du Sureau

NOTES: Credit cards accepted: A MasterCard; B Visa; C American Express; D Discover; E Diner's Club; F Other; 2 Personal checks accepted; 3 Lunch available; 4 Dinner available; 5 Open all year; 6 Pets welcome;

Yosemite's River Resort

11399 Cherry Lake Road, Groveland, 95321
(209) 962-7408; (800) 626-7408
FAX (209) 962-7400; e-mail: LMR@sonnet.com
www.sonnet.com/usr/yosemite/

Yosemite's River Resort, formerly Lee's Middle Fork Resort, is on SR 120, just 150 miles from San Francisco and 11 miles from the Big Oak Flat entrance to Yosemite National Park, the most direct route into the park and the most scenic. For anglers, the Middle Fork of the Tuolumne River is well stocked with pan-size trout, and the river flows right through the resort. Other nearby activities include whitewater rafting on the Tuolumne, hiking, swimming, and panning for gold, and in the winter downhill skiing. Nonsmoking rooms available.

Hosts: Roland and Robin Hilarides
Rooms: 20 (PB) $69-89
Full and Continental Breakfasts
Credit Cards: A, B, C, D, E
Notes: 3, 4, 5, 8, 9, 11, 12, 13, 14, 15

YOUNTVILLE

Bed & Breakfast California

P.O. Box 2247, Saratoga, 95070
(408) 867-9662; (800) 872-4500
FAX (408) 867-0907; e-mail: info@bbintl.com
www.bbintl.com

French country inn that is a perfect base from which to explore the Napa Valley. Thirteen guest rooms in three vine-covered, brick buildings. The lobby of the main building has a welcoming fireplace and is reminiscent of a farmhouse in Provence. Seven rooms in this building have views of the vineyards. Rooms in the Old Bakery and Carriage House buildings have rooms with fireplaces. There is a pool available during the summer months as well as outdoor spa tub. $110-200.

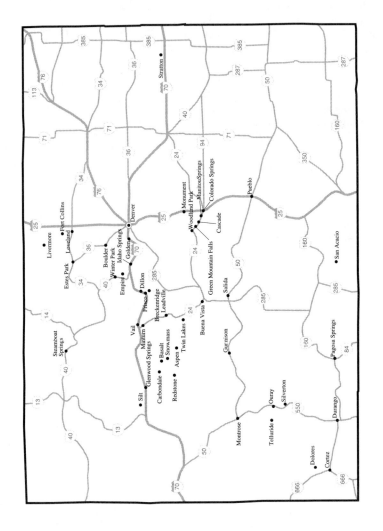

Colorado

Colorado

ANTONITO

Conejos River Guest Ranch

25390 Highway 17, 81120
P.O. Box 175, Conejos, 81129 (mailing address)
(719) 376-2464; e-mail: info@conejosranch.com
www.conejosranch.com

For more than 100 years, the Conejos Ranch has been the traveler's choice in south central Colorado. Nestled in the Rio Grande National Forest on 12 parklike acres, the lodge has classy western decor, a gift shop, and an exterior wraparound deck. Add six comfortable cabins on a mile of river frontage, and guests will find the perfect place to relax—revive—renew. Cumbres and Toltec Narrow Gauge Railroad nearby; great fishing and hiking; fabulous food; extraordinary hospitality. Boxed lunches available. Golf is 42 miles away and skiing is an hour and a half away. Handicapped accessibility is limited.

Host: Shorty Fry (ranch foreman)
Rooms: 8 (PB) $79-95
Full Breakfast
Credit Cards: A, B, D
Notes: 2, 4, 6, 8, 9, 12, 14, 15

Conejos River Guest Ranch

ASPEN

Boomerang Lodge

500 West Hopkins Avenue, 81611
(970) 925-3416; (800) 992-8852
www.boomeranglodge.com

This unique lodge in the quiet West End is within walking distance to downtown, Aspen Mountain ski gondola, or the Aspen Music Festival. All guest rooms and fireplace apartments have a sunny terrace or balcony, thanks to the handsome design influenced by the owner-architect's teacher, Frank Lloyd Wright. Thoughtful touches include pool, whirlpool, and sauna. Additional winter amenities include afternoon tea and town courtesy van. Discover why devoted guests return to the Boomerang.

Hosts: Charles and Fonda Paterson
Rooms: 35 (PB) $105-280
Continental Breakfast
Credit Cards: A, B, C
Notes: 5, 7, 8, 10, 12, 13, 14

Christmas Inn

232 West Main Street, 81611
(970) 925-3822; (800) 625-5581
FAX (970) 925-3328

Aspen...the affordable way! This comfortable inn features attractive rooms, all with private baths, direct-dial telephones, color cable TV, and sun deck. Amenities include whirlpool and sauna (winter only), daily housekeeping,

---

NOTES: Credit cards accepted: A MasterCard; B Visa; C American Express; D Discover; E Diner's Club; F Other; 2 Personal checks accepted; 3 Lunch available; 4 Dinner available; 5 Open all year; 6 Pets welcome; 7 No smoking; 8 Children welcome; 9 Social drinking allowed; 10 Tennis nearby; 11 Swimming nearby; 12 Golf nearby; 13 Skiing nearby; 14 May be booked through a travel agent; 15 Handicapped accessible.

complimentary full breakfast, and afternoon refreshments. Walk to the quaint shops and restaurants of Aspen or utilize the free shuttle service to the Music Tent (summer), to all four ski mountains, and around town.

Host: Lynn Durfee
Rooms: 24 (PB) $56-140
Full Breakfast
Credit Cards: A, B, C
Notes: 5, 8, 9, 10, 11, 12, 13, 14

Hotel Lenado

200 South Aspen Street, 81611
(970) 925-6246; (800) 321-3457
FAX (970) 925-3840; e-mail: hotlsard@rof.net

The Hotel Lenado welcomes guests with award-winning architecture and a warmth and style all its own. Nineteen guest rooms, each with a four-poster hickory or carved applewood bed, some with wood-burning stoves, wet bars, and whirlpool baths. A complimentary full breakfast is served every day. Spend the afternoon relaxing in the rooftop hot tub with its magnificent view of Aspen Mountain or enjoying complimentary hors d'oeuvres in Marham's Bar.

Rooms: 19 (PB) $95-570
Full Breakfast
Credit Cards: A, B, C, E
Notes: 2, 8, 9, 10, 11, 12, 13, 14

Sardy House

128 East Main Street, 81611
(970) 920-2525; (800) 321-3457
FAX (970) 920-4478; e-mail: hotlsard@rof.net

The Sardy House is a beautiful Victorian bed and breakfast hotel with 14 guest rooms and six suites. All rooms have four-poster cherry-wood beds and armoires, terry-cloth robes, feather comforters, and whirlpool baths. The pool, Jacuzzi, and sauna area are perfect for relaxing in the afternoon. The garden area is a great spot for enjoying the complimentary breakfast. An elegant dinner or early evening cocktails are available in the bar and dining room. Inquire about accommodations for pets.

Rooms: 20 (PB) $110-950
Full Breakfast
Credit Cards: A, B, C, E
Notes: 2, 4, 8, 9, 10, 11, 12, 13, 14

BASALT

Shenandoah Inn

600 Frying Pan Road, Box 560, 81621
(970) 927-4991

Contemporary western Colorado bed and breakfast is on two riverfront acres on the Frying Pan River, one of North America's premier trout streams, in the heart of the White River National Forest. The inn is only 20 minutes from Aspen and Glenwood Hot Springs; year-round access to the best of Colorado's numerous outdoor activities. Enjoy the riverside hot tub, the warm, friendly atmosphere, and the exceptional cuisine.

Hosts: Bob and Terri Ziets
Rooms: 4 (PB) $85-115
Cabin: $165
Full Breakfast
Credit Cards: A, B, C
Notes: 2, 5, 7, 9, 10, 11, 12, 13, 14

BOULDER

Bed & Breakfast at Sunset House

1740 Sunset Boulevard, 80304
(303) 444-0801; (877) 338-8489
FAX (303) 443-9416; e-mail: olson1740@aol.com

Two rooms offered with shared bath and a private entrance. Each room has its own telephone. The family room has a cozy fireplace, small library, and a TV. Outside patios overlook the city to the south and the Flatirons to the west. The Pearl Street Mall is a 10-minute walk away. Taikoo, a Shih Tzu mix, is the resident dog. Sunset House provides a nonsmoking environment.

Hosts: Phyllis and Roger Olson
Rooms: 2 (SB) $80
Full Breakfast
Credit Cards: None
Notes: 2, 5, 7

NOTES: Credit cards accepted: A MasterCard; B Visa; C American Express; D Discover; E Diner's Club; F Other; 2 Personal checks accepted; 3 Lunch available; 4 Dinner available; 5 Open all year; 6 Pets welcome;

Briar Rose

Briar Rose Bed & Breakfast

2151 Arapahoe Avenue, 80302
(303) 442-3007; FAX (303) 786-8440
e-mail: brbbx@aol.com

Nine unique guest rooms in this English country cottage inn each have private baths, telephones, and most have queen-size beds. Two rooms have fireplaces. A delicious breakfast of fresh fruit, homemade granola, yogurt, croissants, and freshly baked muffins or nut bread with freshly squeezed orange juice, coffee, and tea is served. In the afternoon, tea and cookies are served to guests in the garden or in the privacy of their room. Near the CU campus, about one mile from Pearl Street Mall, and within walking distance of many good restaurants.

Hosts: Bob and Margaret Weisenbach
Rooms: 9 (PB) $99-190
Continental Breakfast
Credit Cards: A, B, C
Notes: 2, 5, 7, 9, 10, 11, 12, 14

BRECKENRIDGE

Allaire Timbers Inn

9511 Highway 9, South Main Street, 80424
(970) 453-7530; (800) 624-4904
www.allairetimbers.com

An award-winning log bed and breakfast combining contemporary and rustic log furnishings in an intimate setting. Guest rooms have a private bath and deck with mountain views. Suites offer a private fireplace and hot tub. Great room has fireplace, sunroom, loft, and outdoor hot tub. All have spectacular views of the Colorado Rockies. Hearty breakfast and afternoon refreshments. Featured on the Travel channel's *Romantic Inns in America*.

Hosts: Jack and Kathy Gumph
Rooms: 10 (PB) $135-400
Full Breakfast
Credit Cards: A, B, C, D
Notes: 2, 5, 7, 9, 10, 11, 12, 13, 14, 15

Bed & Breakfasts on North Main Street

303 North Main Street, P.O. Box 2454, 80424
(970) 453-2975; (800) 795-2975 (outside Colorado)
FAX (970) 453-5258; e-mail: bnb@imageline.com
www.breckenridge-inn.com

Guests are encouraged to enjoy themselves while staying in one of the three inns, along the Blue River in Breckenridge's historic district. Featured on the travel channel's *Romantic Inns of America*, the 1885 Williams House provides Victorian splendor and the exceptionally private 1880 Willoughby Cottage inspires romance. The post-and-beam 1997 Barn Above the River offers spectacular mountain and river views. Private baths. Scrumptious breakfast. Refreshments. Outdoor spa. Some rooms: fireplace, whirlpool for two, balcony, TV, telephone. Nonsmoking.

Hosts: Fred Kinat and Diane Jaynes
Rooms: 11 (PB) $95-185
Cottage: 1 (PB) $175-235
Full Breakfast
Credit Cards: A, B, C, D
Notes: 2, 5, 7, 9, 10, 11, 12, 13, 14

North Main Street

7 No smoking; 8 Children welcome; 9 Social drinking allowed; 10 Tennis nearby; 11 Swimming nearby; 12 Golf nearby; 13 Skiing nearby; 14 May be booked through a travel agent; 15 Handicapped accessible.

Evans House

Evans House

102 South French Street, P.O. Box 387, 80424
(970) 453-5509; e-mail: evans@imageline.com
www.colorado-bnb.com/evanshse

In the heart of beautiful, historic Breckenridge, the Evans House is a restored 1886 Victorian traditional bed and breakfast with a full view of the 10-mile range. A delicious seven-day-menu breakfast and afternoon refreshments are served. Winter activities are available at the front door via the free bus. Evening activities and restaurants are two blocks away. Spring, summer, and fall events, and sports make this area unforgettable. Supervised children welcome. Limited handicapped accessibility. AAA-approved. New! Hot tub! Two suites!

Hosts: Pete and Georgette Contos
Rooms: 4 (PB) $63-114
Suites: 2 (PB) $77-140
Full Breakfast
Credit Cards: A, B, C, D, E
Notes: 2, 5, 7, 9, 10, 11, 12, 13, 14

Little Mountain Lodge

98 Sunbeam Drive, P.O. Box 2479, 80424
(970) 453-1969; (800) 468-7707 (outside the state)
FAX (970) 453-1919; e-mail: lml@colorado.net

Luxury, loge lodge situated on three acres offers 10 uniquely designed rooms, each with private bath, private deck, TV, VCR, and telephone. Fresh coffee brought to guests' room before a delicious, two-course gourmet breakfast served in the dining room. Enjoy afternoon refreshments by the fireplace or on the deck. Amenities include ski storage room with boot dryer, hot tub, pool table, video library, handicapped accessible, small conference facilities, on ski shuttle route and close to town.

Hosts: Lynn and Truman Esmond
Rooms: 10 (PB) $130-270
Full Breakfast
Credit Cards: A, B, C, D
Notes: 2, 5, 7, 9, 10, 12, 13, 14, 15

The Walker House

211 East Lincoln Avenue, P.O. Box 5107, 80424
(970) 453-2426

An 1875 historic residence with original Victorian furnishings. Informal, quiet, and intimate. Two upstairs bedrooms with great views. Special foods on request. Dinners can be ordered "in." In the historic section of Breckenridge, one-half block from restaurants and shops, on free shuttle route. Catered dinner available.

Hosts: Sue Ellen and the Contos
Rooms: 2 (1 PB; 1 SB) $89-118
Full Breakfast
Credit Cards: B
Notes: 2, 7, 10, 11, 12, 13

The Wellington Inn

200 North Main Street, P.O. Box 5890, 80424
(970) 453-9464; (800) 655-7557
FAX (970) 453-0149; e-mail: welingtn@sni.net
www.thewellingtoninn.com

This Victorian inn is on historical Main Street within walking distance to many shops and restaurants and a short trolley ride to the ski area. Each guest room enjoys a balcony with breathtaking views of the mountain range and downtown Breckenridge. All rooms include whirlpool baths, goose-down comforters, complimentary sherry, coffee makers with complimentary beverages, and a hearty breakfast. The Wellington Inn's romantic restaurant specializes in fine dining nightly, featuring beef

---

NOTES: Credit cards accepted: A MasterCard; B Visa; C American Express; D Discover; E Diner's Club; F Other; 2 Personal checks accepted; 3 Lunch available; 4 Dinner available; 5 Open all year; 6 Pets welcome;

Carbondale, CO 189

The Wellington Inn

Wellington. Sunday brunch available during the summer months.

Rooms: 4 (PB) $139-249
Full Breakfast
Credit Cards: A, B, C, D
Notes: 2, 4, 5, 7, 9, 10, 12, 13, 14

BUENA VISTA

The Adobe Inn

303 North Highway 24, 81211
(719) 395-6340
www.bbonline.com/co/adobe//

Capture the flavor of an Old Southwest adobe hacienda. Three rooms and two suites provide a delightful range of styles and amenities. Each room has a private bath and color TV and guests can relax in the two-person Jacuzzi. In the upper Arkansas River Valley, home of the majestic Collegiate Peaks Range. Featured in AAA (three diamonds), Fodor's, and Mobil guides.

Hosts: Paul, Marjorie, and Michael Knox
Rooms: 5 (PB) $59-89
Full Breakfast
Credit Cards: A, B
Notes: 2, 3, 4, 5, 7, 8, 10, 11, 12, 13, 14

CARBONDALE

The Ambiance Inn

66 North 2nd Street, 81623
(303) 963-3597; (800) 350-1515
e-mail: ambiancein@aol.com
www.ambianceinn.com

Enjoy Aspen, Glenwood Springs, and the beautiful Crystal Valley from this spacious chalet-style home featuring vaulted ceilings throughout. The 1950s ski lodge decor of the very large Aspen Suite or the Victorian elegance of the Sonoma Room featuring a romantic four-poster bed are ideal for getaways. The Santa Fe Room is alive with the warmth of the Southwest. The Kauai Room features special atmosphere and a two-person Jacuzzi. All rooms adjoin the library-sitting room.

Hosts: Norma and Robert Morris
Rooms: 4 (PB) $60-90
Full Breakfast
Credit Cards: A, B
Notes: 2, 5, 7, 8, 9, 10, 11, 12, 13, 14

Mt. Sopris Inn

P.O. Box 126, 81623
(970) 963-2209; (800) 437-8675
FAX (970) 963-8975
e-mail: mt.soprisinn@juno.com
www.colorado.bnb.com/mtsopris

For a special relaxing treat stay at the Mt. Sopris Inn, central to Aspen, Redstone, and Glenwood Springs.

Rooms: 14 (PB) $85-175
Full Breakfast
Credit Cards: A, B
Notes: 5, 7, 11, 12, 13, 15

Van Horn House at Lions Ridge

0318 Lions Ridge Road, 81623
(970) 963-3605; (888) 453-0395
FAX (970) 963-1681; e-mail: jlaatsch@aol.com

Enjoy hiking, biking, trout fishing, and skiing in the Roaring Fork Valley. Hosts offer the comfort of home away from home, featuring antiques, queen-size beds, and country charm; the lounge features satellite TV, VCR, books, movies, games, puzzles, and homemade cookies. Great views of Mount Sopris from the balconies, and a relaxing hot tub beckons. Full deluxe breakfast. Near Aspen, Snowmass, Redstone, and Glenwood Springs. Great restaurants nearby.

---

7 No smoking; 8 Children welcome; 9 Social drinking allowed; 10 Tennis nearby; 11 Swimming nearby; 12 Golf nearby; 13 Skiing nearby; 14 May be booked through a travel agent; 15 Handicapped accessible.

Hosts: Susan and John Laatsch
Rooms: 4 (2 PB; 2 SB) $65-80
Full Breakfast
Credit Cards: A, B
Notes: 2, 5, 7, 9, 12, 13, 14

CASCADE

Black Bear Inn of Pikes Peak

5250 Pikes Peak Highway, 80809
(719) 684-0151

The Black Bear Inn of Pikes Peak is between the North Pole and the Pikes Peak tollgate. Guests enjoy breathtaking mountain views from each bedroom. At the end of a wooded trail guests are invited to enjoy the very private hot tub. Relax, read a book, or have special meetings or gatherings in the large common area. Hiking and nature trails are right outside the inn. "We will be happy to arrange banquets." Three cabins with two fireplaces available. Children 10 or older welcome. Skiing is two hours away.

Host: Christi Heidenreich
Room: 9 (PB) $75-85
Suites: $90
Cabins: 3-$110
Full Breakfast
Credit Cards: A, B, D
Notes: 2, 5, 7, 9, 10, 11, 12, 14, 15

COLORADO SPRINGS

Black Forest Bed & Breakfast

11170 Black Forest Road, 80908
(719) 495-4208; FAX (719) 495-0688
e-mail: blackforestbandb@msn.com
www.blackforestbb.com

Massive log home on 20 acres of pine overlooking city lights and Rocky Mountains rustic romantic retreat with whirlpool tubs, fireplaces, indoor lap pool, and kitchens. Ideal for business travelers with in-room telephones, modem jacks, TV/VCRs, and fax. Family-friendly facility with suites, kitchens, free laundry, and fenced playyard.

Black Forest

Host: Robert and Susan Putnam
Rooms: 5 (PB) $75-200
Continental Breakfast
Credit Cards: A, B, C, D
Notes: 2, 5, 7, 8, 9, 10, 11, 12, 13, 14, 15

Eastholme in the Rockies

4445 Haggerman Avenue, P.O. Box 98, Cascade, 80809
(719) 684-9901; (800) 672-9901

Listed in the National Register of Historic Places, this charming 1885 Victorian is nestled in the mountain village of Cascade. Close to all Colorado Springs attractions. Winner of Colorado's Historic Preservation award and a Ute Pass landmark, it offers a spectacular view of Pike National Forest. Graciously and comfortably decorated in antiques, with fine fabrics, lace, and oriental rugs. A bountiful breakfast is served each morning. There are also two romantic cottages that offer privacy and a whirlpool tub and fireplace.

Hostess: Terry Thompson
Rooms: 8 (5 PB; 2 SB) $70-140
Full Breakfast
Credit Cards: A, B, C, D
Notes: 2, 5, 7, 8, 9, 10, 11, 12, 13, 14

Eastholme in the Rockies

NOTES: Credit cards accepted: A MasterCard; B Visa; C American Express; D Discover; E Diner's Club; F Other; 2 Personal checks accepted; 3 Lunch available; 4 Dinner available; 5 Open all year; 6 Pets welcome;

Holden House

Holden House— 1902 Bed & Breakfast Inn

1102 West Pikes Peak Avenue, 80904
(719) 471-3980; FAX (719) 471-4740
e-mail: holdenhouse@worldnet.att.net
www.bbonline.com/co/holden/

A 1902 Victorian, a 1906 carriage house, and adjacent 1898 Victorian are filled with antiques and heirlooms. Immaculate accommodations in a residential area near historic district and central to the Pikes Peak region. Enjoy the parlor, living room with fireplace, or veranda with mountain views. Guest suites boast private sitting areas, fireplaces, and more. Complimentary refreshments and in-room telephones/modem add convenience. AAA- and Mobil-rated. Inquire about minimum-stay requirements. Friendly resident cats, Mingtoy and Muffin.

Hosts: Sallie and Welling Clark
Suites: 5 (PB) $125-140
Full Breakfast
Credit Cards: A, B, C, D, E, F
Notes: 2, 5, 7, 9, 10, 11, 12, 14, 15

Our Hearts Inn Old Colorado City

2215 West Colorado Avenue, 80904
(719) 473-8684; (800) 533-7095
e-mail: hearts2@gateway.net
www.bbonline.com/co/ourhearts

Visit this 1895 country Victorian bed and breakfast two blocks from the historic district of Old Colorado City. Hand-stenciled interiors are furnished with antiques complimenting the home's 100-year-old character offering three guest rooms. Choose the private 1920s cottage for a romantic getaway or honeymoon. Amenities include fireplaces, jetted Jacuzzi and garden tubs, air conditioning, private baths, telephones, and TVs. Fresh coffee beans, grinder, and pot provided in cottage's kitchenette. In the main house, freshly brewed coffee awaits guests just outside their door. "BB," the friendly parakeet, reminds those with allergies to cats and kittens that this is a cat-free bed and breakfast. Children welcome, separate beds available, and discounts may apply—inquire. Corporate/government rates honored.

Hosts: Andy and Pat Fejedelem
Rooms: 4 (PB) $85-150
Full Breakfast
Credit Cards: A, B, C, D, E
Notes: 2, 5, 7, 8, 9, 10, 11, 12, 14

The Painted Lady Bed & Breakfast Inn

1318 West Colorado Avenue, 80904
(719) 473-3165; (800) 370-3165
FAX (719) 635-1396
e-mail: innkeepers@paintedladyinn.com

An 1894 Victorian Inn in historic west side. Spacious suites with telephone, TV/VCR, CD, refrigerators, work areas, and multiple bed capabilities. Some with fireplaces, two-person tubs or kitchenette. Private outdoor hot tub and deck or balcony and porch beckon guests to the outdoors. A hearty breakfast readies guests for business or pleasure in the Pikes Peak Region. Close to attractions, dining, Colorado College, US Air Force Academy. Resident cats; no smoking; air conditioned. Children over four welcome.

Host: Valerie Maslowski
Rooms: 3 (PB) $90-150
Full Breakfast
Credit Cards: A, B, C, D, E
Notes: 2, 5, 7, 8, 9, 10, 11, 12, 13, 14

---

7 No smoking; 8 Children welcome; 9 Social drinking allowed; 10 Tennis nearby; 11 Swimming nearby; 12 Golf nearby; 13 Skiing nearby; 14 May be booked through a travel agent; 15 Handicapped accessible.

Room at the Inn

618 North Nevada Avenue, 80903
(719) 442-1896; (800) 579-4621 (reservations)
FAX (719) 442-6802

Experience a peek at the past in this 1896 Victorian. Enjoy...the charm of a classic three-story turreted antique-filled Queen Anne featuring original wall murals, oak staircase, and pocket doors...the romance of fireplaces, plush robes, and whirlpool tubs for two...and gracious hospitality featuring full breakfasts, afternoon tea, and turndown service. Conveniently near downtown and Colorado College. A romantic retreat in the heart of the city. Three-star rating from Mobil.

Hosts: Jan and Chick McCormick
Rooms: 7 (PB) $89-145
Full Breakfast
Credit Cards: A, B, C, D, E
Notes: 2, 5, 7, 9, 10, 11, 12, 14, 15

Serenity Pines

True Colorado getaway on acres of pines. Guest house sleeps six. Full-size kitchen, stocked and equipped with new appliances, including dishwasher. Continental breakfast plus supplies are provided for guests to prepare a full breakfast at their leisure. Bed-and-breakfast-style pampering. Private sun deck, hot tub, picnic, barbecue area. Parklike setting. Cable, video library, telephone, answering machine, crib, fax, copier. Also bed-and-breakfast room sleeps two with private bath and entrance, refrigerator, microwave, coffee pot, cable TV/VCR. Within 30 minutes of area attractions.

Hosts: Kathy and Bob
Suites: 2 (PB) $69-129
Continental Breakfast
Credit Cards: A, B, C
Notes: 2, 3, 4, 5, 7, 8, 9, 10, 11, 12, 13, 14, 15

COLORADO SPRINGS/PIKES PEAK AREA

Silver Wood Bed & Breakfast at Divide

463 County Road 512, Divide, 80814
(719) 687-6784

Silver Wood is a tastefully decorated country home built in 1990 in a wooded area with abundant hiking trails and fantastic views of mountains and meadows. An ideal getaway from city life, yet near Colorado Springs and Cripple

Room at the Inn

Serenity Pines Guest House

11910 Windmill Road, 80908
(877) 737-3674; FAX (719) 495-7141
e-mail: serenpines@aol.com
http: //colorado-bnb.com/serenpines

NOTES: Credit cards accepted: A MasterCard; B Visa; C American Express; D Discover; E Diner's Club; F Other; 2 Personal checks accepted; 3 Lunch available; 4 Dinner available; 5 Open all year; 6 Pets welcome;

Creek. Two friendly resident cats, Lucy and Frisco. A country gourmet breakfast is served in the dining room. Enjoy country hospitality.

Hosts: Larry and Bess Oliver
Rooms: 2 (PB) $69-120
Full Breakfast
Credit Cards: A, B, C, D
Notes: 2, 5, 7, 8, 9, 14

CORTEZ

A Bed & Breakfast on Maple

P.O. Box 327, 81321
(970) 565-3906; (800) 665-3906
e-mail: maple@fone.net
www.subee.com/maple/home.htm/

"Where you get spoiled and pampered." Nine miles to Mesa Verde, 45 minutes to Durango. Antiques mixed with country charm. Queen-size beds, hot tub, fitness center, water garden. Big appetite? Big breakfast! Downtown proximity—walk to restaurants, shopping, movies, and Indian dances. Sack lunch available. Limited handicapped accessibility.

Hosts: Nonnie and Roy Fahsholtz
Rooms: 4 (PB) $69-119
Full Breakfast
Credit Cards: A, B, C, D
Notes: 2, 5, 7, 8, 9, 10, 11, 12, 13, 14

Grizzly Roadhouse Bed & Breakfast

3450 Highway 160 South, 81321
(970) 565-7738; (800) 330-7286
e-mail: grizbb@fone.net
www.subee.com/grizzly/home.html

On 30 acres of evergreen-studded hills and canyons, this newly remodeled country-style bed and breakfast and guest cottage provides a place to relax, expand, and be at peace. The "bear" necessities include walking trails, spa, uninterrupted views of the stars, native storytelling, and "hibernation" spiritual retreats. Dine on a full "gourbear" breakfast featuring authentic native foods from family recipes. Each room has its own private bath and sitting area with TV/VCR and privacy.

Rooms: 4 (PB) $69-125
Full Breakfast
Credit Cards: A, B, C
Notes: 2, 3, 5, 7, 8, 9, 10, 11, 12, 13

DENVER

Capitol Hill Mansion

1207 Pennsylvania Street, 80203
(303) 839-5221; (800) 839-9329
FAX (303) 839-9046
www.capitolhillmansion.com

This 1891 Victorian borders downtown Denver on historic east side. Walk to capitol, convention center, business offices, Pedestrian Mall, restaurants, museums, and shops. Eight guest rooms. Three suites. Two balconies. Three whirlpools. Private baths. Air conditioning. Flowers. Antiques. Modem-ready telephone/jacks. Fax machine. Xerox machine available. Desks. TV. Hot breakfast. Evening beverages. Parking. Knowledgeable innkeepers.

Hosts: Bill and Wendy Pearson
Rooms: 9 (PB) $85-175
Full Breakfast
Credit Cards: A, B, C, D, E
Notes: 2, 5, 7, 8, 9, 10, 11, 12, 13, 14, 15

Capitol Hill Mansion

---

7 No smoking; 8 Children welcome; 9 Social drinking allowed; 10 Tennis nearby; 11 Swimming nearby; 12 Golf nearby; 13 Skiing nearby; 14 May be booked through a travel agent; 15 Handicapped accessible.

Castle Marne

1572 Race Street, 80206
(303) 331-0621; (800) 92 MARNE

Come, fall under the spell of one of Denver's grandest historic mansions. Built in 1889, the Marne is on both the local and national historic registers. Guests' stay is a unique experience in pampered luxury. Three rooms with private balconies and hot tubs for two. Two rooms with Jacuzzi tubs for two. Minutes from the finest cultural, shopping, sightseeing attractions, and the convention center. Lunch and dinner available by special arrangements. Ask about the candlelight dinners.

Hosts: The Peiker Family
Rooms: 9 (PB) $85-220
Full Breakfast
Credit Cards: A, B, C, D, E
Notes: 2, 5, 7, 9, 10, 11, 12, 13, 14

Castle Marne

Haus Berlin

1651 Emerson Street, 80218
(303) 837-9527; (800) 659-0253
e-mail: haus.berlin@worldnet.att.net
www.hausberlinbandb.com

Century-old Victorian on a safe, quiet tree-lined street just minutes from downtown Denver. European decor with original paintings and pieces of art. Off-street parking. Superior bed and bath linens. Telephones, TV, alarm radios, air dryers, fresh flowers add to guests'

Haus Berlin

comfort and convenience. Hosts are urbane, friendly, and comfortable, just like their guests.

Hosts: Christiana and Dennis Brown
Rooms: 4 (PB) $95-135
Full Breakfast
Credit Cards: A, B, C
Notes: 2, 5, 7, 9, 10, 12, 13, 14

Merritt House
Bed & Breakfast Inn

941 East 17th Avenue, 80218
(303) 861-5230; (877) 861-5230
FAX (303) 861-9009

"Come visit spacious Merritt House. Fresh flowers, homemade cookies, and a gracious relaxed atmosphere...await you." Offering 10 guest rooms decorated in a Victorian manner with the conveniences of cable TV, telephone and voice mail, private bath (shower or Jacuzzi tubs). Guests are encouraged to tempt their palates from the full breakfast menu. Special event and business meetings welcome. In-house catering. Minutes to downtown and Cherry Creek shopping district. Excellent restaurants within walking distance.

Host: Cathy Kuykendall
Rooms: 10 (PB) $100-140

NOTES: Credit cards accepted: A MasterCard; B Visa; C American Express; D Discover; E Diner's Club; F Other; 2 Personal checks accepted; 3 Lunch available; 4 Dinner available; 5 Open all year; 6 Pets welcome;

Full Breakfast
Credit Cards: A, B, C, D, E
Notes: 2, 5, 7, 8, 9, 10, 11, 12, 13, 14

The Queen Anne Bed & Breakfast Inn

2147 Tremont Place, 80205
(303) 296-6666; (800) 432-INNS
FAX (303) 296-2151
e-mail: queenanne@bedandbreakfastinns.org
www.bedandbreakfastinns.org/queenanne

Experience history, elegance, and warm hospitality in side-by-side Victorians facing a quiet park within walking distance of downtown Denver's pedestrian mall, state capitol, shops, museums, restaurants, convention center, businesses. Enjoy a hot breakfast, period furnishings, private baths, chamber music, fresh flowers, telephones, evening Colorado wine, free parking. Choose from 14 individually decorated rooms, including four "gallery suites." Honors include 10 most romantic, 10 best nationally, and Best of Denver. Inspected and rated by motor clubs and state associations.

Hosts: The King Family
Rooms: 14 (PB) $75-175
Full Breakfast
Credit Cards: A, B, C, D, E, F
Notes: 2, 5, 7, 9, 10, 12, 13, 14

The Queen Anne

DENVER AREA

Bed & Breakfast Reservation Agency of Colorado at Vail

2488 Garmisch Drive, Vail, 81657
(970) 476-0792; (800) 748-2666
FAX (970) 476-0711; e-mail: bbresser@vail.net
www.vail.net/lodging/bnb/bbres

Urban settings downtown to suburban serenity. Decor depicting the history of Denver. The perfect setting for weddings, holidays, or that special occasion. King- or queen-size beds, private baths, some jetted tubs, hot tub. Full or Continental breakfast. $69-165.

DILLION

Bed & Breakfast Reservation Agency of Colorado at Vail

2488 Garmisch Drive, Vail, 81657
(970) 476-0792; (800) 748-2666
FAX (970) 476-0711; e-mail: bbresser@vail.net
www.vail.net/lodging/bnb/bbres

Summit County provides the recreation in its four ski areas; the hosts provide the comforts of home with many extras. Private bath, full or Continental breakfast. Close to shuttle. $65-250.

DOLORES

Historic Rio Grande Southern

101 South Fifth Street, P.O. Box 516, 81323
(970) 882-7527; (800) 258-0434

The Rio Grande Southern hotel was built for the railroad in 1893 and has been in continuous service as a hostelry ever since. The eight guest rooms are decorated in turn-of-the-century antiques with antique claw-foot high-backed tubs. The restaurant is still a popular stop for southwestern cuisine and setting. The hotel is in the national and state of Colorado lists of historic places. Inquire about accommodations for pets.

---

7 No smoking; 8 Children welcome; 9 Social drinking allowed; 10 Tennis nearby; 11 Swimming nearby; 12 Golf nearby; 13 Skiing nearby; 14 May be booked through a travel agent; 15 Handicapped accessible.

Hosts: Fred and Cathy Green
Rooms: 8 (3 PB: 4 SB) $50-130
Full Breakfast
Credit Cards: A, B, D
Notes: 2, 3, 7, 8, 9, 10, 11, 12, 13, 14

Mountain View Bed & Breakfast

28050 County Road P, 81323
(970) 882-7861; (800) 228-4592
e-mail: bdunn@fone.net
www.subee.com/mtnview/home.html

Mountain View is in the Four Corners area one mile from the gateway to the San Juan Skyway, a nationally designated 238-mile scenic loop, 12 miles from the entrance to Mesa Verde National Park, and 4 miles from McPhee Lake, Colorado's second largest lake. On 22 acres, this ranch-style inn has porches, decks, and hot tub with marvelous mountain views. Eight guest rooms/suites, cabin, private baths, full breakfast, laundry. Singles, families, and groups welcome.

Hosts: Brenda and Cecil Dunn
Rooms: 8 (PB) $60-90
Full Breakfast
Credit Cards: A, B, D
Notes: 2, 5, 7, 8, 10, 11, 12, 13, 14, 15

DURANGO

Apple Orchard Inn

7758 Country Road 203, 81301
(970) 247-0751; (800) 426-0751

The Apple Orchard Inn is a newly constructed farmhouse-style home with six country cottages on four and one-half acres of orchards and gardens. From private covered porch enjoy views of surrounding mountains. Inside, be pampered with fresh flowers, fireplaces, quality furnishings and linens, feather beds with down comforters, private baths, and Jacuzzi tubs. A scrumptious full hot breakfast is included and gourmet lunches and dinners are available with advance reservations. Convenient to town and skiing.

Apple Orchard Inn

Hosts: Celeste and John Gardiner
Rooms: 10 (PB) $70-165
Full Breakfast
Credit Cards: A, B, C, D
Notes: 2, 5, 7, 8, 9, 10, 11, 12, 13, 14, 15

Lightner Creek Inn

999 CR 207, 81301
(970) 259-1226; (800) 268-9804
FAX (970) 259-9526; e-mail: lci@frontier.net
www.lightnercreekinn.com

Convenient to town but with a country feeling on 26 pristine acres with pond and stream. Enjoy the privacy and comfort of a king-size feather bed in the carriage house or be spoiled with down comforters and king- or queen-size beds in the other 10 rooms of the main house.

Lightner Creek Inn

NOTES: Credit cards accepted: A MasterCard; B Visa; C American Express; D Discover; E Diner's Club; F Other; 2 Personal checks accepted; 3 Lunch available; 4 Dinner available; 5 Open all year; 6 Pets welcome;

Durango, CO   197

This 1903 home has been lovingly renovated with country charm and attention to detail. Be pampered with gourmet breakfasts served in the sunroom with a view. Ask to hear the player piano. Children over 10 welcome.

Hosts: Suzy and Stan Savage
Rooms: 10 (PB) $85-185
Full Breakfast
Credit Cards: A, B, C, D
Notes: 2, 5, 7, 9, 10, 12, 13, 14, 15

Logwood Bed & Breakfast

35060 US Highway 550 North, 81301
(970) 259-4396; (800) 369-4082

Luxurious red cedar log home is a well-designed bed and breakfast lodge. View the beauty of the upper Animas River and mountains through the guest rooms' large windows. Every room has its own private bath. Suite with fireplace. Lounge on the 700-square-foot deck or the yard hammock, fish on the river while enjoying the views, or walk through the five acres of property while deer and bird watching. Full country breakfasts and evening award-winning desserts are served. Kitchen facilities available if entire lodge is rented. Children are welcome, but based on room availability.

Hosts: The Windmueller's
Rooms: 8 (PB) $85-135
Suite: 1
Full Breakfast
Credit Cards: A, B, C
Notes: 2, 3, 4, 5, 7, 9, 11, 12, 13, 14

River House

River House Bed & Breakfast

495 Animas View Drive, 81301
(970) 247-4775; (800) 254-4775

River House is a large, sprawling southwestern home facing the Animas River. Guests eat in a large atrium filled with plants, a fountain, and eight skylights. Antiques, art, and artifacts from around the world decorate the seven bedrooms, snooker, and music rooms. Enjoy a soak in the hot tub before a relaxing massage or retiring to the living room to watch a favorite video on the large screen TV, and enjoy the warmth of the fire in the beautiful stone and brass fireplace. Comfort, casualness, and fun are themes. New honeymoon cottage available.

Hosts: Crystal Carroll; Kate and Lars Enggren
Rooms: 9 (PB) $80-170
Full Breakfast
Credit Cards: A, B, C, D
Notes: 2, 5, 7, 10, 11, 12, 13

Scrubby Oaks Bed & Breakfast Inn

P.O. Box 1047, 81302
(970) 247-2176
www.southwesterninns.com/scrubby.htm

On 10 acres overlooking the spectacular Animas Valley and surrounding mountains. Three miles from downtown Durango. Rooms are

Logwood

---

7 No smoking; 8 Children welcome; 9 Social drinking allowed; 10 Tennis nearby; 11 Swimming nearby; 12 Golf nearby; 13 Skiing nearby; 14 May be booked through a travel agent; 15 Handicapped accessible.

spacious and furnished with antiques, art works, and good books. Beautiful gardens and patios frame the inn outside, with large sitting areas inside for guests' use. Closed November through April.

Host: Mary Ann Craig
Rooms: 7 (3 PB; 4 S2B) $70-80
Full Breakfast
Credit Cards: None
Notes: 2, 7, 8, 9, 10, 11, 12, 14

EMPIRE

The Peck House

83 Sunny Avenue, P.O. Box 428, 80438
(303) 569-9870; FAX (303) 569-2743
e-mail: thepeckhouse@yahoo.com

Built in 1862, the 10 Victorian rooms of this Colorado hotel abound with antiques, some original. Located in a small mountain town, the hotel is close to Denver, many historic districts and attractions, and many ski areas. The Signature restaurant of the owner/chef is considered one of the finest in Colorado. A finalist for *Uncle Ben's 10 Best Country Inns of the Year Award*. Winner of the *Colorado Governor's Award for Fine Colorado Cuisine*.

Hosts: Gary and Sally St. Clair
Rooms: 10 (9 PB; 1 SB) $45-85
Continental Breakfast
Credit Cards: A, B, C, D
Notes: 4, 5, 8, 9, 10, 11, 13, 14

The Peck House

ESTES PARK

The Anniversary Inn Bed & Breakfast

1060 Mary's Lake Road, 80517
(970) 586-6200

The Anniversary Inn is a turn-of-the-century two-story log home one mile from Rocky Mountain National Park. The living room with its beamed ceiling and moss rock fireplace provides a romantic and restful setting. Breakfast on the glass-enclosed porch starts the day with fruit, freshly baked breads, and a hearty entrée. Specially brewed coffee and a choice of juice complete the meal. The town of Estes Park is nearby and features quaint shops and many fine restaurants. Cross-country skiing, hiking, and fishing nearby.

Hosts: Norma and Harry Menke
Rooms: 4 (PB) $95-160
Full Breakfast
Credit Cards: A, B, C, D
Notes: 2, 5, 7, 9, 10, 12, 13, 14

The Anniversary Inn

Eagle Cliff House

2383 Highway 66, P.O. Box 4312, 80517
(970) 586-5425; (800) 414-0922
FAX (970) 577-0132
e-mail: m.conrin@worldnet.att.net

A warm and friendly facility is nestled in ponderosa pines at the base of Eagle Cliff Mountain. Relax in the comfort of soft colors native to southwestern decor, combined with the beautiful woods used in American antiques, which create warmth and hospitality. Two fireplaces, a hot tub, and a Jacuzzi are available. The abundant breakfast and never empty cookie jar keep guests ready for a full day of activities in the heart of Colorado's most spectacular landscapes.

Hosts: Nancy and Mike Conrin
Rooms: 3 (PB) $80-135
Full Breakfast
Credit Cards: None
Notes: 2, 5, 7, 8, 9, 10, 11, 12, 14

FORT COLLINS

The Edwards House

The Edwards House Bed & Breakfast

402 West Mountain Avenue, 80521
(970) 493-9191; (800) 281-9190
FAX (970) 484-0706
e-mail: edshouse@edwardshouse.com
www.edwardshouse.com

The Edwards House bed and breakfast has been restored to capture the warmth of the Victorian era without sacrificing modern conveniences. All eight rooms feature a gas fireplace, private telephone, shower, and TV/VCR. Central air conditioning. The rooms with private baths also feature a Jacuzzi or claw-foot tub. Afternoon refreshments are provided. Near the historic Old Town shopping and restaurant district and Colorado State University. Conference center and weekend cooking schools. Children over 10 welcome.

Host: Greg Belcher
Rooms: 8 (7 PB; 1 SB) $85-145
Full Breakfast
Credit Cards: A, B, C, D
Notes: 2, 4, 5, 7, 9, 10, 11, 12, 13, 14

FRISCO

Bed & Breakfast Reservation Agency of Colorado at Vail

2488 Garmisch Drive, Vail, 81657
(970) 476-0792; (800) 748-2666
FAX (970) 476-0711; e-mail: bbresser@vail.net
www.vail.net/lodging/bnb/bbres

Whether one prefers an inn or a secluded private home, this reservation service has the perfect place for that getaway to the playgrounds of Summit County. Hike, bike, walk, ski, snowboard—it's all here. $79-160.

Galena Street Mountain Inn

First Avenue and Galena, Box 417, 80443
(800) 248-9138; FAX (970) 668-1569
www.colorado-bnb.com/galena

Fifteen beautifully furnished guest rooms with private baths, down comforters, cable TV, and

Galena Street Mountain Inn

---

7 No smoking; 8 Children welcome; 9 Social drinking allowed; 10 Tennis nearby; 11 Swimming nearby; 12 Golf nearby; 13 Skiing nearby; 14 May be booked through a travel agent; 15 Handicapped accessible.

in-room telephones. Large windows with window seats frame mountains so close guests can feel them. The inn provides easy access to Summit County's famous ski areas in winter and for cycling, hiking, or boating in the summer. The breakfasts include freshly baked breads, homemade granola, and an entrée served in the spacious dining room. Indoor hot tub and sauna also included.

Hosts: John and Sandy Gilfillan
Rooms: 15 (PB) $75-140
Full and Continental Breakfast
Credit Cards: A, B, C, D
Notes: 5, 7, 8, 12, 13, 14, 15

The Lark Mountain Inn

The Lark Mountain Inn Bed & Breakfast

109 Granite Street, 80443-1646
(970) 668-5237; (800) 668-5237
FAX (970) 668-1988
e-mail: smlark@oneimage.com
www.toski.com/lark

The Lark is Frisco's largest log and timber inn. Long known as the skier's bed and breakfast, host can help guests with all their needs—skiing, snowmobiling, nordic skiing, ice fishing. Summer is great fun for hiking, biking, fishing, golfing, a romantic getaway or retreat for 18. The Lark accommodates all of guests' vacation needs! Within minutes of Cooper Mountain, Breckenridge, Keystone, Arapahoe Basin, and nearby Vail Resort. Children over 8 welcome.

Host: Sheila Morgan
Rooms: 7 (4 PB; 1 SB) $90-170
Full Breakfast
Credit Cards: A, B
Notes: 5, 7, 9, 12, 14

GLENWOOD SPRINGS

The Bed & Breakfast on Mitchell Creek

1686 Mitchell Creek Road, 81601-2588
(970) 945-4002; e-mail: carole@rof.net
www.bbinternet.com/mitchell

This contemporary log home on Mitchell Creek in the mountains offers one spacious, romantic suite—private entrance, private bath, king-size bed, and living/dining area. Privacy, solitude, and romance await guests. Personal service is assured. Hiking trails and lower patio with fire pit. Horseback riding and hot mineral springs and spa minutes away. "Let us pamper you." Credit cards accepted only to hold reservation. In-state personal checks accepted.

Hosts: Stan and Carole Rachesky
Rooms: 1 (PB) $90
Full Breakfast
Credit Cards: None
Notes: 5, 7, 8, 9, 10, 11, 12, 13

GOLDEN

The Dove Inn

711 14th Street, 80401-1906
(303) 278-2209; FAX (303) 273-5272

Charming Victorian inn is in the west Denver vicinity in the small-town atmosphere of

The Dove Inn

NOTES: Credit cards accepted: A MasterCard; B Visa; C American Express; D Discover; E Diner's Club; F Other; 2 Personal checks accepted; 3 Lunch available; 4 Dinner available; 5 Open all year; 6 Pets welcome;

Golden. Close to Coors tours and Rocky Mountain National Park; one hour to ski areas. Children welcome. No pets.

Hosts: Tim and Connie Sheffield
Rooms: 6 (PB) $65-90
Full Breakfast
Credit Cards: A, B, C, D
Notes: 2, 5, 7, 8, 9, 10, 11, 12, 14

The Jameson House Bed & Breakfast Inn

1704 Illinois Street, 80401
(303) 278-0200; (888) 880-4448
e-mail: relax@jamesonhouse.com
www.jamesonhouse.com

Experience the romantic charm of this turn-of-the-century English country inn. The Jameson House features dormered bedroom suites, a sunroom for afternoon tea, an antique-filled sitting room with fireplace, library, an English garden set in a shady courtyard, and a full-course breakfast served each morning in the dining room. The Jameson House provides visitors with all the romance charm and comfort of a perfect Colorado vacation.

Hosts: James and Carolyn Durgin
Rooms: 4 (2 PB; 2 SB) $80-120
Full Breakfast
Credit Cards: A, B, C
Notes: 2, 5, 7, 9, 10, 11, 12, 13

GREEN MOUNTAIN FALLS

Outlook Lodge

6975 Howard Street, P.O. Box 586, 80819
(877) 684-7800

This 1889 Victorian lodge is nestled on the slopes of Pikes Peak in the quaint alpine village of Green Mountain Falls. Relax on the large front porch. Hike in nearby Pike National Forest. Escape to another time.

Rooms: 7 (PB) $75-95
Full Breakfast
Credit Cards: A, B, C, D
Notes: 2, 5, 7, 8, 10, 11, 12

GUNNISON

The Eagle's Nest

206 North Colorado, 81230
(970) 641-4457

Originally built in 1923, this Early American former judge's home features stained glass and interior maple woodwork. Gunnison is an attractive place to visit in all four seasons. There is skiing at nearby Crested Butte, hunting in the fall, and fishing in either Blue Mesa Lake or the Gunnison River. During the gorgeous summer weather, there are numerous attractions: rafting, the Gunnison Rodeo, and Crested Butte Wildflower Festival. Credit cards accepted for reservations.

Hosts: Jane and Hugh McGee
Suite: 1 (PB) $45
Full and Continental Breakfast
Credit Cards: None
Notes: 2, 5, 7

Mary Lawrence Inn

601 North Taylor Street, 81230
(970) 641-3343; (800) 445-3861
www.gunnison.co.comm/main/lodging/maryl.htm

Make this Victorian home the center of excursions through Gunnison Country. The mountains, rivers, and lakes are extraordinary. Golf, swimming, rafting are accessible. The inn is furnished with antiques and collectibles. Breakfasts are bountiful and imaginative. Special fly-fishing weekends. Great ski package offered for Crested Butte skiing. Children welcome.

---

7 No smoking; 8 Children welcome; 9 Social drinking allowed; 10 Tennis nearby; 11 Swimming nearby; 12 Golf nearby; 13 Skiing nearby; 14 May be booked through a travel agent; 15 Handicapped accessible.

Hosts: Beth and Doug Parker
Rooms: 4 (PB) $69-85
Suites: 3 (PB) $99-129
Full Breakfast
Credit Cards: A, B
Notes: 2, 5, 7, 8, 9, 10, 11, 12, 13, 14

IDAHO SPRINGS

Riverside Bed & Breakfast

2130 Riverside Drive, P.O. Box 1535, 80452
(303) 567-9032; (303) 987-7450

The Riverside offers a friendly, comfortable stay. Guests can relax in the courtyard or the hot tub and view the nearby mountain scenery. Take a walk along Clear Creek River to Main Street and enjoy the many restaurants, museums, and galleries. If guests are adventurous, there is skiing, hiking, or rafting. Inquire about restrictions on social drinking.

Host: Theresa Gonzales
Rooms: 4 (1 PB: 3 S2B) $54-74
Full Breakfast
Credit Cards: A, B
Notes: 2, 5, 7, 13

Riverside

St. Mary's Glacier Bed & Breakfast

336 Crest Drive, 80452
(303) 567-4084; e-mail: stmgbb@oneimage.com
www.coloradovaction.com/bed/stmary/index.html

Highest bed and breakfast in North America at 10,500 feet. Surrounded by snowcapped Conti-

St. Mary's Glacier

nental Divide peaks, waterfall, mountain lakes, borders the Arapohoe National Forest, short hike to the southern-most glacier in North America. Snowshoe year-round. This is a romantic hideaway rich with opportunities for fun. Kitchen available for guests' use. Three spacious suites with king-size bed and private deck.

Rooms: 7 (PB) $89-159
Full Breakfast
Credit Cards: A, B, C, D, E, F
Notes: 2, 5, 7, 8, 9, 13

LEADVILLE

The Apple Blossom Inn

120 West 4th Street, 80461
(719) 486-2141; (800) 982-9279

This beautiful 1879 banker's home has been featured on two Victorian home tours. Recipient of 1998 Award of Excellence. Decorated with antiques, charm, and a flair for comfortable spaces. Breakfast is fully delicious. Free recreation center passes. Feather beds, fireplaces, home-baked goodies make guests' stay most memorable.

Host: Maggie Senn
Rooms: 5 (PB) $89-128
Full Breakfast
Credit Cards: A, B, C, D, E
Notes: 2, 3, 5, 7, 8, 9, 10, 11, 12, 13, 14

NOTES: Credit cards accepted: A MasterCard; B Visa; C American Express; D Discover; E Diner's Club; F Other; 2 Personal checks accepted; 3 Lunch available; 4 Dinner available; 5 Open all year; 6 Pets welcome;

The Ice Palace Inn

813 Spruce Street, 80461
(719) 486-8272; (800) 754-2840
FAX (719) 486-0345; e-mail: ipalace@sni.net
www.colorado-bnb.com/icepalace

This gracious Victorian inn was built at the turn of the century, using the lumber from the famous Leadville Ice Palace. Romantic guest rooms, elegantly decorated with antiques, feather beds and quilts, each with an exquisite private bath, are named after the original rooms of the Ice Palace. Begin the day with a delicious gourmet breakfast served at individual tables in this historic inn. Afternoon teas and goodies are available every day. Turndown service in the evening. Hot tub.

Hosts: Giles and Kami Kolakowski
Rooms: 6 (PB) $79-119
Full Breakfast
Credit Cards: A, B, C, D
Notes: 2, 5, 7, 8, 9, 10, 11, 12, 13, 14

Wood Haven Manor

with sitting rooms, fireplaces, whirlpool, TV/VCR. Full gourmet breakfast. Hospitality, service, and wonderful atmosphere are just a few reasons pampered guests keep returning.

Rooms: 3 (PB) $79-129
Full Breakfast
Credit Cards: A, B, C, D
Notes: 2, 3, 4, 5, 7, 8, 9, 10, 11, 12, 13, 14

The Ice Palace Inn

Wood Haven Manor Bed & Breakfast

809 Spruce, 80461
(800) 748-2570; FAX (719) 486-0210
e-mail: woodhavn@rmi.net
www.colorado-bnb.com/woodhavn

Casual elegance in Victorian fashion. Furnished with finest antiques. Romantic suites

LIVERMORE

Cherokee Park Dude Ranch

436 Cherokee Hills Drive, 80536
(970) 493-6522; FAX (970) 493-5802
e-mail: cpranch@gateway.net

Nestled in the Colorado Rockies, Cherokee Park Ranch is only two hours from Denver. During the 1880s the ranch was a stage-coach stop, and much of the furnishings are from the ranch beginnings. Activities include horseback riding, river rafting, fishing, sightseeing trips. Home-cooked meals are served family style. The ranch offers counseled programs for 3- to 12-year olds, creating a terrific place for kids to experience the West on a genuine dude ranch.

Hosts: Dickey and Christine Prince and family
Rooms: 12 (PB) $900-1100 weekly
Full Breakfast
Credit Cards: A, B
Notes: 2, 3, 4, 7, 8, 9, 11

---

7 No smoking; 8 Children welcome; 9 Social drinking allowed; 10 Tennis nearby; 11 Swimming nearby; 12 Golf nearby; 13 Skiing nearby; 14 May be booked through a travel agent; 15 Handicapped accessible.

LOVELAND

The Lovelander Bed & Breakfast Inn

217 West 4th Street, 80537
(970) 669-0798; (800) 459-6694 (reservations)
FAX (970) 669-0797

Nestled against the Rocky Mountain foothills, minutes from Rocky Mountain National Park, the Lovelander is a rambling Victorian-style inn. Its beauty and elegance are characteristic of the turn of the century, when the home was built. Near restaurants, shops, museums, and art galleries, the Lovelander is a haven for business and leisure travelers and a retreat for romantics. Meeting and reception facilities are available. Children over 10 are welcome. "We guarantee you will have a memorable stay, or your next stay is on us!"

Hosts: Lauren and Gary Smith
Rooms: 11 (PB) $100-150
Full Breakfast
Credit Cards: A, B, C, D
Notes: 2, 3, 5, 7, 9, 10, 11, 12, 14, 15

MANITOU SPRINGS

The Cliff House Inn

306 Cañon Avenue, 80829
(719) 685-3000; (888) 212-7000
FAX (719) 685-3913; e-mail: canon306@aol.com
www.TheCliffHouse.com

The Cliff House Inn was opened in 1873 and today is still a premier resort inn in the heart of Manitou Springs. This national historic landmark boasts 57 rooms. Each room is individual in character, and may include special features such as gas fireplaces, two-person spa tubs, steam showers, heated toilet seats, towel warmers, mountain views, and more. Close by are many hiking trails, most ski areas (not more than two hours away), the Pikes Peak Cog Railway, and Toll road, shopping and activities for the entire family, restored mineral springs from which to drink refreshing mineral water, art galleries, and all the many charms of Manitou Springs.

Hosts: Craig and Donna Hartman
Rooms: 57 (PB) $129-289
Full Breakfast
Credit Cards: A, B, C, D, E
Notes: 2, 3, 4, 5, 7, 8, 9, 10, 11, 12, 13, 14, 15

Gray's Avenue Hotel

711 Manitou Avenue, 80829
(719) 685-1277; (800) 294-1277
FAX (719) 685-1847
www.spectroweb.com/graysb&b.htm

This bed and breakfast is in the Manitou Springs Historic Preservation District. It was built in 1886 and opened as the Avenue Hotel, one of the original seven hotels in this resort town. Within minutes of most tourist attractions and easy walking distance of many shops and restaurants. Children over 10, please. Outdoor hot tub. Family suites. Small groups welcome. Fifteen dollars for extra person.

Hosts: Tom and Lee Gray
Rooms: 7 (3 suites) $60-80
Full Breakfast
Credit Cards: A, B, C, D
Notes: 2, 5, 7, 10, 11, 12, 13, 14

Rockledge Country Inn

328 El Paso Boulevard, 80829
(719) 685-4515; (888) 685-4515
FAX (719) 685-1031
e-mail: rockinn@webcom.com

Rockledge Country Inn, in the historic Rockledge Manor House, is on three and one-half fenced and gated acres of stone terraces with panoramic views of Pikes Peak and surrounding foothills. All suites are spacious with king-size feather beds, entertainment centers, some with fireplace and spa—all have spectacular views. Guests may enjoy large common areas which include two fireplaces, an 1875 Steinway grand piano, library, parlor games, solarium, patios and outdoor spa. A multi-course gourmet breakfast is served each morning and Colorado wines and hors d'oeuvres each

---

NOTES: Credit cards accepted: A MasterCard; B Visa; C American Express; D Discover; E Diner's Club; F Other; 2 Personal checks accepted; 3 Lunch available; 4 Dinner available; 5 Open all year; 6 Pets welcome;

evening. Fresh cookies and chocolates are always at hand.

Hosts: Hartman and Nancy Smith
Rooms: 4 (PB) $195-250
Full Breakfast
Credit Cards: A, B, C, D
Notes: 2, 4, 5, 7, 9, 10, 11, 12, 13, 14

MONTROSE

Annie's Orchard Historic Bed & Breakfast

14963 6300 Road, 81401
(970) 249-0298; e-mail: mneedham@montrose.net

Comfortably elegant country Tudor built in 1909. Quiet, romantic setting on two-acre estate just outside Montrose in western Colorado. Three unique rooms, all with luxuriously appointed private baths and antique furnishings. Romantic fireplace suite with cozy feather bed. Hot tub under the stars. Central to Black Canyon, San Juan Mountains, Telluride, Ouray Hot Springs, and Grand Mesa. Hiking, skiing, fishing, jeeping nearby. Participant inn-to-inn bicycling. Full gourmet breakfast and afternoon tea.

Host: Mary Needham
Rooms: 3 (PB) $60-85
Full Breakfast
Credit Cards: A, B, C, D
Notes: 2, 5, 7, 9, 10, 11, 12, 13, 14

OURAY

Main Street Bed & Breakfasts

322 Main Street, P.O. Box 641, 81427
(303) 325-4871

Two superbly renovated, turn-of-the-century residences offer three suites, three rooms, and a two-story cottage. All accommodations have private baths, queen-size beds, and cable TV. Six of the units have decks with spectacular views of the San Juan Mountains. Three units have fully equipped modern kitchens. Guests who stay in rooms without kitchens are served a full breakfast on antique china. Guests who stay in kitchen suites are provided with supplies for a hearty breakfast.

Hosts: Lee and Kathy Bates
Rooms: 8 (PB) $68-125
Full Breakfast
Credit Cards: A, B, C
Notes: 2, 7, 8, 9, 10, 11, 12, 14

St. Elmo Hotel

426 Main Street, P.O. Box 667, 81427
(303) 325-4951

Listed in the National Register of Historic Places and established in 1898 as a miners' hotel, St. Elmo's is now fully renovated with stained glass, antiques, polished wood, and brass trim throughout. An outdoor hot tub and aspen-lined sauna are available, as well as a cozy parlor and a breakfast room.

Hosts: Sandy and Dan Lingenfelter
Rooms: 9 (PB) $65-102
Full Breakfast
Credit Cards: A, B, C, D
Notes: 4, 5, 7, 8, 9, 10, 11, 12, 13, 14

PAGOSA SPRINGS

Be Our Guest, A Bed & Breakfast/Guesthouse

19 Swiss Village Drive, SJRV, 81147
(902) 264-6814; FAX (920) 246-6953 (call first)
e-mail: beourguest@pagosa.net
www.pagosa.net/beourguest.

Welcome to your place in Colorado. The warm, inviting atmosphere of this lodge-like home greets you as you pull off Hwy. 160, six miles east of town. Ample parking. Views, San Juan River and National Forest. Comfortable theme rooms. Lower level provides family or group privacy, kitchen, and three baths. Sleeps 16. Great common areas have satellite, VCRs, games, warm fires, awesome views. Delightful breakfast with most accommodations. Take one room or the whole house (30). Great group rate. Inquire about accommodations for pets.

---

7 No smoking; 8 Children welcome; 9 Social drinking allowed; 10 Tennis nearby; 11 Swimming nearby; 12 Golf nearby; 13 Skiing nearby; 14 May be booked through a travel agent; 15 Handicapped accessible.

Hosts: Tom and Pam Schoemig, with Skoshi, Dulce, and Elvira
Rooms: 5 (3 PB; 2 SB) $55-80
Full Breakfast
Credit Cards: None
Notes: 2, 3, 4, 5, 7, 8, 9, 10, 11, 12, 13, 14

Echo Manor Inn

3366 Highway 84, 81147
(970) 264-5646; e-mail: widmer@frontier.net

Beautiful country Dutch Tudor manor with towers, turrets, and gables, set in the majestic San Juan Mountains and described by many as a "fairy tale castle." This lovely bed and breakfast offers a honeymoon suite, gourmet-style breakfast, hot tub, horseback riding, rafting, snowmobiling, fishing, hunting, and boating nearby. Airport shuttle. Across the street is beautiful Echo Lake. Guests are invited to enjoy cozy wood stoves and fireplaces. Children over 10 welcome.

Hosts: Maureen and John Widmer
Rooms: 10 (PB) $70-175
Suite: 1
Full Breakfast
Credit Cards: A, B, C, D
Notes: 2, 5, 7, 9, 10, 11, 12, 13, 14

Abriendo Inn

Listed in the National Register of Historic Places, this distinctive bed and breakfast is in a park-like setting in the heart of Pueblo and one mile off I-25. Bask in the style and luxury of the past in rooms with all the comforts of today. All rooms have king- or queen-size beds, TVs, telephones, and air conditioning. Some have whirlpool tubs. Restaurants, shops, galleries, golf, tennis, and other attractions are all within five minutes of the inn. Children over seven welcome.

Host: Kerrelyn Trent
Rooms: 10 (PB) $64-120
Full Breakfast
Credit Cards: A, B, C, E
Notes: 2, 5, 7, 9, 10, 11, 12, 14

REDSTONE

Crystal Dreams Bed & Breakfast

0475 Redstone Boulevard, 81623
(970) 963-8240; e-mail: redstone@rof.net
www.net-unlimited.com/crystaldreams

Romantic country Victorian house on the Crystal River, in the historical town of Redstone. A perfect getaway in the Rockies. Guests receive special care and attention. Mini-spa available. Year-round sports activities for any enthusiast. Candlelight breakfast offered. Fly-fishing outside the back yard. Luxury at an affordable price. Picnic basket lunches are available.

PUEBLO

Abriendo Inn

300 West Abriendo Avenue, 81004
(719) 544-2703; e-mail: abriendo@rmi.net

NOTES: Credit cards accepted: A MasterCard; B Visa; C American Express; D Discover; E Diner's Club; F Other; 2 Personal checks accepted; 3 Lunch available; 4 Dinner available; 5 Open all year; 6 Pets welcome;

Hosts: Lisa and Stephen Wagner
Rooms: 3 (PB) $100-110
Full Breakfast
Credit Cards: F
Notes: 2, 5, 7, 10, 11, 12, 13

SALIDA

Gazebo Country Inn

507 East Third Street, 81201
(719) 539-7806; (800) 565-7806
FAX (719) 539-6971

This 1901 Victorian home, updated with a comfortable country charm, is nestled in a quiet neighborhood. Salida's historic district is a short walk away. Pick a favorite spot on the sunny second-floor deck, charming backyard gazebo, or shady front porch to take in the mountain views, sunshine, or starry nights. Plan a luxurious soak in the backyard hot tub. Hearty breakfasts each morning. Outdoor activities galore year-round.

Hosts: Sharon and Jeff Rowe
Rooms: 3 (PB) $75-85
Full Breakfast
Credit Cards: A, B, C
Notes: 2, 4, 5, 7, 8, 9, 11, 12, 13, 14

Gazebo Country Inn

River Run Inn Bed & Breakfast

8495 County Road 160, 81201
(719) 539-3818; (800) 385-6925
e-mail: riverrun@amigo.net

Comfort and luxury await guests in this historic home on the Arkansas River. Seven rooms, many with mountain views, plus a dorm for groups. Hearty breakfast, afternoon refreshments and homemade cookies, brandy and sherry in the evenings. Relax on the front porch, sit by the river, enjoy the beautiful views. Lunch and dinner available upon request. Children over 12 welcome.

Host: Virginia Nemmers
Rooms: 8 (4 PB; 4 SB) $60-80
Full Breakfast
Credit Cards: A, B, C
Notes: 2, 5, 7, 9, 10, 11, 12, 13, 14

The Thomas House

The Thomas House Bed & Breakfast

307 East First Street, 81201
(719) 539-7104; (888) 228-1410

The Thomas House reflects the comfortable, homey atmosphere that has earned the house a strong reputation among travelers for many years. The guest rooms have private baths and the suite has its own kitchenette. The home is furnished with many family heirlooms, antiques, and collectibles, mixed with some modern pieces and hand-me-downs to provide a truly eclectic experience. An outdoor hot tub and spacious decks provide guests areas for relaxation.

Hosts: Tammy and Steve Office
Rooms: 6 (PB) $55-100
Continental Breakfast
Credit Cards: A, B, C, D
Notes: 2, 5, 7, 8, 9, 10, 11, 12, 13, 14

---

7 No smoking; 8 Children welcome; 9 Social drinking allowed; 10 Tennis nearby; 11 Swimming nearby; 12 Golf nearby; 13 Skiing nearby; 14 May be booked through a travel agent; 15 Handicapped accessible.

The Tudor Rose

6720 Paradise Road, P.O. Box 89, 81201
(719) 539-2002; (800) 379-0889
www.bbonline.com/co/tudorose

Stately country manor, high on a piñon hill overlooking the Arkansas River valley, is built on 37 acres of an 1890s homestead. Six distinctive rooms, including the Henry Tudor suite with its private Jacuzzi tub room, highlight the inn. A formal Queen Anne living room, relaxing Wolf's Den, deck with sunken spa, and a full hearty breakfast are complimentary. Facilities include a barn, fenced paddocks, access to thousands of federal acres, and outdoor dog accommodations.

Hosts: Jon and Terré Terrell
Rooms: 6 (PB) $60-145
Full Breakfast
Credit Cards: A, B, D
Notes: 2, 3, 5, 6, 7, 8, 9, 11, 12, 13, 14

The Tudor Rose

SAN ACACIO

The Depot Historical Bed & Breakfast

Route 1, Box 186, 81150
(719) 672-3943; (719) 379-0349 (cell phone)
(800) 949-3943

Quiet, spacious lawns, great vistas. Casual, affordable getaway for families, couples, groups, and individuals in the last standing monument to the San Luis Southern Railroad. Built in 1910, the Depot today maintains much of its original character with its freight room, bank

vault, ice house, and railroad memorabilia. The Depot is near Ski Rio, Cumbres-Toltec train, national forest lands, historic San Luis, Great Sand Dunes, and the southwestern culture of Taos, New Mexico. Excellent hiking, hunting, and fishing nearby. State historical register.

Host: Neil Fletcher
Rooms: 4 (2-3 PB; 2 SB) $44-59
Full Breakfast
Credit Cards: B
Notes: 2, 5, 6, 7, 8, 9, 11, 12, 13

SILVERTON

Wyman Hotel & Inn

1371 Greene Street, P.O. Box 780, 81433
(970) 387-5372; (800) 609-7845
FAX (970) 387-5745

Built in 1902; listed in the National Register of Historic Places. Recently featured as the historic hotel in Silverton on the Travel Channel's *Historic Traveler*. Antiques throughout. All rooms have private bathrooms, telephones, TVs, VCRs, and comforters. Some rooms have canopied beds, and/or private whirlpool tubs. Gourmet breakfast and afternoon tea with homemade cookies included. Free videos from the 550 plus collection. AAA three-diamond rated. Step back in time by spending time at the Wyman Hotel and Inn!!

Host: Lorraine Lewis
Rooms: 17 (PB) $95-175
Full Breakfast
Credit Cards: A, B, C, D
Notes: 3, 5, 6, 7, 8, 9, 11, 13, 14, 15

NOTES: Credit cards accepted: A MasterCard; B Visa; C American Express; D Discover; E Diner's Club; F Other; 2 Personal checks accepted; 3 Lunch available; 4 Dinner available; 5 Open all year; 6 Pets welcome;

SNOWMASS

Starry Pines Bed & Breakfast

2262 Snowmass Creek Road, 81654
(800) 527-4202

A contemporary luxurious bed and breakfast home on a 35-acre ranch 20 minutes from Aspen or Snowmass Village. Enjoy the trout stream, picnic area, spectacular mountain views, hot tub under the stars, cathedral ceiling, stone fireplace, and movie selection for VCR. Two guest rooms have private bath with shared shower and tub in between. Apartment sleeps three to four, private bath and entrance. Ski on four world-class mountains, hike, bike, or horseback trek into the wilderness. Boarding for horses available. Children over 10 welcome.

Host: Shelley Burke
Rooms: 3 (3 PB; 2 SB) $80-120
Continental Breakfast
Credit Cards: None
Notes: 2, 5, 7, 9, 10, 12, 13, 14

STEAMBOAT SPRINGS

Bed & Breakfast Reservation Agency of Colorado at Vail

2488 Garmisch Drive, Vail, 81657
(970) 476-0792; (800) 748-2666
FAX (970) 476-0711; e-mail: bbresser@vail.net
www.vail.net/lodging/bnb/bbres

Mountainside ski lodges to Old Town private homes. Experience Steamboat at its best year-round. Single rooms and suites. Private bath, full or Continental breakfast, hot tub, pool, walk or take the free shuttle. $89-200.

Iron Horse Inn

333 South Lincoln Avenue (Highway 40), P.O. Box 771873, 80477
(970) 879-6505; (800) 856-6505
FAX (970) 879-6219

The accommodations at the Iron Horse Inn are clean, comfortable, and spacious. Whether guests' preference is a standard hotel room or a more spacious suite, complete with kitchenette, the hosts can make sure that guests feel right at home. Regardless of your choice of room at the inn, guests will enjoy a scenic view from the window while relaxing in comfort.

Rooms: 52 (PB) $49-122
Continental Breakfast
Credit Cards: A, B, C, E
Notes: 5, 7, 8, 9, 10, 11, 12, 13, 14, 15

Steamboat Valley Guest House

1245 Crawford Avenue, P.O. Box 773815, 80477
(970) 870-9017; (800) 530-3866
www.steamboatvalley.com

On spacious grounds, this western log house has spectacular views of skiing and Old Town. Family treasures and antiques accent log walls and lovely wallpapers. English and Scandinavian decor includes lace at every window. Great room features a fireplace, grand piano, and large sunny windows. Seasonal hot tub. Easy walk to restaurants, shops, bike path, river activities, and historic sites. Covered parking. Ski area is easily reached by town bus.

Hosts: George and Alice Lund
Rooms: 4 (PB) $85-160
Full Breakfast
Credit Cards: A, B, C, D, E
Notes: 2, 5, 7, 9, 11, 12, 13, 14

STRATTON

The Claremont Inn

800 Claremont Drive, P.O. Box 3, 80836
(719) 348-5125; (888) 291-8910
FAX (719) 348-5948
e-mail: www@claremont inn.com

Quiet surroundings 150 miles east of Denver. Perfect for travelers going to the Colorado Rocky Mountains. The luxurious guest rooms have private baths with whirlpool tubs. Cooking classes offered. Enjoy a weekend of fun at one of the murder mystery weekends. Saturday dinners are available. Enjoy dinner during the

---

7 No smoking; 8 Children welcome; 9 Social drinking allowed; 10 Tennis nearby; 11 Swimming nearby; 12 Golf nearby; 13 Skiing nearby; 14 May be booked through a travel agent; 15 Handicapped accessible.

The Claremont Inn

week in the wine cellar during the winter months or a gourmet picnic during the summer months. Lovely candlelight setting. Each room decorated differently. Theater, walking parks, gardens for guests' enjoyment. Enjoy breakfast on the terrace.

Hosts: Dave and Sharon Dischner
Rooms: 7 (PB) $119-299
Full Breakfast
Credit Cards: A, B, C, D, E
Notes: 2, 5, 7, 10, 11, 12, 14

TELLURIDE

Alpine Inn Bed & Breakfast

440 West Colorado Avenue, P.O. Box 2398, 81435
(970) 728-6282; (800) 707-3344

Enjoy the charm and spectacular views at this restored Victorian inn in the historic district of Telluride. The inn is within walking distance of ski lifts, hiking trails, and festivals. Each room captures a Victorian serenity with antiques and soft colors. Enjoy breakfast with views from the sunroom or sun deck. Relax on the porch by the wildflower garden, read a good book by the fire, or enjoy sunsets from the hot tub.

Hosts: Denise and John Weaver
Rooms: 7 (PB) $85-230
Full Breakfast
Credit Cards: A, B, D
Notes: 2, 5, 7, 9, 10, 11, 12, 13, 14

Bear Creek Bed & Breakfast

221 East Colorado Avenue, P.O. Box 2369, 81435
(970) 728-6681; (800) 338-7064
FAX (970) 728-3636; e-mail: colleenw@lynx.sni.net
www.bearcreektelluride.com

European ambiance coupled with Old West hospitality. A steam room, cedar-lined dry sauna, and a rooftop terrace with a hot tub and panoramic views of the San Juan Mountains welcome guests after a day of outdoor activities. The inn has nine lovely guest chambers on the second and third floors of a red brick, Victorian-style structure on the sunny side of Telluride's historic Main Street opposite its namesake, Bear Creek Canyon. The location is ideal; close to summer festivals, dining, shopping, hiking, biking, skiing, the river trail, and jeeping. Children 12 and older welcome.

Hosts: Tom and Colleen Whiteman
Rooms: 9 (PB) $80-195
Full Breakfast
Credit Cards: A, B, D
Notes: 5, 7, 9, 10, 11, 12, 13, 14

Johnstone Inn

403 West Colorado, Box 546, 81435
(970) 728-3316; (800) 752-1901
FAX (970) 728-0724; e-mail: bschiff@rmii.com
www.johnstoneinn.com

A true 100-year-old restored Victorian boarding house in the center of Telluride and the

Johnstone Inn

NOTES: Credit cards accepted: A MasterCard; B Visa; C American Express; D Discover; E Diner's Club; F Other; 2 Personal checks accepted; 3 Lunch available; 4 Dinner available; 5 Open all year; 6 Pets welcome;

spectacular San Juan Mountains. Rooms are warm and romantic with Victorian marble and brass private baths. Full breakfast is served. Winter season includes après-ski refreshments. A sitting room with fireplace and outdoor hot tub complete guests' amenities. Nordic and alpine skiing, hiking, and jeep tours are within walking distance of the inn.

Host: Bill Schiffbauer
Rooms: 8 (PB)
Full Breakfast
Credit Cards: A, B, C
Notes: 2, 7, 9, 12, 13, 14

Pennington's Mountain Village Inn

100 Pennington Court, P.O. Box 2428, 81435
(970) 728-5337; (800) 543-1437
FAX (970) 728-5338
e-mail: telluridemm.com/penn.html

Pennington's Mountain Village Inn sits like a jewel in the majestic San Juan Mountains. The 12 rooms all have private decks, private bath, cable TV, telephone, private lockers, and breathtaking views. Convenient, free transportation provided to and from the slopes and the gondola. Gourmet breakfasts and fun happy hours, while enjoying the best views in Telluride, are some of the reasons Pennington's was named "Best Bed and Breakfast Inn in Colorado." Pennington's closes the first three weeks in May and November.

Hosts: Michael and Judy MacLean
Rooms: 12 (PB) $140-300
Full Breakfast
Credit Cards: A, B, C
Notes: 2, 7, 8, 9, 10, 11, 12, 13, 14, 15

TWIN LAKES

Mt. Elbert Lodge & Cabins

10764 Highway 82, P.O. Box 40, 81251-0040
(719) 486-0594; (800) 381-4433
e-mail: mtelbert@amigo.net
www.colorado-bnb.com/mtelbert

Mt. Elbert Lodge

Nestled in the Rockies, Mt. Elbert Lodge is a wonderful escape from the often hectic pace of everyday life. Beautiful mountain scenery and serenity will surround guests as they fish, hike, or just relax on the porch. In the center of a triangle created by Buena Vista, Leadville, and Aspen, guests are able to explore Colorado from its mining history to its glittery present. Please note, the access to Aspen is closed November through May.

Hosts: Scott and Laura
Room: 5 (3 PB; 2 SB) $59-84
Full Breakfast
Credit Cards: A, B, C, D
Notes: 2, 5, 6, 7, 8, 9, 12, 13, 14

VAIL

The Minturn Inn

442 Main Street, Minturn, 81645
(970) 827-9647; (800) MINTURN
FAX (970) 827-5590; www.minturninn.com

Discover the Minturn Inn, an authentic Rocky Mountain lodge nestled between Vail and Beaver Creek resorts in Minturn. Enjoy this mountain retreat in a completely refurbished 1915 hewn-log home. The distinctive accommodations feature custom-made log beds, antler chandeliers, river rock fireplaces, hardwood floors, and an elegant rustic atmosphere. Whether the ideal vacation consists of snuggling up by the fire with a good book, meandering through an alpine meadow in search of wildflowers, or skiing home on the famous

---

7 No smoking; 8 Children welcome; 9 Social drinking allowed; 10 Tennis nearby; 11 Swimming nearby; 12 Golf nearby; 13 Skiing nearby; 14 May be booked through a travel agent; 15 Handicapped accessible.

Minturn Mile Backcountry Trail, the innkeepers look forward to sharing the secrets of the Vail Valley with guests, helping to make their stay at the Minturn Inn memorable. Recommended by *New York Times*, *Denver Post*, *Travel and Leisure*, and Fodor's.

Hosts: Tom and Cathy Sullivan; Mick Kelly
Rooms: 10 (8 PB; 2 SB) $65-219
Full Breakfast
Credit Cards: A, B, C, D, E
Notes: 2, 5, 7, 9, 10, 11, 12, 13, 14

VAIL (BEAVER CREEK)

Bed & Breakfast Reservation Agency of Colorado at Vail

2488 Garmisch Drive, 81657
(970) 476-0792; (800) 748-2666
FAX (970) 476-0711; e-mail: bbresser@vail.net
www.vail.net/lodging/bnb/bbres

Alpenhaus. This Austrian-flavored home is one bus stop from Vail Village on the golf course. Great views from each bedroom, one overlooking the Gore Range and Vail Village; the other looks out on tall pines and aspens. Common gathering room available for après-ski with TV, VCR, and library. Kitchenette with microwave oven and refrigerator. No smoking. $105-115.

Alpine Creek. This beautiful house is on Alpine, just minutes from downtown. Two rooms with private baths are offered in this home. Elegantly decorated with European flair. Guests wake up to the rippling sound of the creek and the smell of freshly brewed coffee. A delicious breakfast starts off each day of winter skiing or summer recreation. $85-125.

At Home Suite. A lovely private apartment/suite. Charming handmade trim and decor with one bedroom, a sleeper sofa, efficiency kitchen, private bath. Close to bus route, four people maximum. Strictly nonsmoking. Prepare own light breakfast or afternoon snacks. Lots of privacy. $135-150.

Beaver Mountain. Newest bed and breakfast in the Vail area. Three rooms offer king-size beds, private baths, TV, and Continental plus breakfast. Five minutes from lifts at Beaver Creek. Free bus service to slopes and shops. Soaring windows offer views of the surrounding mountains as guests enjoy the fireplace and the ambiance. Nonsmoking. No pets. $140-250.

The Eclectic Artist. Midway between Vail and Beaver Creek with bus service to both. Two bedrooms with private baths, full breakfast, and the serenity of the nearby Eagle River. Delightful long-time local hosts make guests' visit one to remember. $110-135.

Elk View. This gorgeous townhome nestled on the hillside of Beaver Creek boasts five levels with a breathtaking view of Beaver Creek Mountain. Beautifully decorated, each room has a charm of its own, and the house is impeccably furnished. In summer, breakfast can be enjoyed on one of the three outside decks, and in the winter, after a long day of skiing, relax in the outside hot tub. This property is perfect for honeymoon couples and guests wanting to relax with the locals. $85.

Intermountain Bed and Breakfast. This new home, nestled in a corner lot, offers a great view and serenity. Bedroom is spacious with TV, refrigerator, and a great view. Host is a ski instructor. Continental breakfast. $80-95.

Lodge in the Pines. This comfortable log duplex features one guest room with a large full bath including a jetted tub for guests' use. The outdoor hot tub is the perfect place to settle after a hard day of skiing or hiking. The large guest room is ideal for a family, as the hosts include two young children. Sleeps up to six. No smoking or pets, please. $135-200.

Snowed In. For affordable luxury, this home on an 18-hole golf course welcomes guests summer or winter. It is perfect for golfers, and

---

NOTES: Credit cards accepted: A MasterCard; B Visa; C American Express; D Discover; E Diner's Club; F Other; 2 Personal checks accepted; 3 Lunch available; 4 Dinner available; 5 Open all year; 6 Pets welcome;

in the winter, cross-country skiing is right out the back door. The guest rooms have a sitting room with TV, refrigerator, microwave, and dry bar right outside the door. Guests look forward to returning each season to sample the hospitality that reigns in this comfortably formal home. Breakfasts are unbeatable! Beaver Creek and Arrowhead Mountains are minutes away. $100-125.

Sportsman's Haven. Surrounded by pine trees and nestled on a creek, this home is a warm, spacious mountain home that beckons guests to snuggle in during the winter, or lounge on the sunny, private sun decks in summer. The hosts offer a ski home with two rooms. One is bright and cheery with pine trees outside every window, and the downstairs room has a private bath with a sauna and offers an adjoining family room with TV, pool table, shuffleboard, and fireplace. The home is within easy walking distance to the free bus. Discounted parking tickets available if guests should decide to drive. $79-95.

Suite Retirement. In beautiful, quiet East Vail, just 5 minutes from the free town bus and only 15 minutes from the center of Vail Village, this private home-stay bed and breakfast will allow guests to relax with their hosts in the large, pine-ceilinged living room prior to retiring to the very private bedroom and bath. The unique furniture represents the host's international taste and lifestyle. The resident dog will happily greet guests at the door. No smoking. No pets. $115-150.

WINTER PARK

Alpen Rose Bed & Breakfast

244 Forest Trail, P.O. Box 769, 80482
(303) 726-5039

Fantastic mountain view surrounded by aspens and pine on three acres. Only 10 minutes' walking distance to town. Two miles from Winter Park Ski Area with Rocky Mountain National Park nearby. An outdoor lover's paradise. Handmade quilts, down puffs, and Austrian furnishings. Memorable, hearty breakfast with Austrian specialities. Crackling fire and hot tea and cookies in the afternoon. Owner is from Salzburg, Austria, and the inn reflects his love for his Austria.

Hosts: Robin and Rupert Sommerauer
Rooms: 6 (PB) $70-130
Full Breakfast
Credit Cards: A, B, C, D
Notes: 2, 5, 7, 9, 10, 11, 12, 13, 14

The Bear Paw Inn

871 Bear Paw Drive, P.O. Box 334, 80482
(970) 887-1351 (phone/FAX)
e-mail: bearpaw@rkymtnhi.com
www.bestinns.net/usa/co/bearpaw.html

The Bear Paw Inn is a hand-hewn log lodge nestled among the pines and aspens high in the Colorado Rockies. Enjoy spectacular panoramic views from every window. Luxurious rooms feature feather beds and European down comforters, private decks, swings, Jacuzzis, and refrigerators. Easy access from Denver International Airport and Winter Park's world-class skiing. Summer activities include golf at Colorado's number one golf course, 600 miles of bike trails, boating, rodeos, music festivals, and spectacular Trail Ridge Road through Rocky Mountain National Park. "Our cool mountain air and crystal clear skies will

---

7 No smoking; 8 Children welcome; 9 Social drinking allowed; 10 Tennis nearby; 11 Swimming nearby; 12 Golf nearby; 13 Skiing nearby; 14 May be booked through a travel agent; 15 Handicapped accessible.

have you convinced it is truly paradise." Voted "outstanding hospitality."

Hosts: Rick and Susan Callahan
Rooms: 2 (PB) $140-175
Full Breakfast
Credit Cards: A, B, C
Notes: 2, 5, 7, 9, 10, 11, 12, 13, 14

Outpost Inn Bed & Breakfast

P.O. Box 41, 80482
(970) 726-5346; (800) 430-4538

The Outpost offers skiers a powder paradise at Winter Park and is a mountain lover's dream in the summer. The inn, on a quiet 40-acre ranch, serves a full, elegant candlelight breakfast with hot homemade bread. Amenities include an atrium hot tub, a loft with TV, VCR, and CD player, games, books, and cards. Ten-minute drive to golf and just out the door for cross-country skiing, mountain biking, or hiking. The Outpost is just 40 minutes from Rocky Mountain National Park. Guests turn and return to the Outpost for the comfort, the food, but most of all the hospitality. Lunch is available for groups in the winter. Dinner available on winter weekdays.

Hosts: Ken and Barbara Parker
Rooms: 7 (PB) $85-120
Full Breakfast
Credit Cards: A, B, C, D
Notes: 2, 5, 7, 8, 9, 10, 12, 13, 14

WOODLAND PARK

The Lion & the Rose Castle

547 Douglas Fir Drive, 80863
(888) 536-4564; FAX (719) 687-1944
e-mail: LRCastle@ix.netcom.com

The Lion and the Rose Castle sits alone on 20 mountaintop acres near the heart of the Pikes Peak region near Colorado Springs. The Castle is the quintessential luxury bed and breakfast with elegant period furnishings and ornate gilded interior trim. It evokes memories of a bygone era of opulence, nobility, and refinement in a setting of solitude and scenic beauty. The Castle is just two hours from Denver, yet worlds apart.

Hosts: Eric and Nancy Glanzer
Rooms: 3 (PB) $250-550
Credit Cards: A, B, C, D
Notes: 2, 5, 7, 9, 12, 14

Woodland Inn Bed & Breakfast

159 Trull Road, 80863-9027
(719) 687-8209; (800) 226-9565
FAX (719) 687-3112
e-mail: woodlandbb@aol.com
www.bbonline.com/co/woodland/

Come to a cozy country inn in the heart of the Rocky Mountains where guests enjoy a relaxing homelike atmosphere and fantastic views. Peacefully secluded on 12 private acres of woodlands, the inn is convenient to a variety of attractions in the Pikes Peak region. The hosts will prepare a picnic lunch for a day of hiking, biking, or skiing, or guests may join the hosts in a morning of hot-air ballooning.

Hosts: Frank and Nancy O'Neil
Rooms: 7 (PB) $70-100
Full Breakfast
Credit Cards: A, B, C, D
Notes: 2, 5, 7, 8, 9, 10, 11, 12, 13, 14

NOTES: Credit cards accepted: A MasterCard; B Visa; C American Express; D Discover; E Diner's Club; F Other; 2 Personal checks accepted; 3 Lunch available; 4 Dinner available; 5 Open all year; 6 Pets welcome;

Hawaii

HAWAII—CAPTAIN COOK

The Rainbow Plantation

P.O. Box 122, 96704
(808) 323-2393; (800) 494-2829
FAX (808) 323-9445
e-mail: konabnb@aloha.net
www.aloha.net/~konabnb
wwte.com/hawaii/rainbow.htm

Relax at Rainbow Plantation. Explore the peaceful surroundings. Stroll in the shade of the enchanting macadamia forest among coffee trees, tropical plants, and flowers. Listen to the birds and gentle breezes. Enjoy a tasty tropical breakfast on the ocean-view lanai overlooking koi ponds. Just seven miles south of Kona, near Kealakekua Bay, a marine sanctuary. Private entrances, private baths, TV, and refrigerators. Kayak rentals on premises. *On parle français; wir sprechen Deutsch.* No smoking in rooms.

Hosts: Marianna and Reiner Schrepfer
Rooms: 5 (PB) $65-95
Continental Breakfast
Credit Cards: A, B, C
Notes: 5, 6, 9, 11, 12, 14

HAWAII—HILO

Bed & Breakfast Honolulu (Statewide)

3242 Kaohinani Drive, Honolulu, 96817
(808) 595-7533; (800) 288-4666
FAX (808) 595-2030
e-mail: rainbow@hawaiibnb.com
www.hawaiibnb.com

BBHS 2. Two miles outside of Hilo on a cliff overlooking Hilo Bay, this Hawaiian-type home has a private yard with lovely pool. Charming, long-time resident offers two bedrooms. A full bath and a half-bath are reserved for and shared by the guests. The yard is beautifully landscaped, and a charming tea house is by the pool. Children over 12 welcome. Smoking outside. From $60.

BBHS 8. Just five minutes into Hilo in lush tropical surroundings and comfortably furnished. Host offers a spacious and private guest studio. Separate from the main home over the garage, the studio contains a queen-size bed, two twin beds, a queen-size sleeper-sofa, private bath with shower, color cable TV and VCR, stereo, and kitchenette sink, refrigerator, microwave, and hot plate for light cooking. Guests are provided a Continental breakfast each morning. Only minutes away from the Rainbow Falls, Lyman house museum, and Hilo's farmer's market. Children and non-smokers welcome. From $65.

BBHS 28. In cool upper Hilo on a quiet cul-de-sac overlooking Hilo Bay and the city lights. Fifteen minutes to airport and five minutes to downtown, restaurants, supermarkets and stores, and Hilo Bay. Host offers two rooms, each with private entrance and bath and guest living room. Queen-size bed, refrigerator, and microwave in both rooms. Both are wheelchair accessible. Continental breakfast of tropical fruits and juices, Hawaiian breads and coffee, tea and herbal teas provided in the morning. Five-dollar surcharge for less than three night's stay. From $65.

BBHS 185. Two luxury oceanfront units only 25 feet from the ocean. Both units have king-size beds, private baths with tub/shower, refrigerator, microwave, toaster, coffee maker. A telephone is available in the common area. Private lanais and

---

7 No smoking; 8 Children welcome; 9 Social drinking allowed; 10 Tennis nearby; 11 Swimming nearby; 12 Golf nearby; 13 Skiing nearby; 14 May be booked through a travel agent; 15 Handicapped accessible.

Hawaii

TV. Continental breakfast served daily. Children welcome. No smoking on the property. One-nighter accepted. From $95.

BBHS 202. Built in 1939. Elegant two-story, old country-style manor set on one-half acre of lovely grounds. Only a two-minute walk to Richardson Beach State Park and four miles from downtown Hilo. The hosts offer three bed and breakfast rooms. All rooms are on the second floor. Blue Ginger is very large and has a private bath, ceiling fan, and sweeping ocean view. Bamboo Room is medium size and has ceiling fan and overlooks the lanai. This room shares a very nice bathroom with the Hibiscus room. The Hibiscus Room is a smaller room with ceiling fan and garden and ocean views. Continental breakfast is served in guests' room or out on the lanai. Smoking permitted outside only. Children welcome by prior arrangement only. $55-75.

Wild Ginger Inn

100 Puueo, 96720
(800) 882-1887; FAX (808) 969-1225

The Wild Ginger Inn is a Hawaiian plantation-style inn. Garden, creek, bamboo stands. Near historic downtown Hilo. Room rate includes Continental breakfast.

Rooms: 24 (PB) $43-70
Continental Breakfast
Credit Cards: A, B, E
Notes: 5, 8, 9, 10, 11, 12, 14, 15

HAWAII—HOLUALOA

The Kona Escape Bed & Breakfast

78-7025 Mamalahoa Highway, P.O. Box 197, 96725
(808) 322-3295 (phone/FAX)
e-mail: BandBkona@aol.com
www.cyberpathways.com/kona-escape

A newly built house on seven and one-half acres is designed with the guests' needs in mind. A large lanai encircles the main house where guests can have breakfast while enjoying the expansive view of the ocean. A grass courtyard separates the main house from the guest buildings. Each room has a private entrance, TV, queen-size or twin beds, full bath, and angled high windows that act as skylights. Relax in the hot tub under an umbrella of stars.

Host: Patricia Barlow; John and Rosanne Lyle
Rooms: $75
Continental Breakfast
Credit Cards: None
Notes: 2, 5, 8, 9, 10, 11, 12, 14, 15

HAWAII—HONAUNAU

Bed & Breakfast Honolulu (Statewide)

3242 Kaohinani Drive, Honolulu, 96817
(808) 595-7533; (800) 288-4666
FAX (808) 595-2030
e-mail: rainbow@hawaiibnb.com
www.hawaiibnb.com

BBHS 3. Above the city of refuge, this host offers a downstairs studio apartment with private entrance, private bath, and color cable TV. In addition to a Continental breakfast, there is also a small refrigerator, microwave, and coffeepot for light cooking. The unit opens out onto a cool, quiet private half-acre of gardens. Only three miles to the closest beach for snorkeling, 25 miles from airport, 15 minutes to Kona village. From $80.

HAWAII—HONOKAA

Bed & Breakfast Honolulu (Statewide)

3242 Kaohinani Drive, Honolulu, 96817
(808) 595-7533; (800) 288-4666
FAX (808) 595-2030
e-mail: rainbow@hawaiibnb.com
www.hawaiibnb.com

BBHS 181. At the 1200-foot level on a five-acre plantation estate with ocean views on

---

NOTES: Credit cards accepted: A MasterCard; B Visa; C American Express; D Discover; E Diner's Club; F Other; 2 Personal checks accepted; 3 Lunch available; 4 Dinner available; 5 Open all year; 6 Pets welcome; 7 No smoking; 8 Children welcome; 9 Social drinking allowed; 10 Tennis nearby; 11 Swimming nearby; 12 Golf nearby; 13 Skiing nearby; 14 May be booked through a travel agent; 15 Handicapped accessible.

three sides, this home offers three luxury accommodations. The master suite has a king-size bed and fireplace, color TV, large lanai, and adjoining double bedroom via the private full baths, color TV, and views of the gardens. The home itself has 12-foot ceilings, a den with color TV, wet bar, adjoining billiard room, and library overlooking the formal garden. After the Continental breakfast, guests may wish to enjoy the basketball or tennis courts. Laundry service and crib available as well. From $105.

HAWAII—KAILUA-KONA

Bed & Breakfast Honolulu (Statewide)

3242 Kaohinani Drive, Honolulu, 96817
(808) 595-7533; (800) 288-4666
FAX (808) 595-2030
e-mail: rainbow@hawaiibnb.com
www.hawaiibnb.com

BBHS 184. One bedroom with queen-size bed, private entrance, and bath. Kitchenette (microwave, refrigerator, coffeepot, etc.), large sitting room with color cable TV. Pool access, use of washer/dryer, all antiques, very deluxe. Sleeps two to four people. Tennis court, hot tub, pool access. Continental breakfast. Futons available. From $100.

Hale Maluhia Country Inn Bed & Breakfast (House of Peace)

76-770 Hualalai Road, 96740
(808) 329-5773; (800) 559-6627
FAX (808) 326-5487
e-mail:hawaii-inns@aloha.net
www.hawaii-bnb.com/halemal.html

Gracious upcountry Swiss Family Robinson living in the heart of the Kona recreational paradise. In beautiful Holualoa coffee land. Breakfast lovers' buffet. Large rooms, private baths, good beds, and Japanese stone spa, deep with massage jets. Old Hawaii living with

Hale Maluhia Country Inn

native woods, open-beam ceilings, koa cabinets, big lanais, four common areas, and a stream with waterfalls and lily ponds. Two and one-half miles from the Kailua-Kona village; easy (KOA) airport access. Cable TV/VCR with movie library.

Hosts: Ken and Sue Smith
Rooms: 5 (PB) From $65
Cottages: 2 (PB) From $125
Full Breakfast
Credit Cards: A, B, C, D
Notes: 2, 5, 7, 8, 9, 10, 11, 12, 13, 15

HAWAII—KAMUELA

Bed & Breakfast Honolulu (Statewide)

3242 Kaohinani Drive, Honolulu, 96817
(808) 595-7533; (800) 288-4666
FAX (808) 595-2030
e-mail: rainbow@hawaiibnb.com
www.hawaiibnb.com

BBHS 9. On Kalaki Road, this beautiful two-bedroom suite borders the ranch lands of Mauna Kea. The two-bedroom guest unit is on the first floor with its own private entrance, fireplace, full bath, and full kitchen. Two-night minimum. Smoking outside only. The home was built in 1988, and is three miles from Kamuela town center and 14 miles from the island's best white-sand beaches and Waipio Valley. From $70.

BBHS 210. Stunning views, quiet, and immaculate. Watch the sunrise off of Mauna Kea and

NOTES: Credit cards accepted: A MasterCard; B Visa; C American Express; D Discover; E Diner's Club; F Other; 2 Personal checks accepted; 3 Lunch available; 4 Dinner available; 5 Open all year; 6 Pets welcome;

the sunset into the ocean. This separate two-room suite can be rented as one unit if the guests prefer a private bath or as two separate bed and breakfast rooms that would share the full bath. The Steam room has a refrigerator, microwave, TV, and telephone. The Sunset Room has a TV and telephone. Coffee maker can be available for both rooms. Continental breakfast. Nonsmokers only. Beach is 15 minutes away. Kona airport is approximately 45 minutes away. Each additional person is $15. Inquire about rates for unit booked as a private room. $60-65.

HAWAII—KEALAKEKUA

Bed & Breakfast Honolulu (Statewide)

3242 Kaohinani Drive, Honolulu, 96817
(808) 595-7533; (800) 288-4666
FAX (808) 595-2030
e-mail: rainbow@hawaiibnb.com
www.hawaiibnb.com

BBHS 204. On two acres at the 1500-foot elevation, host offers two bed and breakfast rooms. One private full bath is across the hall and the other full bath is further down the hall. An 80 foot screened-in lanai has a wet bar, furniture, 180-degree panoramic unobstructed view of the Pacific Ocean. A secluded side yard features lounge furniture, hot tub spa that allows an ocean view. A delightful breakfast featuring a chef's daily special. One-nighters accepted. TV in each room. Three miles from beach. From $85.

HAWAII—KEALAKEKUA-KONA

Merryman's Bed & Breakfast

P.O. Box 474, 96750
(808) 323-2276; (800) 545-4390
FAX (808) 323-3749

Beautiful and quiet ocean-view upcountry estate in Kealakekua/Captain Cook. Minutes from the best snorkeling, historical sites, activities. Enjoy spacious, charming rooms, pretty linens, fresh flowers, cable TV. Complimentary Hawaiian breakfast, Jacuzzi. AAA-rated three diamonds.

Hosts: Don and Penny Merryman
Rooms: 4 (2 PB; 2 SB) $75-125
Full Breakfast
Credit Cards: A, B, D
Notes: 2, 5, 9, 10, 11, 12, 14

HAWAII—KONA

Bed & Breakfast Honolulu (Statewide)

3242 Kaohinani Drive, Honolulu, 96817
(808) 595-7533; (800) 288-4666
FAX (808) 595-2030
e-mail: rainbow@hawaiibnb.com
www.hawaiibnb.com

BBHS 13. Kona Sundown is conveniently three miles from Kailua-Kona, off Aii'i Drive. The hosts offers three units. One studio has light cooking, twin beds, TV, and an ocean view. The second studio has a double bed, light cooking. There is also a two-bedroom apartment, one room with queen-size bed, the other with twin beds. Full kitchen, large living/dining area. All units have access to a washer/dryer. Beautiful sunsets. Less than two miles to a swimming beach, but only one-half mile to the ocean. Host speaks German. From $55.

BBHS 182. The detached 480-square-foot cottage is one-half mile from the quaint village of Kailua-Kona. Equipped with full-size refrigerator, microwave, toaster oven, coffee maker, blender, queen-size bed, queen-size Hide-a-Bed, TV, and stereo. The cottage will sleep four comfortably as well as provide a lovely garden setting to enjoy the Continental breakfast that is provided as well. Tennis courts available in subdivision. Children welcome. From $65.

---

7 No smoking; 8 Children welcome; 9 Social drinking allowed; 10 Tennis nearby; 11 Swimming nearby; 12 Golf nearby; 13 Skiing nearby; 14 May be booked through a travel agent; 15 Handicapped accessible.

HAWAII—KUKUIHAELA

Bed & Breakfast Honolulu (Statewide)

3242 Kaohinani Drive, Honolulu, 96817
(808) 595-7533; (800) 288-4666
FAX (808) 595-2030
e-mail: rainbow@hawaiibnb.com
www.hawaiibnb.com

BBHS 11. On more than four acres overlooking majestic Waipio Bay and the Hamakua Cliffs, waterfalls, and tropical valleys. Host offers two new units. Both units have a private bath with tub, private entrance, wraparound lanai, kitchenette with two-burner range, refrigerator, sink, microwave, and coffee supplies. Continental breakfast fixings are stocked in kitchen area. Both have living/dining areas with ceiling fan. There are many nearby trails and swimming at the nearby black-sand beach. From $85.

HAWAII—MOUNTAIN VIEW

Bed & Breakfast Honolulu (Statewide)

3242 Kaohinani Drive, Honolulu, 96817
(808) 595-7533; (800) 288-4666
FAX (808) 595-2030
e-mail: rainbow@hawaiibnb.com
www.hawaiibnb.com

BBHS 1. Experience authentic rural Hawaii from this four-acre floral nursery set halfway between Hilo and Volcano National Park. Enjoy the rich cultural surroundings of the spacious home of a well-known island artist couple. These hosts offer four guest rooms to the bed and breakfast traveler. The Plumeria and Lehua Rooms share a bath. The Cherry Blossom Room has a private bath and a spectacular view of Mauna Kea and Mauna Loa. The Heliconia room has a private bath. A gourmet breakfast of fresh island fruits, breads, and kona coffee. Jog the 430-yard lane which encircles the estate. Must have own crib. From $65.

HAWAII—OCEAN VIEW

Bougainvillea Bed & Breakfast

P.O. Box 6045, 96737
(808) 929-7089 (phone/FAX); (800) 688-1763
e-mail: peaceful@interpac.net

"Nights and Breakfasts to Remember." A unique bed and breakfast with romantic-styled rooms featuring therapeutic beds, VCR movies, private baths and entrances. Historic location commands view of ocean and southpoint—the landing place of first Polynesians in Hawaii. Pavillion area offers barbecue grill, swimming pool, hot tub, and awesome stargazing at night. Snorkel at the nearby green- and black-sand beaches, and enjoy golf, tennis, restaurants, Volcano National Park. Quiet, peaceful, and restful!

Hosts: Martie Jean Nitsche, CT.C. and Don Nitsche
Rooms: 4 (PB) $65
Breakfast
Credit Cards: A, B, C, D, E
Notes: 2, 5, 8, 9, 10, 11, 12, 14

HAWAII—PAAUILO

Suds' Acres Bed & Breakfast

43-1973 Paauilo Mauka Road, P.O. Box 277, 96776
(808) 776-1611 (phone/FAX); (800) 735-3262
e-mail: aphesis@interpac.net
www.hawaii-bnb.com/sudsac.html

Suds' Acres Bed and Breakfast is on a six-acre macadamia nut farm on the Hamakua coast of the Big Island of Hawaii. There is a cozy two-bedroom rustic cottage that sleeps five. In the main house the privacy of the ground floor is available for up to seven people, with a private entrance, kitchenette, bath, fireplace, and wheelchair accessibility. The upstairs includes a separate bedroom with double bed and private bath. Continental breakfast. Color TVs. Smoking permitted outside only.

Rooms: 3 (PB) $65
Continental Breakfast
Credit Cards: A, B, C, D, E, F
Notes: 5, 7, 8, 10, 11, 12, 14, 15

NOTES: Credit cards accepted: A MasterCard; B Visa; C American Express; D Discover; E Diner's Club; F Other; 2 Personal checks accepted; 3 Lunch available; 4 Dinner available; 5 Open all year; 6 Pets welcome;

HAWAII—PAHOA

Bed & Breakfast Honolulu (Statewide)

3242 Kaohinani Drive, Honolulu, 96817
(808) 595-7533; (800) 288-4666
FAX (808) 595-2030
e-mail: rainbow@hawaiibnb.com
www.hawaiibnb.com

BBHS 7. A beautiful new home in the Puna rain forest, 23 miles from Hilo. Four miles to Pahoa, a historic mill town. Many fruit farms in the area. Host is very friendly and invites guests to enjoy a cup of Kona coffee or a tropical fruit drink in the comfort of her living room or enjoy the spa. Spacious bedrooms with either two double beds or a double bed and a twin bed. Both with private bath. Breakfast includes locally grown fruit as well as a wide selection of breakfast foods. From $60.

BBHS 186. The budget traveler has a choice of two bed and breakfast rooms. One room has an attached full bathroom. The second room shares a bath with the hosts. There is a microwave on the guest lanai. Guests may use hosts' refrigerator (limited space). Twenty-five miles from Hilo. Smoking outside only. TV shared with hosts. Hosts are Unitarians. Full breakfast. From $45.

HAWAII—PAPAIKOU

Our Place Papaikou's Bed & Breakfast

P.O. Box 469, 96781-0469
(808) 964-5250; (800) 245-5250
e-mail: rplace@aloha.net
www.best.com/~ourplace

A private, lush, tropical retreat. Four miles north of Hilo, Our Place Papaikou's Bed and Breakfast is a cedar home set amid a lush tropical garden overlooking Kapua stream. The great room, splendid with its cathedral ceiling, has a library, fireplace, grand piano, and cable

TV for guests to enjoy. Four rooms share a Hawaiian-style lanai that looks out over Kapua stream. Nearby attractions include surfing and snorkeling at beaches and ocean parks, the Hawaii Tropical Botanical Garden, Akaka Falls, and Hawaii Volcanoes National Park. Continental plus breakfast. Children over 12 welcome. Smoking permitted on lanai only.

Hosts: Ouida Trahan and Sharon Miller
Rooms: 4 (1 PB; 3 SB) $55-90
Continental Breakfast
Credit Cards: A, B
Notes: 2, 5, 7, 9, 10, 11, 12, 13, 14

HAWAII—SOUTH POINT

Bed & Breakfast Honolulu (Statewide)

3242 Kaohinani Drive, Honolulu, 96817
(808) 595-7533; (800) 288-4666
FAX (808) 595-2030
e-mail: rainbow@hawaiibnb.com
www.hawaiibnb.com

BBHS 180. Midway between Kona and Volcano on the Big Island of Hawaii, this bed and

---

7 No smoking; 8 Children welcome; 9 Social drinking allowed; 10 Tennis nearby; 11 Swimming nearby; 12 Golf nearby; 13 Skiing nearby; 14 May be booked through a travel agent; 15 Handicapped accessible.

breakfast offers guests comfortable, attractive, quiet rooms. The host offers one room with a private bath and entrance with a private porch, and a second room with a private bath. Enjoy a full breakfast on the wraparound lanai and take in the flowers and view of South Point and the ocean. Explore Kalae (South Point) site of the first Polynesian landings in the islands. Enjoy spectacular views of the cliffs and shoreland. Hike to famous green-sand beaches from South Point road. About one and one-half hours south of the Kona airport. From $55.

HAWAII—WAIOHINU

Hawaii South Point Banyan Tree House

Mamalahoa Highway
(888) 451-0880

This unique guest house is nestled up inside a huge Chinese banyan tree in the picturesque and historic village of Waiohinu. The South Point Banyan Tree House is next to a pastoral, manicured church grounds on the corner of Pinao Street and the Mamalahoa Highway. This luxury designer studio features a unique Lexan see-through roof, giving an airy, open feeling as guests look up into the dense canopy of the massive banyan tree by day or enjoy the subtle lighting of its splendor at night. The tree house is convenient to Hawaii Volcanoes National Park, the massive cliffs, and the green-sand beach of South Point, as well as Punalu'u's black-sand beach where snorkelers enjoy swimming among the giant sea turtles.

Host: Terri Remuler
Rooms: 1 (PB) $110
Continental Breakfast
Credit Cards: None
Notes: 2, 5, 8, 9, 10, 11, 12, 14

HAWAII—VOLCANO

Bed & Breakfast Honolulu (Statewide)

3242 Kaohinani Drive, Honolulu, 96817
(808) 595-7533; (800) 288-4666
FAX (808) 595-2030
e-mail: rainbow@hawaiibnb.com
www.hawaiibnb.com

BBHS 19. Positively charming, restored turn-of-the-century two-bedroom guest cottage with wood-burning fireplace. Nestled on two and one-half acres of beautifully landscaped property. One bedroom has a four-poster bed and the other has two twin beds. Some breakfast fixings provided. TV/VCR, beautifully furnished and maintained. Smoking permitted outside only. Two-night minimum stay. From $85.

BBHS 121. At the 3,800-foot elevation, this historic missionary home, built about 1886, has a large botanical garden that blooms year-round. The main house has a room on each of the floors. All guests share the two and one-half baths, Hawaiian library, and living room with TV. The host can provide picnic coolers, flashlights, and specially prepared maps and hiking guides for day or night trips. Their specialty is a full "all you can eat" breakfast and all the macadamia nuts guests can eat (in season). Children, smokers, and one-night stays welcome. Cat in residence. From $65.

BBHS 183. Cedar 2, in a rain forest setting, is a three-bedroom, two-bath home with queen-size beds in the bedrooms, three queen-size sofas in the living room, and dining room. Unit has full kitchen stocked with breakfast fixings. Families welcome. Three-night minimum. Also on the property is a small cottage for two with private bath. Three is a queen-size bed, TV, kitchenette which includes microwave, hot plate, and refrigerator. There are a table and chair, and a covered lanai. From $65-125.

NOTES: Credit cards accepted: A MasterCard; B Visa; C American Express; D Discover; E Diner's Club; F Other; 2 Personal checks accepted; 3 Lunch available; 4 Dinner available; 5 Open all year; 6 Pets welcome;

Kilauea Lodge

Kilauea Lodge

P.O. Box 116, 96785
(808) 967-7366; FAX (808) 967-7367
e-mail: stay@kilauea-lodge.com
www.kilauea-lodge.com

Charming mountain lodge one mile from Volcanoes National Park. Award-winning restaurant with excellent wine list. Full breakfast readies guests for an active day of hiking and viewing the wonders of Pele, the volcano goddess. Private baths. Central heat. Some rooms and cottages have fireplaces and bath robes. Common area.

Rooms: 14 (PB) $95-145
Full Breakfast
Credit Cards: A, B
Notes: 2, 4, 5, 7, 8, 9, 12, 15

HAWAII—WAIMEA

Bed & Breakfast Honolulu (Statewide)

3242 Kaohinani Drive, Honolulu, 96817
(808) 595-7533; (800) 288-4666
FAX (808) 595-2030
e-mail: rainbow@hawaiibnb.com
www.hawaiibnb.com

BBHS 206. Luxury Mediterranean-style home designed to maximize the sweeping view of the lush green Parker Ranch pasturelands and the famous Kohala gold coast sunsets from every room. Three guest rooms with private marble bathrooms. Guest rooms are on the second floor along with a family room used as a gathering place for the guests. Breakfast is served downstairs in the formal dining room. Smoking permitted outside only. Each additional adult in room is $25. Fifteen dollars for each child. From $65.

KAUAI—ANAHOLA

Bed & Breakfast Honolulu (Statewide)

3242 Kaohinani Drive, Honolulu, 96817
(808) 595-7533; (800) 288-4666
FAX (808) 595-2030
e-mail: rainbow@hawaiibnb.com
www.hawaiibnb.com

BBHS 60. This host has a two-bedroom, one-bath cottage. There is a fully equipped kitchen. Living room has a garden view. There is a large deck. This property is a two-minute walk to a long sandy beach. Also on this property are two 500-square-foot one-bedroom apartments with kitchenette, living room, private bath. Ocean view from one of these, mountain view from the other. Both of the apartments have use of a large gazebo and an indoor/outdoor kitchen, wet bar, and barbecue. Ocean view from the gazebo. From $85.

BBHS 63. Enjoy a peaceful vacation or a romantic honeymoon in this completely private studio. Color cable TV. Laundry facilities, mini-refrigerator, wet bar, complete kitchenette. Continental breakfast fixings provided for guests to have at their leisure. The bath has a tub/shower combo. Central on the island for easy access to all sightseeing and touring. The beach is directly across the road. Reef protected for beautiful swimming or sunning on the white sands. Sit in own private yard and enjoy the tropical birds, flowers, trees, and the beautiful mountain view, or take a walk in the hills and valleys just behind the home. Adults preferred. Smoking outside only. The host has no pets. From $85.

BBHS 176. Luxury bed and breakfast on a seven-acre estate with tropical fruit and flower garden with breathtaking ocean views and elegantly furnished suites with Indonesian art and

---

7 No smoking; 8 Children welcome; 9 Social drinking allowed; 10 Tennis nearby; 11 Swimming nearby; 12 Golf nearby; 13 Skiing nearby; 14 May be booked through a travel agent; 15 Handicapped accessible.

furniture. Aloha Mana is just steps away from the Allomanu Bay beach and a short drive away from recreational activities. Accommodates one to five people in the guest house with ocean view, and the farm house suite with lovely garden/waterfall view is for one to two people only. Units each have a private balcony, telephone, TV/VCR, kitchenette. Homegrown Continental breakfast. Use of outdoor Jacuzzi. From $100.

KAUAI—HANALEI

Bed & Breakfast Honolulu (Statewide)

3242 Kaohinani Drive, Honolulu, 96817
(808) 595-7533; (800) 288-4666
FAX (808) 595-2030
e-mail: rainbow@hawaiibnb.com
www.hawaiibnb.com

BBHS 73. Breathtaking views of lush mountains, tropical jungles, cascading waterfalls, and Hanalei Bay just 100 yards away. This host offers three guest rooms in her elegantly decorated home. On the second floor are two rooms, one with a private bath off the hall and the other with a private bath and TV. On the third floor is the honeymoon suite with extra-large private bath. All are welcome to enjoy the views from the 1,000-square-foot wraparound, second-floor lanai. Continental breakfast. Two-night minimum stay. From $75.

KAUAI—KALAHEO

Bed & Breakfast Honolulu (Statewide)

3242 Kaohinani Drive, Honolulu, 96817
(808) 595-7533; (800) 288-4666
FAX (808) 595-2030
e-mail: rainbow@hawaiibnb.com
www.hawaiibnb.com

BBHS 70. Minutes from the quaint town of Kalaheo, surrounded by open meadows with bananas and palm trees that frame the ocean views. This host offers two private units in her lovely home. The Seaview Suite is a spacious one bedroom with a complete kitchen. There is a queen-size and a single bed in the extra-large, tiled bedroom. Also, cable TV/VCR, stereo, and telephone. Can be combined with the Ti Room for larger parties. Extra futons are available. From $60.

BBHS 203. Three delightful, self-contained, cottages adjacent to a custom-built home on landscaped half-acre. These unique cottages feature antique stained and leaded windows from New Zealand, plus all the comforts of home. Fully furnished, carpeted, full kitchens, TV. Seven minutes by car to the golden beaches and playground of the sunny south shores of Poipu. Five minutes to Kukulolono golf course atop a prime vista point in Kalaheo, with unobstructed ocean views. Enjoy an afternoon in the hot tub after touring. Tennis and golf nearby. From $75.

KAUAI—KAPAA

Bed & Breakfast Honolulu (Statewide)

3242 Kaohinani Drive, Honolulu, 96817
(808) 595-7533; (800) 288-4666
FAX (808) 595-2030
e-mail: rainbow@hawaiibnb.com
www.hawaiibnb.com

BBHS 23. Nestled behind the Sleeping Giant mountain on a lovely landscaped one-half acre, this host offers six guest rooms in her bed and breakfast home, all with private baths. Three of the rooms are off the common area with cable TV, VCR, and kitchenette for light cooking. In the other wing of the home are three other rooms with private entrances. One room has cable TV, and all three have refrigerators, microwaves, dishes, etc. Continental breakfast. From $65.

NOTES: Credit cards accepted: A MasterCard; B Visa; C American Express; D Discover; E Diner's Club; F Other; 2 Personal checks accepted; 3 Lunch available; 4 Dinner available; 5 Open all year; 6 Pets welcome;

BBHS 71. In a friendly neighborhood, atop a country mountainside plateau, this host offers two units. The first unit has private bath and entrance, shower/tub, living room with sofa bed. Both units have lanais, mini-wet bars, refrigerators, microwave ovens, and color TV. A gazebo with a Jacuzzi and sauna is available for guests' relaxation. No smoking. Ten dollars for each additional guest. From $70.

BBHS 171. Adjacent to Opaeka'a Falls is one of the most beautiful bed and breakfast homes on the island. It has three wonderfully appointed rooms and a studio. Two guest rooms share a bath. The third room has a private bath. All units have ceiling fans, full carpeting, and are tastefully decorated with original artwork. Continental breakfast. The studio has a kitchenette, TV, and ceiling fan. Hot tub. Children over 16 welcome. From $70.

BBHS 207. Spacious one-bedroom apartment. Unit has a very complete kitchenette. Tropical garden just outside the living room and bedroom. Halfway between the Na Pali coast and Waimea Canyon. Only three miles to beaches. Host provides breakfast fixings for the first morning only. Ten dollars for children. $70.

KAUAI—KILAUEA

Bed & Breakfast Honolulu (Statewide)

3242 Kaohinani Drive, Honolulu, 96817
(808) 595-7533; (800) 288-4666
FAX (808) 595-2030
e-mail: rainbow@hawaiibnb.com
www.hawaiibnb.com

BBHS 64. This magnificent split-level home is overlooking a fresh-water stream and pond on five acres. The Pineapple Room features a seven-foot round bed and a private full bath; the Guava Room has a canopied bed, sitting area with table/chairs, private bath and entrance; the Mango Room has two beds and a shared bath; and the Papaya Room has a shared full bath. Each room has TV and telephone. Continental breakfast. Kitchen privileges. Washer/dryer, surf and boogie boards, snorkel gear, and gas barbecue. Fifteen-minute walk to secret beach. From $65.

BBHS 174. Spacious, cozy one-bedroom apartment hideaway on the edge of the Kilauea River valley. Telephone, washer/dryer, TV/VCR. Kitchenette is fully equipped with the exception of a cook top/oven. Beautiful valley views. Continental breakfast served daily. Two miles to beaches. Smoking outside only. One-nighters accepted at $90. From $80.

Kai Mana Bed & Breakfast

P.O. Box 612, 96754
(808) 828-1280; (800) 837-1782
FAX (808) 828-6670; e-mail: km@kai-mana.com
www.kai-mana.com

Shakti Gawain's home on Kauai. Magnificent suites and cottages with kitchen and bath on five luscious acres overlooking secluded beach. Completely remodeled and comfortable. Massage, acupuncture, etc., on-site. Trail to Secret Beach!

Hosts: Sara Cash and Chris Mildwater
Rooms: 4 (PB) $100-175
Continental Breakfast
Credit Cards: A, B
Notes: 2, 5, 7, 9, 10, 11, 12, 14

KAUAI—KOLOA

Bed & Breakfast Honolulu (Statewide)

3242 Kaohinani Drive, Honolulu, 96817
(808) 595-7533; (800) 288-4666
FAX (808) 595-2030
e-mail: rainbow@hawaiibnb.com
www.hawaiibnb.com

BBHS 67. Only four miles from sunny Poipu, this 500-square-foot one-bedroom garage apartment tropically decorated with rattan furniture has beamed ceilings, a wraparound lanai with panoramic views of Poipu and Black Mountain. The bedroom has a bed and the living room has a sofa bed. A full kitchen is stocked with breakfast fixings, TV/VCR, cassette stereo, telephone, snorkel gear, beach chairs, cooler, boogie boards, and golf clubs. Outdoor shower. From $65.

BBHS 131. This host is between the two ends of the island for easy sightseeing. The host offers a guest room with twin beds, private bath and entrance. Continental breakfast is provided. Small refrigerator, color TV, private patio. The sandy beaches of Poipu are an easy 15-20 minute walk away. Two-night minimum stay. Outside cat. Smokers welcome. From $55.

KAUAI—LAWAI

Bed & Breakfast Honolulu (Statewide)

3242 Kaohinani Drive, Honolulu, 96817
(808) 595-7533; (800) 288-4666
FAX (808) 595-2030
e-mail: rainbow@hawaiibnb.com
www.hawaiibnb.com

BBHS 62. Victoria Place overlooks thick jungle, whispering cane fields, and the beckoning Pacific. It's an oasis of pampered comfort and privacy for travelers. Three guest rooms in one wing of the spacious skylit home open directly through glass doors onto a pool surrounded by flowering walls. The Calla Lilly Room has a full bath off the hallway and makes an ideal romantic getaway. The Raindrop Room is for one person with a private half-bath. The Shell Room has a private bath and a portable ramp for wheelchair use. Non-smoking house. From $75.

BBHS 170. Just 10 minutes from beautiful Poipu Beach. Terrific one-bedroom cottage with full kitchen, living room, dining area, and telephone. Mountain view from dining area. Covered lanai. Continental breakfast provided in unit. Smoking permitted. From $65.

BBHS 172. Secluded high up in the Lawai Valley, these hosts offer three suites in their home. All three suites have private entrances, queen-size beds, private baths, small refrigerators, ceiling fans. A telephone and a fax are available for guests' use. There is a reading room with TV/VCR and plenty of videos. Island delights are served each morning, fresh from local suppliers. Prepared as available or to suit guests' own dietetic or nutritional needs. There is no cooking. One-nighters accepted. Smoking outside only. Only 20 minutes to Poipu Beach, and 25 minutes to the airport. From $75.

KAUAI—POIPU

Bed & Breakfast Honolulu (Statewide)

3242 Kaohinani Drive, Honolulu, 96817
(808) 595-7533; (800) 288-4666
FAX (808) 595-2030
e-mail: rainbow@hawaiibnb.com
www.hawaiibnb.com

BBHS 173. The beautiful Harbor Room has a ceiling fan, stereo, TV/VCR, refrigerator, and private bath. Sitting right on the water's edge with panoramic views of the ocean, boat harbor, Spouting Horn, Mt. Kahill, Black Mountain, and lush cane fields, all from guests' own private balcony. A wonderful breakfast served daily. No smoking on premises. Rates slightly lower for stay of three nights. From $130.

BBHS 205. This bed and breakfast offers two rooms. Both rooms have private baths, lanais, a single futon for a third person, and private entrances. There is a pool and a hot tub. One and one-half blocks to Shipwreck beach. Breakfast supplies stocked. Smoking permitted outside only. From $85.

NOTES: Credit cards accepted: A MasterCard; B Visa; C American Express; D Discover; E Diner's Club; F Other; 2 Personal checks accepted; 3 Lunch available; 4 Dinner available; 5 Open all year; 6 Pets welcome;

KAUAI—WAILUA

Bed & Breakfast Honolulu (Statewide)

3242 Kaohinani Drive, Honolulu, 96817
(808) 595-7533; (800) 288-4666
FAX (808) 595-2030
e-mail: rainbow@hawaiibnb.com
www.hawaiibnb.com

BBHS 66. Wailua country bed and breakfast offers guests a personal touch of Hawaiian country hospitality. On two acres tucked behind the famous Sleeping Giant mountain. This host offers several guest rooms, studio apartment, and a two-bedroom cottage. Both private units have been newly redecorated. Breakfast is served daily. Fifteen minutes from the airport, five minutes to swimming beaches, restaurants, golf courses, shopping. From $65.

BBHS 74. Mohala Ke Ola is high above the lush Wailua River. It offers three spacious guest rooms with Continental breakfast. Private and shared baths. The magnificent mountain and waterfall views wait to greet guests. Relax around the pool and Jacuzzi. Enjoy the gardens and valley views. Host speaks Japanese and does professional massage. One-quarter mile to Opaeka'a Falls. Three-minute drive to the beach. Nonsmoking home. From $65.

LANAI—LANAI CITY

Bed & Breakfast Honolulu (Statewide)

3242 Kaohinani Drive, Honolulu, 96817
(808) 595-7533; (800) 288-4666
FAX (808) 595-2030
e-mail: rainbow@hawaiibnb.com
www.hawaiibnb.com

BBHS 141. This host offers two bed and breakfast rooms with private baths. Continental breakfast. The guests are welcome to use the TV in the living room and the kitchen. Ten minutes from the airport, 15 minutes from the beach, and within walking distance of the community recreation center with pool. There is a shuttle to this home from airport. From $65.

MAUI—HAIKU

Bed & Breakfast Honolulu (Statewide)

3242 Kaohinani Drive, Honolulu, 96817
(808) 595-7533; (800) 288-4666
FAX (808) 595-2030
e-mail: rainbow@hawaiibnb.com
www.hawaiibnb.com

BBHS 48. Designed along the line of the old gracious Hawaiian-style plantation homes, this is a lovely cottage that can sleep three. There is a glass sitting room and an adjacent screened in veranda. King-size bed and double bed in the glass room. Kitchenette. Continental breakfast included first morning. Beautiful, peaceful, open and airy. From $105.

BBHS 164. On a peaceful two-acre farm with macadamia, coconut, avocado, citrus, and banana trees. Off the beaten path, it is a tropical setting with a gazebo which overlooks the ocean. The bedrooms each have queen-size beds and refrigerators. Gourmet teas and coffee served with European charm for breakfast. German is spoken by the West German host. Only international squash court in Hawaii on premises. Minutes to international wind surfing beach and Haleakala crater district. From $60.

Haikuleana Bed & Breakfast Plantation

555 Haiku Road, 96708-5884
(808) 575-2890 (reservations); (808) 575-7459 (guests' use); FAX (808) 575-9177
e-mail: blumblum@maui.net

Fully licensed, Haikuleana is the gateway to upcountry. Built in the 1870s amid Cook Island pines and lush foliage. Renovated in 1992. Elegant and relaxing. Hawaiian and New England

---

7 No smoking; 8 Children welcome; 9 Social drinking allowed; 10 Tennis nearby; 11 Swimming nearby; 12 Golf nearby; 13 Skiing nearby; 14 May be booked through a travel agent; 15 Handicapped accessible.

antiques, beautiful fabrics, and fresh orchids enhance traditional fretwork of Colonial architecture. Convenient to Hana and Haleakala Crater. Ceiling fans. Private guest telephones. Cable TV and VCR. Gourmet breakfast. True aloha atmosphere. Children over seven are welcome. Additional charge for third person. Smoking outside only. Ten-person whirlpool hot tub.

Hosts: Ralph H. and Jeanne Elizabeth Blum
Rooms: 4 (PB) $100-135
Full Breakfast
Credit Cards: None
Notes: 2, 5, 9, 11, 12, 14

Halfway to Hana House

P.O. Box 675, 96708
(808) 572-1176; FAX (808) 572-3609
e-mail: gailp@maui.net; www.maui.net/~gailp

This cozy private studio, with its spectacular location, is nestled in lush seclusion 20 minutes from Paia town on the Hana road. Sparkling clean, airy, with a minikitchen and private bath and entrance, it features a breakfast patio overlooking a tropical valley with panoramic ocean views. Freshwater pools and waterfalls are nearby. The hostess, a long-time Maui resident and avid outdoor enthusiast, delights in graceful touches like chocolate-covered macadamia nuts by the pillow and dazzling floral arrangements. She's helpful with restaurant and adventure tips and might invite guests to go snorkeling or kayaking on a Sunday morning.

Host: Gail Pickholz
Room: 1 (PB) $70
Continental Breakfast
Credit Cards: None
Notes: 5, 7, 8, 9, 11, 14

MAUI—HANA

Affordable Accommodations Maui

2825 Kauhale Street, Kihei, 96753
(808) 879-7865; FAX (808) 874-0831
e-mail: info@affordablemaui.com
www.affordablemaui.com

1. Bed and breakfast in Hana town. Fifteen-minute walk to Hana Bay. Three comfortable, spacious rooms with queen-size and twin beds in each. Private baths. Two rooms have decks looking out to the garden area with fruit trees and tropical plants. In-room refrigerator. Outdoor kitchenette and barbecue available to guests. Additional guests $10 each. $55-65.

MAUI—KIHEI

Affordable Accommodations Maui

2825 Kauhale Street, Kihei, 96753
(808) 879-7865; FAX (808) 874-0831
e-mail: info@affordablemaui.com
www.affordablemaui.com

Listing bed and breakfast accommodations throughout Maui and the outer islands. Some bed and breakfasts may include pools and/or Jacuzzis. There are more than 50 available listings, which include guest rooms, studios, and cottages. Continental breakfast. Open year-round. $50-150.

1. Lovely Hawaiian pole-style home in garden setting with barbecue and picnic table available for guests. Tiki torches give that wonderful Hawaiian feeling. Two spacious one-bedroom one-bath suites, one studio suite, and a master bedroom. One with ocean view. Nicely furnished. Warm hosts offer breakfast on their lanai with sweeping ocean views. $75-95.

2. Enchanting bed and breakfast right above Wailea. Immaculately clean. Garden Room with private bath, queen-size bed. Huge master bedroom with king-size bed, private bath, and entrance. Property has many fruit trees, a courtyard for relaxing and reading a book, and a lovely gazebo with a koi pond and waterfall to sit and reflect on the wonders of Maui. Charming hostess to help guests with all their needs. $75-95.

NOTES: Credit cards accepted: A MasterCard; B Visa; C American Express; D Discover; E Diner's Club; F Other; 2 Personal checks accepted; 3 Lunch available; 4 Dinner available; 5 Open all year; 6 Pets welcome;

3. Large, light airy room with king-size bed, private bath in south Kihei home. Three blocks from the beach. TV, refrigerator. Breakfast served on ocean-view lanai, weather permitting. $50-60.

4. Private, set apart one-bedroom one-bath deluxe cottage bordering Wailea. Small ocean view. Full kitchen equipped with everything guests need. TV, VCR, tape deck, radio/CD player. Washer and dryer, air conditioned for those warm summer days. Skylight in the bedroom for viewing the stars at night. $80-90.

5. A tropical haven in North Kihei. Lush, tropical gardens with waterfall. Three units each with private entrance and bath. Oversize rooms. Two of the rooms are wheelchair accessible. Kitchenettes. A short stroll to long sandy beach. $95-110.

Aloha Bed & Breakfast

811 South Kihei Road, #1F, 96753
(808) 875-4517; (800) 484-6748 ext. 5582

Enjoy magical Maui at this beautiful condominium resort. For guests' pleasure there is a near-Olympic-size swimming pool, hot tub, 18-hole putting green, and two tennis courts. Across the street there is a five-mile-long beach where guests can enjoy walks, swimming, or watching beautiful sunsets. Enjoy the luscious breakfast in the elegant dining area or on the airy lanai that is surrounded by lovely tropical flowers. Double room available.

Hosts: Eric and Karen Miller
Rooms: 1 (PB) $65
Full Breakfast
Credit Cards: F
Notes: 5, 7, 9, 10, 11, 12, 14

Aloha Pualani

15 Wailana Place, 96753
(808) 874-9265; (800) PUALANI
FAX (808) 874-9127

"Our heavenly flowers welcome you." Experience the best of both worlds—a bed and breakfast and a condominium. Five private suites surround a tropically landscaped courtyard and heated swimming pool. Best of all, Aloha Pualani is just across the street from beautiful Maalaea Bay and the longest sandy beach on Maui. Enjoy spectacular sunsets from either guests' private ocean-view lanai or from the beach only 100 feet away. Centrally placed on the island for convenient sightseeing.

Hosts: Marina and Keith Dinsmoor
Rooms: 5 (PB) $89-119
Continental Breakfast
Credit Cards: A, B, C, D, E
Notes: 2, 5, 7, 8, 9, 10, 11, 12, 14

Bed & Breakfast Honolulu (Statewide)

3242 Kaohinani Drive, Honolulu, 96817
(808) 595-7533; (800) 288-4666
FAX (808) 595-2030
e-mail: rainbow@hawaiibnb.com
www.hawaiibnb.com

BBHS 46. From a house overlooking Maaiaea Bay, this host offers two guest rooms to the bed and breakfast traveler. Both rooms have a private bath, cable TV, and a lanai. Although there is a private telephone in each unit, the line is shared between the rooms. Continental breakfast is served each morning. Only an eight-minute walk to beautiful Mai Poina Oe la'U beach park. Host provides beach towels, sand chairs, and ice chest. No smoking. From $65.

BBHS 49. Less than 1,000 feet from Mai Poina 'Oe la'U Beach that stretches for three miles. Beautiful three-story plantation-style home in north Kihei. Offers three guest rooms on the second floor. One unit has a private bath and the other two units share a bath. Ocean and mountain views from every room. Climb the open stairway to a third-story sitting area with lanai, perfect for whale watching or spectacular sunset views. Continental breakfast. Some refrigerator space available for snacks and

---

7 No smoking; 8 Children welcome; 9 Social drinking allowed; 10 Tennis nearby; 11 Swimming nearby; 12 Golf nearby; 13 Skiing nearby; 14 May be booked through a travel agent; 15 Handicapped accessible.

drinks. Smoking permitted outside only. Children over 14 welcome. $60-70.

BBHS 52. At the top of Maui meadows, just above Wailea, overlooking the islands of Lanai, Molokini, and Kahoolawe. The home is divided into four living sections, one which is occupied by the owner. The studio has one bedroom, a full kitchen, and private bath. The apartment has two bedrooms, private bath, and kitchenette. The cottage is separate and has one bedroom, living room with sofa bed, full kitchen, and wraparound lanai. Kitchens are stocked with breakfast foods. Minutes from beaches, golf courses, shopping. From $90.

BBHS 54. Only one-half mile stroll to Kamaole II beach. Guests may select from four exceptional units in this beautiful pole home with lovely grounds. Beach gear is provided. Four units with private baths. One unit has a full kitchen and two units have kitchenettes. All units include a full breakfast served family style. Air conditioning, hot tub, barbecue, telephone, TV/VCR. From $75-95.

BBHS 163. Walled and gated for privacy, three bed and breakfast rooms. Large outdoor entertainment area with large Jacuzzi and gas barbecue. Continental breakfast. Smoking outside only. One room has a private bath and the other two rooms share a bath. Short walk to beach. From $55-65.

BBHS 166. Only one-half mile up the street from Kamaole III beach and adjoining the beautiful Wailea resort area. Host offers a bed and breakfast suite with private bath with shower and private entrance. A coffee maker and small refrigerator are in the suite. Continental breakfast. Smoking outside only. Ten dollars for additional person over five. From $85.

BBHS 208. The host thought of everything they wanted in a vacation place and created it.... The Palm Cottage has a spacious living/dining room, large bedroom, TV, stereo, telephone, and fully equipped kitchen. Four-night minimum. Smoking permitted outside only. Fifteen dollars for each additional person. From $80.

MAUI—KUAU

Affordable Accommodations Maui

2825 Kauhale Street, Kihei, 96753
(808) 879-7865; FAX (808) 874-0831
e-mail: info@affordablemaui.com
www.affordablemaui.com

1. Just past Paia guests will find a charming bed and breakfast with the feel of old Hawaii. Beautifully decorated with Hawaiian fabrics of the 40s and touches of Hawaiiana everywhere guests look. The property has a large grass area for lounging around and listening to the birds sing. Walk a few steps and guests will be in a private cove with the waves lapping at the shore. A five-minute walk will take guests to several sandy beaches. Two bed and breakfast rooms are offered with private baths and a dining/relaxing area. World-famous windsurfing beach, Hookipa, is just minutes away. $85.

MAUI—KULA

Bed & Breakfast Honolulu (Statewide)

3242 Kaohinani Drive, Honolulu, 96817
(808) 595-7533; (800) 288-4666
FAX (808) 595-2030
e-mail: rainbow@hawaiibnb.com
www.hawaiibnb.com

BBHS 81. Host offers several accommodations in a recently renovated ranch home. This home has six bedrooms with private baths. Guests are invited to use the kitchen. The bunkhouse is a U-shaped building with five small apartments. These units all have kitchens and one has a fireplace for cooler evenings. The Lahaina cottage is the honeymoon suite. It has an old wood-burning stove, complete kitchen, king-

---

NOTES: Credit cards accepted: A MasterCard; B Visa; C American Express; D Discover; E Diner's Club; F Other; 2 Personal checks accepted; 3 Lunch available; 4 Dinner available; 5 Open all year; 6 Pets welcome;

size bed, a big red bathtub with ocean views. Families and one-nighters welcome. Smoking outside only. From $85.

BBHS 167. On the slopes of Haleakala with beautiful views of the west Maui mountains and the Kihei coastline sits a lovely home that offers two bed and breakfast rooms. The master bedroom has a private bath with views of pasture lands, ferns, orchids, and anthurium flowers. The second bedroom shares a bath with the host only. There is a very large lanai to relax and just enjoy the gorgeous surroundings. Breakfast is served in the dining room. From $65.

Kula View

Kula View Bed & Breakfast

140 Holopuni Road, P.O. Box 322, 96790
(808) 878-6736

Glorious sunrise and sunsets, sweeping ocean, mountain, and garden views from every guest room. Raised 2,000 feet above sea level on the slopes of the dormant volcano Haleakala, Kula View is surrounded by two acres of lush greenery, fruits, flowers, banana and coffee trees, and yet is close to the Kahului airport, shopping centers, hiking parks, and beaches. The upper-level suite has a private entrance, deck, and private bath luxuriously appointed with a queen-size bed, reading area, wicker breakfast nook, and mini-refrigerator. Kula View offers personal old-fashioned Maui upcountry-style hospitality. Two-night minimum stay required.

Host: Susan Kauai
Room: 1 (PB) $85
Continental Breakfast
Credit Cards: None
Notes: 5, 7, 9, 10, 11, 12

MAUI—LAHAINA

Affordable Accommodations Maui

2825 Kauhale Street, Kihei, 96753
(808) 879-7865; FAX (808) 874-0831
e-mail: info@affordablemaui.com
www.affordablemaui.com

1. Large home with six accommodations. Amenities include pool, barbecue area, large lanai with tables to watch the sunset. All tile floors. Guests share exclusive kitchen. Delicious full breakfast served each morning. Air conditioned for those warm Lahaina days. Hosts with worldly interests. Rooms and suites include queen-size bed, mini-refrigerator, and private baths. $85-125.

2. Just a short walk to Lahaina town, Lahaina Harbor, and the beach from this bed and breakfast on a quiet street in Lahaina. Friendly hostess happy to share her knowledge about this historic town. Rooms with queen-size or twin beds share a bath in this quaint home. $55-70.

Bed & Breakfast Honolulu (Statewide)

3242 Kaohinani Drive, Honolulu, 96817
(808) 595-7533; (800) 288-4666
FAX (808) 595-2030
e-mail: rainbow@hawaiibnb.com
www.hawaiibnb.com

BBHS 39. Hosts offer two units in their luxurious waterfront home. The oceanfront room has a private bath and entrance with lanai. The ocean-view room has a private bath and

---

7 No smoking; 8 Children welcome; 9 Social drinking allowed; 10 Tennis nearby; 11 Swimming nearby; 12 Golf nearby; 13 Skiing nearby; 14 May be booked through a travel agent; 15 Handicapped accessible.

entrance. Both have TV and refrigerator. Continental breakfast. The beach is ideal for snorkeling, kayaking, or wind surfing. A great swimming beach is just moments away. Nonsmokers welcome. From $85.

BBHS 53. This recently remodeled 7,000-square-foot residence offers six spacious guest rooms, five with outside access. Guest lounges, pool with slide and separate Jacuzzi. A full complimentary breakfast served in the main dining room or on the terrace. Guests also have the convenience of a separate kitchen. Four rooms accommodate up to four persons. Private baths. Smoking outside only. From $95.

BBHS 130. Each unit has a queen-size bed, plus a pull-out single or twin, a private Jacuzzi or hot tub, air conditioning, color TV, ceiling fan, small refrigerator, private bath, and private lanai. Relax around the large pool, join other guests in the family room for the latest videos or just relax in the quiet comfort of the living room. Continental breakfast provided and use of the kitchen is permitted. Outstanding accommodations at a modest price. From $115.

Old Lahaina House

P.O. Box 10355, 96761
(808) 667-4663; (800) 847-0761
FAX (808) 667-5615
www.mauiweb.com/maui/olhouse/

This convenient, relaxing place from which to visit Maui allows guests to enjoy the romantic, secluded ambiance of a private pool in a tropical courtyard. Only steps from a serene beach and convenient walking distance to dining and shopping in historic Lahaina town, a culturally rich and diverse old whaling town. Old Lahaina House is a home away from home, a special retreat, an intimate piece of paradise! Special tropical breakfast by the pool. Laundry facilities available. Smoking permitted outside.

Hosts: John and Sherry Barbier and Family
Rooms: 4 (PB) $69-95
Continental Breakfast
Credit Cards: A, B, C, D
Notes: 2, 5, 7, 8, 9, 10, 11, 12, 14

MAUI—MAKAWAO

Affordable Accommodations Maui

2825 Kauhale Street, Kihei, 96753
(808) 879-7865; FAX (808) 874-0831
e-mail: info@affordablemaui.com
www.affordablemaui.com

1. Charming plantation-style home in upcountry Makawao. Two lovely rooms and one suite decorated with antiques. The suite has a TV, refrigerator, and private bath which includes a shower and the original claw-foot tub. Room one is decorated in collectible Hawaiana and has an antique brass bed with a private bath. The second room is spacious and comfortable and features a queen-size bed and private bath. The newest addition is a two-bedroom suite complete with a sleeper-sofa and private bath. Rambling country kitchen perfect for families. Walk to Makawao, the paniolo (Hawaiian cowboy) town of the past. The gracious hostess serves breakfast on the sideboard. $60-130.

2. Cozy one-bedroom, 700-square-foot cottage, walking distance to Makawao. Queen-size bed in bedroom and sofa bed in living area. Covered patio, nice garden. Amenities include TV, VCR. Decorated with a romantic flair. Ten dollars for each additional person. $75-85.

MAUI—MAUI MEADOWS

Bed & Breakfast Honolulu (Statewide)

3242 Kaohinani Drive, Honolulu, 96817
(808) 595-7533; (800) 288-4666
FAX (808) 595-2030

NOTES: Credit cards accepted: A MasterCard; B Visa; C American Express; D Discover; E Diner's Club; F Other; 2 Personal checks accepted; 3 Lunch available; 4 Dinner available; 5 Open all year; 6 Pets welcome;

e-mail: rainbow@hawaiibnb.com
www.hawaiibnb.com

BBHS 30. Above Wailea, this redwood pole house sits on an acre and is surrounded by 75 fruit trees and large tropical garden. It has a lanai that wraps around the home for beautiful ocean views. There are two accommodations offered. The guest rooms have private entrances and baths. On the garden level is the two-bedroom apartment with a full bath, kitchen, and private lanai. Less than a mile to the beach and shopping. Continental breakfast. Twelve miles from the airport. The Swedish-born hostess is a great help with coolers, snorkeling gear, beach mats, and lounge chairs. From $60.

BBHS 40. In a quiet residential area above Wailea. This host has two studios with private baths and entrances. These large studios have light cooking facilities with refrigerator, coffee maker, and microwave. The host stocks breakfast fixings for guests to use when they want. There is an ocean view from the lanai above the units. Just a short drive to the beaches, shopping, and restaurants. Three-night minimum stay. From $65.

MAUI—PAIA

Bed & Breakfast Honolulu (Statewide)

3242 Kaohinani Drive, Honolulu, 96817
(808) 595-7533; (800) 288-4666
FAX (808) 595-2030
e-mail: rainbow@hawaiibnb.com
www.hawaiibnb.com

BBHS 201. Built in 1939, this plantation house sits on three-quarters of an acre with two gigantic monkey pods and one rubber tree. There are two bed and breakfast units with private baths and ceiling fans. Refrigerator-freezer and washer/dryer available for guests.

Large living room and dining room separate from the family living area. Continental breakfast. Six miles from airport. Five- to eight-minute walk to beach. Children over six welcome. Smoking permitted outside only. Rates will be higher December 21 through March 31. From $85.

MAUI—SPRECKELSVILLE

Affordable Accommodations Maui

2825 Kauhale Street, Kihei, 96753
(808) 879-7865; FAX (808) 874-0831
e-mail: info@affordablemaui.com
www.affordablemaui.com

1. Charming studio attached to a beautiful old plantation-style home with kitchenette/ full refrigerator, lovely lanai to sit in and view the garden. Private bath, TV, VCR, and telephone. Just a few steps to baby beach and the Maui Country Club. Gracious hostess. $65-75.

MAUI—UPCOUNTRY

Bed & Breakfast Honolulu (Statewide)

3242 Kaohinani Drive, Honolulu, 96817
(808) 595-7533; (800) 288-4666
FAX (808) 595-2030
e-mail: rainbow@hawaiibnb.com
www.hawaiibnb.com

BBHS 161. Walking distance to charming Makawao. Gracious old plantation home built in 1924. Host offers three bed and breakfast rooms, all with private baths. Each room is furnished with Old World charm. TV in the main common area and the Rose Room. Continental breakfast. Refrigerator, microwave, and coffee maker available for guests. Smoking permitted outside only. Children welcome. One-nighters welcomed. From $70-80.

---

7 No smoking; 8 Children welcome; 9 Social drinking allowed; 10 Tennis nearby; 11 Swimming nearby; 12 Golf nearby; 13 Skiing nearby; 14 May be booked through a travel agent; 15 Handicapped accessible.

MAUI—WAILUKU

Bed & Breakfast Honolulu (Statewide)

3242 Kaohinani Drive, Honolulu, 96817
(808) 595-7533; (800) 288-4666
FAX (808) 595-2030
e-mail: rainbow@hawaiibnb.com
www.hawaiibnb.com

BBHS 162. Built in 1924 by a wealthy island banker. Down to the smallest detail it represents 1920s Hawaii at its best intertwined with the conveniences and luxuries modern travelers expect. Seven gracious rooms each named for an island flower. Each room has a private bath, telephone, and an heirloom Hawaiian quilt. A few of the rooms have a whirlpool bath. Full gourmet breakfast is served. Smoking permitted outside only. Twenty dollars for each additional guest. From $120-180.

OAHU—AIEA

Rainbow Inn

98-1049 Mahola Place, 96701
(808) 488-7525 (phone/FAX)
e-mail: gsmith3777@aol.com

This beautiful bed and breakfast has easy access to sights and airport, yet is in a secluded tropical setting with marvelous views of Pearl Harbor, mountains, and the entire south coast of Oahu. Private garden apartment, separate entrance, private pool, beautiful private bath. In one of Oahu's nicest executive neighborhoods on valley filled with rainbows. Fully furnished, plenty of extras: refrigerator, microwave, air conditioning, color cable TV, many interesting books on Hawaii. Use of washer/dryer. Stores, ethnic restaurants, theaters nearby.

Hosts: Cdr. (Ret) USN Gene and Betty Smith
Rooms: 1 (PB) $65
Full Breakfast
Credit Cards: None
Notes: 2, 5, 7, 9, 10, 11, 12, 14

OAHU—EWA BEACH

Bed & Breakfast Honolulu (Statewide)

3242 Kaohinani Drive, Honolulu, 96817
(808) 595-7533; (800) 288-4666
FAX (808) 595-2030
e-mail: rainbow@hawaiibnb.com
www.hawaiibnb.com

BBHS 158. If one yearns to get away from the crowds and find an uncrowded white-sand beach, then come to Oahu's southern shore. This home offers four bedrooms and two baths. Full kitchen. Common area. TV. More than one family could share this home. Full breakfast. Views of the shoreline and Diamond Head. Nonsmoking property. From $60.

OAHU—HAWAII KAI

Bed & Breakfast Honolulu (Statewide)

3242 Kaohinani Drive, Honolulu, 96817
(808) 595-7533; (800) 288-4666
FAX (808) 595-2030
e-mail: rainbow@hawaiibnb.com
www.hawaiibnb.com

BBHS 79. The hosts, mother and daughter, are originally from England where bed and breakfast started. The upstairs guest room has a private bath, TV, refrigerator. The downstairs room has a private bath, TV, VCR, microwave. A hearty Continental breakfast served. Ten-minute drive to swimming beaches and Hanauma Bay (famous for snorkeling). No smoking. Adults only. Two-night minimum. Hosts have a dog. From $65-75.

BBHS 150. This host offers two newly renovated guest rooms with shared bath. Each room has a private entrance through a private patio/garden area. Both have TV, radio-alarm clock, ceiling fan, and small refrigerator. Guests may also eat and sunbathe on the marina side of the house where there is a gas grill. Convenient

---

NOTES: Credit cards accepted: A MasterCard; B Visa; C American Express; D Discover; E Diner's Club; F Other; 2 Personal checks accepted; 3 Lunch available; 4 Dinner available; 5 Open all year; 6 Pets welcome;

to Hanauma Bay, Sandy Beach, shopping centers, and many restaurants. It is nine miles to Waikiki, 11 miles to Ala Moana shopping center. Continental breakfast. Smoking permitted outside. From $55.

BBHS 151. Luxurious marina waterfront property. Foyer has moss rock waterfall with fish pool. Enjoy a beautiful lagoon-shaped pool with waterfalls. A four-poster brass bed. Private full bath, small refrigerator, TV, air conditioning, Continental breakfast. Smoking permitted outside only. From $85.

BBHS 160. This home on Mariners Ridge, in an executive community, has many pluses. The large deck offers marvelous ocean views, and has a patio table which is a perfect place to have breakfast or just relax in the early evening. Swimming pool available for guests' use. These hosts offer two rooms in their home with a shared bathroom. The king-size room has an ocean view, while the room with twin beds has its own TV and looks out on a small tropical garden. This bed and breakfast is minutes from Hanauma Bay and other beaches, shopping centers, and restaurants. Also, there is absolutely no smoking. From $60.

OAHU—HONOLULU

Bed & Breakfast Honolulu (Statewide)

3242 Kaohinani Drive, Honolulu, 96817
(808) 595-7533; (800) 288-4666
FAX (808) 595-2030
e-mail: rainbow@hawaiibnb.com
www.hawaiibnb.com

BBHS 101. In Foster Village, about two miles from Pearl Harbor and the Arizona Memorial. This home has two bed and breakfast rooms. Kitchen privileges with microwave and regular ovens, freezer, refrigerator, range, laundry facilities, and color TV. Not directly on the bus line, so a car is probably necessary. Children and smokers welcome. Two blocks from Tripler Hospital busline. From $50.

OAHU—KAILUA

All Islands Bed & Breakfast

463 Iliwahi Loop, 96734-1837
(808) 263-2342; (800) 542-0344 (U.S. & Canada)
FAX (808) 263-0308
e-mail: carlina001@hawaii.rr.com
www.hawaiialohaspirit.com/alisbnb

Experience the real Hawaii! More than 700 private accommodations on all Hawaiian islands. Rooms in private homes average $55-75. Studios average $65-85. Ohana cottages average $75-95. Excellent rental car and interisland air rates. Free brochure. Continental breakfast is provided at some of the bed and breakfasts.

Rooms: 1,500 (900 PB; 100 SB) $55-300
Cards: A, B, C
Notes: 2, 5, 7, 8, 9, 10, 11, 12, 14

Bed & Breakfast Honolulu (Statewide)

3242 Kaohinani Drive, Honolulu, 96817
(808) 595-7533; (800) 288-4666
FAX (808) 595-2030
e-mail: rainbow@hawaiibnb.com
www.hawaiibnb.com

BBHS 89. Walk to Kailua town and only one-half mile to gorgeous Kailua Beach. Beautiful tropical yard with pool. The bed and breakfast unit has private entrance and bath, TV, coffee maker, refrigerator, microwave, toaster, and ceiling fan. The large private studio is also equipped for light cooking. Futons can be used for additional guests. Both units are given Continental breakfast fixings for the first day only. Children welcome. Smoking permitted outside only. From $75.

BBHS 91. Only 200 yards from the ocean. Host offers two units with private entrances and baths. Each unit has built-in microwave, coffee maker, and refrigerator for light cooking. The host provides breakfast fixings in the unit for the first morning only. Air conditioning. Swimming pool for guests' use. The property is enclosed and very private. Children over 16

---

7 No smoking; 8 Children welcome; 9 Social drinking allowed; 10 Tennis nearby; 11 Swimming nearby; 12 Golf nearby; 13 Skiing nearby; 14 May be booked through a travel agent; 15 Handicapped accessible.

welcome. Smokers welcome. Host has an Irish setter. Three-night minimum. From $70.

BBHS 96. Welcome to this beautiful open Hawaiian-style home enhanced by gorgeous flower arrangements in all rooms. Back yard is picture perfect with a large pool and gentle stream that empties into the ocean two blocks away. Lovely golf course rimmed by mountains completes the view. Room offers a private bath, TV, chair, ceiling fan, and refrigerator. Inquire about nonbreakfast option. Two aloof cats on premises. From $65.

BBHS 153. This host offers two guest rooms, with private baths, in her newly decorated home furnished with oriental art gathered from around the world. It's a three and one-half-minute walk to Kailua Beach. Both have TVs and share the guest refrigerator off the hall between the rooms. The common rooms are large and spacious with a lovely garden in the back of the house. Continental breakfast. Entrance is through an oriental arch. Husband fluent in Chinese and some Japanese. Nonsmokers welcome. From $60.

BBHS 154. Enjoy this oceanfront unit sitting right on the breakers of Kailua Beach—not for swimming due to lava rock. Five-minute walk to a swimming area. Attached to single-family home. Hosts offer studio with king-size or twin beds. Futon available for extra guest. TV in room along with light cooking facilities. Breakfast fixings stocked for guests' convenience. Private entrance and full bath. Golden retriever on property. From $85-90.

BBHS 155. Just four houses from Kailua Beach is a small studio with private entrance. It has a private bath, microwave, refrigerator, and small eating area. The host serves a bountiful Continental breakfast. Relax at the pool or in the small, private sitting area adjacent to the studio. There is a convenient right of away to the beach available. From $65.

BBHS 159. Away from the clamor of Waikiki on a quiet dead end street, Kailua Beach park is a one-half mile walk. This host offers two guest rooms. Both share the guest bath with shower/tub combo. Continental breakfast. Guests are welcome to use the coolers, beach mats, and beach chairs. On bus line. Dog on premises. Smoking permitted on lanai only. Adults only. Two-night minimum. From $55.

BBHS 200. This secluded apartment on Kailua Beach, one of Hawaii's most beautiful white-sand beaches. One-bedroom apartment furnished with cable TV, dining counter, large closets, and ceiling fan. There is a connecting private bath and a delightful kitchenette separate from the bedroom area. Private entrance. In a quiet residential neighborhood. Only 30 minutes from Honolulu, Waikiki, and airport. Second bedroom available upon request. Monthly rates available. No children under 14. Nonsmokers only. No view from the unit. $85.

BBHS 211. An enchanted lake studio cottage. Two stories, main living space on the top and a laundry area on the bottom. The top story includes a spacious bedroom, a bathroom, and a kitchenette. Microwave, full-size refrigerator, stove top, sink, toaster, coffee maker, TV, telephone, and a pool. This unit is near Kailua and Lanikai beaches, shopping center, theatres, and a bus stop. From $70.

Papaya Paradise

395 Auwinala Road, 96734
(808) 261-0316 (phone/FAX)

Private, quiet, tropical, and near all attractions. Enjoy the pool. Relax in the Jacuzzi. Stroll Kailua Beach. Savor breakfast on the lanai surrounded by Hawaiian plants, trees, and flowers with Mount Olomana in the background. Rooms with private bath, private entry, refrigerator, air conditioning, telephone, and TV. Tennis, golf, and all kinds of water sports nearby. Just 20 miles from Waikiki and the Honolulu airport.

NOTES: Credit cards accepted: A MasterCard; B Visa; C American Express; D Discover; E Diner's Club; F Other; 2 Personal checks accepted; 3 Lunch available; 4 Dinner available; 5 Open all year; 6 Pets welcome;

Minimum three-night stay. Personal checks accepted for deposit only. AAA-approved.

Hosts: Bob and Jeanette Martz
Rooms: 2 (PB) $75-80
Continental Breakfast
Credit Cards: None
Notes: 5, 8, 9, 10, 11, 12

OAHU—KANEOHE

Bed & Breakfast Honolulu (Statewide)

3242 Kaohinani Drive, Honolulu, 96817
(808) 595-7533; (800) 288-4666
FAX (808) 595-2030
e-mail: rainbow@hawaiibnb.com
www.hawaiibnb.com

BBHS 95. On the bay. This host has two guest rooms with private baths and entrance. The King room has an adjacent sitting room with a twin daybed (fine for third person), microwave, coffee maker, refrigerator, and TV. The Queen room has a small dinette, coffee maker, toaster oven (refrigerator also available). Guests can enjoy sitting poolside. Picture postcard views available from the lanai or the boatdock. Near village shopping center, supermarket, cinema, and nice restaurants. Two miles to one of the loveliest beaches on the island. Fifteen miles from airport. Smoking outside only. From $65.

OAHU—LANIKAI

Bed & Breakfast Honolulu (Statewide)

3242 Kaohinani Drive, Honolulu, 96817
(808) 595-7533; (800) 288-4666
FAX (808) 595-2030
e-mail: rainbow@hawaiibnb.com
www.hawaiibnb.com

BBHS 94. A lovely 350-square-foot studio two blocks from gorgeous Lanikai Beach. Queen-size and twin beds. Bath with tub/shower, TV, coffee maker, toaster oven, refrigerator, bath towels, and beach chairs. Recessed on the lower part of hosts property. Very secluded and private. No smoking on property. There are 16 steps down to the property. Breakfast fixings in the unit for guests to prepare at their leisure. No use of telephone except for emergency calls. No children. No laundry facilities. Two-night minimum. From $85.

OAHU—MANOA

Bed & Breakfast Honolulu (Statewide)

3242 Kaohinani Drive, Honolulu, 96817
(808) 595-7533; (800) 288-4666
FAX (808) 595-2030
e-mail: rainbow@hawaiibnb.com
www.hawaiibnb.com

BBHS 82. In Manoa Valley (known for its rainbows and waterfalls), this host offers two comfortably decorated units to the bed and breakfast traveler. One bedroom has a private bath with shower only. The second room has a private half-bath and shared shower/tub. Entry is connected to the room. Continental breakfast. A 5- to 10-minute drive to beaches of Waikiki, hike to Manoa Falls, or visit Lyon Arboretum. Children welcome. Smoking permitted outside only. From $75.

OAHU—NIU VALLEY

Bed & Breakfast Honolulu (Statewide)

3242 Kaohinani Drive, Honolulu, 96817
(808) 595-7533; (800) 288-4666
FAX (808) 595-2030
e-mail: rainbow@hawaiibnb.com
www.hawaiibnb.com

BBHS 157. In the lower middle portion of quiet Niu Valley this host offers two bed and breakfast rooms at very modest prices making this an exceptional value. Room one has twin beds and room for a futon, TV, and small refrigerator. Room two has a ceiling fan and a double bed.

---

7 No smoking; 8 Children welcome; 9 Social drinking allowed; 10 Tennis nearby; 11 Swimming nearby; 12 Golf nearby; 13 Skiing nearby; 14 May be booked through a travel agent; 15 Handicapped accessible.

The rooms share a bath. Continental breakfast. Three blocks to bus. Thirty minutes to airport. Nonsmokers only. No pets. From $55.

OAHU—NUUANU

Bed & Breakfast Honolulu (Statewide)

3242 Kaohinani Drive, Honolulu, 96817
(808) 595-7533; (800) 288-4666
FAX (808) 595-2030
e-mail: rainbow@hawaiibnb.com
www.hawaiibnb.com

BBHS 78. These units are in the home/office of the owners of this service. It's 10 minutes to downtown Honolulu, 20 minutes to Waikiki, or the airport. Each unit has color TV, private telephone, coffee maker, toaster, refrigerator, table, chairs, dishes, and private shower bath. The second-floor unit has a small bedroom. The first floor unit also has a small dining area and a daybed. Microwave and hot plate available nearby, so only an aloha welcome basket is provided for the first day. Three blocks to bus stop. One-nighters welcome, but surcharge, if fewer than three. Smokers and children welcome. Hosts have dogs in the main house and outdoor cats. Fax, e-mail, and copying available for a modest fee. From $55.

OAHU—WAIANAE

Bed & Breakfast Honolulu (Statewide)

3242 Kaohinani Drive, Honolulu, 96817
(808) 595-7533; (800) 288-4666
FAX (808) 595-2030
e-mail: rainbow@hawaiibnb.com
www.hawaiibnb.com

BBHS 156. Nine-tenths of a mile from Pokai Beach and Waianae Army Beach. Twenty-two miles from airport. Continental breakfast. Smoking permitted outside only. Two-night minimum. Two rooms with either shared or private bath. From $60-65.

OAHU—WAIKIKI

Bed & Breakfast Honolulu (Statewide)

3242 Kaohinani Drive, Honolulu, 96817
(808) 595-7533; (800) 288-4666
FAX (808) 595-2030
e-mail: rainbow@hawaiibnb.com
www.hawaiibnb.com

BBHS 109. Only two blocks to Waikiki Beach, this host offers one guest room in his two-bedroom, air-conditioned condo. This room has a queen-size bed with private bath. Enjoy the view of downtown, Waikiki, the beach in the daytime, and the beautiful stars and sunsets in the evening. Continental breakfast. Easy walking distance to shopping and restaurants. Guests may use the kitchen. Smoking permitted outside on the lanai only. Parking on street. From $60.

OAHU—WAIMANALO

Bed & Breakfast Honolulu (Statewide)

3242 Kaohinani Drive, Honolulu, 96817
(808) 595-7533; (800) 288-4666
FAX (808) 595-2030
e-mail: rainbow@hawaiibnb.com
www.hawaiibnb.com

BBHS 92. This host offers a separate cottage with light cooking. Refrigerator, microwave, and coffee maker available. Host provides some breakfast materials. The cottage has a queen-size bed. There is a tub/shower combination and air conditioning is available. The main house fronts the ocean and the cottage is a distance behind the house. There is no ocean view from the cottage, although there is direct access to the beach which is about 100 feet away. Bus service is two blocks away. Telephone in unit shares host's line. Three-night minimum. Two people maximum. From $70.

NOTES: Credit cards accepted: A MasterCard; B Visa; C American Express; D Discover; E Diner's Club; F Other; 2 Personal checks accepted; 3 Lunch available; 4 Dinner available; 5 Open all year; 6 Pets welcome;

Idaho

ATHOL

The Ponderosa

2555 Brunner Road, 83801
(208) 683-2251; (888) 683-2251
FAX (208) 683-5112; e-mail: pondrosa@ior.com
www.onlinenow.com/theponderosa/

A breathtaking log home nestled on a 10-acre wooded estate with beautiful mountain views. Three rooms have queen-size log beds; one room has twin beds. Country atmosphere. Complimentary wine tasting in hosts' 2,000-bottle wine cellar. Each room has "His and Her" robes for the walk to the enclosed whirlpool tub. Area attractions include Silverwood Theme Park (May thru October), Farragut State Park, shopping malls, antique shops, and numerous outdoor activities.

Hosts: Jack and Betty Bonzey
Rooms: 4 (PB) $85-125
Full Breakfast
Credit Cards: A, B
Notes: 2, 5, 7, 9, 10, 11, 12, 13

BEAR LAKE

Bear Lake Bed & Breakfast

500 Loveland Lane, Fish Lake, 83287
(208) 945-2688

Guests are encouraged to make themselves at home in this spacious secluded log home. Sitting on the deck guests can absorb the peace and beauty of the turquoise blue lake below. The national forest is half a mile behind the bed and breakfast. Each guest room is decorated in a different style. Guests will find total hospitality here and yummy aromas coming

Bear Lake

from the kitchen each morning. Children over 13 are welcome.

Host: Esther Harrison
Rooms: 5 (1 PB; 3 SB) $79-89
Full Breakfast
Credit Cards: A, B
Notes: 2, 5, 7, 9, 10, 11, 12, 13

BOISE

Idaho Heritage Inn

109 West Idaho, 83702
(208) 342-8066
www.idheritageinn.com

This inn was a former governor's mansion and home to the late Sen. Frank Church. In

Idaho Heritage Inn

---

7 No smoking; 8 Children welcome; 9 Social drinking allowed; 10 Tennis nearby; 11 Swimming nearby; 12 Golf nearby; 13 Skiing nearby; 14 May be booked through a travel agent; 15 Handicapped accessible.

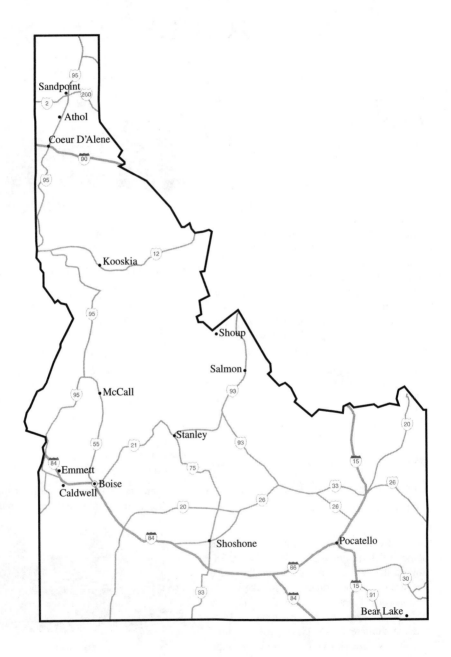

Idaho

the historic Warm Springs district, the inn enjoys the convenience of natural geothermal water. The inn is surrounded by other distinguished turn-of-the-century homes and is also within walking distance of downtown, beautiful parks, museums, and Boise's famous Greenbelt river walkway. All rooms have been comfortably and charmingly appointed with private baths, period furniture, and crisp linens.

Hosts: Phyllis and Tom Lupher
Rooms: 6 (PB) $60-105
Full Breakfast
Credit Cards: A, B, C, D
Notes: 2, 5, 7, 9, 10, 11, 12, 13, 14

CALDWELL

Harvey House Bed & Breakfast

13466 Highway 44, 83605
(208) 454-9874

Big Sky Country hospitality at its best! Circa 1910 home furnished is comfortable—with a capital C. Fresh flowers, complimentary local wines, as well as fruit and cheese plate upon arrival. Spacious rooms furnished in antiques. In addition, rooftop decking which overlooks mountains. Hot tub under the stars. Near golf courses, ski area, antiques. White-water rafting and vineyards.

Hosts: Bill and Angela Cyr
Rooms: 3 (1 PB; 2 SB) $85-110
Full Breakfast
Credit Cards: A, B, C
Notes: 2, 3, 4, 5, 7, 8, 9, 11, 12, 13

COEUR D'ALENE

Berry Patch Inn Bed & Breakfast

1150 North Four Winds Road, 83814
(208) 765-4994; FAX (208) 667-7336
www.bbhost.com/berrypatchinn

Nationally acclaimed by *National Geographic Traveler* as "One of the 20 Best Inns in the Rockies," and featured by Nordstrom stores. Private, elegant mountaintop chalet, backed to pristine forest. Only three and one-half miles to dining and shopping. Lakes, golf, and skiing. Heart-healthy delicious full breakfast with berries from the garden. Down comforters for sweet sleep. Tea and wine complimentary. Gift certificates. Adults only. Honeymoons. Air conditioned. Parking for boat trailers and RVs.

Host: Ann M. Caggiano
Rooms: 3 (PB) $125-150
Full Breakfast
Credit Cards: A, B
Notes: 2, 5, 7, 9, 10, 11, 12, 13

Gregory's McFarland House Bed & Breakfast

601 Foster Avenue, 83814
(208) 667-1232; (800) 335-1232
www.bbhost.com/mcfarlandhouse

Surrender to the elegance of this award-winning historical home, circa 1905. Breakfast is gourmet, the cookie jar always full. Guests will find an ideal blending of beauty, comfort, and clean surroundings. Jerry Hulse of the *Los Angeles Times* says, "Entering Gregory's McFarland House is like stepping back 100 years to an unhurried time when four-posters were in fashion, and lace curtains fluttered at the windows." Air conditioning. Small, intimate and/or church weddings available.

Hosts: Winifred, Carol, and Stephen
Rooms: 5 (PB) $85-150
Full Breakfast
Credit Cards: A, B, D
Notes: 2, 5, 7, 10, 11, 12, 13, 14

NOTES: Credit cards accepted: A MasterCard; B Visa; C American Express; D Discover; E Diner's Club; F Other; 2 Personal checks accepted; 3 Lunch available; 4 Dinner available; 5 Open all year; 6 Pets welcome; 7 No smoking; 8 Children welcome; 9 Social drinking allowed; 10 Tennis nearby; 11 Swimming nearby; 12 Golf nearby; 13 Skiing nearby; 14 May be booked through a travel agent; 15 Handicapped accessible.

Katie's Wild Rose Inn

Katie's Wild Rose Inn

East 5150 Coeur d' Alene Lake Drive, 83814
(208) 765-WISH (9474)
www.dmi.net/idaho-bandb/

Katie's welcomes all who enjoy a cozy, warm atmosphere. The house is decorated country cottage style, offering four guest rooms. The suite includes a view of the lake from its deck, large spa bathtub, and queen-size bed. Three and one-half miles east of Coeur d'Alene, it is on the Centennial Trail for hikers and bicyclists. Relax and enjoy the library, TV, or a game of pool. Weddings are a specialty.

Hosts: Lee and Joisse Knowles
Rooms: 4 (2 PB; 2 SB) $55-117 plus tax
Full Breakfast
Credit Cards: A, B, C
Notes: 2, 5, 7, 9, 10, 11, 12, 13, 14

Kingston 5 Ranch Bed & Breakfast

42297 Silver Valley Road, P.O. Box 130, Kingston, 83839
(208) 682-4862; (800) 254-1852
FAX (208) 682-9445; e-mail: k5ranch@nidlink.com
www.nidlink.com/~k5ranch

This picturesque New England style farmhouse offers a quiet, relaxing retreat or a wonderful romantic getaway. Room amenities include fireplaces, private baths with Jacuzzi tubs, and personal outdoor spas for each room. Lazy mornings begin with the wonderful tastes and smells of country home cooking. Enjoy such specialties as eggs dijon, strawberry crêpes and waffles, and our special huckleberry French toast topped with a fresh huckleberry sauce. Located south of I-90 on the way to Glacier National Park...one hour east of Spokane, Washington; two hours west of Missoula, Montana; 25 minutes east of Coeur d'Alene, Idaho.

Hosts: Walt and Pat Gentry
Rooms: 2 (PB) $99-125
Full Breakfast
Credit Cards: A, B
Notes: 2, 5, 7, 9, 10, 11, 12, 13, 14

EMMETT

Frozen Dog Digs

4325 Frozen Dog Road, 83617
(208) 365-7372

Frozen Dog Digs is as unique as its name. Nestled in the foothills and surrounded by fruit orchards, the Digs offers a panoramic view of the Emmett Valley. Sunsets viewed from the romantic gazebo are an artist's dream. Amenities the owner designed and built include a racquetball court, chip-and-putt golf greens, landscaped gardens with secluded spa, and sports bar. For the adventuresome, world-famous recreational areas and white-water rapids are within an echo and beckon.

Host: Jon Elsberry
Rooms: 4 (2 PB; 2 SB) $59-99
Full Breakfast
Credit Cards: A, B, D
Notes: 2, 5, 7, 9, 10, 11, 12, 13

KOOSKIA

Dream's Bed & Breakfast

Milepost 86 US Hwy. 12, P.O. Box 733, 83539
(208) 926-7540; e-mail: dreams@camasnet.com

On the Lewis-Clark Highway (US 12) which parallels the route of the famous explorers

---

NOTES: Credit cards accepted: A MasterCard; B Visa; C American Express; D Discover; E Diner's Club; F Other; 2 Personal checks accepted; 3 Lunch available; 4 Dinner available; 5 Open all year; 6 Pets welcome;

Captains Lewis and Clark. Panoramic river view—total privacy—country breakfast. Dream's 18 acres are part of the Wild and Scenic corridor along the middle fork of the Clearwater River. With the assistance of local guides, explore some of the endless wilderness mountains—or just relax in the hot tub under the sky.

Hosts: Gene and Helga Tennies
Rooms: 2 (PB) $65
Full Breakfast
Credit Cards: A, B
Notes: 2, 5, 7, 9, 11, 15

The Looking Glass Inn

HCR 75, Box 32, 83539
(208) 926-0855; (888) 926-0855
FAX (208) 926-7860; www.lookingglassinn.com

A small country inn on 10 private acres overlooking the wild and scenic middlefork of the Clearwater River near the Selway Bitterroot Wilderness. Recently renovated guest house has seven spacious rooms. Homey family room with full kitchen, hot tub under the stars, and casual outdoor areas for guests. On the Lewis and Clark Trail, the Looking Glass Inn is perfect for small groups. On scenic byway US Highway 12, 11 miles east of Kooskia.

Hosts: Ruth and Jim May
Rooms: 7 (PB) $65-75
Full Breakfast
Credit Cards: A, B
Notes: 2, 4, 5, 7, 9

Three Rivers Bed & Breakfast

Highway 12, HC 75, Box 61, 83539
(208) 926-4430

In the heart of the Idaho wilderness these bed and breakfast cabins sit high on the hill in privacy. A log cabin with grand open-beam A-frame. The view is spectacular. Each cabin has a fireplace, a Jacuzzi, and an antique brass bed in a mountain paradise.

Hosts: Mike and Marie Smith
Rooms: 15 (PB) $45-97.50

Full Breakfast
Credit Cards: A, B, C, D, E
Note: 2, 3, 4, 5, 6, 8, 9, 11

MCCALL

Northwest Passage Bed & Breakfast

201 Rio Vista, P.O. Box 4208, 83638
(208) 634-5349; (800) 597-6658
FAX (208) 634-4977

The Northwest Passage Bed and Breakfast is in the Rocky Mountain town of McCall on the shores of Payette Lake. The Northwest Passage was originally built to house the cast of the 1938 MGM movie *Northwest Passage*. The hostess serves a full breakfast, the menu changing daily. Complimentary wines and sherry in the afternoon also available. The McCall area is a full service four-season resort destination but still maintains its small-town ambiance and affordability. Winter activities include alpine and cross-country skiing, ice skating, and snowmobiling. Summer activities include all water sports, fishing, golf, and hiking.

Hosts: Steve and Barbara Schott
Rooms: 6 (PB) $65-85
Full Breakfast
Credit Cards: A, B, C
Notes: 2, 5, 9, 11, 12, 13, 14

POCATELLO

Z Bed & Breakfast

620 South 8th Avenue, 83201
(208) 235-1095; (888) 235-1095

This beautifully renovated 1915 home is just one-half block from Idaho State University campus. A warm welcome awaits guests. The guest rooms feature queen-size brass beds, colorful comforters, and private baths. The cozy fireplace, screened sunroom, shady patio, and spacious front porch all invite guests to relax. Guests will enjoy the friendly hospitality, fine food, and quiet, comfortable atmosphere of Z

---

7 No smoking; 8 Children welcome; 9 Social drinking allowed; 10 Tennis nearby; 11 Swimming nearby; 12 Golf nearby; 13 Skiing nearby; 14 May be booked through a travel agent; 15 Handicapped accessible.

Z Bed and Breakfast

Bed and Breakfast. "We are looking forward to meeting you!" Children 12 and older welcome.

Hosts: Greg and Naoni Zervas
Rooms: 3 (PB) $75
Full Breakfast
Credit Cards: A, B, C, D
Notes: 2, 5, 7, 12, 13

SALMON

Greyhouse Inn Bed & Breakfast

HC 61, Box 16, 83467
(800) 348-8097

Built in 1894, this fully restored Victorian farmhouse is near the Frank Church-River of No Return Wilderness. Surrounded by the Bitteroot, Beaverhead, and Salmon Mountains. Fishing, hiking, hot springs, white-water rafting, and skiing are just a few of the things to do while staying at the Greyhouse Inn. The rooms are furnished with antiques and wonderfully comfortable beds in every room. A full breakfast will be ready for guests each morning with homemade muffins and scones.

Hosts: Dave and Sharon Osgood
Rooms: 4 (2 PB: 2 SB) $65-80
Full Breakfast
Credit Cards: A, B
Notes: 2, 3, 4, 5, 7, 8, 9, 11, 12, 13

SANDPOINT

The Coit House Bed & Breakfast

502 North Fourth Avenue, 83804
(208) 265-4035

Walk through the doors and experience the magnificent beauty of a restored 1907 Victorian manor. All rooms feature private baths, air conditioning, and are uniquely decorated with antiques. Enjoy mountain hospitality with the full homemade breakfast. Conveniently one block from downtown shopping, dining, and City Beach. An easy drive to Schweitzer Mountain Ski area. Open year-round. AAA-approved, three diamonds.

Hosts: Julie and Seth Coit
Rooms: 4 (PB) $90
Full Breakfast
Credit Cards: A, B
Notes: 2, 5, 7, 10, 11, 12, 13, 14

SHOSHONE

Governor's Mansion Bed & Breakfast Inn

315 South Greenwood, P.O. Box 326, 83352
(208) 886-2858

First occupied in 1906, the Governor's Mansion was built by the Gooding family. It was owned by Thomas Gooding, older brother of Frank Gooding, once governor of Idaho. Come to a small-town atmosphere 55 miles from Sun Valley and near many Idaho attractions, including

Greyhouse Inn

NOTES: Credit cards accepted: A MasterCard; B Visa; C American Express; D Discover; E Diner's Club; F Other; 2 Personal checks accepted; 3 Lunch available; 4 Dinner available; 5 Open all year; 6 Pets welcome;

Shoshone Falls and the Craters of the Moon. Host offers a friendly, homelike atmosphere and breakfast to guest's order. Air conditioned.

Host: Edith Collins
Rooms: 7 (2 PB; 5 SB) $45-65
Full Breakfast
Credit Cards: None
Notes: 2, 5, 6, 8, 9

Idaho Rocky Mountain Ranch

SHOUP

Smith House Bed & Breakfast

49 Salmon River Road, 83469
(208) 394-2121; (800) 238-5915

The perfect place to relax and let the stress of city life slide by. Caters to small groups—birthdays, reunions, anniversaries, weddings. Guest house sleeps 10 and has separate living and dining rooms from the log home. Hiking, fishing, rafting, photography, and more both off and on the property. Delightful Continental plus breakfast served. One small house pet allowed for additional charge. Smoking outside only and children are always welcome. The outdoor hot tub and front lawn are natural gathering spots.

Hosts: Aubrey and Marsha Smith
Rooms: 5 (1 PB; 4 SB) $35-55
Continental Breakfast
Credit Cards: A, B
Notes: 2, 7, 8, 9, 11, 13, 14

STANLEY

Idaho Rocky Mountain Ranch

HC 64, Box 9934, 83278
(208) 774-3544; FAX (208) 774-3477
e-mail: idrocky@cyberhighway.net

Summer. One of Idaho's oldest and finest guest ranches, offering charming lodge and cabin accommodations. Delightful breakfast and dinner meals. Breathtaking Sawtooth Mountain vistas. Natural hot springs swimming pool, hiking, fishing, horseback riding, mountain biking, and wildlife viewing on ranch. Rafting, ghost towns, additional outdoor adventure opportunities in the area. One thousand acres in the Sawtooth National Recreation area. In the National Register of Historic Places. Open mid-June through mid-September.

Winter. Stay in a charming log cabin studio or three-bedroom home nestled in the Sawtooth Mountains on the Salmon River, and enjoy unlimited ski touring on the ranch's 1,000 acres and adjacent forest lands. Soothing natural hot springs swimming pool, spectacular mountain vistas and abundant wintering wildlife provide relaxation Idaho-style. Full kitchens and wood-burning stoves add a homey touch. Groomed ski trails available nearby; alpine skiing one and one-half hours away. Two-night minimum, three nights during holidays. Open Thanksgiving through March. Fifty miles north of Sun Valley in the Sawtooth National Recreation area. Brochure available. Weekly available. Notes and credit cards are seasonal.

Hosts: Bill Leavell and Sandra Bakwith
Rooms: 21 (PB) $145-240
Cabins: 2 (PB) $85-140
Credit Cards: A, B, D
Notes: 2, 3, 4, 7, 8, 9, 11, 13

---

7 No smoking; 8 Children welcome; 9 Social drinking allowed; 10 Tennis nearby; 11 Swimming nearby; 12 Golf nearby; 13 Skiing nearby; 14 May be booked through a travel agent; 15 Handicapped accessible.

Montana

Montana

Burggraf's Countrylane

BIGFORK

Burggraf's Countrylane Bed 'n' Breakfast on Swan Lake

Rainbow Drive, 59911
(406) 837-4608; (800) 525-3344
FAX (406) 837-2468
e-mail: burggraf@digisys.net

Custom-made log home on seven acres beside Swan Lake with panoramic view. Forty-five miles south of Glacier National Park. "All you can eat" breakfast. Complimentary wine, fruit and cheese upon arrival. All rooms with private bath and walk-in showers. King-, queen-, or single-size beds. Lawn croquet; free use of canoes, or paddle and fishing boat rental. Cabin by the lake. Honeymoon suite with Jacuzzi/whirlpool tubs. Children over 12 welcome.

Hosts: Natalie and R. J. Burggraf
Rooms: 5 (PB) $95-130
Full Breakfast
Credit Cards: A, B
Notes: 2, 3, 6, 7, 9, 10, 11, 12, 13, 14, 15

BILLINGS

The Josephine Bed & Breakfast

514 North 29th Street, 59101
(406) 248-5898; (800) 552-5898

The Josephine Bed and Breakfast offers an oasis within walking distance of downtown Billings. Relax in the Josephine's parlor, complete with cable TV and VCR, an upright piano and cozy seating, or sink into a comfy chair in our study. The Josephine offers five individually decorated guest rooms, each with telephone with data port, and its own private bath. Two are suites with sitting rooms. Enjoy complimentary snacks, health club guest passes, and delicious gourmet breakfasts.

Hosts: Doug and Becky Taylor
Rooms: 5 (PB) $68-98
Full Breakfast
Credit Cards: A, B, C, D
Notes: 2, 5, 7, 9, 10, 11, 12, 13, 14

The Josephine

NOTES: Credit cards accepted: A MasterCard; B Visa; C American Express; D Discover; E Diner's Club; F Other; 2 Personal checks accepted; 3 Lunch available; 4 Dinner available; 5 Open all year; 6 Pets welcome; 7 No smoking; 8 Children welcome; 9 Social drinking allowed; 10 Tennis nearby; 11 Swimming nearby; 12 Golf nearby; 13 Skiing nearby; 14 May be booked through a travel agent; 15 Handicapped accessible.

BOZEMAN

Fox Hollow Bed & Breakfast at Baxter Creek

545 Mary Road, 59718
(406) 582-8440; (800) 431-5010
www.bozeman-mt.com

A country setting in the heart of the Gallatin River Valley. Enjoy panoramic views of majestic mountain ranges from the wraparound deck or hot tub. This 1993 country-style home offers spacious guest rooms with plush queen-size beds and private baths. Wake to full gourmet breakfasts every morning. Montana is a traveler's paradise. Choose from world-famous fly-fishing, hiking, mountain biking, or alpine and cross-country skiing. Yellowstone National Park is only 90 minutes away.

Hosts: Michael and Nancy Dawson
Rooms: 5 (PB) $79-120
Full Breakfast
Credit Cards: A, B, C, D
Notes: 2, 5, 7, 9, 10, 11, 12, 13, 14

The Lehrkind Mansion Bed & Breakfast

719 North Wallace Avenue, 59715
(406) 585-6932; (800) 992-6932
e-mail: lehrkindmansion@imt.net
www.bozemanbedandbreakfast.com

As the center of Bozeman's historic brewery district, this 1897 brewer's mansion offers one of Montana's finest examples of Victorian Queen Anne architecture. This enchanting home is furnished throughout with period antiques and an abundance of live plants. A full gourmet breakfast is served in the elegant dining room. A large hot tub soaks away aches of an active day and comfortable queen-size beds with down comforters provide the perfect rest in this peaceful setting. Only one and one-half hour's drive from Yellowstone National Park, the Lehrkind serves as an excellent base for exploring Montana's Big Sky Country.

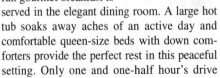

Hosts: Jon Gerster and Christopher Nixon
Rooms: 5 (3 PB; 2 SB) $78-158
Full Breakfast
Credit Cards: A, B, C
Notes: 2, 5, 7, 8, 9, 10, 11, 12, 13, 14

Torch & Toes

Torch & Toes Bed & Breakfast

309 South Third Avenue, 59715
(406) 586-7285; (800) 446-2138

Set back from the street, it looks much as it did when it was built in 1906. A tall, trim brick-and-frame house in the Colonial Revival style. Just enough lace curtains and turn-of-the-century furniture to remind guests that this is a house with a past. Smells of blueberry muffins, coddled eggs, and fresh fruit will entice guests to breakfast in the oak-paneled dining room with the wood-burning fireplace.

Hosts: Ronald and Judy Hess
Rooms: 4 (PB) $70-100
Full Breakfast
Credit Cards: A, B, C
Notes: 2, 5, 7, 8, 9, 10, 11, 12, 13, 14

NOTES: Credit cards accepted: A MasterCard; B Visa; C American Express; D Discover; E Diner's Club; F Other; 2 Personal checks accepted; 3 Lunch available; 4 Dinner available; 5 Open all year; 6 Pets welcome;

Voss Inn Bed & Breakfast

319 South Wilson, 59715
(406) 587-0982

Magnificently restored Victorian inn in the historic district with elegant guest rooms and private baths. A delightful gourmet breakfast is served in the privacy of guests' rooms or family style in guest parlor. Bozeman is 90 miles north of Yellowstone Park, near skiing, fishing, hiking, and snowmobiling. Full afternoon tea. Airport transportation available. Children over five welcome.

Hosts: Bruce and Frankee Muller
Rooms: 6 (PB) $95-110
Full Breakfast
Credit Cards: A, B, C
Notes: 2, 5, 7, 9, 10, 11, 12, 13, 14

Voss Inn

COLUMBIA FALLS

Bad Rock Country Bed & Breakfast

480 Bad Rock Drive, 59912
(888) 892-2829

For the visitor to Glacier National Park. On 30 rolling country acres. Spectacular views of nearby Rocky Mountains. Three rooms in the house; Old West antiques; four rooms in two new square-hewn log buildings with handmade lodgepole pine furniture. Selected one of 1995's 12 top inns in U.S. and Mexico by *Country Inns* magazine. Inspected and approved by AAA and Mobil, and the Montana Bed and Breakfast Association.

Hosts: Jon and Susie Alper
Rooms: 7 (PB) $120-169
Full Breakfast
Credit Cards: A, B, C, D, E
Notes: 2, 5, 7, 9, 12, 13, 14

EMIGRANT

Paradise Gateway Bed & Breakfast & Guest Log Cabin

P.O. Box 84, 59027
(403) 333-4063; (800) 541-4113
e-mail: paradise@gomontana.com

Paradise Gateway Bed and Breakfast, nestled in the majestic Absaroka Mountains, is just minutes away from scenic Yellowstone National Park. The bed and breakfast offers quiet, comfortable guest rooms. Each room has a private bath and a large, relaxing parlor in between for reading, music, and conversation. The surrounding area boasts many activities including hiking, horseback riding, fishing, rafting, sightseeing, and much more. Also available: two-bedroom log cabin on 26 acres next to the Yellowstone River. Very private with mountain views. Homemade Continental breakfast served at the cabin. The bed and breakfast receives a full breakfast. Inquire about accommodations for pets. Children welcome in cabin only.

Hosts: Pete and Carol Reed
Rooms: 4 (PB) $85-110
Cabin: $150
Full and Continental Breakfast
Credit Cards: A, B
Notes: 2, 5, 7, 9, 10, 11, 12, 13, 14, 15

Yellowstone Riverview Lodge

186 East River Road, 59027
(406) 848-2156; (888) 848-2550
e-mail: riverview@imt.net
www.wtp.net/go/riverview

The Yellowstone Riverview Lodge is a beautiful hand-hewn log home overlooking the

---

7 No smoking; 8 Children welcome; 9 Social drinking allowed; 10 Tennis nearby; 11 Swimming nearby; 12 Golf nearby; 13 Skiing nearby; 14 May be booked through a travel agent; 15 Handicapped accessible.

Yellowstone River, minutes from Yellowstone National Park. Nestled between the Absaroka and Gallatin Mountains in the spectacular Paradise Valley, it offers breathtaking views, blue-ribbon fly-fishing and endless outdoor activities. The home, which sits on 20 wild acres, provides guests with an entire floor to themselves: four bedrooms, private entrance, lounge, kitchenette/dining area, and patio. Open year-round.

Hosts: Steve Koester and Bill Wagner
Rooms: 4 (2 PB; 2 SB) $70-110
Full Breakfast
Credit Cards: A, B
Notes: 2, 3, 4, 5, 6, 7, 8, 9, 11, 13

ESSEX

Paola Creek Bed & Breakfast at Glacier National Park

HC 36, Box 4C, 59916
(406) 888-5061; (888) 311-5061
FAX (406) 888-5063; e-mail: paola@in-tch.com
www.wtp.net/go/paola

The rustic luxury of Glacier National Park's premier bed and breakfast accommodation is the ultimate base camp for the active traveler. Paola Creek is a handcrafted larch-log home. The Great Room is dominated by a river-rock fireplace while the reading and dining rooms offer unequaled views of Glacier National Park's St. Nicholas. Centrally located at the southern edge of Glacier National Park for quick access to hiking, rafting, and relaxing. Inquire about accommodations for children. Limited handicapped accessible.

Hosts: Kelly and Les Hostetler
Rooms: 4 (PB) $90-120
Full Breakfast
Credit Cards: A, B
Notes: 2, 3, 4, 5, 7, 9, 12, 13, 14

GLENDIVE

The Hostetler House Bed & Breakfast

113 North Douglas Street, 59330
(377) 365-4505; (800) 965-8456
FAX (377) 365-8456

Two blocks from downtown shopping and restaurants, the Hostetler House is a charming 1912 historic Frank Lloyd Wright Prairie School home with two comfortable guest rooms, sitting room filled with books, enclosed sun porch, gazebo, and hot tub. Casual country decor mixes with handmade and heirloom furnishings and many special touches. Full gourmet breakfast is served on Grandma's china. On I-94 and the Yellowstone River, close to parks, antique shops, churches, and Makoshika State Park.

Hosts: Craig and Dea Hostetler
Rooms: 2 (SB) $50
Full Breakfast
Credit Cards: A, B, D
Notes: 2, 5, 7, 9, 10, 11, 12, 13, 14

The Hostetler House

GREAT FALLS

The Old Oak Inn

709 Fourth Avenue North, 59401
(406) 727-5782; (888) 727-5782

Home-style comfort is what guests will find when they visit the Old Oak Inn bed and

---

NOTES: Credit cards accepted: A MasterCard; B Visa; C American Express; D Discover; E Diner's Club; F Other; 2 Personal checks accepted; 3 Lunch available; 4 Dinner available; 5 Open all year; 6 Pets welcome;

breakfast. This restored Victorian mansion built in 1908 has two rooms with shared bath and one room and two suites with private bath. Enjoy the beautiful Montana sky from the large front porch where smoking is permitted. While here guests are only five blocks from the C.M. Russel Museum and the Rivers Edge Trail and within walking distance of downtown and fine dining.

Host: Judy Vance
Rooms: 5 (3 PB; 2 SB) $60-95
Full Breakfast
Credit Cards: A, B, C, D
Notes: 2, 5, 6, 7, 8, 9, 11, 12, 13

HAMILTON

Deer Crossing Bed & Breakfast

396 Hayes Creek Road, 59840
(406) 363-2232; (800) 763-2232
e-mail: deercros@bitterroot.net
www.wtp.net/go/deercrossing

Old West charm and hospitality at its best. Deer Crossing is on 25 acres of pines and pasture overlooking the beautiful Bitterroot Valley. After watching the sun rise over the Sapphire Mountains, enjoy a hearty ranch breakfast and plan the day. Visit historic sites, explore on horseback, hike, or fly-fish in one of the numerous sparkling creeks. Inspected and approved by Montana Bed and Breakfast Association and Mobil Travel Guide. "Kick off your boots, hang your hat, and make yourself at home!" Guests' horses are welcome.

Deer Crossing

Host: Mary Lynch
Rooms: 5 (4 PB; 1 SB) $80-115
Full Breakfast
Credit Cards: A, B, C
Notes: 2, 5, 7, 8, 9, 10, 11, 12, 13, 14, 15

HARDIN

Kendrick House Inn

Kendrick House Inn Bed & Breakfast

206 North Custer Avenue, 59034
(406) 665-3035

The Kendrick House Inn was built in 1914 as a boarding house. In 1988 the boarding house was restored as a bed and breakfast and now is in the historic register. The inn's five guest rooms feature comfy antique beds, dressers, and a sink, true to the boarding houses of yesteryear. Shared bathrooms are unique with antique tubs, showers, and pull-chain toilets. The common areas include two glassed-in verandas, a library, and a parlor. A full Montana breakfast is served in the formal dining room. Within 15 miles of the Little Bighorn Battlefield National Monument. Inquire about accommodations for pets.

Hosts: Steve and Marcie Smith
Rooms: 6 (1 PB; 5 SB) $65-85
Full Breakfast
Credit Cards: A, B, F
Notes: 2, 7, 9, 10, 11, 12, 14

---

7 No smoking; 8 Children welcome; 9 Social drinking allowed; 10 Tennis nearby; 11 Swimming nearby; 12 Golf nearby; 13 Skiing nearby; 14 May be booked through a travel agent; 15 Handicapped accessible.

HELENA

The Sanders— Helena's Bed & Breakfast

328 North Ewing, 59601
(406) 442-3309

This 1875 Victorian mansion offers elegant accommodations steeped in Helena's historic past. Appointed with original furnishings, each spacious guest room has a private bath, TV, and telephone and data port. Brass beds, high ceilings, and ornately framed paintings radiate the quiet charm of days past. In the heart of Helena and listed in the national register, the Sanders combines friendly hospitality with grand turn-of-the-century living.

Hosts: Rock Ringling and Bobbi Uecker
Rooms: 7 (PB) $85-105
Full Breakfast
Credit Cards: A, B, C, D, E
Notes: 2, 5, 7, 8, 9, 10, 11, 12, 13

The Sanders

HOBSON

Meadow Brook Bed & Breakfast Inn

Box 271, 59452
(800) 318-6423

Waiting for guests to relax and enjoy is this restored 1908 original Montana ranch house. It is made of concrete block, finished to look like stone. People are impressed by its three-story grandeur. The hosts serve a full breakfast of Belgian waffles and local chokecherry syrup. The house has been furnished with antiques and family memorabilia. The hosts have spent years restoring it back to almost its original so guests can enjoy a bit of Montana history. A registered historical site.

Rooms: 5 (5 S2B) $55
Full Breakfast
Credit Cards: None
Notes: 2, 5, 6, 7, 8, 9, 11, 15

HUSON

The Schoolhouse & the Teacherage

18815 Remount Road, 59846
(406) 626-5879

The Schoolhouse and the Teacherage is 27 miles northwest of Missoula. The bed and breakfast, built by the Anaconda Company in early 1900 for the loggers' children, has four guest rooms with featherbeds, down comforters, and handmade quilts plus a separate guest house. Each room has a different theme: Amish, Swedish, Dutch, and Montana. Reasonable rates, full breakfast. Owners are craftsmen, designers, and Hanneke is a published author.

Hosts: Les and Hanneke Ippisch
Rooms: 5 (5 SB) $70
Full Breakfast
Credit Cards: None
Notes: 2, 5, 7, 8, 9, 12, 13, 15

KALISPELL

Bonnie's Bed & Breakfast

265 Lake Blaine Road, 59901
(406) 755-3776; (800) 755-3778
www.wtp.net/go/montana/sites/bonnie.html

An English Tudor with Montana hospitality. Minutes to Glacier Park and Flathead Lake.

NOTES: Credit cards accepted: A MasterCard; B Visa; C American Express; D Discover; E Diner's Club; F Other; 2 Personal checks accepted; 3 Lunch available; 4 Dinner available; 5 Open all year; 6 Pets welcome;

Hiking, white-water rafting, antiquing, fine dining, and skiing nearby. Member of the Montana Bed and Breakfast Association.

Hosts: Leonard and Bonnie Boles
Rooms: 3 (2 PB; 2 SB) $85-120
Full Breakfast
Credit Cards: A, B
Notes: 2, 5, 7, 8, 9, 12, 13, 14

LINCOLN

Lumberjack Inn Bed & Breakfast

Conifer Lane, 59639
(406) 362-4001; (406) 362-4815
FAX (406) 362-4827

Guest rooms feature spectacular mountain views and log beds. Country furnishings and antiques make each room special and unique. Relax with a book from the guest library and let the world pass you by at the Lumberjack Inn Bed and Breakfast.

Hosts: Brent and Carla Anderson
Rooms: 3 (1 PB; 2 SB) $75-95
Full Breakfast
Credit Cards: A, B
Notes: 2, 5, 7, 8, 9, 14

LIVINGSTON

The River Inn on the Yellowstone

4950 Highway 89 South, 59047
(406) 222-2429; FAX (406) 222-2625
e-mail: riverinn@wtp.net
www.wtp.net/go/riverinn

Bed and breakfast, rustic cabin, and sheepherder's wagon. A beautifully restored historic farmhouse, 30 feet from the Yellowstone River. Secluded old cottonwoods on five acres with plenty of riverfront to meander or fish. Three fine bedrooms offer private baths. Spectacular river and mountain views. Guided canoe, hiking, and biking trips. Exceptional dining.

The River Inn on the Yellowstone

Twenty-six miles east of Bozeman and just minutes from Livingston, a lively Old West town. Children nine and older are welcome. Cats on premises.

Hosts: DeeDee VanZyl and Ursula Neese
Rooms: 3 (PB) $70-90
Full Breakfast
Credit Cards: A, B
Notes: 2, 3, 4, 7, 9, 11, 12, 13, 14

MISSOULA

Foxglove Cottage Bed & Breakfast

2331 Gilbert Avenue, 59802
(406) 543-2927

Foxglove Cottage is a cozy 100-year-old house surrounded by a lovely garden just seven minutes from downtown Missoula, the University of Montana, and the Rattlesnake Wilderness National Recreation Area. Swimming pool, sun room, TVs, VCRs, 500-tape video library, croquet, and horseshoes available.

Hosts: John Keegan and Anthony Cesare
Rooms: 3 (1 PB; 2 SB) $65-95
Continental Breakfast
Credit Cards: None
Notes: 2, 7, 9, 10, 11, 12, 13

---

7 No smoking; 8 Children welcome; 9 Social drinking allowed; 10 Tennis nearby; 11 Swimming nearby; 12 Golf nearby; 13 Skiing nearby; 14 May be booked through a travel agent; 15 Handicapped accessible.

RED LODGE

Inn on the Beartooth, Inc.

6648 Highway 212 South, P.O. Box 1515, 59068
(406) 446-3555 (phone/FAX); (888) 222-7686

This western retreat log bed and breakfast offers an awesome view of the Beartooth Mountains. Each guest room is tastefully furnished in lodgepole pine furniture and cozy comforters. The great room is very inviting with a wood-burning stone fireplace to warm guests when the nights are chilly or after a long day skiing. Jan serves a wonderful full gourmet breakfast that prepares guests for a delightful trip over the Beartooth Mountains to Yellowstone National Park or biking, fishing, horseback riding, or hiking in the mountains. The inn has a smoke-free environment, cable TV, and all guest rooms have private baths. Reservations requested. Inquire about accommodations for children.

Hosts: Jan and Bob Goehringer
Rooms: 6 (PB) $60-95
Full Breakfast
Credit Cards: A, B, C, D
Notes: 2, 5, 7, 9, 10, 11, 12, 13, 14

Willows Inn

224 South Platt Avenue, P.O. Box 886, 59068
(406) 446-3913

Spectacular mountain scenery surrounds this delightful turn-of-the-century inn. Flanked by giant evergreens and colorful flower beds, it is reminiscent of a bygone era, complete with white picket fence, gingerbread trim, and a porch swing. Guest rooms have brass-and-iron and four-poster beds. Delicious home-baked pastries and afternoon refreshments are served. Close to hiking, fishing, and Yellowstone Park. Video movies, books, games, and a large sun deck are available. Two storybook cottages are ideal for families.

Hosts: Kerry, Carolyn, and Elven Boggio
Rooms: 5 (3 PB: 2 SB) $50-75
Cottages: 2; $80-110

Full Breakfast
Credit Cards: A, B, D
Notes: 2, 5, 7, 8, 9, 10, 11, 12, 13, 14

SEELEY LAKE

The Emily A. Bed & Breakfast

P.O. Box 350, 59868
(406) 677-3474 (phone/FAX)
e-mail: SLK3340@montana.com
www.theemilya.com

Grand 11,000-square-foot log home overlooking the headwaters of the Clearwater River. Private lake and fishing dam. Fourth-generation Montana family will share stories and adventures. Hiking, fishing, wildlife viewing on the 160 acres. Family antiques and a remarkable western art collection.

Hosts: Marilyn and Keith Peterson
Rooms: 5 (2 PB: 3 SB) $95-150
Full Breakfast
Credit Cards: A, B
Notes: 2, 5, 7, 8, 9, 10, 11, 12, 13, 14

STEVENSVILLE

Big Creek Pines Bed & Breakfast

2986 Highway 93 North, 59870
(406) 642-6475; (888) 300-6475
e-mail: bcp1@cybernet1.com
www.wtp.net/go/bigcreek

Guests love how treasured family mementos have been used in decorating this warm, friendly bed and breakfast. Fresh flowers and a candlelight full breakfast await you. Spacious rooms with private baths and large windows with window seats for guests to enjoy the quiet, peaceful setting with creek, meadow, and mountain views. Just 27 miles south of Missoula on the Lewis and Clark Trail with convenient access to any of Montana's outdoor activities and historical sites.

Hosts: Rosemary and Joe Beason
Rooms: 4 (PB) $80
Full Breakfast

NOTES: Credit cards accepted: A MasterCard; B Visa; C American Express; D Discover; E Diner's Club; F Other; 2 Personal checks accepted; 3 Lunch available; 4 Dinner available; 5 Open all year; 6 Pets welcome;

Credit Cards: A, B
Notes: 2, 5, 7, 9, 12, 14

THREE FORKS

Sacajawea Hotel

Box 648, 59752
(406) 285-6515; (800) 821-7326

Since William Howard Taft was president, guests have enjoyed the gracious hospitality of the Sacajawea Hotel. Come savor the casual elegance of this landmark which is listed in the National Register of Historic Places. Graced by rocking chairs, a large front porch welcomes guests to a spacious lobby and newly renovated nostalgic guest rooms. One hundred miles from Yellowstone, the hotel is a perfect spot from which to explore the Gallatin Valley. The Missouri headwaters are filled with Lewis and Clark history and are less than five miles from the hotel.

Host: Scott Pirraglio
Rooms: 32 (PB) $60-120
Credit Cards: A, B, C, D
Notes: 4, 5, 7, 8, 9, 12, 14, 15

VIRGINIA CITY

Bennett House Country Inn

115 East Idaho, P.O. Box 96, 59755
(877) 843-5220; e-mail: stay@bennetthouseinn.com
www.bennetthouseinn.com

The inn, an 1879 Queen Anne Victorian home, is in the wild west town of Virginia City, just 80 miles northwest of Yellowstone National Park. Virginia City and nearby Nevada City are well-preserved mining towns that sprang up with the discovery of gold in 1863. In addition to the haunting beauty of the century-plus old buildings, guests can enjoy melodrama and vaudeville performances by the Virginia City Players, take a ride on the narrow gauge train and so much more.

Hosts: Karla Boyd and Nancy Allen
Rooms: 6 (6 SB) $55-75
Full Breakfast
Credit Cards: A, B, C
Notes: 2, 5, 7, 12, 13, 14

WEST GLACIER

Mountain Timbers Wilderness Lodge Bed & Breakfast

P.O. Box 127, 59936
(406) 387-5830; (800) 841-3835
FAX (406) 387-5835; e-mail: mtntmbrs@digisys.net

Tucked in the heart of the Rocky Mountains of northwest Montana stands Mountain Timbers—a magnificent hand-hewn hideaway which provides wilderness, wildlife, and spectacular vistas into Glacier National Park. Inside the spacious lodge guests will find massive rock and stone fireplaces, comfortable sitting areas, a fully stocked library, and outstanding views from almost every room. Nearby is whitewater rafting, fishing, horseback riding, hiking, big game hunting, and cross-country and downhill skiing. Enjoy the spectacular views into Glacier National Park while soaking in the hot tub.

Hosts: David and Betty Rudisill
Rooms: 6 (4 PB; 2 SB) $75-135
Full Breakfast
Credit Cards: A, B, C
Notes: 2, 5, 7, 8, 9, 11, 12, 13, 14

WHITEFISH

Gasthaus Wendlingen

700 Monegan Road, 59937
(406) 862-4886 (phone/FAX); (800) 811-8002
www.whitefishmt.com

A place for all seasons and sports! Barbara and Bill welcome guests with German-western

---

7 No smoking; 8 Children welcome; 9 Social drinking allowed; 10 Tennis nearby; 11 Swimming nearby; 12 Golf nearby; 13 Skiing nearby; 14 May be booked through a travel agent; 15 Handicapped accessible.

hospitality. Enjoy a full breakfast with homemade specialties. The off-highway location, two miles from Whitefish center, has a real Montana setting on eight acres. Spectacular views of Big Mountain and Blacktail ski areas to the gateway of Glacier National Park. The spacious bedrooms with private baths view Haskell Creek and Whitefish River. Sit by the fire or relax on the porch or patio. Smoking permitted outside only.

Hosts: Barbara and Bill Klein
Rooms: 3 (2 PB; 1 SB) $70-125
Full Breakfast
Credit Cards: A, B
Notes: 2, 5, 7, 8, 9, 10, 11, 12, 13, 14

Good Medicine Lodge

537 Wisconsin Avenue, 59937
(800) 860-5488; FAX (406) 862-5489
www.wtp.net/go/goodrx

This classic Montana getaway hewn from solid cedar timbers has nine guest rooms with private baths, direct-dial telephones, balconies, mountain views, custom-made lodgepole beds, hearty breakfasts, laundry, and ski room. Only minutes from guests' favorite outdoor activity, shopping, dining, the airport, and Amtrak. Relax in front of a fireplace or unwind in the outdoor spa. AAA-rated three diamonds. Handicapped accessible.

Hosts: Christopher and Susan Ridder
Rooms: 9 (PB) $85-125
Full Breakfast
Credit Cards: A, B, C, D
Notes: 2, 5, 7, 8, 9, 10, 11, 12, 13, 14, 15

Kandahar Lodge

3824 Big Mountain Road, 59937
(406) 862-6098; (877) 862-1505
FAX (406) 862-6095; e-mail: kandahar@digisys.net
www.kanduharlodge.com

Kandahar Lodge blends the virtues of an intimate country inn with the indulgences of a grand European hotel. The personalized service and amenities plus the location in the village area of the Big Mountain ski and summer resort make the Kandahar a popular destination.

Hosts: Buck and Mary Pat Love
Rooms: 48 (PB) $125-380
Credit Cards: A, B, C, D
Notes: 2, 4, 7, 8, 9, 10, 12, 13, 14

WHITE SULPHUR SPRINGS

Sky Lodge Bed & Breakfast

4260 Highway 12 East, P.O. Box 428, 59645
(406) 547-3999; (800) 965-4305

Sky Lodge is a spacious log lodge that provides affordable luxury and homelike accommodations in large, comfortable guest rooms with private baths. There are large common areas—a game room with pool table and Ping-Pong, two living rooms for reading, TV and VCR movies, and a deck with awesome views of the surrounding mountains. In the beautiful Smith River valley of central Montana. Outdoor recreation: hiking, bicycling, skiing, fishing, and hunting. Deluxe hot tub outdoors with great view of mountains.

Hosts: Marc and Debbie Steinberg
Rooms: 4 (PB) $65-78
Full Breakfast
Credit Cards: A, B
Notes: 4, 5, 7, 8, 9, 11, 13

NOTES: Credit cards accepted: A MasterCard; B Visa; C American Express; D Discover; E Diner's Club; F Other; 2 Personal checks accepted; 3 Lunch available; 4 Dinner available; 5 Open all year; 6 Pets welcome;

Nevada

CARSON CITY (WASHOE VALLEY)

Deer Run Ranch Bed & Breakfast

5440 Eastlake Boulevard, 89704
(775) 882-3643

Western ambiance in a unique timber-framed ranch house on this family-owned and -operated alfalfa ranch. Private guest wing with two comfortable rooms, private baths, a sitting room and library, all with its own private entry. Twenty minutes south of Reno, 10 minutes north of Carson City, and a half-hour to Lake Tahoe or Virginia City. The ranch is adjacent to Washoe Lake State Park and affords lots of privacy and wildlife viewing.

Hosts: David and Muffy Vhay
Rooms: 2 (PB) $80-105
Full Breakfast
Credit Cards: A, B, C, D
Notes: 2, 5, 7, 9, 11, 12, 13

EAST ELY

Steptoe Valley Inn

P.O. Box 151110, 220 East 11th Street, 89315-1110
(775) 289-8687 (June-September)
(702) 435-2860 (October-May)
www.nevadaweb.com/steptoe

Elegantly reconstructed in 1990 from the Ely City Grocery of 1907, this inn is one-half block from the Nevada Northern Railway Museum with its weekend train excursions, and 70 miles from the Great Basin National Park. Its individually decorated guest rooms are on the sec-

Steptoe Valley Inn

ond floor and have private balconies with views of the mountains and valley or the gazebo and rose garden. Guests have use of the veranda, Victorian living/dining room, and library. Open June through September.

Hosts: Jane and Norman Lindley
Rooms: 5 (PB) $84-90
Full Breakfast
Credit Cards: A, B, C
Notes: 2, 7, 10, 12, 14

GENOA

The Genoa House Inn Bed & Breakfast

180 Nixon Street, P.O. Box 141, 89411
(702) 782-7075

The Genoa House Inn is an authentic Victorian home listed in the National Register of Historic Places. The house has been restored to the charm and tranquility of an earlier time. Take a romantic step into the past, and enjoy the gracious accommodations accented by antiques and collectibles. Wine in the afternoon; a coffee

---

7 No smoking; 8 Children welcome; 9 Social drinking allowed; 10 Tennis nearby; 11 Swimming nearby; 12 Golf nearby; 13 Skiing nearby; 14 May be booked through a travel agent; 15 Handicapped accessible.

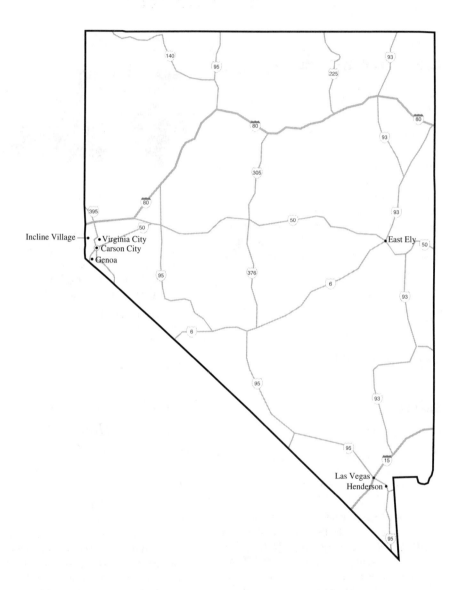

Nevada

Genoa House Inn

tray delivered to room, followed by a full breakfast. A discount for Walley's Hot Springs spa nearby. Inquire about accommodations for pets. Inquire about accommodations for children. Smoking is not permitted indoors.

Hosts: Bob and Linda Sanfilippo
Rooms: 3 (PB) $110-175
Full Breakfast
Credit Cards: A, B, D
Notes: 2, 5, 7, 9, 10, 11, 12, 13, 14

HENDERSON

Mi Casa Su Casa/Old Pueblo Homestays Bed & Breakfast Reservation Service

P.O. Box 950, Tempe, AZ 85280-0950
(602) 990-0682; (800) 456-0682
FAX (602) 990-3390
e-mail: micasa@primenet.com
www.azres.com

7321. Couple welcomes guests to their two-story 1996 Spanish-style house in a quiet, residential, gated community. Easy driving distance to Las Vegas, Boulder Dam, and Lake Mead. Two second-floor guest rooms share a full hall bath. Only one party accepted at a time. Guests welcome in the living room with fireplace, cable TV and VCR. Bicycles to loan. Full breakfast. No smoking. No children. No pets. $65.

INCLINE VILLAGE

Haus Bavaria

P.O. Box 9079, 89452
(775) 831-6122; (800) 731-6222
FAX (775) 831-1238

Haus Bavaria is a European-style guest house, built in 1980. Each of the five upstairs guest rooms opens onto a balcony, offering a view of the surrounding mountains, while the living room, with its rustic wood paneling and collection of German bric-a-brac, retains an alpine charm. Breakfast is served in the cozy dining room downstairs and includes freshly baked goods, seasonal fruits and juices, freshly ground coffee, and a selection of teas. Children over 12 welcome.

Host: Bick Hewitt
Rooms: 5 (PB) $85-225
Full Breakfast
Credit Cards: A, B, C, D
Notes: 2, 5, 7, 9, 10, 11, 12, 13, 14

LAS VEGAS

Mi Casa Su Casa/Old Pueblo Homestays Bed & Breakfast Reservation Service

P.O. Box 950, Tempe, AZ 85280-0950
(602) 990-0682; (800) 456-0682
FAX (602) 990-3390
e-mail: micasa@primenet.com
www.azres.com

7332. Near the hub of Las Vegas activity, this cottage-style home is in a quiet area with beautiful, mature landscaping. The house interior has been recreated to reflect Las Vegas in the 50's. Three neat and homey guest rooms share a bath with tub and shower in the hall. Guests are welcome to use the living room with cable TV and VCR or enclosed back yard. Bicycles to loan. Airport and convention site pick-up possible. Computer/fax service and picnic baskets available for reasonable charge. Smoking permitted

---

NOTES: Credit cards accepted: A MasterCard; B Visa; C American Express; D Discover; E Diner's Club; F Other; 2 Personal checks accepted; 3 Lunch available; 4 Dinner available; 5 Open all year; 6 Pets welcome; 7 No smoking; 8 Children welcome; 9 Social drinking allowed; 10 Tennis nearby; 11 Swimming nearby; 12 Golf nearby; 13 Skiing nearby; 14 May be booked through a travel agent; 15 Handicapped accessible.

outside. No pets. Children six and older welcome. Full breakfast. Weekly rates. $60.

7331. This large 1950 home with a southwestern-style exterior is in an established quiet neighborhood within two miles of the Strip. Antiques, blended with other lovely furnishings, give this bed and breakfast a romantic touch. Two guest rooms each with private hall bath, TV, and telephone. Bicycles are also on hand for guests to use. Heated spa. Prefer two-night minimum stay on weekends. Full breakfast. Smoking permitted outside only. No pets. Airport pickup available. Inquire about accommodations for children. $60.

VIRGINIA CITY

Gold Hill Hotel

Highway 342, P.O. Box 710, 89440
(775) 847-0111; FAX (775) 847-0604

The Gold Hill Hotel is Nevada's oldest hotel, circa 1859. This country inn is a wonderful combination of luxury and rustic charm, placed in a setting that is fascinating for its history, beauty, and personalities. Guests enjoy a range

Gold Hill Hotel

of accommodations: all rooms have private baths and four very spacious rooms have fireplaces and balconies. All rooms are decorated with period antiques. Special luxury honeymoon house available. Fabulous dinners accented with a choice of over 160 wines create a memorable escape. The cozy bar with its stone and dark wood decor and forge-like fireplace is reminiscent of Old World country inns.

Hosts: Carol and Bill Fain
Rooms: 14 (PB) $45-200
Continental Breakfast
Credit Cards: A, B
Notes: 2, 4, 5, 8, 9, 10, 11, 12, 13, 14, 15

NOTES: Credit cards accepted: A MasterCard; B Visa; C American Express; D Discover; E Diner's Club; F Other; 2 Personal checks accepted; 3 Lunch available; 4 Dinner available; 5 Open all year; 6 Pets welcome;

New Mexico

ALBUQUERQUE

Brittania and W.E. Mauger Estate Bed & Breakfast

701 Roma Avenue Northwest, 87102
(505) 242-8755; (800) 719-9189
FAX (505) 842-8835
www.thuntek.net/tc_arts/mauger

This wonderful 1897 Queen Anne Victorian in the National Register of Historic Places has eight unique rooms with private baths, robes, TV/VCR, and down comforters. The property features a wonderful front porch for enjoying New Mexico summer evenings. Within walking distance of Old Town, downtown, convention center, and many restaurants. Elegant and gracious, this is the place to stay for leisure or business travel. Earn InnPoints for every stay.

Hosts: Mark Brown and Keith Lewis
Rooms: 8 (PB) $89-179
Full Breakfast
Credit Cards: A, B, C, D, E
Notes: 2, 5, 6, 7, 8

Mi Casa Su Casa/Old Pueblo Homestays Bed & Breakfast Reservation Service

P.O. Box 950, Tempe, AZ 85280-0950
(602) 990-0682; (800) 456-0682
FAX (602) 990-3290
e-mail: micasa@primenet.com
www.azres.com

6011. Just 20 minutes from downtown Albuquerque, this southwestern-style home is in a quiet residential neighborhood, decorated in a delightful mix of antiques, handmade collectibles, and family memorabilia. Surrounded by fruit trees with a large vegetable garden in the corner side yard, this bed and breakfast brings a taste of the country to a convenient city location. Four rooms with private or shared baths available. Dogs in residence. Smoking restricted. Full breakfast is served. $50-60.

6012. By the beautiful Sandia Mountains, this house, on one acre in a quiet neighborhood, offers panoramic views of the city lights by night. Five minutes from the ski slopes and walking distance to a winery. Two very private spacious suites each have private entrances, small refrigerator, microwave, TV, telephone, and private baths, one with a whirlpool tub. Continental plus breakfast. Children under 12 free, other additional guests $10 each. Smoking outside, small guest dog or a horse possible. $62-74.

6013. Warm hospitality and comfortable Southwestern decor await you in this two-story contemporary home. Antiques and collectibles from traveling and teaching in Africa are sprinkled throughout. Near to hiking, skiing, ballooning, art galleries and museums, Indian pueblos, and golf. The two guest accommodations share a bath and have scenic balcony views. Continental breakfast and afternoon tea. No pets or smoking. Children welcome. $75

6151. The only bed and breakfast accommodation in Old Town proper, this spacious mansion with shaded garden courtyard is visible from

---

7 No smoking; 8 Children welcome; 9 Social drinking allowed; 10 Tennis nearby; 11 Swimming nearby; 12 Golf nearby; 13 Skiing nearby; 14 May be booked through a travel agent; 15 Handicapped accessible.

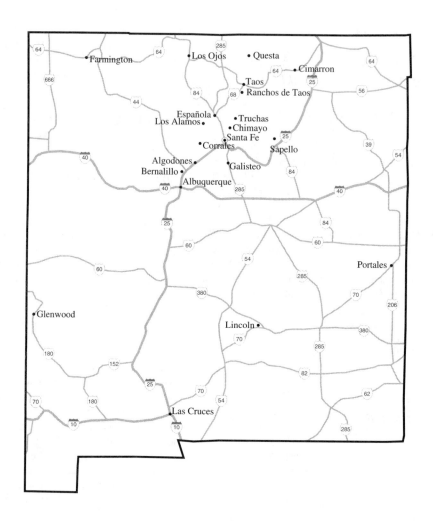

New Mexico

the plaza. In the National Register of Historic Places, the 1912 Victorian mansion was built in four-square style and is unusual when compared to most of Old Town's architecture. The decor, food, and hospitality reflect the Indian, Spanish, and Anglo cultures of the area. Three sets of accommodations are available, each with private bath. Full breakfast. No pets. Smoking restricted. Two night stay on weekends preferred. $89-99.

6152. In one of Albuquerque's most beautiful areas, this working pottery shop is within walking distance of the Rio Grande Nature Conservancy and eight miles to the airport. Walking and riding paths criss-cross this North Valley area. In one wing of the house is a Southwestern guest suite with a private entrance and bath by the flower-filled courtyard. The Quilt Room is in the same wing with a private hall bath. There is a large enclosed sun room for lounging which is available for guests. Smoking outside. "Memorable" Continental plus breakfast. $75-85.

6153. An elegant 1897 three-story Queen Anne historic landmark with a Victorian sitting room and a living room with an organ and a fireplace. Eight charming suites have private baths, small refrigerator, air conditioning, coffee maker, TVs, and all the comforts of a luxury inn. Laser disc player available with 200 movies. Walk to the Convention Center, downtown business center, shops, restaurants, Old Town and the Indian Cultural Center. Six miles from the airport. Full gourmet breakfast, evening treats. Additional guests $15. Inquire about rates for children. Small pet with special arrangement permitted in one room only, $30. Health club privileges. Indoor/outdoor dining room. German and Spanish spoken. $79-159.

6154. Territorial 1880 adobe home with southwestern decor. There is an outdoor kiva fireplace. Seven rooms or suites in the main house and the guest house, each with a private bath,
fireplace and many amenities. The largest suite is perfect for families. Afternoon refreshments. Sumptuous full breakfast includes local specialties. Full air conditioning, TV, hot tub. Smoking outdoors only, no pets, children 5 and older welcome. Three-night minimum stay during the Balloon Fiesta. For business travelers, fully equipped office, meeting room and catered meals. Additional person $20. $99-139.

6155. Step into this 200-year old hacienda and the rich history of Spanish Colonial times. Four spacious rooms and one suite offer warm hospitality, antique furnishings, kiva fireplaces and private baths. Amenities include a courtyard with a pool, hot tub, and peaceful gardens. The full breakfasts often include southwestern specialties. Two small dogs live here. No smoking, no pets. Children under 12 free, other additional guests $25 each. $95-125.

Old Town Bed & Breakfast

707 Seventeenth Street Northwest, 87104
(505) 764-9144; (888) 900-9144
www.virtualcities.com

Beautiful adobe home, quiet residential area a few blocks from historic Old Town. Charming upstairs guest room, queen-size bed, private bath, provides views of Sandia Mountains and tree-lined neighborhood streets. Spacious first-floor suite has king-size bed, kiva fireplace, adjacent Jacuzzi bath shared with owner only. Single beds, additional sleeping accommodations available. Enjoy a short walk to museums, shops, restaurants, or relax on the premises in secluded garden setting. Generous breakfast. Gracious hospitality. Children five and older welcome.

Host: Nancy Hoffman
Rooms: 2 (1 PB; 1 SB) $70-85

NOTES: Credit cards accepted: A MasterCard; B Visa; C American Express; D Discover; E Diner's Club; F Other; 2 Personal checks accepted; 3 Lunch available; 4 Dinner available; 5 Open all year; 6 Pets welcome; 7 No smoking; 8 Children welcome; 9 Social drinking allowed; 10 Tennis nearby; 11 Swimming nearby; 12 Golf nearby; 13 Skiing nearby; 14 May be booked through a travel agent; 15 Handicapped accessible.

Continental Breakfast
Credit Cards: None
Notes: 2, 5, 7, 8, 9, 10, 12, 13, 14

No resident pets. Smoking outside. Rollaway bed available. $79-109.

ALGODONES
B&B of New Mexico

P.O. Box 2805, Santa Fe, 87504
(505) 982-3332; e-mail: santafebnb@nets.com
www.nets.com/santafebnb

106. This hacienda just 30 miles south of Santa Fe offers the grace and elegance of historic New Mexico. It is decorated with antique furniture. Each room has its own handmade kiva fireplace. The tranquility offered there complements the peace and serenity found in the hacienda courtyard and garden. The largest room is the Wagner Room with Jacuzzi bathtub, fireplace, sitting area, and queen-size bed. The Peña Room has a queen-size bed. Both the Piñon and Pueblo Rooms have full-size beds and private baths. $79-109.

Mi Casa Su Casa/Old Pueblo Homestays Bed & Breakfast Reservation Service

P.O. Box 950, Tempe, AZ 85280-0950
(602) 990-0682; (800) 456-0682
FAX (602) 990-3390
e-mail: micasa@primenet.com
www.azres.com

6210. Gracious hosts welcome guests to a delightful 200-year-old spacious hacienda halfway between Albuquerque and Santa Fe. The Hacienda Vargas is full of light, has polished tile floors, southwestern art, Indian arts and crafts, and a nice mix of antiques. Guests are welcome in the living room or library. The chef presents special full breakfasts. Six guest rooms each have kiva fireplace, private bath, and private entrance to courtyard or hot tub. The large Wagner Room has a whirlpool tub.

ALGODONES/SANTA FE
Hacienda Vargas

P.O. Box 307, 87001
(505) 867-9115; (800) 261-0006

Romantic, secluded, and historic. Elegantly renovated. Amid the majestic New Mexico mesas, beside the Rio Grande, and lined by cottonwood trees. Seven rooms with fireplaces, private baths, and private entrances. Four suites with two-person Jacuzzi. Barbecue. Thirty minutes south of Santa Fe and north of Albuquerque. Romance packages available. A place of enchantment in the land of enchantment. Children over 12 welcome.

Hosts: Pablo and Julia De Vargas
Rooms: 7 (PB) $79-149
Full Breakfast
Credit Cards: A, B
Notes: 2, 5, 7, 9, 12, 13, 14

BERNALILLO
Mi Casa Su Casa/Old Pueblo Homestays Bed & Breakfast Reservation Service

P.O. Box 950, Tempe, AZ 85280-0950
(602) 990-0682; (800) 456-0682
FAX (602) 990-3390
e-mail: micasa@primenet.com
www.azres.com

6231. Magnificent 250-year-old Spanish hacienda built around a central courtyard. Full gourmet breakfast with a southwestern flair. Six guest rooms with private baths; one has a double whirlpool tub. Five rooms have beehive-shaped kiva fireplaces and ceilings with vigas. Coffee is served to guests in their room

---

NOTES: Credit cards accepted: A MasterCard; B Visa; C American Express; D Discover; E Diner's Club; F Other; 2 Personal checks accepted; 3 Lunch available; 4 Dinner available; 5 Open all year; 6 Pets welcome;

in the morning. Afternoon refreshments available. Romance packages with intimate dinners for two can be arranged. The hacienda is available for special events or business meetings. Air conditioning. Telephones, TVs, and a VCR are available. Downhill and cross-country skiing less than a half-hour away. Golfing, fishing, boating and swimming are just minutes from the inn. Rated three-diamonds by AAA. No smoking inside. No pets. Meals other than breakfast by special arrangement. $99-129.

CHIMAYO

Casa Escondida

P.O. Box 142, 87522
(505) 351-4805; (800) 643-7201
FAX (505) 351-2575

Casa Escondida, "The Hidden House," nestled on six acres of secluded land is an intimate and serene inn built in the Spanish Colonial adobe style, typical of northern New Mexico. The rooms are tastefully decorated in the American Arts and Crafts style, intimate and comfortable. Full breakfast awaits guests upon rising. Fireplaces fill the inn with warmth and fragrance of Piñon wood. Relax in the hot tub at the end of the day.

Host: Irenka Taurek
Rooms: 8 (PB) $75-130
Full Breakfast
Credit Cards: A, B, C
Notes: 2, 5, 6, 7, 8, 9, 13, 14

Mi Casa Su Casa/Old Pueblo Homestays Bed & Breakfast Reservation Service

P.O. Box 950, Tempe, AZ 85280-0950
(602) 990-0682; (800) 456-0682
FAX (602) 990-3390
e-mail: micasa@primenet.com
www.azres.com

6251. The inn is 30 miles north of Santa Fe, within a half-hour's drive of several Indian pueblos, national forests and archaeological sites. On six acres, surrounded by mountains, this is a serene home in a Spanish Colonial adobe style, typical of Northern New Mexico. Five rooms all have private full baths and are decorated with American arts and crafts. Living area includes a full kitchenette with microwave oven. Hot tub available. Full breakfast. Smoking outside. No pets. VISA, Mastercard. Weekly rates. $85-150.

CIMARRON

Casa del Gavilan

Highway 21 South, P.O. Box 518, 87714
(505) 376-2246; (800) GAVILAN
FAX (505) 376-2247

Nestled in the majestic foothills of the Sangre de Cristo Mountains, the Casa del Gavilan is a place of spirit where hawk and eagle soar. Secluded turn-of-the-century adobe villa. Enjoy elegant hospitality and breathtaking views in a historic setting. Four guest rooms with private baths, plus a two-room suite. "Come join us—and experience the uncommon tranquility of Casa del Gavilan."

Host: Isabel Lloyd
Rooms: 6 (4 PB; 2 SB) $75-105
Full Breakfast
Credit Cards: A, B, C, D
Notes: 2, 4, 5, 7, 8, 9, 13, 14, 15

Casa del Gavilan

---

7 No smoking; 8 Children welcome; 9 Social drinking allowed; 10 Tennis nearby; 11 Swimming nearby; 12 Golf nearby; 13 Skiing nearby; 14 May be booked through a travel agent; 15 Handicapped accessible.

CORRALES

Mi Casa Su Casa/Old Pueblo Homestays Bed & Breakfast Reservation Service

P.O. Box 950, Tempe, AZ 85280-0950
(602) 990-0682; (800) 456-0682
FAX (602) 990-3390
e-mail: micasa@primenet.com
www.azres.com

6271. This traditional adobe inn was built in 1986 around an inner courtyard with flowers and hummingbirds. Navajo rugs, kachina dolls, carved santos, and pueblo pottery reflect the richness of New Mexico's cultural and artistic background. Within a short walk the visitor will encounter the Bosque (cottonwood forest) of the Rio Grande, several fine restaurants and art galleries. All of the six guest rooms have TV, fireplace, private entrances, and full baths. A hot tub and meeting rooms/facilities are available. Rates include a full breakfast, afternoon snacks, complimentary wine or sherry. No smoking, no pets, children possible. $75-95.

6272. This bed and breakfast is a secluded adobe hacienda hidden behind traditional New Mexico walls. An old wooden turquoise gate leads visitors to a shaded patio, intimate gardens and a hot tub. The suite has a bedroom, sitting room, sofa bed, TV, and kitchenette. Two guest rooms have private baths and TV. Enjoy memorable breakfasts on the patio. Fourteen miles from the Albuquerque Airport, 45 miles to Santa Fe. No smoking or pets. Rates for extended stays and business travelers. Fax available. Children 12 and older welcome. $75-150.

6274. This contemporary adobe overlooks twinkling city lights and mountain views. The four guest rooms have private baths, fireplaces, cable TV, and radios. A morning coffee tray is placed outside the door, and a warm delectable breakfast is on the buffet. There are comfy robes for relaxing and for the hot tub. Loaner mountain bikes. For business guests, conference areas available. Short pleasant distance from Intel and other area businesses. Telephones, fax available. Smoking restricted, no children. Extra guest $10. $98.

ESPAÑOLA

Mi Casa Su Casa/Old Pueblo Homestays Bed & Breakfast Reservation Service

P.O. Box 950, Tempe, AZ 85280-0950
(602) 990-0682; (800) 456-0682
FAX (602) 990-3390
e-mail: micasa@primenet.com
www.azres.com

6291. Hostess welcomes guests to this handsome New Mexico-style home, an easy drive to many places of interest, such as Santa Fe, Taos Los Alamos, and Bandelier National Monument. Two guest rooms, each with private bath and TV, are available. Guests are welcome in the large living room with a fireplace, ceramic tile floors, and log-beamed ceilings. Afternoon refreshments. Seasonal lap pool. Hot tub. Full breakfast offers New Mexican specialties. Smoking outside. No children, please. Two-night minimum stay. $90.

FARMINGTON

B&B of New Mexico

P.O. Box 2805, Santa Fe, 87504
(505) 982-3332; e-mail: santafebnb@nets.com
www.nets.com/santafebnb

108. A traditional northern New Mexico adobe on the cliffside confluence of the San Juan and La Plata Rivers on the outskirts of Farmington. This bed and breakfast suite includes bedroom with queen-size bed, living room/dining room with two twin day beds, bathroom with Mexican tile shower, kitchen, and hot tub. $65-80.

NOTES: Credit cards accepted: A MasterCard; B Visa; C American Express; D Discover; E Diner's Club; F Other; 2 Personal checks accepted; 3 Lunch available; 4 Dinner available; 5 Open all year; 6 Pets welcome;

GALISTEO

The Galisteo Inn

HC 75, Box 4, 87540
(505) 466-4000; e-mail: galisteoin@aol.com

Visit this 250-year-old adobe hacienda in the beautiful countryside of northern New Mexico, 23 miles southeast of Santa Fe. Enjoy the hot tub, sauna, pool, bicycles, horseback riding, and massage. The dinners feature creative southwestern cuisine nightly, except Monday and Tuesday. Reservations required for accommodations and dining. A buffet breakfast is offered. Smoking in designated areas only.

Hosts: Joanna Kaufman and Wayne Aarniokoski
Rooms: 12 (9 PB; 3 SB) $115-190
Full Breakfast
Credit Cards: A, B, D
Notes: 2, 3, 4, 9, 10, 11, 13, 14, 15

The Galisteo Inn

GLENWOOD

Los Olmos Guest Ranch

P.O. Box 127, 88039
(505) 539-2311

A quiet country inn nestles in a narrow valley amidst a bulky mountain range in a popular outdoor recreation area; hiking, bird watching, and fishing abound. Guest recreation room is in the main building, and guest accommodations are in individual stone cottages with private baths. A swimming pool, spa, and horseback riding are all available. Pets welcome with a $5 fee.

Hosts: Jerry and Tiffany Hagemeier
Rooms: 13 (PB) $65-80
Full Breakfast
Credit Cards: A, B, C, D
Notes: 2, 4, 7, 8, 9, 11

GREATER SANTA FE/ESPAÑOLA/ABIQUIU

Casa del Rio

P.O. Box 92, Española, 87532
(505) 753-2035 (phone/FAX)
e-mail: casadelr@roadrunner.com
www.fourcorners.com/nm/inns/casadelrio
www.virtualcities.com/ons/nm/s/nms6702.htm

Casa del Rio, a small ranch on the Chama River, amidst Georgia O'Keeffe's red cliffs. Horses, sheep, hand-carved furniture, local crafts—gracious, genuine, and understated. For an enchanted getaway or a romantic rendezvous, with Casa del Rio as the hub guests can enjoy a wide variety of attractions—hiking, bird watching, biking, skiing, white-water rafting, gambling, fishing, hot springs, horseback riding. This bed and breakfast is in the heart of it all midway between Santa Fe and Taos. Extravagant breakfasts, spectacular view.

Hosts: Eileen Sopanen and Mel Vigil
Rooms: 4 (PB) $95-125
Full Breakfast
Credit Cards: A, B
Notes: 2, 5, 7, 9, 11, 13, 14

Casa del Rio

---

7 No smoking; 8 Children welcome; 9 Social drinking allowed; 10 Tennis nearby; 11 Swimming nearby; 12 Golf nearby; 13 Skiing nearby; 14 May be booked through a travel agent; 15 Handicapped accessible.

LAS CRUCES

Hilltop Hacienda Bed & Breakfast

2600 Westmoreland, 88012
(505) 382-3556; FAX (505) 382-0308
e-mail: hilltop@zianet.com

Just minutes from downtown, Hilltop Hacienda is an unusual two-story adobe dwelling of Spanish Moors architecture offering spectacular views of the city, river valley, and mountains. Guests stay comfortable in the summer and winter and enjoy spectacular sunrises, sunsets, and skies full of stars. Guest quarters are filled with heirlooms, paintings, and southwestern craft collectibles. Bob and Teddi are full of tips on how to spend time productively. Smoking outside only. Inquire about accommodations for pets. Children 12 and older welcome. Skiing is two hours away.

Hosts: Bob and Teddi Peters
Rooms: 3 (PB) $75-85
Full Breakfast
Credit Cards: A, B, C, D
Notes: 2, 5, 7, 9, 10, 11, 12, 14, 15

Mi Casa Su Casa/Old Pueblo Homestays Bed & Breakfast Reservation Service

P.O. Box 950, Tempe, AZ 85280-0950
(602) 990-0682; (800) 456-0682
FAX (602) 990-3390
e-mail: micasa@primenet.com
www.azres.com

6342. A romantic desert hideaway, this unique two-story adobe in Spanish Moorish design is perched atop 20 acres 10 minutes from downtown. Enjoy spectacular sunrises and sunsets on the wide patios or be warmed by the fireside in the sitting room with cable TV, videos, and a southwest library. Four spacious first floor rooms each have private bath, telephone, writing desk, and garden views. Early coffee and treats in advance of a full breakfast. Smoking outside, pets possible. $75-85.

LOS ALAMOS

Casa del Rey

305 Rover Street, 87544
(505) 672-9401

Quiet residential area, friendly atmosphere. In White Rock, minutes from Los Alamos and 40 minutes from Santa Fe. Excellent recreational facilities and restaurants nearby. The area is rich in Indian and Spanish history. Breakfast features homemade granola and breads served on the sun porch overlooking flower gardens, with views of the mountains. Children over five welcome. Resident cat.

Host: Virginia King
Rooms: 2 (SB) $45
Continental Breakfast
Credit Cards: None
Notes: 2, 5, 7, 9, 10, 11, 12, 13

LINCOLN

Mi Casa Su Casa/Old Pueblo Homestays Bed & Breakfast Reservation Service

P.O. Box 950, Tempe, AZ 85280-0950
(602) 990-0682; (800) 456-0682
FAX (602) 990-3390
e-mail: micasa@primenet.com
www.azres.com

6371. The prominent vigas, high ceilings and Mexican tiled baths add to the charm of this (circa 1860) historic home. All accommodations have private baths. There are three guest rooms in the main house. In the Old Trail House the two rooms each have private entrance, porch, wet bar and fireplace, and one has whirlpool tub. Also available are two guest casitas, one with kitchenette and one with coffee maker and small refrigerator. Full country breakfast in main house and Old Trail House, Continental plus in casitas. Smoking outdoors, no pets. Additional persons $10 each. $84-117.

NOTES: Credit cards accepted: A MasterCard; B Visa; C American Express; D Discover; E Diner's Club; F Other; 2 Personal checks accepted; 3 Lunch available; 4 Dinner available; 5 Open all year; 6 Pets welcome;

LOS OJOS

Mi Casa Su Casa/Old Pueblo Homestays Bed & Breakfast Reservation Service

P.O. Box 950, Tempe, AZ 85280-0950
(602) 990-0682; (800) 456-0682
FAX (602) 990-3390
e-mail: micasa@primenet.com
www.azres.com

6391. Nine miles south of Chama, this historic beautifully converted adobe residence was built in 1859 and has been in the same family for several generations. Choose from four second floor guest rooms, all with private bath or one large first floor guest suite with a private bath and fireplace. There is a small conference room and gift shop. There are no telephones or TVs. Attractions in the area include train rides over the Rocky Mountains, fishing, hunting and cross-country skiing. Full breakfast. No smoking or pets. Age restrictions may apply for children. Weekly and monthly rates available. Open February through October. Possible handicapped accessibility. AAA three-diamond-rated. $85-125.

PORTALES

Mi Casa Su Casa/Old Pueblo Homestays Bed & Breakfast Reservation Service

P.O. Box 950, Tempe, AZ 85280-0950
(602) 990-0682; (800) 456-0682
FAX (602) 990-3390
e-mail: micasa@primenet.com
www.azres.com

4861. This bed and breakfast is a rustic, comfortable two-bedroom guest house in a wooded area with a living room, dining room, kitchen, and full bath. One room has a double bed and a twin bed; the other room has one double bed. There is a double sofa-bed in the living room, and camp cots are available for a large group.

There is an excellent library of regional books, video tapes, field guides, and maps. There is also a screened-in front porch and a patio area with picnic table and a barbecue grill. Laundry facilities. The breakfast is stocked in the kitchen and is self-serve. Smoking outside. Partially handicapped possible. Very good bird watching area. Inquire about accommodations for pets. $85.

QUESTA

B&B of New Mexico

P.O. Box 2805, Santa Fe, 87504
(505) 982-3332; e-mail: santafebnb@nets.com
www.nets.com/santafebnb

109. Large, cozy, rustic log home is waiting for travelers at the base of the Sangre de Cristo Mountains with three bedrooms, two baths, hot tub, and sauna. Area is quiet and restful with close access to the Rio Grande. Wild-river hiking, wilderness area, three major ski resorts, wildlife, and shopping in Taos are all at guests' disposal. Continental breakfast, southwestern style. Rent whole house at $250 per day. Can accommodate eight adults and three children. $40-70.

RANCHOS DE TAOS

Mi Casa Su Casa/Old Pueblo Homestays Bed & Breakfast Reservation Service

P.O. Box 950, Tempe, AZ 85280-0950
(602) 990-0682; (800) 456-0682
FAX (602) 990-3390
e-mail: micasa@primenet.com
www.azres.com

6411. This 160-year-old adobe home is on four acres of pines, fruit trees, and pasture on the tranquil outskirts of Taos. Fifteen minutes to the Rio Grande Gorge and 25 minutes to Taos Ski Valley. All four luxurious, romantic guest rooms in the main house and one guest cottage

---

7 No smoking; 8 Children welcome; 9 Social drinking allowed; 10 Tennis nearby; 11 Swimming nearby; 12 Golf nearby; 13 Skiing nearby; 14 May be booked through a travel agent; 15 Handicapped accessible.

have private entrances, baths, fireplaces. Two-night minimum stay on weekends. Smoking restricted. No pets. Children over 12 welcome. Major credit cards accepted. Full gourmet breakfast. An additional $20 for third person in room. $95-145.

6463. This two-story B&B is on a large property and has three very private large guest rooms with private baths. There is a wraparound "coyote fence," flower beds, a fountain, fish pond, deck and portal. The living room has a fireplace and baby grand piano. Fourteen miles to a world-class ski area. Continental breakfast. No smoking or pets. Children welcome. Handicapped possible. $75-95.

SANTA FE

Adobe Abode

202 Chapelle, 87501
(505) 983-3133; FAX (505) 986-0972

Just three blocks from the plaza, this is a historic adobe home restored into an inviting and intimate inn. Decorated with flair and authentic southwestern charm, the inn has private baths, telephones, and TVs in all guest rooms. There are two guest rooms and a two-room suite in the main house, plus three detached casitas with fireplaces, private entrances, and landscaped patios, all in pure Santa Fe style. Complimentary sherry, cookies, and morning newspaper are offered in the stylish guest living room with fireplace. A full gourmet breakfast is served.

Host: Pat Harbour
Rooms: 6 (PB) $120-160
Full Breakfast
Credit Cards: A, B, D
Notes: 2, 5, 7, 8, 9, 10, 11, 12, 13, 14

Alexander's Inn

Alexander's Inn

529 East Palace, 87501
(505) 986-1431

Enjoy the luxury of this award-winning historic inn near the plaza, surrounded by beautiful gardens of roses and lilacs. The sun-filled rooms are lovingly decorated with antiques, lace, and stenciling. Guests are pampered by hosts with home-baked goodies, a hot tub under the stars, and incredible personal service. Pets welcome. Cottages for families.

Host: Carolyn Lee
Rooms: 16 (14 PB; 2 SB) $75-160
Continental Breakfast
Credit Cards: A, B, D
Notes: 2, 5, 6, 7, 8, 9, 10, 11, 12, 13, 14, 15

B&B of New Mexico

P.O. Box 2805, 87504
(505) 982-3332; e-mail: santafebnb@nets.com
www.nets.com/santafebnb

100. New Santa Fe pueblo-style home with 15-foot covered ceilings with large vigas and large open rooms. Sunny and cozy half-moon banco breakfast nook in which guests can sit and relax. Shepherd's fireplace in living room, Saltillo tile floors throughout, and carpeted

Adobe Abode

NOTES: Credit cards accepted: A MasterCard; B Visa; C American Express; D Discover; E Diner's Club; F Other; 2 Personal checks accepted; 3 Lunch available; 4 Dinner available; 5 Open all year; 6 Pets welcome;

bedrooms. Master suite has king-size canopied bed, kiva fireplace, TV, huge tiled double-head shower room, and step-into tiled whirlpool tub with garden window. Attached but private sitting room with two twin beds and TV is available at an additional cost. Cozy room with Santa Fe queen-size bed, TV, and private bath. $90-110.

101. Beautiful pueblo-style home in the foothills of the Sangre de Cristo Moun-tains. Gorgeous sunsets and views of the city lights at night. Jogging trails behind the house. Very quiet except for the sounds of nature. Only 15 minutes to ski basin, 10 minutes to the plaza. Patio for sunning; living room and dining room have high-beamed ceiling and fireplace. Master bedroom has king-size bed, dressing area, walk-in closet, private bath, and views of the foothills. Smaller bedroom has two twin beds, large closet, and private bath. Cat in residence. No smoking. $75-90.

102. Beautiful two-story home less than one mile from the plaza. Large downstairs bedroom with queen-size bed, refrigerator, lots of closet space, and a private bath and shower. Upstairs room has twin beds, walls covered with watercolors, and private three-quarter bath. Breakfast upstairs in dining room with view of hills filled with piñon trees. Living room has views of Sangre de Cristo Mountains, beamed ceilings, and kiva fireplace. Spanish tile in kitchen and hallways. No smoking. $50-75.

103. Romantic guest suite in the heart of Santa Fe's historic east side. This adobe residence is at the end of a narrow lane, secluded and quiet, surrounded by rock walls, coyote fence, and adobe walls, yet minutes to Canyon Road, galleries, shops, and restaurants. Features include sun-filled bedroom, queen-size four-poster bed, kiva fireplace, vigas, and clerestory windows so guests can watch the stars. Also available are a cozy sitting room and cable TV, with both rooms opening onto patio. $90.

104. Small, cozy adobe home two blocks from Canyon Road and five blocks from downtown plaza. Kiva fireplace in living room, enclosed courtyard in front. Door from guest room opens onto back garden area. Host very knowledgeable about activities in Santa Fe. Private full bath down the hall and king-size bed. No smoking. $75.

105. Simply elegant, this restored 100-year-old spacious adobe features fireplace, hardwood floors, plastered walls, full furnishings, custom kitchen cabinets, washer and dryer, CD, and cable TV. Eight blocks from the plaza. Queen-size four-poster bed $150 for two persons; queen-size pullout beds $175 for four persons; $225 for five persons.

Dunshee's

986 Acequia Madre, 87501
(505) 982-0988

A romantic adobe getaway in the historic east side, about a mile from the Plaza. Guests can choose either a two-room suite or a two-bedroom guest house with kitchen. Both units have kiva fireplaces, antiques, folk art, fresh flowers, homemade cookies, telephone, TV, pretty linens, private bath, patio, and great breakfasts. Two-night minimum stay weekends and holidays.

Host: Susan Dunshee
Rooms: 2 (PB) $125
Full or Continental Breakfast
Credit Cards: A, B
Notes: 2, 5, 7, 8, 9, 13

El Paradero

220 West Manhattan, 87501
(505) 988-1177; e-mail: elparadero@nets.com

Just a short walk from the busy Plaza, this 200-year-old Spanish farmhouse was restored as a charming southwestern inn. Enjoy a full gourmet breakfast, caring service, and a relaxed, friendly atmosphere. The inn offers

---

7 No smoking; 8 Children welcome; 9 Social drinking allowed; 10 Tennis nearby; 11 Swimming nearby; 12 Golf nearby; 13 Skiing nearby; 14 May be booked through a travel agent; 15 Handicapped accessible.

El Paradero

lots of common space and a patio for afternoon tea and snacks. Pets welcome by prior arrangements. AAA- and Mobil-rated.

Hosts: Thom Allen and Ouida MacGregor
Rooms: 14 (10 PB; 4 SB) $65-140
Full Breakfast
Credit Cards: A, B
Notes: 2, 5, 6, 7, 8, 9, 10, 11, 12, 13, 14

Four Kachinas Inn

512 Webber Street, 87501
(505) 982-2550; (800) 397-2564
FAX (505) 989-1323
e-mail: info@fourkachinas.com
www.fourkachinas.com

Four Kachinas Inn, a short walk from Santa Fe's historic Plaza, offers six rooms with private baths. The rooms are furnished with Navajo rugs, Hopi kachina dolls, and handcrafted wooden furniture. Three rooms have individual garden patios, while an upstairs room offers a view of the Sangre de Cristo Mountains. Two rooms are in the 1910 landmark cottage. A Continental plus breakfast, including award-winning baked goods, is served in the room. The old adobe guest lounge features afternoon tea and cookies. One room and the guest lounge are handicapped accessible. Children 10 and older welcome. Member of Bread Bakers Guild of America.

Hosts: John Daw and Andrew Beckerman
Rooms: 6 (PB) $75-149
Continental Breakfast
Credit Cards: A, B, D
Notes: 7, 9, 10, 11, 12, 13

Grant Corner Inn

Grant Corner Inn

122 Grant Avenue, 87501
(505) 983-6678; (800) 964-9003

An exquisite Colonial manor home in downtown Santa Fe. Just two blocks from the historic plaza, the inn is nestled among intriguing shops, restaurants, and galleries. Each room is individually appointed with antiques and treasures from around the world: quilts, brass and four-poster beds, armoires, and art. Private telephones, cable TV, and ceiling fans.

Host: Louise Stewart
Rooms: 12 (10 PB; 2 SB) $70-165
Full Breakfast
Credit Cards: A, B, C
Notes: 2, 3, 5, 7, 10, 11, 12, 13, 14, 15

Four Kachinas Inn

NOTES: Credit cards accepted: A MasterCard; B Visa; C American Express; D Discover; E Diner's Club; F Other; 2 Personal checks accepted; 3 Lunch available; 4 Dinner available; 5 Open all year; 6 Pets welcome;

Santa Fe, NM 273

La Tienda Inn

La Tienda Inn

445-447 West San Francisco Street, 87501
(505) 989-8259; (800) 889-7611
FAX (505) 820-6931; e-mail: info@latiendabb.com
www.latiendabb.com

Just four blocks from the Santa Fe Plaza, the compound includes a turn-of-the-century Territorial-style house and a meandering adobe building which began as a small neighborhood market—La Tienda. Individually decorated guest rooms, some with fireplaces and all overlooking a courtyard or garden area. Private entrances, private bathrooms, cable color TV, and telephones are provided in each room. Enjoy the refreshing afternoon tea in the Old Store Common Room and a generous Continental plus breakfast delivered to guests' room in the morning—or in the garden in summer.

Hosts: Leighton and Barbara Watson
Rooms: 7 (PB) $90-160
Continental Breakfast
Credit Cards: A, B
Notes: 2, 5, 7, 10, 11, 12, 13, 14, 15

Mi Casa Su Casa/Old Pueblo Homestays Bed & Breakfast Reservation Service

P.O. Box 950, Tempe, AZ 85280-0950
(602) 990-0682; (800) 456-0682
FAX (602) 990-3390
e-mail: micasa@primenet.com
www.azres.com

6431. Santa Fe Territotial-style unhosted accommodation on the Canyon Road Historic District, a mixed zoning area of shops, restaurants, and residences. Guests can choose from two separate accommodations sharing a courtyard behind a shop. The suite consists of a bedroom, a sitting room with futon and fireplace, full bath, and kitchenette. The compact casita has a bedroom, kitchenette, and bath. Santa Fe furnishings, quality linens and toiletries, original art, and Mexican tile floors. Self-catered Continental breakfast. Two-week minimum stay. Call for rates.

6432. This two-story, 1903 Craftsman inn and cottage has a friendly, romantic atmosphere. In keeping with the turn-of-the-century style, inside are found hardwood floors, fireplaces, antiques, quilts, and stenciling. In the main house, three guest rooms have private baths and two share one bath. Three separate suites have private baths. Continental plus breakfast served. Garden hot tub, mountain bikes, health club guest privileges, concierge services. French spoken. Two-night minimum stay on weekends. No smoking inside. Children six and older welcome in main house, children all ages welcome in suites. Well-behaved pets welcome. $75-200.

6433. Constructed in 1948, this small, two-bedroom New Mexico Territorial-style house is in a residential historic neighborhood in an excellent location. There is one guest room available with a private bath in the hall. Near public transportation. Two-night minimum stay weekends. Handicapped accessible. Full breakfast. Smoking outside. An infant or small child welcome. Upon request, hostess will arrange for a crib. Pets welcome with prior arrangement. Weekly rates available. Less in off-season except during holidays. $65-75.

6434. This bed and breakfast is in a hilly area and has beautiful city and mountain views. Walk to the Plaza in 15 minutes. Guests are welcome in the living room where there are a TV, fireplace, VCR, radio, and many books. The large guest room has a full bath en suite, door to outside patio. The extra large room has a private full hall bath. Roll-away beds are

---

7 No smoking; 8 Children welcome; 9 Social drinking allowed; 10 Tennis nearby; 11 Swimming nearby; 12 Golf nearby; 13 Skiing nearby; 14 May be booked through a travel agent; 15 Handicapped accessible.

available. Six guests maximum. Continental plus breakfast. Cats in residence. Two-night minimum preferred. Smoking outside. No pets. No children. German, a little Spanish, and French spoken. For a stay of more than two weeks, 10 percent less. $70-85.

6436. Between the stream-like Santa Fe River and a wooded area, this old adobe main house and the attached guest house have been carefully refurbished by the artist-hostess. The cottage has a private entrance and patio, private bath, and a fully furnished kitchenette. Continental plus breakfast stocked in kitchen. Two night minimum stay. Smoking outside. No pets. $85.

6437. Close to the heart of historic Santa Fe Plaza, this territorial style bed and breakfast offers the charm and intimacy of a small European inn, yet has the convenience and accessibility of a downtown hotel. Each of the 11 rooms and the four suites has private bath with cheerful Mexican tile, hardwood floors, central air conditioning, telephone, and cable TV. Continental plus breakfast. No smoking. Fifteen dollars for each extra person in room. Rates slightly lower November through February. $69-159.

Preston House

106 Faithway Street, 87501
(505) 982-3465; (888) 877-7622
FAX (505) 988-2397
e-mail: prestonhouse@aol.com

Santa Fe's first bed and breakfast is a historically plaqued Queen Anne-style house built in 1886 offering eight guest rooms, furnished with antiques and sumptuous, individually chosen linens and lace. The inn is comfortably on a quiet street near the Plaza and Canyon Road. Gardens, fireplaces, stained-glass windows, fresh breads and pastries, personalized service, and an English afternoon tea make Preston House the premier inn of Santa Fe. Continental plus breakfast served. Children and pets welcome. Back garden hot tub.

Host: Carolyn Lee
Rooms: 8 (6 PB; 2 SB) $65-165
Continental Breakfast
Credit Cards: A, B, D
Notes: 2, 5, 6, 7, 8, 9, 10, 11, 12, 13, 14

Pueblo Bonito Bed & Breakfast Inn

138 West Manhattan Avenue, 87501
(505) 984-8001; (800) 461-4599
FAX (505) 984-3155

Historic adobe estate in downtown Santa Fe, three blocks south of the Plaza. Eighteen guest rooms, each with private bath, kiva fireplace, telephone, TV, and 12-inch-thick adobe walls. While the rooms vary in size, the decor is enchantingly Santa Fe—boasting hand-carved wooden furniture and southwestern attire. A bountiful Continental "create your own" breakfast buffet and afternoon tea (including margaritas) are the perfect complement to any visit. Hot tub facility on premises.

Rooms: 18 (PB) $70-150
Continental Breakfast
Credit Cards: A, B, C, D
Notes: 2, 5, 7, 8, 9, 10, 11, 12, 13, 14, 15

Spencer House Inn

222 McKenzie Street, 87501
(800) 647-0530; www.spencerhse-santafe.com

Spencer House Inn is a five-bedroom cozy and charming traditional bed and breakfast inn. Recipient of the 1994 Historical Preservation award by the Santa Fe Historical Board for restoring the property. Just three blocks from the downtown plaza near the finest restaurants, galleries, and retail stores. Fine bed linens, pri-

Spencer House

NOTES: Credit cards accepted: A MasterCard; B Visa; C American Express; D Discover; E Diner's Club; F Other; 2 Personal checks accepted; 3 Lunch available; 4 Dinner available; 5 Open all year; 6 Pets welcome;

vate baths, and a full breakfast served by the innkeeper. A cozy retreat in downtown Santa Fe. Fully air-conditioned. Children over 12 welcome.

Rooms: 5 (PB) $95-167
Full Breakfast
Credit Cards: A, B, C
Notes: 2, 5, 7, 9, 10, 11, 12, 13, 14

Water Street Inn

427 West Water Street, 87501
(505) 984-1193; (800) 646-6752
FAX (505) 984-6235; e-mail: h2ostin@ibm.net
www.waterstreetinn.com

An award-winning adobe restoration, the Water Street Inn is centrally located two blocks from the Plaza, surrounded by fine restaurants, galleries, and shops. The authentic and beautifully appointed spacious rooms all have private baths, TV, telephone, voice mail, with fireplaces in most rooms. The defining quality to the Water Street Inn is the full hospitality and friendly relaxed environment. The evening "Happy Hour" features New Mexico wines, hors d'oeuvres, and great company—our guests!

Rooms: 12 (PB) $95-200
Continental Breakfast
Credit Cards: A, B, C, D
Notes: 2, 6, 7, 8, 12, 13, 14, 15

SAPELLO

Star Hill Inn

P.O. Box 1A, 87745
(505) 425-5605; e-mail: info@starhillinn.com
www.starhillinn.com

An astronomy retreat in the Rockies, located one hour from Santa Fe. Open year-round, an ideal place for vacation and retreat for family, friends, receptions, and workshops. Private, charming cottages with kitchens (everything except food), private baths, living rooms, bedroom, fireplaces, porches. Located on 200 acres of peaceful pines. Hiking trails, mountain meadow labyrinth, meditation garden. Ten telescopes, private star tours available. Astronomy, art, bird watching workshops scheduled throughout the year.

Rooms: 7 (PB) $90-140
Credit Cards: None
Notes: 2, 5, 7, 8, 9, 10, 11, 12, 13, 14, 15

TAOS

American Artists Gallery House

132 Frontier Road, P.O. Box 584, 87571
(505) 758-4446; (800) 532-2041
e-mail: aagh@taosnm.com
www.taosbedandbreakfast.com

One of Taos most romantic bed and breakfast inns. Discover the magic of Taos at this delightful southwest hacienda. Taos Mountain provides a commanding backdrop for an array of metal sculpture planted in the flower-filled garden. Enjoy in-room Jacuzzi tubs for two, wood-burning fireplaces, stargaze from the hot tub, and savor a delicious gourmet breakfast. Let hosts arrange a historical walking tour to round out a visit to Taos. "Step into our world and re-create...."

Hosts: LeAn and Charles Clamurro
Rooms: 10 (PB) $85-185
Full Breakfast
Credit Cards: A, B
Notes: 2, 5, 7, 9, 10, 11, 12, 13, 14

American Artists Gallery House

---

7 No smoking; 8 Children welcome; 9 Social drinking allowed; 10 Tennis nearby; 11 Swimming nearby; 12 Golf nearby; 13 Skiing nearby; 14 May be booked through a travel agent; 15 Handicapped accessible.

The Brooks Street Inn

119 Brooks Street, P.O. Box 4954, 87571
(505) 758-1489; (800) 758-1489
e-mail: brooks@taos.newmex.com
www.brooksstreetinn.com

"One of the Ten Best Inns of North America!"—*Country Inns* magazine. A short walk from Taos Plaza, discover this adobe home, the perfect mix of comfort and elegance, a place of southwestern history, style, and warmth. Enjoy local art, fireplaces, cozy reading nooks, spacious gardens. Indulge in gourmet breakfasts and specialty coffees from the espresso bar. Like Taos itself, the host offers a tradition of gracious hospitality. Children over 10 welcome. Limited handicapped accessibility.

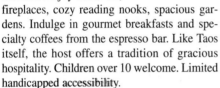

Host: Carol Frank
Rooms: 6 (PB) $80-110
Full Breakfast
Credit Cards: A, B, C
Notes: 2, 5, 7, 9, 10, 11, 12, 13, 14

Casa Europa Inn & Gallery

840 Upper Ranchito Road, HC 68 Box 3F, 87571
(505) 758-9798; (888) 758-9798

Spacious 17th-century pueblo-style inn rests under giant cottonwoods a little over one mile from Taos Plaza. Surrounded with open pastures, grazing horses, and majestic mountain views. Seven elegant guest rooms offer fireplaces, private baths (two with hot tubs), and comfortable furnishings of European antiques and southwestern style. Full gourmet breakfasts and European pastries or evening hors d'oeuvres included. Walled courtyards with flowers, fountains, hot tub, and Swedish sauna. Enjoy the best of the Southwest! America's Favorite Inn Award 1997, Mobil-rated three stars.

Hosts: Rudi and Marcia Zwicker
Rooms: 7 (PB) $75-165
Full Breakfast
Credit Cards: A, B, C
Notes: 2, 5, 7, 8, 9, 10, 11, 12, 13, 14

Cottonwood Inn Bed & Breakfast

HCR 74, Box 24609, 87529
(800) 324-7120; FAX (505) 776-1141
e-mail: cottonbb@taos.newmex.com
www.taos-cottonwood.com

Relax in adobe elegance at the Cottonwood Inn, surrounded by original art and artifacts of the Southwest. This country inn is serenely set at the foot of the Sangre de Cristo Mountains amidst a grove of cottonwoods. Each of the inn's seven rooms is distinctive, offering spectacular views and a range of amenities from private spa and whirlpool bath to private deck and kiva fireplace. The inn provides a savory full breakfast and evening appetizers. AAA three-diamonds; Mobil three-stars.

Hosts: Bill and Kit Owen
Rooms: 7 (PB) $85-155
Full Breakfast
Credit Cards: A, B
Notes: 2, 5, 7, 8, 9, 10, 11, 12, 13, 14, 15

Cottonwood Inn

NOTES: Credit cards accepted: A MasterCard; B Visa; C American Express; D Discover; E Diner's Club; F Other; 2 Personal checks accepted; 3 Lunch available; 4 Dinner available; 5 Open all year; 6 Pets welcome;

Dreamcatcher Bed & Breakfast

416 La Lomita, P.O. Box 2069, 87571
(505) 758-0613; FAX (505) 751-0115
e-mail: dream@taosnm.com
www.taoswebb.com/hotel/dreamcatcher

Dreamcatcher is easy walking distance to historic Taos Plaza, the perfect location from which to explore town. After experiencing Taos return to enjoy afternoon social and snacks. Unwind on a lazy summer afternoon in a hammock in the wooded courtyard or snuggle up with a book near a crackling fire on a chilly winter evening. Delight in one of Taos' many fine restaurants, then return "home" to stargaze and relax in the hot tub.

Hosts: Bob and Jill Purtee
Rooms: 7 (PB) $79-104
Full Breakfast
Credit Cards: A, B, C, D
Notes: 2, 5, 7, 9, 10, 11, 12, 13, 14, 15

Hacienda del Sol

P.O. Box 177, 87571
(505) 758-0287; e-mail: sunhous@newmex.com
www.taoshaciendadelsol.com

A 190-year-old historic, charming, quiet adobe with fireplaces, viga ceilings, surrounded by century-old trees. Guest rooms have down comforters, carefully selected furnishings, and fine art. Enjoy an unobstructed view of the mountains from the deck of the outdoor hot tub. Generous breakfasts are served by a crackling fire in the winter, or on the patio in the summer. Chosen by *USA Weekend* as one of America's 10 most romantic inns. One mile north of Taos Plaza. Mobil-rated three stars.

Hacienda del Sol

Host: Dennis Sheehan
Rooms: 10 (PB) $85-155
Full Breakfast
Credit Cards: A, B
Notes: 2, 5, 7, 8, 9, 10, 11, 12, 13, 14, 15

La Posada de Taos

309 Juanita Lane, P.O. Box 1118, 87571
(800) 645-4803; FAX (505) 751-3294
e-mail: laposada@taos.newmex.com
www.taosnet.com/laposada/

Escape to a romantic, secluded adobe inn, two and one-half blocks from Plaza in the historic district. First bed and breakfast in Taos. Walk to galleries, museums, restaurants, shops. Return to casual elegance of country pine antiques, handmade quilts, private baths, courtyards, fireplaces. Savor a delicious full breakfast. Two rooms with whirlpool tubs. Separate honeymoon house. Local knowledge of shops and nearby mountains. *New York Times* on Taos "Where to Stay." AAA three-diamond-rated.

Hosts: Bill Swan and Nancy Brooks-Swan
Rooms: 6 (PB) $85-135
Full Breakfast
Credit Cards: A, B, C
Notes: 2, 5, 7, 9, 10, 11, 12, 13, 14, 15

Mi Casa Su Casa/Old Pueblo Homestays Bed & Breakfast Reservation Service

P.O. Box 950, Tempe, AZ 85280-0950
(602) 990-0682; (800) 456-0682
FAX (602) 990-3390
e-mail: micasa@primenet.com
www.azres.com

6461. This inn is on a secluded acre surrounded by an adobe wall in the heart of Taos. Each of the inn's five guest rooms has a private entrance and private bath plus a welcoming kiva fireplace and a lot of privacy. Listed in the national and state historic registries. The living room offers TV, stereo, and a library of more than 500 classical and jazz CDs. Guided fishing trips are available upon request. Continental and full breakfasts. Afternoon refreshments. Smoking outdoors. No pets. Fifteen dollars for each additional guest. $95-130.

6462. This updated and enlarged adobe sits in a valley just below town and is very private, yet only a 15-minute walk to the famed Taos Plaza. Nearby to skiing, galleries, rafting, and fabulous eateries. Three guest rooms, two of which can be combined as a suite. Each room has private bath, kiva fireplace, and separate outside entrance. Gourmet Continental breakfast. Smoking in portals only. No pets. Small additional charge for children or one night stays. $75-155.

The Willows Inn

The Willows Inn

412 Kit Carson Road at Dolan Street
Box 6560 NDCBU, 87571-6223
(505) 758-2558; (800) 525-TAOS (8267)
(505) 758-5445 (guestline/FAX)
e-mail: willows@newmex.com
www.willows-taos.com

Nestled under two of America's largest willow trees is this national historic register estate. The walled adobe estate was the home and studio of E. M. Hennings, member of the elite 1920s Taos Society of Artists. The innkeeper/owners share their hospitality beginning with a gourmet, family-style breakfast and visiting over lavish afternoon refreshments. Each of the inn's guest rooms has an outside entrance, private bath, queen-size bed, and year-round kiva fireplace. Each individual room's decor reflects cultures special to Taos. Guided fly-fishing trips available. Walk to the plaza. Limited handicapped accessibility.

Hosts: Janet and Doug Camp
Rooms: 5 (PB) $95-140
Full Breakfast
Credit Cards: A, B, C, D
Notes: 2, 5, 7, 8, 9, 10, 11, 12, 13, 14

TRUCHAS

Rancho Arriba

P.O. Box 338, 87578
(505) 689-2374
www.redbay.com/web/rancho

A European-style bed and breakfast with an informal and tranquil atmosphere, this traditional adobe hacienda is on a historic Spanish land grant. Spectacular mountain view in every direction, amid colonial villages featuring traditional arts and architecture. Adobe churches, hand weaving, wood carving, and quilting. Smoking in designated areas only.

Host: Curtiss Frank
Rooms: 4 (SB) $70
Full Breakfast
Credit Cards: A, B
Notes: 2, 4, 5, 8, 9, 13

Oregon

ASHLAND

Ashland's English Country Cottage

271 Beach Street, 97520
(541) 488-4428; (800) 760-4428
e-mail: bwallace@edsnet.net
www.ahslandbb.com

A Tudor-style home decorated in the country English style. Five rooms named after flowers with an outside deck overlooking lush flower gardens are offered. Queen-size or twin beds are available with down comforters, quilts, and private baths en suite. The English garden theme is maintained throughout the home, providing a warm and relaxing vacation experience. Relax in the lush garden or on the deck, and play the conservatory grand piano.

Hosts: Brian and Shirley Wallace
Rooms: 5 (PB) $89-109
Full Breakfast
Credit Cards: A, B, D
Notes: 2, 5, 7, 9, 11, 12, 13, 14, 15

Country Willows Bed & Breakfast Inn

1313 Clay Street, 97520
(541) 488-1590; (800) WILLOWS
FAX (541) 488-1611; www.willowsinn.com

Combine Ashland's theatrical attractions with a peaceful rural setting at Country Willows. Guest rooms have views of the Siskiyou and Cascade Mountains. Guests may relax in the Jacuzzi, on the inn's porches, or in the Willows's swing. Hiking trails are also available. The five-acre, 1896 farmhouse was remodeled in 1985 for maximum comfort. Rooms are in the main house, a separate guest cottage, and in an 1899 barn. The swimming pool is heated spring through fall. Rates include a full breakfast served at individual tables on the porch or in the sunroom. Guests looking for a special romantic getaway will love the two barn suites with king-size beds, fireplaces, and Jacuzzis for two.

Host: Dan Durant
Suite: 9 (PB) $95-195
Full Breakfast
Credit Cards: A, B, C, D
Notes: 2, 5, 7, 9, 10, 11, 12, 13, 14, 15

Cowslip's Belle Bed & Breakfast

159 North Main Street, 97520
(541) 488-2901; (800) 888-6819
FAX (541) 482-6138; e-mail: stay@cowslip.com
www.cowslip.com/cowslip

Teddy bears, chocolate truffles, sweet dreams, and scrumptious breakfasts can be enjoyed here. Just three blocks to the heart of town. Beautiful 1913 Craftsman bungalow and carriage house. Three queen/twin rooms with private baths and entrances and one king/twin suite. Featured in *McCall's* "Most Charming Inns in America," *Weekends for Two in the*

Cowslip's Belle

---

7 No smoking; 8 Children welcome; 9 Social drinking allowed; 10 Tennis nearby; 11 Swimming nearby; 12 Golf nearby; 13 Skiing nearby; 14 May be booked through a travel agent; 15 Handicapped accessible.

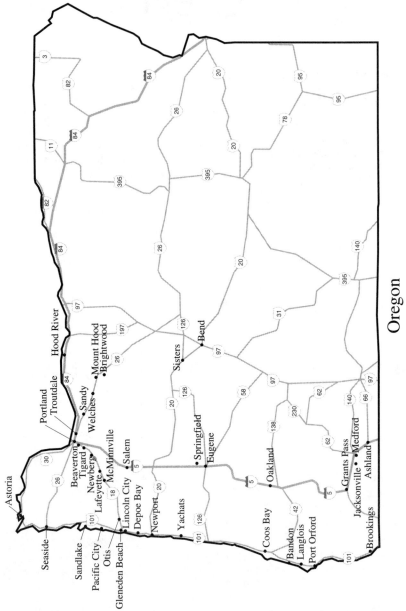

Pacific Northwest—50 Romantic Getaways, Best Places to Kiss in the Northwest, and *Northwest Best Places*. Country accents. "A garden of many splendored delights." Member of the Oregon Bed and Breakfast Guild. Children over nine welcome.

Hosts: Jon and Carmen Reinhardt
Rooms: 4 (PB) From $105
Full Breakfast
Credit Cards: None
Notes: 2, 5, 7, 9, 10, 11, 12, 13, 14

The Iris Inn

59 Manzanita Street, 97520
(541) 488-2286; (800) 460-7650
FAX (541) 488-3709; e-mail: irisinnbb@aol.com
www.irisinnbb.com

A favorite since 1982. A 1905 Victorian furnished with antiques. Elegant breakfasts feature gourmet delights such as eggs Benedict with smoked salmon, fresh-baked breads, gourmet coffee. Afternoon refreshments. Mountain views, quiet neighborhood. Near the Oregon Shakespeare Festival and the Rouge River for rafting. Cross-country and downhill skiing also nearby. The Oregon Cabaret Theater operates year-round and the Britt Music Festival is enjoyed during the summer. Children over seven welcome.

Host: Vicki and Greg Capp
Rooms: 5 (PB) $110
Full Breakfast
Credit Cards: A, B
Notes: 2, 5, 7, 10, 11, 12, 13

Morical House Garden Inn

668 North Main Street, 97520
(541) 482-2254; (800) 208-0960
FAX (541) 482-1775; e-mail: moricalhse@aol.com
www.garden-inn.com

Eastlake Victorian farmhouse on two acres of gardens with mountain views, ponds, and stately trees provides rural setting only seven blocks from Oregon Shakespeare Festival. Some guest rooms feature fireplaces, wet bars, and double

Morical House Garden Inn

whirlpool tubs. All have private baths. Superb breakfasts served at individual tables in dining room or on sun porch. AAA-rated three diamonds, ABBA-rated three crowns.

Hosts: Gary and Sandye Moore
Rooms: 7 (PB) $88-160
Full Breakfast
Credit Cards: A, B, C, D
Notes: 2, 5, 7, 9, 10, 11, 12, 13, 14, 15

The Mousetrap Inn

312 Helman Street, 97520
(541) 482-9228; (800) 460-5453
www.mousetrapinn.com

Contemporary art and antiques compliment this charming and comfortable 1890s restored country home. Only four blocks to the theaters, it offers guests a quiet escape yet easy access to the center of activity. Six rooms with private baths, queen/double beds, air conditioning, English garden. Enjoy full hearty breakfasts and afternoon refreshments on the deck or by the fire. Children welcome.

Hosts: Johnny and Amy Ma
Rooms: 6 (PB) $73-105
Full Breakfast
Credit Cards: A, B, D
Notes: 2, 5, 7, 8, 9, 12, 13, 14

NOTES: Credit cards accepted: A MasterCard; B Visa; C American Express; D Discover; E Diner's Club; F Other; 2 Personal checks accepted; 3 Lunch available; 4 Dinner available; 5 Open all year; 6 Pets welcome; 7 No smoking; 8 Children welcome; 9 Social drinking allowed; 10 Tennis nearby; 11 Swimming nearby; 12 Golf nearby; 13 Skiing nearby; 14 May be booked through a travel agent; 15 Handicapped accessible.

Neil Creek House

Neil Creek House Bed & Breakfast

341 Mowetza Drive, 97520
(541) 482-6443; (800) 460-7860
FAX (541) 482-1074; e-mail: neilcrk@mind.net
www.mind.net/neilcrk

Nestled in the foothills of the Siskiyou Mountains with magnificent views of the Cascades is this country retreat. Leave the noisy "real world" behind as you enter a new world of tranquility where Neil Creek meanders lazily through the property. The guest room opens on to a private patio with an expansive lawn and is just steps away from the gazebo that overlooks the creek. Merely six picturesque miles from the Shakespearean experience and many other exciting activities including the Britt Music Festival. Service dogs are welcome.

Hosts: Paul and Gayle Negro
Rooms: 2 (PB) $85-175
Full Breakfast
Credit Cards: None
Notes: 2, 4, 5, 7, 9, 10, 11, 12, 13, 14

Oak Hill Country Bed & Breakfast

2190 Siskiyou Boulevard, 97520
(541) 482-1554; (800) 888-7434
FAX (541) 482-1378; e-mail: oakhill@mind.net
www.bbonline.com/or/oakhill

This charming 1910 farmhouse, minutes from the Oregon Shakespeare Festival, offers the convenience of the city with the ambiance and tranquillity of the country. An old-fashioned veranda, spacious living room, gardens, deck, and bicycles provide variety for guests' relaxation. Each of the inn's six air-conditioned bedrooms has a queen-size bed and a private bath. The delicious family-style breakfast served in the sunny dining room is truly the main event at Oak Hill. AAA two-diamonds- and Mobil two-stars-rated. Children 12 and older welcome. "What a terrific find—charming, immaculate, warm, and inviting, absolutely wonderful food, and a loving and generous innkeeper."

Rooms: 6 (PB) $75-115
Full Breakfast
Credit Cards: A, B
Notes: 2, 3, 5, 7, 9, 10, 11, 12, 13, 14

Oak Hill

The Wood's House Bed & Breakfast Inn

333 North Main Street, 97520
(541) 488-1598; (800) 435-8260
FAX (541) 482-8027
e-mail: woodshse@mind.net
www.mind.net/woodshouse/

In the historic district, four blocks from the Shakespeare theaters, Lithia Park, restaurants, and shops, this 1908 Craftsman-style home offers six sunny and spacious guest rooms. Simple furnishings of warm woods, antique furniture, fine linens, watercolors, oriental carpets, leather books, and private-label amenities create a sophisticated comfortable ambiance. The one-half-acre terraced English gardens provide many areas for guests to relax, read, and socialize. Golf, swimming, hiking, biking, and river rafting are nearby.

NOTES: Credit cards accepted: A MasterCard; B Visa; C American Express; D Discover; E Diner's Club; F Other; 2 Personal checks accepted; 3 Lunch available; 4 Dinner available; 5 Open all year; 6 Pets welcome;

The Wood's House

Hosts: Françoise and Lester Roddy
Rooms: 6 (PB) $75-120
Full Breakfast
Credit Cards: A, B, D
Notes: 2, 5, 7, 9, 11, 12, 13, 14

ASTORIA

Astoria Inn Bed & Breakfast

3391 Irving Avenue, 97103
(503) 325-8153; (800) 718-8153

Relax and be pampered in the comfort of an 1890s Victorian. Magnificent views of the Columbia River. Hiking trails in the forest behind the inn. Beautifully decorated guest rooms with private baths. Full breakfast and daily snacks. Beautiful, quiet residential neighborhood just three minutes from shopping and restaurants.

Host: Mickey Cox
Rooms: 4 (PB) $60-85
Full Breakfast
Credit Cards: A, B, D
Notes: 2, 5, 7, 9, 10, 11, 12, 14

Columbia River Inn Bed & Breakfast

1681 Franklin Avenue, 97103
(503) 325-5044; (800) 953-5044

A five-star Victorian charmer. Elegant "painted lady" when guests enter. Built in the late 1870s. Nearby, Columbia River Maritime Museum and Captain George Flavel House. Ocean is five miles away. Full breakfast, river view, off-street parking available. Enjoy Stairway to the Stars, a unique terraced garden. Gazebo available for outdoor weddings and parties; write and ask for details and prices. New seafood lab. New aquatic center two blocks away. During the summer and holidays a two-night minimum stay is required. Children 10 and older welcome.

Host: Karen N. Nelson
Rooms: 4 (PB) $75-125
Full Breakfast
Credit Cards: A, B, C, D
Notes: 2, 5, 7, 9, 11, 12

Columbia River Inn

Franklin Street Station Bed & Breakfast

1140 Franklin Street, 97103
(503) 325-4314; (800) 448-1098

This Victorian home is rated one of the finest bed and breakfast establishments by many publications. Five rooms, all with private baths (two suites), and three rooms with views of the Columbia River. Try the Captain's Quarters, with a fabulous view, wet bar, fireplace, TV, VCR, stereo, and luxurious bath. Full breakfast. Close to downtown and within walking distance of museums. Make reservations in advance, if possible.

---

7 No smoking; 8 Children welcome; 9 Social drinking allowed; 10 Tennis nearby; 11 Swimming nearby; 12 Golf nearby; 13 Skiing nearby; 14 May be booked through a travel agent; 15 Handicapped accessible.

Hosts: Maurizio Bassini and Darcy Urell
Rooms: 5 (PB) $80-135
Full Breakfast
Credit Cards: A, B
Notes: 2, 7, 9, 10, 11

Grandview

Grandview Bed & Breakfast

1574 Grand Avenue, 97103
(503) 325-0000; (503) 325-5555; (800) 488-3250
E-FAX (707) 982-8790
e-mail: grandviewbedandbreakfast@usa.net
www.pacifier.com/~grandview
www.bbonline.com/or/grandview/

Wonderful views of the Columbia River; close to the best maritime museum on the West Coast and other museums, churches, and Victorian homes. Domestic and foreign ships in port. Light, airy three-story Victorian with hardwood floors.

Hostess: Charleen Maxwell
Rooms: 9 (7 PB; 2 SB) $45-98
Full Breakfast
Credit Cards: A, B, D
Notes: 5, 7, 11, 12

Pacific Bed & Breakfast Agency

P.O. Box 46894, Seattle, WA 98146
(206) 439-7677; (800) 684-2932
FAX (206) 431-0932; e-mail: pacificb@nwlink.com
www.seattlebedandbreakfast.com

193. Victorian home. Ornate craftsmanship describes this Victorian home built in 1900 by a shipbuilder for his son. Three of the five rooms have views of the Columbia River and feature claw-foot tubs for a relaxing, quiet getaway from the daily routine. Seasonal rates.

BANDON

Beach Street Bed & Breakfast

200 Beach Street, 97411-0217
(541) 347-5124; (888) 355-1076
e-mail:sharon@beach-street.com
www.beach-street.com

Beach Street Bed and Breakfast is a tranquil retreat in beautiful Bandon by the sea. From the ocean-view room and private deck guests will experience the many moods of the Pacific. Walk the unspoiled, secluded beach. Or just relax in the quiet of the spa tub. Pamper yourself and getaway from it all. Rooms feature two-person spa tubs, fireplaces, and pillowtop king- or queen-size beds. Breakfast is of guests' choosing or let Sharon surprise you. "Come join us. We will have a cup of cheer and a sunset waiting."

Rooms: 6 (PB) $100-145
Full Breakfast
Credit Cards: A, B, C
Notes: 2, 5, 7, 9, 12

Beach Street

Lighthouse Bed & Breakfast

650 Jetty Road, P.O. Box 24, 97411
(541) 347-9316

The gateway of the Pacific Ocean meets the mouth of the Coquille River with the Bandon

---

NOTES: Credit cards accepted: A MasterCard; B Visa; C American Express; D Discover; E Diner's Club; F Other; 2 Personal checks accepted; 3 Lunch available; 4 Dinner available; 5 Open all year; 6 Pets welcome;

historical lighthouse illuminating the scene. Walking distance to historical old downtown Bandon or the beach and surf. Unsurpassed views. Five guest rooms, two king-size with whirlpool and fireplace. Full breakfast. Children over 12 welcome by prior arrangement. Complimentary wine.

Host: Shirley Chalupa
Rooms: 5 (PB) $95-155
Full Breakfast
Credit Cards: A, B
Notes: 2, 5, 7, 9, 11, 12

Sea Star Guesthouse

370 First Street, 97411
(503) 347-9632

This guest house is a comfortable, romantic coastal getaway with European ambiance. It is on the harbor and provides harbor, river, and ocean views. The shops, galleries, theater, and other sights of the Oldtown Harbor District are just a step away. The newly decorated rooms offer a warm, private retreat. Some rooms have skylights, open-beam ceilings, and fireplaces; all have decks. All rooms have refrigerators, toaster ovens, and in-room coffee and tea service.

Host: Eileen Goff
Rooms: 4 (PB) $40-85
Credit Cards: A, B, D
Notes: 5, 7, 8, 9, 10, 11, 12

BEND

Juniper Acres Bed & Breakfast

65220 Smokey Ridge Road, 97701
(541) 389-2193 (phone/FAX)
e-mail: verndella@prodigy.net

Vern and Della built this lodge-style log home as a bed and breakfast facility in 1991. Each room has a private bath, sitting area, and TV. Guests are encouraged to use the great room which overlooks a fantastic seven-mountain vista. This bed and breakfast has a very private country set-

Juniper Acres

ting only seven minutes from mall shopping. Guests are provided a delicious breakfast each morning at a time convenient to them.

Host: Della Bjerk
Rooms: 2 (PB) $75
Full Breakfast
Credit Cards: None
Notes: 2, 5, 7, 9, 12, 13, 14

BEAVERTON

The Yankee Tinker Bed & Breakfast

5480 Southwest 183rd Avenue, 97007
(503) 649-0932; (800) 846-5372
e-mail: yankeetb&b@aol.com
www.yankeetinker.com

Easy access to Beaverton, Hillsboro businesses, 10 miles west of Portland, in Washington County wine country. Comfortable home operating as bed and breakfast since 1988, filled with family heirlooms, antiques, quilts, and flowers. Private yard and gardens. Spacious deck. Quiet retreat, perfect for a day or a week. Fireplace in guest sitting room. Fully air conditioned. Acclaimed breakfasts, timed and scaled to meet guests' needs, utilize the abundant variety of locally grown fruits and berries. Featured in *Hidden Oregon*.

Hosts: Jan and Ralph Wadleigh
Rooms: 3 (2 PB; 1 SB) $65-75
Full Breakfast
Credit Cards: A, B, C, D, E
Notes: 2, 5, 7, 9, 10, 11, 12, 14

---

7 No smoking; 8 Children welcome; 9 Social drinking allowed; 10 Tennis nearby; 11 Swimming nearby; 12 Golf nearby; 13 Skiing nearby; 14 May be booked through a travel agent; 15 Handicapped accessible.

BRIGHTWOOD

Pacific Bed & Breakfast Agency

P.O. Box 46894, Seattle, WA 98146
(206) 439-7677; (800) 684-2932
FAX (206) 431-0932; e-mail: pacificb@nwlink.com
www.seattlebedandbreakfast.com

149. East of Portland, on two acres on historic Barlow Trail and surrounded by a clear mountain stream and tall firs is guests' very own guest house with its own Japanese water garden for that special getaway. A complimentary gourmet breakfast can accommodate special diets if there is advanced notice. A variety of bikes, books, videos, games, and puzzles are provided. Make sure to make reservations for lodging early for this lovely spot.

BROOKINGS

Brookings South Coast Inn

516 Redwood Street, 97415
(541) 469-5557; (800) 525-9273
FAX (541) 469-6615; e-mail: scoastin@wave.net
www.virtualcities.com

A 1917 vintage home designed in the Craftsman style by Bernard Maybeck. Restored and furnished with antiques and treasures, this home has a happy, warm feeling. Large parlor, indoor hot tub/sauna, in-room TV/VCRs, spacious bedrooms upstairs. Ocean view. Just a few blocks from the river and harbor. Gourmet breakfast includes Norwegian waffles. A private garden cottage is also available. Fully licensed. AAA-approved and *Northwest Best Places*. Children over 12 are welcome.

Hosts: Ken and Keith
Rooms: 4 (PB) $84-94
Full Breakfast
Credit Cards: A, B, C, D
Notes: 2, 5, 7, 9, 10, 11, 12, 14

Chetco River Inn

Chetco River Inn

21202 High Prairie Road, 97415
(541) 670-1645
(800) 327-2688 (Pelican Bay Travel)
FAX (503) 469-4341; www.chetcoriverinn.com

Relax in the peaceful seclusion of 35 forested acres. Near the seacoast town of Brookings. The inn is small, so guest numbers are limited. Surrounded on three sides by the lovely Chetco River, the inn uses alternative energy, but it will offer guests all modern amenities. Delicious big meals. River fishing, swimming, hiking, bird watching, mushrooming, and just plain relaxing. Smoking in designated areas. Inquire about accommodations for children. Social drinking permitted if self-provided. Swimming (no lifeguard) is available in the river. May book through a travel agent if called direct.

Host: Sandra Brugger
Rooms: 5 (PB) $115-135
Full Breakfast
Credit Cards: A, B, C, D
Notes: 2, 3, 4, 5, 11

COOS BAY

Blackberry Inn Bed & Breakfast

843 Central, 97420
(541) 267-6951; (800) 500-4657

On the southern Oregon coast, this charming bed and breakfast offers the elegant atmosphere of an old Victorian home. Since the inn is separate

---

NOTES: Credit cards accepted: A MasterCard; B Visa; C American Express; D Discover; E Diner's Club; F Other; 2 Personal checks accepted; 3 Lunch available; 4 Dinner available; 5 Open all year; 6 Pets welcome;

Blackberry Inn

from the hosts' residence, guests can enjoy the hospitality and have privacy, too. A quick walk to several restaurants, stores, a theater, an art museum, and the city park, with its lovely Japanese gardens, tennis courts, and picnic areas.

Hosts: John and Louise Duncan
Rooms: 4 (3 PB; 1 SB) $35-50
Continental Breakfast
Credit Cards: A, B
Notes: 2, 5, 7, 8, 9, 10, 11, 12

Pacific Bed & Breakfast Agency

P.O. Box 46894, Seattle, WA 98146
(206) 439-7677; (800) 684-2932
FAX (206) 431-0932; e-mail: pacificb@nwlink.com
www.seattlebedandbreakfast.com

148. Built in 1912, this Colonial-style house has an open-air banister that surrounds the second floor, and the detailed woodworking throughout the entire home makes for a warm and inviting atmosphere. Choose from five rooms with private or shared baths. A Continental plus breakfast is included in the room rate.

DEPOE BAY

The Channel House Inn, Inc.

35 Ellingson, P.O. Box 56, 97341
(541) 765-2140; (800) 477-2140
FAX (541) 765-2191; www.channelhouse.com

The Channel House Inn is perched on a cliff high above the rugged coastline of Oregon's Depoe Bay. Enjoy spectacular views of the Pacific Ocean, with abundant whale watching and captivating winter storms. Charter fishing and whale watching cruises are available. Whirlpool tubs for two on private oceanfront decks and cozy gas log fireplaces make Channel House the perfect romantic getaway. Two and one-half hours southwest of Portland, just off Highway 101. Buffet breakfast served.

Host: Vicki Mix and Carl Finseth
Rooms: 14 (PB) $80-235
Continental Breakfast
Credit Cards: A, B, C, D
Notes: 2, 5, 7, 12, 14

The Channel House Inn

Pacific Bed & Breakfast Agency

P.O. Box 46894, Seattle, WA 98146
(206) 439-7677; (800) 684-2932
FAX (206) 431-0932; e-mail: pacificb@nwlink.com
www.seattlebedandbreakfast.com

168. Endless ocean views. Built high above the rocky shore of the bay and with views of the ocean, this modern home was designed with the sea in mind. Of the six rooms and three suites, two of the large oceanfront suites have kitchens, fireplaces, and whirlpool baths for that special getaway. Enjoy the breakfast in the first-floor dining room or in the privacy of guests' suite. This bed and breakfast offers all the comforts of a first-class resort with the congeniality of a small ocean hideaway.

---

7 No smoking; 8 Children welcome; 9 Social drinking allowed; 10 Tennis nearby; 11 Swimming nearby; 12 Golf nearby; 13 Skiing nearby; 14 May be booked through a travel agent; 15 Handicapped accessible.

EUGENE

Kjaer's House in the Woods

814 Lorane Highway, 97405
(541) 343-3234; (800) 437-4501
FAX (541) 343-0623

A 1910 Craftsman-style bungalow designated as a city historic landmark, the Young-Pallett House, in a peaceful wooded setting with abundant wildlife. Near jogging, biking, and hiking trails. Furnished with comfortable antiques, oriental carpets, square grand piano, music and reading libraries. This home offers urban convenience with suburban tranquility. Full breakfasts with careful attention to dietary needs served at guests' convenience. No smoking or pets. Inquire about accommodations for children. Fax/modem data port.

Rooms: 2 (PB) $65-80
Full Breakfast
Credit Cards: None
Notes: 2, 5, 7, 10, 11, 12, 14

Kjaer's House in the Woods

The Oval Door

988 Lawrence at Tenth, 97401
(541) 683-3160; FAX (541) 485-5339
www.ovaldoor.com

Recently built as a bed and breakfast inn, this 1920s farmhouse-style home in the heart of Eugene has a wraparound porch and an inviting front door with an oval glass. Guest rooms are spacious and comfortable, each with large private bathroom. The Tub Room with Jacuzzi for two is a relaxing haven with bubbles, candles, and music. Hearty breakfast with homemade specialties. Guests love the porch swing and cozy library.

Hosts: Nicole Wergeland and Melissa Coray
Rooms: 4 (PB) $75-115
Full Breakfast
Credit Cards: A, B, C
Notes: 2, 5, 7, 8, 9, 12, 14

Pookie's Bed 'n' Breakfast on College Hill

2013 Charnelton Street, 97405
(541) 343-0383; (800) 558-0383
FAX (541) 431-0967
www.travelassist.com

This restored Craftsman home built in 1918 offers distinctive rooms with many antiques. The three rooms with queen-size bed and twin beds are upstairs and share a cozy sitting room. In a quiet, older neighborhood close to the University of Oregon, downtown, shopping, and fine restaurants. The hosts pamper their guests with a full breakfast served in the formal dining room at guests' convenience. Beautiful grounds with rose garden and wonderful yard where guests can relax. This is a nonsmoking facility, but smoking is permitted outside. Children six and older are welcome.

Hosts: Pookie and Doug Walling
Rooms: 3 (2 PB; 1 SB) $70-95
Full Breakfast
Credit Cards: None
Notes: 2, 5, 7, 9, 10, 11, 12, 13, 14

GLENEDEN BEACH

Pacific Bed & Breakfast Agency

P.O. Box 46894, Seattle, WA 98146
(206) 439-7677; (800) 684-2932
FAX (206) 431-0932; e-mail: pacificb@nwlink.com
www.seattlebedandbreakfast.com

151. If one is looking for a peaceful hideaway on the Oregon coast, this is the right place to stay. Guest rooms are native wood structures

NOTES: Credit cards accepted: A MasterCard; B Visa; C American Express; D Discover; E Diner's Club; F Other; 2 Personal checks accepted; 3 Lunch available; 4 Dinner available; 5 Open all year; 6 Pets welcome;

built in harmony with the naturally landscaped surroundings with sheltered, covered walkways, and bridges leading to the main lodge. The ambiance is heightened by the variety and caliber of the Pacific Northwest dining. Play golf, indoor/outdoor tennis, take a swim in the indoor pool or just relax in front of the fireplace. Large conference and social events rooms available. Seasonal rates.

GRANTS PASS

Flery Manor Bed & Breakfast

2000 Jumpoff Joe Creek Road, 97526
(541) 476-3591; FAX (541) 471-2303
e-mail: flery@flerymanor.com
www.flerymanor.com

"Get away from the hurried world...retreat to the comfort and hospitality of Flery Manor." Elegant, romantic, secluded. On seven mountain view acres near the Rogue River. Elegantly decorated bedrooms. Suite has king-size bed, fireplace, Jacuzzi tub, and private balcony. Ponds, paths, waterfall, streams, and gazebo. Library, parlor with piano, two-story high living room, huge balcony, and formal dining room. Three-course gourmet breakfast. Access to private health club/pool. Easy I-5 access. Featured in *Chef* magazine.

Hosts: John and Marla Vidrinskas
Rooms: 4 (PB) $75-125
Full Breakfast
Credit Cards: A, B
Notes: 2, 5, 7, 8, 9, 10, 11, 12, 13, 14

Lawnridge House

Lawnridge House Bed & Breakfast

1304 Northwest Lawnridge, 97526
(541) 476-8518

Since 1984, guests have enjoyed the privacy and peace of this 1909 restored Craftsman two-story. Large rooms, guest friendly antiques, beamed ceilings, and a large wooded lot framed by 200-year-old oak trees are features of this inn. Bedrooms have king- or queen-size canopied beds, TV, VCR, mini-refrigerators, and air conditioning. Northwest regional focus is a specialty, and dietary requests are catered to when possible. The family suite sleeps from two to six people, while the king-size suite is used frequently for honeymoons and anniversary celebrations.

Host: Barbara Head
Rooms: 3 (2 PB; 1 SB) $65-85
Full Breakfast
Credit Cards: None
Notes: 2, 5, 7, 8, 9, 10, 11, 12, 13, 14

Morrison's Rogue River Lodge

8500 Galice Road, Merlin, 97532
(541) 476-3825; (800) 826-1963
FAX (541) 476-4953; www.morrisonslodge.com

Morrison's Rogue River Lodge is in southern Oregon on the famous Rogue River. It was built in the 1940s and has grown from a fishing lodge to a full-service destination resort catering to romantics as well as families, outdoorsmen,

Flery Manor

---

7 No smoking; 8 Children welcome; 9 Social drinking allowed; 10 Tennis nearby; 11 Swimming nearby; 12 Golf nearby; 13 Skiing nearby; 14 May be booked through a travel agent; 15 Handicapped accessible.

rafting enthusiasts, and fishermen. First-class accommodations in cozy river-view cottages with fireplaces or lodge rooms. Well known for its fabulous cuisine. Overnight accommodations include a four-course gourmet dinner and a bountiful country breakfast. Full service conference facilities are available.

Host: Michelle Hanten
Rooms: 13 (PB) $160-260
Full Breakfast
Credit Cards: A, B, D
Notes: 2, 3, 4, 7, 8, 9, 10, 11, 12, 14

Pine Meadow Inn

Pine Meadow Inn Bed & Breakfast

1000 Crow Road, Merlin, 97532-9718
(541) 471-6277 (phone/FAX); (800) 554-0806
e-mail: pmi@pinemeadowinn.com
www.pinemeadowinn.com

A distinctive country retreat on nine acres of meadow and woods near the wild and scenic area of the Rogue River. Enjoy nearby whitewater rafting, Shakespeare Festival, historic Jacksonville, and California redwoods. Wraparound porch with wicker furniture, English cutting and herb gardens, a hot tub under the pines, koi pond. Guest rooms are sunny and well lit for reading, with queen-size, pillow-top mattresses, and private baths. Delicious, healthy breakfasts. Central air. Children over 10 welcome. AAA-rated three diamonds. Winter rates.

Hosts: Maloy and Nancy Murdock
Rooms: 4 (PB) $80-110
Full Breakfast
Credit Cards: A, B, C, D
Notes: 2, 5, 7, 9, 12, 14

Weasku Inn

5560 Rogue River Highway, 97527
(541) 471-8000; (800) 4 WEASKU
e-mail: info@weasku.com

The Weasku Inn is a luxurious legendary Hollywood getaway nestled on the banks of the Rogue River, in southern Oregon. Recently the lodge completed a major renovation. Choose from elegant lodge or river cabins furnished with all modern conveniences. All rooms are decorated with authentic Pacific Northwest furnishings and portray the ambiance of years past. Fishing and rafting guide service available. A wine and cheese reception is served nightly. Relax and enjoy. Take exit 48 off I-5.

Host: Carl Johnson
Rooms: 20 (PB) $85-295
Continental Breakfast
Credit Cards: A, B, C, D, E
Notes: 5, 7, 8, 9, 10, 11, 12, 13, 14, 15

HOOD RIVER

Brown's Bed & Breakfast

3000 Reed Road, 97031
(541) 386-1545

This house is a functioning farmhouse built in the early 1930s and remodeled in 1985. It has a modern kitchen where the large farm-style breakfasts are prepared and a new bathroom that is shared by the two bedrooms. One bedroom has twin beds and overlooks beautiful Mount Hood, the other bedroom has a king-size bed and overlooks the orchard. Nestled in the forest and at the end of the road; the only noise to be heard is that of birds chirping. There are nature trails for hiking or jogging.

Hosts: Al and Marian Brown
Rooms: 2 (SB) $65
Full Breakfast

NOTES: Credit cards accepted: A MasterCard; B Visa; C American Express; D Discover; E Diner's Club; F Other; 2 Personal checks accepted; 3 Lunch available; 4 Dinner available; 5 Open all year; 6 Pets welcome;

Credit Cards: A, B
Notes: 2, 5, 7, 8, 10, 11, 12, 13, 14

Columbia Gorge Hotel

4000 Westcliff Drive, 97031
(541) 386-5566; (800) 345-1921
FAX (541) 387-5414; e-mail: cghotel@gorge.net

The Columbia Gorge Hotel, 60 miles east of Portland, was built in 1921 as a gracious oasis for travelers along the Columbia River Scenic Highway. At the top of a 210-foot waterfall above the majestic Columbia River, the hotel has a national reputation for fine cuisine and elegant surroundings. The hotel boasts 40 unique guest rooms, an award-winning dining room, and exquisite wedding facilities on 11 beautifully landscaped acres. Complimentary "World-Famous Farm Breakfast."

Hosts: Boyd and Halla Graves
Rooms: 40 (PB) $150-250
Full Breakfast
Credit Cards: A, B, C, D, E
Notes: 2, 3, 4, 5, 6, 7, 9, 10, 11, 12, 13, 14

Columbia Gorge Hotel

JACKSONVILLE

Jacksonville Inn

175 East California Street, P.O. Box 359, 97530
(541) 899-1900; (800) 321-9344
e-mail: jvinn@mind.net
www.jacksonvilleinn.com

In the national historic landmark town of Jacksonville, the Jacksonville Inn, built in 1861, offers eight elegantly decorated hotel rooms, modernized for comfort and opulence with whirlpool tubs, steam showers, and air conditioning, as well as three luxurious honeymoon cottages that cater to romance and privacy. An

Jacksonville Inn

award-winning dinner house features gourmet dining with more than 2,000 wines and a full service lounge.

Hosts: Jerry and Linda Evans
Rooms: 11 (PB) $100-245
Full Breakfast
Credit Cards: A, B, C, D, E
Notes: 2, 3, 4, 5, 7, 9, 10, 11, 12, 13, 14

LA GRANDE

Stang Manor Inn

1612 Walnut, 97850
(541) 963-2400; (888) 286-9463
e-mail: innkeeper@stangmanor.com

A historic 1920s timber baron's mansion. Totally renovated and redecorated, all of the manor's rooms have private baths and queen-size beds. Two suites are available, one with a fireplace. A full breakfast is served in the formal dining room—and conversations are

Stang Manor Inn

---

7 No smoking; 8 Children welcome; 9 Social drinking allowed; 10 Tennis nearby; 11 Swimming nearby; 12 Golf nearby; 13 Skiing nearby; 14 May be booked through a travel agent; 15 Handicapped accessible.

superb. The manor sits on an acre of trees, roses, and lawn in a quiet residential area. La Grande is the principal city in one of the most beautiful valleys in Oregon.

Hosts: Margorie and Pat McClure
Rooms: 4 (PB) $80-95
Full Breakfast
Credit Cards: A, B
Notes: 2, 5, 7, 9, 11, 12, 13, 14

LANGLOIS

Floras Lake House by the Sea Bed & Breakfast

92870 Boice Cope Road, 97450
(541) 348-2573; e-mail: floraslk@harborside.com
www.floraslake.com

Seventeen miles south of Bandon, this contemporary cedar home was built in 1991. Four rooms, all have lake and ocean views, vaulted wood ceilings, private baths, and deck entrances. Two with fireplace. Beachcombing, mountain biking, windsurfing lessons and rentals available nearby. Casual buffet-style full breakfast gets guests started for a day of exploring the beautiful southern Oregon coast.

Hosts: Liz and Will Brady
Rooms: 4 (PB) $100-130
Full Breakfast
Credit Cards: A, B
Notes: 2, 7, 8, 9, 10, 11, 12

LINCOLN CITY

Brey House Ocean View Bed & Breakfast Inn

3725 Northwest Keel Avenue, 97367
(541) 994-7123
www.moriah.com/breyhouse

This three-story Cape Cod-style house has a nautical theme that shows throughout the home. Across the street from the ocean, it is a short walk to shops and restaurants. Queen-size beds are in all the rooms, and all rooms have private entrances. Close to sea lion caves and the world's smallest harbor. Lincoln City is also the kite capital of the world. Keiko, the *Free Willy* orca, is 20 miles away in the Oregon Coast Aquarium. Enjoy watching the ocean while eating a fantastic breakfast served by the hosts.

Hosts: Milt and Shirley Brey
Rooms: 4 (PB) $75-135
Full Breakfast
Credit Cards: A, B, D
Notes: 5, 7, 9, 10, 11, 12, 14

Pacific Rest Bed & Breakfast

1611 Northeast 11th, 97367
(541) 994-2337; (888) 405-7378
e-mail: jwaetjen@wcn.net
http://pacificrestbb.hypermart.net/

Journey back to simpler times at this central, peaceful hillside location. Built especially for a bed and breakfast, guests will find respite for the body and the soul. Two spacious suites with private baths and balconies—within walking distance to beach, restaurants, shopping. Full candlelight breakfast and homemade treats. Children welcome. Also available 2 two- to three-bedroom, two baths, fully furnished ocean view guest cottages with fireplaces, decks, and hot tub—sleeps four to seven.

Hosts: Ray and Judy Waetjen; Barbara Beard
Rooms: 2 (PB) $85-150
Full Breakfast
Credit Cards: None
Notes: 2, 5, 7, 8, 10, 11, 12, 14

MCMINNVILLE

Pacific Bed & Breakfast Agency

P.O. Box 46894, Seattle, WA 98146
(206) 439-7677; (800) 684-2932
FAX (206) 431-0932; e-mail: pacificb@nwlink.com
www.seattlebedandbreakfast.com

220. Farmhouse in the hills. Enjoy this French farmhouse on 12 acres in a vineyard. Five bedrooms, all with private baths, two with fireplaces. Full gourmet breakfast. Nonsmoking. $99-150.

NOTES: Credit cards accepted: A MasterCard; B Visa; C American Express; D Discover; E Diner's Club; F Other; 2 Personal checks accepted; 3 Lunch available; 4 Dinner available; 5 Open all year; 6 Pets welcome;

Youngberg Hill Vineyard

Youngberg Hill Vineyard Bed & Breakfast

10660 Southwest Youngberg Hill Road, 97128
(503) 472-2727; FAX (503) 472-1313
e-mail: martin@youngberghill.com
www.youngberghill.com

This magnificent hilltop farmhouse commands breathtaking views across the property's 12 acres of pinot noir vineyards, over the Willamette Valley towards the Cascades and Coast Range. Every room has a romantic view (two have fireplaces), a private bath, lovely oak furnishings, fresh flowers, and bedtime chocolates. Breakfasts are a treat. Among the inn's special attractions are a well-stocked wine cellar with an emphasis on Oregon wines.

Hosts: Kevin and Tasha Byrd
Rooms: 5 (PB) $130-150
Full Breakfast
Credit Cards: A, B
Notes: 2, 5, 7, 9, 10, 11, 12, 14, 15

MEDFORD

Waverly Cottages

305 North Grape, 97501
(541) 779-4716; FAX (541) 732-1718
www.aaaabbcom.

In a historic area just north of downtown Medford, Waverly Cottage offers complete privacy with authentic Victorian charm. Built in 1898, the cottage has been restored to accurately maintain its ornate Queen Anne style. Central heating and air conditioning. Fully furnished suites offer complete privacy, cable TV, private telephones, and ample living areas. This central location is within walking distance of the Craterian Theater, government offices, dozens of restaurants, nightclubs, a microwbrewery, and a historic walking tour. Inquire about accommodations for children and pets. One unit is handicapped accessible. All units have kitchens. On request, the host will do fruit baskets with muffins, coffee, and juice for an additional $10.

Host: David K. Fisse
Rooms: 2 (PB) $40-90
Credit Cards: A, B, C
Notes: 2, 5, 7, 9, 10, 11, 12, 13, 14

Waverly Cottages

MOUNT HOOD

Pacific Bed & Breakfast Agency

P.O. Box 46894, Seattle, WA 98146
(206) 439-7677; (800) 684-2932
FAX (206) 431-0932; e-mail: pacificb@nwlink.com
www.seattlebedandbreakfast.com

150. Mountain lodge/chalet. On the Government Camp Loop Highway of Mount Hood, the architecturally designed lodge/chalet fits into the quiet natural forest and majestic setting of the Cascades. Guests are invited to enjoy all of the common areas of the inn and choose from a variety of guest accommodations. The host and hostess will make guests' stay a memorable one any time during the year and the gourmet meals are a joy to remember. Call for

---

7 No smoking; 8 Children welcome; 9 Social drinking allowed; 10 Tennis nearby; 11 Swimming nearby; 12 Golf nearby; 13 Skiing nearby; 14 May be booked through a travel agent; 15 Handicapped accessible.

availability and be sure you call in advance to reserve your special room. Rates vary.

MOUNT HOOD AREA

Falcon's Crest Inn

87287 Government Camp Loop Highway
P.O. Box 185, 97028
(503) 272-3403; (800) 624-7384
FAX (503) 272-3454

Elegance Mount Hood-style features three rooms and two suites with private baths. Individually decorated with family heirlooms, in-room telephones, bed turndown service, morning refreshment tray. A full breakfast is served in the morning. In the heart of a year-round recreation area. Skiing, hiking, fishing, and golf are all nearby. Corporate, private, and mystery parties. Ski packages, holiday, and special events. Fine evening dining and spirits available.

Hosts: Melody and Bob Johnson
Rooms: 5 (PB) $95-179
Full Breakfast
Credit Cards: A, B, C, D
Notes: 2, 4, 5, 7, 9, 10, 11, 12, 13, 14

NEWBERG

Avellan Inn: A Bed & Breakfast

16900 Northeast Highway 240, 97132
(503) 537-9161

Discover the magic that is Avellan Inn. Twelve acres of grounds invite guests to wander through the gardens, woods, and hazelnut orchard. Gourmet breakfast features Oregon products, homemade breads and jams. Each room offers panoramic view, down featherbed on queen-size mattress, and private bath with bidet. Enjoy the hosts' lavish attention to detail, from the hazelnut truffle on the pillow upon arrival to the "brown bag cookie" on departure. Explore Portland (30 miles northeast), the ocean (60 miles west), the wineries (more than 20 in a 10-mile radius), or simply relax and enjoy the private, country peacefulness. Close to George Fox University and Linfield College. Optional suite available.

Hosts: Ken and Carol Bond Williams
Rooms: 2 (PB) $85-115
Full Breakfast
Credit Cards: A, B
Notes: 2, 5, 6, 8, 9, 14

NEWPORT

Oar House

520 Southwest Second Street, 97365
(541) 265-9571; (800) 252-2358
e-mail: oarhouse@newportnet.com
www.newportnet.com/oarhouse

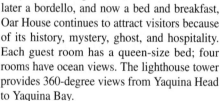

Oar House, a Lincoln County historic landmark in the picturesque Nye Beach area of Newport, has offered comfort and conviviality to guests since the early 1900s. Originally a boarding house, later a bordello, and now a bed and breakfast, Oar House continues to attract visitors because of its history, mystery, ghost, and hospitality. Each guest room has a queen-size bed; four rooms have ocean views. The lighthouse tower provides 360-degree views from Yaquina Head to Yaquina Bay.

Host: Jan LeBrun
Rooms: 5 (PB) $95-125
Full Breakfast
Credit Cards: A, B, D
Notes: 5, 7, 9, 10, 11, 12

Pacific Bed & Breakfast Agency

P.O. Box 46894, Seattle, WA 98146
(206) 439-7677; (800) 684-2932
FAX (206) 431-0932; e-mail: pacificb@nwlink.com
www.seattlebedandbreakfast.com

194. Oceanfront hotel. In this oceanfront book lover's bed and breakfast, each room is individually decorated and is given the name of a different author. Some rooms have fireplaces. Full

---

NOTES: Credit cards accepted: A MasterCard; B Visa; C American Express; D Discover; E Diner's Club;
F Other; 2 Personal checks accepted; 3 Lunch available; 4 Dinner available; 5 Open all year; 6 Pets welcome;

breakfast each morning, dinner is served nightly and hot spiced wine is served in the library each evening. Not suitable for young children. Twenty rooms with reasonable prices.

OAKLAND

Beckley House Bed & Breakfast

338 Southeast Second Street, P.O. Box 198, 97462
(541) 459-9320 (phone/FAX)

The Beckley House is a historic two-story Classical Revival Victorian home listed in the historic register. Reflecting a nostalgic era, the home is comfortably furnished in period-style antiques. Enjoy wine tours, Rochester covered bridge, or the Umpqua River. Two rooms with private baths. Fresh bread, muffins, and a great breakfast are served.

Hosts: Karene and Rich Neuharth
Rooms: 2 (PB) $60-85
Full Breakfast
Credit Cards: A, B, C, D
Notes: 2, 5, 7, 8, 9, 10, 12, 14

OTIS

Salmon River Bed & Breakfast

5622 Salmon River Highway 18, 97368
(541) 994-2639; e-mail: mpegg@wcn.net
www.lincolncity.com/salmonriverb&b

Big breakfasts—golden delicious applesauce or huckleberry pancakes; or roasted hazelnut waffles; or German pancake served with lemon and powdered sugar; meat dish, fruit dish, juice, coffee or tea; homemade fruit syrups. Ten to 15 minutes from beach accesses and shopping. Situated at Lincoln City midway between Newport and Tillamoor. Allow three days, if possible, to explore all three. Closed Thanksgiving and Christmas.

Hosts: Marvin and Pawnee Pegg
Rooms: 4 (2 PB; 2 S1&1/2B) $55-70
Full Breakfast
Credit Cards: A, B, D, E
Notes: 2, 7, 8, 9, 10, 11, 12, 14

PACIFIC CITY

Eagle's View Bed & Breakfast

37975 Brooten Road, P.O. Box 901, 97135
(503) 965-7600; (888) TIME AWAY (846-3292)
www.moriah.com/eaglesview/

The inn is decorated country comfortable including pine vaulted ceiling fans and lots of quilts. This custom-built inn was carved high on a mountain overlooking beautiful Nestucca Bay and River. All rooms have private baths, queen-size beds, a TV, a VCR, a CD player, and direct-dial telephones. Three guest rooms have Jacuzzis. Enjoy a hearty country breakfast in the privacy of own room or dine in the great room.

Hosts: Mike and Kathy Lewis
Rooms: 5 (PB) $95-115
Full Breakfast
Credit Cards: A, B, D. E
Notes: 2, 5, 7, 9, 11, 12, 14, 15

Eagle's View

PORTLAND

General Hooker's Bed & Breakfast

125 Southwest Hooker, 97201
(503) 222-4435; (800) 745-4135
FAX (503) 295-6410
e-mail: ghbandb@teleport.com
www.teleport.com/~ghbandb

In a quiet district and within walking distance of downtown, General Hooker's is a casually

---

7 No smoking; 8 Children welcome; 9 Social drinking allowed; 10 Tennis nearby; 11 Swimming nearby; 12 Golf nearby; 13 Skiing nearby; 14 May be booked through a travel agent; 15 Handicapped accessible.

General Hooker's

classic Victorian townhouse that combines the mellow warmth of the 19th century with the comfort and convenience of the 20th. Knowledgeable host, a fourth-generation Portlander and a charter member of the Oregon Bed and Breakfast Guild, can be a veritable gold mine of information for newcomers to her city. Two-night minimum stay is often required. Sociable Abyssinian cat in residence. AAA- and Mobil-approved. Continental plus breakfast included in rates.

Host: Lori Hall
Rooms: 4 (2 PB; 2 SB) $75-125
Continental Breakfast
Credit Cards: A, B, C
Notes: 5, 7, 9, 10, 11, 12

Georgian House Bed & Breakfast

1828 Northeast Siskiyou, 97212
(503) 281-2250; (888) 282-2250 (toll-free)
FAX (503) 281-3301

Step back in time to charming Olde England at this restored, handsome brick Georgian Colonial featured in *Better Homes and Gardens*

magazine. Relax on the sun deck or in the gazebo. Stroll through the colorful rose garden or the quiet, historic Irvington neighborhood. Close to shopping, restaurants, theaters; easy freeway access to I-5, I-205, and I-84. Close to convention center, coliseum, Lloyd Center Mall, downtown, and MAX Light Rail. Winding staircase to second floor, hardwood floors, and antiques. Rooms are air conditioned.

Host: Willie Ackley
Rooms: 4 (2 PB: 2 SB) $65-85
Full Breakfast
Credit Cards: A, B
Notes: 2, 5, 7, 9, 10, 11, 12, 13

Georgian House

Pacific Bed & Breakfast Agency

P.O. Box 46894, Seattle, WA 98146
(206) 439-7677; (800) 684-2932
FAX (206) 431-0932; e-mail: pacificb@nwlink.com
www.seattlebedandbreakfast.com

142. Villa on the Butte. On a volcanic cone above the city this host home has wonderful views of Mount St. Helens, Mount Hood, and the Columbia River Gorge. One suite is offered to guests and there is a king-size bed and private bath, TV, and VCR for guests' enjoyment. A special exercise room is available for guests' morning workout followed by a full breakfast. Seasonal rates.

143. Georgian Colonial. This is one of only three true Georgian Colonial homes in Port-

NOTES: Credit cards accepted: A MasterCard; B Visa; C American Express; D Discover; E Diner's Club; F Other; 2 Personal checks accepted; 3 Lunch available; 4 Dinner available; 5 Open all year; 6 Pets welcome;

land. There are several gold coins placed in the house foundation for good luck. Leaded windows, a winding staircase, and oak floors have been lovingly restored. Three bedrooms give guests the choice of shared or private bath and king- or queen-size bed. Full breakfast served. $70-100.

144. Elegant historic landmark. Six rooms all with private baths featuring claw-foot tubs make this historic home a special place for a romantic weekend or business trip. Guests will enjoy the friendly atmosphere in a quiet residential area. Continental buffet breakfast is served in the formal dining room. Room rates vary.

145. City and mountain views. A garden-level suite with a private entrance can be guests' home-away-from-home just 10 minutes by car from the city center. This two-room suite has a choice of king-size or twin beds and has a Hide-a-Bed to accommodate a total of four persons. A fireplace, TV, and VCR are provided and a full breakfast is served in the dining room. Call for prices and availability.

Pittock Acres Bed & Breakfast

103 Northwest Pittock Avenue, 97210
(503) 226-1163; (800) 769-9774
FAX (503) 226-6116
www.bbhost.com/pittockacres

Delightful contemporary home with a "touch" of elegance in scenic historic urban area one and one-half miles from downtown Portland. Stroll to historic Pittock Mansion. Walk/jog beautiful forested trails to the Hoyt Arboretum, Oregon Zoo, World Forestry Center, and the beautiful Japanese and Rose Test Gardens. Experience nearby Nob Hill's exciting boutiques, art galleries, and wonderful restaurants from our atmosphere of peace and tranquility.

Air conditioned. Tea. Small dog. Children 14 and older welcome. ABBA-rated Excellent.

Hosts: Linda and Richard Matson
Rooms: 3 (2 PB; 1 SB) $95
Full Breakfast
Credit Cards: A, B, C, D
Notes: 2, 5, 7, 10, 12

Portland Guest House

Portland Guest House

1720 Northeast Fifteenth Street, 97212
(503) 282-1402; e-mail: pgh@teleport.com
www.teleport.com/~pgh/

This 1890 Victorian is in the historic Irvington neighborhood. All rooms have telephones, antiques, heirloom linens, and great beds. Luscious breakfasts. Family suite with three beds, two rooms with two beds, and five rooms with private baths. Herb, vegetable, and flower gardens. Closest bed and breakfast to convention center. Convenient transit to downtown. Walk to restaurants, delis, coffee shops, and boutiques. Central air conditioning. Mount Hood is 50 miles away.

Host: Susan Gisvold
Rooms: 7 (5 PB; 2 SB) $70-100
Full Breakfast
Credit Cards: A, B
Notes: 2, 5, 7, 8, 10, 11, 12

---

7 No smoking; 8 Children welcome; 9 Social drinking allowed; 10 Tennis nearby; 11 Swimming nearby; 12 Golf nearby; 13 Skiing nearby; 14 May be booked through a travel agent; 15 Handicapped accessible.

Portland, OR

Portland White House

Portland White House Bed & Breakfast Inn

1914 Northeast Twenty-second Avenue, 97212
(503) 287-7131; (800) 272-7131
FAX (503) 249-1641; e-mail: pdxwhi@aol.com
www.portlandswhitehouse.com

Listed in the National Register of Historic Places, this stately home and Carriage House have been restored to its original splendor with circular drive and classic Greek columns. Romantic elegance with bronze and crystal chandeliers, fountains, grand dining room, and period furnishings. The inn is in the historic Irvington district, convenient to Broadway shops, downtown Portland, convention center, fine dining, and local sights. Nine elegantly furnished rooms, all with private baths, private telephone, data ports, and air conditioning. Full gourmet breakfast.

Rooms: 9 (PB) $98-159
Full Breakfast
Credit Cards: A, B, C, D
Notes: 5, 7, 8, 9, 14

PORT ORFORD

Home by the Sea Bed & Breakfast

444 Jackson Street, P.O. Box 606, 97465-0606
(541) 332-2855; www.homebythesea.com

The hosts built their contemporary wood home on a spit of land overlooking a dramatic stretch of Oregon Coast. Queen-sized Oregon myrtle-wood beds and cable TV are featured in both accommodations. Romantic dining and the harbor are close by. Short walk to the beach for agate hunting, beachcombing, storm and whale watching. Shuttle service available to the Cape Blanco lighthouse for bird watchers and beach walkers. Amenities include laundry privileges and telephone jacks in rooms.

Hosts: Alan and Brenda Mitchell
Rooms: 2 (PB) $95-105
Full Breakfast
Credit Cards: A, B
Notes: 2, 5, 7, 8, 9, 12

Home by the Sea

SALEM

Marquee House

333 Wyatt Court Northeast, 97301
(503) 391-0837; (800) 949-0837
FAX (503) 391-1713; e-mail: rickiemh@open.org
www.marqueehouse.com/rickiemh

A 1930s Mount Vernon Colonial with a park-like setting on beautiful Mill Creek. Walking distance to the capitol, Willamette University, historic districts; convenient for wine country tours. Data ports available for business use. Antique-furnished rooms have comedy movie themes. Murder mystery weekends. Nightly

Marquee House

NOTES: Credit cards accepted: A MasterCard; B Visa; C American Express; D Discover; E Diner's Club; F Other; 2 Personal checks accepted; 3 Lunch available; 4 Dinner available; 5 Open all year; 6 Pets welcome;

film showing with bottomless popcorn bowl. Full breakfast featuring Northwest ingredients.

Host: Rickie Hart
Rooms: 5 (3 PB; 2 SB) $63-90
Full Breakfast
Credit Cards: A, B, D, E
Notes: 2, 5, 7, 8, 9, 10, 11, 12, 14

SANDLAKE (PACIFIC CITY)

Sandlake Country Inn

8505 Galloway Road, Cloverdale, 97112
(503) 965-6745

It's a secret hideaway on the awesome Oregon coast—a private, peaceful place for making memories. This 1894 shipwreck-timbered farmhouse on the Oregon historic register is tucked into a bower of old roses. Hummingbirds, Mozart, cookies at midnight, fireplaces, whirlpools for two, honeymoon cottage, breakfast en suite, vintage movies, no smoking, wheelchair accessible. Togetherness baskets available.

Hosts: Femke and David Durham
Rooms: 4 (PB) $90-135
Full Breakfast
Credit Cards: A, B, C, D
Notes: 2, 7, 12, 14, 15

SANDY

Brookside Bed & Breakfast

45232 SE Paha Loop, P.O. Box 1112, 97055
(503) 668-4766
e-mail: brooksidesandy@hotmail.com

Brookside is three miles east of Sandy, just off Highway 26. A small brook runs through the property. Read a book from the large variety. Sit on the deck and enjoy the view of Mount Hood. Easy commute to skiing, hiking, fishing, golfing, or sightseeing in the Mount Hood area. A stop-over for the traveler; a relaxing getaway. A large country breakfast is served to start the day off right.

Hosts: Jack and Barbara Brooks
Rooms: 5 (1 PB; 4 S2B) $50-65
Full Breakfast
Credit Cards: None
Notes: 2, 5, 6, 7, 8, 12, 13

SEASIDE

Pacific Bed & Breakfast Agency

P.O. Box 46894, Seattle, WA 98146
(206) 439-7677; (800) 684-2932
FAX (206) 431-0932; e-mail: pacificb@nwlink.com
www.seattlebedandbreakfast.com

146. Oceanfront bed and breakfast hotel. With breathtaking ocean views, this small inn has 14 rooms. Room sizes range from cozy hideaway to large penthouse suites and family units with kitchens. Chef-prepared meals, jetted tubs, individual heating and air conditioning, private baths, and maybe a fireplace become a special retreat for guests. There is a wide range of prices.

147. Share the charm. This turn-of-the- century bed and breakfast has two rooms, each with a private bath, and one room is spacious enough to accommodate two children. Wake up each morning to hot beverages delivered to guests' room followed by a full breakfast featuring homemade breads and delicious fruits. Just made available is a cottage separate from the host home for those who prefer more privacy. Affordable rates.

Riverside Inn

430 South Holladay Drive, 97138
(503) 738-8254; (800) 826-6151
FAX (503) 738-7375; e-mail: river@seasurf.com
www.riversideinn.com

On the Necanicum River, two to five blocks from restaurants, shopping, and the beach. All rooms/suites have private entrances. Breakfast is served on the deck or in the dining room. A large array of tempting entrées. "We're here to

---

7 No smoking; 8 Children welcome; 9 Social drinking allowed; 10 Tennis nearby; 11 Swimming nearby; 12 Golf nearby; 13 Skiing nearby; 14 May be booked through a travel agent; 15 Handicapped accessible.

make your visit to Seaside one you will remember fondly."

Hosts: Judy and Larry Heth
Rooms: 11 (PB) $55-99
Full Breakfast
Credit Cards: A, B, C, D
Notes: 2, 5, 7, 8, 9, 10, 11, 12, 14

Summer House— A Bed & Breakfast

1221 North Franklin Street, 97138
(503) 738-5740; (800) 745-BEST (2378)
FAX (503) 738-0172
e-mail: summerhs@seasurf.com

Summer House is a special home, decorated with possessions from a lifetime of travels. There are five cozy guest rooms, each with its own spotless, private, attached bath. Summer House is one block from the beach, right off the north end of the Prom, in a residential neighborhood. The breakfasts have been described as a feast for the eye as well as the palate. Join the hosts to compare travels with their guests from around the world. Non-smoking guests only. Children over 12 welcome.

Hosts: Jack and Lesle Palmeri
Rooms: 5 (PB) $69-129
Full Breakfast
Credit Cards: A, B, C, D, E
Notes: 5, 7, 9, 10, 11, 12, 14

SISTERS

Conklin's Guest House

69013 Camp Polk Road, 97759
(541) 549-0123; (800) 549-4262
FAX (541) 549-4481

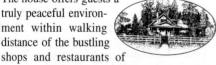

The house offers guests a truly peaceful environment within walking distance of the bustling shops and restaurants of Sisters. All guests are served evening refreshments and a full country breakfast in the morning. Trout ponds are stocked for catch and release fishing, the swimming pool is heated, and there are plenty of places around the grounds to relax in privacy. Groups, reunions, parties, and weddings are welcome. Children over 12 welcome.

Rooms: 5 (PB) $90-140
Full Breakfast
Credit Cards: None
Notes: 2, 5, 7, 10, 11, 12, 13, 14, 15

SPRINGFIELD

Park View Bed & Breakfast

1311 "G" Street, 97477
(541) 744-1642; (877) 860-2100 PIN 199-033
www.moriah.com/parkview

In the center of Springfield. Enjoy a stay in this beautifully decorated home. The peaceful quiet rooms include an upstairs suite with queen-size bed, cathedral windows, view of park, ponds, waterfall, trees, and flowers. Large sitting area, TV, writing table, balcony. Two rooms on the main floor. Choice of king-size, double, or twin beds. Whirlpool bathtub with shower. Delicious homemade breakfast. Easy freeway access. Ten minutes to University of Oregon, Autzen Stadium. Near shopping and restaurants.

Hosts: Wanda and Erik Berglund
Rooms: 3 (PB) $65-150
Full Breakfast
Credit Cards: None
Notes: 2, 5, 7, 10, 11, 14

TIGARD

Woven Glass Inn

14645 Beef Bend Road, 97224
(503) 590-6040; e-mail: wovenglass@jps.net
www.jps.net/wovenglass

A large rambling historic country home in the heart of the wine country just 12 miles south of Portland. The house abounds with stained-glass windows of unique design and purpose in every room. The Garden Suite (queen-size bed) and the French Room (four-poster bed) both

NOTES: Credit cards accepted: A MasterCard; B Visa; C American Express; D Discover; E Diner's Club; F Other; 2 Personal checks accepted; 3 Lunch available; 4 Dinner available; 5 Open all year; 6 Pets welcome;

Woven Glass Inn

have private baths and are tastefully decorated, complete with down comforters, luxurious linens, and seasonal flowers. Two fireplaces entice peaceful relaxation, or stroll through the sunken garden and rose gardens.

Hosts: Renée and Paul Giroux
Rooms: 2 (PB) $65-75
Full Breakfast
Credit Cards: A, B, C
Notes: 2, 5, 7, 11

TROUTDALE

McMenamins Edgefield

2126 Southwest Halsey Street, 97060
(503) 669-8610; FAX (503) 665-4209
e-mail: edge@mcmenamins.com

Formerly a poor farm, this 25-acre estate now features a hotel, fine dining restaurant, brewery, distillery, winery and tasting room, pub, beer garden, four bars, golf course, movie theater, artisans, gardens, retreat facilities, and special events. A favorite gathering place for both locals and travelers. Listed in the National Register of Historic Places. Smoking is not permitted inside.

Rooms: 103 (3 PB; 100 SB) $85-120
Full Breakfast
Credit Cards: A, B, C, D
Notes: 3, 4, 5, 7, 8, 9, 12, 13, 15

WELCHES

Doublegate Inn Bed & Breakfast

26711 East Welches Road, 97067
(503) 622-4859; e-mail: dgatebnb@teleport.com
www.mthoodlodging.com

A storybook cottage among towering cedars at the edge of Mount Hood National Forest at the foot of Mount Hood. Romantic rooms, each a world of its own with spa or soak tubs and cozy queen-size beds. A yummy full breakfast served fireside in the dining room with view of Salmon River. Great location for all Mount Hood activities and wonderful restaurants. "Honeymooners, love us!"

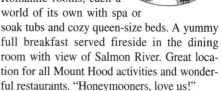

Hosts: Gary and Charlene Poston
Rooms: 3 (PB) $95-120
Full Breakfast
Credit Cards: A, B, C, D
Notes: 2, 5, 7, 9, 11, 12, 13, 14

Old Welches Inn Bed & Breakfast

26401 East Welches Road, 97067
(503) 622-3754; FAX (503) 622-5370
e-mail: oldwelchesinn@bbdirectory.com
www.innsandouts.com/property/
   old_welches_inn.html

Spectacular views of the Salmon River and Hunchback Mountain will keep guests spellbound. Discover what *Northwest Best Places* and *Sunset* magazine have known for years. Awake to the tantalizing aromas of a full gourmet breakfast served in elegant surroundings. Linger over a special coffee blend and plan a busy day of hiking, golf, antiquing, fishing, skiing, or just reading a book down by the river. Enjoy afternoon tea, and after a great dinner at one of the nearby restaurants, come back and indulge in a wonderful dessert at the inn. Member of PAII and the Associated B & Bs of

---

7 No smoking; 8 Children welcome; 9 Social drinking allowed; 10 Tennis nearby; 11 Swimming nearby; 12 Golf nearby; 13 Skiing nearby; 14 May be booked through a travel agent; 15 Handicapped accessible.

Old Welches Inn

Mount Hood, and OLA. Innkeepers of fine hospitality.

Hosts: Judith and Ted Mondun
Rooms: 4 (2 PB; 2 SB) $85-130
Full Breakfast
Credit Cards: A, B, C, D
Notes: 2, 5, 7, 8, 9, 10, 11, 12, 13, 14

YACHATS

The Kittiwake

95368 Highway 101 South, 97498
(541) 547-4470
e-mail: holidays@kittiwakeBandB.com
www.KittiwakeBandB.com

A calm ambiance of personal relaxation and restoration permeates this romantic two-story, 4,000-square-foot contemporary home on the ocean. This grown-ups' place for grown-up people was completed in 1993. Amenities include two guest rooms with breathtaking ocean views, queen-size beds, afghans, down comforters, window seats, decks, and private baths with double whirlpool tubs. Guest reading/whale watching room; coffee bar. Fantastic European breakfasts. The Germans have a word for the Kittiwake's warmth: *gemütlichkeit*.

Hosts: Brigitte and Joseph Szewc
Rooms: 2 (PB) $125-140
Full and Continental Breakfast
Credit Cards: A, B, C, D
Notes: 2, 5, 7, 9, 10, 11, 12, 14

NOTES: Credit cards accepted: A MasterCard; B Visa; C American Express; D Discover; E Diner's Club; F Other; 2 Personal checks accepted; 3 Lunch available; 4 Dinner available; 5 Open all year; 6 Pets welcome;

Texas

ABILENE

BJ's Prairie House Bed & Breakfast

508 Mulberry Street, 79601
(915) 675-5855; (800) 673-5855

Nestled in the heart of Abilene is a 1902 home furnished with antiques and modern luxuries combined to create a warm, homelike atmosphere. Downstairs, there are high ceilings and hardwood floors. The living room invites cozy conversation or curling up with a book in comfortable recliners or watching TV or movies. Upstairs are four unique bedrooms (Love, Joy, Peace, and Patience), each beautifully decorated. Breakfast includes homemade breads, fresh fruits, and other scrumptious delights and is served in the dining room that is decorated with a collection of blue-and-white china collected from around the world.

Hosts: BJ and Bob Fender
Rooms: 4 (2 PB; 2 SB) $65-75
Continental Breakfast
Credit Cards: A, B, C, D
Notes: 2, 5, 7, 9, 12

AMARILLO

Parkview House Bed & Breakfast

1311 South Jefferson, 79101
(806) 373-9464; FAX (806) 373-3166
e-mail: parkviewbb@aol.com
www.members.aol.com/parkviewbb

This 1908 Prairie Victorian in the heart of the Texas panhandle has been lovingly restored

Parkview House

by the present owners to capture its original charm. It is furnished with antiques and comfortably updated. Guests may relax, read, or engage in friendly conversation on the wicker-filled front porch; browse through the garden; or soak leisurely in the romantic hot tub under stars. Convenient to biking, jogging, tennis, hiking, and the award-winning musical drama *Texas* in Palo Duro State Park. Old Route 66, antique shops, restaurants, various museums, and West Texas A&M University are nearby. Continental plus breakfast. Smoking outside only. Inquire about accommodations for children.

Hosts: Nabil and Carol Dia
Rooms: 5 (3 PB; 2 SB) $65-85
Cottage: $135
Continental Breakfast
Credit Cards: A, B, C
Notes: 2, 5, 7, 9, 10, 12, 14

---

7 No smoking; 8 Children welcome; 9 Social drinking allowed; 10 Tennis nearby; 11 Swimming nearby; 12 Golf nearby; 13 Skiing nearby; 14 May be booked through a travel agent; 15 Handicapped accessible.

Texas

AUSTIN

Austin-Lake Travis Bed & Breakfast

4446 Eck Lane, 78734
(512) 266-3386; (888) 764-LTBB (5822)
  (reservations only)
e-mail: LTBINNB@aol.com
www.laketravisbb.com

This unique waterfront retreat is a 20-minute drive from downtown Austin. Cliffside location, crystal water, hills, and expansive view provide the setting for a luxurious getaway. The natural beauty of the surroundings is reflected in the hill country home with each of the four guest suites having a deck with view of the lake. "Intimate resort" describes the amenities available: private boat dock, pool, hot tub, fitness center, massage and spa services, and sailing/boat charters. Inside is a stone fireplace, game room, pool table, and library/theater. Nearby are a boat and Jet Ski rentals, horseback riding, bicycling, hiking, steam train, and wineries to tour. Breakfast is served in bed.

Hosts: Judy and Vic Dwyer
Rooms: 4 (PB) $145-195
Full Breakfast
Credit Cards: A, B, C
Notes: 5, 7, 9, 10, 11, 12, 14

Austin's Wildflower Inn

1200 West 22 1/2 Street, 78705
(512) 477-9639; FAX (512) 474-4188
e-mail: kjackson@io.com

Austin's Wildflower Inn

Austin's Wildflower Inn, built in the early 1930s, is a lovely Colonial-style two-story home tucked away in a very quiet neighborhood of tree-lined streets in the center of Austin. Convenient to the University of Texas, the state capitol, and the downtown shopping and entertainment district. Every room has been carefully restored to create an atmosphere of warmth and comfort. "I invite you to come and relax here and enjoy our beautiful grounds and have one of our special breakfasts in our lovely back garden. I wish you happiness and prosperity, and may your road lead to mine."

Host: Kay Jackson
Rooms: 4 (2 PB; 2 SB) $79-94
Full Breakfast
Credit Cards: A, B, C
Notes: 2, 5, 7, 9, 10, 11, 12

Bed & Breakfast Texas Style

4224 West Red Bird Lane, Dallas, 75237
(972) 298-8586; (800) 899-4538
FAX (972) 298-7118; e-mail: bdtxstyle1@aol.com
www.bnbtexasstyle.com

Bed and Breakfast on Castle Hill. This very private, one-bedroom efficiency is tucked between the trees and gardens behind the large residence and is very centrally located. There is a king-size bed, nice sitting area, and beautiful built-in kitchen. Perfect setting for business travelers or visitors to Austin who want peace and solitude, as well as convenience. Breakfast goodies are provided. $95.

Carter Lane Bed and Breakfast. This large sprawling residence in a quiet area of bustling Austin has two guest areas, a well-stocked fish pond, pool, picnic area, and a weight and exercise room. The home is newly decorated with upscale furnishings; each guest room has a

---

NOTES: Credit cards accepted: A MasterCard; B Visa; C American Express; D Discover; E Diner's Club; F Other; 2 Personal checks accepted; 3 Lunch available; 4 Dinner available; 5 Open all year; 6 Pets welcome; 7 No smoking; 8 Children welcome; 9 Social drinking allowed; 10 Tennis nearby; 11 Swimming nearby; 12 Golf nearby; 13 Skiing nearby; 14 May be booked through a travel agent; 15 Handicapped accessible.

private bath. Guests are encouraged to relax in the hammock by the lake, or work out while watching a video in the exercise room. Weekday breakfasts are Continental. On weekends guests will be served a full breakfast with all the trimmings. The lucky guest who lands a bass from the lake may enjoy having it for breakfast. The host will also prepare vegetarian and healthy recipes. $75-85.

The Brook House

The Brook House Bed & Breakfast

609 West 33rd Street, 78705
(512) 459-0534

The Brook House was built in 1922 and restored to its present country charm. It is seven blocks from the University of Texas with easy access to local restaurants and live music. Enjoy one of six guest rooms, each of which has a private bath, TV, and telephone. A full breakfast is served daily in the dining room which has a fireplace or, weather permitting, outside on the veranda. No smoking in rooms. Partial handicapped accessibility.

Host: Barbara Love
Rooms: 6 (PB) $72-99
Full Breakfast
Credit Cards: A, B, C, D, E, F
Notes: 2, 5, 6, 8, 9, 10, 11, 12

Carrington's Bluff

1900 David Street, 78705
(800) 871-8908; e-mail: governorstan@earthlink

Carrington's Bluff is Austin's "Country Inn in the City." Inside this 1877 English country house, guests will find rooms filled with English and American antiques, accented with English country fabrics and decor. The smell of fresh-brewed gourmet coffee beckons from the kitchen. Full breakfast of fresh fruit, homemade granola, choice of yogurts, bakery items, and the hot house specialty entrée, all served on fine china. A 500-year-old native oak is visible from spacious porch. A few minutes away is the University of Texas, the state capitol, parks, museums, fine shopping, excellent restaurants, and Austin's famous Sixth Street. Featured in *Innstyle* magazine, March 1998.

Host: Lisa Kloss
Rooms: 8 (PB) $59-119
Full Breakfast
Credit Cards: A, B, C, D, E, F
Notes: 2, 5, 6, 7, 8, 9, 10, 11, 12, 14

Carrington's Bluff

Gregg House & Gardens

4201 Gregg Lane, 78744
(512) 448-0402; FAX (512) 462-0512
e-mail: jhayes@qsigroup.com

Two in-town country retreats on three acres of wood property await guests 10 minutes from downtown Austin. Two fish ponds, a beautiful waterfall, decks, a huge patio, hardwood floors, stone fireplace, swimming pool, and hot

---

NOTES: Credit cards accepted: A MasterCard; B Visa; C American Express; D Discover; E Diner's Club; F Other; 2 Personal checks accepted; 3 Lunch available; 4 Dinner available; 5 Open all year; 6 Pets welcome;

tub. LBJ presidential library and shopping 15 minutes away. Full kitchen, TV rooms, living/dining, and laundry available for guests' use. Bus stop at corner of property; airport 10 minutes. Hosts will help guests with their special interests and provide directions and maps. Large organic gardens.

Hosts: Nelda and Jim Haynes
Rooms: 4 (PB) $50-60; 2 (SB) $40-45
Credit Cards: None
Notes: 2, 4, 5, 7, 9, 10, 11, 12

The McCallum House

The McCallum House

613 West 32nd Street, 78705
(512) 451-6744; FAX (512) 451-4752
e-mail: McCallum@austinTx.net

Six blocks from UT, two miles from the capitol and downtown, and located in a historic residential area. There are three guest rooms and a suite in the main house, and a large suite in an adjoining building on the grounds. All accommodations have private baths, kitchen facilities, color TVs, private telephones with answering machines, private verandas, hair dryers, irons and ironing boards, sitting and working areas. Suites have VCRs and one has a whirlpool tub.

Hosts: Roger and Nancy Danley
Rooms: 5 (PB) $94-149
Full Breakfast
Credit Cards A, B, D
Notes: 2, 5, 7, 9, 10, 11, 12, 13

BEN WHEELER

Bed & Breakfast Texas Style

4224 West Red Bird Lane, Dallas, 75237
(972) 298-8586; (800) 899-4538
FAX (972) 298-7118; e-mail: bdtxstyle1@aol.com
www.bnbtexasstyle.com

The Arc Ridge Guest Ranch. This 600-acre ranch in East Texas near Canton and Tyler has its own lake. Three guest houses have two bedrooms, living room, complete kitchen, and shower. Fishing and paddleboats are available. No hunters allowed in this environmentally protected area. Breakfast will be left in the refrigerator for guests to prepare themselves. Family rates will be considered. Two-night minimum stay. $95.

BOERNE

Guadalupe River Ranch

605 F.M. 474, 78006
(830) 537-4837; (800) 460-2005
FAX (830) 537-5249; e-mail: grranch@gvtc.com
www.guadaluperiverranch.com

The main lodge was built in 1929 (formerly owned by actress Olivia de Havilland) and restored to its original elegance. With 360 acres, the ranch provides one of the most spectacular views in the Texas Hill Country. The Guadalupe River Ranch is known for its memorable cuisine, fine wines, Vintner Events, and it also offers a variety of activities: river tubing, canoeing, horseback riding, body treatments and pampering spa services, and hiking trails. If one is seeking rest and relaxation, find a hammock, or the overlook swing. Enjoy the peace and serenity.

Host: Elisa McClure
Rooms: 43 (PB) $219-309
Full Breakfast
Credit Cards: A, B, C, D
Notes: 2, 3, 4, 7, 8, 9, 12, 14, 15

---

7 No smoking; 8 Children welcome; 9 Social drinking allowed; 10 Tennis nearby; 11 Swimming nearby; 12 Golf nearby; 13 Skiing nearby; 14 May be booked through a travel agent; 15 Handicapped accessible.

BRADY

Brady House

Brady House

704 South Bridge, 76825
(915) 597-5265; (888) 272-3901
e-mail: bradyhs@centex.net

Brady is at the geographic center of Texas: the northern gateway to the Hill Country, the southern door to the Texas plains, and the portal to West Texas. Six blocks south of the square, Brady House, amid its acre of landscaped grounds has three spacious guest rooms, each with private bath. The Craftsman-style home built in 1908 is furnished to reflect not only the period but also family collections.

Hosts: Bobbie and Kelly Hancock
Rooms: 3 (PB) $85-95
Full Breakfast
Credit Cards: A, B, C, D
Notes: 3, 4, 5, 7, 10, 11, 12

BRECKENRIDGE

Bed & Breakfast Texas Style

4224 West Red Bird Lane, Dallas, 75237
(972) 298-8586; (800) 899-4538
FAX (972) 298-7118; e-mail: bdtxstyle1@aol.com
www.bnbtexasstyle.com

The Keeping Room Bed and Breakfast. This large two-story brick inn is a place for comfort and refuge from the busy world. It was built in 1929 and has been faithfully restored to "better than original" condition. There are two large suites, Bluebonnet and Walker, that each have a sitting room, a bedroom with queen-size beds and matching day bed, and a private bath. The other two rooms, Goodwin and Rustic, also have queen-size beds and share a hall bath. All rooms have TVs. Guests will be pampered with a hearty breakfast of biscuits, sausage, eggs, muffins, juice, and coffee. $65-75.

BROADDUS

Sam Rayburn Lake Bed & Breakfast "The Cole House"

Route 1 Box 258, 75929
(409) 872-3666

Within the piney woods of deep East Texas is this cozy guest house, bed and breakfast, that has been in operation since 1984. All electric home, with full kitchen, including microwave, everything furnished, central heating and cooling, and carpeted throughout. Five-room cottage with a great view of Sam Rayburn Lake. Charcoal grill and other facilities available. Rental boats available at near-by marina, also launching for private boats.

Hosts: Gene and Jean Cole
Rate for House: $55
Continental Breakfast
Notes: 2, 5, 7, 8, 9, 11, 13, 14, 15

Sam Rayburn Lake

NOTES: Credit cards accepted: A MasterCard; B Visa; C American Express; D Discover; E Diner's Club; F Other; 2 Personal checks accepted; 3 Lunch available; 4 Dinner available; 5 Open all year; 6 Pets welcome;

BRYAN

Bed & Breakfast Texas Style

4224 West Red Bird Lane, Dallas, 75237
(972) 298-8586; (800) 899-4538
FAX (972) 298-7118; e-mail: bdtxstyle1@aol.com
www.bnbtexasstyle.com

Wilderness Bed and Breakfast. This charming home is at the end of a cul-de-sac just three miles from Texas A&M University. There are three bedrooms, two with queen-size beds, one with twin beds, and a private sitting room with a sleeper-sofa. The master suite downstairs has a private bath; the two rooms upstairs share a hall bath. Breakfast may be Continental with homemade breads or muffins, lots of fruit and cereals, or it may be a traditional Canadian/Texan-style breakfast. This is a nonsmoking facility. Children over 15 years welcome. $75-85.

Cardinal's Retreat. This lovely home is on acreage that attracts birds and critters for fun viewing out the back patio. A visit with Reba and Bob will be the highlight of your trip, as they share one hall bath. Many antiques are found throughout the home, also a lovely angel collection that fills a large glass cabinet in the cozy den. breakfast will be homemade bread or muffins, fruit, cereal, and beverages, coffee, tea, and juice. There is a siamese cat in the residence. The George Bush Library is very near this Bed and Breakfast. $75.

CANTON

Heavenly Acres Guest Ranch

660 Van Zandt Circle, Box 2816, 75147
(800) 283-0341; (903) 887-3016

Heavenly Acres fits many guests' personal visions of what Heaven must be like. An 83-acre East Texas ranch between Dallas and Tyler. Just 12 miles southwest of Canton, known for its First Monday Trade Days. There are five cabins which are designed to be guests'

very own "home-away-from-home" and have the capacity of 41 beds. All kitchens are fully equipped and stocked with breakfast items for guests to prepare at their own convenience.

Hosts: Diana and Bruce Avellanet
Rates: $35-95
Full or Continental Breakfast
Credit Cards: A, B, C, D
Notes: 2, 3, 4, 5, 7, 8, 9, 11, 12, 15

Bed & Breakfast Texas Style

4224 West Red Bird Lane, Dallas, 75237
(972) 298-8586; (800) 899-4538
FAX (972) 298-7118; e-mail: bdtxstyle1@aol.com
www.bnbtexasstyle.com

Lacy Creek Bed and Breakfast. This large style home sits on a farm just outside Canton and has four bedrooms available for guests that wish a quiet retreat in the country. There is a pool for relaxing in the summer, and a large game room with a wood-burning stove for fall and winter evenings. The bedroom upstairs has its own private entrance and sitting area. The other rooms are great for families or groups of ladies. Children are welcome here. Hearty breakfast of sausage and egg casserole, hash browns, homemade muffins, and fruit, or stuffed French toast with strawberry syrup. Smoking only on deck or porches. $75-95.

Texas Star Bed & Breakfast

Route 1, Box 187, Edgewood, 75117
(903) 896-4277; FAX (903) 896-7061
e-mail: ohohm@aol.com

Enjoy a peaceful day in the country nestled among large oaks, cedar trees, and green pasturelands in the gently rolling hills of East Texas. Each of the six rooms reflects a different theme of Texas history—Spanish, Native American, Old West, German, Texas country. Private baths, private entrances, and private patios are available. Full course country breakfasts. Five minutes from the world-famous First Monday Trade Days in Canton. Dinner

---

7 No smoking; 8 Children welcome; 9 Social drinking allowed; 10 Tennis nearby; 11 Swimming nearby; 12 Golf nearby; 13 Skiing nearby; 14 May be booked through a travel agent; 15 Handicapped accessible.

for groups is available by advance request. Capacity up to 20. Private cabin now available.

Hosts: David and Marie Stoltzfus
Rooms: 6 (4 PB; 2 SB) $65-85
Full Breakfast
Credit Cards: A, B, C, D
Notes: 2, 4, 5, 7, 12

CASTROVILLE

Bed & Breakfast Texas Style

4224 West Red Bird Lane, Dallas, 75237
(972) 298-8586; (800) 899-4538
FAX (972) 298-7118; e-mail: bdtxstyle1@aol.com
www.bnbtexasstyle.com

Le Parc Bed and Breakfast. This wonderful historic town with the Medina River running through it can now boast of a recently opened bed and breakfast cottage and a Tea Room next door. The cottage has three bedrooms with private baths, a lovely sitting room, and front porch with a swing and patio. Two have private entrances. Each room has a TV with VCR. Full breakfast served in Tea Room. A fourth bedroom upstairs in the Tea Room has a private bath. Enjoy the park, town square across the street, and the French restaurant just two blocks away. Jaye and Gene are veterans of the bed and breakfast industry and are eager for guests to enjoy their special hospitality. Castroville is just 22 miles from the Riverwalk in downtown San Antonio and convenient to Sea World and Fiesta Texas. No children. No pets. Smoking on the porch. $80-95.

CLEBURNE

Bed & Breakfast Texas Style

4224 West Red Bird Lane, Dallas, 75237
(972) 298-8586; (800) 899-4538
FAX (972) 298-7118; e-mail: bdtxstyle1@aol.com
www.bnbtexasstyle.com

Cleburne Guest House. This lovely historical Queen Anne Victorian house was built near the turn of the century and is near downtown Cleburne. There are four guest rooms, two with private baths and two sharing a hall bath. All rooms have color TVs and fresh flowers. Coffee bar and refrigerator upstairs for guests' needs. A Continental breakfast will be served in the main dining room or out on the New Orleans-style patio. Area attractions include antiquing, candlewalk, Springfest, and Hot Air Balloon Festival. Walk to antique malls, tearoom, and shopping. $95-115.

CLIFTON

Bed & Breakfast Texas Style

4224 West Red Bird Lane, Dallas, 75237
(972) 298-8586; (800) 899-4538
FAX (972) 298-7118; e-mail: bdtxstyle1@aol.com
www.bnbtexasstyle.com

The Sweetheart Cottage. A historic home, once damaged in a tornado, now restored for a perfect weekend getaway. A loft room has a queen-size bed, and a pull-out sofa is available downstairs. Country breakfast fare is left in the complete kitchen for the guests to prepare. No smoking. Two-night minimum stay required. $85-125.

COLLEGE STATION

Bed & Breakfast Texas Style

4224 West Red Bird Lane, Dallas, 75237
(972) 298-8586; (800) 899-4538
FAX (972) 298-7118; e-mail: bdtxstyle1@aol.com
www.bnbtexasstyle.com

Country Gardens. A sense of peace and tranquility will descend on guests as they enter this little country hideaway on four acres. Stroll through the wooded glen, fruit orchard, grapevines, and berry patches and enjoy the birds and wildflowers. The hosts will prepare a delicious breakfast of wheat pancakes or homemade bread; coffee, tea, or milk; and fruit in season. $65-75.

NOTES: Credit cards accepted: A MasterCard; B Visa; C American Express; D Discover; E Diner's Club; F Other; 2 Personal checks accepted; 3 Lunch available; 4 Dinner available; 5 Open all year; 6 Pets welcome;

Crystal Lake Cottage. Nestled in the woods on a large private lake is this two-bedroom guesthouse just behind the owner's home. It has a private entrance, off-street parking, walking trails around the lake, and lovely gardens. There is a nice sitting room, small kitchen, and a full bath in the cottage. Patty and Byron want to interact with their guests and will invite them into the main residence for a full breakfast of homemade rolls, omelets, and sausage. Fruit and coffee, tea or milk will also be served. She is a teacher, and Byron is with TAMU. About one-half mile to the University. No smoking. Double $125.

COMFORT

The Comfort Common

717 High Street, P.O. Box 539, 78013
(830) 995-3030
e-mail: comfortcommon@hctc.net
www.bbhost.com/comfortcommon

Historic limestone hotel, circa 1880, listed in the National Register of Historic Places. Rooms and suites are furnished with antiques. The downstairs of the hotel features numerous shops filled with American antiques. A stay at the Comfort Common will put guests in the heart of the Texas Hill Country with Fredericksburg, Kerrville, Boerne, Bandera, and San Antonio all a brief 15-30 minutes away. Fiesta Texas theme park is only 20 minutes away. Featured in *Southern Living* and *Travel &*

The Comfort Common

Leisure magazines. Also selected by *Fodor's Travel Publications* as one of the Best Bed and Breakfasts.

Hosts: Jim Lord and Bobby Dent
Rooms: 9 (PB) $65-110
Full Breakfast
Credit Cards: A, B, C, D
Notes: 2, 5, 7, 9, 12

CORPUS CHRISTI

Bay Breeze

Bay Breeze Bed & Breakfast

201 Louisiana Parkway, 78404
(361) 882-4123; (887) 882-4123
e-mail: baybreeze@baybreezebb.com
www.baybreezebb.com

Within view of the sparkling bay waters, this fine older home features bedroom suites with private baths that radiate the charm and ambiance of days gone by. Less than a five-minute drive from the business district and city marinas, where sea vessels of every description are berthed. One can enjoy fine dining, recreation, or purchase shrimp direct from the net. Travel only a short distance to the Bayfront Convention Center, art and science museums, the Columbus ships, the preservation homes of Heritage Park, and the Harbor Playhouse Community Theater. Beach nearby.

Hosts: Frank and Perry Tompkins
Rooms: 4 (PB)
Full Breakfast
Credit Cards: A, B
Notes: 2, 5, 7, 9, 10, 11, 12

---

7 No smoking; 8 Children welcome; 9 Social drinking allowed; 10 Tennis nearby; 11 Swimming nearby; 12 Golf nearby; 13 Skiing nearby; 14 May be booked through a travel agent; 15 Handicapped accessible.

The Ginger Rose Bed & Breakfast

7030 Dunsford Drive, 78413
(361) 992-0115; (877) 894-8109
e-mail: ginrose@flash.net
www.GingerRose.com

The Ginger Rose is easily accessible to all bayfront activities and the beach, but allows the guest to escape the tourist traffic for a quiet night's sleep. There is a private pool and a tennis court. Rooms have private baths, cable TV, stained glass, and antiques. A typical breakfast might be blackberry pancakes with Grand Marnier syrup. Arrangements with several of the best restaurants, tourist attractions, and merchants in town allow special discounts for guests.

Hosts: Peg and Pete Braswell
Rooms: 2 (PB) $60-75
Full Breakfast
Notes: 2, 5, 7, 9, 10, 11, 14

Sand Dollar Hospitality

3605 Mendenhall Drive, 78415
(361) 853-1222; (800) 528-7322
FAX (361) 814-1285
e-mail: bednbreakfast@aol.com
www.ccinternet.net/sand-dollar

Bay Breeze. Within view of the sparkling bay waters, this fine older home offers four accommodations, all with private baths. Guests are invited to enjoy the large sunroom, the 1930s billiard table, watch TV, or just relax. A five-minute drive to the business district and city marinas, where guests can enjoy fine dining and recreation or purchase shrimp direct from the net. It is only a short stroll to the city's finest bayfront park and fishing pier. Resident cat. Full breakfast. Smoking permitted outside only. $65-90.

Colley House (formerly the Seagull). New England antiques collected by the hosts, a retired navy couple, add to the charm and ambiance of this lovely home. Only one block from Corpus Christi Bay, this 50-year-old home is in a quiet up-scale neighborhood just a five-minute walk from the city's largest bayside park. Guests are invited to relax in the enclosed patio/den with TV, wet bar, and cozy surroundings. Two bedrooms with private baths are available. Older children are welcome. Full breakfast. Smoking permitted outside only. $75.

Ginger Rose. Within a quiet gated community, reminiscent of the medieval cities of Provence, this scenic home offers a guest room with private bath, a heated pool, and access to nearby tennis courts. This charming French Provincial-style home is midway between downtown and the gulf beaches—driving time being 25 minutes in either direction. A full gourmet breakfast served. Smoking permitted outside only. $70-75.

Smith Place. A colorfully landscaped back yard with pool and hot tub is the setting for two charming guest houses—the Garden Room and the Lodge. The sleeping accommodations for the Garden Room include a queen-size bed in the bedroom and a queen-size sofa bed in the adjoining sitting room. The Lodge has just a queen-size bed and easy chair. Other amenities include private entrances, off-street parking, refrigerator, microwave, coffee center, and cable TV. Breakfast provisions are brought in daily. Small pets permitted. $90.

DALLAS

Bed & Breakfast Texas Style

4224 West Red Bird Lane, Dallas, 75237
(972) 298-8586; (800) 899-4538
FAX (972) 298-7118; e-mail: bdtxstyle1@aol.com
www.bnbtexasstyle.com

Artist's Haven. This private home offers two upstairs guest rooms with lovely amenities and shared bath. One room has twin beds, and the other room has a king-size bed. Breakfast is Continental plus, with fruit, pastries, and bev-

---

NOTES: Credit cards accepted: A MasterCard; B Visa; C American Express; D Discover; E Diner's Club; F Other; 2 Personal checks accepted; 3 Lunch available; 4 Dinner available; 5 Open all year; 6 Pets welcome;

erages. Cat in residence. No smoking. Children are welcome. $85.

The Cloisters. This lovely home is one block from White Rock Lake in a secluded area of Dallas. There are two guest rooms, each with a private bath. Both rooms have double beds, one with an antique Mexican headboard that is a conversation piece. Breakfast will be lots of protein, eggs, and/or blueberry pancakes. A bicycle is available for riding around the lake. No smoking. $85.

Fan Room. The antique fan displayed in this lovely twin bedroom is the focal point and was the start of a large collection of fans. The home is near Prestonwood, Marshall Fields, and the Galleria Mall. Southfork Ranch is a 15-minute drive north. A full country breakfast includes jalapeño muffins for first-time Texas visitors. Second bedroom near the kitchen with a double bed and private bath. $70.

The Southern House. A new three-story modified prairie-style home fits right in with the large historic homes in the State-Thomas area, in the Arts District of Dallas. The two bed and breakfast rooms share one bath; the Heritage Room is exquisitely decorated with a full-size bed, the luxurious bath features a black antique-footed tub and shower. The Artist's Room has a queen bed and is the owner's actual studio and office. The computer and fax machine are available for guests' use. The McKinney Trolley and Hard Rock Café are two blocks away. The Myerson Symphony Hall and Art Museum are walking distance away. $125-150.

Tudor Mansion. Built in 1933 in an exclusive neighborhood in the shadow of downtown, this Tudor-style mansion offers queen-size bed and private bath. A full gourmet breakfast of cheddar on toast, Texas-style creamed eggs with jalapeño, or fresh vegetable omelet is served. The bus line is three blocks away. Spanish and French are spoken. Three miles from downtown. Close to a public golf course. $80.

DEL RIO

The 1890 House

609 Griner Street, 78840
(830) 775-8061; (800) 282-1360
FAX (830) 775-4667; www.1890house.com

Nestled in the heart of Del Rio guests will find this magnificent turn-of-the-century Victorian home. It boasts five charming guest rooms, private soaking tubs, and Jacuzzi. Intimate and elegant. Fireplaces, verandas, and candlelight breakfasts. Make this visit an international event by traveling three miles south of the border to Acuna, Mexico.

Hosts: Alberto and Laura Galvan
Rooms: 5 (PB)
Full Breakfast
Credit Cards: A, B, C, D
Notes: 5, 7, 8, 9, 10, 11, 12

EL PASO

Cowboys & Indians Board & Bunk

P.O. Box 13752, 79913
(505) 589-2653; www.softaid.net/cowboys

Lie back and enjoy the wonderful panoramic view of Franklin Mountains and desert sunsets of southern New Mexico. Bunk down in one of the four theme rooms that are comfortable and decorated to make guests feel like they are a part of the Old West. Relax in the large gathering room. The grub is the best in southwestern- and chuckwagon-style cooking. Special packages for year-round golf, horseback riding, sightseeing, seminars, and workshops. Lunch and dinner available but catered only. Smoking permitted outside only. Children over 12 welcome. One room is handicapped accessible.

Hosts: Irene and Don Newlon
Rooms: 4 (PB) $67-89 per night
Full and Continental Breakfast

---

7 No smoking; 8 Children welcome; 9 Social drinking allowed; 10 Tennis nearby; 11 Swimming nearby; 12 Golf nearby; 13 Skiing nearby; 14 May be booked through a travel agent; 15 Handicapped accessible.

Credit Cards: A, B, C, E
Notes: 2, 4, 5, 7, 8, 9, 10, 11, 12, 15

FORT DAVIS

The Veranda Country Inn

210 Court Avenue, P.O. Box 1238, 79734
(888) 383-2847; e-mail: info@veranda.com
www.theveranda.com

The Veranda is a spacious historic inn built in 1883. This unique adobe building, with 2-foot-thick walls and 12-foot ceilings, has fourteen large rooms and suites furnished with antiques and collectibles. Its walled gardens and quiet courtyards provide travelers with a change of pace and lifestyle in mile-high Fort Davis. A large, separate Carriage House is next to the gardens in the shade of a large pecan tree. The Veranda is within minutes of sites renowned for astronomy, historical forts and buildings, and scenic hiking, biking, and bird watching.

Hosts: Paul and Kathie Woods
Rooms: 14 (PB) $80-120
Carriage House: $100-145
Full Breakfast
Credit Cards: A, B, D
Notes: 2, 5, 7, 9,

The Veranda Country Inn

FORT WORTH

Bed & Breakfast at the Ranch

8275 Wagley Robertson Road, 76131
(817) 232-5522; (888) 593-0352
e-mail: bbranch@flash.net
www.fortworthians.com/bbranch

Bed & Breakfast at the Ranch

A true taste of Texas on 15 acres. Bed and Breakfast at the Ranch offers four spacious rooms with their own private baths. Two rooms have special tubs—a Jacuzzi and antique claw-foot tub. Three rooms have their own private patio. The spacious living room offers a stone fireplace, TV with video library, board games, upright grand piano, and library of books. Enclosed patio room is complete with hot tub, patio furniture, wet bar, guest refrigerator, and free pinball. Gourmet breakfast served by resident innkeeper—full on weekends and Continental on weekdays. Grounds offer tennis, putting green, gazebo, swing, and smokehouse. Unique!

Hosts: Scott and Cheryl Stewart
Rooms: 4 (PB) $85-159
Full or Continental Breakfast
Credit Cards: A, B, C
Notes: 2, 4, 5, 7, 8, 9, 10, 12, 14, 15

Bed & Breakfast Texas Style

4224 West Red Bird Lane, Dallas, 75237
(972) 298-8586; (800) 899-4538
FAX (972) 298-7118; e-mail: bdtxstyle1@aol.com
www.bnbtexasstyle.com

Bloomsbury House. Escape to this beautifully restored 1908 two-story Queen Anne home in one of Texas's largest historic neighborhoods, just south of downtown. Guests will be pampered in one of the four guest bedrooms; each room has its own private bath. Enjoy desserts upon arrival and full home-cooked breakfast in the morning. Attractions in Fort Worth include the Sundance Square, Kimbell Art Museum, and Billy Bob's (famous "kicker dance" club). $99-110.

NOTES: Credit cards accepted: A MasterCard; B Visa; C American Express; D Discover; E Diner's Club; F Other; 2 Personal checks accepted; 3 Lunch available; 4 Dinner available; 5 Open all year; 6 Pets welcome;

The Texas White House

1417 Eighth Avenue, 76104
(817) 923-3597; (800) 279-6791
FAX (817) 923-0410

This historically designated, award-winning country-style home has been restored to its original 1910 grandeur of simple, yet elegant decor. Within five minutes of downtown, medical center, Fort Worth zoo, the cultural district, botanic gardens, water gardens, and Texas Christian University. Three guest rooms with sitting areas and private baths with claw-foot tubs. Breakfast served in either the dining room or sent to guests' room. Amenities include telephone, TV, early morning coffee service, afternoon snacks and beverages, secretarial services, laundry service for extended stays, and off-street parking.

Hosts: Jamie and Grover McMains
Rooms: 3 (PB) $100-125
Full Breakfast
Credit Cards: A, B, C, D
Notes: 2, 5, 7, 9, 10, 11, 12, 14

FREDERICKSBURG

Das College Haus

106 West College, 78624
(830) 997-9047; (800) 654-2802
www.dascollegehaus.com

Visit historic Fredericksburg and stay at Das College Haus, just three blocks from downtown. Spacious rooms with private baths; all have access to the porches, balcony with porch swing, and wicker rockers, where guests can relax and visit. Das College Haus is beautifully

Das College Haus

appointed with comfortable period furniture and original art for a wonderful "at home" atmosphere. Enjoy a full breakfast served in the old-fashioned dining room. Central heat and air, cable TV, VCR, and a collection of movies. Coffee makers and refrigerators in rooms.

Host: Myrna Dennis
Rooms: 4 (PB) $95-110
Full Breakfast
Credit Cards: A, B
Notes: 2, 5, 7, 9, 10, 11, 12, 15

Magnolia House

101 East Hackberry, 78624
(800) 880-4374; FAX (830) 997-0766
e-mail: magnolia@hctc.net
www.magnolia-house.com

Built circa 1923 and restored in 1991, this inn exudes southern hospitality in a grand and gracious manner. Outside magnolias, a bubbling fishpond with waterfall set a soothing mood. Inside, a beautiful living room, formal dining room, and sunroom provide areas for guests to mingle. Two beautiful suites, with fireplaces, and three romantic rooms have been decorated thoughtfully with antiques. Beautiful, bountiful breakfast and complimentary beverages make this a memorable experience.

Hosts: Joyce and Patrick Kennard
Rooms: 5 (PB) $95-140
Full Breakfast
Credit Cards: A, B, C, D
Notes: 2, 5, 7, 9, 10, 11, 12

Moonbeam Cottage

514 West Austin Street, 78624
(830) 997-5612

Completely private cottage located in the historic district one block off Main Street offering city convenience and country charm in the shadow of a 1904 home surrounded by beautiful country gardens. Central heat and air, full kitchen, microwave. One bedroom with luxuries, both with shower for two. Queen sofa bed can accommodate two extra people. Front

7 No smoking; 8 Children welcome; 9 Social drinking allowed; 10 Tennis nearby; 11 Swimming nearby; 12 Golf nearby; 13 Skiing nearby; 14 May be booked through a travel agent; 15 Handicapped accessible.

porch swing and rocker. Telephone, cable TV, and Continental breakfast included. Contact Gastehaus Schmidt.

Hosts: Judy Vincent
Rooms: 1 (PB) $85 per night
Continental Breakfast
Notes: 5, 7, 12, 14

Schmidt Barn Bed & Breakfast

Gästehaus Schmidt Reservation Service
231 West Main, 78624
(210) 997-5612; FAX (210) 997-8282
e-mail: gasthaus@ktc.com
www.fbglodging.com

The remnants of an 1860s limestone barn were lovingly saved to turn it into a guest house. Stone walls, brick floors, timber beams maintain century-old charm. Bathroom invites guests to a long soak in a sunken tub. Quilts, antique linens, samplers, and a collection of toys enliven the wooden-beamed loft bedrooms. Hosts live next door. Featured in *Country Living* and *Travel and Leisure*. German Continental plus breakfast is left for guests to enjoy at their leisure.

Hosts: Charles and Loretta Schmidt
Rooms: 1 (PB) $90
Continental Breakfast
Credit Cards: A, B
Notes: 2, 5, 6, 8, 9, 10, 11, 12, 14

GAINESVILLE

Alexander Bed & Breakfast Acres, Inc.

3692 C.R. 201, 76240-7819
(903) 564-7440; (800) 887-8794
e-mail: abba@texoma.net
www.bbhost.com/alexanderbbacres

Three-story Queen Anne Victorian home on 65 peaceful acres of woods and meadows. Large wraparound porch for lounging; walking trails; near two large lakes, antiques, country farms, and zoo. Each bedroom decorated with different theme: western, antique, canopied, or Amish. Full breakfast included. Separate conference room and extra lodging on third floor. Two-story guest cottage offers three bedrooms sharing one and one-half baths, kitchen, laundry, living area, and large screened porch. Children welcome in cottage only. Dinner available by arrangement.

Hosts: Jim and Pamela Alexander
Rooms: 8 (5 PB; 3 SB) $60-125
Full Breakfast
Credit Cards: A, B, C, D
Notes: 2, 4, 5, 7, 9, 11, 12, 14

GALVESTON

Inn at 1816 Postoffice

1816 Postoffice Street, 77550
(409) 765-9444; e-mail: INN1816@aol.com
www.bbonline.com/tx/1816

Built in 1886, this beautiful Victorian home is located in Galveston's East End Historic District and has been lovingly restored and furnished with antiques and fine furniture. Five separate and unique rooms, all with private baths. Guests can walk to Strand Shopping District, Galveston Arts District, Grand Opera House, many casual and fine restaurants, historic trolley station, and Galveston Bay Harbor. Accommodations include game room with pool table and board games and use of bicycles for touring purposes. Gourmet breakfast served in dining room with fresh coffee and tea. Appetizers and refreshments in afternoon. Gourmet picnic baskets available for extra fee.

Rooms: 5 (PB) $125-195
Full Breakfast
Credit Cards: A, B, C, D
Notes: 2, 5, 7, 9, 11, 12

The Queen Anne Bed & Breakfast

1915 Sealy Avenue, 77550-2312
(409) 763-7088; (800) 472-0930

This home is a four-story Queen Anne-style Victorian in the historic home district, built in

---

NOTES: Credit cards accepted: A MasterCard; B Visa; C American Express; D Discover; E Diner's Club; F Other; 2 Personal checks accepted; 3 Lunch available; 4 Dinner available; 5 Open all year; 6 Pets welcome;

1905. Stained-glass windows, beautiful floors, large rooms, pocket doors, and 12-foot ceilings with transom windows; beautifully redecorated in 1991. Walk to the historic shopping district, restaurants, 1894 opera house, and museums. A short drive to the beach. A visit to Queen Anne is to be anticipated, relished, and long-remembered.

Hosts: Ron and Jackie Metzger
Rooms: 5 (3 PB; 2 SB) $90-150
Full Breakfast
Credit Cards: A, B, C
Notes: 2, 5, 7, 9, 10, 11, 12, 13, 14

GALVESTON ISLAND

Bayview Inn with Hot Tub and Boatpier

P.O. Box 1326, 77553
(409) 741-0705

Waterfront casual luxury and elegance in a romantic setting complete with huge swaying palms, exotic waterfowl, and hot tub. Water views from all rooms with private baths; furnished with fabulous rare antiques from world travels. Boat dock. Golf course and beach two minutes away. Ms. Pat is an island character well worth meeting. Her specialty is adult getaways. Nearby are flight and car museums, historical homes, IMAX, rainforest-pyramid, trolley, fishing, beach, boating; 45 minutes to Houston. Discount for weekly or monthly rates.

Host: Ms. Pat Hazlewood
Rooms: 3 (PB) $65-145
Continental Breakfast
Credit Cards: F
Notes: 2, 5, 7, 9, 10, 11, 12, 13

GARLAND

Bed & Breakfast Texas Style

4224 West Red Bird Lane, Dallas, 75237
(972) 298-8586; (800) 899-4538
FAX (972) 298-7118; e-mail: bdtxstyle1@aol.com
www.bnbtexasstyle.com

Catnip Creek. Right on Spring Creek, the hot tub on the deck overlooks a wooded creek. The guest room has a queen-size bed, private bath, and private entrance. Breakfast has granola and cinnamon-raisin biscuits or other homemade muffins and breads. Weekend guests are treated to a healthy quiche or pancakes. Herbal teas and specially blended coffees are offered. Bicycles are provided. Just 30 minutes from downtown Dallas and very near Hypermart, the newest tourist attraction of the metroplex. Also near Southfork Ranch. $60-75.

GEORGETOWN

Claibourne House

912 Forest, 78626
(512) 930-3934; (512) 913-2272 (voice mail)
FAX: (512) 869-0202

Claibourne House is three blocks west of the historic courthouse square in the heart of old Georgetown. Built in 1896, this spacious Victorian residence was restored during 1987-88 and adapted as a bed and breakfast inn. Guests are graciously accommodated in four bedrooms, each with private bath. An intimate upstairs sitting room and downstairs grand hall and parlor and wraparound porch are available for guests. The guest rooms are handsomely furnished with treasured family furniture, antiques, and distinctive fine art.

Host: Clare Easley
Rooms: 4 (PB) $85-125
Continental Breakfast
Credit Cards: A, B
Notes: 2, 5, 7, 9

Heron Hill Farm Bed & Breakfast

1350 County Road 143, 78626
(512) 863-0461; (800) 439-3828

New, old-fashioned Texas farmhouse built in 1996 especially for bed and breakfast. House sits high on a hill overlooking 13 acres of wildlife habitat and a large vegetable garden.

---

7 No smoking; 8 Children welcome; 9 Social drinking allowed; 10 Tennis nearby; 11 Swimming nearby; 12 Golf nearby; 13 Skiing nearby; 14 May be booked through a travel agent; 15 Handicapped accessible.

Heron Hill Farm

Pick own veggies in season. The four guest rooms, each with private bath, are on the second floor. Rooms feature country decor which mixes new and antique furniture. Three rooms have queen-size beds, one room has two twin antique white iron beds. Full breakfast served daily. Enjoy antiquing, hiking, biking, and swimming and boating at local lake; golf also available nearby. Inner Space Caverns and Lady Bird Johnson Wildflower Center make good day trips.

Hosts: Ed and Linda Devine
Rooms: 4 (PB) $80
Full Breakfast
Credit Cards: A, B
Notes: 2, 5, 7, 8, 9, 11, 12

GLADEWATER

Honeycomb Suites

111 North Main Street, 75647
(800) 594-2253; FAX (903) 845-2448
e-mail: sho4go@internetwork.net
www.honeycombsuites.com

Specializing in romantic getaways, offering seven suites, each in a different motif. Five suites are above scratch-recipe bakery in the antique district of Gladewater. Two suites (including the honeymoon suite) are in an adjacent building. Four suites have whirlpool tubs for two. Saturday evenings, candlelight dinners with horse-drawn carriage rides are available by reservation. Romance packages and gift certificates are available. Gladewater is 120 miles east of Dallas or 60 miles west of Shreveport.

Hosts: Bill and Susan Morgan
Rooms: 7 (PB) $85-150
Full Breakfast
Credit Cards: A, B, C, D
Notes: 2, 3, 4, 5, 7, 9, 10, 11, 12

GLEN ROSE

Bed & Breakfast Texas Style

4224 West Red Bird Lane, Dallas, 75237
(972) 298-8586; (800) 899-4538
FAX (972) 298-7118; e-mail: bdtxstyle1@aol.com
www.bnbtexasstyle.com

Hummingbird Lodge. The motto of the owners for this extraordinary bed and breakfast is "Come find the trees and streams, the deer and the birds, the peace. Come find yourself." Just about two miles south of Glen Rose off the beaten path, surrounded by cedar trees and small hills, a weary city dweller will find complete serenity. There are large porches and decks with rocking chairs; the "hummers" are most entertaining; or just curl up with a book down by the hot tub in the swinging hammock. There are well-marked walking trails, a waterfall, and a pond for the energetic fisherman. There are six guest rooms, all with private baths. A full gourmet breakfast is provided. $85-115.

Bussey's Something Special

202 Hereford Street, P.O. Box 1425, 76043
(817) 897-4843; (877) 426-2233

Relax in a private country cottage in downtown Glen Rose historic district. Family-friendly with crib upstairs. Enjoy hand-crafted lounges, artwork, books, games, and toys. Seashell and oak bathroom with shower (no tub). Experience the Early American decor in a private cozy cottage with tropical bath, whirlpool jet

---

NOTES: Credit cards accepted: A MasterCard; B Visa; C American Express; D Discover; E Diner's Club; F Other; 2 Personal checks accepted; 3 Lunch available; 4 Dinner available; 5 Open all year; 6 Pets welcome;

GRANBURY

Dabney House Bed & Breakfast

106 South Jones, 76048
(817) 579-1260; (800) 566-1260

Craftsman-style home built in 1907 boasts its original hardwood floors, ceiling beams, stained and beveled glass, and fixtures. Long-term business rates available per request as well as a whole-house rental discount. Hosts offer a candlelight romantic dinner or group lunches per reservation only. Custom special occasion baskets available by advance order only. Special discounts for certified peace officers and firefighters.

Hosts: John and Gwen Hurley
Rooms: 4 (PB) $60-105
Full Breakfast
Credit Cards: A, B, C
Notes: 2, 5, 7, 9, 10, 11, 12, 14

Bussey's Something Special

tub/shower, and small kitchen. Both cottages have a king-size bed. Continental plus breakfast, private front porches, and attractive decor. Sweetheart packages available upon request. No hosts on premises

Hosts: Susan and Morris Bussey
Cottage: 2 (PB) $80-100
Continental Breakfast
Credit Cards: A, B, C, D
Notes: 2, 5, 7, 8, 10, 11, 12, 14

Ye Ole Maple Inn

1509 Van Zandt, P.O. Box 1141, 76043
(254) 897-3456; texasguides.com/mapleinn.html

Built circa 1950, the inn is decorated with several antique pieces throughout. Two rooms, each with its own private bath. Den with a grand fireplace and small library for reading pleasure. Breakfast includes fresh fruit or fruit compote, breakfast sausage or Black Forest Ham, orange juice and coffee or tea with an entree such as Oatmeal waffles, Maple Baked Eggs or Egg-Sausage-Apple Casserole. Dessert is served every evening. Area activities include the Fossil Rim Wildlife Refuge, Creation Museum, Dinosaur State Park, Texas Amphitheatre, and the Somervell Country Golf Course. No pets, children, or smoking.

Host: Roberta Maple
Rooms: 2 (PB) $80-85
Credit Cards: A, B, C
Notes: 2, 5, 7, 12, 15

Pearl Street Inn Bed & Breakfast

319 West Pearl Street, 76048
(817) 579-7465; (888) PEARL ST

Relax and reminisce in the stately, stylish comfort of a 1912 Prairie-style home. Three blocks from Granbury's historic square, this tastefully restored historical home features antique furnishings, two porches, cast-iron tubs, pocket doors, outdoor hot tub, and scrumptious breakfasts. Enjoy live theater, state parks, drive-in

Pearl Street Inn

---

7 No smoking; 8 Children welcome; 9 Social drinking allowed; 10 Tennis nearby; 11 Swimming nearby; 12 Golf nearby; 13 Skiing nearby; 14 May be booked through a travel agent; 15 Handicapped accessible.

movies, antique shopping, or festivals in a charming country setting, 30 miles south of the Dallas/Fort Worth metroplex. Enjoy overnight accommodations in a delightful home "where days move gently in all seasons."

Host: Danette D. Hebda
Rooms: 5 (PB) $59-109
Full Breakfast
Credit Cards: None
Notes: 2, 5, 7, 9, 10, 11, 12, 14

HOUSTON

The Lovett Inn

501 Lovett Boulevard, 77006
(713) 522-5224; (800) 779-5224
FAX (713) 528-6708; e-mail LovettInn@aol.com
www.lovettinn.com

Once the home of Houston mayor and federal court judge Joseph C. Hutcheson, the Lovett Inn has all of the amenities of a first-class hotel. Within walking distance to some of the city's finest restaurants, clubs, and shopping. The George R. Brown Convention Center, downtown, Greenway Plaza, Texas Medical Center, Hobby Airport, and the Galleria are also nearby. Each room has been comfortably decorated to evoke the inn's historic past, while adding such modern amenities as in-room telephones, remote color TV, and private bathrooms. To accommodate the most discriminating traveler, suite accommodations, meeting rooms, fax service, and in-room whirlpool are available.

Host: Tom Fricke
Rooms: 9 (8 PB; 1 SB) $85-150
Continental Breakfast
Credit Cards: A, B, C, D
Notes: 5, 6, 7, 8, 9, 10, 11, 12, 14

Patrician Bed & Breakfast Inn

1200 Southmore Boulevard, 77004-5826
(713) 523-1114; (800) 553-5797;
FAX (713) 523-0790; e-mail: southmor@swbell.net
www.texasbnb.com

Visitors can relax in this immense, three- story mansion built in 1919. The inn is centrally

Patrician

located and less than 2 miles south of downtown Houston. Take a short walk to Hermann Park, Museum of Fine Arts, and Rice University. The breakfast is served gourmet-style and may include creamy French toast slathered with cream cheese and orange marmalade, orange mandarin coffee cake, fresh fruit, and orange juice.

Host: Patricia Thomas
Rooms: 5 (PB) $90-135
Full Breakfast
Credit Cards: A, B, C, D, E
Notes: 5, 7, 9, 12, 14

Robin's Nest

4104 Greeley, 77006
(713) 528-5821; (800) 622-8343
FAX (713) 521-2154; www.houstonbnb.com

Historic, circa 1898, two-story wooden Queen Anne. Feather beds atop fine mattresses, convenience of central location, and a full breakfast make the stay worthwhile. The rooms are spacious, furnished in eclectic Victorian with custom-made drapes, bed covers, etc. Robin's Nest is decoratively painted in concert with her sister "painted ladies." In the Museum and Arts district, surrounded by museums, art galleries, downtown, excellent restaurants, and the theater district. Inquire about accommodations for pets and children.

NOTES: Credit cards accepted: A MasterCard; B Visa; C American Express; D Discover; E Diner's Club; F Other; 2 Personal checks accepted; 3 Lunch available; 4 Dinner available; 5 Open all year; 6 Pets welcome;

Host: Robin Smith
Rooms: 4 (PB) $75-120
Full Breakfast
Credit Cards: A, B, C, D
Notes: 2, 5, 7, 9, 10, 11, 12, 13

Sara's

Sara's Bed & Breakfast Inn

941 Heights Boulevard, 77008
(713) 868-1130; (800) 593-1130

This Queen Anne Victorian is in the historic Heights district of Houston, only four miles from downtown, a neighborhood of historic homes, many of which are in the National Register of Historic Places. Each bedroom is uniquely furnished, having either single, double, queen-, or king-size beds. The balcony suite consists of two bedrooms, two baths, kitchen, living area, and balcony. Children welcome only in balcony suite.

Hosts: Donna and Tillman Arledge
Rooms: 14 (12 PB; 2 SB) $70-150
Continental Breakfast
Credit Cards: A, B, C, D, E, F
Notes: 2, 5, 7, 8, 9, 10, 11, 12, 14

INGRAM

Lazy Hills Guest Ranch

P.O. Box G, 78025
(800) 880-0632; (830) 367-5600;
FAX (830) 367-5667; e-mail: lhills@ktc.com

Surrounded by the panoramic beauty of the Texas Hill Country, Lazy Hills has a wide variety of fun activities, comfortable accommodations, and delicious, family meals. Guest rooms are furnished with comfortable twin or queen beds and will sleep from four to six people comfortably. Electric heat, air conditioning, bathrooms with showers, and pleasant porches. Some have fireplaces. Breakfast, lunch, and dinner served daily. Accommodations include swimming pool, game room, tennis courts, a community telephone and community TV, and coin-operated laundry facilities. Activities include horseback riding, hiking, bird watching, golf, and fishing. No pets. Children are welcome.

Hosts: Bob and Carol Steinruck and family
Rooms: 25 (PB) $75-95
Full Breakfast
Credit Cards: A, B
Notes: 7, 8, 10, 11, 12, 14

JEFFERSON

1st Bed & Breakfast in Texas—Pride House

409 Broadway, 75657
(800) 894-3526; (903) 665- 2675;
FAX (903) 665-3901; e-mail: jefftx@mind.net
www.jeffersontexas.com

Breathtaking Victorian mansion in historic steamboat port, Texas' favorite small town where a weekend is never enough. Luxurious accommodations, luscious interiors, and legendary breakfasts. Within driving distance of Shreveport and Texarkana. Eleven rooms, each with private bath. Mobil rated, HAT approved, member TH&MA. Hot and cold drinks and snacks included and available around the clock. German and English spoken. No pets. Smoking outside only.

Hosts: Carol Abernathy and Christel Frederick (innkeepers); Sandy Spalding (owner)
Rooms: 11 (PB) $75-150
Full Breakfast
Credit Cards: A, B, C, D
Notes: 2, 5, 7, 8, 9, 10, 12, 14

---

7 No smoking; 8 Children welcome; 9 Social drinking allowed; 10 Tennis nearby; 11 Swimming nearby; 12 Golf nearby; 13 Skiing nearby; 14 May be booked through a travel agent; 15 Handicapped accessible.

Jefferson, TX

McKay House

McKay House Bed & Breakfast Inn

306 East Delta Street, 75657
(903) 665-7322
(800) 468-2627 (reservations 9 A.M.-5 P.M.)

Jefferson is a riverport town from the frontier days of the Republic of Texas. It has historical mule-drawn tours, 30 antique shops, boat rides on the Big Cypress Bayou, and a mysterious lake made famous by Walt Disney. The McKay House, an 1851 Greek Revival cottage, offers period furnishings, cool lemonade, porch swings, and fireplaces. Seven rooms that vary from the keeping room to the garden suite (with his and her antique footed tubs). A full gentleman's breakfast is served in the garden conservatory. Victorian nightclothes are laid out for guests. VIP guests have included Lady Bird Johnson, Alex Haley, and Fabio. Mobil Travel Guide.

Owner: Peggy Taylor
Innkeepers: Lisa and Roger Cantrell
Rooms: 4 (PB) $139 weekend; $89 weekday
Suites: 3 (PB) $169
Full Breakfast
Credit Cards: A, B, C
Notes: 2, 5, 7, 8, 11, 12

Old Mulberry Inn

209 Jefferson Street, 75657
(903) 665-1945; (800) 263-5319;
FAX (903) 665-9123;
e-mail: mulberry@jeffersontx.com
www.jefferson.com/oldmulberryinn

A gracious new inn in the style of Jefferson's fine antebellum homes offers guests the best of the old and the new. Adding to the charm are antique heartpine floors, tastefully eclectic furnishings, and designer touches throughout. Soak in a footed tub, relax by the fireplace in the library, or swing on the spacious porch. Five unique rooms. Private baths. Cable TV. Gourmet breakfast. 24-hour refreshments. Walk to tour homes, shopping, museums.

Hosts: Donald and Gloria Degn
Rooms: 5 (PB) $100-125
Full Breakfast
Credit Cards: A, B, C, D
Notes: 5, 7, 9, 11, 12, 14

Urquhart House of Eleven Gables

Urquhart House of Eleven Gables

301 East Walker Street, 75657
(903) 665-8442; (888) 922-8442

The Urquhart House of Eleven Gables is an experience of luxuries and historical elegance. Turn-of-the-century quality of life comes alive with period decor and antiques. Further creating the yesteryear ambiance are equestrian carriages and wagons clip-clopping the street that fronts the wraparound porch of this expansive 1890 Queen Anne house. Antique wicker swing and furniture occupy the abundantly pleasant wraparound porch inviting guests to come and "sit a spell." Gourmet breakfast served with antique linens, crystal, and china.

NOTES: Credit cards accepted: A MasterCard; B Visa; C American Express; D Discover; E Diner's Club; F Other; 2 Personal checks accepted; 3 Lunch available; 4 Dinner available; 5 Open all year; 6 Pets welcome;

Host: Joyce Jackson
Rooms: 2 (PB) $125
Full Breakfast
Credit Cards: A, B, C, D, E
Notes: 2, 5, 7, 8, 9, 12, 14

KINGSLAND

The Antlers Hotel

Route 2, Box 430, 78639
(800) 383-0007; FAX (915) 388-6488
www.theantlers.com

Historic, lakeside hotel built by the railroad in 1901. All antique-filled rooms and suites are luxurious with private entrances off wide porches. Game room with TV/VCR, pool table, and treadmill. Fifteen acres of grounds include nature trails, orchard, and over a thousand feet of waterfront for swimming, fishing, and boating. Boat slips available. Listed on National Register of Historic Places. Great weather, wildflowers, bird watching, and golfing in the Texas Hill Country.

Hosts: Lori and Anthony Mayfield
Rooms: 6 (PB) $120-140
Continental Breakfast
Credit Cards: A, B, C, D
Notes: 2, 3, 4, 5, 7, 9, 11, 12, 15

KINGSVILLE

B Bar B Ranch Inn

325 East County Road 2215, 78363
(361) 296-3331; FAX (361) 296-3337
e-mail: bbarb@rivnet.com
www.b-bar-b.com

Quietly nestled beneath the rippling leaves of a south Texas mesquite grove, this 80-acre working ranch is host to a wide variety of native plants and wildlife. Originally part of the historic King Ranch, the B Bar B is a bird watching hot spot. The hosts also offer fishing and hunting trips. Their gourmet restaurant is sure to tempt guests' taste buds.

Hosts: Luther and Patti Young
Rooms: 16 (PB) $85-125

Full Breakfast
Credit Cards: A, B, D
Notes: 2, 4, 5, 11, 12, 14

LEANDER

Trails End Bed & Breakfast

12223 Trail End Road, #7, 78641
(512) 267-2901

Trails End Bed and Breakfast located near Austin and Lake Travis in Texas Hill Country. Our quiet country setting is elegant and entertaining. We offer fine food, quaint hospitality, decks, nature hikes, pool, monogrammed robes, telephones in rooms, and gardens. Take home happy memories and a gift from the Bed and Breakfast Store. Fishing, water sport, and golfing close by. Much exploring in nearby quaint town.

Hosts: JoAnn and Tom Patty
Rooms: 3 (PB) $75-185
Full Breakfast
Notes: 2, 3, 4, 5, 7, 8, 9, 10, 11, 12, 13, 14

Trails End

MASON

Hasse House Ranch

P.O. Box 779, 76856
(888) 41-HASSE (414-2773)

The Hasse House, circa 1883, is where country quality lives in historical architecture laced

---

7 No smoking; 8 Children welcome; 9 Social drinking allowed; 10 Tennis nearby; 11 Swimming nearby; 12 Golf nearby; 13 Skiing nearby; 14 May be booked through a travel agent; 15 Handicapped accessible.

Hasse House Ranch

with modern conveniences. Complete with period furniture, microwave, dishwasher, washer-dryer, central air, two bedrooms, two baths, living room, and complete kitchen. Guests may explore the 320-acre ranch with two-mile nature trail and abundant wildlife. Owner lives in town so party will be only one in the house. "Let us invite you to the complete peace of rural living."

Host: Laverne Lee
Rooms: 2 (PB) $95
Continental Breakfast
Credit Cards: A, B
Notes: 2, 5, 8, 9, 12

MINEOLA

The Lott Home Bed & Breakfast Cottages

311 East Kilpatrick Street, 75773
(888) 232-LOTT (5688); e-mail: lotthomecottages@tyler.net

The Lott Home Cottages, circa 1918, offers old-fashioned southern hospitality at its best. The charming, romantic cottages include queen-size beds, private baths, cable TV, antique furnishings, and a kitchen, with microwave, refrigerator, and coffee maker, fully stocked with refreshments and snacks. Each cottage has its own private porch with wooden rockers for guests to relax and view a beautiful East Texas sunset. Treat oneself to an unforgettable night, relive a moment in time and take home wonderful memories at the Lott Home Bed and Breakfast Cottages.

Hosts: Mark and Sharon Chamblee
Rooms: 2 (PB) $95
Full Breakfast
Credit Cards: A, B, D
Notes: 2, 5, 7, 9, 10, 12, 14, 15

NEW BRAUNFELS

Gruene Homestead Inn

832 Gruene Road, 78130
(830) 606-0216; FAX (830) 625-6390
e-mail: homestead@compuvision.com

The inn's 20 guest suites are housed in several historic homes and cottages, dating from the late 1860s, that have been carefully restored and decorated in unique styles ranging from elegant Victorian to "Texas Country." Relaxation and romance are the keys to the graceful beauty of this hill country inn. On eight acres and less then two minutes from historic Gruene and the Guadalupe River. One room is handicapped accessible.

Hosts: Ed and Billie Miles
Rooms: 18 (PB) $95-135
Credit Cards: A, B, D
Notes: 2, 5, 7, 9, 11, 12, 15

Karbach Haus Bed & Breakfast

487 West San Antonio Street, 78130
(830) 625-2131; (800) 972-5941;
FAX (830) 629-1126; www.bbhost.com/karbach

Meticulously restored turn-of-the-century mansion on an acre estate in downtown New Braunfels. Walk to fine restaurants, museums, antique stores, local attractions. Experience *Gemutlichkeit* of a German *Gasthaus* with amenities of a small resort. Spacious guest rooms have private tile baths (some with Jacuzzis), queen- or king-size beds, cable TV, VCR, robes, ceiling fans, down quilts, and many antiques. Central heat/air conditioning, swimming pool and spa, video library, butler's pantry with guest refrigerator, ice machine. World-class German-style breakfasts. Long-term rentals available. Owner/hosts on premises.

NOTES: Credit cards accepted: A MasterCard; B Visa; C American Express; D Discover; E Diner's Club; F Other; 2 Personal checks accepted; 3 Lunch available; 4 Dinner available; 5 Open all year; 6 Pets welcome;

Hosts: Captain Ben Jack Kinney, USN (retired) and Kathleen Karbach Kinney, Ph.D.
Rooms: 6 (PB) $105-175
Full Breakfast
Credit Cards: A, B, D
Notes: 2, 5, 7, 9, 10, 11, 12, 14

Prince Solms Inn

295 East San Antonio Street, 78130
(800) 625-9169; FAX (830) 625-9169

100-year-old landmark in historic New Braunfels. Gateway to the breathtaking Texas Hill Country. Rated ninth best historic inn by *Texas Highways* Magazine. Two blocks from museum, water sports, and shopping. Ideal for family gatherings, small weddings, and corporate retreats. Romance Package which includes dinner in renowned Wolfgang's Keller Restaurant, rated one of the ten most romantic restaurants by *Ultra* Magazine. Country breakfast served. Restaurant on premises. Smoking permitted in courtyard only.

Hosts: Larry Patton, Carmen Morales, and Beverly Talbot
Rooms: 10 (PB) $95-159
Four-Room Cottage: $229
Continental Breakfast
Credit Cards: A, B, C, D
Notes: 2, 4, 5, 7, 8, 9, 10, 11, 12, 14

PADRE ISLES

Sand Dollar Hospitality

35 Mendenhall Drive, Corpus Christi, 78415
(512) 853-1222; (800) 528-7782
FAX (512) 814-1285
www.ccinternet.net/sand-dollar

Coguina Bay. Two great suites, each with a king-size bed, private bath, ceiling fan with view of pool and hot tub offered on this canal home in Padre Isles. The host, an accomplished mariner also offers sailing charters on his 33 foot sail boat. Jet ski rentals are also available. A full buffet-style breakfast is served in the dining room overlooking the water. $120.

Fortuna Bay. This enchanting hideaway on Texas's North Padre Island is cradled between the Laguna Madre and the Gulf of Mexico. A unique bed and breakfast inn, Fortune Bay presently consists of three one-bedroom fully furnished condominiums in a 10-unit complex. Each unit has a living room with cable TV, a bedroom with a queen-size bed, a fully equipped kitchen with microwave, and a washer and dryer. There is also an outside grill near the pool. The three-story, red-tile-roof structure is at the intersection of five canals. Provisions for a Continental plus breakfast are supplied. A complimentary boat ride through the canal system is offered. Weekly and monthly rates are available. $96.

Island Retreat. Overlooking a major canal on North Padre Island, this attractive two-bedroom, two-bath home is available in total for families or couples traveling together. The home can accommodate six people in air-conditioned comfort. One bedroom has sleeping room for four. The refrigerator is stocked with fruit and other breakfast provisions for guests to self serve. There are two decks, one with a hammock, the other built out over the water. Children are welcome. Also small, well-behaved pets are permitted with a $50 damage deposit. The gulf beaches are just minutes away, across the island. Ten dollars for each additional person school-age or older. $150.

Sunrise on the Water. This bright and beautiful white stucco home is on one of the major canals on North Padre Island and is just 5 minutes from the gulf beaches. The larger of the two guest suites faces the water and has a balcony large enough for seating. A second bedroom has twin beds and its own private bath. Both rooms have their own TVs and telephones. $90-110.

---

7 No smoking; 8 Children welcome; 9 Social drinking allowed; 10 Tennis nearby; 11 Swimming nearby; 12 Golf nearby; 13 Skiing nearby; 14 May be booked through a travel agent; 15 Handicapped accessible.

ROCKPORT

Sand Dollar Hospitality

35 Mendenhall Drive, Corpus Christi, 78415
(361) 853-1222; (800) 528-7782
FAX (361) 814-1285
www.ccinternet.net/sand-dollar

Anthony's by the Sea. The innkeepers at Anthony's offer four guest bedrooms in the guest wing of the residence plus two guest cottages. All units throughout the inn include a refrigerator, cable TV and VCR. A spacious plant-filled patio with lounge chair and tables connects the main house and the two guest cottages. There guests will also find a barbecue grill for guests' use. Off to the side is a swimming pool and hot tub. A full breakfast is served. The renowned Aransas Wildlife Refuge is less than an hour's drive away. Group, weekly, and monthly rates available. $66-95.

The Blue Heron. This Federal-style brick home was built in 1890 and after withstanding the hurricane of 1919 was reconstructed with the addition of porches and verandas in the 1930s. Great accommodations include four suites, two with half-baths and two with full. Outside, the rose and herb garden invites visitors to sit and relax under the massive live-oak tree. A full buffet style breakfast is served in the formal dining room. $95-105.

Chandler House. The upper-level veranda of this 123-year-old house offers a view of the gulf and the town's shopping area with its many specialty shops and galleries. Each of the two large upstairs bedrooms has two queen-size beds and its own private bath. The downstairs bedroom has a king-size bed, a private attached bath, fireplace, and TV. The common area includes a great room with fireplace and parlor games and a spacious breakfast room. Lunch is also available and open to the public at the unique Chandler House Tea Room. Children over 12 welcome at $25 per each child. $100-150.

Cygnet. A cozy, secluded country cottage on 16 acres with a double bed, top of the line queen-size sleeper sofa, kitchenette, TV/VCR, and country Jacuzzi outside. This delightful country retreat is about five miles south of Rockport and was designed to provide guests with privacy and comfort. Guests will be provided with farm-fresh eggs, homemade bread, cereals, milk, and fresh fruit. Five dollars for each additional person. $70.

The Habitat. A unique haven of seven plus acres, in the heart of the Lamar Peninsula and near the Aransas Wildlife Refuge, this bed and breakfast consists of four log cabins. Each cabin has a fully stocked kitchen, screened front porch, and outdoor grill. Bird watchers will have a chance to identify and photograph a myrid of bird life in and around the two-acre lake that fronts each cabin. Self-serve Continental breakfast. No pets. $70.

Hoope's House. Elegant but casual, this lovely home combines modern luxury with Old World charm. With its gleaming hardwood floors, twelve-foot ceilings with crown molding, this home is one of the oldest and most illustrious homes in the area. Commanding a panoramic view of Rockport Harbor, the inn is also within walking distance of museums, shops, and galleries. There are four guest rooms in the main house, each with a private bath. In addition there are four garden rooms across from the pool and hot tub. These too, have private bath, telephone, and TV.

ROCKWELL

Bed & Breakfast Texas Style

4224 West Red Bird Lane, Dallas, 75237
(972) 298-8586; (800) 899-4538
FAX (972) 298-7118; e-mail: bdtxstyle1@aol.com
www.bnbtexasstyle.com

Barton on Boydstun. Individual cottage suites are on this large property right near downtown

---

NOTES: Credit cards accepted: A MasterCard; B Visa; C American Express; D Discover; E Diner's Club; F Other; 2 Personal checks accepted; 3 Lunch available; 4 Dinner available; 5 Open all year; 6 Pets welcome;

Rockwall. Other buildings are an art gallery, working studio, and the Bois d'Arc Chapel. The cottages are new and built specifically for guests. Each one has its own screened porch and small kitchen. Perfect place for a small wedding or honeymoon retreat. Breakfast is a prepared treat that is left in the cottage for guests to zap in the microwave. $110-140.

ROUND TOP

The Settlement at Round Top

2218 Hartfield Road, P.O. Box 176, 78954
(406) 249-5015; (888) ROUNDTOP
FAX (409) 249-5587
e-mail: stay@thesettlement.com
www.thesettlement.com

The Settlement at Round Top is a luxurious pioneer-era adult retreat on 35 picturesque acres. This charming little complex includes 10 private guest rooms and suites in wonderfully restored log cabins and Berman cottages and houses including porches with rockers, fireplaces, private whirlpools, original art, fine linens, towering oaks, antique roses, miniature horses, and wildflowers in season. Featured in *Country Living, Country Home,* and *The Dallas Morning News.* Full breakfast on weekends and Continental weekdays.

Hosts: Karen and Larry Beevers
Rooms: 10 (PB) $95-200
Full Breakfast
Credit Cards: A, B, C, D
Notes: 2, 3, 4, 5, 7, 9, 10, 11, 12, 14

The Settlement at Round Top

SAN ANTONIO

Beckmann Inn & Carriage House

222 East Guenther Street, 78204
(210) 229-1449; (800) 945-1449
FAX (210) 229-1061; www.beckmanninn.com

This elegant Victorian inn is in the heart of San Antonio in the King William Street Historic District. The wraparound porch welcomes guests to this beautiful home. All rooms are colorfully decorated, featuring ornately carved Victorian queen-size beds, antiques, private baths, TVs, telephones, refrigerators, desks, and robes. Ride the trolley or take the Riverwalk to the Alamo, restaurants, shops, Mexican market, and much more. Guests receive gracious and warm hospitality during their stay. Gourmet breakfast with a breakfast dessert. AAA three-diamond-rated, Mobil three-star-rated, and IIA-rated excellent.

Hosts: Betty Jo and Don Schwartz
Rooms: 5 (PB) $99-140
Full Breakfast
Credit Cards: A, B, C, D, E
Notes: 2, 5, 7, 8, 9, 11, 12, 14

Beckmann Inn

The Belle of Monte Vista

505 Belknap Place, 78212
(210) 732-4006; FAX (210) 732-4006

J. Riley Gordon designed this Queen Anne-style Victorian as a model home. Built in 1890 with limestone, the house has been beautifully

---

7 No smoking; 8 Children welcome; 9 Social drinking allowed; 10 Tennis nearby; 11 Swimming nearby; 12 Golf nearby; 13 Skiing nearby; 14 May be booked through a travel agent; 15 Handicapped accessible.

restored and is located in the elegant Monte Vista historic district just two miles from the Alamo and Riverwalk. Inside, guests will find eight fireplaces, stained-glass windows, a hand-carved oak staircase, and Victorian furnishings. The host, Jim Davis, serves a full southern breakfast and will help guests plan their day.

Hosts: Jim Davis and Jeanette Duval
Rooms: 5 (2 PB; 3 SB) $50-85
Full Breakfast
Credit Cards: A, B, C
Notes: 2, 5, 7, 8, 9, 10, 12

Bonner Garden Bed & Breakfast

145 East Agartia, 78212
(800) 396-4222; FAX (210) 733-6129
e-mail: noels@onr.com
www.travelbase.com

An award-winning replica of an Italian Renaissance villa built in 1910 for internationally known artist Mary Bonner. The original villa was built in Italy in the early 1600s. Fireplaces, tile, fixtures, etc., were imported from Italy. A large swimming pool and a rooftop patio provide enjoyable respites for guests. Guest rooms have private baths, some with Jacuzzi, TVs, VCRs, and telephones. A film library and Texarkana library are available for guests' enjoyment. A full gourmet breakfast is served.

Hosts: Jan and Noel Stenoien
Rooms: 5 (PB) $85-115
Full Breakfast
Credit Cards: A, B, C, D, E
Notes: 2, 5, 7, 9, 10, 11, 12, 14

Bonner Garden

Brackenridge House

Brackenridge House: A Bed & Breakfast Inn

230 Madison, 78204
(210) 271-3442; (800) 221-1412
FAX (210) 226-3139; e-mail: benniesueb@aol.com
www.brackenridgehouse.com

Native Texan owners and innkeepers will guide guests through their visit to this beautiful Greek Revival home in historic King William. Gourmet breakfast served in formal dining room or veranda, hot tub, private baths, and country Victorian decor add to guests' comfort and pleasure. Pets and children are welcome in the carriage house. AAA-, Mobil-, and HAT-rated.

Owners and Innkeepers: Bennie and Sue Blansett
Rooms: 5 (PB) $89-200
Guest house: 2 (PB) $125-250
Full Breakfast
Credit Cards: A, B, D, E
Notes: 2, 5, 6, 7, 8, 9, 10, 11, 12, 14

The Columns on Alamo

1037 South Alamo, 78210
(800) 233-3364
www.bbonline.com/tx/columns

Resident innkeepers welcome guests to their gracious 1892 Greek Revival home and guest house in the historic King William area. Blocks from Riverwalk, restaurants, shopping, conven-

---

NOTES: Credit cards accepted: A MasterCard; B Visa; C American Express; D Discover; E Diner's Club; F Other; 2 Personal checks accepted; 3 Lunch available; 4 Dinner available; 5 Open all year; 6 Pets welcome;

San Antonio, TX

The Columns on Alamo

tion center, and Alamo; short drive to Sea World and Fiesta Texas. Marvelous antiques and period reproductions, queen- and king-size beds, Jacuzzis, fireplace, telephones, TVs, large common areas, verandas, gardens, off-street parking. Full gourmet breakfast is served in the main house. Smoke free except for verandas, outdoors. Two-night minimum Saturday.

Hosts: Ellenor and Art Link
Rooms: 11 (PB) $89-155
Full Breakfast
Credit Cards: A, B, C, D, E, F
Notes: 5, 7, 9, 10, 12, 14

Noble Inns

107 Madison Street, 78204
(210) 225-4045; (800) 221-4045
FAX (210) 227-0877; e-mail: nobleinns@aol.com
www.nobleinns.com

Noble Inns

Noble Inns operates two luxury Victorian properties in downtown San Antonio's King William historic district. Meticulously restored, the 1890-era bed and breakfasts are decorated with period antiques and offer full modern amenities. All accommodations feature private, marble bath with two-person Jacuzzi or claw-foot tub; antique mantel gas fireplace; sumptuous fabrics, wallpapers; color cable TV with HBO; telephone with data port and voice mail. Full and Continental breakfasts. Beautiful patios, outdoor pool and heated spa or indoor swim spa. Transportation in classic 1960 Rolls Royce available.

Hosts: Don and Liesl Noble
Rooms: 9 (PB) $130-185
Full and Continental Breakfast
Credit Cards: A, B, C, D, E, F
Notes: 2, 5, 7, 9, 10, 11, 12, 14

The Ogé House on the Riverwalk

209 Washington Street, 78204
(800) 242-2770; FAX (210) 226-5812
e-mail: ogeinn@swbell.net; www.ogeinn.com

Elegant historic antebellum mansion shaded by massive pecans and oaks, on one and one-half landscaped acres along the banks of the famous San Antonio Riverwalk in the King William Street historic district. The inn, beautifully decorated with antiques, has large verandas and a grand foyer. All rooms have air conditioning, telephones, and TVs, many with fireplaces. Dining, entertainment, convention centers, trolley, and the Alamo are steps away. Featured in the *New York Times*, *Glamour*, *Victoria*, *Southern Living*, Travel channel. IIA-rated excellent, Mobil three-star-rated. Complimentary *Wall Street Journal*, *New York Times*, and *San Antonio Express News*. Smoking restricted. Gourmet breakfast.

Hosts: Patrick and Sharrie Magatagan
Rooms: 10 (PB) $145-205
Full Breakfast
Credit Cards: A, B, C, D, E
Notes: 2, 5, 9, 10, 12, 14

---

7 No smoking; 8 Children welcome; 9 Social drinking allowed; 10 Tennis nearby; 11 Swimming nearby; 12 Golf nearby; 13 Skiing nearby; 14 May be booked through a travel agent; 15 Handicapped accessible.

Riverwalk Inn

329 Old Gailbeau Road, 78204
(210) 212-8300; (800) 254-4440
FAX (210) 229-9422

The Riverwalk Inn is five two-story log homes, circa 1840, that have been restored on the San Antonio Riverwalk and are tastefully decorated in period antiques. Amenities include fireplaces, refrigerators, private baths, telephones, balconies, 80-foot porch, and conference area. Continental plus breakfasts and desserts served. Swimming nearby. Smoking permitted outside only. No children.

Hosts: Johnny Halpenny; Jan and Tracy Hammer
Rooms: 11 (PB) $110-175
Continental Breakfast
Credit Cards: A, B, C, D
Notes: 2, 5, 10, 11, 12, 14

The Victorian Lady Inn

421 Howard Street, 78212
(210) 224-2524; (800) 879-7116
www.viclady.com

This 1898 historic mansion offers spacious guest rooms furnished with period antiques. High-back beds, claw-foot tubs, fireplaces, and verandas complete guests' pampered retreat. Savor a fabulous full breakfast each morning. Relax in the outdoor hot tub or in-ground pool surrounded by tropical palms and banana trees. The Alamo, Riverwalk, convention center, and trolley are just blocks away. Package plans, corporate rates, and meeting space available.

Hosts: Joe and Kathleen Bowski
Rooms: 8 (PB) $79-135
Full Breakfast
Credit Cards: A, B, C, D
Notes: 2, 5, 7, 9, 10, 11, 12, 14

The Victorian Lady Inn

A Yellow Rose

229 Madison, 78204
(210) 229-9903; (800) 950-9903
www.bbonline.com/tx/yellowrose/

A Yellow Rose bed and breakfast is an 1878 Victorian home in the King William Street Historic District. It has five wonderful guest rooms appointed with antiques, and each has private bath, cable TV, and queen-size bed. Off-street, covered parking is also provided. Breakfast is served daily in the elegant 18th-century dining room, and afterwards or in the afternoon or evening guests will enjoy relaxing on the veranda. Two blocks from the Riverwalk, one block from the 50¢ trolley, five blocks from the Alamo and convention center, and within three blocks three of the finest restaurants in San Antonio.

Hosts: Deb Field-Walker and Kit Walker
Rooms: 5 (PB) $95-140
Full Breakfast
Credit Cards: A, B, C, D
Notes: 5, 7, 9, 12, 14

SANDIA

Sand Dollar Hospitality

35 Mendenhall Drive, Corpus Christi, 78415
(361) 853-1222; (800) 528-7782
FAX (361) 814-1285
www.ccinternet.net/sand-dollar

Knolle Farm and Ranch Bed and Breakfast. A true Texas ranch experience with sufficient "citified" amenities to make for a comfortable and enjoyable stay. There are four guest rooms. There are eight stalls as well as outside paddock and arena. Additional attractions and/or

NOTES: Credit cards accepted: A MasterCard; B Visa; C American Express; D Discover; E Diner's Club; F Other; 2 Personal checks accepted; 3 Lunch available; 4 Dinner available; 5 Open all year; 6 Pets welcome;

activities include canoeing, fishing, skeet shooting, and bird watching. Ten dollars for each additional person. $125.

SEABROOK

Bed & Breakfast Texas Style

4224 West Red Bird Lane, Dallas, 75387
(972) 298-8586; (800) 899-4538
FAX (972) 298-7118; e-mail: bdtxstyle1@aol.com
www.bnbtexasstyle.com

Crew's Quarters. Right on Galveston Bay at the channel where shrimp boats and ocean liners go in and out, this Cape Cod-style cottage is available for families or romantic getaways. It will sleep seven to nine people with two bedrooms downstairs, each with a private bath. A loft room upstairs with two double beds and a twin bed has a half-bath. A large deck with chairs is perfect for sunning and watching birds and boats. Continental breakfast. $75-95.

SMITHVILLE

Katy House Bed & Breakfast

201 Ramona Street, P.O. Box 803, 78957
(512) 237-4262; (800) 843-5289;
FAX (512) 237-2239; e-mail thekatyh@onr.com
www.katyhouse.com

Consider this an invitation to visit the Katy House, named for the M-K-T Railroad. In the beautiful old road town of Smithville, Texas, this charming turn-of-the-century residence is handsomely decorated in American antiques and railroad memorabilia. All guest rooms offer a queen-size bed and private bath. Smithville is also the hometown of the movie, *Hope Floats.*

Hosts: Bruce and Sallie Blalock
Rooms: 5 (PB) $68-115
Full Breakfast
Credit Cards: A, B, C
Notes: 2, 5, 7, 12, 14

Bed & Breakfast Texas Style

4224 West Red Bird Lane, Dallas, 75387
(972) 298-8586; (800) 899-4538
FAX (972) 298-7118; e-mail: bdtxstyle1@aol.com
www.bnbtexasstyle.com

The Doll House. A private guest area on the second level of this residence in the Lost Pines area near Bastrop is available for visitors. The large sitting-bedroom is furnished with lovely antiques and collectibles and has its own private bath. There is a small kitchen area with refrigerator and microwave. If guests prefer to eat in, Continental fixings will be left in the room. A hearty breakfast downstairs in the dining area will be served by the gracious hosts. Two decks are available for bird watching or sunning. A lovely patio is a few steps down the trail. The state park is a few miles away. Two public golf courses are within a 10-minute drive. $110-125.

SOUTH PADRE ISLAND

Brown Pelican Inn

207 West Aries, P.O. Box 2667, 78597
(956) 761-2722

The Brown Pelican Inn is a place to relax, make oneself at home, and enjoy personalized service. The porches are a great spot to sit and watch the sun set over the bay. The inn is comfortably furnished with European and American antiques; all guest rooms have private baths, and most rooms have spectacular bay views. Breakfast in the parlor includes freshly baked bread or muffins, fresh fruit, cereal, juice, and gourmet coffee or tea. Children over 12 welcome.

Hosts: Vicky and Ken Conway
Rooms: 8 (PB) $73-108
Continental Breakfast
Credit Cards: A, B
Notes: 2, 5, 7, 9, 10, 11, 12, 14, 15

---

7 No smoking; 8 Children welcome; 9 Social drinking allowed; 10 Tennis nearby; 11 Swimming nearby; 12 Golf nearby; 13 Skiing nearby; 14 May be booked through a travel agent; 15 Handicapped accessible.

TEXARKANA

Mansion on Main Bed & Breakfast Inn

802 Main Street, 75501
(903) 792-1835; www.bbonline.com/tx/mansion/

Historic Victorian mansion accented with 14 Ionic columns around the veranda. Six romantic rooms and suites, each with private bath. Cross the threshold to timeless values, comfortable lodging for business and leisure travelers, and hospitality that confirms the city of Texarkana's motto of "Twice as Nice." Guests enjoy luxury beds in rooms and suites authentically furnished with period antiques and pleased amenities. A classic "Gentleman's Breakfast" served in the dining room, prepared by a trained chef. Visitors will drive right past any motel to get to luxury lodging, fine food, and southern hospitality.

Hosts: Inez and Lee Hayden
Rooms: 6 (PB) $60-109
Full Breakfast
Credit Cards: A, B, C
Notes: 2, 5, 7, 8, 12, 14, 15

Mansion on Main

TYLER

Bed & Breakfast Texas Style

4224 West Red Bird Lane, Dallas, 75237
(972) 298-8586; (800) 899-4538
FAX (972) 298-7118; e-mail: bdtxstyle1@aol.com
www.bnbtexasstyle.com

Vintage Farm Home. This newly renovated, circa 1836-1864, home, once an original dogtrot plantation home, sits in the piney woods of East Texas. Catch the morning sun or evening breeze on the large veranda where rocking chairs and a swing invite relaxation. Take a stroll through the trails during dogwood or fall foliage season. The guest room has a king-size bed and private bath. Breakfast is served downstairs in the cozy nook. $85-125

Rosevine Inn Bed & Breakfast

415 South Vine, 75702
(903) 592-2221; e-mail: rosevine@iamerica.net
www.bbonline.com/tx/rosevine

Rosevine Inn is in the historic Brick Street district. Come rest and relax at Rosevine Inn. Amenities include a lovely courtyard with fountain and fireplace. There are also an outdoor hot tub and game room complete with billiards for guests' enjoyment. There are now two suites available. A full gourmet breakfast is served, and picnic lunches are available. The hosts look forward to meeting guests and welcoming them to the Rose Capital of the World. A picnic lunch is available. Children more than two-years-old welcome.

Hosts: Bert and Rebecca Powell
Rooms: 7 (PB) $85-150
Full Breakfast
Credit Cards: A, B, C, D, E
Notes: 2, 3, 5, 7, 8, 9, 10, 11, 12, 14

VICTORIA

Friendly Oaks Bed & Breakfast

210 East Juan Linn Street, 77901
(512) 575-0000; e-mail: innkprbill@aol.com
www.bbhost.com/friendlyoaks

In the shelter of ancient live oaks, history comes alive at the Friendly Oaks Bed and Breakfast in a preservation area of 200 restored Victorian homes. Each of four guest rooms has a private bath, its own individual decor reflecting the preservation efforts of Victoria. A conference room provides a quiet setting for retreats, meetings, seminars, parties, showers,

---

NOTES: Credit cards accepted: A MasterCard; B Visa; C American Express; D Discover; E Diner's Club; F Other; 2 Personal checks accepted; 3 Lunch available; 4 Dinner available; 5 Open all year; 6 Pets welcome;

and small weddings. Here "Bed means Comfortable, Breakfast means Scrumptious."

Hosts: Bill and Cee Bee McLeod
Rooms: 4 (PB) $55-80
Full Breakfast
Credit Cards: A, B, C, D
Notes: 2, 5, 7, 9, 10, 11, 12, 14, 15

WACO

The Judge Baylor House

908 Speight Avenue, 76706
(888) JBAYLOR; FAX (817) 756-0711
e-mail: jbaylor@iamerica.net
www.eyeweb.com/jbaylor

Two blocks from Baylor University and its Armstrong Browning Library, five minutes from Waco Convention Center. A two-story red brick home with five spacious and beautifully appointed guest rooms. All have private baths and either king-, queen-size, or twin beds. Sitting in the swing hanging from a large ash tree in the front lawn, playing the grand piano, or enjoying a new book, guests are sure to relax and feel at home.

Hosts: Bruce and Dorothy Dyer
Rooms: 5 (PB) $69-89
Full Breakfast
Credit Cards: A, B, C
Notes: 2, 6, 7, 8, 9, 10, 12, 14, 15

WAXAHACHIE

BonnyNook Inn

414 West Main Street, 75163
(972) 938-7207

Queen Anne Victorian Painted Lady. Elaborate gardens with a bit of whimsy. Elegant décor but not frilly. Refined furnishings yet comfy. Graceful candlelight table with wholesome food. Friendly hosts with the CVB thrown in. In all, more than a place to rest, relax, and reflect. Old World elegance with 20th-century comforts.

Hosts: Bonnie and Vaughn Franks
Rooms: 5 (PB) $85-115
Full Breakfast
Credit Cards: A, B, C, D, E
Notes: 2, 4, 5, 7, 8, 9, 10, 12, 14

WIMBERLEY

Rancho Cama Bed & Breakfast

2595 Flite Acres Road, 78676-5706
(512) 847-2596; (800) 594-4501
FAX (512) 847-7135
e-mail: ranchocama@aol.com

Romantic getaway in charming Guest House. Queen bed, sitting area, electric organ, private bath. Cozy Bunk House comfortably sleeps six, featuring extra-long twin beds, double bed, and bunk beds with shared bath. Both houses have color/cable TV, courtesy telephone, refrigerator, coffee maker, air conditioning, and ceiling fans. Homemade breakfast. Pool, hot tub, swings, rockers. On a miniature horse and donkey ranch, with Nigerian Dwarf Goats, and lots of deer. Live oak setting with unobscured view of the Hill Country.

Hosts: Curtis and Nell Cadenhead
Rooms: 3 (1 PB; 2 SB) $70-90
Full Breakfast
Notes: 2, 5, 7, 9, 11, 12

Rancho Cama

---

7 No smoking; 8 Children welcome; 9 Social drinking allowed; 10 Tennis nearby; 11 Swimming nearby; 12 Golf nearby; 13 Skiing nearby; 14 May be booked through a travel agent; 15 Handicapped accessible.

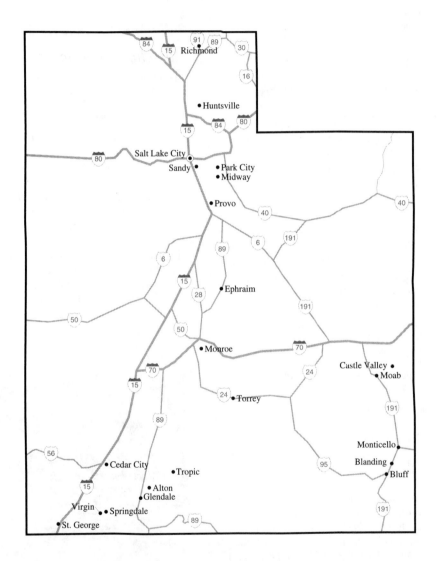

Utah

Utah

ALTON

Mi Casa Su Casa/Old Pueblo Homestays Bed & Breakfast Reservation Service

P.O. Box 950, Tempe, AZ 85280-0950
(602) 990-0682; (800) 456-0682
FAX (602) 990-3390
e-mail: micasa@primenet.com; www.azres.com

7011. Within a 30-minute drive of Zion and Bryce National Parks, these two extra large A-frame buildings sit on a heavily wooded five-acre lot. The master suite on the main floor has a private bath. The three first-floor rooms share one bath in the hall. Weather permitting, a campfire held each night overlooking the meadow. Exercise equipment, satellite TV and VCR, barbecue, and fireplace. Kitchen privileges. Business center with computer and fax. Full breakfast. Smoking outside. Pets possible. Children welcome. Unique RV garage houses up to a 32-foot RV with complete hookups. $65-110.

BLANDING

Grayson Country Inn Bed & Breakfast

118 East 300 South, 84511
(801) 678-2388; (800) 365-0868

Grayson Country Inn sits in the heart of San Juan County, known for Lake Powell, Monument Valley, Canyonlands, Arches, Rainbow Bridge, and Natural Bridges. The inn is off Main Street near a pottery factory and gift shops. Great hiking in the back country. Grayson has 11 guest rooms, each with private bath and TV. Welcome singles, couples, families. Three-bedroom cottage available for groups. The hosts specialize in home cooking and home atmosphere.

Hosts: Dennis and Lurlene Gutke
Rooms: 11 (PB) $42-59
Full Breakfast
Credit Cards: A, B, C
Notes: 2, 5, 7, 8, 11, 12, 13, 14

BLUFF

Calf Canyon Bed & Breakfast

Seventh Street East at Black Locust Avenue, 84512
(435) 672- 2470; (888) 922-2470
e-mail: duke@calfcanyon.com
www.calfcanyon.com

Intimate, homey, artistic, cozy, bright, private, cheerful, and tasty. Three bedrooms, each a corner room upstairs. Bluff is the jump-off point for endless southwest adventures in the four corners/Colorado Plateau area. New home constructed in the style of 1880s Mormon pioneer rock houses. Navajo rugs and original art.

Calf Canyon

NOTES: Credit cards accepted: A MasterCard; B Visa; C American Express; D Discover; E Diner's Club; F Other; 2 Personal checks accepted; 3 Lunch available; 4 Dinner available; 5 Open all year; 6 Pets welcome; 7 No smoking; 8 Children welcome; 9 Social drinking allowed; 10 Tennis nearby; 11 Swimming nearby; 12 Golf nearby; 13 Skiing nearby; 14 May be booked through a travel agent; 15 Handicapped accessible.

Views of the bluffs. Fabulous night skies. Rock art, river runs, Anasazi ruins.

Hosts: Duke and Sarah Hayduk
Rooms: 3 (PB) $ 65-85
Full Breakfast
Notes: 2, 7, 9

CASTLE VALLEY

Castle Valley Inn Bed & Breakfast

HC64 Box 2602, 424 Amber Lane, 84532-9607
(435) 259-6012; FAX (435) 259-1501
e-mail: castle@lasal.net; www.castlevalleyinn.com

Castle Valley Inn treats its guests to uninhibited views of the Utah Canyonlands. In a dramatic high desert valley at 5,000 feet; the skyline immediately south of the inn is dominated by the lofty La Sal Mountains. Five minutes to the north, the Colorado River cuts its serpentine canyons. In this peaceful, quiet setting, the inn offers guests a place to relax and unwind in informal comfort. Eleven acres of grounds are maintained in orchard, lawn, gardens, and fields to provide guests the "elbow room" expected in a landscape of such immensity. The distractions of city life happily, seem far away indeed.

Hosts: Robert Ryan and Hertha Wakefield
Rooms: 8 (PB) $95-155
Full Breakfast
Credit Cards: A, B, D
Notes: 2, 7, 9

Castle Valley Inn

CEDAR CITY

The Garden Cottage Bed & Breakfast

16 North 200 West, 84720
(435) 586-4919

Charming English cottages circa 1920s, surrounded by an old-fashioned garden. Four antique-filled, romantic rooms with queen-size beds and private baths await guests at the top of an inviting winding staircase. One room with private entrance, connecting rooms available. Closest bed and breakfast to Utah Shakespearean Festival. Air conditioned. Full breakfast.

Hosts: Gary and Diana Simkins
Rooms: 4 (PB) $65-90
Full Breakfast
Credit Cards: A, B, C
Notes: 2, 5, 7, 10, 11, 12, 13

Mi Casa Su Casa/Old Pueblo Homestays Bed & Breakfast Reservation Service

P.O. Box 950, Tempe, AZ 85280-0950
(602) 990-0682; (800) 456-0682
FAX (602) 990-3390
e-mail: micasa@primenet.com; www.azres.com

7021. Old-fashioned charm and warm hospitality await guests at this lovingly restored turn-of-the-century two-story brick farmhouse. The main floor master bedroom (available summer only) and the three upper floor rooms are furnished with a lifetime collection of antiques. Continental plus breakfast. Inquire about accommodations for children. Smoking permitted in designated areas only. No pets. Seasonal rates. $49-65.

EPHRAIM

Ephraim Homestead Bed & Breakfast

135 West 100 North (43-2), 84627
(801) 283-6367

NOTES: Credit cards accepted: A MasterCard; B Visa; C American Express; D Discover; E Diner's Club; F Other; 2 Personal checks accepted; 3 Lunch available; 4 Dinner available; 5 Open all year; 6 Pets welcome;

Ephraim Homestead

Ephraim Homestead offers lodging in a pioneer log cabin or a rustic barn. Both are furnished with antiques and surrounded by old-fashioned gardens under a canopy of trees. Breakfast is cooked on a century-old Monarch stove and served privately to guests in the cabin; others are served in the hosts' dining room. A delicious nighttime treat is also provided. Truly a unique and memorable experience. Smoking permitted outside only. Cross-country skiing nearby.

Hosts: Sherron and McKay Andreasen
Log Cabin: 1 (PB) $85
Barn: 2 (SB) $55-65
Full Breakfast
Credit Cards: None
Notes: 2, 5, 7, 8, 10, 11, 12, 13

GLENDALE

Arizona Trails Bed & Breakfast Reservation Service

P.O. Box 18998, Fountain Hills, AZ 85269-8998
(480) 837-4284; (888) 799-4284
FAX (480) 816-4224
e-mail: aztrails@arizonatrails.com
www.arizonatrails.com

AZ 056. This four-room bed and breakfast sits amidst 13 acres and is the perfect tranquil, romantic getaway and great for those touring the national park areas. Half way between Bryce and Zion Canyons and only two hours to the north rim of the Grand Canyon. All rooms have private baths, two with fireplaces. Each is decorated with a unique collection of artifacts and art collected from around the world. Full breakfast. Children welcome. $79-107.

Eagle's Nest Bed & Breakfast

500 Lydia's Canyon Road, P.O. Box 160, 84729
(435) 648-2200; (800) 293-6378
FAX (435) 648-2221
e-mail: innkeeps@eaglesnestbb.com
www.eaglesnestbb.com

Enjoy the tranquility of Lydia's Canyon in the heart of southwest Utah off US Highway 89. Zion, Bryce, and Grand Canyon National Parks and Cedar Breaks National Monument are easily accessible. Every room is detailed to provide a relaxed and romantic setting with unique furnishings from around the world. Enjoy a full gourmet breakfast in the sunlit, antique-filled dining room. Soak carelessly in the spa. All rooms have private baths, two with fireplaces. Extra amenities.

Hosts: Shanoan and Dearborn Clark
Rooms: 4 (PB) $69-117
Full Breakfast
Credit Cards: A, B, D
Notes: 2, 5, 7, 9, 12, 14

Mi Casa Su Casa/Old Pueblo Homestays Bed & Breakfast Reservation Service

P.O. Box 950, Tempe, AZ 85280-0950
(602) 990-0682; (800) 456-0682
FAX (602) 990-3390
e-mail: micasa@primenet.com; www.azres.com

7031. Half way between Zion and Bryce National Parks, this romantic bed and breakfast is nestled on 13 acres in a side canyon of Lydia's Canyon, in what is known as the Grand Circle of the Southwest, America's highest concentration of scenic national parks and monuments, including the Grand Canyon and Lake Powell. Four guest rooms all have private baths, two have fireplaces. A full gourmet

---

7 No smoking; 8 Children welcome; 9 Social drinking allowed; 10 Tennis nearby; 11 Swimming nearby; 12 Golf nearby; 13 Skiing nearby; 14 May be booked through a travel agent; 15 Handicapped accessible.

breakfast is served and special dietary needs are accommodated with prior notice. Smoking permitted outside. No pets. Inquire about accommodations for children. Twenty dollars for each additional guest. $68-107.

Smith Hotel

Smith Hotel

295 North Main Street, P.O. Box 106, 84429
(435) 648-2156

This historic hotel-boarding house was built in 1927 by Mormon settlers. Enjoy western charm. Screened porch overlooking the hills of southern Utah's beautiful Long Valley. Close to the scenic wonders of Zion, Bryce, and Grand Canyon National Parks and the recreational facilities of Lake Powell. All rooms have private baths. Late 1800s private family cemetery on property. Continental plus breakfast served in family dining room. Meet other guests from all over the world. Easy to find, right on Highway 89.

Hosts: Rochelle and Bunny
Rooms: 7 (PB) $37-74
Continental Breakfast
Credit Cards: A, B
Notes: 5, 7, 9, 12, 14, 15

HUNTSVILLE

Jackson Fork Inn

7345 East 900 South, 84317
(801) 745-0051; (800) 255-0672
www.bbchannel.com

The Jackson Fork Inn was originally a dairy barn built in the 1930s. It was converted in 1980 to an inn and restaurant. All rooms have private bathrooms and some rooms have Jacuzzis. Restaurant serves steaks, chicken, and fish dinners. Non-smoking. Pets welcome for a fee and kept on a leash.

Host: Vicki Petersen
Rooms: 8 (PB) $50-115
Continental Breakfast
Credit Cards: A, B, C, D
Notes: 2, 4, 5, 7, 8, 9, 11, 12, 13, 14

MIDWAY

The Homestead

700 North Homestead Drive, P.O. Box 99, 84049
(800) 327-7220; (435) 654-1102
FAX (435) 654-5087
e-mail: info@homesteadresort.com

The original Scheitter Family Hotel at the historic Homestead Resort. Eight Victorian rooms individually appointed with antiques, linens, and special amenities. Adjacent solarium and whirlpool. This AAA four-diamond resort offers golf, swimming, horseback riding, tennis, fitness room, elegant dining, sleigh rides, cross-country skiing, snowmobiling, snowshoeing, yard games, game room, scuba diving, and complete meeting and banquet facilities. No smoking.

Host: Britt Mathwich
Rooms: 8 (PB) $139-159
Breakfast Voucher
Credit Cards: A, B, C, D, E, F
Notes: 2, 3, 4, 5, 9, 10, 12, 13, 14

MOAB

Canyon Country Bed & Breakfast

590 North 500 West, 84532
(435) 259-5262; (888) 350-5262
www.canyoncountryBB.com

The bed and breakfast is nestled between the snow-capped La Sal Mountains and the red

---

NOTES: Credit cards accepted: A MasterCard; B Visa; C American Express; D Discover; E Diner's Club; F Other; 2 Personal checks accepted; 3 Lunch available; 4 Dinner available; 5 Open all year; 6 Pets welcome;

rock canyons of the Colorado River. Minutes from Arches National Park and Canyon Lands National Park. This ranch-style house has five rooms, most with private baths; all rooms have log-frame beds. In a quiet residential neighborhood within walking distance to local shops, museums, art galleries, and restaurants. A full gourmet breakfast awaits guests in the morning, as do the gardens and hot tub.

Hosts: Samuel Smith and Chad Beyer
Rooms: 5 (4 PB; 1 SB) $75-125
Full Breakfast
Notes: 2, 5, 6, 7, 8, 9, 10, 11, 12, 13, 14

Mi Casa Su Casa/Old Pueblo Homestays Bed & Breakfast Reservation Service

P.O. Box 950, Tempe, AZ 85280-0950
(602) 990-0682; (800) 456-0682
FAX (602) 990-3390
e-mail: micasa@primenet.com; www.azres.com

7041. Casual atmosphere in a ranch-style home nestled between the snow-capped La Sal Mountains and the red-rock canyons of the Colorado River. Mountain biking, white-water challenging, and downhill or cross-country skiing are nearby. This home is a perfect place to relax at the end of the day. Three guest rooms with private baths. Two rooms share a bath. Cable TV, hot tub. Maximum 14 guests. Full breakfast. Bicycles to rent. Resident dogs. No smoking. Inquire about accommodations for children. Rollaway beds are available. Weekly and seasonal rates. $62-79.

7042. The host couple has renovated the original adobe farmhouse built about 100 years ago, added extra rooms and a cozy country cottage. There are six rooms including two two-bedroom units. Some rooms have air conditioning and telephones. All rooms have private baths and video cassette players. Adventure library, outdoor hot tub, lush gardens, patios, barbecue. Three blocks from downtown. Outstanding breakfast buffet. No smoking. No pets. Children welcome by prior arrangement. Twenty dollars for each additional person. Seasonal rates. $95-145.

Sunflower Hill Bed & Breakfast

185 North 300 East, 84532
(435) 259-2974; (800) MOABSUN
FAX: (435) 259-3065
e-mail: innkeeper@sunflowerhill.com

Moab's only AAA four-diamond inn. This premiere country retreat features two beautifully restored buildings set amidst an acre of wooded pathways and flower gardens. Eleven elegant guest rooms offer private baths, air conditioning, TV, and antique beds. Deluxe rooms feature Jacuzzis and private balconies or patios. Amenities include a Great Room with adventure library, evening refreshments, outdoor hot tub, terry-cloth robes, guest laundry, bike storage. Quiet location, three blocks from Main Street.

Host: Gregg Stucki
Rooms: 11 (PB) $95-165
Full Breakfast
Credit Cards: A, B, C, D
Notes: 2, 3, 5, 7, 11, 12, 14

Westwood Guest House

81 East 100 South, 84532
(801) 259-7283; (800) 526-5690

Seven uniquely decorated condos. Reasonable; clean. Living room, bathroom, bedroom, kitchen with do-it-yourself breakfast food (eggs, bagels, pancakes, coffee, tea, milk, and juice). Sleeps two to eight comfortably. Telephones, TV, hot tub in private back yard, decks, patios. Visitor center, museum, tennis courts, ball park, shopping, bars, restaurants in immediate area. Golf course within four miles, the river within two miles, city park with pool within five blocks. Mild winters. Jeep trails, all directions, are about seven to eight blocks away. Biking and hiking near town, seven to eight blocks to the Sleckrock trails. Hunting is 30 minutes to mountains. Skiing is 40 miles from Moab.

---

7 No smoking; 8 Children welcome; 9 Social drinking allowed; 10 Tennis nearby; 11 Swimming nearby; 12 Golf nearby; 13 Skiing nearby; 14 May be booked through a travel agent; 15 Handicapped accessible.

Host: Betty Beck
Rooms: 7 (PB) $59
Continental Breakfast
Credit Cards: A, B, C, D
Notes: 2, 5, 7, 8, 9, 11, 12, 14

MONROE

Mi Casa Su Casa/Old Pueblo Homestays Bed & Breakfast Reservation Service

P.O. Box 950, Tempe, AZ 85280-0950
(602) 990-0682; (800) 456-0682
FAX (602) 990-3390
e-mail: micasa@primenet.com; www.azres.com

7051. Halfway between Denver and Los Angeles, a considerate hostess, who is known for her cookbooks and cooking skills, offers three guest rooms. Room one has a private entrance, private bath with shower, small refrigerator, and coffee maker. Room two, which adjoins room one, has small TV and children's games. The third room has a full bath across the hall, TV, and refrigerator. Private, fully fenced yard. A 100-year-old apple tree provides ample shade. Easy driving distance to five national parks and four national forests. Full breakfast. No smoking. Well-behaved children $10 extra. $65.

MONTICELLO

Mi Casa Su Casa/Old Pueblo Homestays Bed & Breakfast Reservation Service

P.O. Box 950, Tempe, AZ 85280-0950
(602) 990-0682; (800) 456-0682
FAX (602) 990-3390
e-mail: micasa@primenet.com; www.azres.com

7161. This saltbox structure was built in 1933 at the foot of the Blue Mountains. The three-story building was originally known as the Old Monticello Flour Mill. Six beautiful suites, all with private baths. Several attractions are within driving distance, including the Four Corners area, Lake Powell, Natural Bridges National Monument, Canyonlands and Arches National Parks, and Monument Valley. Guests are welcome to enjoy the sitting room with fireplace, the library with a view of the Blue Mountains, the TV room, the deck, and the whirlpool. There is a local golf course. No smoking. No pets. Inquire about accommodations for children. Seasonal rates. $72-92.

PARK CITY

The Blue Church Lodge

424 Park Avenue, P.O. Box 1720, 84060
(435) 649-8009; (800) 626-5467
FAX (435) 649-0686; e-mail: bcl@ditell.com

Listed in the Utah and the national historic registers, the church was originally built in 1897. A Victorian-era church on the outside. Inside, the lodge houses seven charmingly quaint and cozy, distinctively different condominiums, ranging from a room with a private bath up to a four-bedroom suite. Amenities include indoor spa, game room, laundry, private telephones, cable TV, VCR, CD player, private parking, ski lockers, maid service, and gas-burning fireplaces.

Host: Nancy Schmidt
Rooms: 7 (PB) $110-340
Continental Breakfast
Credit Cards: A, B
Notes: 2, 7, 8, 9, 13, 14

1904 Imperial Hotel, A Bed & Breakfast Inn

221 Main Street, P.O. Box 1628, 84060-1628
(435) 649-1904; (800) 669-8824
FAX (435) 645-7421
e-mail: stay@1904imperial.com
www.1904imperial.com

On historic Main Street in Park City, the 1904 Imperial Hotel warmly captures the spirited charm and hospitality of Park City's illustrious past. Although it once boarded weary miners, served as a hospital, and was known to be a house of ill-repute, the 1904 Imperial Hotel's

---

NOTES: Credit cards accepted: A MasterCard; B Visa; C American Express; D Discover; E Diner's Club; F Other; 2 Personal checks accepted; 3 Lunch available; 4 Dinner available; 5 Open all year; 6 Pets welcome;

1904 Imperial Hotel

10 guest rooms have since been restored with period decor and furnishings, many featuring oversized tubs. Breakfast greets guests in the morning and a revitalizing hot tub welcomes them back in the afternoon.

Hosts: Nancy McLaughlin and Karen Hart
Rooms: 10 (PB) $65-245
Full Breakfast
Credit Cards: A, B, C, D
Notes: 2, 5, 7, 8, 9, 10, 11, 12, 13, 14

The Old Miners' Lodge

615 Woodside Avenue, Box 2639, 84060
(435) 645-8068; (800) 648-8068
FAX (435) 645-7420;
e-mail: stan@oldminerslodge.com
www.oldminerslodge.com

A restored 1889 miners' boarding house in the national historic district of Park City, with 12 individually decorated rooms filled with antiques and older pieces. Close to historic Main Street, with the Park City ski area in its back yard, the lodge is "more like staying with friends than at a hotel!" A non-smoking inn. Minimum-stay requirements Christmas and some special events.

Hosts: Susan Wynne and Liza Simpson
Rooms: 12 (PB) $70-265
Full Breakfast
Credit Cards: A, B, C, D, E
Notes: 2, 5, 7, 8, 9, 10, 11, 12, 13, 14

Old Town Guest House

1011 Empire Avenue, Box 162, 84060
(435) 649-2642; (800) 290-6423 ext. 3710
FAX (435) 649-3320
e-mail: dlovci@compuserve.com
www.oldtownguesthouse.com

This beautiful, historically registered home is the perfect place for active skiers, hikers, and bikers. Guests may walk to the ski area as well as the historic Main Street. All the rooms are furnished with lodgepole pine furniture. Afternoon snacks are available for when guests return from their active day and there is a hot tub to soothe any aching muscles.

Host: Deb Lovci
Rooms: 4 (2 PB; 2 SB) $75-175
Full Breakfast
Credit Cards: A, B, C
Notes: 2, 5, 7, 9, 12, 13

Washington School Inn

543 Park Avenue, P.O. Box 536, 84060
(435) 649-3800; (800) 824-1672

Historic restoration of an old schoolhouse, decorated with modified Victorian furnishings. Hot tub and sauna on the property. Full breakfast and afternoon tea service included in rates. In downtown historic Park City, close to Salt Lake area airport (45 minutes) and some of the best skiing in the world.

Hosts: Nancy Beaufait and Delphine Covington
Rooms: 15 (PB) $100-300
Full Breakfast
Credit Cards: A, B, C, D
Notes: 5, 7, 9, 10, 11, 12, 13, 14

---

7 No smoking; 8 Children welcome; 9 Social drinking allowed; 10 Tennis nearby; 11 Swimming nearby; 12 Golf nearby; 13 Skiing nearby; 14 May be booked through a travel agent; 15 Handicapped accessible.

PROVO

Hines Mansion Luxury Bed & Breakfast

383 West 100 South, 84601
(801) 374-8400; (800) 428-5636
FAX (801) 374-0823

Hines Mansion Bed and Breakfast is housed in a 100-year-old Victorian mansion. Much of the original decor such as wood moldings, brick walls, and stained glass has been left in place. The nine bedrooms are decorated with antique and reproduction furniture from the period, using a variety of themes. King- and queen-size beds, with a two-person whirlpool tub and private bath in each room. Full gourmet breakfast, complimentary cookies and fruit and Martinelli apple cider.

Hosts: Sandi and Gene Henderson
Rooms: 9 (PB) $99-199
Full Breakfast
Credit Cards: A, B, C
Notes: 2, 5, 7, 11, 12, 13, 14

Hines Mansion

RICHMOND

Clint's Bed & Breakfast

165 North State Street, 84333
(435) 258-3768 (Bed and Breakfast)
FAX (435) 258-4572; e-mail: clintbb@aol.com
http://members.aol.com/clintbb

Enjoy the beautiful countryside of Cache Valley in northern Utah on US Highway 91.

Clint's

Guests will appreciate the peaceful quiet in the small rural community of Richmond. Guest suite with separate entrance, baths, kitchen, dining room, laundry. Living room with fireplace, satellite TV, VCR, and recliner. Perfect for small groups, for families who want to enjoy a home setting, or for the privacy of a honeymoon suite. Will board animals. Great home. Cooked food. Great home-cooked food.

Hosts: Clint and Bonnie Groll
Rooms: 4 $45-75
Full Breakfast
Credit Cards: A, B
Notes: 5, 6, 7, 8, 9, 10, 11, 12, 13

ST. GEORGE

Mi Casa Su Casa/Old Pueblo Homestays Bed & Breakfast Reservation Service

P.O. Box 950, Tempe, AZ 85280-0950
(602) 990-0682; (800) 456-0682
FAX (602) 990-3390
e-mail: micasa@primenet.com; www.azres.com

7261. In the historic district of St. George, across from the Brigham Young home, guests will find traditional western hospitality in this inn, which has two buildings. One is an 1873 Colonial with three stories. The other is an 1883 Victorian Colonial with two stories. Decorated with antiques collected in America and Europe, some of the bedrooms are named after each of the seven wives of an ancestor of the innkeepers, who really did have seven wives. All 13 guest rooms have private baths, two with whirlpool tubs. Some have wood-burning stoves and most have outside doors to downstairs porches or

---

NOTES: Credit cards accepted: A MasterCard; B Visa; C American Express; D Discover; E Diner's Club; F Other; 2 Personal checks accepted; 3 Lunch available; 4 Dinner available; 5 Open all year; 6 Pets welcome;

upstairs balconies. Pool. No smoking. No pets. Credit cards accepted. $50-100.

Quicksand and Cactus Bed & Breakfast

346 North Main Street, 84770
(435) 674-1739; (800) 381-1654
e-mail: quiksand@infowest.com
www.infowest.com/quicksand/

This historic pioneer home is where the renowned author and historian, Juanita Brooks, lived and wrote. On the North Main Street hill, there is a great view of the city with the entire downtown historic district within walking distance. The original two rooms of this house were built by George Brooks, with chips and irregular stones from the cleanup of the temple and tabernacle construction sites. Rooms have private baths and TV/VCRs. Covered porches abound.

Host: Carla Fox
Rooms: 3 (PB) $55-85
Full Breakfast
Credit Cards: A, B, D
Notes: 5, 7, 9, 10, 11, 12, 14

SALT LAKE CITY

The Anton Boxrud Bed & Breakfast Inn

57 South 600 East, 84102
(801) 363-8035; (800) 524-5511
FAX (801) 596-1316

This "Grand Old Home" is a half-block from the governor's mansion and six blocks from Temple Square and city center. The Anton Boxrud Bed and Breakfast Inn is within walking distance to many restaurants and the ski bus. Whether enjoying a cozy fire, a soothing soak in the hot tub after a great day of skiing, or simply relaxing on a cool summer evening on the front porch after a day of sightseeing, guests find life at the Anton Boxrud truly

The Anton Boxrud

uncomplicated—an invitation to relax and unwind. Lunches and dinners available by special arrangement. Fifteen dollars extra per additional person.

Host: Jane E. Johnson
Rooms: 7 (5 PB; 2 SB) $69-140
Full Breakfast
Credit Cards: A, B, C, D, E
Notes: 2, 3, 4, 5, 7, 8, 9, 10, 11, 12, 13, 14

Armstrong Mansion

667 East 100 South, 84102
(801) 531-1333; (800) 708-1333
FAX (801) 531-0282
e-mail: armstrong@vii.com
www.armstrong-bb.com

The Armstrong Mansion was built in 1893 in fulfillment of a wedding-day promise by Francis Armstrong made to his wife, Isabel. This grand Queen Anne-style Victorian mansion was the scene of many gala affairs hosted by Francis Armstrong, one of the first mayors of Salt Lake City. Thirteen magnificently restored rooms come alive under the reflections of the beautiful stained-glass windows and the ornate woodwork.

Hosts: Dave and Judy Savage
Rooms: 13 (PB) $99-229
Full Breakfast
Credit Cards: A, B, C, D, E
Notes: 2, 5, 7, 8, 12, 13, 14, 15

---

7 No smoking; 8 Children welcome; 9 Social drinking allowed; 10 Tennis nearby; 11 Swimming nearby; 12 Golf nearby; 13 Skiing nearby; 14 May be booked through a travel agent; 15 Handicapped accessible.

Mi Casa Su Casa/Old Pueblo Homestays Bed & Breakfast Reservation Service

P.O. Box 950, Tempe, AZ 85280-0950
(602) 990-0682; (800) 456-0682
FAX (602) 990-3390
e-mail: micasa@primenet.com; www.azres.com

7201. Well known for its superior luxury and hospitality, this inn, a beautifully preserved 1915 home, takes great pride in providing its guests with one of the most beautiful settings in the Southwest. Secluded canyon close to hiking trails, ski resorts. Six accommodations house a maximum of 16 guests. One two-bedroom unit. Some rooms have air conditioning, kitchens, telephones, cable TVs. Outstanding full breakfasts. No smoking. No pets. Children 10 and older welcome. Credit cards accepted. AAA-rated four diamonds. Twenty dollars for each additional person. $70-175.

7202. The Salt Lake City Historic Society has recognized this two and one-half story brick house as one of Salt Lake's "Grand Old Homes." The beveled-glass windows and beautiful woodwork have been carefully restored according to the original 1901 plans. Rooms are furnished with antiques, including a hand-carved German dining table where a full breakfast is served. Close to the governor's mansion, downtown, University of Utah, and Temple Square. Seven guest rooms on the second and third floors have private and shared baths. Hot tub. Smoking outside. Seasonal rates. $49-109.

7203. Welcoming guests with homegrown hospitality has become a tradition at this oldest continuously operating bed and breakfast in Utah. Antiques from the 19th and early 20th century have been placed so the decor is simple and comfortable. In a residential area of Salt Lake City within minutes of the Utah State Capitol, Tempe Square, the Genealogy Library, and Symphony Hall. Seven ski resorts are within a 40-minute drive. There are five rooms and three baths in the main house. There are two cottages with full facilities. Refreshments. Full breakfast. $55-120.

Saltair Bed & Breakfast

164 South 900 East, 84102
(801) 533-8184; (800) 733-8184
e-mail: saltair@saltlakebandb.com
www.saltlakebandb.com

Antiques and charm complement queen-size brass beds, Amish quilts, and period lamps. A full breakfast featuring house juice and wake-up favorites such as pumpkin-walnut waffles and Saltair mc(muffins) greet each guest. Hospitality offered by innkeepers includes snacks and use of parlor, dining room, TV, and telephone. Close to the University of Utah, historic downtown, skiing, canyons, and seasonal recreation.

Hosts: Jan Bartlett and Nancy Saxton
Rooms: 5 (2 PB; 3 SB) $55-105
Full Breakfast
Credit Cards: A, B, C, D, E
Notes: 2, 5, 7, 9, 11, 12, 13, 14

SANDY

Mountain Hollow Bed & Breakfast Inn

10209 South Dimple Dell Road, 84092
(801) 942-3428; (800) 757-3428
FAX (801) 733-7187; e-mail: skye@aros.net
www.mountainhollow.com

Nestled in the exclusive Granite Hills of Sandy, Utah, Mountain Hollow is on a two-acre, wooded estate. This 10-room inn reflects the charm of a small European inn with a western kick. The inn includes a breakfast buffet, an outdoor hot tub, and a game room. Just 15 minutes from world-class ski resorts, hiking, mountain biking, and shopping. Mountain Hollow offers serenity, quiet, and comfort to guests, honeymooners, and travelers.

Hosts: Kathy and Doug Larson
Rooms: 10 (5 PB: 5 SB) $75-175

NOTES: Credit cards accepted: A MasterCard; B Visa; C American Express; D Discover; E Diner's Club; F Other; 2 Personal checks accepted; 3 Lunch available; 4 Dinner available; 5 Open all year; 6 Pets welcome;

Mountain Hollow

Continental Breakfast
Credit Cards: A, B, C, D
Notes: 2, 5, 7, 9, 10, 11, 12, 13, 14

SPRINGDALE

Mi Casa Su Casa/Old Pueblo Homestays Bed & Breakfast Reservation Service

P.O. Box 950, Tempe, AZ 85280-0950
(602) 990-0682; (800) 456-0682
FAX (602) 990-3390
e-mail: micasa@primenet.com; www.azres.com

7251. Built in 1988 in a contemporary pioneer ranch style, this two-story inn is on a quiet dead-end street less than one mile from the south entrance to Zion National Park. Comfortable, clean, and bright with a contemporary interior, original artwork, and collectibles. Suite on the first floor and three rooms on the second floor all have private baths. Complimentary beverages. Breakfast is a culinary event! Hot tub. Children six and older are welcome by prior arrangement. No smoking. Credit cards are accepted. AAA-rated three diamonds. Fifteen dollars for each additional person. $90-190.

7252. At this two-story bed and breakfast, guests can choose one of 10 rooms, each with private bath, telephone, and TV. In the center of a panoramic arc of spectacular red rock mountains, this inn is within walking distance of shops and restaurants. The entrance to Zion National Park is about a mile away, and Cedar City's Shakespeare Festival or the shops of St. George are about an hour away. English-style afternoon tea. Gourmet breakfast. Handicapped accessible. AAA-rated three diamonds. Seasonal rates. $85-105.

TORREY

Mi Casa Su Casa/Old Pueblo Homestays Bed & Breakfast Reservation Service

P.O. Box 950, Tempe, AZ 85280-0950
(602) 990-0682; (800) 456-0682
FAX (602) 990-3390
e-mail: micasa@primenet.com; www.azres.com

7271. This two-story Territorial-style house is on 75 acres seven miles west of Capitol Reef National Park. The six guest rooms have private baths, VCRs, antiques, art furniture, and folk sculpture. Some have telephones, a private deck or patio. One unit has a private hot tub on an enclosed open-air deck. There are interior and exterior corridors. No smoking. Near bicycling and hiking trails. Full breakfast. Credit cards accepted. AAA-rated four diamonds. Fifteen dollars per each additional person. $87-125.

TROPIC

Mi Casa Su Casa/Old Pueblo Homestays Bed & Breakfast Reservation Service

P.O. Box 950, Tempe, AZ 85280-0950
(602) 990-0682; (800) 456-0682
FAX (602) 990-3390
e-mail: micasa@primenet.com; www.azres.com

7281. In tiny picturesque Tropic, this bed and breakfast is within walking distance of Bryce

---

7 No smoking; 8 Children welcome; 9 Social drinking allowed; 10 Tennis nearby; 11 Swimming nearby; 12 Golf nearby; 13 Skiing nearby; 14 May be booked through a travel agent; 15 Handicapped accessible.

Canyon National Park's eastern boundary. The house was built in the early 1930s and a two-story addition was built in 1990. There are wraparound decks with spectacular views. Five spacious guest rooms, private bath, and picture windows. The new guest cottage has a living room, bedroom, kitchen. Children are welcome. Full breakfast. No smoking. Ten dollars for each additional person in room. $77-110.

7282. This bed and breakfast is a modern log two-story home with flower gardens. It is a working farm of 10 acres that produces grain and hay. Farm animals. Nine miles from Bryce Canyon Park entrance and a few miles from Kodachrome Basin. The three rooms all have private baths. Enclosed spa. Children welcome. Full breakfast. No smoking. No pets. Possible handicapped accessibility. Ten dollars for each additional person in room. Seasonal rates. $60-70.

VIRGIN

Snow Family Guest Ranch Bed & Breakfast

Zion Canyon, 633 East Highway 9, P.O. Box 790190, 84779
(435) 635-2500; (800) 308-7669
FAX (435) 635-2758; www.snowfamilyranch.com

The Snow Family Guest Ranch is just east of the town of Virgin, on the north side of Highway 9. This beautiful horse ranch lies in a picturesque setting just 15 minutes from entrance to Zion National Park, on 12 acres of lush green pastures, surrounded by white-rail fencing. Area attractions include Zion National Park, Bryce Canyon, the North Rim of the Grand Canyon, and Lake Powell. The ranch has very mild winters, and year-round activities are plentiful. The western hospitality of the ranch provides a quiet, private atmosphere. It is perfect for a relaxing peaceful getaway. Pool, spa, trail rides on site.

Hosts: Steve and Shelley Penrose
Rooms: 9 (PB) $85-150
Full Breakfast
Credit Cards: A, B, C, D
Notes: 5, 7, 11, 12, 14

NOTES: Credit cards accepted: A MasterCard; B Visa; C American Express; D Discover; E Diner's Club; F Other; 2 Personal checks accepted; 3 Lunch available; 4 Dinner available; 5 Open all year; 6 Pets welcome;

Washington

Cooney Mansion

ABERDEEN (COSMOPOLIS)

Cooney Mansion

Box 54, 1705 Fifth Street, Cosmopolis, 98537
(360) 533-0602; (800) 9 SPRUCE
www.techline.com/~cooney/

This historically registered Craftsman-style lumber baron's retreat features original furniture and private baths. Relax in the Jacuzzi, exercise room, or sauna. Play golf, tennis, or curl up with a book from the extensive library. Sit in the rose garden or amble through Mill Creek Park with its bridges and waterfalls. The Cooney Mansion exudes an old-fashioned warmth and relaxed atmosphere. The Cooney Suite features fireplace, sitting areas, and original rainfall shower. Two-minutes' drive from Aberdeen and Hoquiam. Close to beaches, antique shops, and historic seaport. Serving national award-winning breakfast.

Hosts: Judi and Jim Lohr
Rooms: 8 (5 PB; 3 SB) $75-165
Full Breakfast
Credit Cards: A, B, D, E, F
Notes: 5, 7, 10, 12

ANACORTES

Albatross Bed & Breakfast

5708 Kingsway West, 98221
(360) 293-0677; (800) 622-8864

Across from the Skyline Marina, this 1927 Cape Cod-style home features delicious full breakfasts, king- and queen-size beds, private baths, fine art, antiques, and island views. The marina offers charter boats, a deli, and fine dining. Nearby are Washington Park and ferries to the San Juan Islands and Victoria, British Columbia. AAA-approved.

Hosts: Linda and Lorrie Flowers
Rooms: 4 (PB) $75-95
Full Breakfast
Credit Cards: A, B, C
Notes: 2, 5, 6, 7, 8, 9, 10, 11, 12, 13, 14, 15

Albatross

---

7 No smoking; 8 Children welcome; 9 Social drinking allowed; 10 Tennis nearby; 11 Swimming nearby; 12 Golf nearby; 13 Skiing nearby; 14 May be booked through a travel agent; 15 Handicapped accessible.

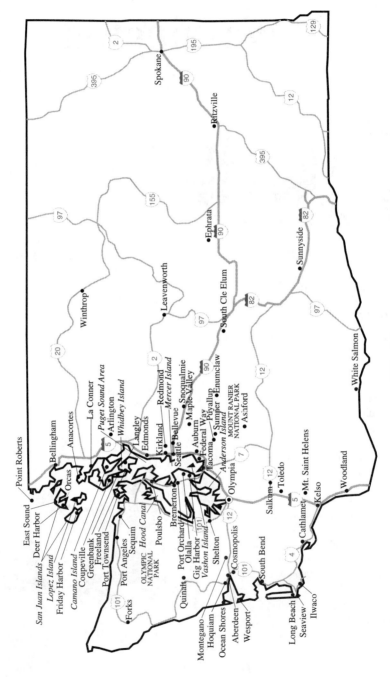

Old Brook Inn

7270 Old Brook Lane, 98221
(360) 293-4768; (800) 503-4768
FAX (360) 299-9720; www.oldbrookinn.com

"Seclusion" is the best way to describe the Old Brook Inn. The inn is actually three miles outside of Anacortes in a sheltered valley of woods and meadows green the year-round. The inn itself is nestled within an heirloom orchard planted in 1868. A small brook meanders alongside, from which the Inn derives its name. The inn's 10 acres are surrounded by even more open and forested parcels of land, creating a haven of tranquility and discovery.

Host: Dick Ash
Rooms: 2 (PB) $80-90
Continental Breakfast
Credit Cards: A, B
Notes: 2, 5, 6, 7, 8, 9, 10, 11, 12, 14

Pacific Bed & Breakfast Agency

P.O. Box 46894, Seattle, 98146
(206) 439-7677; (800) 684-2932
FAX (206) 431-0932; e-mail: pacificb@nwlink.com
www.seattlebedandbreakfast.com

118. 1902 Host Home. This Victorian home, designed and built for an Italian count in 1902, is a lovely bed and breakfast furnished with antiques in each room. Just a few minutes from the San Juan Islands ferry dock, guests have views of Puget Sound and Guemes Channel. Each room has its own special decor and private bath. In the Rose Cottage guests will find two rooms with fireplaces and jetted tubs for that special occasion. The outdoor hot tub is nearby and is for all the guests to enjoy. A wonderful, homemade, gourmet breakfast is served in the dining room and will start guests' day perfectly. $79-109.

119. Anacortes Marina. With 52 rooms, a guest spa and Jacuzzi rooms, this modern inn will accommodate any guest or group of guests.
Cable TV/VCRs and a Continental breakfast that will satisfy even the most seasoned traveler for a night or a longer stay. Rates are seasonal. $55-85.

158. Restored Farmhouse. Originally built in 1915, this two-story farmhouse was moved and completely restored in 1990. The atmosphere is relaxed and quiet with warm hospitality. The acreage is small but wooded, affording the ambiance of a peaceful spot for a getaway bed and breakfast. The master bedroom has a private bath with claw-foot tub and the other two rooms share a very large bath. Full breakfast.

173. Hotel, bistro, and pub. Dating from 1889, this small, grand hotel will welcome guests with friendly and personalized service. The 23 unique rooms are furnished with antiques and down comforters, soaking tubs, wet bars, and have view decks. A Continental breakfast is complimentary. A Victorian Pub and banquet and meeting rooms are available.

Sunset Beach Bed & Breakfast

100 Sunset Beach, 98221
(360) 293-5428; (800) 359-3448

On the exciting Rosario Strait overlooking seven of the San Juan Islands, this bed and breakfast invites guests to enjoy the water scenery that includes water birds, deer, fishing boats, and more. Take a stroll and enjoy the scenic view of the Olympic Mountains, or amble down the beach. Close to the ferry, marina, and excellent restaurants, and adjacent to Washington Park. Full breakfasts, queen-size beds, and private baths. Hot tub on request.

Hosts: Joann and Hal Harker
Rooms: 3 (PB) $82-95
Full Breakfast
Credit Cards: A, B
Notes: 2, 5, 7, 9, 11, 12, 13, 14

NOTES: Credit cards accepted: A MasterCard; B Visa; C American Express; D Discover; E Diner's Club; F Other; 2 Personal checks accepted; 3 Lunch available; 4 Dinner available; 5 Open all year; 6 Pets welcome; 7 No smoking; 8 Children welcome; 9 Social drinking allowed; 10 Tennis nearby; 11 Swimming nearby; 12 Golf nearby; 13 Skiing nearby; 14 May be booked through a travel agent; 15 Handicapped accessible.

ANDERSON ISLAND

A Greater Tacoma Bed & Breakfast Reservation Service

3312 North Union Avenue, Tacoma, 98407
(253) 759-4088; (800) 406-4088
FAX (253) 759-4025
e-mail: reservations@tacoma-inns.org
e-mail: tacomabnbs@aol.com
www.tacoma-inns.org

E. Burg's Landing. A real Northwest treat. This majestic waterfront log home overlooks Mount Ranier with lots of modern comforts, a hot tub, skylight, and deck. Four guest rooms with private or shared baths. (WBBG) Full breakfast. $75-115

The Inn at Burg's Landing

8808 Villa Beach Road, 98303
(206) 884-9185; (206) 488-8682

Catch the ferry from Steilacoom to stay at this contemporary log homestead built in 1987. It offers spectacular views of Mount Rainier, Puget Sound, and Cascade Mountains. The inn has a private beach. Collect seashells and agates, swim in one of the two freshwater lakes nearby, or enjoy a game of tennis or golf. Tour the scenic island by bicycle or on foot. Relax in the hot tub. Families are welcome.

Hosts: Ken and Annie Burg
Rooms: 3 (2 PB; 1 SB) $77-110
Full Breakfast
Credit Cards: A, B
Notes: 2, 5, 7, 8, 9, 10, 11, 12, 13

ARLINGTON

Mt. Higgins House

29805 State Route 530 Northeast, 98223
(360) 435-8703; (888) 296-3777
FAX (360) 435-9752

A secluded retreat on a 70-acre farm in the Stillaguamish River Valley 17 miles east of Arlington and 11 miles West of Darrington. All rooms with mountain views. A large deck overlooks a stocked trout pond. The common areas include the living room with a river rock fireplace, piano, satellite TV and CD player; a large dining area and a cozy library. Enjoy birding, fishing, and hiking with river access; Adults only. Smoke-free. A generous buffet breakfast is included.

Host: Renee Ottersen
Rooms: 2 (PB) $85-105
Full Breakfast
Credit Cards: A, B
Notes: 2, 5, 7, 12, 14

ASHFORD

Mountain Meadows Inn Bed & Breakfast

28912 State Route 706 East, P.O. Box 291, 98304-0291
(360) 569-2788

Built in 1910 as the home of a lumber mill superintendent, Mountain Meadows Inn is on 11 acres of serene cedar groves amid the grandeur of the northwestern landscape. Guests enjoy forested trails, private outdoor hot tub garden, evening campfires, and an impressive Northwest Coast Native American artifact collection. The nature library of more than 1,000 books includes a John Muir archive. The large comfortable rooms are highlighted with a gourmet country breakfast. Smoking permitted outside only.

Hosts: Harry and Michelle Latimer
Rooms: 6 (PB) $85-135
Full Breakfast
Credit Cards: A, B
Notes: 2, 5, 7, 8, 9, 11, 12, 13, 14

Pacific Bed & Breakfast Agency

P.O. Box 46894, Seattle, 98146
(206) 439-7677; (800) 684-2932
FAX (206) 431-0932; e-mail: pacificb@nwlink.com
www.seattlebedandbreakfast.com

067. Country Inn near Mount Rainier. The original register of this inn includes such

---

NOTES: Credit cards accepted: A MasterCard; B Visa; C American Express; D Discover; E Diner's Club; F Other; 2 Personal checks accepted; 3 Lunch available; 4 Dinner available; 5 Open all year; 6 Pets welcome;

famous names as Presidents Theodore Roosevelt and William Howard Taft. Built in 1912 and restored in 1984, it features 11 newly renovated rooms, 6 with private baths. Guests will enjoy the handmade quilts, the antiques, Tiffany lamps, and stained-glass windows. Also at this inn is a critically acclaimed restaurant that serves delicious food in a relaxed, genteel fashion by a big stone fireplace. Join in for a fun country experience. Seasonal rates. $104.31-148.23.

AUBURN

Pacific Bed & Breakfast Agency

P.O. Box 46894, Seattle, 98146
(206) 439-7677; (800) 684-2932
FAX (206) 431-0932; e-mail: pacificb@nwlink.com
www.seattlebedandbreakfast.com

063. Ranch-style Experience. This authentic 21-acre family ranch is home to the hostess and her family and their pets, two horses, a pony, and two dogs. The bed and breakfast accommodation offered is a two-bedroom suite with two baths (one with a one-person jetted tub). There is a scenic bicycle route, and a wide array of activities are offered for guests' enjoyment while visiting this unique host home. Continental plus breakfast served. $125.

064. A Step Back in Time. Choose either a king-size bedroom with private bath or a double bedroom with shared bath. The ample vegetarian breakfasts include homemade breads and granola, waffles with fruit topping or real maple syrup. A special feature is an hour-long Swedish massage at an additional charge. $70-90.

BELLEVUE

Pacific Bed & Breakfast Agency

P.O. Box 46894, Seattle, 98146
(206) 439-7677; (800) 684-2932
FAX (206) 431-0932; e-mail: pacificb@nwlink.com
www.seattlebedandbreakfast.com

044. Host Home. Hospitable retired hosts offer guests a suite with two bedrooms, each with private bath, living room, kitchenette, and private entrance. Self-serve breakfast. Super handy location. $85.

045. Bellevue Square. Secluded, yet near downtown Bellevue, this modern home offers either king/twin- or queen-size bedroom sharing one bath. Enjoy the hot tub on the deck during the summer. Full breakfast. $65.

047. British-Style Bed and Breakfast. The British hostess welcomes guests to her lovely contemporary home. Two rooms with a shared bath are available. Guests are welcome to use the sitting room with TV and VCR. Full breakfast. $60-65.

BELLINGHAM

Pacific Bed & Breakfast Agency

P.O. Box 46894, Seattle, 98146
(206) 439-7677; (800) 684-2932
FAX (206) 431-0932; e-mail: pacificb@nwlink.com
www.seattlebedandbreakfast.com

134. Victorian. A restored Victorian that overlooks the bay is proudly shared with guests by the innkeepers. Two rooms only, each with a private bath. The house is decorated with stained glass and etchings crafted by the hostess. Lots of advice and friendly help are given by the hosts who have lived in the area a long time. Guests are assured of a warm welcome. Full breakfast served. No smoking in house. No small children. $59-69.

135. Historic Queen Anne Mansion. In the national register, the inn is a unique and very special bed and breakfast that offers guests splendid views over Bellingham Bay and 10 rooms from which to choose. A Steinway grand piano adorns the entry, and music suggests names for each room. A variety of bed sizes and private or shared bath accommodations will meet the needs of any traveler. Full breakfast. $50-89.

---

7 No smoking; 8 Children welcome; 9 Social drinking allowed; 10 Tennis nearby; 11 Swimming nearby; 12 Golf nearby; 13 Skiing nearby; 14 May be booked through a travel agent; 15 Handicapped accessible.

Schnauzer Crossing

4421 Lakeway Drive, 98226
(360) 733-0055; (800) 562-2808;
FAX (360) 734-2808; e-mail: schnauzerx@aol.com
www.schauzercrossing.com

Schnauzer Crossing is a luxury bed and breakfast between Seattle and Vancouver, British Columbia, and a destination bed and breakfast, with its lakeside ambiance, outdoor hot tub, and one-and-a-half-acres of gardens. A garden suite and new cottage boast Jacuzzi, fireplace, and king-size bed. New this year, a Japanese garden with koi pond.

Hosts: Vermont and Donna McAllister
Rooms: 3 (PB) $120-200
Full Breakfast
Credit Cards: A, B, D
Notes: 2, 5, 7, 8, 9, 10, 11, 12, 13, 15

BREMERTON

Pacific Bed & Breakfast Agency

P.O. Box 46894, Seattle, 98146
(206) 439-7677; (800) 684-2932
FAX (206) 431-0932; e-mail: pacificb@nwlink.com
www.seattlebedandbreakfast.com

115. High Society. "An opulent retreat to yesteryear" is the description of this stately mansion built in 1936 and it became the hub of high society on the Canal in 1937. The Gable Room is named for Clark Gable who was a frequent visitor. Six rooms, all with private baths, offer wonderful choices for guests' stay. Breakfast is a special treat. The mansion has an interesting history and special spaces to explore. Two night minimum on weekends. $115-175.

CAMANO ISLAND

Peifferhaus

1462 East Larkspur Lane, 98292
(360) 629-4746; (877) 623-8497
FAX (360) 629-4785
www.peifferhaus.com

This country-style home on Camano Island is designed for relaxing. Enjoy the panoramic view from the room or on the wraparound covered porch. There are five and one-half acres of beautiful grounds and flower gardens. A short drive from Seattle, this island retreat has the charisma of the San Juan Islands, without the ferry lines and expenses. Gourmet breakfasts are served in a peaceful country setting. Enjoy lawn games and mini-golf course on-site.

Hosts: Tom and Mary Ann Peiffer
Rooms: 4 (PB) $85-95
Full Breakfast
Credit Cards: A, B, D
Notes: 2, 3, 4, 5, 7, 8, 9, 11, 12, 13, 14

CATHLAMET

Redfern Farm Bed & Breakfast

277 Crossdike Road, 98612
(360) 849-4108

In the lower Columbia River estuary and on rural Puget Island, Redfern Farm is about two hours from Portland, Oregon, and Olympia. There is easy access by bridge from Cathlamet or by the historic ferry from Westport, Oregon. The 1940s farmhouse has two second-story guest rooms, each with queen-size beds and private bath. Furnishings are an eclectic mix of old and new. Enjoy the quiet of the country garden and outdoor spa; walk, hike, bicycle, and bird watch on this portion of Columbia White-tailed Deer Refuge.

Host: Winnie
Rooms: 2 (PB) $55
Full Breakfast
Credit Cards: None
Notes: 2, 5, 7, 12

COSMOPOLIS

Pacific Bed & Breakfast Agency

P.O. Box 46894, Seattle, 98146
(206) 439-7677; (800) 684-2932
FAX (206) 431-0932; e-mail: pacificb@nwlink.com
www.seattlebedandbreakfast.com

NOTES: Credit cards accepted: A MasterCard; B Visa; C American Express; D Discover; E Diner's Club; F Other; 2 Personal checks accepted; 3 Lunch available; 4 Dinner available; 5 Open all year; 6 Pets welcome;

110. **Lumber Baron's Mansion.** A circular driveway leads guests to the portico of this lumber baron's mansion built in 1908. In the state and national registers. Guests will find that old-fashioned charm and warmth are tangible qualities here. Five rooms have private baths and four additional rooms with shared baths are offered. The first-floor living room, dining room, and two parlors are all available for ceremonies and receptions and on the lower level, the ballroom is ideal for banquets for large groups. Jacuzzi, sauna, and exercise rooms are an added bonus. $65-115.

COUPEVILLE

The Compass Rose

508 South Main Street, 98239
(360) 678-5318; (800) 237-3881
FAX (360) 678-5318

This bed and breakfast on Whitbey Island, is idyllically placed in Coupeville, the heart of Ebey's Landing National Historical Reserve. This fine 1890 Queen Anne Victorian home, on the National Register of Historic Places, is now an elegant two room bed and breakfast, furnished with antiques and glorious things from around the globe. The hosts serve afternoon tea upon arrival, and, at guests' convenience in the morning, a sumptuous breakfast, presented on exquisite china, crystal, silver, linen, and lace.

Hosts: Captain and Mrs. Marshall W. Bronson
Rooms: 2 (SB)
Full Breakfast
Credit Cards: None
Notes: 2, 5, 7, 9, 10, 12

Pacific Bed & Breakfast Agency

P.O. Box 46894, Seattle, 98146
(206) 439-7677; (800) 684-2932
FAX (206) 431-0932; e-mail: pacificb@nwlink.com
www.seattlebedandbreakfast.com

130. **Two Victorian Host Homes.** Two lovely Victorian host homes sit side-by-side and offer a truly unique stay in a bygone era. Dating from 1887 and 1891 and restored in a loving manner, the rooms will give guests the feeling of days long gone. All six rooms have private baths with claw-foot tubs and either king- or queen-size beds. The master rooms have a gas fireplace and Jacuzzi. $65-125.

DEER HARBOR (ORCAS ISLAND)

Palmer's Chart House

Box 51, 98243
(360) 376-4231

The first bed and breakfast on Orcas Island (since 1975) with a magnificent water view. The 33-foot private yacht *Amante* is available for a minimal fee with Skipper Don. Low-key, private, personal attention makes this bed and breakfast unique and attractive. Well-traveled hosts speak Spanish. Children over 10 welcome.

Hosts: Majean and Donald Palmer
Rooms: 2 (PB) $60-80
Full Breakfast
Credit Cards: None
Notes: 2, 5, 9, 10, 11, 12, 14

Palmer's Chart House

EASTSOUND (ORCAS ISLAND)

Kangaroo House Bed & Breakfast

P.O. Box 334, 98245-0334
(360) 376-2175; (888) 371-2175
FAX (360) 376-3604
e-mail: InnKeeper@KangarooHouse.com
www.kangaroohouse.com

A centrally positioned base for enjoying all that Orcas Island has to offer, Kangaroo House

---

7 No smoking; 8 Children welcome; 9 Social drinking allowed; 10 Tennis nearby; 11 Swimming nearby; 12 Golf nearby; 13 Skiing nearby; 14 May be booked through a travel agent; 15 Handicapped accessible.

Kangaroo House

provides comfortable accommodations, relaxed, and unpretentious atmosphere, and fine breakfasts. Large guest living room, stone fireplace, garden hot tub. Families welcome. Walk to village shops, restaurants, and beach. Panoramic view from nearby Moran State Park.

Hosts: Peter and Helen Allen
Rooms: 5 (2 PB; 3 SB) $75-125
Full Breakfast
Credit Cards: A, B, C, D
Notes: 2, 5, 7, 8, 9, 10, 11, 12, 14

Turtleback Farm Inn and the Orchard House at Turtleback Farm

1981 Crow Valley Road, 98243
(360) 376-4914; (800) 376-4914
FAX (360) 376-5329; www.turtlebackinn.com

This meticulously restored farmhouse has been described as a "marvel of bed and breakfastmanship decorated with country finesse and a sophisticated sense of the right antiques." Two buildings house 11 bedrooms with private baths. Award-winning breakfasts. Lunch and dinner available by special arrangements. Children eight and older welcome. Inquire about handicapped accessibility.

Hosts: William and Susan Fletcher
Rooms: 11 (PB) $80-210
Full Breakfast
Credit Cards: A, B, D
Notes: 2, 5, 7, 9, 10, 11, 12, 14

EDMONDS

Harrison House

210 Sunset Avenue, 98020
(206) 776-4748

New waterfront home with sweeping view of Puget Sound and the Olympic Mountains. Many fine restaurants within walking distance. Each spacious room has private bath, private deck, TV, wet bar, telephone, and king-size bed. University of Washington is nearby.

Hosts: Jody and Harve Harrison
Rooms: 2 (PB) $55-65
Continental Breakfast
Credit Cards: None
Notes: 2, 5, 7, 9, 10, 11, 12

ENUMCLAW

Pacific Bed & Breakfast Agency

P.O. Box 46894, Seattle, 98146
(206) 439-7677; (800) 684-2932
FAX (206) 431-0932; e-mail: pacificb@nwlink.com
www.seattlebedandbreakfast.com

138. Magnificent Mansion. This 1922 Colonial mansion has 22 rooms and took two years to build. Master craftsmen decorated the interior with beautiful millwork using old-growth Honduran mahogany and oak. Four guest rooms are offered, all with private bath. Awaken to the aroma of freshly brewed coffee and a gourmet breakfast. $85-95.

EPHRATA

Ivy Chapel Inn Bed & Breakfast

164 D Street Southwest, 98823
(509) 754-0629; e-mail: ivychapel@hotmail.com
www.quikpage.com/I/ivychapel

The inn is in the former Presbyterian church. The original brick building was built in the 1940s and refurbished in 1994. The inn features six unique theme rooms including the Blue Suite, the Outdoorsman's Room, the

---

NOTES: Credit cards accepted: A MasterCard; B Visa; C American Express; D Discover; E Diner's Club; F Other; 2 Personal checks accepted; 3 Lunch available; 4 Dinner available; 5 Open all year; 6 Pets welcome;

Safari Room, the Southwest Room, the Ivy Room, and the Bridal Room. Each room has a private bath. A large parlor, breakfast room, deck with hot tub, and the 1,800-square-foot chapel complete the inn.

Hosts: Kirk and Cheryl McClelland
Rooms: 6 (PB) $75-100
Full Breakfast
Credit Cards: A, B, C
Notes: 2, 5, 7, 9, 11, 12

FEDERAL WAY

A Greater Tacoma Bed & Breakfast Reservation Service

3312 North Union Avenue, 98407
(253) 759-4088; (800) 406-4088
FAX (253) 759-4025
e-mail: reservations@tacoma-inns.org
www.tacoma-inns.org

Palisades Bed & Breakfast. An elegant European-style home with beautiful landscaping and water. Mountain views. A very large private suite with canopied queen-size bed, fireplace, TV/VCR, and marbled Jacuzzi. WBBG. Full breakfast. $185-195.

FORKS

Miller Tree Inn

654 East Division Street, P.O. Box 1565, 98331
(360) 374-6806; FAX (360) 374-6807
e-mail: milltree@ptinet.net
www.northolympic.com/millertree

Wonderful 1916 country homestead. Near Pacific beaches, Hoh Rain Forest, and five fish-filled rivers. Breakfast is served 7:30-9:00 A.M., consisting of fresh fruit, cereal, and pastry bar followed by mouth-watering entrée. Two living rooms, hot tub, and warm hospitality. For the fisherman: guide and trailer shuttle referrals, pre-dawn breakfasts (October through April), secure off-street parking, and river reports. American Automobile Association two-diamond, 14 years *NW Best Places.*

Hosts: Bill and Susan Brager
Rooms: 7 (3 PB; 4 SB) $60-125
Full Breakfast
Credit Cards: A, B
Notes: 2, 5, 7, 8, 9

Pacific Bed & Breakfast Agency

P.O. Box 46894, Seattle, 98146
(206) 439-7677; (800) 684-2932
FAX (206) 431-0932; e-mail: pacificb@nwlink.com
www.seattlebedandbreakfast.com

117. Rustic Getaway on the Ocean. Go as far west as one can where the wilderness meets the sea and guests will find a complex of rustic main lodges with full restaurant, motel-style accommodations, and house-keeping cabins. Walk on the beach (there are seven beaches in six miles), watch the sun go down, and listen to the waves while falling asleep each night. This is the ultimate getaway. Be sure to specify desired accomodations. Rates are seasonal.

FREELAND (WHIDBEY ISLAND)

Cliff House & Seacliff Cottage

727 Windmill Drive, Whidbey Island, 98249
(360) 331-1566
e-mail: wink@whidbey.com
www.whidbey.com/cliffhouse

On Whidbey Island, a setting so unique there is nothing anywhere quite like Cliff House. In a private world of luxury, this stunning home and/or cottage is the guests' alone. Secluded in a forest on the edge of Puget Sound. Views are breathtaking. Stone fireplace, spa, and miles of driftwood beach. Gourmet kitchen. No commission included if booked through a travel agent. Two-night minimum stay required. Children 14 and older or tiny babies.

Hosts: Peggy Moore and Walter O'Toole
House: $410
Cottage: $165
Continental Breakfast
Credit Cards: None
Notes: 2, 5, 7, 9, 12, 14

---

7 No smoking; 8 Children welcome; 9 Social drinking allowed; 10 Tennis nearby; 11 Swimming nearby; 12 Golf nearby; 13 Skiing nearby; 14 May be booked through a travel agent; 15 Handicapped accessible.

FRIDAY HARBOR

Pacific Bed & Breakfast Agency

P.O. Box 46894, Seattle, 98146
(206) 439-7677; (800) 684-2932
FAX (206) 431-0932; e-mail: pacificb@nwlink.com
www.seattlebedandbreakfast.com

126. Victorian Inn. Enjoy the hospitality and the relaxed days of yesteryear where quaintness, comfort, and charm await guests at this Victorian inn at Friday Harbor. Each guest room reflects the nostalgic atmosphere of days gone by, and the old-fashioned garden provides fresh flowers each day. Shared and private bath accommodations have reasonable rates.

States Inn

2039 West Valley Road, 98250
(360) 378-6240; FAX (360) 378-6241
e-mail: paschal@rockisland.com
www.karuna.com/statesinn

In a scenic valley seven miles from town, States Inn is on a 60-acre horse ranch on the west side of San Juan Island. It is a fully updated 10-room inn (including a three-room suite) originally built circa 1910. Each guest room is decorated with a theme from a different state. Consistently AAA three-diamond-rated since it opened in 1991, the top rating for San Juan Islands bed and breakfast inns.

Hosts: Alan and Julia Paschal
Rooms: 10 (8 PB; 2 SB) $85-135

States Inn

Full Breakfast
Credit Cards: A, B
Notes: 2, 5, 7, 14, 15

Tower House

Tower House Bed & Breakfast

1230 Little Road, 98250
(360) 378-5464; (800) 858-4276
e-mail: towerhouse@san-juan-island.com
www.san-juan-island.com

This Queen Anne-style home on 10 acres overlooks the San Juan Valley. Two suites offer a blend of Victorian spirit and contemporary comfort. Retreat to the library and the sunroom or watch sunsets through stained glass from the window seat of the Tower Room. Cherished old linens, china, and crystal recall the ceremony of the past as guests enjoy breakfast. Play the piano or view a movie by the fire in the paneled parlor. Vegan breakfast (no animal products) available with advance notice.

Hosts: Chris and Joe Luma
Rooms: 2 (PB) $115-130
Full Breakfast
Credit Cards: A, B, C, D
Notes: 2, 5, 7, 12, 14

Tucker House Bed & Breakfast with Cottages

260 B Street, 98250
(800) 965-0123; FAX (360) 378-6437
e-mail: tucker@rockisland.com
www.san-juan.net/tucker

NOTES: Credit cards accepted: A MasterCard; B Visa; C American Express; D Discover; E Diner's Club; F Other; 2 Personal checks accepted; 3 Lunch available; 4 Dinner available; 5 Open all year; 6 Pets welcome;

This 1898 Victorian home has three upstairs bedrooms with queen-size beds, TV/VCRs, accent furniture plus three self-contained cottages with private baths, queen-size beds, wood stoves/electric heat, kitchenettes, TV/VCR. An outdoor hot tub. A full gourmet breakfast in the solarium. One block from ferry landing. Families welcome in the cottage. Small dogs permitted in cottages with prior arrangement and extra charge. Gift certificates available.

Hosts: Skip and Annette Metzger
Rooms: 5 (3 PB; 2 SB) $85-210
Full Breakfast
Credit Cards: A, B, C, D
Notes: 2, 5, 6, 7, 8, 9, 10, 11, 12, 14

GIG HARBOR

A Greater Tacoma Bed & Breakfast Reservation Service

3312 North Union Avenue, Tacoma, 984067
(253) 759-4088; (800) 406-4088
FAX (253) 759-4025
e-mail: reservations@tacoma-inns.org
e-mail: tacomabnbs@aol.com
www.tacoma-inns.org

A. Olalla Orchard B&B. Savor quiet rural country charm in a modern home with mountain views. An orchard and pond beautify the grounds. Suite with private bath and Jacuzzi. Full breakfast $85.

B. Sunny Bay Cottage. Private and relaxing, this one-bedroom cottage overlooks Puget Sound and the Olympics. Bath with shower, sitting room with wood stove, TV/VCR, kitchen, and outdoor hot tub. Self-serve Continental breakfast. $125.

C. Rosedale Bed & Breakfast. A welcoming, homey atmosphere in this large, contemporary home. Enormous waterfront suite with fireplace, TV and VCR, and private bath. Second floor room has a private bath. WBBG. Full breakfast. $95.

D. Beachside Bed & Breakfast. Relax on the beach of this waterfront English Tudor-style home with private entrance. A large suite with private full bath, fireplace, TV/VCR, kitchen, and hot tub. WBBG. Self-serve Continental breakfast. $95.

GREENBANK

Guest House Log Cottages

24371 State Route 525, 98253
(360) 678-3115; e-mail: guesthse@whidbey.net
www.whidbey.net/logcottages

A couple's romantic retreat, this AAA four-diamond-rated bed and breakfast hideaway offers five storybook cottages and one log mansion in cozy settings on 25 acres. Fireplaces, VCRs, more than 400 complimentary movies, in-room Jacuzzis, kitchens, country antiques, and wildlife pond. Continental plus breakfast. Pool and spa. Privacy, peace, and pampering. Near winery. Special midweek rates October 31 through March 15. Minimum-stay requirements for weekends and holidays.

Hosts: Don and Mary Jane Creger
Cottages: 6 (PB) $125-285
Full Breakfast
Credit Cards: A, B, C, D
Notes: 2, 5, 7, 9, 10, 11, 12, 14

Guest House Log Cottages

---

7 No smoking; 8 Children welcome; 9 Social drinking allowed; 10 Tennis nearby; 11 Swimming nearby; 12 Golf nearby; 13 Skiing nearby; 14 May be booked through a travel agent; 15 Handicapped accessible.

HOQUIAM

Pacific Bed & Breakfast Agency

P.O. Box 46894, Seattle, 98146
(206) 439-7677; (800) 684-2932
FAX (206) 431-0932; e-mail: pacificb@nwlink.com
www.seattlebedandbreakfast.com

109. Elegant Inn. Much more than an elegant inn, it is a gallery, museum, and workshop where furniture, collectibles, and antiques can be purchased. Each room at the inn is uniquely furnished with queen-size beds and a choice of shared or private bath accommodations. Freshly brewed coffee starts the day and a full buffet breakfast awaits guests in the dining room. $75-140.

ILWACO

Kola House Bed & Breakfast

211 Pearl, P.O. Box 646, 98624
(360) 642-2819; e-mail: ljl@willapa.org

Walk to fishing, plenty of parking for boat trailers. View of Columbia River and Astoria. Suite has fireplace and sauna. Pool table in basement. Cabin with kitchen available. Quaint 1919 home. Quiet neighborhood. Rates available for groups and winter. Kitty on premises.

Host: Linda Luokkala
Rooms: 5 (PB) $65-75
Full Breakfast
Credit Cards: A, B
Notes: 2, 5, 7, 9, 10, 11, 12

KELSO

Longfellow House Bed & Breakfast Cottage

203 Williams Finney Road, 98626
(360) 423-4545; e-mail: lngfelhs@pacifier.com
www.pacifier.com/~lngfelhs

Longfellow House is the ideal private destination for that special occasion or business trip. A secluded cottage for two in a rural setting one mile east of I-5. The main floor is guests' alone. Enjoy the 1913 player piano and collection of works by and about Henry Wadsworth Longfellow. Sleep as long as you like. Wake to the smell of gourmet coffee and the breakfast guests selected being prepared. Off-street parking, telephone, modem jack, and business services. Visit Mount St. Helens, Pacific beaches, and Columbia Gorge.

Hosts: Richard and Sally Longfellow
Rooms: 1 (PB) $89
Full Breakfast
Credit Cards: None
Notes: 2, 5, 7, 10, 12

KIRKLAND

Pacific Bed & Breakfast Agency

P.O. Box 46894, Seattle, 98146
(206) 439-7677; (800) 684-2932
FAX (206) 431-0932; e-mail: pacificb@nwlink.com
www.seattlebedandbreakfast.com

054. Historic Mansion. The mansion has eight wonderfully appointed bed and breakfast rooms, each with a queen-size bed and private bath. An inviting buffet breakfast is served in the dining room, complemented with candles and flowers. Each evening there are homemade goodies with beverages as the season suggests. Children over 12 welcome. $70-105.

Shumway Mansion

11410 99th Place Northeast, 98033
(425) 823-2303

Overlook Lake Washington from this award-winning 23-room mansion dating from 1909. Eight individually decorated guest rooms with private baths. Variety-filled breakfast. Complimentary use of athletic club. Short distance to all forms of shopping; 20 minutes to downtown Seattle. Water and snow recreation close at hand. Children over 12 welcome.

Hosts: Richard and Salli Harris
Rooms: 8 (PB) $70-105

NOTES: Credit cards accepted: A MasterCard; B Visa; C American Express; D Discover; E Diner's Club; F Other; 2 Personal checks accepted; 3 Lunch available; 4 Dinner available; 5 Open all year; 6 Pets welcome;

La Conner, WA 359

Shumway Mansion

Full Breakfast
Credit Cards: A, B, C
Notes: 2, 5, 7, 9, 10, 11, 12, 13, 14

LA CONNER

Benson Farmstead

10113 Avon-Allen Road, Bow, 98232
(206) 757-0578; (800) 441-9814
www.bbhost.com/bensonbnb

The Benson Farmstead is a 1914 restored 17-room farmhouse with antiques, quilts, and a cozy decor. It is surrounded by flower gardens and farmland and is just off I-5 near La Conner, Burlington, Chuckanut Drive, and the tulip fields. Third-generation Skagit Valley farmers Jerry and Sharon are friendly hosts who serve a full country breakfast every morning and dessert and coffee in the evening.

Hosts: Jerry and Sharon Benson
Rooms: 4 (PB) $80-90
Full Breakfast
Credit Cards: A, B
Notes: 2, 5, 7, 8, 9, 10, 11, 12, 13

Pacific Bed & Breakfast Agency

P.O. Box 46894, Seattle, 98146
(206) 439-7677; (800) 684-2932
FAX (206) 431-0932; e-mail: pacificb@nwlink.com
www.seattlebedandbreakfast.com

128. Country Inn. A beautiful Victorian-style country inn at the entrance to La Conner with views over fields, meadows, and mountains offers guests 10 rooms, each with a private bath. Some rooms feature fireplace and view. Telephone and TV in each room. The honeymoon suite has a Jacuzzi. An outdoor hot tub invites guests to relax their cares away. Continental breakfast included. $69-155.

157. Samish Bay Guest Houses. On a bluff above Samish Bay are these two Cape Cod-style guest houses. Views of Samish Bay and the Canadian mountains. Individual rooms can be rented as well as an entire house. Decks, outdoor spa, breakfast in the morning. From $100.

185. Historic Bed and Breakfast. Relax in the serenity of country living at this turn-of-the-century farmhouse with sweeping views of the farmlands and Mount Baker. Relax in the hot tub on the back deck or gather in the parlor around the wood-burning ceramic fireplace. There are eight rooms to choose from with a variety of personal touches and either shared or private bath accommodations. Breakfasts are satisfying and wholesome served on the windowed front porch or in the dining room.

The White Swan

The White Swan Guest House

15872 Moore Road, Mount Vernon, 98273
(360) 445-6805; www.cnw.com/~wswan/

The White Swan is a "storybook" farmhouse only six miles from the historic waterfront town of La Conner. Fine restaurants, great antiquing, and interesting shops are all available in Washington's favorite artist's community. Just an hour north of Seattle and 90 miles

7 No smoking; 8 Children welcome; 9 Social drinking allowed; 10 Tennis nearby; 11 Swimming nearby; 12 Golf nearby; 13 Skiing nearby; 14 May be booked through a travel agent; 15 Handicapped accessible.

south of Vancouver. Separate honeymoon cottage available. Gardens seen in *Country Home* magazine. Two stars in *Northwest Best Places*. Children welcome in cottage.

Host: Peter Goldfarb
Rooms: 4 (1 PB; 3 SB) $65-85
Cottage: $125-150
Continental Breakfast
Credit Cards: A, B
Notes: 2, 5, 7, 12

LANGLEY

Island Tyme Bed & Breakfast Inn

4940 South Bayview Road, 98260
(360) 221-5078; (800) 898-8963
e-mail: islandty@whidbey.com

Peaceful, elegant country Victorian on secluded estate. Five rooms, all with private baths, Jacuzzis, fireplaces, decks, gourmet breakfasts, beverage bars, homemade cookies. Friendly pygmy goats. Near Langley, a quaint village by the sea, a popular tourist attraction. Local art, antiques, fine dining, golf, beaches, parks, wineries, and microbrewery tours. AAA-rated three diamonds. Pets welcome in one room. Inquire about accommodations for children. One room is handicapped accessible.

Hosts: Cliff and Carol Wisman
Rooms: 5 (PB) $95-140
Full Breakfast

Island Tyme

Credit Cards: A, B, C, D
Notes: 2, 5, 6, 7, 8, 9, 10, 11, 12, 14, 15

Log Castle

4693 Saratoga Road, 98260
(360) 221-5483

On Whidbey Island, 30 miles north of Seattle. Log lodge on secluded beach. Big stone fireplace, turret bedrooms, panoramic views of Puget Sound and the Cascade Mountains. The lodge's breakfast is a legend. Watch for bald eagles, seals, and herons from the widow's walk. Two-night minimum stay required for holidays.

Owners: Representative Jack and Norma Metcalf
Innkeepers: Karen and Phil Holdsworth
Rooms: 4 (PB) $95-120
Full Breakfast
Credit Cards: A, B, D
Notes: 2, 5, 7, 10, 11, 12, 13, 14

Pacific Bed & Breakfast Agency

P.O. Box 46894, Seattle, 98146
(206) 439-7677; (800) 684-2932
FAX (206) 431-0932; e-mail: pacificb@nwlink.com
www.seattlebedandbreakfast.com

197. Haven in the Woods. A private guest suite includes a private outside stairway and a large deck. The main sleeping room has a queen-size bed and windows on three sides and there is additional sleeping space in the loft. The special amenities include a walk-in dressing area and private bath with tiled soaking tub. A Continental breakfast waits for guests outside their doors each morning. Pricing is according to the number of guests.

LANGLEY (WHIDBEY ISLAND)

Heron Haven Bed & Breakfast

513 Anthes Avenue, 98260
(360) 221-9121; FAX (360) 221-7506
e-mail: sybil@whidbey.com

A 1930s Cape Cod cottage on beautiful Whidbey Island, 30 minutes north of Seattle, plus a short ferry ride. View of water and mountains. Enjoy beautiful antiques and luscious gardens. Full breakfast is served in dining room, on the deck, or under wisteria-covered arbor. Walk to everything in town—antique shops, restaurants, and performing arts center. Queen-size beds, private half-baths in rooms and shared shower, common area, TV, fireplace, spectacular views.

Host: Sybil Yates
Rooms: 2 (2 P1/2B; 2 SB) $90
Full Breakfast
Credit Cards: A, B
Notes: 2, 5, 7, 9, 10, 12

Pacific Bed & Breakfast Agency

P.O. Box 46894, Seattle, 98146
(206) 439-7677; (800) 684-2932
FAX (206) 431-0932; e-mail: pacificb@nwlink.com
www.seattlebedandbreakfast.com

129. New Victorian Style. The inn is newly built in the Victorian style and is wheelchair accessible. Five guest rooms are offered and all have private baths; two have fireplaces and one has a Jacuzzi. Full breakfast. Children welcome. $95-140.

133. Modern Inn. Built into a bluff overlooking the sound, each of the 24 rooms has a 180-degree waterfront view. Each room features a wood-burning fireplace, refrigerator, coffee maker, and Jacuzzi facing both the fireplace and the water view. Continental breakfast is served. Rates start at $189-279.

161. Saratoga Modern View Inn. New inn in Langley, features 15 guest rooms each with a fireplace and views of Saratoga Passage or the Cascade Mountains. All private baths, oversize showers, breakfast, and afternoon tea with appetizers. Also available is a cabin suite with private deck, fireplace, kitchen, and antique tub. From $140-275.

LEAVENWORTH

Pacific Bed & Breakfast Agency

P.O. Box 46894, Seattle, 98146
(206) 439-7677; (800) 684-2932
FAX (206) 431-0932; e-mail: pacificb@nwlink.com
www.seattlebedandbreakfast.com

140. Bavarian Inn. A perfect place for business or pleasure. Ample space, courteous staff, and restaurant on premises are features guests will enjoy as they come home from exploring the many recreational activities of this unique town. Exercise room, spa, and pool available. Continental breakfast. Seasonal rates.

141. European-style Country Inn. The brochure for this unique inn tells guests that they will find a bit of the Alps in the foothills of the Cascades, two minutes from the center of Leavenworth and a world away from daily cares. Settle into one of 10 comfortable, cozy rooms in the main house or stay in a snug chalet with kitchen. This location is perfect any time of the year with a special festival during the holidays. Full country breakfast. $65-160.

Run of the River Bed & Breakfast

9308 East Leavenworth Road, P.O. Box 285, 98826
(509) 548-7171; (800) 288-6491

Imagine the quintessential northwestern log bed and breakfast inn. Spacious rooms feature private baths and hand-hewn log beds. The suite has its own wood stove, jetted Jacuzzi surrounded by river rock, and a bird's-eye loft. View Icicle River, surrounding bird refuge, and the Cascade peaks, appropriately named the Enchantments. Take a spin on complimentary mountain bikes. A delicious hearty northwestern breakfast sets the day in motion! The inn is an ideal base for side trips to Winthrop, Lake Chelan, and Grand Coulee.

Hosts: Monty and Karen Turner
Rooms: 5 (PB) $100-155
Full Breakfast
Credit Cards: A, B, D
Notes: 2, 5, 7, 9, 10, 11, 12, 13, 14

---

7 No smoking; 8 Children welcome; 9 Social drinking allowed; 10 Tennis nearby; 11 Swimming nearby; 12 Golf nearby; 13 Skiing nearby; 14 May be booked through a travel agent; 15 Handicapped accessible.

LONG BEACH

Boreas Bed & Breakfast Inn

607 North Ocean Beach Boulevard
P.O. Box 1344, 98631
(360) 642-8069; (888) 642-8069
e-mail: boreas@boreasinn.com
www.boreasinn.com

This 1920s beach house, remodeled in eclectic style, skillfully combines art and antiques with comfort and casualness. Romantic ocean-view bedrooms and spacious living rooms with stereo, musical instruments, and marble fireplace. A custom-designed cedar-and-glass gazebo houses a state-of-the-art spa facing the dunes. Delicious full breakfast is served. Walk or bike to the boardwalk, shopping, and restaurants. Ten minutes to lighthouses and beautiful state parks for hiking, kayaking, and the many other outdoor activities Washington has to offer.

Hosts: Susie Goldsmith and Bill Verner
Rooms: 5 (PB) $120-135
Full Breakfast
Credit Cards: A, B, C, D, E
Notes: 2, 5, 7, 9, 10, 11, 12, 14

Boreas

LOPEZ ISLAND

Edenwild Inn

P.O. Box 271, 132 Lopez Road, 98261
(360) 468-3138; FAX (360) 468-4080
e-mail: edenwildinn@msn.com
www.edenwildinn.com

Elegant Victorian country inn in pastoral Lopez Valley. Eight large bedrooms all with private baths, some with fireplaces, water and garden views. Wonderful full breakfasts with award-winning baked goods. Within walking distance to shops, restaurants, hiking and kayaking. Ideal for small receptions, banquets, and group events. Gift certificates available. No smoking or pets.

Rooms: 8 (PB) $110-165
Full Breakfast
Credit Cards: A, B, C, D
Notes: 2, 5, 7, 9, 10, 12, 14, 15

MacKaye Harbor Inn

949 MacKaye Harbor Road, 98361
(360) 468-2253

The ideal beachfront getaway. Lopez's only bed and breakfast on a low-bank sandy beach. Kayak and mountain bike rentals and/or instruction. This 1927 Victorian home has been painstakingly restored. Guests are pampered in comfortable elegance. Eagles, deer, seals, and otters frequent this Cape Cod of the Northwest. Commendations from *Sunset, Pacific Northwest* magazine, the *Los Angeles Times,* and *Northwest Best Places.*

Hosts: Mike and Robin Bergstrom
Rooms: 5 (3PB), (1 DB), (1 SB) $79-159
Full Breakfast
Credit Cards: A, B
Notes: 2, 5, 7, 9, 10, 11, 12, 14

MERCER ISLAND

Pacific Bed & Breakfast Agency

P.O. Box 46894, Seattle, 98146
(206) 439-7677; (800) 684-2932
FAX (206) 431-0932; e-mail: pacificb@nwlink.com
www.seattlebedandbreakfast.com

048. Lakefront Cottage. This lovely two-bedroom cottage is just steps from Lake Washington. The large private yard gives guests a relaxed and peaceful setting. The hostess provides a Continental breakfast each day and

---

NOTES: Credit cards accepted: A MasterCard; B Visa; C American Express; D Discover; E Diner's Club; F Other; 2 Personal checks accepted; 3 Lunch available; 4 Dinner available; 5 Open all year; 6 Pets welcome;

guests will have a full kitchen, bath, living room, and study, and TV and VCR. No smoking. No pets. Children welcome. $125.

049. View Home. This contemporary home has three different bed and breakfast spaces for the folks with different needs. The first is a garden-level two-room suite with private bath; the second has a private bath and is on the main floor. On the top floor guests can choose a one-bedroom apartment with private deck. Breakfast is a special occasion and is served in the dining room by the German hostess. No pets. No smoking. Inquire about accommodations for children. $65-80.

050. Tudor with a View. On Mercer Island with easy access to the I-90 bridge, guests can be in Seattle in about 10 minutes. Two rooms that share a bath are offered. Breakfast is served by the hostess. No smoking. No pets. Inquire about accommodations for children. Private bath. $130.

051. Ivy Lane Bed and Breakfast. Totally furnished private suite with private parking and private entrance is at garden level for those folks who need to avoid steps. Very private with TV and telephone just one minute from I-90 and into Seattle in 10 minutes. Self-serve breakfast. No pets. No smoking. Inquire about accommodations for children. $75-95.

052. Lakeview Bed and Breakfast. This bed and breakfast, in a lovely neighborhood just minutes away from downtown Seattle, has four bedrooms with private or shared baths. Continental breakfast. No smoking. No pets. Inquire about accommodations for children. $75-125.

053. Modern View Home. This English hostess welcomes guests to her lovely home. There is one room with a private bath. This room has its own sitting area for guests' comfort. Full breakfast. No smoking, pets, or children. $60-90.

201. Colonial Style Home. If guests prefer freshly baked organic food, this hostess offers a varied menu to suit. Two rooms are available, one with a private half-bath. Private entrance for easy access and convenience. A 25-minute drive from downtown Seattle in an easy-to-find location. $65-85.

MONTESANO

The Abel House Bed & Breakfast

117 Fleet Street South, 98563
(360) 249-6002; (800) 235-ABEL

Large Victorian-style home, surrounded by a garden. Five rooms, one with a private bath. Rec Room, pool table, baby grand piano, sauna, and bikes to use. Full country breakfast. No pets. Smoking permitted on porch. Decorated in antiques and period decor. Private dining room will seat up to 12 people. Warm and friendly.

Hosts: Jerry and Beth Reeves
Rooms: 5 (1 PB, 4 SB) $75-95
Full Breakfast
Credit Cards: A, B, C, D
Notes: 2, 3, 4, 5, 7, 8, 9, 12, 14

MOUNT ST. HELENS

Pacific Bed & Breakfast Agency

P.O. Box 46894, Seattle, 98146
(206) 439-7677; (800) 684-2932
FAX (206) 431-0932; e-mail: pacificb@nwlink.com
www.seattlebedandbreakfast.com

219. Mount St. Helens Bed & Breakfast. The introduction to this bed and breakfast says it has "an awesome view of Mount St. Helens and Silver Lake." Built in the style of a lodge, the inn has seven rooms all with private baths and one is equipped for handicapped access. One bath has a two-person Jacuzzi. Each room has a balcony overlooking the mountain and lake. Other amenities include hot tub, two large living rooms, and a koi pond along the balcony. Breakfast and dinner are included in the room rate. Seasonal rates. $125-195.

---

7 No smoking; 8 Children welcome; 9 Social drinking allowed; 10 Tennis nearby; 11 Swimming nearby; 12 Golf nearby; 13 Skiing nearby; 14 May be booked through a travel agent; 15 Handicapped accessible.

163. Bed & Breakfast in Salkum. This 5,000-square-foot country home is newly built and is nestled among tall trees with acres of seclusion and a view of the Cowlitz Valley and the rolling hills beyond. The five guest rooms feature private or shared baths, one with a two-person Jacuzzi. The full breakfast includes Wild Huckleberry crêpes. The hostess will try to accommodate anyone with a special diet request. Call for availability and rates.

OCEAN SHORES

Pacific Bed & Breakfast Agency

P.O. Box 46894, Seattle, 98146
(206) 439-7677; (800) 684-2932
FAX (206) 431-0932; e-mail: pacificb@nwlink.com
www.seattlebedandbreakfast.com

107. On the Beach. The ocean is just outside the door and the view is spectacular. There are fireplaces in each room and Jacuzzi suites are available. Many amenities are offered to make guests' stay very personal and special with exercise room, indoor pool and spa, and color TV and VCR. Continental breakfast. $99-209.

108. Ocean View Elegance. In the national register. Much more than an elegant inn, it is a gallery, museum, and workshop where furniture, collectibles, and antiques can be purchased. Each room at the inn is uniquely furnished with a choice of shared or private bath accommodations. Freshly brewed coffee starts the day and a full buffet breakfast awaits guests in the dining room. $125-140.

OLALLA

Pacific Bed & Breakfast Agency

P.O. Box 46894, Seattle, 98146
(206) 439-7677; (800) 684-2932
FAX (206) 431-0932; e-mail: pacificb@nwlink.com
www.seattlebedandbreakfast.com

164. Orchard Bed & Breakfast. This lovely bed and breakfast in an orchard was built in 1984 on three acres of rural land south of Bremerton, about 90 minutes from Seattle. The large guest room features a private bath that welcomes guests to relax in the two-person whirlpool tub. Views of Mount Rainier can be seen from the living room and dining room. What a perfect spot for a quiet country getaway! Seasonal rates.

OLYMPIA

Pacific Bed & Breakfast Agency

P.O. Box 46894, Seattle, 98146
(206) 439-7677; (800) 684-2932
FAX (206) 431-0932; e-mail: pacificb@nwlink.com
www.seattlebedandbreakfast.com

061. Historic Mansion. Built in 1893, this stately Queen Anne/Eastlake mansion is an Olympia landmark, listed in both the city and state historical registers. Guests are invited to relax with a hot or cold beverage in the drawing room or stroll among the inn's half-acre of gardens and orchard. Four rooms with private baths and a honeymoon suite with jetted tub. Full breakfast. $85-115.

Puget View Guesthouse

7924 61st Avenue Northeast, 98516
(360) 413-9474

Classic Puget Sound. This quaint waterfront guest cottage suite sleeps four and is on the shore of Puget Sound next to the hosts' log home. Gorgeous and expansive marine-mountain view is breathtaking. Breakfast is served privately in the cottage. Great for a special honeymoon or romantic retreat. Near Tolmie State Park, only five minutes off I-5, just north of downtown Olympia.

Hosts: The Yunkers
Cottage: 1 (PB) $99-119
Continental Breakfast
Credit Cards: A, B
Notes: 2, 5, 6, 8, 9, 11, 12, 14

NOTES: Credit cards accepted: A MasterCard; B Visa; C American Express; D Discover; E Diner's Club; F Other; 2 Personal checks accepted; 3 Lunch available; 4 Dinner available; 5 Open all year; 6 Pets welcome;

Swantown Inn

1431 11th Avenue Southeast, 98501
(360) 753-9123
www.olywa.net/swantown

Welcome to the Swantown Inn, an 1893 Queen Anne/Eastlake Mansion listed on both the city and state historical registers. Guests are invited to relax near the fire in the drawing room, or wander the Inn's half-acre of gardens, orchard, and gazebo. The inn is close to the state capital campus, Olympia Farmers' Market, downtown shops and restaurants, and waterfront boardwalk. Further afield, the Olympic Peninsula, Mount St. Helens, Mount Rainier, and the city of Seattle are all an easy day's trip. Children over 11 welcome.

Hosts: Ed and Lillian Peeples
Rooms: 4 (PB) $75-115
Full Breakfast
Credit Cards: A, B
Notes: 2, 3, 4, 5, 7, 9, 14

ORCAS ISLAND

Pacific Bed & Breakfast Agency

P.O. Box 46894, Seattle, 98146
(206) 439-7677; (800) 684-2932
FAX (206) 431-0932; e-mail: pacificb@nwlink.com
www.seattlebedandbreakfast.com

120. Resort. Guests are invited to step back in time, when life was simple and service was expected. This lovely mansion was built by a Seattle industrialist as a place to regain his failing health and enjoy the quiet beauty. On the surrounding grounds, Guests will find relaxing pools, modern accommodations, convention facilities, dining room, and lounge. A variety of room arrangements are available, and the spa is an added pleasure. $100 and up.

121. Log Inn. This modern log inn is on a hill with a view over Puget Sound looking to the west to give guests the bonus of lovely sunsets. Eight rooms all have private baths. A full restaurant is on the main floor for guests' convenience and a self-serve breakfast will be delivered to guests' room. Three cottages also available. $100.

122. Historic Waterfront Inn. On the water on Orcas Island, the inn looks as if it had been transplanted from the coast of Maine. A private beach, small pond, and flower gardens welcome guests to relax and forget the busy city. Ask about its colorful history beginning in 1888. Choose from 30 different rooms with private or shared baths or select a suite for a stay. Seasonal rates.

127. Hotel Orcas. Ask about the history of this lovely old Victorian hotel built between 1900 and 1904 and listed in the National Registry of Historic Places. The 12 rooms are decorated with a collection of antiques and lovely log cabin quilts made by Orcas quilters. Moderately priced rooms share the baths Victorian style, a few rooms have half-baths, and the "romantic" rooms have Jacuzzis and views overlooking Harney Channel. Seasonal rates. $69-170.

POINT ROBERTS

Maple Meadow Bed & Breakfast

101 Goodman Road, 98281
(360) 945-5536; FAX (360) 945-2855
e-mail: mplmedbb@whidbey.com
www.travel-wise.com/maple/index.html

Maple Meadow

---

7 No smoking; 8 Children welcome; 9 Social drinking allowed; 10 Tennis nearby; 11 Swimming nearby; 12 Golf nearby; 13 Skiing nearby; 14 May be booked through a travel agent; 15 Handicapped accessible.

Discover a geographical quirk: Point Roberts, five square miles of peninsula which guests can reach by land only through Canada or via water through Juan de Fuca. The 1910 farmhouse and Old Pump House cottage offer a romantic getaway one block from the tidal beaches of Boundary Bay. Great crabbing, hiking, bike trails, and restaurants await guests. Enjoy the hearty breakfast with a view of the horses grazing under the landmark maple tree.

Rooms: 4 (2 PB; 2 SB) $65-140
Full Breakfast
Credit Cards: A, B
Notes: 2, 5, 7, 9, 11, 12

BJ's Garden Gate

PORT ANGELES

Angeles Inn Bed & Breakfast

1203 East Seventh Street, 98362-0012
(360) 417-0260; (888) 552-4263
FAX (360) 457-4269; e-mail: james@olypen.com
www.northolympic.com/angeles

Better Homes and Gardens-featured, award-winning, contemporary dwelling. On a quiet dead-end street with ground-level rooms. King-size beds, private and shared baths. Full breakfast. Smoke free. Children five and over are welcome.

Hosts: Al and June James
Rooms: 4 (2 PB; 2 SB) $65-95
Full Breakfast
Credit Cards: A, B
Notes: 2, 5, 7, 10, 11, 12, 13, 14

BJ's Garden Gate Bed & Breakfast

397 Monterra Drive, 98262
(800) 880-1332; FAX (360) 417-5098
e-mail: www.bjgarden@olympen.com
www.bjgarden.com

Waterfront new Victorian estate. Five antique-themed rooms with private baths, Jacuzzi for two, hot tub, fireplace, TV, CD player, VCR, and telephone. Full, savory breakfast and evening dessert. All rooms have panoramic water views overlooking exquisite gardens. Close to Gateway to Olympic National Park, Hoh Rain Forest, beaches, hiking, golf, whale watching, minutes to the ferry to Victoria, B.C.

Host: BJ Paton
Rooms: 5 (PB)
Full Breakfast
Credit Cards: A, B, C
Notes: 2, 5, 7, 9, 10, 11, 12, 13, 14

Domaine Madeleine

146 Wildflower Lane, 98362
(360) 457-4174; FAX (360) 457-3037
www.domainemadeleine.com

Four-star rating from Mobil Travel Guide. Secluded, elegant, five-acre waterfront estate with water and mountain views. Four rooms with Jacuzzis for two. All rooms have fireplaces. Monet garden replica. Lawn games; whale, eagle, and deer watching; golf and skiing nearby. Breakfast so good that the inn pays if guests have lunch before 2:00 P.M. Practice languages with the hostess. Take a nature walk with the botanist host.

Hosts: Madeleine and John Chambers
Rooms: 5 (PB) $145-185
Full Breakfast
Credit Cards: A, B, C, D
Notes: 2, 5, 7, 9, 10, 11, 12, 13, 14

Pacific Bed & Breakfast Agency

P.O. Box 46894, Seattle, 98146
(206) 439-7677; (800) 684-2932
FAX (206) 431-0932; e-mail: pacificb@nwlink.com
www.seattlebedandbreakfast.com

NOTES: Credit cards accepted: A MasterCard; B Visa; C American Express; D Discover; E Diner's Club; F Other; 2 Personal checks accepted; 3 Lunch available; 4 Dinner available; 5 Open all year; 6 Pets welcome;

105. Chalet-style Lodging. The inn is a delightful chalet nestled in the foothills of the Olympic Alps with a view of the harbor. The rooms will have a private bath and comfortable beds with down comforters. A bountiful breakfast is served or guests may ask for an early breakfast to be on the ferry for the early sailing to Victoria. Cheerful hospitality. $80-95.

The SeaSuns Bed & Breakfast Inn

1006 South Lincoln Street, 98362
(360) 452-8248; (800) 708-0777
FAX (360) 417-0465
www.seasuns.com

Peaceful gardens with towering evergreens surround this elegant 1926 Dutch Colonial home with antique period furnishings, water and mountain views. Five minutes to Olympic National Park and a short walk to downtown and ferry dock. Pacific Northwest breakfast and pleasant memories are the specialty. AAA-approved. Mobil Travel Guide. *N.W. Best Places to Kiss* and *Best Places to Stay.*

Hosts: Bob and Jan Harbick
Rooms: 5 (3 PB; 2 SB) $60-115
Full Breakfast
Credit Cards: A, B, C
Notes: 2, 3, 5, 7, 9, 10, 11, 12, 13, 14

Tudor Inn

1108 South Oak, 98362
(360) 452-3138
www.tudorinn.com

Between the mountains and the sea, this half-timbered Tudor home was built by an Englishman in 1910 and has been tastefully restored and furnished with European antiques and an English garden. Five rooms, all with private baths, one with fireplace and balcony. Two-night minimum stay required for weekends July through September and for holidays. Children over 12 welcome.

Host: Jane Glass
Rooms: 5 (PB) $75-125
Full Breakfast
Credit Cards: A, B, C, D
Notes: 2, 5, 7, 9, 10, 11, 12, 13

PORT ORCHARD

"Reflections"– A Bed & Breakfast Inn

3878 Reflection Lane, East, 98366
(360) 871-5582; e-mail: jimreflect@hurricane.net

Reflections is a Colonial home filled with New England antiques. Four rooms, each with a gorgeous view of Puget Sound. Relax in the hot tub, or enjoy the view from the gazebo on two and one-half acres of landscaped grounds. Gateway to the Olympic Peninsula; scenic ferry ride to Seattle. Full gourmet breakfast is served. Antique shopping in Port Orchard. Quality golf courses nearby. Children over 14 welcome.

Hosts: Jim and Cathy Hall
Rooms: 4 (2 PB; 2 SB) $60-95
Credit Cards: A, B
Notes: 2, 5, 7, 8, 9, 12

PORT TOWNSEND

Bishop Victorian Guest Suites

714 Washington Street, 98368
(360) 385-6122; (800) 824-4738

This Victorian hotel built in 1890 has been restored and is in the heart of downtown Port Townsend. The lower floor of the building is used as a storefront and a flight of steps leads to the main lobby. Thirteen suites are furnished with period pieces and offer private baths, sitting areas, full kitchens, and one or two bedrooms. Eight suites have fireplaces and two have soaking tubs. Off-street parking and athletic club facilities are available.

Rooms: 13 (PB) $79-150
Continental Breakfast
Credit Cards: A, B, C, D
Notes: 2, 5, 7, 8, 9, 10, 12, 14

---

7 No smoking; 8 Children welcome; 9 Social drinking allowed; 10 Tennis nearby; 11 Swimming nearby; 12 Golf nearby; 13 Skiing nearby; 14 May be booked through a travel agent; 15 Handicapped accessible.

Lizzie's Victorian

Lizzie's Victorian Bed & Breakfast

731 Pierce Street, 98368
(360) 385-4168; (800) 700-4168
e-mail: wickline@olympus.net

An 1888 Victorian mansion within walking distance of shops and restaurants. The inn is decorated in antiques and some original wallpaper. Parlors are comfortable retreats for reading or conversation. Gateway to the Olympic Mountains, San Juan Islands, and Victoria. Wonderful breakfasts! Children over 10 welcome.

Hosts: Bill and Patti Wickline
Rooms: 7 (PB) $70-135
Full Breakfast
Credit Cards: A, B, D
Notes: 2, 5, 7, 9, 10, 12

Manresa Castle

Seventh and Sheridan, P.O. Box 564, 98368
(360) 385-5750; (800) 732-1281

This historic landmark, listed in the National Register of Historic Places, now houses 40 Victorian-style guest rooms, an elegant dining room, and an Edwardian-style lounge set atop Castle Hill. Almost all rooms, including the dining room and lounge, have spectacular views of the town, harbor, marina, and/or Olympic Mountains. The guest rooms offer private baths, direct dial telephones, TVs, and Continental breakfast.

Hosts: Lena and Vernon Humber
Rooms: 40 (PB) $70-175
Continental Breakfast
Credit Cards: A, B, D
Notes: 2, 4, 5, 8, 9, 10, 11, 12, 14

Pacific Bed & Breakfast Agency

P.O. Box 46894, Seattle, 98146
(206) 439-7677; (800) 684-2932
FAX (206) 431-0932; e-mail: pacificb@nwlink.com
www.seattlebedandbreakfast.com

096. 1876 Victorian. Experience elegant hospitality with an eclectic flair, sumptuous cuisine garnished by the live magic melodies of the classical concert harp. Five superbly appointed guest accommodations with private baths, down comforters, and feather beds. Enjoy luxurious ambiance accented by art and antiques. Full breakfast. $95-135.

097. Romantic Cabin. The perfect spot for a honeymoon, this 800-square-foot cabin with arched ceilings has two murals in the peaks depicting pristine views of Mount Rainier and the early days of Port Townsend. Lots of northwestern woods and tiles accent the floor-to-ceiling fireplace facing the king-size bed, jetted tub, full kitchen, TV/VCR, and washer/dryer. Breakfast is self-serve Continental with some food provided by the hostess. Inquire about special honeymoon package and weekly rates. $165.

098. Classic Seaport Inn. Experience the joy of awakening to a golden sunrise over the water as boats of all descriptions glide by on the bay. A gourmet breakfast plus a morning concert on the Steinway grand will give guests' day the best possible start. Eight rooms with private baths. $67-175.

099. 1892 Castle. This castle sits on a hill with commanding marine views. It features rooms with private baths and Victorian decor; lovely gardens. The landmark mansion is in the national register and was totally restored to former glory in 1973, yet the historic character was retained. Enjoy this splendid luxury while

NOTES: Credit cards accepted: A MasterCard; B Visa; C American Express; D Discover; E Diner's Club; F Other; 2 Personal checks accepted; 3 Lunch available; 4 Dinner available; 5 Open all year; 6 Pets welcome;

in Port Townsend. The honeymoon suite in the tower is a favorite for all romantics. Continental breakfast is served in the restaurant. $75-175.

100. Grand Dame. On the bluff overlooking mountains and Puget Sound, the lovingly restored grand mansion epitomizes the soul of historic Port Townsend. It is known for its classic Victorian architecture with a spiral staircase leading to a unique domed ceiling. Nine delightful rooms are individually decorated and offer private or shared baths. Rates are seasonal and a full breakfast is included. Two night minimum on weekends.

101. Victorian Grandeur. Today, historic preservation has allowed visitors in this town a chance to relive a time when lumber tycoons and ship captains built their futures. This Italianate-Victorian inn was built in 1883 on a hill overlooking a broad farming valley and the Olympic Mountains. The five guest rooms have private baths. A cozy gazebo in the garden offers guests a quiet spot or they may prefer a few relaxed minutes in the hot tub. $85-115.

The Palace Hotel

1004 Water Street, 98368
(360) 385-0773; (800) 962-0741 (US only)

Awarded again this year as a Northwest Best Place to Stay, the Palace Hotel on Water Street is a beautifully restored Victorian hotel in the heart of Port Townsend's historic district. Close to galleries and shops, it offers convenient off-street parking and is within blocks of ferry and bus services. Accommodations range from superior rooms with fabulous views and beautiful baths, to family-style suites with equipped kitchens to the most economical Continental-style bedrooms. Any stay at the Palace includes a complimentary Continental breakfast. All rooms have cable TVs, coffee, and tea. Two nonsmoking rooms are available. Pets and children are welcome. Off-season discounts offered during the winter.

Rooms: 15 (12 PB; 3 SB) $65-129
Continental Breakfast
Credit Cards: A, B, C, D
Notes: 2, 3, 4, 5, 6, 7, 8, 9, 10, 11, 12, 14

Quimper Inn, Ltd.

Quimper Inn, Ltd.

1306 Franklin Street, 98368
(360) 385-1060; (800) 557-1060

This 1886 mansion in the historic uptown district offers lovely water and mountain views. Four comfortable bedrooms, plus a two-room suite with a sitting room and bath. Antique period furniture, lots of books, and two porches for relaxation. A short walk to historic downtown with its many shops and restaurants. A wonderful breakfast is served. Off-season rates October through May.

Hosts: Ron and Sue Ramage
Rooms: 5 (3 PB; 2 SB) $70-140
Full Breakfast
Credit Cards: A, B
Notes: 2, 5, 7, 9, 10, 11, 12

Swan Hotel

Water and Monroe Street, 98368
(360) 385-1718; (800) 776-1718
e-mail: swan@waypt.com
www.waypt.com/bishop

Enjoy views of the Olympic and Cascade Mountains and the sea from a one-bedroom suite with kitchen and TV. Charming garden cottages offer queen-size beds, minikitchenettes, and TVs. The penthouse has an expansive

---

7 No smoking; 8 Children welcome; 9 Social drinking allowed; 10 Tennis nearby; 11 Swimming nearby; 12 Golf nearby; 13 Skiing nearby; 14 May be booked through a travel agent; 15 Handicapped accessible.

reception and dining area with four bedrooms, fully equipped kitchen, and a large Jacuzzi. Guests are welcome to a complimentary Continental breakfast at the Bishop Victorian.

Hosts: Joe and Cindy Finnie
Rooms: 9 (PB) $65-200
Continental Breakfast
Credit Cards: A, B, C
Notes: 2, 5, 7, 8, 9, 10, 11, 12, 14, 15

Water Street Hotel

635 Water Street, 98368
(360) 385-5467; (800) 735-9810
www.virtualwebdesign.com/hotel/home.htm

Built in 1889 and completely renovated in 1990, the Water Street Hotel is in a secluded waterfront community. It combines the Old World charm of historic downtown Port Townsend with a panoramic view of Puget Sound and the majestic Olympic Mountains. It's within walking distance of downtown shops, restaurants, and the Keystone ferry. A Continental breakfast is served across the street at the bakery. Only in-state personal checks accepted. Pets welcome at an additional charge. No smoking available.

Hosts: Mary Hewitt and Dawn Pfeiffer
Rooms: 16 (11 PB; 5 SB) $45-125
Continental Breakfast
Credit Cards: A, B, C, D
Notes: 5, 8, 10, 11, 12

POULSBO

Pacific Bed & Breakfast Agency

P.O. Box 46894, Seattle, 98146
(206) 439-7677; (800) 684-2932
FAX (206) 431-0932; e-mail: pacificb@nwlink.com
www.seattlebedandbreakfast.com

114. Hospitality. This elegant bed and breakfast overlooks the picturesque Scandinavian town, the bay, and the marina. A variety of rooms are available with shared or private baths, and a combination of rooms can be arranged for a group of adults for a special occasion. Full breakfast. $59-140.

PUYALLUP

A Greater Tacoma Bed & Breakfast Service

3312 North Union Avenue, Tacoma, WA 98407
(253) 759-4088; (800) 406-4088
FAX (253) 759-4025; e-mail: tacomabnbs@aol.com
e-mail: reservations@tacoma-inns.org
www.tacoma-inns.org

Q. Tayberry Victorian Cottage. Minutes from both Puyallup and Tacoma, this graceful Victorian-style home overlooks a quiet farm area. Three charming rooms with antiques, queen-size beds, TV/VCR, private baths, and nice atmosphere. Elevator available. WBBG. Full breakfast. $65-95.

R. Murphy's Corner Bed & Breakfast. A darling Victorian home just two blocks from quaint downtown Puyallup shops and the fairgrounds. Two lovely rooms with queen-size beds and private baths, one with a Jacuzzi. Full breakfast. $65-75.

REDMOND

Pacific Bed & Breakfast Agency

P.O. Box 46894, Seattle, 98146
(206) 439-7677; (800) 684-2932
FAX (206) 431-0932; e-mail: pacificb@nwlink.com
www.seattlebedandbreakfast.com

055. Host Home. Welcome to a private woodland cottage. It is large, self-contained, furnished with antiques, and includes a private entrance, queen-size bed, private bath, TV, and telephone. The large deck and wooded picnic area will give guests privacy, and breakfast will be brought to guests' suite. This is a smoke- and alcohol-free environment. No pets or children. $85.

NOTES: Credit cards accepted: A MasterCard; B Visa; C American Express; D Discover; E Diner's Club; F Other; 2 Personal checks accepted; 3 Lunch available; 4 Dinner available; 5 Open all year; 6 Pets welcome;

RITZVILLE

The Portico Bed & Breakfast

502 South Adams, 99169
(509) 659-0800; e-mail: portico@ritzcom.net
www.porticobandb.com

The Portico Bed and Breakfast is in a lovely 1902 house in the National Register of Historic Places. Gleaming oak woodwork and turn-of-the-century wallpaper and lighting are part of the rich detail. The rooms are comfortable and well appointed—a discreet TV to catch guests up on the news. Rest on the porch, relax in the hot tub, enjoy the gardens. Easy access to I-90 and Highway 395. "Come refresh yourself—We're on your way!"

Rooms: 4 (PB) $59-85
Full Breakfast
Credit Cards: A, B, C, D
Notes: 2, 5, 7, 9, 10, 11, 12, 14

SALKUM

The Shepherd's Inn

168 Autumn Heights Drive, 98582
(800) 985-2434

Experience warm hospitality in a quiet country setting between Mount St. Helens and Mount Rainier. The inn is nestled among the trees on 40 wooded acres. The 5,000-square-foot home features a wraparound deck for star gazing and enjoying the sunsets over the Cowlitz Valley and the rolling hills beyond. Enjoy bird watching and deer grazing in the morning and evening. Relax with music in the private double Jacuzzi. Individual tables to dine privately or for large groups in the main dining room. Feast on a full breakfast featuring the inn specialty of wild huckleberry crêpes, and more. Take exit 68 from I-5, go 13 miles east on highway 12, turn right on Fischer Road and follow signs. WBBG. A Northwestern hidden treasure. All major credit cards accepted.

Hosts: Richard and Ellen Berdan
Rooms: 5 (3 PB; 2 SB) $65-85

Full Breakfast
Credit Cards: A, B, C, D
Notes: 2, 5, 7, 11, 12, 13, 14

SAN JUAN ISLAND

Pacific Bed & Breakfast Agency

P.O. Box 46894, Seattle, 98146
(206) 439-7677; (800) 684-2932
FAX (206) 431-0932; e-mail: pacificb@nwlink.com
www.seattlebedandbreakfast.com

124. On the Water. Guests can enjoy the experience of staying in a 60-foot sailboat at the harbor on San Juan Island. Two cabins are available, one with double bed and bunk beds, shared bath, the other with queen-size bed and private bath. Breakfasts here are special. Two-night minimum stay. $90-95.

SEATTLE

Bacon Mansion

959 Broadway East, 98102
(206) 329-1864; (800) 240-1864
FAX (206) 860-9025
www.baconmansion.com

This is one of Seattle's most gracious mansions, within two blocks of the Broadway

Bacon Mansion

---

7 No smoking; 8 Children welcome; 9 Social drinking allowed; 10 Tennis nearby; 11 Swimming nearby; 12 Golf nearby; 13 Skiing nearby; 14 May be booked through a travel agent; 15 Handicapped accessible.

shopping district. The Bacon Mansion is in the Harvard-Belmont historic district. Most of the rooms have their own private baths. There are a beautiful grand staircase and a turn-of-the-century library in the house; breakfast is served in the formal dining room.

Host: Daryl King
Rooms: 11 (9 PB; 2 SB) $79-149
Continental Breakfast
Credit Cards: A, B, C, D
Notes: 2, 5, 7, 8, 9, 10, 15

Chambered Nautilus

Chambered Nautilus

5005 22nd Avenue Northeast, 98105
(206) 522-2536; (800) 545-8459
FAX (206) 528-0898
e-mail: chamberednautilus@msn.com

Enjoy the gracious ambiance of the classic Chambered Nautilus inn, an elegant 1915 Georgian Colonial perched on a peaceful hill in the university district overlooking the Cascade Mountains. Ten minutes from downtown attractions and a short walk to University of Washington. Relax by the living room fireplace or in the large guest rooms. Sip afternoon tea on the sun porches. Sumptuous full breakfast features house specialties, such as stuffed French toast or northwestern breakfast pie.

Hosts: Joyce Schulte and Steven Poole
Rooms: 6 (PB) $89-124
Full Breakfast
Credit Cards: A, B, C
Notes: 2, 5, 7, 9, 10, 11, 12

Chelsea Station on the Park Bed & Breakfast Inn

4915 Linden Avenue North, 98103
(206) 547-6077; (800) 400-6077
FAX (206) 632-5107
e-mail:info@bandbseattle.com
www.bandbseattle.com

Refresh your spirit! Feel the welcome of the warm and comfortable mood in one of Seattle's finest neighborhood inns. Built in 1929, Chelsea Station offers unique rooms including large suites with mountain views. Relax in Mission-style furniture and enjoy antiques throughout. Stroll to Woodland Park, the zoo, the rose garden, and wonderful restaurants. Ten minutes to the heart of downtown and city activities. Sumptuous breakfasts, a bottomless cookie jar, and smoke-free comfort. Guests will want to return. Children over 12 welcome.

Hosts: Eric and Carolanne Watness
Rooms: 9 (PB) $75-135
Full Breakfast
Credit Cards: A, B, D, E
Notes: 2, 5, 7, 9, 10, 11, 12

Chelsea Station on the Park

Gaslight Inn

1727 15th Avenue, 98122
(206) 325-3654; FAX (206) 328-4803
e-mail: innkeepr@gaslight-inn.com
www.gaslight-inn.com

This beautifully restored turn-of-the-century home is on Capitol Hill in downtown Seattle. Oak paneling, fireplaces, decks, and a heated in-ground pool make the Gaslight a very spe-

---

NOTES: Credit cards accepted: A MasterCard; B Visa; C American Express; D Discover; E Diner's Club; F Other; 2 Personal checks accepted; 3 Lunch available; 4 Dinner available; 5 Open all year; 6 Pets welcome;

Gaslight Inn

cial place for the guests, whether they are visiting for pleasure or business. Guests may choose among nine rooms and seven suites.

Hosts: Steve Bennett and Trevor Logan
Rooms: 16 (11 PB; 3 SB) $78-178
Continental Breakfast
Credit Cards: A, B, C
Notes: 2, 5, 7, 10, 11, 12, 13

Green Gables Guesthouse

1503 Second Avenue West, 98119
(206) 282-6863; FAX (206) 286-8525
www.greengablesseattle.com

A tranquil, in-city retreat on historic Queen Anne Hill. Walk to many restaurants, shops, the Space Needle, and performing arts. Built in 1904, this home is filled with antiques and family heirlooms. Spectacular box-beam ceilings and leaded-glass windows make for a truly vintage setting. A private garden leads to a 1906 Sears, Roebuck kit house, offering longer stays. Guests are served generous family-style breakfasts. Private telephones, fax, and TV/VCR.

Hosts: Reonn Rabon; David and Lila Chapman
Rooms: 8 (3 PB; 2 SB) $79-149
Houses: 2 @ 8 (6 PB; 2 SB)
Full Breakfast
Credit Cards: A, B, C, D
Notes: 2, 5, 7, 8, 9, 11

Hill House Bed & Breakfast

1113 East John Street, 98102
(206) 720-7161; (800) 720-7161
FAX (206) 323-0772
e-mail: hillhouse@seattlebnb.com

This 1903 Victorian is just minutes from downtown Seattle. Featuring superb gourmet breakfasts served on china and crystal and seven rooms, tastefully appointed with antiques. All rooms have queen-size beds with down comforters and cotton sheets, fresh flowers, handmade soaps, and terry robes. Walk to numerous shops and restaurants just blocks away. A 15-minute walk to downtown attractions, the convention center, and Pike Place Market. Close to transportation, off-street parking. AAA-rated three diamonds, *Best Places to Kiss in the Northwest*, Seattle Bed and Breakfast Association.

Hosts: Herman and Alea Foster
Rooms: 7 (5 PB; 2 SB) $80-165
Full Breakfast
Credit Cards: A, B, C, D, E
Notes: 4, 5, 7, 10, 12, 13, 14

Mildred's Bed & Breakfast

1202 15th Avenue East, 98112
(206) 325-6072

A traditional 1890 Victorian gem in an elegant style. Old-fashioned hospitality awaits. Red carpets, lace curtains, fireplace, grand piano, and wraparound porch. Across the street is the Seattle Asian Art Museum, flower conservatory, and historic 44-acre Volunteer Park. Electric trolley at the front door. Minutes to city center, freeways, and all points of interest.

Green Gables Guesthouse

---

7 No smoking; 8 Children welcome; 9 Social drinking allowed; 10 Tennis nearby; 11 Swimming nearby; 12 Golf nearby; 13 Skiing nearby; 14 May be booked through a travel agent; 15 Handicapped accessible.

Mildred's

Hosts: Mildred Sarver and Melodee Sarver
Rooms: 3 (PB) $85-130
Full Breakfast
Credit Cards: A, B, C
Notes: 2, 5, 7, 8, 9, 10, 11, 12, 14

Pacific Bed & Breakfast Agency

P.O. Box 46894, Seattle, 98146
(206) 439-7677; (800) 684-2932
FAX (206) 431-0932; e-mail: pacificb@nwlink.com
www.seattlebedandbreakfast.com

001. New Elegant Bed & Breakfast. Recently opened, Seattle's newest downtown luxury bed and breakfast featuring rooms with fireplaces, Jacuzzis, turndown service, afternoon tea and hors d'oeuvres, and full country breakfasts. It also offers exercise facilities, lap pool, 24-hour front desk, and morning newspapers. One block to the waterfront shops and restaurants and three blocks to Pike Place Market. $160-200.

002. New View Bed & Breakfast. Just opened! Five blocks north of the Pike Place Market and three blocks east of the Victoria Clipper Terminal. This location features 20 rooms, some with views of Elliott Bay or the Space Needle, all with private baths, some kitchen units, TV, telephones. Continental plus breakfast served. $100-135.

005. 1920s Hotel. Conveniently close to everything downtown, this hotel was completely renovated a few years ago but retains the original tiled bathrooms of the 1920s. Double, twin, or queen-size beds, private baths, TVs, telephones, and Continental breakfast. Smoking permitted in designated areas only. No pets. Children welcome. $74-99.

007. Cruising. Enjoy the life of the rich and famous aboard a 56-foot Chris Craft motor yacht. Guests will leave Seattle on Friday night, spend the night in Port Orchard. Saturday, cruise to the Scandinavian village of Poulsbo. Return to Seattle on Sunday afternoon. Breakfast and lunch aboard the boat are included in the price. Two private staterooms, huge salon with queen-size sleepersofa. The yacht is fully equipped. Well-behaved children are welcome. Some holiday weekends not available; moorage and docking fees are extra (approximately $18 per night). No smoking or pets. $600.

008. Room with a View. Enjoy the view of Puget Sound from private deck while having a Continental breakfast. The large guest room has a private bath, TV, and telephone. Small refrigerator for guests' convenience. $75.

009. Romantic Apartment with a View. Small unit in a triplex that has a great view looking over Elliott Bay to the southwest, ferry traffic, Vashon Island, Blake Island, Duwamish Head, and the tip of Bainbridge Island. Beautifully decorated studio apartment, full kitchen, private entrance, TV, telephone, and balcony. Hostess provides food for self-serve breakfast. Bus is at the front door and two and one-half miles to downtown. $90.

011. Historic 1904 Mansion. Laura Ashley prints and original artwork greet guests at this stunning bed and breakfast on Queen Anne Hill about five minutes' drive from downtown Seattle. Four bedrooms and one suite have either a private or shared bath. This home has

---

NOTES: Credit cards accepted: A MasterCard; B Visa; C American Express; D Discover; E Diner's Club; F Other; 2 Personal checks accepted; 3 Lunch available; 4 Dinner available; 5 Open all year; 6 Pets welcome;

been featured in many publications around the U.S. and is one that is unique. Full breakfast. Smoking permitted outside only. Inquire about accommodations for pets. Children welcome. $59-105.

021. Victorian Charm. A true Victorian, built in 1890, with stained-glass windows, fine period furniture, original woodwork, and an ambiance that is unequaled. All the little touches that make that special bed and breakfast experience for guests happen here. The breakfasts are legendary. Come and experience this personally. Three rooms with private baths. No smoking, pets, or children. $130.

023. Beacon Hill-View. Two miles south of downtown on Beacon Hill with Spanish decor and serving either American or Spanish-style breakfasts. Five rooms with private baths. Views out over the Kingdome, Elliott Bay, and the Olympic Mountains from the two west rooms and from the dining room. Inquire about accommodations for children. No pets. Smoking permitted outside only. $60-95.

024. Seward Park. With a view of Lake Washington, this suite has two bedrooms and can accommodate a family. The kitchenette is small but convenient for making snacks and lunches. The hostess offers a self-serve breakfast in the refrigerator. No smoking, pets, or children. $50-55.

025. Lake Washington View Home. A contemporary host home with a spectacular view from the exclusive guest room is one's accommodation in this south Seattle location. A large room with a king-size bed and four-piece private bath will wrap guests in luxury and give guests the privacy they want for that special day in Seattle. Full breakfast is served. No smoking, pets, or children. $100.

026. Park View. Up on a hill, this room with a view shows guests the Seattle skyline and sunsets over the Olympic Mountains. The suite has private bath, TV, private entrance, and private parking. Pick-up from the train or plane for an additional $7. Full breakfast. No pets. Children welcome. $49.

027. Betty's Place. This 1930s brick home is on a quiet cul-de-sac in the Magnolia area of the city. The upstairs room has an in-room TV and a private bath with a large shower. Breakfast is served in the dining room. Two-night minimum stay. No smoking or pets. Children welcome. $65.

028. Discovery Park Bed & Breakfast. Northwest of downtown Seattle, in a woodsy setting by a stream frequently visited by local wildlife, is this Tudor-style bed and breakfast featuring the master suite with king-size bed, fireplace, French doors opening to the balcony with a view of the forest and Puget Sound, private bath, dressing room, TV, telephone, and full gourmet breakfast. Also four other rooms with private or shared bath. Smoking permitted outside. No pets or children. $60-100.

029. Bed & Breakfast. On a quiet neighborhood street, this lovely Tudor host home offers six rooms, four with shared baths and two with full private bath. This home is perfect for a visiting family and does welcome children. Smoking permitted outside only. No pets. Full breakfast. $55-65.

030. Private Guest Suite. In the Ballard neighborhood, this garden-level suite features a living room, full kitchen, separate bedroom with queen-size bed and three-quarter bath, TV, and telephone. Some staple foods are provided for guests' convenience. Two-night minimum stay required. $65.

031. Crown Hill Suite. This host home offers guests a private suite with private entrance, queen-size bed, private bath, TV, telephone,

---

7 No smoking; 8 Children welcome; 9 Social drinking allowed; 10 Tennis nearby; 11 Swimming nearby; 12 Golf nearby; 13 Skiing nearby; 14 May be booked through a travel agent; 15 Handicapped accessible.

Pacific Bed & Breakfast Agency (cont.)

and a self-serve breakfast. Two-night minimum stay. No smoking, pets, or children. $85.

033. Cottage. West of the university and north of Lake Union is this stand-alone cottage beside the main house. On a quiet residential street within two blocks of the bus line. Features private bath, full kitchen, TV, telephone, and even a piano. Hostess provides food so that guests can make their own breakfast. Smoking permitted outside only. No pets. Children welcome. Two-night minimum stay. $65.

034. Mr. Monroe's 85th Street Guest House. For family or business groups nothing compares to the comfort and convenience of a fully equipped house with separate bedrooms, full kitchen, full bath, and staple foods for breakfast. This house has the capability of expanding to accommodate up to 16 persons with extra bedrooms and other half-bath. Children welcome and there is a crib available. Two color TVs, two VCRs, movies for everyone, toys for the children, and other pleasant surprises to make a stay here enjoyable. Fifteen dollars for each additional person. $95.

036. Luxury Suite. The four-room guest suite has a vaulted ceiling bedroom with a four-poster queen-size bed, private bath, kitchenette, and sitting room. Relax in the private sauna and enjoy the partially enclosed sunrise deck with outdoor shower. TV/VCR and library with books-on-tape are there for guests to enjoy. Continental breakfast. Smoking permitted outside only. No pets or children. $85-125.

038. Bed & Breakfast. Contemporary northwestern home on a wooded greenbelt area north of the university campus. Gracious hostess who will make guests' stay a delight. Two-night minimum. Full breakfast. No smoking, pets, or children. $75-85.

040. Alki Beach. If guests like to walk, jog, play at the beach, enjoy sunrises, sunsets, and spectacular views of the sound and downtown the Alki Beach area will fit their needs. This apartment is one-half block from the beach. Fully equipped and furnished two bedroom unit, full kitchen, TV, telephone, and food provided for self-serve breakfast. Three-day minimum. Ten dollars for each additional person. Weekly rates available. $100.

041. Beach Drive. On Beach Drive in west Seattle, one-half mile from Lincoln Park, is a small bed and breakfast with views of the sound, mountains, and ship traffic. One room features a queen-size bed, a ship's bunk bed/window seat, four-head European shower, TV, telephone. Two-night minimum stay. Full breakfast. No smoking or pets. Inquire about accommodations for children. $85.

043. Ultimate Luxury Suite. Beautiful suite featuring open-canopied bed, fireplace, large marbled Jacuzzi, double shower, bidet, terry-cloth robes, TV/VCR, sitting room with hand-painted ceiling, separate office, French doors opening to the balcony, views of the Olympic Mountains and Puget Sound, waterfront on a bluff with wooded trail leading to the beach. Full gourmet breakfast served. Smoking permitted outside only. Please, no pets or children. $180-195.

136. The 85th Street Apartments. Just behind the main guest house are five furnished apartments that can be available on short notice for last-minute lodging accomodations. All include private baths, telephones, and stocked kitchens so guests can prepare their own breakfast. $55-75.

137. Room with a View. On the west side of Queen Anne Hill is a condominium unit where the owner has converted the first floor into stu-

---

NOTES: Credit cards accepted: A MasterCard; B Visa; C American Express; D Discover; E Diner's Club; F Other; 2 Personal checks accepted; 3 Lunch available; 4 Dinner available; 5 Open all year; 6 Pets welcome;

dio apartment with a kitchen, queen bed, private bath, TV, and telephone. Hostess provides breakfast with gourmet touches for guests to prepare at their convenience. The view is spectacular, looking out over Elliott Bay, Pier 91, Magnolia Bluff and Marina, and westward to the Olympic Mountains. Two-and-a-half miles north of Pike Place Market. $75-85.

183. Luxury Yacht. Guests can rent a private yacht to visit the scenic Northwest or Alaska. Built in 1959, this 80-foot luxury yacht sleeps six overnight guests and can accommodate 30 day guests, with a crew of three. Three staterooms all have a private head with shower and the master stateroom has one each head for him and her. This yacht can also be available for dock-side lodging with Continental breakfast and is perfect for the visiting executive with conference space in the salon.

199. Bed & Breakfast at North Richmond Beach. With a breathtaking view of Puget Sound and the Olympic Mountains, this Bed and Breakfast consists of a large living room with fireplace, sound system, and cable TV. The kitchen is fully equipped, the two bedrooms each have queen-size beds, and there is a full bath. Enjoy the private courtyard and the fantastic sunsets. Call for availability. $85-120.

202. Residence Apartment. With a private entrance, this one-bedroom apartment is a great home for guests visiting Seattle. The hostess welcomes extended stays and offers an affordable rate. Queen-size bed, single bed, kitchen (stocked with breakfast foods and milk), fireplace, full bath, TV, telephone, and washer/dryer. The outside pool adds a special touch for those summer evenings.

208. Private Suite. A private suite now available on Capitol Hill with a private entrance giving guests complete privacy. A king-size bed, with TV nearby, a private bath, and sitting area add comfort, and a full kitchen, including washer and dryer, are there for convenience. Hostess provides food for self-serve Continental breakfast. In the sitting area there is an open-out sofa to accommodate extra guests. Adults only. No smoking. Two-night minimum. $125.

212. Lake View Inn. Just opened in October is this 180-room inn at the base of Capitol Hill and overlooking Lake Union. Some suites feature views of the seaplanes and boat activity on the lake, fireplaces and in-room spas. Complimentary breakfast, guest laundry facilities, and parking. In-room refrigerators, coffee makers, voice mail, microwaves, irons, and full size ironing boards. Two miles to downtown, walking distance to lakefront restaurants and attractions. Indoor and outdoor swimming pools and whirlpool tub. $99.

213. Lynnwood Suites. The brochure for this inn says they offer comfortable rooms and delightful breakfasts that turn a first-time visitor into a frequent guest. Add that there is a swimming pool, spa, and a well-equipped exercise facility and you can see why folks will return. A perfect option for guests whose business or pleasure travelling takes them just north of Seattle. Inquire about availability and rates.

214. Bed & Breakfast at Kenmore. High on the hills above Kenmore near the Burke-Gillman Trail for the hikers or bikers we have a recently added bed and breakfast offering three rooms with queen-size beds, one has a private bath with a whirlpool tub, and the other two rooms share a bath. The decor is a combination of contemporary and antique furnishings. Breakfast is prepared by the host and served in the dining room. Host knows various European tongues. $65.

217. Campus Suites. Almost on the University of Washington campus are these four suites for short- or long-term visits. Private entrances, living room with TV/VCR, separate bedrooms with queen-size beds and down comforters,

---

7 No smoking; 8 Children welcome; 9 Social drinking allowed; 10 Tennis nearby; 11 Swimming nearby; 12 Golf nearby; 13 Skiing nearby; 14 May be booked through a travel agent; 15 Handicapped accessible.

desks with private telephone lines and modem access, tastefully decorated with a mix of antiques and contemporary furnishings and a Continental breakfast basket. Rates vary with length of stay. $109.

Pioneer Square Hotel

77 Yesler Way, 98104
(206) 340-1234; FAX (206) 467-0707
e-mail: info@pioneersquare.com
www.pioneersquare.com

Seventy-five beautifully appointed rooms and suites with private, tiled bathrooms with brass fixtures, individual room climate controls, and color cable remote control TVs. Computer data port, guest room telephones. Board room meeting facility. Tratoria Michelli and al Bocalino restaurants adjacent to hotel. The Pioneer Square Saloon and Juice and Java coffee bar within the hotel building. Walk to the ferry terminal, Pike Place Market, the Kingdome, Amtrak station, and historic Pioneer Square's shopping, restaurants, nightlife, and tourist attractions.

Rooms: 75 (PB) $99-209
Continental Breakfast
Credit Cards: A, B, C, D, E, F
Notes: 3, 4, 5, 7, 8, 9, 10, 11, 12, 13, 14, 15

Queen Anne Hill Bed & Breakfast

1835 Seventh Avenue West, 98119
(206) 284-9779

Just minutes from downtown Seattle and historic Pike Place Market with many rooms with views of Olympic Mountains and Puget Sound. Set on a quiet, residential street, this hospitable bed and breakfast is the oldest family-run one in Seattle since 1981. During the blooming months, gardens surround the home. Come take in the friendliness of this bed and breakfast.

Rooms: 5 (3PB; 2 SB) $79-110
Credit Cards: A, B
Notes: 2, 5, 7, 8, 10, 11, 12, 13

Shafer-Baillie Mansion Bed & Breakfast

907 14th Avenue East, 98112
(206) 322-4654; (800) 922-4654
FAX (206) 329-4654; e-mail: smansion.sprynet.com
www.shaferbaillie.com

Fifteen thousand square feet of romance, mystery, and elegance. The Shafer-Baillie Mansion is the largest estate on historic Millionaire Row on Seattle's Capitol Hill. Offering 13 guest rooms and suites, most with private baths, telephones, TVs, and refrigerators. Antiques are abundant throughout the mansion, along with beautiful period furnishing in the bedrooms and day rooms. A romantic place for weddings, receptions, and dinners. Great English gardens lit at night to enjoy. Five minutes from downtown. One block from bus line. AAA-rated.

Hosts: Matthew, Erv, Mike, and Rick
Rooms: 13 (11 PB; 3 SB) $89-145
Continental Breakfast
Credit Cards: A, B
Notes: 2, 5, 7, 8, 9, 10, 11, 14

SEAVIEW

Pacific Bed & Breakfast Agency

P.O. Box 46894, Seattle, 98146
(206) 439-7677; (800) 684-2932
FAX (206) 431-0932; e-mail: pacificb@nwlink.com
www.seattlebedandbreakfast.com

111. Seaview/Long Beach Peninsula. A three- to four-hour car ride from Seattle will take guests to this lovely, often undiscovered area of the state where the Colombia River meets the Pacific Ocean. The best beachcombing, clam digging, salmon fishing, and relaxation can be found here. One of the few surviving Victorian inns in southwestern Washington. Each of the twelve rooms is furnished in antiques as a reminder of gentler times. An award-winning restaurant on the premises allows guests to experience innovative and regional cuisine based on local produce. $70-160.

The Shelburne Inn

The Shelburne Inn

P.O. Box 250, 98644-0250
(360) 642-2442; FAX (360) 642-8904

The Shelburne Inn, established in 1896, is a true American classic. It has offered travelers warm hospitality, wonderful food, and comfortable shelter for more than a century. A relaxing retreat for city dwellers, a sublime sanctuary for nature lovers, this country inn houses 15 thoughtfully appointed, antique-filled guest rooms, all with private baths, and most with a private deck.

Hosts: David Campiche and Laurie Anderson
Rooms: 15 (PB) $109-179
Full Breakfast
Credit Cards: A, B, C
Notes: 2, 3, 4, 5, 7, 8, 10, 12, 14, 15

SEQUIM

Glenna's Cuthrie Cottage Bed & Breakfast— Antique & Gift Shop

10083 Old Olympic Highway, 98382
(360) 681-4349; (800) 930-4349

Historic farmhouse viewing the snow-capped Olympic Mountains and the Olympic National Park. Hosts invite guests to come and visit them while exploring the area. Suites with private baths and private outside entrance, cable TV, and RV and boat parking. Enjoy the friendly service, hot tub under the stars,

gourmet breakfast. Cooking classes, fax, and bikes available. With the mild winters, golf and other sports are enjoyed year-round. Great shopping and colorful attractions nearby.

Rooms: 4 (PB) $60-100
Full Breakfast
Credit Cards: A, B, C, D
Notes: 5, 7, 8, 9, 10, 11, 12, 13, 14, 15

Pacific Bed & Breakfast Agency

P.O. Box 46894, Seattle, 98146
(206) 439-7677; (800) 684-2932
FAX (206) 431-9267; e-mail: pacificb@nwlink.com
www.seattlebedandbreakfast.com

102. A 100-Year-Old Victorian. Sequim is called "the Banana Belt" of the Northwest, known for its good weather, protected by the Olympic Mountains. The inn was built at the turn of the century and the original decor remains. The five guest rooms have queen- or king-size beds and offer private or shared bath accommodations. Most rooms have TV/VCRs. Breakfast is served in the dining room. $85-110.

103. Craftsman-style. Set in the rural quiet north of Sequim, this bed and breakfast is tastefully decorated with English antiques in comfortable elegance. Three rooms have queen-size beds, lace curtains, and a peek-a-boo view of the Strait of Juan de Fuca. Breakfast is served at 8:30 A.M. and the menu is varied, with egg and sausage main dishes, fruit, breads, coffee, tea, and dessert. Hot beverages and snacks are offered in the evening. $85-95.

178. Golf and Lodging in Sunny Sequim. Stay in sunny Sequim with affordable rates starting at $75 for two to $100 for deluxe suites. Golf, lodging, and meal packages start at $80 per person double occupancy for two nights lodging, two rounds of golf, and two food vouchers in the winter, to $121 in the summer. Restaurants, lounge, and putting course on premises.

---

7 No smoking; 8 Children welcome; 9 Social drinking allowed; 10 Tennis nearby; 11 Swimming nearby; 12 Golf nearby; 13 Skiing nearby; 14 May be booked through a travel agent; 15 Handicapped accessible.

SHELTON

Twin River Ranch Bed & Breakfast

5730 Highway 3, 98584
(360) 426-1023

A 1915 manor house on the Olympic Peninsula. Beamed ceilings, stone fireplace, antiques. Granny rooms tucked under eaves overlooking the garden and stream. One hundred forty acres of pasture surrounded by old-growth trees. Puget Sound laps the marsh, and gulls, blue heron, and eagles circle overhead in season. By reservation only. No smoking upstairs.

Hosts: Phlorence and Ted Rohde
Rooms: 2 (SB) $59
Full Breakfast
Credit Cards: A, B
Notes: 2, 12

SNOQUALMIE

Pacific Bed & Breakfast Agency

P.O. Box 46894, Seattle, 98146
(206) 439-7677; (800) 684-2932
FAX (206) 431-0932; e-mail: pacificb@nwlink.com
www.seattlebedandbreakfast.com

139. Historic Inn at Snoqualmie Falls. Overlooking the spectacular Snoqualmie Falls, the lodge offers a unique combination of comfort, privacy, and style, in an elegant setting. Each room has a woodburning fireplace and a whirlpool tub, and guests may request breakfast to be brought to their rooms from the famous, world-class restaurant. Guests looking for quiet refuge with charm and beauty will be pleasantly gratified. Seasonal rates. $349-749.

198. Private Luxury Chateau at Snoqualmie Falls. This lovely Swiss hideaway includes six bedrooms on three floors, four baths (one with whirlpool tub, marble floors, and gold fixtures), three fireplaces, and many other special accommodations for a stay in the mountains.

There is a fully equipped kitchen, all the housewares and table service for 12, all the linens, living room, rec room, and family room. Decks, gazebo, barbeque area, TVs, VCRs, stereos, and laundry. Well suited for an unforgettable family reunion. One-hour drive from Seattle. Four ski resorts within one mile. Two-night minimum. Children welcome. Call for pricing and availability.

SOUTH BEND

The Russell House

902 East Water Street, P.O. Box F, 98586
(360) 875-6487; (888) 484-6907
e-mail: srown@willapabay.org

A Queen Anne Victorian bed and breakfast, built in 1891. Furnished and decorated elegantly with antiques. Enjoy a lavish breakfast served in the dining room. Birds and deer are plentiful. Lots of history in the town. John Russell is the architect of this beautiful building and several others in town. One hour from beach, one hour from shopping mall. No smoking inside.

Hosts: Sylvia and Steve Rowan
Rooms: 3 (PB) $65-75
Full Breakfast
Credit Cards: A, B, C, D, E, F
Notes: 2, 3, 4, 5, 6, 8, 9, 12, 14

SOUTH CLE ELUM

The Iron Horse Inn Bed & Breakfast

526 Marie Avenue, P.O. Box 629, 98943
(509) 674-5939

Former 1909 Milwaukee Railroad crew hotel, now offering 12 bright and airy rooms ranging from economical to exquisite, including two genuine cabooses and a bridal suite with jetted tub. Now in the national

---

NOTES: Credit cards accepted: A MasterCard; B Visa; C American Express; D Discover; E Diner's Club; F Other; 2 Personal checks accepted; 3 Lunch available; 4 Dinner available; 5 Open all year; 6 Pets welcome;

historic register, the inn has a museum-like atmosphere with an extensive collection of railroad memorabilia and artifacts. Nestled in the Cascade Mountain foothills, the Iron Horse is close to cross-country skiing, hiking, biking, rafting, fishing, horseback riding, and also fine dining. Only 90 minutes east of Seattle.

Hosts: Mary and Doug Pittis
Rooms: 12 (6 PB; 6 SB) $50-125
Full Breakfast
Credit Cards: A, B
Notes: 2, 5, 7, 8, 9, 12, 13, 14

SPOKANE

Angelica's Bed & Breakfast

West 1321 Ninth Avenue, 99204
(509) 624-5598; (800) 987-0053
www.angelicasbb.com

Romantic 1907 Craftsman mansion. Listed in the Local and National Register of Historical Places. Elegant atmosphere. Peaceful setting. Queen-size beds. Down comforters. Luxurious linens. Private baths. Savor freshly ground gourmet coffee and assorted teas in the sunroom. Full breakfast served in the dining room or outside on the veranda. Continental breakfast served in privacy of room. Close to dining, shopping, museum, Spokane arena, Spokane Falls, Riverfront Park, golf, and biking trails.

Hosts: Lynette and Arielle White
Rooms: 4 (2 PB; 2 SB) $85-115
Full Breakfast
Credit Cards: A, B
Notes: 2, 5, 7, 12, 13, 14

Angelica's

The Fotheringham House

The Fotheringham House

2128 West Second Avenue, 99204
(509) 838-1891; FAX (509) 838-1807
e-mail: innkeeper@fotheringham.net
www.fotheringham.net

This 1891 Victorian home of the city's first mayor features beautiful hand-carved woodwork, tin ceilings, and an open, curved staircase. The recent award-winning restoration of the exterior and grounds returns this inn to its rightful place as one of the finest homes in historic Browne's Addition. Period furniture, wraparound porch, player piano, evening tea, and nearby antique shops will delight all guests. Museum and excellent restaurants are within walking distance.

Hosts: Jackie and Graham Johnson
Rooms: 4 (1 PB; 3 SB) $80-95
Full Breakfast
Credit Cards: A, B, C, D
Notes: 2, 5, 7, 9, 10, 12, 13, 14

Marianna Stoltz House

East 427 Indiana, 99207
(509) 483-4316; (800) 978-6587
FAX (509) 483-6773
www.aimcomm.com/stoltzhouse

Established in 1987, the Marianna Stoltz House has earned a reputation for pampering its guests. This 1908 historic landmark is beautifully decorated. Private baths with a tub for two, air conditioning, cable TV, secure on-site

---

7 No smoking; 8 Children welcome; 9 Social drinking allowed; 10 Tennis nearby; 11 Swimming nearby; 12 Golf nearby; 13 Skiing nearby; 14 May be booked through a travel agent; 15 Handicapped accessible.

Marianna Stoltz House

parking, and a hearty breakfast each morning are just a few of the amenities that await guests. Minutes from I-90, downtown, Spokane Arena, Opera House, Convention Center, Centennial Trail, and Gonzaga University.

Host: Phyllis Maguire
Rooms: 4 (2 PB; 2 SB) $69-99
Full Breakfast
Credit Cards: A, B, C, D
Notes: 2, 5, 7, 9, 10, 11, 12, 13, 14

Pacific Bed & Breakfast Agency

P.O. Box 46894, Seattle, 98146
(206) 439-7677; (800) 684-2932
FAX (206) 431-0932; e-mail: pacificb@nwlink.com
www.seattlebedandbreakfast.com

156. Victorian Inn. Here is a romantic 1907 Craftsman style mansion that is listed on the National Register of Historic Places. Queen-size beds, down comforters, and luxurious linens give guests a sense of calm and quiet nights away from their busy schedule. Private or shared bath accommodations are offered. Breakfast is served in the dining room at your private table or outside on the veranda.

SUNNYSIDE

Sunnyside Inn Bed & Breakfast

804 East Edison Avenue, 98944
(509) 839-5557; (800) 221-4195

In the heart of Washington wine country with more than 20 wineries and 300 days of sunshine. Seven of the rooms have in-room double Jacuzzis. All rooms have cable TVs, telephones, and private baths. A full country breakfast is served as well as popcorn, cookies, and ice cream for snacks. Come enjoy a stay that is a cut above the common experience.

Hosts: Karen and Donavon Vlieger
Rooms: 10 (PB) $50-90
Full Breakfast
Credit Cards: A, B, C, D
Notes: 2, 5, 7, 8, 9, 10, 11, 12, 14

TACOMA

Commencement Bay Bed & Breakfast

3312 North Union Avenue, 98407
(253) 752-8175; FAX (253) 759-4025
e-mail: greatviews@aol.com
www.bestinns.net/sa/wa/cb.html

From its elevated perch above the scenic waterfront, this stately Colonial home affords breathtaking views of Mount Rainier, Puget Sound, and the Cascades. Three elegantly appointed guest  rooms, all with private baths, TVs, VCRs, and telephones with data ports. A variety of common areas offer a fireplace, hot tub, game room, and office area for business travelers. Full breakfasts and gourmet coffees daily. Exercise room and bikes available. Ten minutes to state historical museum. Special rates for winter. AAA three-diamond-rated and Mobil-approved. Featured on NBC's *Evening Magazine* and in *Northwest Best Places*, 11th edition. Children over 12 welcome.

NOTES: Credit cards accepted: A MasterCard; B Visa; C American Express; D Discover; E Diner's Club; F Other; 2 Personal checks accepted; 3 Lunch available; 4 Dinner available; 5 Open all year; 6 Pets welcome;

Hosts: Bill and Sharon Kaufmann
Rooms: 3 (PB) $85-125
Full Breakfast
Credit Cards: A, B, C, D
Notes: 2, 5, 7, 9, 10, 11, 12, 14

A Greater Tacoma Bed & Breakfast Reservation Service

3312 North Union Avenue, 98407
(253) 759-4088; (800) 406-4088
FAX (253) 759-4025
e-mail: reservations@tacoma-inns.org
www.tacoma-inns.org

F. The Lafayette House. A Colonial home with fabulous views and a private deck. One room with king-size bed, private bath, TV/VCR, antiques. Walk to nearby beaches. Full breakfast. $125.

G. Sally's Bear Tree Cottage. A brass bed and crackling fireplace make this secluded private cottage in the woods warm and inviting. Private bath, small kitchen area with refrigerator and microwave. Golf nearby. Continental breakfast. $85.

H. Thornewood Castle Bed & Breakfast. On American Lake and has five large elegant suites all with private baths—some with fireplaces and whirlpool bath. Enjoy lovely sunken English gardens, a stroll on the beach or the romantic sunsets. WBBG. Full breakfast. $150-200.

I. Fern Hill Bed & Breakfast. A cute farmhouse furnished with period antiques and two theme guest rooms, both with queen bed, shared bath, and TV. Outdoor hot tub, private grotto, lovely gardens. Walk to antique shops and espresso bar. Continental breakfast. $75.

J. Oakes Street Barn Bed and Breakfast. This Dutch Colonial home offers country decor and great hospitality. Two bedrooms with private or shared baths, a large sitting area with TV/VCR, and an outdoor hot tub. Close to shopping. Full breakfast. $65.

K. Hillcrest Bed & Breakfast. A modern home offering great Mount Rainier views. Two rooms with private baths, double or twin beds. Full breakfast. $75.

L. Blue Willow Cottage. Enjoy country charm minutes from the university area or downtown. Main floor suite with private bath and private garden deck, or upstairs room with shared bath. Full breakfast. $75-95.

M. Plum Duff House Bed and Breakfast. A warm and charming 1901 house near downtown in the historic Stadium District. Three large rooms with private baths, TVs, and telephones. Afternoon tea, evening desserts, fax/modem available. Full breakfast. $80-100.

N. Commencement Bay Bed and Breakfast. This award-winning Colonial home features elegant decor, dramatic bay and mountain views, hot tub, fireplace, game and exercise rooms, three rooms, all with bay views, private baths, telephones, TVs, and VCRs. Business guest service. Full breakfast. $80-125.

Keenan House

2610 North Warner, 98407
(206) 752-0702

Clean, comfortable, attractive rooms. Complimentary full breakfast. Seven blocks from University of Puget Sound. Ten minutes from Point Defiance Park. Five minutes from Commencement Bay with a fine selection of restaurants. Just off I-5 and near Highway 16.

Host: Lenore Keenan
Room: 4 (2 PB; 2 SB) $60-70
Full Breakfast
Credit Cards: A, B
Notes: 2, 5, 7, 8, 9, 10, 12, 14

---

7 No smoking; 8 Children welcome; 9 Social drinking allowed; 10 Tennis nearby; 11 Swimming nearby; 12 Golf nearby; 13 Skiing nearby; 14 May be booked through a travel agent; 15 Handicapped accessible.

Pacific Bed & Breakfast Agency

P.O. Box 46894, Seattle, 98146
(206) 439-7677; (800) 684-2932
FAX (206) 431-0932; e-mail: pacificb@nwlink.com
www.seattlebedandbreakfast.com

057. Victorian Guest Houses. Ten minutes from Point Defiance Park and near the University of Puget Sound, on a tree-lined street, these two Victorian host homes offer a variety of rooms with shared or private baths. Decorated with comfortable country-style furnishings. Guests will find a relaxed atmosphere. Full breakfast. $45-65.

058. On the national registry. With echoes of the drama of the historical Pantages Theatre, the master suite of this true Victorian home has views of the harbor from the bay window, queen-size bed, and private bath with Jacuzzi. The second suite also features a fireplace. The Garden Room has a queen-size bed and private bath with claw-foot tub. A two-story cottage is also available with two suites, each with private bath, queen-size bed, and a small kitchenette. $85-200.

059. Secluded Cottage. For that cozy, comfortable place of one's own for a getaway, consider this small cottage in a wooded setting. The cottage has a queen-size bed, private bath with sunken tub, kitchenette, and Swedish fireplace. Breakfast is self-serve. $85.

TOLEDO

Pacific Bed & Breakfast Agency

P.O. Box 46894, Seattle, 98146
(206) 439-7677; (800) 684-2932
FAX (206) 431-0932; e-mail: pacificb@nwlink.com
www.seattlebedandbreakfast.com

112. The Farm. Nestled in the foothills of Mount St. Helens, this 80-acre farm is home to a herd of cashmere goats, livestock, guard dogs, horses, geese, ducks, and chickens. The farm borders Salmon Creek where guests can find arrowheads, agates, and copperlight. The host and hostess maintain this working farm and the chef prepares a memorable farm breakfast to start the day off right. Five guest rooms, all with private baths with showers. $85.

VASHON ISLAND

A Greater Tacoma Bed & Breakfast

3312 North Union Avenue, 98407
(253) 759-4088; (800) 406-4088
FAX (253) 759-4025
e-mail: reservations@tacoma-inns.org
e-mail: tacomabnbs@aol.com
www.tacoma-inns.org

P. Angels of the Sea Bed & Breakfast. Guests are in heaven at this 1917 country church bed and breakfast. Three rooms, queen-size or twin beds, private or shared baths, one with Jacuzzi. Enjoy harp music during breakfast by the hostess. TV/VCR, golf and pool available. Children welcome. WBBG. Full breakfast. $75-125.

Pacific Bed & Breakfast Agency

P.O. Box 46894, Seattle, 98146
(206) 439-7677; (800) 684-2932
FAX (206) 431-0932; e-mail: pacificb@nwlink.com
www.seattlebedandbreakfast.com

216. Emerald Cottage. Take a short ferry ride from Seattle, Tacoma, or the Peninsula to this private cabin on Vashon Island. The island offers scenic beaches and parks as well as numerous art galleries, studios, antique stores, and restaurants. Features include green canopied bed, claw-foot tub, gas stove fireplace, skylights, surround-sound music system, TV/VCR, kitchenette, artist-designed furniture, and the meadow view with an occasional deer as visitor. Children welcome to the queen-size hideaway bed in the living room. No smoking. Pets allowed with prior approval and damage deposit. $100.

NOTES: Credit cards accepted: A MasterCard; B Visa; C American Express; D Discover; E Diner's Club; F Other; 2 Personal checks accepted; 3 Lunch available; 4 Dinner available; 5 Open all year; 6 Pets welcome;

WESTPORT

Pacific Bed & Breakfast Agency

P.O. Box 46894, Seattle, 98146
(206) 439-7677; (800) 684-2932
FAX (206) 431-0932; e-mail: pacificb@nwlink.com
www.seattlebedandbreakfast.com

106. Historic Mansion. Westport is a lovely town on the ocean where the salmon fishing is great. Stay in a historic mansion built in 1898 on eight acres two blocks from the ocean. Choose from five bedrooms in the inn, all with private baths, or choose one of five unique cottages (no breakfasts for cottage guests). Robert Kennedy and his party stayed here. Lace curtains, brass queen-size beds, bay windows, and fine period furnishings make this inn a popular choice for a getaway. Cottages can accommodate larger groups of up to 14 people. Hot tub, barbeque and picnic areas, volleyball, and badminton. $75.

WHITE SALMON

Llama Ranch Bed & Breakfast

1980 Highway 141, 98672
(509) 395-2786; (877) 800-LAMA

This inn stands between two snow-capped mountains. The hosts offer hands-on experience with llamas, including guided llama walks through the woods. Get better acquainted with these beautiful, intelligent animals. The bedrooms have queen-size beds and spectacular views. Nearby are refreshing waterfalls and natural lava bridges. Other activities in the area include white-water rafting, golf, plane trips over Mount St. Helens, fishing, hunting, hiking, cave exploration, and huckleberry picking. Cross-country skiing and snowmobiling in the winter. Close to nice restaurants.

Hosts: Jerry Stone and Dee Kern
Rooms: 7 (2 PB; 5 SB) $79-99
Full Breakfast
Credit Cards: A, B, C, D
Notes: 2, 5, 6, 7, 8, 9, 12, 13

WINTHROP

Dammann's Bed & Breakfast

716 Highway 20, 98862
(509) 996-2484

Two antique-filled guest rooms are on the banks of the Methow River. Winthrop has been westernized and all buildings look old. Also board sidewalks. It is a real tourist attraction. The valley is a recreation paradise for photography, seasonal hunting, fishing, hiking, camping, and skiing. Eight lakes within six to eight miles; right at the foot of the Cascade Mountains.

Hosts: Hank and Jean Dammann
Rooms: 2 (PB) $55
Continental Breakfast
Credit Cards: None
Notes: 2, 7, 9, 10, 11, 12, 13

WOODINVILLE

A Big Red Barn Bed & Breakfast

16560 140th Place NE, 98072
(425) 806-4646; FAX (425) 488-7446
www.abigredbarnbandb.com

Enjoy a relaxed "country" atmosphere, close to Seattle and area attractions. This pristine bed and breakfast was, indeed, a barn built in 1939 in the Gothic Gambrel style. The stunning architecture lent naturally to convert this massive 40-x-80-foot barn into a luxurious, rustic dwelling. The former hayloft boasts a 35-x-40-foot living room with a 17-foot ceiling, a massive wood-burning fireplace, and a 12-foot picture window. Decorated with country themes, folk art and Native American artwork. Full farm breakfast served. Telephone, fax, TV/VCR, whirlpool tub. Offering longer stays.

Hosts: David and Lila Chapman
Rooms: 6 (5PB; 1 SB) $69-139
Houses: 2 @ 6 (4 PB; 1 SB; 1 PB)
Full Breakfast
Credit Cards: A, B, C
Notes: 2, 5, 7, 8, 9, 10, 11, 12

---

7 No smoking; 8 Children welcome; 9 Social drinking allowed; 10 Tennis nearby; 11 Swimming nearby; 12 Golf nearby; 13 Skiing nearby; 14 May be booked through a travel agent; 15 Handicapped accessible.

WOODLAND

Grandma's House

4551 Lewis River Road, 98674-9305
(360) 225-7002; e-mail: gmasbb@pacifier.com

Bed and breakfast featuring country charm in a three-bedroom 1917 farmhouse on 35 secluded acres overlooking the north fork of the Lewis River. Relax on the deck and view the river and occasional deer and eagle. Private boat launch. Salmon and steelhead fishing. Eight miles east of Woodland and I-5 and 20 miles west of Cougar on Highway 503, scenic route to Mount St. Helen's National Monument. Full country breakfast.

Hosts: Warren and Louise Moir
Rooms: 2 (SB) $55-64
Full Breakfast
Credit Cards: A, B
Notes: 2, 5, 7, 8, 9, 10, 11, 12

YAKIMA

Birchfield Manor Country Inn

2018 Birchfield Road, 98902
(509) 452-1960; (800) 375-3420

Enjoy a relaxing getaway with dinners prepared by professional chef/owners served in the casual, warm atmosphere of a gracious home. Park-like grounds surround the outdoor pool. Some rooms with fireplace, two-person tub, and panoramic views. Hosts can personalize guests' tour of local wineries, direct them to roadside stands for fresh fruit and vegetables, or establish tee times at the best golf courses. Mobil and AAA three-diamond-rated.

Hosts: Masset Family and Tim Newbury
Rooms: 11 (PB) $95-195
Full Breakfast
Credit Cards: A, B, C, E
Notes: 2, 4, 5, 7, 9, 11, 12, 14, 15

NOTES: Credit cards accepted: A MasterCard; B Visa; C American Express; D Discover; E Diner's Club; F Other; 2 Personal checks accepted; 3 Lunch available; 4 Dinner available; 5 Open all year; 6 Pets welcome;

Wyoming

BIG HORN

Spahn's Bighorn Mountain Bed and Breakfast

Box 579, 82833
(307) 674-8150

Towering log home and secluded guest cabins on the mountainside in whispering pines. Borders one million acres of public forest with deer and moose. Gracious mountain breakfast served on the deck with binoculars to enjoy the 100-mile view. Owner was a Yellowstone ranger. Just 15 minutes from Sheridan and I-90. Wildlife trips. Mobil- and AAA-approved: three-diamond rating.

Hosts: Ron and Bobbie Spahn
Rooms: 4 (PB) $80-135
Full Breakfast
Credit Cards: A, B
Notes: 4, 5, 7, 8, 9

CHEYENNE

The Howdy Pardner

1920 Tranquility Road, 82009
(307) 634-6493; FAX (307) 634-2822
e-mail: janp9999@aol.com
www.cruising-america.com/howdy.html

Western atmosphere with a Big Wyoming Welcome. A ranch-style home on 10 acres in a serene country setting perched high on a hill with spectacular views all around that invite walkabouts. Only 10 minutes from Frontier Park, Interstates 25 and 80, and the airport. All rooms have queen-size beds, private baths, telephones, and TV/VCR. Afternoon refreshments await guests' arrival, and a full gourmet country breakfast will start guests off the next morning in the true western tradition. Gather in the evening to gaze at the ever-changing sunset. Join other guests at a game of pool or Ping Pong. Belly-up to the bar on tractor-seat stools. Tour the sheepherder's wagon, sit by the Lucky Horseshoe Pond. Children and pets welcome. Resident cat provides companionship at no additional charge.

Hostess: Jan Peterson
Rooms: 3 (PB) $65-105
Full Breakfast
Credit Cards: A, B
Notes: 2, 5, 6, 7, 8, 9, 10, 11, 12, 14

The Howdy Pardner

7 No smoking; 8 Children welcome; 9 Social drinking allowed; 10 Tennis nearby; 11 Swimming nearby; 12 Golf nearby; 13 Skiing nearby; 14 May be booked through a travel agent; 15 Handicapped accessible.

Wyoming

Nagel Warren Mansion

Nagle Warren Mansion Bed and Breakfast

222 East 17th Street, 82001
(307) 637-3333; (800) 811-2610
FAX (307) 638-6835

This 1888 national historic register mansion has been newly restored to its original glory with all of today's necessities. On the quiet edge of downtown, it is convenient to all of Cheyenne, especially for business people. Public areas include parlor, sitting room, library, conference rooms, workout room, and the tower. All rooms are spacious and individually appointed. Luxuriate in the Victorian elegance while exploring the public spaces and private places.

Hosts: Jim and Jacquie Osterfoss
Rooms: 12 (PB) $85-125
Full Breakfast
Credit Cards: A, B, C
Notes: 2, 5, 7, 9, 10, 12, 14, 15

CHEYENNE (LARAMIE)

A. Drummond's Ranch Bed and Breakfast

399 Happy Jack Road, State Highway 210, 82007
(307) 634-6042 (phone/FAX)
e-mail: adrummond@juno.com

Quiet, gracious retreat on 120 acres; 20 minutes to Cheyenne or Laramie, by national forest. Mountain bike, hike, rock climb, llama trek, cross-country ski, or relax. Bring own horse and train at 7,600 feet. Boarding for horses and pets in transit. "Adventure at your pace" packages. Private outdoor Jacuzzis. Suite with fireplace, sauna, private deck with Jacuzzi, and pantry closet kitchen. Privacy with personalized attention. Featured in *Country Inns* and *Sunset* magazines. Superb breakfast, fine dining. Beverages, fresh fruit, and homemade snacks always available. AAA- and Mobil-approved. Reservations required. Partially handicapped accessible.

Host: Taydie Drummond
Rooms: 4 (2 PB; 2 SB) $65-175
Full Breakfast
Credit Cards: A, B, D
Notes: 2, 3, 4, 5, 6, 7, 8, 9, 12, 13, 14

CODY

Lockhart Bed & Breakfast Inn

109 West Yellowstone Avenue, 82414
(307) 587-6074; (800) 377-7255
FAX (307) 587-8644
e-mail: cbaldwin@wyoming.com
www.coltorbay.com/lockhart

Historic home overlooking Shoshone River. Private baths, TV, telephone, full breakfsat, Victorian decor, parlor with piano, games, dining with "always available" beverages. "Cozy, just like grandma's house."

Hosts: Don and Cindy Kraemer
Rooms: 7 (PB) $68
Full Breakfast
Credit Cards: A, B, D, E
Notes: 2, 3, 7, 8, 9, 10, 11, 12, 13, 14, 15

EVANSTON

Pine Gables Inn Bed and Breakfast

1049 Center Street, 82930
(307) 789-2069; (800) 789-2069

NOTES: Credit cards accepted: A MasterCard; B Visa; C American Express; D Discover; E Diner's Club; F Other; 2 Personal checks accepted; 3 Lunch available; 4 Dinner available; 5 Open all year; 6 Pets welcome; 7 No smoking; 8 Children welcome; 9 Social drinking allowed; 10 Tennis nearby; 11 Swimming nearby; 12 Golf nearby; 13 Skiing nearby; 14 May be booked through a travel agent; 15 Handicapped accessible.

Pine Gables Inn

Framed by majestic pine trees, historic Pine Gables was built in 1883 and is an ideal location for a romantic getaway, celebration, or travel. This Eastlake Victorian-style mansion offers four lovely guest rooms, dining room, and formal parlor with hand-painted murals and walls. Relax in newly redecorated antique-filled rooms. Cross-country skiing in winter; hiking and fishing in the summer. Private baths, color TVs, and telephones in all rooms. A full homemade breakfast is served. Visit soon.

Hosts: Nephi and Ruby Jensen
Rooms: 4 (PB) $50-80
Full Breakfast
Credit Cards: A, B, C, D
Notes: 2, 5, 7, 10, 11, 12, 13, 14

JACKSON

The Alpine House

285 North Glenwood, Box 20245, 83001
(307) 739-1570; (800) 753-1421
FAX (307) 734-2850
e-mail: alpinhouse@compuserve.com

The Alpine House is a little bit of Scandinavia in the heart of Jackson Hole. It is a new timber-frame lodge that is bright and airy. Light and spotless guest rooms, each with its own private bath, await guests' arrival. Each of the seven rooms has a private balcony with French doors leading to it, heated tile floors, down comforters, plush towels, and simple country antique furniture. A full healthy homemade breakfast served each morning. Brand new hot tub in 1999.

Hosts: Hans and Nancy Johnstone
Rooms: 7 (PB) $80-120
Full Breakfast
Credit Cards: A, B
Notes: 2, 5, 7, 9, 10, 11, 12, 13, 14, 15

Bentwood Bed & Breakfast

4250 Raven Haven Road, P. O. Box 561, 83001
(307) 739-1411; FAX (307) 739-2453
e-mail: bentwood@blissnet.com

In the heart of a cottonwood grove, just casts from the Snake River lies Bentwood, a magnificent and inviting log lodge. Enjoy the rustic elegance of one of the five beautifully detailed guest rooms, each equipped with a fireplace, deck, and full bath with Jacuzzi. Named one of the "top ten inns of the year" (*Country Inns* magazine, February 1998) and featured in *Log Home Living* (January 1999), Bentwood offers its guests a comfortable and casual vacation experience.

Hosts: Nell and Bill Fay
Rooms: 5 (PB) $145-285
Full Breakfast
Credit Cards: A, B, C, D
Notes: 2, 5, 7, 8, 9, 10, 11, 12, 13, 14, 15

The Huff House Inn Bed & Breakfast

240 East Deloney, P.O. Box 1189, 83001
(307) 733-4164; FAX (307) 739-9091
e-mail: huffhousebnb@blissnet.com
http: //jacksonwyomingbnb.com

Innkeepers Jackie and Weldon Richardson have dedicated themselves to retaining the characteristics that make this lovely home special. Old-fashioned kitchen cupboards with pull-out flour bins, beveled-glass doors, original light fixtures, fine antiques, and pedestal sinks. At the same time, they have added the

---

NOTES: Credit cards accepted: A MasterCard; B Visa; C American Express; D Discover; E Diner's Club; F Other; 2 Personal checks accepted; 3 Lunch available; 4 Dinner available; 5 Open all year; 6 Pets welcome;

amenities that bed and breakfast guests appreciate, such as whirlpool tubs, in-room telephones, TVs, and outdoor hot tub.

Hosts: Jackie and Weldon Richardson
Rooms: 9 (PB) $109-199
Full Breakfast
Credit Cards: A, B, D
Notes: 2, 5, 7, 8, 9, 10, 11, 12, 13, 14

The Wildflower Inn

P.O. Box 11000, 83002
(307) 733-4710

A lovely log home with five sunny guest rooms, this bed and breakfast is on three acres of land only 5 minutes from the Jackson Hole ski area, 10 minutes from the town of Jackson, and 15 minutes from Grand Teton.

Hosts: Ken and Sherrie Jern
Rooms: 5 (PB) $140-260
Full Breakfast
Credit Cards: A, B
Notes: 2, 5, 7, 8, 9, 10, 11, 12, 13, 14

The Wildflower Inn

JACKSON HOLE

Teton Tree House

6175 Heck of a Hill Road, Box 550, 83014-0550
(307) 733-3233

A gem of an inn that is way out on a mountainside in the quiet and solitude and only 3/4 mile from town. Add the opportunity to retreat up 95 steps and one finds guests and innkeepers

Teton Tree House

who are vibrant and adventuresome and funny and certainly worth spending time with. "Please help us celebrate our 15th year providing exceptional hospitality." Featured in *New York Times* Travel Section, *National Geographic Traveler*, *Country Inns* magazine, and *Snow Country*. Children 10 and older welcome.

Host: Denny Becker
Rooms: 6 (PB) $125-180
Full Breakfast
Credit Cards: A, B, D
Notes: 2, 5, 7, 9, 10, 11, 12, 13, 14

LARAMIE

Annie Moore's Guest House

819 University Avenue, 82072
(307) 721-4177; (800) 552-8992

Restored Princess Anne home with three individually decorated guest rooms with sinks. Large, sunny common living rooms, second-story sun deck. Across the street from the University of Wyoming; two blocks from the Laramie Plains Museum; six blocks from downtown shops, galleries, and restaurants. Just 15 minutes from skiing, camping, biking, and fishing in uncrowded wilderness areas.

---

7 No smoking; 8 Children welcome; 9 Social drinking allowed; 10 Tennis nearby; 11 Swimming nearby; 12 Golf nearby; 13 Skiing nearby; 14 May be booked through a travel agent; 15 Handicapped accessible.

Annie Moore's Guest House

Hosts: Ann Acuff and Joe Bundy
Rooms: 3 (SB) $55-72
Continental Breakfast
Credit Cards: A, B, C, D
Notes: 2, 5, 7, 9, 12, 13

Vee Bar Guest Ranch

2091 State Highway 130, 82070
(307) 745-7036; (800) 483-3227
FAX (307) 745-7433

The historic Vee Bar Guest Ranch is nestled in the shadows of the beautiful Snowy Range mountains where the Little Laramie River winds its way through the Centennial Valley. The riverside cabins have decks, gas fireplaces, access to the hot tub, and are decorated in country-western comfort. Guests at the Vee Bar enjoy a wonderful blend of western tradition, contemporary comfort, and personal, old-fashioned service. Activities are varied and there is something for everyone on this year-round ranch.

Hosts: Jim "Lefty" and Carla Cole (owners)
Rooms: 9 (PB) $100-150
Full Breakfast
Credit Cards: A, B
Notes: 2, 4, 5, 7, 8, 9, 12, 13, 14, 15

NEWCASTLE

EVA—Great Spirit Ranch Bed and Breakfast

1262 Beaver Creek Road, 82701
(307) 746-2537; e-mail: rspilln@trib.com

Secluded log home on historic Cheyenne/Deadwood stagecoach route. On 525 acres of scenic grounds in the beautiful Black Hills. Roomy bedrooms, private baths, full country breakfast. Great room with fireplace, movie and reading libraries, board games and puzzles. An outdoor gas grill and kitchen are available to guests. Hiking, exploring, cross-country skiing, wildlife, serenity. Adjoins national forest. Hunting packages are available. Fishing, horseback riding, rock climbing, snowmobile trails are all within minutes. Mount Rushmore, Devil's Tower, Crazy Horse Mountain, Deadwood gaming, and more are within 90 minutes' drive. Dog in residence.

Host: Irene Spillane
Rooms: 4 (2 PB; 2 SB) $50-80
Full Breakfast
Credit Cards: A, B
Notes: 2, 5, 7, 9, 11, 12, 13, 15

4W Ranch Recreation

1162 Lynch Road, 82701
(307) 746-2815

Looking for the unbeaten path? Spend a few days on this working cattle ranch with 20,000 acres of diversified rangeland to explore at leisure. Rates include three meals a day.

Hosts: Bob and Jean Harshbarger
Rooms: 2 (SB) $100-125 (American plan)
Full Breakfast
Credit Cards: None
Notes: 2, 3, 4, 7, 8, 9, 11

NOTES: Credit cards accepted: A MasterCard; B Visa; C American Express; D Discover; E Diner's Club; F Other; 2 Personal checks accepted; 3 Lunch available; 4 Dinner available; 5 Open all year; 6 Pets welcome;

PINEDALE

Window on the Winds

10151 Highway 191, Box 996, 82941
(307) 367-2600; (888) 367-1345

The McClains invite guests to this rustic log home. The hosts offer lodgepole pine queen-size beds, a large common room, all decorated in western and Plains Indian decor. Enjoy the breathtaking view of the Winds or relax in the hot tub. Only minutes from year-round mountain adventures such as hiking, fishing, skiing, and snowmobiling, and less than two hours from Jackson and Yellowstone. The perfect base for a western Wyoming vacation.

Host: Leanne McClain
Rooms: 4 (SB) $60-95
Full Breakfast
Credit Cards: A, B
Notes: 2, 3, 4, 5, 6, 7, 8, 9, 11, 12, 13, 14

SARATOGA

Hotel Wolf

P.O. Box 1298, 82331
(307) 326-5525

The historic Hotel Wolf, built in 1893, served as a stagecoach stop. During its early years, the hotel was the hub of the community and noted for its fine food and convivial atmosphere. The same holds true today. The dining room is acclaimed as one of the finest in the region. Nearby is a mineral hot spring and excellent fishing. On the North Platte River.

Hosts: Doug and Kathleen Campbell
Rooms: 6 (PB) $30-47
Suites: 3 (PB) $58-105
Credit Cards: A, B, C, E
Notes: 2, 3, 4, 5, 7, 8, 9, 10, 11, 12, 13, 14

---

7 No smoking; 8 Children welcome; 9 Social drinking allowed; 10 Tennis nearby; 11 Swimming nearby; 12 Golf nearby; 13 Skiing nearby; 14 May be booked through a travel agent; 15 Handicapped accessible.

Canada

Alberta

Eleanor's House

BANFF

Eleanor's House

125 Kootenay Avenue, P.O. Box 1553, T0L 0C0
(403) 760-2457; FAX (403) 762-3852
e-mail: info@bbeleanor.com; www.bbeleanor.com

Banff's finest guest home reflects mid-century elegance for the discerning traveler. Spacious superior bedrooms have private full bathrooms. Mountain views from all windows. In a quiet, prestigious neighborhood, walking distance from the town center or the famous Banff Springs Hotel. The hosts provide guests with an individual daily itinerary to make the best of their days in the area. Together they have more than 50 years' experience in mountain hospitality and national park management. Closed November, December, and January.

Hosts: Eleanor House and Rick Kunelius
Rooms: 2 (PB) $135 Canadian
Full Breakfast
Credit Cards: A, B
Notes: 2, 7, 9, 10, 11, 12, 13, 14

Pension Tannenhof Inn

121 Cave Avenue, Box 1914, T0L 0C0
(403) 762-4636; (877) 999-5011
FAX (403) 762-5660;
e-mail: riedinger@hotmail.com
www.pensiontannenhof.com

Tannenhof, meaning "Lodge in the Pine Trees," is a beautiful English-style mansion built in 1942 with an elegant yet homey atmosphere, set in the majestic Rocky Mountains in world-famous Banff. The surroundings let guests enjoy the beauty of nature at their own pace—hiking up mountain trails, fishing, rafting, and horseback riding. The history of Banff will unfold at the Cave and Basin hot springs—only a short walk from the Pension Tannenhof. Children over six welcome. Seasonal rates.

Hosts: Herbert and Fanny Riedinger
Rooms: 10 (8 PB; 2 SB) $95-165
Full Breakfast
Credit Cards: A, B
Notes: 2, 3, 5, 7, 10, 11, 12, 13, 14

Valley Bed & Breakfast

117 Spray Avenue, Box 184, T0L 0C0
(403) 762-2846; e-mail: spraybb@telus

"A home away from home" close to the famous Banff Springs Hotel Conference Center and Banff Course. Lots of wild life. Restaurants close by. Downtown center only a five minute walk. Hostess is knowledgeable of the area and

---

NOTES: Credit cards accepted: A MasterCard; B Visa; C American Express; D Discover; E Diner's Club; F Other; 2 Personal checks accepted; 3 Lunch available; 4 Dinner available; 5 Open all year; 6 Pets welcome; 7 No smoking; 8 Children welcome; 9 Social drinking allowed; 10 Tennis nearby; 11 Swimming nearby; 12 Golf nearby; 13 Skiing nearby; 14 May be booked through a travel agent; 15 Handicapped accessible.

will help with your itineraries. Sitting room with fireplace, cable TV, and library outside patio. Hostess is a toastmaster, enjoys good conversation, speaks English and German. Come and enjoy breathtaking scenery and quiet atmosphere. No pets please, dog in residence. Smoke free environment. Canada Select two-and-a-half stars rating. Cash and traveler's checks accepted.

Hostess: Marvelyne Yarmoloy
Rooms: 3 (2 PB; 1 suite) $65-125
Continental Breakfast
Credit Cards: None
Notes: 5, 7, 10, 11, 12, 13, 14

CALGARY

Along River Ridge Bed & Breakfast

1919 52nd Street Northwest, T3B 1C3
(403) 247-1330; (888) 434-9555
FAX (403) 247-1328
e-mail: riveredg@hotmail.com

Along River Ridge Bed and Breakfast (a Canada Select Four-Star Rated bed and breakfast) is a peaceful retreat on the Bow River in Calgary, Alberta, Canada. Experience "A touch of country in the city." A 1300-square-foot guest area awaits guests. Fireplace, hot tub, billiards table, microwave, refrigerator. Two bedrooms, each with en suite bath, TV/VCR, and queen-size bed. Private entrance and parking. Magnificent breakfast. Calgary is home of the world famous Calgary Stampede and Exhibits, Spruce Meadow International World Class Equestrian Venue, and Olympic venues. The Bow River offers world class fly-fishing. One hour from the majestic Canadian Rocky Mountains.

Hosts: Dianne Haskell
Rooms: 2 (2 PB; 1 extra bath) $75-90
Full Breakfast
Credit Cards: A, B, C
Notes: 3, 4, 5, 7, 9, 10, 11, 12, 13

Bed & Breakfast at Harrison's

6016 Thornburn Drive NW, T2K 3P7
(403) 274-7281; FAX (403) 531-0069

Harrison's is a cozy bungalow in a quiet residential area of Calgary. Fifteen minutes to Calgary International Airport and city center. Good access to public transit. Guests share comfortable living room and sheltered patio with host. Two main-floor rooms: queen-size bedroom and twin-size bedroom, each with private bath. Children over 10 welcome. Smoking outside only.

Host: Susan Harrison
Rooms: 2 (PB) $60-70 Canadian
Full Breakfast
Credit Cards: None
Notes: 2, 5, 7, 9, 12, 13, 14

Big Springs Bed & Breakfast

Rural Route 1, T4B 2A3
(403) 948-5264; FAX (403) 948-5851
e-mail: bigsprings@bigsprings-bb.com
www.bigsprings-bb.com

Peaceful country setting. Excellent access to Calgary (15 minutes), airport (22 minutes), Kananaskis Country, Banff, Lake Louise, and famous Calgary Stampede. This 5,500-square-foot home is on 35 acres overlooking a valley. Elegantly appointed rooms: Manor, Victorian, Arbour, Bridal Suite with Thermomasseur tub. Secluded English Garden sitting room. Gourmet breakfast experience. Patios, hot tub, sauna, fireplace, piano, and nature path. Evening snacks. Romantic package, self-guided day trips available. Extra personal touches. Canada Select three-and-a-half stars.

Hosts: Earle and Carol Whitaker
Rooms: 4 (PB) $90-125
Full Breakfast
Credit Cards: A, B
Notes: 5, 7, 8, 10, 11, 12, 13, 14

NOTES: Credit cards accepted: A MasterCard; B Visa; C American Express; D Discover; E Diner's Club; F Other; 2 Personal checks accepted; 3 Lunch available; 4 Dinner available; 5 Open all year; 6 Pets welcome;

Hilltop Ranch Bed & Breakfast

Box 54, Priddis, T0L 1W0
(800) 801-0451; (403) 931-2639
FAX (403) 931-3426
e-mail: hilltopr@cybersurf.net

A hobby ranch in the foothills. Mountain view. All rooms with private bathrooms. Guest lounge with TV, VCR, fireplace, and private deck. Fifteen minutes southwest of Calgary. A beautiful spot. "If you are coming to Calgary, you should have a western bed and breakfast experience."

Hosts: Gary and Barb Zorn
Rooms: 3 (PB) $60-105
Full Breakfast
Credit Cards: A, B, C
Notes: 5, 6, 7, 8, 9, 10, 11, 12, 13, 14

Paradise Acres Bed & Breakfast

243105 Paradise Road, Box 20, Site 2, Rural Route 6, T2M 4L5
(403) 248-4748; FAX (403) 235-3916

On Paradise Road just minutes away from the Calgary International Airport. Guests can enjoy a beautiful lake, golf course, shopping, and recreation nearby. Hosts have five rooms fitted with queen-size beds. Three baths en suite and two private baths. Relax next to a luxurious marble fireplace or enjoy the city or mountain view. Inquire about accommodations for children. CAA- and AAA-approved. Skiing 80 miles away.

Hosts: Brian and Char Bates
Rooms: 4 (PB) $67.50-82.50 Canadian
Full and Continental Breakfast
Credit Cards: A, B, C
Notes: 5, 7, 10, 11, 12, 14

CANMORE

The Georgetown Inn

1101 Bow Valley Trail T1W 1N4
(403) 678-3439; (800) 657-5955
FAX (403) 678-6909
e-mail: gtowninn@banff.net
www.georgetowninn.ab.ca

At the eastern gateway to Banff National Park, a Tudor-style 24-bedroom inn with private dining room and a licensed guest lounge. All bedrooms have private baths, antique furnishings, TVs, telephones, and majestic mountain views. Each room is individually decorated, several with gas fireplaces, and some with jetted tubs. Easy to find and close to all conveniences. Smoking is permitted in the snug and the outdoor patios. Doreen and Barry built the inn in 1993 from scratch, patterning it after those in their native England.

Hosts: Barry and Doreen Jones and Family
Rooms: 24 (PB) $79-169 Canadian
Full Breakfast
Credit Cards: A, B, C, D
Notes: 2, 5, 8, 9, 10, 11, 12, 13, 14, 15

EDMONTON

Barratt House Bed & Breakfast

4204-115 Street, T6J 1P4
(780) 437-2568; FAX (780) 439-1669
e-mail: longley@telusplanet.net
www.bbcanada.com/1349.html

In quiet residential area of southwest Edmonton, 20 minutes from airport and downtown, 10 minutes to famous West Edmonton Mall. Parks and walking trails nearby. Beautifully appointed upstairs bedrooms with ceiling fans. Relax and unwind with cool drink and home-baking in family room with TV, VCR, or on flower-filled deck. Beverage trays in rooms. Delicious, gourmet-style breakfast served in sunny dining room. Laundry facilities available. Cat in residence. Canada Select three-and-a-half stars. Member Alberta Bed and Breakfast Association.

Hosts: Doug and Joan Longley
Rooms: 2 (PB) $65-70
Full Breakfast
Credit Cards: A, B
Notes: 2, 5, 7, 11, 12

---

7 No smoking; 8 Children welcome; 9 Social drinking allowed; 10 Tennis nearby; 11 Swimming nearby; 12 Golf nearby; 13 Skiing nearby; 14 May be booked through a travel agent; 15 Handicapped accessible.

HINTON

Black Cat Guest Ranch

Box 6267, T7V 1X6
(403) 865-3084; FAX (403) 865-1924

Historic Albertan guest ranch celebrated its 60th anniversary in 1995. Guests are offered guided trail rides, hiking, line dancing, rafting in the summer, and cross-country skiing in the winter. Relaxation year-round. Home-style meals and sociable surroundings in a beautiful mountain setting one hour's drive from Jasper townsite.

Hosts: Amber and Perry Hayward
Rooms: 16 (PB) $73-139 Canadian
Full Breakfast
Credit Cards: A, B
Notes: 2, 3, 4, 5, 8, 9, 13, 14

Black Cat Guest Ranch

OKOTOKS

The Ranch

Rural Route 1, T0L 1T0
(403) 938-5109 (phone/FAX)

The folks at The Ranch pamper guests at this working ranch home in the Rocky Mountain foothills. Wild life, star gazing, mountain view, wild flower walks. Guest privacy.

Hosts: Lynn and Jim Willoughby
Rooms: 3 (SB) $75
Full Breakfast
Notes: 2, 3, 4, 5, 8, 9, 12, 13, 14

NOTES: Credit cards accepted: A MasterCard; B Visa; C American Express; D Discover; E Diner's Club; F Other; 2 Personal checks accepted; 3 Lunch available; 4 Dinner available; 5 Open all year; 6 Pets welcome;

British Columbia

BRENTWOOD BAY

Sea S Cape Oceanfront Bed & Breakfast

740 Sea Drive, V8M 1B1
(250) 652-9628 (phone/FAX); (888) 791-1192
e-mail: seascape@bctravel.com

Contemporary waterfront home in a country setting only three minutes from Butchart Gardens. Private baths, queen-size beds, antique furnishings, outstanding views from every room, private decks, guest lounges, hearty breakfasts (muffins, scones, marvelous breads, preserves—all homemade). Government-approved luxurious accommodations. Relax on dock, swim, boat, and fish. Watch seals, otters, bird life, and sunsets. Deep-water moorage available. Close to fine dining. Twenty minutes to Victoria.

Hosts: Ray and Judith Sam
Rooms: 3 (2 PB; 1 SB) $95-150 Canadian
Full Breakfast
Credit Cards: A, B
Notes: 2, 5, 7, 10, 11, 12

CAMPBELL RIVER

Arbour's Guest House

375 South Murphy Street, V9W 1Y8
(250) 287-9873; FAX (250) 287-2353

Reservations suggested, seasonal, five minutes from downtown and all amenities. Complimentary glass of wine on arrival, antique decor, with spectacular view of the mountains, ocean, and fishing grounds from large treed property. TV room. Golf course close by. Boat rental arrangements made and experienced guides available for saltwater salmon fishing. No smoking or pets, please. Adult oriented. "Hospitality is our business, in the sport fishing capital of the world." Weekly rates available.

Hosts: Sharon and Ted Arbour
Rooms: 2 (1 PB; 1 SB) $70-95
Continental Breakfast
Credit Cards: A, B
Notes: 2, 5, 7, 9, 10, 11, 12, 13, 14

Campbell River Lodge

Campbell River Lodge, Fishing, and Adventure Resort

1760 Island Highway, V9W 2E7
(250) 287-7446; (800) 663-7212
e-mail: crlodge@oberon.ark.com
www.vquest.com/crlodge/

Small, intimate fishing lodge on the banks of the famous Campbell River. Originally constructed of logs in 1948, the lodge is the oldest and most unique in the area. Offers Old World charm and modern conveniences. Dine in the Riverside Cafe or English-style pub. Relaxing outdoor hot tub overlooking Campbell River. Light Continental breakfast served daily.

---

7 No smoking; 8 Children welcome; 9 Social drinking allowed; 10 Tennis nearby; 11 Swimming nearby; 12 Golf nearby; 13 Skiing nearby; 14 May be booked through a travel agent; 15 Handicapped accessible.

British Columbia

Rooms: 28 (PB) $50-94
Continental Breakfast
Credit Cards: A, B
Notes: 3, 4, 5, 6, 7, 8, 9, 10 ,11, 12, 14

CHEMAINUS

At the Sea-Breeze Bed & Breakfast

2912 Esplanade Street, P.O. Box 1362, V0R 1K0
(250) 246-4593 (phone/FAX)

Turn-of-the-century home just steps from the beach and boat ramp in picturesque Chemainus. Play park and picnic area at the beach. Beautiful views from every room. Lighthouse and island view. Full breakfast is served on linen with silver and candles. English and German spoken. Smoking in designated areas only. Chemainus is on Vancouver Island, just one hour north of Victoria.

Hosts: John and Christa Stegemann
Rooms: 4 (PB) $55-60 Canadian
Full Breakfast
Credit Cards: None
Notes: 5, 6, 7, 8, 9, 10, 11, 12, 14

DUNCAN

Garden City Bed & Breakfast Reservation Service

660 Jones Terrace, Victoria, V8Z 2L7
(250) 479-1986; FAX (250) 479-9999
gardencity@bc-bed-breakfast.com
www.bc-bed-breakfast.com

K-23. Eighteen acres with a lake that is a bird sanctuary. The hosts take pride in offering one of the most unique bed and breakfasts on the island. Furnished with antiques and gardens replete with swans and winding walkways, the Tudor-style mansion designed by architect Samuel Maclure has two bedrooms with en suite private bathrooms, queen-size beds, and incredible views of the lake. These world-wide travelers are splendid host and hostess and invite guests also to enjoy their TV sitting room with billiards, games, piano, etc. Everything guests could possibly hope for. From $185.

FORT STEELE

Emery's Mountain View Bed & Breakfast

183 Wardner Fort Steele Road, P.O. Box 60, V0B 1N0
(250) 426-4756 (phone/FAX)

Three hours from Banff, Alberta; four hours from Spokane, Washington; and five minutes from Fort Steele historic town. On 37 scenic acres above a creek and a marsh where wild animals and birds live and feed. This new home and cabins have porches and patios where guests can relax and enjoy views of the Rocky Mountains. Enjoy mountain hiking trails, hot springs, historic sites, golf courses, and ski hills. Smoking permitted on porches only.

Hosts: John and Joanna Emery
Rooms: 3 (PB) $60-110 Canadian
Full Breakfast
Credit Cards: B
Notes: 5, 7, 8, 9, 11, 12, 13, 14

HALFMOON BAY

Lord Jim's Resort Hotel

Rural Route 2, Ole's Cove Site, C-1, V0N I4O
(604) 885-7038; FAX (604) 885-7036
e-mail: lordjims_resorthotel@sunshine.net
www.cybercites.com/lordjims.html

Modern facilities on beautiful Sunshine Coast on nine acres of prime waterfront property. Two hours by car and ferry from Vancouver. The full-facility resort offers deluxe accommodations (room or suite,) cozy log cabins, meeting rooms, restaurant, and lounge, game room complete with pool table and sauna, and heated outdoor swimming pool (seasonal.) Recreational activities include golfing, kayaking, nature tours, Heli fly-fishing, scenic boat tours, and scuba diving. Lord Jim's specializes in

---

NOTES: Credit cards accepted: A MasterCard; B Visa; C American Express; D Discover; E Diner's Club; F Other; 2 Personal checks accepted; 3 Lunch available; 4 Dinner available; 5 Open all year; 6 Pets welcome; 7 No smoking; 8 Children welcome; 9 Social drinking allowed; 10 Tennis nearby; 11 Swimming nearby; 12 Golf nearby; 13 Skiing nearby; 14 May be booked through a travel agent; 15 Handicapped accessible.

Salmon Charters. Both package and à la carte prices are offered.

Hosts: Hugh and Catherine Gadsby
Rooms: 25 (PB) $ 80-205
Credit Cards: A, B, C
Notes: 3, 4, 5, 7, 8, 9, 10, 11, 12, 14

KAMLOOPS

Father's Country Inn

Tod Mountain Road, c/o Box 152, V0E 1Z0
(250) 578-7308; (800) 578-7322
FAX (250) 578-7334
e-mail: mmfathers@bc.sympatico.ca
www.mwsolutions.com/fathersbb

Quiet, spacious home nestled in the mountains with breathtaking view of farm lands below and the snow-covered mountains. Relax in the indoor pool and hot tub surrounded by tropical plants. In-room four-poster queen-size beds, fireplaces, candlelit Jacuzzi tubs, guest lounges, one fireside. Heated ski room with locker, drying racks and benches for waxing skies. In summer guided trail rides, fishing in nearby lakes, golf, and hiking. Halfway between Vancouver and Jasper or Banff. Exit off of Highway 5, north of Kamloops at Heffley Creek, follow sign. Easy to find.

Hosts: Brenda and David
Rooms: 5 (PB) $65-120
Full Breakfast
Credit Cards: A, B
Notes: 4, 5, 7, 9, 10, 12, 13, 14

LIGHTHOUSE COUNTRY

Garden City Bed & Breakfast Reservation Service

660 Jones Terrace, Victoria, V8Z 2L7
(250) 479-1986; FAX (250) 479-9999
e-mail: gardencity@bc-bed-breakfast.com
www.bc-bed-breakfast.com

K-Bowser. The hosts welcome guests to a very special place in Lighthouse Country, just halfway between Parksville and Courtenay. An attractive self-contained suite, set away from the highway, offers peaceful, quiet living quarters with private entrance and large sun deck overlooking a brook with mini-waterfall. The bright living room has a skylight and fully equipped kitchenette with deluxe range and fridge. Bedroom has a luxurious queen-size bed and en suite bathroom. Laundry facilities available. Every activity imaginable is within a short drive and a sandy beach, stores, shops, post office, restaurants, and service station only a few minutes away. Sorry—no smoking, no children, no pets. From $70.

MAYNE ISLAND

Oceanwood Country Inn

630 Dinner Bay Road, V0N 2J0
(250) 539-5074; FAX (250) 539-3002
e-mail: oceanwood@gulfislands.com
www.oceanwood.com

Overlooking the water, Oceanwood has 12 charming guest rooms, most with fireplaces and soaking tubs, plus a comfortable living room, well-stocked library, and cozy games room. The intimate 30-seat waterfront restaurant, open for dinner every day, serves Pacific northwestern cuisine. The extensive wine list features the best from British Columbia, Washington, Oregon, and California. Large outdoor hot tub and sauna are available. Bicycles for guests' use. Ocean kayaking nearby.

Oceanwood Country Inn

NOTES: Credit cards accepted: A MasterCard; B Visa; C American Express; D Discover; E Diner's Club; F Other; 2 Personal checks accepted; 3 Lunch available; 4 Dinner available; 5 Open all year; 6 Pets welcome;

Breakfast and afternoon tea included. Closed December to February. Golf available on the adjacent island.

Host: Jonathan Chilvers
Rooms: 12 (PB) $109-299
Full Breakfast
Credit Cards: A, B
Notes: 4, 7, 9, 10, 11, 12, 14

METCHOSIN

Garden City Bed & Breakfast Reservation Service

660 Jones Terrace, Victoria, V8Z 2L7
(250) 479-1986; FAX (250) 479-9999
e-mail: dwensley@vanisle.net
www.bctravel.com/gardencity/html

L-8. Victoria's countryside home. Exquisite log home, built by the owners, features cozy dining room, friendly informative hosts, and beautiful guest's quarters. Queen-size beds, en suite private bathroom, on-going beverage bar, and own private hot tub. Guests' comfort, privacy, enjoyment are the major concerns in this home. Only 30 minutes drive to city center or in 20 minutes in the opposite direction, guests can enjoy the amenities of Sooke with world-class fishing, museum, and Sooke Harbor House with its wonderful herb gardens. From $110.

MILL BAY (VANCOUVER ISLAND)

Garden City Bed & Breakfast Reservation Service

660 Jones Terrace, Victoria, V8Z 2L7
(250) 479-1986; FAX (250) 479-9999
e-mail: gardencity@loc-bed-breakfast.com
www.bc-bed-breakfast.com.

K-3. Oceanfront, country home on 2.5 acres, 35 minutes north of Victoria, 50 minutes south of Nanaimo. All guests are special—they will have been "spoiled" by the time they leave. Beachcombing, boating, canoeing, tea-for-two in the gazebo or by the fireplace, or ocean-gazing from the swimming pool. Dot's breakfasts include garden-fresh fruits. Activities include Farmgate Winery, cidery tours. Specialty shopping Mill Bay, Shawnigan Lake, Cobble Hill. Nearby are Duncan and the Native Heritage Centre, Cowichan Bay and the Marine Ecology Station, Chemainus, and possibility of a fishing trip with Jim. Accommodations include a suite: lounge (refrigerator, kettle, microwave), queen-size bedroom, private bath, and a room with a twin bed with private bath. Excellent for families. From $80.

NANAIMO

Garden City Bed & Breakfast Reservation Service

660 Jones Terrace, Victoria, V8Z 2L7
(250) 479-1986; FAX (250) 479-9999
e-mail: gardencity@bc-bed-breakfast.com
www.bc-bed-breakfast.com

K-31. Majestic panoramic view of Strait of Georgia and snowcapped mountains with a bonus of fantastic sunsets—all this awaits guests in this lovely, peaceful, home five-minutes' drive from Nanaimo city center. Simmons mattresses on king- or queen-size beds. Families welcome and spacious rooms equipped for children. From $55.

NANOOSE BAY

Garden City Bed & Breakfast Reservation Service

660 Jones Terrace, Victoria, V8Z 2L7
(250) 479-1986; FAX (250) 479-9999
e-mail: gardencity@bc-bed-breakfast.com
www.bc-bed-breakfast.com

K-1. Charming contemporary West Coast-style home on two acres of quiet paradise just 20 minutes from Nanaimo's Departure Bay ferry terminal. This is a beautifully unique setting where sunsets color the mountains and sparkle on the ocean below. Only minutes from golfing, boating, strolling nature trails. One guest

---

7 No smoking; 8 Children welcome; 9 Social drinking allowed; 10 Tennis nearby; 11 Swimming nearby; 12 Golf nearby; 13 Skiing nearby; 14 May be booked through a travel agent; 15 Handicapped accessible.

room has a private en suite bathroom plus a fireplace and sun deck. The other guest room has a private bathroom and sun deck. $75-85.

The Lookout at Schooner Cove

3381 Dolphin Drive, V9P 9H7
(250) 468-9796 (phone/FAX)
e-mail: mwilkie@webtv.net
www.pixsell.bc.ca/bb/116q.htm

A great base for touring Vancouver Island, this contemporary cedar home is about two hours from Victoria and Tofino. It is in a quiet park-like setting with an awesome view of Georgia Strait and the mountains beyond. The challenging Fairwinds Golf Course is one-half mile away—just one of many 18-hole courses in the area. Schooner Cove Resort and Marina is 500 yards away. Fishing, sailing, kayaking, swimming, riding stables, tennis, and hiking nearby.

Hosts: Marj and Herb Wilkie
Rooms: 3 (2 PB; 1 SB) $60-90
Full Breakfast
Credit Cards: None
Notes: 2, 7, 9, 10, 11, 12, 14

NELSON

Willow Point Lodge

Rural Route 1, S21 C31, 2211 Taylor Drive, V1L 5P4
(250) 825-9411; (800) 949-2211

A 1920 elegant country inn on the mountainside overlooking the west arm of Kootenay Lake. There is an inviting hot tub in the garden and walking trails lead to creek and forest

Willow Point Lodge

glades. Abundance of wildlife activity in the forest. Nelson, the tour guide (and golden retriever), is always happy to stroll the trails with guests.

Hosts: Florent and Anni
Rooms: 6 (5 PB) $75-150
Full Breakfast
Credit Cards: A, B
Notes: 5, 7, 8, 9, 11, 12, 13

NEW WESTMINSTER

Chambres d'hôtes Sunflower Bed & Breakfast

1110 Hamilton Street, New Westmister, V3M 2M9
(604) 522-4186; FAX (604) 522-4176
e-mail: yourhost@sunflower-bnb.com
http://www.sunflower-bnb.com

Guests are invited to appreciate the comfort and tranquility of this heritage house, just minutes away from downtown Vancouver and Vancouver International Airport. The bedrooms are tastefully decorated and the breakfasts are unforgettable. Weekly and monthly rates, no pets, cancellation 72 hours notice. Hostess speaks English, Français, and Italiano.

Hostess: Rosina Iantosca
Rooms: 2 (SB) $70 Canadian
Full Breakfast
Notes: 5, 7, 8, 9, 10, 11, 12, 13, 14

NORTH VANCOUVER

Grand Manor Guest House Bed & Breakfast

1617 Grand Boulevard, V7L 3Y2
(604) 988-6082; FAX (604) 988-4596
e-mail: donna@helix.net
http: //users.imag.net/.sry.donna

This four-story stone Edwardian home is one of the original mansions of the Grand Boulevard, the widest in Canada. In the heart of North Vancouver, close to shopping, skiing, swimming, tennis, Londsdale Market, and 20 minutes from downtown Vancouver. Rooms

NOTES: Credit cards accepted: A MasterCard; B Visa; C American Express; D Discover; E Diner's Club; F Other; 2 Personal checks accepted; 3 Lunch available; 4 Dinner available; 5 Open all year; 6 Pets welcome;

Grand Manor Guest House

have been renovated and are clean and comfortable with mountain and ocean views, decorated in antiques. Grand Manor is a place to relax and enjoy new friends and a warm, comfortable informal atmosphere. A two-bedroom carriage house is on two levels and has all cooking facilities and will sleep six people.

Host: Donna Patrick and family
Rooms: 4 (2 PB; 2SB) $75-130
Full or Continental Breakfast
Credit Cards: B
Notes: 5, 7, 8, 9, 10, 11, 12, 13, 14

Norgate Parkhouse Bed & Breakfast

1226 Silverwood Crescent V7P 1J3
(604) 986-5069; FAX (604) 986-8810
e-mail: relax@oldenglishbandb.bc.ca

Gardeners' delight. Relax in the large, lush, green West Coast garden. Experience hospitality Vancouver style. Have a quiet sleep and enjoy delicious breakfasts in the morning. Telephones in guest rooms. Guest lounge with TV, books, and fireplace. Close to public transit. Only 12 minutes to Vancouver center. Near British Columbia Rail Station and all amenities.

Host: Vicki Tyndall
Rooms: 3 (1 PB; 2 SB) $95-115
Full Breakfast
Credit Cards: A, B
Notes: 5, 7, 9, 10, 11, 12, 13, 14

Old English Bed & Breakfast Registry

1226 Silverwood Crescent, V7P 1J3
(604) 986-5069; FAX (604) 986-8810
e-mail: relax@oldenglishbandb.bc.ca
www.oldenglishbandb.bc.ca

Ambleside Beach in West Vancouver is a traditional gabled home. This bed and breakfast is surrounded by a rambling English garden. The accommodation is a very large self-contained bed/sitting room. It has a small cooking area for light meals, private bath, private entrance with sliding glass doors that open to a patio deck overlooking the garden. This is a terrific location, near to all amenities, great restaurants, buses to downtown, ocean beachfront, golfing, boating, upscale shopping, etc. Minutes to downtown Vancouver. $150.

Deep Cove II. This large, deluxe Victorian Manor is set on the side of the North Shore Mountains. It has a terrific ocean view of Burrard Inlet including Simon Fraser University on the far side. Twenty-five minutes from downtown Vancouver in a very quiet residential area, close to restaurants, mountain trails, beach walks, canoeing, kayaking, and golf and country club. Room one has a large bed/sitting room with TV and fireplace. Private patio deck with ocean view. The large bathroom has a shower and Jacuzzi tub for two. Rooms two and three share a four-piece bathroom. These rooms look out over the forest. The hosts will rent out one of these rooms with a private bath,

Norgate Parkhouse

---

7 No smoking; 8 Children welcome; 9 Social drinking allowed; 10 Tennis nearby; 11 Swimming nearby; 12 Golf nearby; 13 Skiing nearby; 14 May be booked through a travel agent; 15 Handicapped accessible.

if requested. There is a guest TV available for use. $175.

Deep Cove III is the ideal getaway weekend for two. The unbelievable view from this ocean-front property will have guests wanting to put their feet up and stay awhile. The accommodation is a one-bedroom suite, complete with en suite shower, a sitting room comfortably furnished and with a color TV. French doors open onto private waterfront patio. This modern home is on the side of a mountain. This is an adult-oriented, non-smoking home. Deep Cove offers guests peace, tranquility, beautiful scenery, salmon fishing, canoeing, kayaking, hiking, and fine dining. Yet guests are only 20 minutes to downtown Vancouver. $175.

Lonsdale Quay. A Victorian-style home beautifully furnished with antiques. Each room features a harbor view of Vancouver. Two rooms share a bathroom and one room has a private en suite bath. Close to all amenities and a short walk to the Lonsdale Quay. $95-105.

Norgate Park. Relax in a lush, quiet garden. This bed and breakfast has intriguing nooks and crannies that are filled with interesting items from around the world. Three guest rooms, one with private en suite bath. There is a guest sitting room with TV and fireplace. Twelve minutes to downtown and close to public transit. $95-115.

Pemberton Heights. A wonderful old English-style garden surrounds this bed and breakfast. The accommodation is comfy, casual, and relaxing. The guest area centers around the sitting room and sunroom that open directly to the garden. The sitting room is equipped with a very large TV, piano, fireplace, a juice bar, and a telephone. Close to public transit and 12 minutes to Vancouver center. $125.

Sue's Victorian Guest House

Sue's Victorian Guest House— Circa 1904

152 East Third, V7L 1E6
(604) 985-1523; (800) 776-1811

This lovely smoke-free home just four blocks from the harbor, SeaBus terminal, and Lonsdale Quay market is close to restaurants, shops, and transportation. Home is circa 1909 and was originally renovated in 1949. Featuring Victorian soaker baths (no showers). Each room is individually keyed and offers a TV, a local-call telephone, fan, and video player. Long-term stays encouraged. Visa accepted for deposit only. Recently expanded to accommodate four fully furnished and serviced apartments. Guest refrigerator, shared kitchen available from 4:00 P.M. until 10:00 A.M. Make own food or eat out.

Hosts: Jen Lowe and Sue Chalmers
Rooms: 3 (1 PB; 2 SB) $50-75 Canadian
No Breakfast
Credit Cards: None
Notes: 5, 7

NOTES: Credit cards accepted: A MasterCard; B Visa; C American Express; D Discover; E Diner's Club; F Other; 2 Personal checks accepted; 3 Lunch available; 4 Dinner available; 5 Open all year; 6 Pets welcome;

PARKSVILLE

Garden City Bed & Breakfast Reservation Service

660 Jones Terrace, Victoria, V8Z 2L7
(250) 479-1986; FAX (250) 479-9999
e-mail: gardencity@bc-bed-breakfast.com
www.bc-bed-breakfast.com

K-2. Welcome to a cozy, midisland home. Relax and enjoy (seasonally) heated pool, or slate-bed pool table. Get into comfortable shoes and stroll the many nature trails along the Nature Trust Estuary. It is a beautiful, easy trip to the west coast and Tofino area. Five golf courses within a 15-minute drive. A few minute's walk to shops, beach, tennis, miniature golf, and restaurants. Two guest rooms, both with private baths, one en suite. Full breakfast served. Adult-oriented home where small pets are welcome with prior arrangement. $60-70.

PEMBERTON

Alpen View Bed & Breakfast

P.O. Box 636, 7406 Larch Street, V0N 2L0
(604) 894-6787; FAX (604) 894-2026
e-mail: ceinarson@bigfoot.com
www.netadssell.com/bandb

Guests are warmly welcomed by Fred and Christine Einarson to their quiet air conditioned/fireside home at the foot of the Coast Mountains and on Circle Route tours. Magnificent snowcapped mountain views are seen from the hot tub, summer jetpool, on the ten-minute stroll to the village and restaurants, or from the bedrooms. Over breakfast, guests share their experiences of Pemberton's all-season activities: golf, hiking, fishing, snowmobiling, and cross-country skiing, plus skiing and snowboarding at neighboring Whistler. Ten percent discount if booked through a travel agent. Well-behaved children welcome. Traveler's checks accepted.

Hosts: Fred and Christine Einarson
Rooms: 3 (1 PB; 2 SB) $75-95
Full or Continental Breakfast

Credit Cards: None
Notes: 5, 7, 8, 9, 10, 11, 12, 13, 14

PENDER ISLAND

The Cliffside Inn

4230 Armadale Road, Box 50, V0N 2M0
(604) 629-6691; www.penderisland.com

Cliffside Inn, offering affordable tranquility, is nestled on three acres of secluded oceanfront, in the heart of the Canadian islands. View whales, otters, and other wildlife from our decks and beach. Dine on the finest of fresh foods in our incredible oceanfront dining room. Cliffside is perfect for that romantic interlude and escape from the stress of city life.

Rooms: 4 (PB) $129-229 Canadian ($99-149 U.S.)
Full Breakfast
Credit Cards: B
Notes: 4, 5, 6, 7, 9, 11, 12

PRINCE GEORGE

Beaverly Bed & Breakfast

12725 Miles Road, V2N 5C1
(250) 560-5255; (888)522-2298
FAX (250) 560-5211
www.bbcanada.com./html

30 Kilometers (12 miles) west of Prince George; on Highway 16 follow Blue Bed and Breakfast signs. Park-like setting on four BA (ten acres) of beautiful British Columbia wilderness. The Beaverly Inn offers king-, queen-, and single-size beds and private baths. Enjoy an outside hot tub. A full breakfast is served in our country kitchen or on the outside deck, weather permitting. Many birds to watch. Satellite TV and telephone available. Transportation for guests to and from airport, bus station, or train station is also provided.

Hosts: Anneke and Adrian Van Peenen
Rooms: 3 (2 PB; 1 SB) $50-75
Full Breakfast
Credit Cards: A, B
Notes: 3, 5, 6, 7, 8, 9, 10, 11, 12, 13, 14

---

7 No smoking; 8 Children welcome; 9 Social drinking allowed; 10 Tennis nearby; 11 Swimming nearby; 12 Golf nearby; 13 Skiing nearby; 14 May be booked through a travel agent; 15 Handicapped accessible.

QUALICUM BEACH

Bahari Bed & Breakfast

5101 Island Highway West, V9K 1Z1
(250) 752-9278; (877) 752-9278
FAX (250) 752-9038
e-mail: lhooper@macn.bc.ca
www.baharibandb.com

Rest and repast overlooking Strait of Georgia, watching sea lions cavort and seals bask, shucking oysters on the accessible beach, strolling the philosopher's path, or soaking in the outdoor hot tub—that's Bahari. Conveniently on mid-Vancouver Island, making all the island's attractions a day trip or less away. Each room is a calm oasis where guests will luxuriate under eiderdown and wake to enjoy a gourmet's breakfast. The freedom of a two-bedroom self-catered apartment is also available.

Rooms: 4 (PB) $125-250 Canadian
Full Breakfast
Credit Cards: A, B, C
Notes: 7, 9, 10, 11, 12, 14

Hollyford Bed & Breakfast

106 Hoylake Road East, V9K 1L7
(250) 752-8101; (877) 224-5359
FAX (250) 752-8102; e-mail: mail@hollyford.ca
www.hollyford.ca

Large, single story heritage house, perfect island home base. Central to west and east coast beaches, for touring Tofino, Nanaimo, and Mount Washington. Executive facilities and services. All suites feature private four-piece baths with double shower and soaker tub, gas fireplace, cable/VCR, telephone, clock radio, heated floor, sound-proof facilities, privacy locks, premium mattress, bed linens, towels, robes, private patio, and more. Complimentary 24-hour refreshment sideboard, guest lounge, library, private table in dining room. Private entrance, on-site parking. Special culinary breakfasts, exotic teas and robust coffees, served up in a grand style with sterling, crystal, and china on fine Irish linens. Canada Select five-star award. Member of WCBBIA, Approved BC Tourism Accommodation. Member QB Chamber of Commerce.

Hosts: Jim and Marjorie Ford
Rooms: 3 (PB) $125-165 Canadian ($100-117 US)
Full Breakfast
Credit Cards: A, B
Notes: 5, 7, 9, 10, 11, 12, 13, 14

SIDNEY

Garden City Bed & Breakfast Reservation Service

660 Jones Terrace, Victoria, V8Z 2L7
(250) 479-1986; FAX (250) 479-9999
e-mail: gardencity@bc-bed-breakfast.com
www.bc-bed-breakfast.com

A-1. On the shores of Cordova Channel, about 35 minutes north of Victoria city center, overlooking a panorama of islands, mountains, and ocean. Minutes from the airport, ferries, Sidney, and Butchart Gardens. One acre of sandy beach and oriental gardens offers peace, quiet, and privacy. Guest room one has two bedrooms, private entrance, patio, and hot tub. Large sitting room has a wet bar. En suite bathroom features large Jacuzzi tub. Guest room two is a beach house on the ocean. It has a private hot tub, a bed/sitting room with TV, VCR, movies, slippers and housecoat, plus toiletries. Beverages in refrigerator, coffee maker, tea, etc.

A-2. One acre of incredible forest, lawns, and garden plus a picturesque Tudor-style home with the most beautiful ocean views and a pathway to the beach. Two suites, each with private entrance and en suite private bathroom with tub and shower. Spacious bedrooms. Sitting room with cable TV. The Tudor Suite has a kitchenette and double sofa bed in the sitting room. Ocean View Suite has additional single bed and private patio adjoining the garden. From $95.

A-6. A beautiful Tudor-style home, nestled in beautiful gardens, only a 20-minute walk to

---

NOTES: Credit cards accepted: A MasterCard; B Visa; C American Express; D Discover; E Diner's Club; F Other; 2 Personal checks accepted; 3 Lunch available; 4 Dinner available; 5 Open all year; 6 Pets welcome;

downtown Sidney. After a sumptuous breakfast, meander out the back door to the ocean beach. The queen-size bedroom has an en suite private bathroom with large Jacuzzi tub and ocean view. The other two rooms share a bathroom. From $65-95.

A-7. This incredible executive-style home on the waterfront in a quiet area of Brentwood Bay is only five minutes from Butchart Gardens. After a relaxing sleep in one of the three guest rooms, enjoy a superlative breakfast. Views of ocean and small islands. Guests' sitting room has private entrance, TV, stereo, etc. From $90.

A-3. Drift to sleep to the sound of gently lapping waves in this beautiful seaside home. Step out the back door to a beautiful stretch of clean, sandy beach with incredible views of the gulf and San Juan Islands. Cordova Bay is just a 20-minute drive to Victoria; within walking distance of golf, tennis, shopping, and a wonderful variety of dining places. Room one (honeymoon suite) has an en suite bathroom with extra-large airjet tub and shower, sitting area—all with ocean view. Room two has sweeping ocean views from sun deck and en suite private bathroom. Room three has private bathroom with sunken tub.

SOOKE (VANCOUVER ISLAND)

Garden City Bed & Breakfast Reservation Service

660 Jones Terrace, Victoria, V8Z 2L7
(250) 479-1986; FAX (250) 479-9999
e-mail: gardencity@bc-bed-breakfast.com
www.bc-bed-breakfast.com

L-3. Two beautifully appointed guest rooms in this lovely country home. The hosts offer true English hospitality in their two large rooms with en suite private bathrooms as well as private deck overlooking forest and distant ocean view. Guests' lounge and breakfast room features a large fireplace and just outside the glass doors is a deck with hot tub for guests' relaxation and pleasure. Wild flowers, deer, squirrels abound. From $95.

Ocean Wilderness Inn

Ocean Wilderness Inn & Spa Retreat

109 West Coast Road, Rural Route 2, V0S 1N0
(250) 646-2116; (800) 323-2116
FAX (250) 646-2317; e-mail: ocean@sookenet.com
www.sookenet.com/ocean

Relax, renew, revitalize in the spa facilities in the peaceful surroundings of an ancient coastal rain forest. Ocean Wilderness offers five peaceful, forested acres with beach, a natural haven for romantics. Watch for whales and eagles from the hot tub tucked in the Japanese gazebo. The large, luxurious rooms with private entrances are furnished with antiques and canopied beds. Plant a "memory tree" after a multi-course breakfast served in the rustic log dining room. Pets welcome by prior arrangements.

Host: Marion Rolston
Rooms: 9 (PB) $75-175 Canadian
Full Breakfast
Credit Cards: A, B, C
Notes: 5, 6, 7, 8, 9, 11, 12, 14, 15

Sooke Harbour House

1528 Whiffen Spit Road, V0S 1N0
(250) 642-3421; FAX (250) 642-6988
e-mail: info@sookeharbourhouse.com

Overlooking Sooke Bay, the Sooke Harbour House offers exquisite cuisine, glorious gardens, and restful accommodation. The romantic dining room offers fine service and seductive food that will tantalize the most jaded palate. Accommodations embrace antiques, regional art, cathedral ceilings, fine rugs and carpeting, fireplaces, four-poster beds, fine baths, and ocean views. Amenities include balconies, patios, and sun decks. Some units offer private whirlpools, old claw-foot tubs, or steam showers. This inn receives high marks for its gracious service, romantic atmosphere, and splendid restaurant.

Hosts: Sinclair and Frederique Philip
Rooms: 28 (PB) $125-330
Full or Continental Breakfast
Credit Cards: A, B, C, E, F
Notes: 2, 4, 5, 6, 7, 8, 9, 10, 11, 12, 14, 15

SOUTH SURREY

Crescent Green

3467-141st Street, V4P 1L7
(604) 538-2935; (888) 972-3333
FAX (604) 538-2987; e-mail: surges@direct.ca

Exceptional Canada Select four-star accredited accommodations with an extensive range of facilities, guest amenities, and services. Sprawling rancher on show garden and mature evergreen-forested acreage. Swimming pool, sauna, hot tub. Gourmet breakfast freshly prepared. Near beaches, fine restaurants, and golf. Minutes to U.S. border and 30 minutes to Vancouver. Pamper yourself! Skiing within one hour.

Hosts: Louisa and Keith Surges
Rooms: 4 (PB) $75-120
Full Breakfast
Credit Cards: A, B, C
Notes: 5, 6, 7, 8, 9, 10, 11, 12, 13, 14

TOFINO

Silver Cloud

Box 188, V0R 2Z0
(250) 725-3998; FAX (250) 725-3908
e-mail: silvercloud@mail.Tofino-BC.com
www.tofino-bc.com/silvercloud

Waterfront with quiet privacy and spectacular gardens. View rooms, private baths, one with hot tub. Restful lounge areas; gazebo, waterside decks. Elegant full breakfast served in solarium over the water. Self-contained apartment also available. Silver Cloud is as unique and delightfully surprising as the sea itself. Serving discerning guests for 19 years.

Host: Olivia A. Mae
Rooms: 3 (PB) $95-195
Full Breakfast
Credit Cards: A, B
Notes: 5, 8, 9, 10, 11, 12

Wilp Gybuu (Wolf House) Bed & Breakfast

311 Leighton Way, P.O. Box 396, V0R 2Z0
(250) 725-2330; FAX (250) 725-1205
e-mail: wilpgybu@island.net
www.vancouverisland-bc.com/wilpgybuubb

Adult guests warmly welcomed to this contemporary west coast cedar home. Watch boats travel through beautiful Duffin Passage while enjoying a delicious full breakfast. Walk to Tonquin Beach, galleries, and restaurants. Golf, Pacific Rim National Park's beaches, and rain forest are minutes away by car. Tastefully decorated guest rooms with twin or queen-size beds have private en suite bathrooms. Two rooms with fireplace. Cat in residence. Airport/bus pickup. Recommended by *Northwest Best Places*. Children over 12 welcome.

Hosts: Wendy and Ralph Burgess
Rooms: 3 (PB) $80-95 Canadian
Full Breakfast
Credit Cards: A, B
Notes: 5, 7, 9, 10, 12

NOTES: Credit cards accepted: A MasterCard; B Visa; C American Express; D Discover; E Diner's Club; F Other; 2 Personal checks accepted; 3 Lunch available; 4 Dinner available; 5 Open all year; 6 Pets welcome;

VANCOUVER

A, B, and C Bed & Breakfast Agency

4390 Frances Street, V5C 2P3
(604) 298-8815; (800) 488-1941
FAX (604) 298-5917

This reservation service will help the guest find a splendid home away from home in a clean, comfortable house with especially friendly hosts and hostesses. From modest, to average, to luxurious accommodations. There are also accommodations for film crews, students, and those with long-stay and special requirements. Covering Vancouver, Victoria, and throughout British Columbia. Call for pricing and availability.

Credit Cards: A, B, C
Notes: 5, 7, 10, 11, 12, 13, 14

Albion Guest House Bed & Breakfast

592 West 19th Avenue, V5Z-1W6
(604) 873-2287

This romantic turn-of-the-century guest house is in a quiet neighborhood with only a short walk to some of Vancouver's most beautiful gardens. Twelve minutes from the Vancouver International Airportand and nearby are shops and restaurants. All rooms are appointed with a wrought iron feather bed. Guests will enjoy daily maid service, fresh flowers, fine linens, and down comforters. Available are complimentary soft drinks, juices, tea, bottled water, cookies, fruit, and liqueurs. The morning begins with the daily newspaper, music, coffee and/or a selection of herbal teas. Guests enjoy a three-course breakfast with Swiss brioche, French toast topped with seasonal fruit or homemade compote, and Westcoast eggs Benedict surrounded by homemade tomato chutney.

Hosts: Lise and Richard
Rooms: 3 (1 PB; 2 SB) $110-155
Full Breakfast
Credit Cards: A, B, C
Notes: 5, 7, 8, 9, 10, 11, 12, 13, 14

Albion Guest House

Apricot Cat Guest House

628 Union Street, V6A 2B9
(604) 215-9898; FAX (604) 255-9271
e-mail: info@apricotcat.com; www.apricotcat.com

A charming, comfortable circa 1898 home. Two and one-half minutes to downtown. West coast retreat. Buffet breakfasts in high season. Lively mornings. Refreshingly quiet nights. Friendly, well-loved dog.

Host: Sara Ratner
Full Breakfast
Credit Cards: A, B
Notes: 5, 7, 8, 9, 10, 13

Arbutus House Bed & Breakfast

4470 Maple Crescent, V6J 4B3
(604) 738-6432; FAX (604) 738-6433
e-mail: stay@arbutushouse.com
http: //arbutushouse.com

Stay at one of Vancouver's finest bed and breakfasts in the upscale, historic Shaughnessy neighborhood. This elegant 1922 home is near public transit, 10 minutes to downtown, beaches, and a short walk to Van Dusen Gardens. Spacious, well-appointed guest rooms may include en suite bathrooms, fireplaces, sun

---

7 No smoking; 8 Children welcome; 9 Social drinking allowed; 10 Tennis nearby; 11 Swimming nearby; 12 Golf nearby; 13 Skiing nearby; 14 May be booked through a travel agent; 15 Handicapped accessible.

decks, TV. Delicious full breakfast, afternoon goodies. Bedtime treats. Fragrant guest gardens. Free off-street parking. Wonderful walks through safe neighborhood of lushly gardened estates. Children 12 and older welcome.

Hosts: Gus and Lani Mitchell
Rooms: 5 (3 PB; 2 SB) $85-155
Full Breakfast
Credit Cards: None
Notes: 7, 10, 11, 12, 13, 14

Beautiful

Beautiful Bed & Breakfast

428 West 40th Avenue, V5Y 2R4
(604) 327-1102

Relax in this elegant, clean, new Colonial home with antiques, fresh flowers, views, and quiet. Minutes from downtown. Walk to tennis, golf, Queen Elizabeth Park, VanDusen Gardens, YMCA/YWCA, three cinemas, shopping center, and fine restaurants. Three-quarters of a block from bus to downtown, airport, ferries, and UBC. Breakfast in formal dining room with linens, silver, and fresh flowers. Friendly hosts will assist with travel plans. Children over 14 welcome.

Hosts: Ian and Corinne Sanderson
Rates: $70-150 U.S.
Full Breakfast
Credit Cards: A, B
Notes: 5, 7, 9, 10, 11, 12, 14

Johnson Heritage House Bed & Breakfast

2278 West 34th Avenue, V6M 1G6
(604) 266-4175 (phone/FAX)
e-mail: fun@johnsons-inn-vancouver.com
www.johnsons-inn-vancouver.com

Wonderfully restored Craftsman-style home is furnished with Canadiana antique furniture, carousel horses, and comfy brass and iron beds. Full breakfasts include a main course, fresh fruit, and homemade muffins and jams. The friendly hosts invite guests to stay in one of Vancouver's finest and safest city neighborhoods. The house is a 10-minute drive to downtown or the university and is close to fine restaurants, services, and tourist attractions. Fifteen minutes from the airport. Children 12 and older welcome.

Hosts: Sandy and Ron Johnson
Rooms: 3 (2 PB; 1 SB) $75-155 Canadian
Full Breakfast
Credit Cards: None
Notes: 2, 7, 9, 10, 11, 12, 14

Johnson Heritage House

Kenya Court Ocean Front Guest House

2230 Cornwall Avenue, V6K 1B5
(604) 738-7085

Ocean-view suites on the waterfront in a gracious Heritage building minutes from downtown Vancouver. Across the street are tennis

---

NOTES: Credit cards accepted: A MasterCard; B Visa; C American Express; D Discover; E Diner's Club; F Other; 2 Personal checks accepted; 3 Lunch available; 4 Dinner available; 5 Open all year; 6 Pets welcome;

courts, a large heated saltwater pool, and walking and jogging paths along the water's edge. It is an easy walk to Granville Island, the planetarium, and interesting shops and restaurants. All of the guest suites are spacious and tastefully furnished. The delicious full breakfast is served in a glass solarium with a spectacular view of English Bay. Children over eight are welcome.

Host: Dr. and Mrs. H. R. Williams
Suites: 4 (PB) From $85
Full Breakfast
Credit Cards: None
Notes: 2, 5, 7, 9, 10, 11, 12, 13

Laburnum Cottage

Kenya Court

Laburnum Cottage Bed & Breakfast

1388 Terrace Avenue, North Vancouver, V7R 1B4
(604) 988-4877; FAX (604) 988-4877

Restful, peaceful seclusion at this English country home with leaded-pane windows. Set on one-half acre of award-winning English garden, nestled against a forest, yet only 15 minutes from downtown. Each of the guest rooms in the main house has its own decor, complemented by magnificent garden views. Also two cottages in the garden with remodeled bathrooms with soaking tubs, and new kitchen in larger carriage house cottage. Antiques in main house. Breakfasts are jolly occasions in the big country-house-style kitchen near the cozy AGA cooker or in the breakfast room, where all can enjoy a full three- or four-course meal. Smoking permitted outside only. May be booked through a travel agent, but not encouraged.

Hosts: Delphine Masterton and Karin Essinger (chef/manager)
Rooms: 4 (PB) $95-150 U.S. ($75-195 Canadian)
Cottages: 2
Full Breakfast
Credit Cards: A, B
Notes: 2, 5, 7, 8, 9, 10, 11, 12, 13, 14, 15

The Manor Guest House

345 West 13th Avenue, V5Y 1W2
(604) 876-8494; FAX (604) 876-5763

The Manor Guest House is an Edwardian Heritage mansion in the heart of the city. Choose

The Manor Guest House

---

7 No smoking; 8 Children welcome; 9 Social drinking allowed; 10 Tennis nearby; 11 Swimming nearby; 12 Golf nearby; 13 Skiing nearby; 14 May be booked through a travel agent; 15 Handicapped accessible.

from nine spacious rooms, most with king-size or twin beds and private bath. The self-contained penthouse suite has a loft, kitchen, and private deck, which offers a spectacular view of the city. A generous and delicious healthful breakfast is served, featuring fresh daily baking.

Host: Brenda Yablon
Rooms: 10 (6 PB; 4 SB) $65-125
Full Breakfast
Credit Cards: A, B
Notes: 5, 7, 8, 9, 10, 11, 12, 13, 14

Old English Bed & Breakfast Registry

1226 Silverwood Crescent, North Vancouver, V7P 1J3
(604) 986-5069; FAX (604) 986-8810
e-mail: relax@oldenglishbandb.bc.ca
www.oldenglishbandb.bc.ca

This **Kitsilano** bed and breakfast has one of the best locations in Vancouver. Within walking distance of downtown, just steps away from cafés, bistros, and restaurants, one block from Kitsilano Beach, one-half block to the bus stop, and a 10-minute walk to Granville Market. The bed and breakfast is a restored circa 1900 Heritage home. There are five guest rooms in all. One has a private en suite bath. The other rooms share two, four-piece bathrooms. $105-150.

Shaughnessy. The Canadian Pacific Railway built this Georgian manor in 1913 for its executives. Minutes to the center of the city. The inn has 12 rooms, some with private baths, some with kitchenettes. Each room has its own unique color and design. The inn is set in a wonderful large garden with paths leading to the gazebo. The whole setting is reminiscent of a bygone era. $85-160.

South Vancouver. A warm welcome awaits guests at this budget/backpackers-style bed and breakfast. The hostess provides down-home comfort and big breakfasts. It is in a quiet residential area close to the airport and just a few steps to the busloop to downtown Vancouver. Children are welcome and so are pets. $55-85.

Vancouver Arbutus. The accommodation consists of two good-sized bedrooms. The rooms share a bathroom as well as a very large sitting room. The sitting room is equipped with a wet bar, large TV with VCR, and a library of videos. Fifteen minutes from the airport and downtown Vancouver. Public transit is nearby with two buses going into downtown on a regular basis. A short walk to a unique shopping area of Kerrisdale. $55-85.

West End. The Langtry is a small deluxe apartment in the much sought after area of the city. Each of the large one-bedroom apartments has been beautifully decorated with a mix of Edwardian, Victorian, and Georgian furniture. Great attention to detail. The units are fully furnished and equipped with a business area. Included in the room rate are guests' first morning's breakfast food, free parking, and free local telephone/fax calls. $175-225.

West End II. This one-bedroom fully furnished self-contained suite is a half-block away from Denman Street, a few short blocks from English Bay Beach and Stanley Park, and minutes to the center of downtown Vancouver on foot. Underground parking is provided. The apartment is on the 14th floor of an older high-rise apartment building. There is a bedroom, a bath with a shower and tub, a living room with stereo system, TV, and VCR. The kitchen is completely stocked. The apartment also comes with a telephone/fax for guests' convenience. $145.

Pacific Bed & Breakfast Agency

P.O. Box 46894, Seattle, WA 98146
(206) 439-7677; (800) 684-2932
FAX (206) 431-0932; e-mail: pacificb@nwlink.com
www.seattlebedandbreakfast.com

084. Gourmet Cook. With 100 cookbooks as a source for breakfast ideas, this gourmet cook will make guests' breakfast a special occasion. The private suite with full bath can accommodate four people and has a fireplace, TV, stereo, and is furnished with lovely antiques. Eight

---

NOTES: Credit cards accepted: A MasterCard; B Visa; C American Express; D Discover; E Diner's Club; F Other; 2 Personal checks accepted; 3 Lunch available; 4 Dinner available; 5 Open all year; 6 Pets welcome;

miles from downtown Vancouver, this bed and breakfast is convenient to all sections of the city. $110 Canadian.

085. Tudor. This warm and friendly executive Tudor home is in a natural park setting and has easy access to the city center. Two rooms each with private bath share a wing of this lovely home, and the hostess will serve a gourmet breakfast. Two-night minimum stay. $95 U.S.

086. Cottage. Restful, peaceful seclusion is what this charming home with a Victorian air suggests to guests. Set in a half-acre of beautifully kept garden, surrounded by virgin forest yet 15 minutes from the city center. Two cottages plus rooms in the main house all have private baths and all are decorated to make guests' stay comfortable. The hostess serves a full breakfast with homemade jams. Relax on the patio and enjoy the stream and fountain. Prices vary for each room up to $175 U.S.

087. A cedar-sided rancher with designer nooks and crannies holds intriguing statues and knickknacks from around the world. More than 1,000 square feet of decking opens onto lush gardens. Three guest rooms all share bath accommodations. $90-95 U.S.

088. 1912. In a pretty residential area just minutes to downtown, this 1912 Craftsman-style home offers guests four rooms with either private or shared bath accommodations. It is furnished with antiques brought from England and the stained-glass windows, inlaid oak floors, and wood paneling give this home a warm and cozy ambiance. $81-127 U.S.

089. Neo-Victorian. A bed and breakfast newly built in the traditional Victorian style is near Kitsilano Point just five minutes to downtown. Two enchanting guest bedrooms wrap guests in luxury and have romantic balconies that overlook the beach and secluded garden. Breakfasts are gourmet and served on the antique dining table by the fireplace. Enjoy the private guest library. Two-night minimum in summer. $100 U.S.

090. Kits. Inn designed in the ski chalet style. The hostess has made two suites available for her guests. With queen-size or twin/king-size beds and private or shared bath and private patio and fireplace guests have many choices for their stay at this host home. The Continental self-serve breakfast may include homemade muffins. $75-95 Canadian.

091. Chef. Breakfast will be prepared by a gourmet chef at this Victorian home just minutes away from the heart of the city. One unit with queen-size bed and private bath, TV, and telephone gives guests privacy as well as comfort. $90 U.S.

092. 1920. The hostess warmly welcomes guests to her 1920s-style Tudor cottage where they will enjoy gracious hospitality. Five rooms all with private baths and king-, queen-size, or full beds give guests a wide variety of choices. A gourmet breakfast starts the day. $135-155 Canadian.

196. Fraser View Bed and Breakfast. Overlooking the Fraser River with a nice view of the whole valley, any guests will enjoy the atmosphere of this contemporary home. Two rooms are available sharing the bath or one room with private bath can be arranged. The hostess also has a garden-level suite that can be arranged with private bath. The gourmet breakfast is served in the dining room. Room rates vary with type of accommodations requested and start at $65 U.S.

200. Lakewood Bed and Breakfast. Just reopened is this very convenient and inexpensive bed and breakfast. Shared and private baths, all rooms with cable TV, Continental breakfast. Five minutes east of downtown. Three blocks to the skytrain station, two blocks to lake, park, and tennis courts. *Wir sprechen Deutsch* as well as English and Japanese. $75-95 Canadian.

---

7 No smoking; 8 Children welcome; 9 Social drinking allowed; 10 Tennis nearby; 11 Swimming nearby; 12 Golf nearby; 13 Skiing nearby; 14 May be booked through a travel agent; 15 Handicapped accessible.

206. Guest Suite. In North Vancouver, just a 90-minute drive to the Whistler ski area, the suite is a warm and welcoming accommodation for any traveler. Featured is a separate living area, full bath, and a fully equipped kitchen. The futon in the sitting room can be used for extra sleeping space. Guests may choose to have their own "dine-in" breakfast or let the hostess create a delicious, fresh breakfast for them. Seasonal rates. $70.

211. Pacific Spirit. This home built in 1950 is by Pacific Spirit Park. The hostess offers two rooms sharing the bath or the arrangement can be a suite of two rooms to accommodate a family group or friends traveling together. The sitting room has a TV and fireplace. A full gourmet breakfast will be served in the dining room. There is a hot tub in the garden for the guests to enjoy. $70-120.

Town and Country Bed & Breakfast Reservation Service

P.O. Box 74542, 2803 West Fourth Avenue, V6K 1K2
(604) 731-5942 (phone/FAX)
www.tcbb.bc.ca

Offering bed and breakfast homes in residential areas of Vancouver and Victoria, the listings include some small inns. A few of the listings have waterfront or special views. Private and shared baths available. Some have from one to three guest rooms. Some character homes, some West Coast-style homes or townhouse accommodations. Usually within 15-20 minutes to city center. Booking service only; no lists mailed.

3. This lovely contemporary home has two guest rooms with private baths, one with queen-size bed and patio on the ground level and one room with lovely views. Excellent location for walking to Kitsilano Beach and park, Granville Island with its market, shops, galleries, restaurants, and live theater, all on the waterfront. Bus within one block. Downtown five minutes. $115-125.

5. Vancouver. Not the usual bed and breakfast, this is a private suite one block from bus line with terrific view of mountains, sea, city. Fifteen minutes to downtown. Bedroom with queen-size bed, sitting room with queen-size sofa bed, TV, also kitchen facilities. Suitable for three or four traveling together. No children. Twenty-five dollars for additional persons. $125.

6. North Vancouver. A contemporary home with a view of the city. Nutritious and delicious breakfast. Mountain-view spa. Families welcome, but children should be over eight years old. Walk to Grouse Mountain Skyride. Fifteen minutes to downtown and Stanley Park. Smoking is not permitted. Seasonal rates available. $95-135.

7. West Vancouver. From this bed and breakfast, guests can see Stanley Park, downtown city lights, the Lions Gate Bridge, the mountains, and the cruise ships on their way to Alaska. Queen-size beds and private baths. All the suites overlook the beautiful, secluded gardens. Guests can sit in the gazebo and enjoy the flowers, the birds, the views, and the serenity of this peaceful setting. $150-190.

8. In Kitsilano, one of Vancouver's most popular and safe neighborhoods, a few blocks to first-class beaches and parks; downtown is a 5- to 10-minute drive. This beautifully restored and renovated 1912 home has a sophisticated contemporary interior. Dining/living room for guests on second floor with ocean, city, mountain views. Two bedrooms on second floor share a bath, and the honeymoon suite has a fireplace, double Jacuzzi bath, and en suite bathroom with shower. $115-185.

9. Perfect location for those without a car who like to walk to local buses, shops, restaurants, and cafés, Kitsilano Beach and Park, Granville Island, 5 to 10 minutes to downtown by bus/car. Popular Fourth Avenue area. Heritage-

---

NOTES: Credit cards accepted: A MasterCard; B Visa; C American Express; D Discover; E Diner's Club; F Other; 2 Personal checks accepted; 3 Lunch available; 4 Dinner available; 5 Open all year; 6 Pets welcome;

style home with three bedrooms upstairs; two sharing one bath and one with private bath. $98-120.

10. This lovely restored and updated Heritage home has four guest rooms and suite, all with private baths. On a quiet tree-lined street in popular Kitsilano area, walk to shops, cafés, fine restaurants. Garden level suites suitable for family. $135-185.

12. In a quiet part of Kitsilano, this new four-room bed and breakfast has all the features to make a stay an enjoyable one. Private and shared baths, TV, and telephones. Within walking distance of shops, restaurants, buses. Ten to 15 minutes by car/bus to downtown. $95-140.

The West End Guest House

The West End Guest House

1362 Hard Street, V6E 1G2
(604) 681-2889; FAX (604) 688-8812

Built in 1906 for the Edwards family, the West End Guest House is constructed entirely of straight-grain cedar (meaning it has no knots). The young Edwards men operated the first photography shop in Vancouver, and many of their pictures hang in the inn. In 1985 it was restored as a bed and breakfast, complete with a "painted lady" pink-and-green exterior. Its owner, Evan Penner, has furnished the rooms with Victorian antiques and reproductions, keeping the style elegant and interesting with memorabilia. Rooms include bathroom, TV, telephone, bathrobes and slippers; sun deck has wicker furniture. Sherry served year-round by the fireplace.

Rooms: 7 (PB) $110-250
Full Breakfast
Credit Cards: A, B, C, D
Notes: 2, 5, 7, 9, 10, 11, 12, 13, 14

VERNON

Harbour Lights

135 Joharon Road, V1H 1C1
(250) 549-5117; FAX (250) 549-5162
e-mail: harbourlights@bc.smpatico.ca

Custom-built home on two quiet hillside acres. Three spacious guest rooms, each with en suite bath and picture window offering panoramic view of Lake Oganagan and the mountains. Full gourmet breakfast featuring homemade breads, preserves, local cheese, and hot entrée. "Come and enjoy our tranquil setting."

Hosts: Joyce and Doug Stewart
Rooms: 3 (PB) $75
Full Breakfast
Credit Cards: B
Notes: 7, 9, 10, 11, 12, 13

VICTORIA

Abbey Rose Bed & Breakfast

3960 Cedar Hill X Road, V8P 2N7
(800) 307-7561; FAX (250) 479-5422

Abbey Rose is an English country home convenient to Victoria's downtown Inner Harbour, Butchart Gardens, beautiful beaches, and the University of Victoria. Hike at Mount Doug Provincial Park, bike for miles on the Galloping Goose Trail, golf at Cedar Hill Golf

---

7 No smoking; 8 Children welcome; 9 Social drinking allowed; 10 Tennis nearby; 11 Swimming nearby; 12 Golf nearby; 13 Skiing nearby; 14 May be booked through a travel agent; 15 Handicapped accessible.

Course. Relax in one's own private room with en suite bath and balcony or join the other guests in the sitting room with a cozy warm fireplace. All-you-can-eat delicious home-baked breakfast. Enjoy a cup of tea upon arrival. Come as guests, leave as friends.

Hosts: Joanne and Arnie Davis
Rooms: 2 (PB) $60-80 U.S.
Full Breakfast
Credit Cards: A, B
Notes: 5, 7, 8, 9, 10, 11, 12, 14

Abigail's Hotel

Abigail's Hotel

906 McClure Street, V8V 3E7
(250) 388-5363; (800) 561-6565
FAX (250) 388-7787
e-mail: innkeeper@abigailshotel.com
www.abigailshotel.com

In the tradition of European-style inns, Abigail's has been marvelously transformed into a small luxurious hotel. Exquisite antique furnishings, crystal chandeliers, crackling fireplace, and fresh flowers provide the romantic ambiance. All guest rooms have private baths, fluffy goose down comforters. Many rooms have Jacuzzis and wood-burning fireplaces. The famous gourmet breakfast is included with every stay. Complimentary sherry served in the cozy library. Just three blocks to Victoria's Inner Harbour, downtown shops, restaurants, museums, parks, and ocean. Honeymoon packages available. Canada Select five-star-rated.

Off-season discounts available. Children over 10 welcome.

Hosts: Daniel and Frauke Behune
Rooms: 22 (PB) $179-299 Canadian
Full Breakfast
Credit Cards: A, B, C
Notes: 5, 7, 9, 10, 11, 12, 14

Ambleside Bed & Breakfast

1121 Faithful Street, V8V 2R5
(250) 383-9948; FAX (250) 383-9317
e-mail:hosts@amblesidebb.com
amblesidebb.com

Discover Victoria's charms right from the doorstep. Delightful 1919 Arts and Craft home in downtown Victoria's most scenic, tranquil, and walkable Heritage neighborhood. Stroll to all the attractions through lovely Beacon Hill Park or along irresistible oceanside paths. Spacious, elegant guest rooms offer the comfort and pleasure of fine antique beds, cozy goose-down comforters, deluxe en suite baths. Balconied honeymoon suite with fireplace and TV/VCR. Enjoy convivial gourmet breakfasts and gracious, helpful hospitality. Adult-oriented. Canada Select four and one-half stars.

Hosts: Marilyn Jessen and Gordon Banta
Rooms: 2 (PB) $95-180 Canadian (approx. $65-125 U.S.)
Full Breakfast
Credit Cards: A, B
Notes: 5, 7, 9, 10, 11, 12, 14

Ambleside

NOTES: Credit cards accepted: A MasterCard; B Visa; C American Express; D Discover; E Diner's Club; F Other; 2 Personal checks accepted; 3 Lunch available; 4 Dinner available; 5 Open all year; 6 Pets welcome;

Battery Street Guesthouse

670 Battery Street, V8V 1E5
(250) 385-4632

Comfortable guest house (circa 1898) in downtown Victoria. Beacon Hill Park and the ocean are only one block away. An ample breakfast is served and the hostess speaks Dutch as a first language. Nonsmokers only.

Host: Pamela Verduyn
Rooms: 6 (2 PB; 4 SB) $65-95
Full Breakfast
Credit Cards: B
Notes: 2, 5, 7, 9, 10

Beaconsfield Inn

Beaconsfield Inn

998 Humboldt Street, V8V 2Z8
(250) 384-4044; FAX (250) 384-4052
www.islandnet.com/beaconsfield

The 1995 International Bed and Breakfast winner, this Heritage 1905 English manor with award-winning restoration has nine guest rooms and suites with private bathrooms. Three blocks to downtown and the waterfront. Adult-oriented. Complimentary parking. Highly rated by *Best Places to Kiss in the Northwest,* Fodor's, AAA, *Special Places, Northwest Best Places, Unique NW Country Inns,* and special award-winner: 1995 Bed and Breakfast of the Year by Andrew Harper's *Hideaway Report.* An oceanfront cottage for the ultimate romantic hideaway has two fireplaces, a Jacuzzi for two, hot tub under the stars, self-catering kitchen, TV, and VCR.

Hosts: Con and Judi Sollid
Rooms: 6 (PB) $165-350
Suites: 3 (PB)
Full Breakfast
Credit Cards: A, B
Notes: 5, 7, 10, 11, 12, 14

A B & B at Swallow Hill Farm

4910 William Head Road, V9C 3Y8
(250) 474-4042 (phone/FAX)
e-mail: adgd@swallowhillfarm.com
www.swallowhillfarm.com

Tourism B.C. approved. Canada Select three-star-rated. Guests will find a peaceful country getaway at this little Canadian farm on Vancouver Island's beautiful southwest coast. A short drive from the heart of Victoria, this bed and breakfast offers two suites with queen-size and twin beds, private decks, and a spectacular ocean and mountain sunrise view. Enjoy delicious farm breakfasts and friendly conversation. Wildlife includes deer, eagles, seals, otters, birds. Go whale watching, hiking, kayaking, swimming, cycling, golfing, etc.

Hosts: Gini and Peter Walsh
Rooms: 2 (PB) $85-95 Canadian (subject to change)
Full and Continental Breakfast
Credit Cards: A, B, C, F
Notes: 5, 7, 11, 12, 14

Swallow Hill Farm

---

7 No smoking; 8 Children welcome; 9 Social drinking allowed; 10 Tennis nearby; 11 Swimming nearby; 12 Golf nearby; 13 Skiing nearby; 14 May be booked through a travel agent; 15 Handicapped accessible.

Dashwood Seaside Manor

One Cook Street, V8V 3W6
(604) 658-8879; (800) 667-5517
www.dashwoodmanor.com

Victoria's Heritage inn by the sea welcomes guests warmly. This 1912 Heritage mansion has 14 elegant suites. Close to town, next to lovely Beacon Hill Park, on Victoria's enchanting Marine Drive. Breathtaking views, Old World charm. Some fireplaces, balconies, Jacuzzis. Each suite is complete with private bath and kitchenette. Breakfast supplies are provided for guests to prepare breakfast at their leisure.

Hosts: Derek Dashwood, Family, and Staff
Rooms: 14 (PB) $63-218
Full Breakfast
Credit Cards: A, B, C, D, E
Notes: 2, 5, 6, 7, 8, 10, 11, 12, 14

Garden City Bed & Breakfast Reservation Service

660 Jones Terrace, Victoria, V8Z 2L7
(250) 479-1986; FAX (250) 479-9999
e-mail: gardencity@bc-bed-breakfast.com
www.bc-bed-breakfast.com

F-1. Only five blocks from city center Inner Harbour, the hosts provide two beautiful suites in their 1912 Maclure-built home. Each suite has bathroom, queen-size bedroom, sitting room with fireplace, and discreetly positioned kitchen—appropriately furnished with antiques and memorabilia. Breakfast is served to guests' suite each morning. A grand entrance hall with original wood and stained-glass windows plus beautiful gardens add to luxurious surroundings. From $125.

F-2. Two spacious suites, each with en suite private bathroom and a sofa bed for an extra person. Breakfast is served in guests' suite. Within easy walking distance of shopping plaza, lieutenant governor's residence, and bus service to city center. Twenty-five dollars for extra person. From $110-125.

F-9. Be lulled to sleep by lapping waves in this 1908 character home, which has wonderful views of ocean and is also close to city center and Beacon Hill Park. Old-fashioned claw-foot tub plus many antiques, with beautifully restored hardwood floors and 11-foot ceilings. Ocean and park just across the street. $80.

F-10. Quietly elegant home built in 1915. Impressive open staircase, stained-glass windows, beautiful antiques, and friendly atmosphere. Bright and cheerful dining room. Informed host and hostess assist with itineraries, local sightseeing, etc. Excellent bus service or 25-minute walk to city center. Also a new suite fully furnished with all the comforts and necessities. From $85-90.

I-1. This truly is a gem! A fabulous 1912 Heritage home on one-half acre of ocean inlet. Entering from a large veranda which faces the salt-water bird sanctuary, guests will immediately feel comfortable and relaxed. Spacious rooms have en suite private bathrooms. Many beautiful antiques but all the modern day comforts. From $110.

I-3. This home reflects the beauty and serenity of the Hawaiian Islands. On a salt-water inlet, this bird sanctuary is only 15 minutes from city center. Rooms have water views. Guest sitting area with TV. Extra space for large groups. From $65.

J-1. Elegance and comfort tucked into historic area. Down comforters, bathrobes, Casablanca fans, en suite private bathrooms in each room. Guests' lounge with fireplace. Early morning "silver tray service" of coffee or tea. Also English-style cottage with two bedrooms, bathroom, sitting room, eating area, kitchen, laundry facilities, and private patio/garden. $95-125.

S-3. A lovely modern chalet across from Swan Lake and only three miles to city center. Stroll around the lake or marvel at views from atop Christmas Hill. En suite private bathrooms.

NOTES: Credit cards accepted: A MasterCard; B Visa; C American Express; D Discover; E Diner's Club; F Other; 2 Personal checks accepted; 3 Lunch available; 4 Dinner available; 5 Open all year; 6 Pets welcome;

Breakfast served on the deck or in formal dining room. Excellent menu. From $70.

S-7. A working Norwegian fjord horse farm. Only 20 minutes from city center. Guests are invited to use the living room, dining room, patio, and all outside areas. Families are welcome in the large room with queen-size beds and are very well fed with fresh local produce used in the country breakfasts. Hospitality and peace featured in rural setting of this Christian home. From $95.

The Gatsby Mansion

309 Belleville Street, V8V 1X2
(250) 388-9191; (800) 563-9656
FAX (250) 920-5651

The mansion is poised overlooking the Inner Harbour. Its twinkling crystal chandeliers, stained-glass windows, and hand-frescoed ceilings extend an invitation for guests to come experience this taste from the past. Conveniently across the street from the ferry and custom facilities and next to the legislative buildings. Twenty guest rooms available with full breakfast, restaurant, and martini lounge. Come share the experience.

Host: Rita A. Roy-Wilson
Rooms: 20 (PB) $83-253
Full Breakfast
Credit Cards: A, B, C, D, E
Notes: 3, 4, 5, 7, 8, 9, 10, 11, 12, 14

Heathergate House Bed & Breakfast

122 Simcoe Street, V8V 1K4
(250) 383-0068; (888) 683-0068
FAX (250) 383-4320
e-mail: heathergate@bc.sympatico.ca

Casual elegance in the heart of Victoria, close to the Inner Harbour and Parliament buildings.

Heathergate House

Guest rooms have private baths, bathrobes, down comforters, and Casablanca fans. Guest lounge with fireplace, books, telephone, and TV. Silver tray service for early morning coffee or tea in rooms. Full breakfast served in the dining room in the English tradition. Private two-bedroom cottage also available at the same location with Continental breakfast brought each morning. Enjoy the hospitality of a friendly Canadian home with many of the comforts and antiques of a small English inn. Off-season discount rates available.

Hosts: Ann and Ned Easton
Rooms: 3 (PB) $70-90 U.S.
Cottage: $105 U.S.
Full Breakfast
Credit Cards: A, B
Notes: 2, 5, 7, 10, 11, 12, 14

Heritage House Bed & Breakfast

3808 Heritage Lane, V8Z 7A7
(250) 479-0892; FAX (250) 479-0812
www.victoriabc.com/accom/heritage.html

Beautiful 1910 registered Heritage home on three-quarters of an acre in a country setting. Quiet and secluded with a lounging veranda. Large rooms, guest parlor with fireplace, and library/den. Gourmet breakfasts. Private parking. Convenient to ferries, downtown, and all

---

7 No smoking; 8 Children welcome; 9 Social drinking allowed; 10 Tennis nearby; 11 Swimming nearby; 12 Golf nearby; 13 Skiing nearby; 14 May be booked through a travel agent; 15 Handicapped accessible.

Heritage House

highways. Reservations recommended. Two-day minimum stay. No pets. Inquire about accommodations for children. Cancellation policy of five-day notice. Check-in hours are 4:30-6:30 P.M.

Hosts: Larry and Sandra Gray
Rooms: (PB) $115-125 Canadian
Full Breakfast
Credit Cards: A, B
Notes: 5, 7, 9, 10, 11, 12

Humboldt House Bed & Breakfast

867 Humboldt Street, V8V 2Z6
(250) 383-0152; (888) 383-0327
FAX (250) 383-6402
e-mail: rooms@humboldthouse.com
www.humboldthouse.com

Relax in the romantic luxury of Victoria's most beautiful and private bed and breakfast, built in 1893. Each guest room now features its own unique decor, Jacuzzi, and fireplace. Downtown on a quiet, historic tree-lined street, this splendid Victorian home is just steps away from the Inner Harbour. Highest rating of four kisses by *Best Places to Kiss in the Northwest*. Also featured in *Country Inns* and *Weekends for Two in the Pacific Northwest*.

Hosts: Mila Werbik; David and Vlasta Booth
Rooms: 5 (PB) $87.50-205 U.S.
Full and Continental Breakfast
Credit Cards: A, B
Notes: 5, 7, 9, 10, 11, 14

Markham House Bed & Breakfast

1853 Connie Road, V9C 4C2
(250) 642-7542; (888) 256-6888
FAX (250) 642-7538
e-mail: mail@markhamhouse.com
www/sookenet.com/markham
www.markhamhouse.com

Stroll the gardens and dream; sink into the feather beds and sleep till tomorrow; sip tea on the lawns and dine by the pond or luxuriate in the romantic cottage in the woods featuring private spa and wood stove. The Tudor home is set on 10 truly picturesque acres near the rural village of Sooke, 25 minutes west of Victoria on the way to the spectacular west coast beaches. Excellent bike and hiking trails are nearby and the fishing is superb. Private baths, guest lounge with fireplace, comfortably elegant decor, imaginative breakfasts, and true west coast hospitality will complete a visit. AAA three-diamond-approved. *Best Places to Kiss* 1996/1997. Canada Select four stars.

Hosts: Sally and Lyall Markham
Rooms: 4 (PB) $95-175 Canadian
Full Breakfast
Credit Cards: A, B, C, D, E, F
Notes: 2, 5, 7, 9, 10, 12, 14

Oak Bay Guest House

1052 Newport Avenue in Oak Bay, V8S 5E3
(250) 598-3812; (800) 575-3812
FAX (250) 598-0369
e-mail: oakbay@beds-breakfasts.com
www.beds-breakfasts.com

This historic Tudor design bed and breakfast inn has been looking after travelers since 1922 and is in Victoria's most English and elegant suburb. Designer-decorated rooms, en suite baths, antiques, claw-foot tubs, four-poster beds, guest lounges, library, beautiful gardens. Walking distance to the best restaurants, golf, fishing, ocean walks, and incredible scenery. Sumptuous breakfasts. Seven minutes to town centre. Children 12 and older welcome.

NOTES: Credit cards accepted: A MasterCard; B Visa; C American Express; D Discover; E Diner's Club; F Other; 2 Personal checks accepted; 3 Lunch available; 4 Dinner available; 5 Open all year; 6 Pets welcome;

Hosts: Jackie and Karl Morris
Rooms: 11 (PB) $55-170 Canadian
Full Breakfast
Credit Cards: A, B, C
Notes: 5, 7, 9, 10, 11, 12, 14

Pacific Bed & Breakfast Agency

P.O. Box 46894, Seattle, WA 98146
(206) 439-7677; (800) 684-2932
FAX (206) 431-0932; e-mail: pacificb@nwlink.com
www.seattlebedandbreakfast.com

069. On the national registry. Step back in time to the warmth of the late 1800s and in the morning wake to the aroma of fresh coffee and a gourmet breakfast. Three rooms with private baths. Turndown service and sweet-dream chocolates bring a pleasant close to a memorable day of sightseeing or shopping. $100-150 U.S.

070. Water Views. The property slopes to a bird sanctuary with stunning sunset views from a private balcony. Each large room is reminiscent of a grand past and is uniquely decorated. Full breakfast. No detail is overlooked. Choose from five rooms, all with private baths. $95-150 Canadian.

071. On Antique Row. Built by a prominent local architect, this 1901 Heritage home is within a 15-minute walk to the Inner Harbour. With handicapped accessibility, the hosts can accommodate most special needs requests. The stained-glass windows and many antiques welcome guests for a comfortable stay. Two rooms are available with shared bath (private can be arranged). Full breakfast. $60-89 U.S.

072. Edwardian Mansion. Enjoy the splendor of this grand home and be treated to a sumptuous breakfast served in the elegant dining room. The mansion features rich oak paneling, stained-glass windows, antique furnishings, and a carved-stone terrace overlooking a lovely garden. A variety of accommodations are offered. The Royal Suite with fireplace, canopied bed, Jacuzzi, wet bar, and a bathroom with onyx tub and gold fixtures. Goose down comforters and pillows, fresh flowers, and afternoon tea. $80-200 U.S.

073. Circa 1899. Filled with antiques, this guest house has the atmosphere of genteel hospitality. All woodwork, fireplaces, and floors are restored originals, and wainscoting, pedestal sink, and soaking tub are in keeping with the period. Three rooms on the second floor have private baths. Full breakfast. $125 Canadian.

074. 1908 Character Home. Just one-half block from the ocean and a 20-minute walk to the Inner Harbour, this host home offers three rooms with queen- or king-size beds and all have private baths. The king-size room has a fireplace, lots of windows, and a big claw-foot tub. Breakfasts are creative and served with warm hospitality. $130 Canadian.

075. Near the Inner Harbour. This 1907 historic home has three suites to choose from. Old World charm with New World comfort pampers guests at this guest house. A Continental breakfast is brought to the suite on a tray and special breakfasts can be ordered at the time of booking. $95-105.

076. Near Butchart Gardens. Enjoy the quiet along with a cedar-shaded pond, terrace, and patio. Breakfast can be served on the patio and guests may choose either vegetarian or Continental fare with fresh coffee and country-fresh baked treats. The hostess offers organic products and chemical-free cleaning agents. Shared or private bath accommodations. $55-65 U.S.

077. 1912 Edwardian. A honeymoon suite with a fireplace and kitchen, queen-size bed, and private bath can be guests' for that special trip to the island. Three other rooms with queen-size or double beds and private baths are also available. Just two blocks from ocean beachfront, guests are just four blocks from the heart

---

7 No smoking; 8 Children welcome; 9 Social drinking allowed; 10 Tennis nearby; 11 Swimming nearby; 12 Golf nearby; 13 Skiing nearby; 14 May be booked through a travel agent; 15 Handicapped accessible.

of Victoria. A gourmet breakfast to start the day of sightseeing or shopping. Open for summer seasons only. $95-115 U.S.

078. Rockland District. Beamed ceilings, seven fireplaces, and elegantly furnished rooms will take guests back to a life of high society of the late 1800s. All rooms are generously proportioned in the grand style with simple touches such as handmade quilts and antique furnishings. Breakfast is served in the dining room. Guests are welcome to enjoy the den and browse the hundreds of books. A number of rooms are offered with shared or private baths and rates vary with each accommodation.

079. Waterfront Views. This guest house has views of the water and the snowcapped Olympic Mountains. Seabirds are at the front door and guests might see a whale swimming in the strait. On a bus route, these suites with private baths and private entrances include a full breakfast. All suites have TVs. $115-170 Canadian.

080. Cordova Bay. This contemporary lodge features oversized rooms with private baths, refrigerators, and TVs and some rooms have kitchenettes. The guest lounge and dining room have a fireplace, coffee machine, and microwave oven for heating snacks. Cordova Bay has lovely water views to the east and is in a country-like setting, but is just 15-minute's drive from the heart of Victoria and the ferries, Butchart Gardens, and ocean beaches. Rates vary with accommodations.

082. Heart of the City Hotel. An elegant small hotel in the heart of the city with 40 charming rooms with extra touches including fireplaces, Jacuzzi tubs, and down comforters. A morning paper, coffee, or tea is delivered to guests' room. Breakfast is served in the dining room. Seasonal rates. $79-150 U.S.

184. Tudor House and Romantic Cottage. Imagine a charming Tudor house in a setting of landscaped gardens surrounded by tall trees just a 30-minute drive from Victoria. The main house offers three guest rooms with private baths, feather beds, and down comforters. Breakfast is deliciously designed especially to please each guest. If guests prefer seclusion, the cottage may be their choice with a hot tub and barbecue on the deck. Entering the cottage, guests will discover a feeling of space and coziness with a vaulted ceiling, woodstove, and a tiny kitchen concealed in an antique pine wardrobe. The bedroom has a queen-size bed and private bath en suite. Rates depend on choice of accommodation and season.

190. Manor House. A dramatic curved oak staircase welcomes guests to this traditional Tudor-style home. Three guest rooms on the first and second floors have private baths. Enjoy an elegantly served home-cooked breakfast in the beautiful classical dining room. Relax on the spacious sun deck and enjoy the fresh country air or walk to the beach where there is a lounge with a fireplace and ocean views. From $55 U.S.

191. Tudor-style European Inn. Experience the charm and hospitality of this unique bed and breakfast hotel just a few blocks from the Inner Harbour. There are 16 unique rooms individually decorated and offering Jacuzzi baths and wood-burning fireplaces. Sherry and hors d'oeuvres are served each evening in the library, and in the morning join the other guests for the famous gourmet breakfast in the dining room. Please call for seasonal rates.

192. Turn-of-the-century Manor. Secluded on a quiet, tree-lined residential street near the heart of the city, this registered designated Heritage building was named after a luxurious London hotel. Guests will feel surrounded with Old World charm and turn-of-the-century refinements of period furniture, high-beamed ceilings, and oriental carpets. Enjoy goose-down comforters, wood-burning fireplaces, claw-foot

---

NOTES: Credit cards accepted: A MasterCard; B Visa; C American Express; D Discover; E Diner's Club; F Other; 2 Personal checks accepted; 3 Lunch available; 4 Dinner available; 5 Open all year; 6 Pets welcome;

and Jacuzzi tubs, sherry served in the afternoon, and a full breakfast elegantly served. Choose from a wide range of prices.

Prior House Bed & Breakfast Inn

620 St. Charles Street, V8S 3N7
(250) 592-8847; FAX (250) 592-8223
e-mail: innkeeper@priorhouse.com
www.priorhouse.com

Prior House is a five-star gracious Edward-ian mansion once a private residence for the English crown. Circa 1912. All rooms have cozy fireplaces, some with marble whirlpool tubs. Enjoy Olympic Mountain views or the beautiful English gardens. A sumptuous full breakfast is served in the elegant dining room or in the privacy of guests' room. Enjoy delicious high tea served daily 4:00-6:00 P.M. in the many comfortable common areas. Children 10 and older welcome.

Rooms: 6 (PB) $125-275 Canadian (approx. $90-199 U.S.)
Full Breakfast
Credit Cards: A, B
Notes: 5, 7, 9, 11, 12, 14

Sunnymeade House Inn

1002 Fenn Avenue, V8Y 1P3
(250) 658-1414

Take the scenic route into Victoria to discover this custom-designed, beautifully decorated,

Sunnymeade House Inn

English-style country inn in a village setting by the sea. Steps to beach, shopping, golf, and tennis courts. Pub and restaurants. New special occasion suite with view, whirlpool bath, private dining and sitting room. Lovely English garden. Delicious breakfasts.

Hosts: Jim and Ginny Flanigan
Rooms: 6 (PB) $89-169 Canadian
Full and Continental Breakfast
Credit Cards: None
Notes: 2, 5, 7, 9, 11, 12, 14

Top O' Triangle Mountain

3442 Karger Terrace, V9C 3K5
(250) 478-7853; (800) 870-2255
FAX (250) 478-2245
e-mail: pat@hospitalityvictoria.com
www.hospitalityvictoria.com

As guests arrive, the panoramic view of mountains, ocean, and city will take one's breath away. Enter into the solid cedar log home and immediately be "at home" in the warm and relaxing atmosphere. Add to this sincere hospitality and full, home-cooked breakfasts, lovingly prepared, and one will have the "complete bed and breakfast experience."

Hosts: Pat and Henry Hansen
Rooms: 3 (PB) $70-100
Full Breakfast
Credit Cards: A, B
Notes: 5, 7, 8, 9, 10, 11, 12, 14

Town and Country Bed & Breakfast in British Columbia

2803 West Fourth Avenue, P.O. Box 74542, V6K 1K2
(604) 731-5942 (phone/FAX); www.tcbb.bc.ca

1. Beautiful Edwardian home one block to waterfront road, 10-minute drive to city center. Three rooms, one with private bath and two that share a bathroom. Furnished with antiques and other special touches. Some sea views. $110-135.

---

7 No smoking; 8 Children welcome; 9 Social drinking allowed; 10 Tennis nearby; 11 Swimming nearby; 12 Golf nearby; 13 Skiing nearby; 14 May be booked through a travel agent; 15 Handicapped accessible.

2. The guests are special at Arundel Manor, a 1912 Heritage home on a half-acre of land sloping to Portage Inlet, a bird sanctuary with stunning sunset views. The four large bedrooms have private en suite bathrooms, and two have spacious balconies overlooking the water. The fifth room has twin beds and a private bathroom. A full home-cooked breakfast is served in the elegant dining room. A cheerful, welcoming lounge with fireplace awaits the guests. Check in between 2:00 and 4:00 P.M.; check out 11:00 A.M. No smoking. Not suitable for pets. $145-160.

3. Relax in this beach home with incredible views over the Haro Strait to the San Juan Islands and Mount Baker. Each room has a queen-size bed and private bath. A delicious hearty breakfast is served in the ocean-view dining room. Within walking distance to restaurants, shopping, golfing, and tennis. From $145.

4. This friendly family home, just two blocks to park, beach, buses, country bakery, and restaurant is just a short drive to downtown Victoria. Charming rooms, lovely garden, two rooms in main house plus separate cottage for families. $95-125.

5. Heritage house on historic street has large, nicely furnished rooms with private baths, queen- and king-size beds, TV. Within walking distance to Victoria city center, Beaconhill Park, waterfront. $98-135.

6. This Edwardian-style Heritage home is furnished with antiques and has all the comforts of home. Quiet, yet within easy walking distance to downtown Victoria. $105-125.

Wooded Acres Bed & Breakfast

4907 Rocky Point Road, V9C 4G2
(250) 478-8172
e-mail: cabin@lodgingvictoria.com
e-mail: ekennedy@pacificcoast.net
www.LodgingVictoria.com/countryside

Wooded Acres

Unique countryside log home is secluded in a parklike setting on three acres of forest. Together, the hosts built their log home and have created an authentic old-fashioned bed and breakfast. Suites provide complete privacy, queen-size beds, and sheltered hot tubs to relax amidst the pleasures and relics of bygone times. Breakfast is a feast of specialties baked daily and served at guests' convenience. The elegance of candlelight, lace, and fine china help to provide lasting memories for all special occasions. Adult oriented.

Hosts: Elva and Skip Kennedy
Rooms: 2 (PB) $110
Full Breakfast
Credit Cards: None
Notes: 2, 5, 7, 9, 10, 11, 12, 14

WEST VANCOUVER

Creekside Bed & Breakfast

1515 Palmerston Avenue, V7V 4S9
(604) 926-1861; (604) 328-9400 (cellular)
FAX (604) 926-7545

Quiet, romantic, parklike, casual setting with a creek flowing through this natural garden property. All-you-can-eat home-baked breakfast. Luxurious en suite bath with two-person Jacuzzi in a glass-roofed bathroom. The second bath also has a Jacuzzi tub and skylights. In-room TVs with remotes, stocked mini-refrigerators, and coffee makers. Complimentary wines, beverages, snacks, toiletries, and robes. Ideal honeymoon setting. Commissionable. Fifty percent deposit (non-returnable) required. Half-price coupons available for entertainment and dining. Two-day minimum stay. Pets welcome by prior arrangements. Smoking not permitted indoors.

Hosts: John Boden and Donna Hawrelko
Rooms: 2 (PB) $109-149 Canadian
Full Breakfast
Credit Cards: A, B
Notes: 5, 7, 9, 10, 11, 12, 13, 14

WHISTLER

Golden Dreams Bed & Breakfast

6412 Easy Street, V0N 1B6
(604) 932-2667; (800) 668-7055
FAX (604) 932-7055; e-mail: golden@whistler.net
www.cantravel.ab.ca/goldendr.html

Enjoy this world-class year-round resort just two hours from Vancouver. Be surrounded by nature's beauty and pampered with a wholesome breakfast, homemade jams, and fresh breads. Unique theme rooms feature cozy duvets, sherry decanter. Relax in outdoor hot tub with mountain views. Family room with wood fireplace. Full guest kitchen. Just one mile to village express gondolas. Valley trail system and bus route at doorstep. On-site bike rentals. Many seasonal activities. Now in two locations. Whistler Town Plaza is within walking distance to the express ski lifts, fabulous restaurants, and new shops. These new condos feature gas fireplace, entertainment center, full kitchen, spa access, and underground parking.

Hosts: Ann and Terry Spence
Rooms: 3 (1 PB; 2 SB) $85-125 Canadian ($65-85 U.S.)
Full Breakfast
Credit Cards: A, B
Notes: 2, 7, 8, 10, 11, 12, 13

WHITE ROCK

Dorrington Bed & Breakfast

13851 19A Avenue, V4A 9M2
(604) 535-4408; FAX (604) 535-4409
www.accommodationsbc.com/dorrington.html

Dorrington is a magnificent Canada Select four-star-rated brick-and-stone estate set on one-half acre featuring three themed rooms with four-poster beds, private bathrooms, outdoor hot tub, tennis court, towering cedar trees, pond, and gardens. Full breakfast is served in the Hunt Salon or on the patio overlooking the peaceful gardens. Dorrington is close to the border or ferry terminal to Victoria and 45 minutes from Vancouver.

Host: Pat Gray
Rooms: 3 (PB) $90-110 Canadian
Full Breakfast
Credit Cards: A, B
Notes: 2, 5, 7, 9, 10, 11, 12, 13, 14

---

7 No smoking; 8 Children welcome; 9 Social drinking allowed; 10 Tennis nearby; 11 Swimming nearby; 12 Golf nearby; 13 Skiing nearby; 14 May be booked through a travel agent; 15 Handicapped accessible.

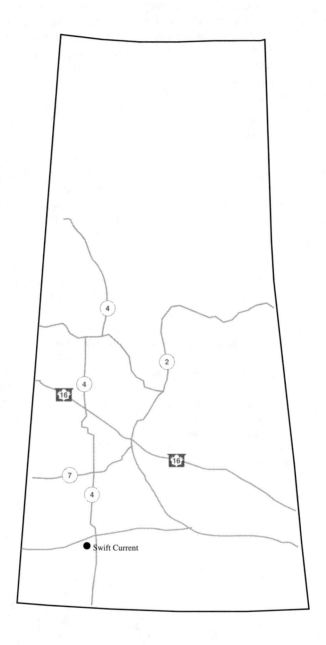

Saskatchewan

Saskatchewan

SWIFT CURRENT

Swift Current Heritage Bed & Breakfast

Box 1301, S9H 3X4
(306) 773-6305; FAX (306) 773-0135
e-mail: DGreen@SCHDB.SK.CA

Less than 1km from town, beautiful ranch house on a working cattle ranch. Rooms have a view of the Swift Current Creek and pastoral hills. Guests can relax on the deck, watch young Appaloosa horses in training or at play, or visit the Swift Current Petroglyph, an ancient boulder with carvings dating back over 3,000 years. The friendly hosts and the peaceful country environment will make guests' stay memorable. Canadian personal checks accepted.

Hosts: Dixie and Dave Green
Rooms: 4 (4 SB) $50-60
Full or Continental Breakfast
Credit Cards: None
Notes: 7, 8, 9, 10, 11, 12

NOTES: Credit cards accepted: A MasterCard; B Visa; C American Express; D Discover; E Diner's Club; F Other; 2 Personal checks accepted; 3 Lunch available; 4 Dinner available; 5 Open all year; 6 Pets welcome; 7 No smoking; 8 Children welcome; 9 Social drinking allowed; 10 Tennis nearby; 11 Swimming nearby; 12 Golf nearby; 13 Skiing nearby; 14 May be booked through a travel agent; 15 Handicapped accessible.

RECOMMENDATION FORM

As *The Annual Directory of American and Canadian Bed & Breakfasts* gains approval from the traveling public, more and more bed and breakfast establishments are asking to be included on our mailing list. If you know of another bed and breakfast which may not be on our list, give them a great outreach and advertising opportunity by providing us with the following information:

1) B&B Name _____

Host's Name _____

Address _____

City _____ State _____ Zip Code _____

Telephone _____ FAX _____

2) B&B Name _____

Host's Name _____

Address _____

City _____ State _____ Zip Code _____

Telephone _____ FAX _____

3) B&B Name _____

Host's Name _____

Address _____

City _____ State _____ Zip Code _____

Telephone _____ FAX _____

Please return this form to: Barbour Publishing, Inc.
P.O. Box 719, Uhrichsville, OH 44683
(740) 922-6045; FAX (740) 922-5948

Planning the perfect vacation?

Find all the best lodging in

The Annual Directory of American and Canadian Bed & Breakfasts

Five volumes in the series:

New England (Volume I)—includes Connecticut, Maine, Massachusetts, New Hampshire, Rhode Island, Vermont, New Brunswick, Nova Scotia, Prince Edward Island, and Quebec. 304 pages, $9.95 ($15.50 in Canada), ISBN 1-57748-771-0

Mid-Atlantic Region (Volume II)—includes Delaware, District of Columbia, Maryland, New Jersey, New York, Pennsylvania, Virginia, Ontario. 272 pages, $9.95 ($15.50 in Canada), ISBN 1-57748-772-9

The South (Volume III)—includes Alabama, Arkansas, Florida, Georgia, Kentucky, Louisiana, Mississippi, North Carolina, South Carolina, Tennessee, Texas, Virginia, West Virginia, Puerto Rico, and the Virgin Islands. 288 pages, $9.95 ($15.50 in Canada), ISBN 1-57748-773-7

The Midwest (Volume IV)—includes Illinois, Indiana, Iowa, Kansas, Michigan, Minnesota, Missouri, Nebraska, North Dakota, Ohio, Oklahoma, South Dakota, Wisconsin, Manitoba, and Ontario. 192 pages, $9.95 ($15.50 in Canada), ISBN 1-57748-774-5

The West (Volume V)—includes Alaska, Arizona, California, Colorado, Hawaii, Idaho, Montana, Nevada, New Mexico, Oregon, Texas, Utah, Washington, Wyoming, Alberta, British Columbia, and Saskatchewan. 448 pages, $12.95 ($19.95 in Canada), ISBN 1-57748-775-3

Available wherever books are sold.
Or order from:
Barbour Publishing, Inc.
P.O. Box 719
Uhrichsville, Ohio 44683
http://www.barbourbooks.com

If you order by mail, add $2.00 to your order for shipping.
Prices subject to change without notice.